# Labor Arbitration

## Cases and Materials for Advocates

## Other BNA Books Authored by the ABA Section of Labor & Employment Law

*Covenants Not to Compete: A State-by-State Survey*

*The Developing Labor Law*

*Employee Benefits Law*

*Employee Duty of Loyalty: A State-by-State Survey*

*Employment Discrimination Law*

*Equal Employment Law Update*

*How Arbitration Works*

*Labor Arbitration: A Practical Guide for Advocates*

*Labor Arbitrator Development: A Handbook*

*Occupational Safety and Health Law*

*The Railway Labor Act*

# Labor Arbitration
## Cases and Materials for Advocates

### William F. Dolson
*Professor of Law*
*University of Louisville School of Law*

### Max Zimny
*General Counsel*
*Union of Needletrades, Industrial and Textile Employees*

### Christopher A. Barreca
*Paul, Hastings, Janofsky & Walker LLP*

Committee on ADR in Labor and Employment Law

Section of Labor and Employment Law
American Bar Association

The Bureau of National Affairs, Inc., Washington, D.C.

Copyright © 1997
American Bar Association
Chicago, IL

**Library of Congress Cataloging-in-Publication Data**

Labor arbitration : cases and materials for advocates / editors,
    William F. Dolson, Christopher A. Barreca, Max Zinmy.
        p.  cm.
    ISBN 1-57018-036-9
      1. Arbitration, Industrial--Unites States--Cases. I. Dolson,
William F. II. Barreca, Christopher A. III. Zimny, Max.
KF3423.L33   1997
344.7301'89143--dc21

                                                97-2056
                                                CIP

Published by BNA Books
1250 23rd St. NW, Washington, DC 20037
International Standard Book Number: 1-57018-036-9
*Printed in the United States of America*

# Foreword

Since 1945 when it began, the ABA Section of Labor and Employment Law has had as its stated purposes (1) to study and report upon continuing developments in the law affecting labor relations, (2) to assist the professional growth and development of practitioners in the field of employment and labor relations law, and (3) to promote justice, human welfare, industrial peace, and the recognition of the supremacy of law in labor-management relations.

Through the publication of books such as *Labor Arbitration: Cases and Materials for Advocates,* and through annual and committee meeting programs designed to provide a forum for the exchange of ideas, the Section has pursued these stated goals. Gradually, the Section has built a library of comprehensive legal works intended for the use of the Section membership as well as the bar generally.

The Section of Labor and Employment Law is pleased to provide this casebook as part of its library of books published by BNA Books, a Division of The Bureau of National Affairs, Inc.

The Section wishes to express its appreciation to the Committee on ADR in Labor and Employment Law, and in particular to the authors, William F. Dolson, Christopher A. Barreca, and Max Zimny, and to Timothy J. Darby for his editorial work. The authors have tried to accomplish two primary objectives: (1) to be equally balanced and nonpartisan in their viewpoints, and (2) to ensure the book is of significant value to the practitioner, student, and sophisticated nonlawyer.

The views expressed herein do not necessarily represent the views of the American Bar Association, or its Section of Labor and Employment Law, or any other organization, but are simply the collective, but not necessarily the individual, views of the authors.

CHRISTOPHER A. BARRECA

*Chair*

ROBERT M. DOHRMANN

*Chair-Elect*

Section of Labor

and Employment Law

American Bar Association

December 1996

# Preface

This casebook is the companion to the textbook LABOR ARBITRATION: A PRACTICAL GUIDE FOR ADVOCATES, edited by Max Zimny, William F. Dolson, and Christopher A. Barreca (BNA Books 1990). That textbook includes a compilation of presentations by nationally recognized arbitrators and experienced advocates on the various aspects of labor arbitration and the grievance procedure, including its history, contract negotiation, practice and procedure, and substantive principles. It also contains articles that deal directly with the advocacy skills with which this casebook is concerned, such as direct examination and cross-examination of witnesses, opening and closing statements, and the preparation of briefs.

The authors believe this casebook is unique, and that when used in conjunction with the companion textbook, it will prove to be a valuable learning experience. Another related title is LABOR ARBITRATOR DEVELOPMENT: A HANDBOOK, edited by Christopher A. Barreca, Anne Harmon Miller, and Max Zimny (BNA Books 1983). It is a valuable reference source for practitioners as well as for arbitrators and arbitrators-to-be.

## Casebook Format

This companion casebook is not like the ordinary casebook used in law schools. The ordinary casebook calls on students to analyze versions of reported cases from appellate courts and arbitrations; rarely are students called on to examine a case at the trial level, much less participate in the trial itself. This casebook requires students to engage in both of these activities: to examine what actually takes place at an arbitration hearing (the equivalent of a case at the trial level), and to take an active part as advocates or arbitrators via role playing or simulation in mock cases. Observing mock arbitrations when they are not participating is also a valuable learning experience for other students in the class.

The cases selected for this casebook are based on actual arbitration cases which have been edited with the time constraints of class scheduling in mind. Transcripts of these cases provide one script of the case-in-chief for the Company and for the Union advocates. Specifically, the scripts comprise the direct testimony (and re-direct in some cases) of each side's witnesses plus the supporting exhibits. While the transcripts have been edited for clarity, balance, and suitability for classroom use, the authors have attempted to retain the authenticity and color of the testimony. Participants should understand that the Q-and-A scripts do not have to be read word for word; the individuals concerned can script their own performances as formally or as informally as they prefer, as long as the pertinent facts are elicited and the examination stays within the parameters of the original script, generally.

Cross-examinations in the original transcripts have been deleted. The authors have tried to provide a valuable learning experience by requiring student advocates in these simulations to develop their own cross-examination styles based on the testimony of the other side's witnesses. Cross-examination hones the true skills of an advocate. It is demanding, but can be rewarding and fun for both participants and observers, if the parties can stay within reasonable bounds in exercising artistic license.

On occasion the casebook contains transcripts of "re-direct" after the opportunity for cross-examination. As will be evident from such "re-direct," often the advocate is in effect adding new evidence through this process, although technically re-direct is supposed to clarify prior evidence, not offer new evidence. Arbitrators generally tend to admit the new material in such a situation. However, users of the casebook might consider weaving the re-direct into the direct examination.

## Pre-Hearing Activities

One requirement pivotal to a successful simulation of an arbitration is that the student advocates from both sides meet prior to the hearing to discuss ground rules, enter into stipulations, and inform each other generally as to what their positions are and how they plan to present their cases. The student arbitrator may be included in their meeting. In actual arbitrations, the arbitrator sometimes facilitates this meeting. Such a meeting usually occurs in actual arbitrations only if the advocates and arbitrator are located in the same town and thus can easily get together in advance of the arbitration date, or if said individuals, while not in the same town, nevertheless all are available for this activity the day before the arbitration. It is also used when the grievance process being utilized for the case is not highly developed. The grievance process itself is not simulated in the exercises although its paper trail is included in the exhibits; accordingly, the pre-arbitration meeting is a substitute for what goes on in the multiple steps of the grievance process, including focusing on what the issue is and exchanging documents. This preliminary activity in actual practice often takes place at the beginning of the arbitration itself, as discussed in LABOR ARBITRATION: A PRACTICAL GUIDE FOR ADVOCATES (Part IV). Pre-hearing arbitration meeting forms found in Appendixes A, B, and C can be used as a guide to structure the students' pre-arbitration process. This meeting can take place in class, so that the other members of the class can observe the process and perhaps improve on it when their turn to participate comes.

The issue involved in the case is not provided in the case materials; framing the issue is part of the student exercise, and this should be one of the topics of the pre-arbitration exercise, using the form in Appendix A. The arbitrator should assist the parties in framing the issue. In actual arbitration, when the parties have been unable to frame the issue at the pre-arbitration meeting, the arbitrator at the beginning of the arbitration hearing usually asks the parties to frame the issue, and assists them in doing so where necessary. Pertinent to the issue are the facts and provisions in the collective bargaining agreement. If the parties are unable to stipulate the issue, the arbitrator indicates what he or she believes the issue to be. (The arbitrator may do this at the end of the hearing, because by then the arbitrator will have had the benefit of being briefed on the facts and the parties' positions and arguments.) This assists the parties in making their arguments and writing their briefs.

The terms "grievance" and "arbitration" are used as terms of art in this casebook. A *grievance* is filed by the Union and/or employee and decided at various steps by the Company, with appeals to the next higher level. A request or demand for an *arbitration* occurs after the grievance is denied at the last step. In some contracts, discharge arbitrations are expedited. Thus, grievance filing forms and disposition results may appear as exhibits in some cases in this casebook, along with requests or demands for arbitration following denial of a grievance at the final step. Usually, the Union makes the determination whether a grievance will be taken to arbitration, depending on what the collective bargaining agreement says. In the cases that follow, relevant excerpts from collective bargaining agreements are included in the joint exhibits.

## Witnesses

Student advocates may be made responsible for obtaining persons to play the part of witnesses in the simulations, or the teacher may assign others in the class to play these parts. It is particularly helpful for a student to be a witness as well as an advocate and arbitrator; it provides students with very helpful insights into the mental processes of a witness. Friends, relatives, and amateur actors can be pressed into service as witnesses also. Having individuals from outside the class participate can increase the feel of authenticity and challenge students to prepare more thoroughly.

More important than who will play the part of a witness, though, is witness preparation. Articles in the companion textbook LABOR ARBITRATION: A PRACTICAL GUIDE FOR ADVOCATES (Part IV) stress this point; as the adage goes, the three most important factors in a successful arbitration are preparation, preparation, and preparation. In a mock proceeding, this becomes even more important. Student advocates must ensure that their witnesses are fully educated in the background of the case. As part of their preparation, witnesses at the start (a) should be given a briefing on the dispute by the advocate who will be doing the direct examination—i.e., what happened, the identity of the individuals involved, and what arguments the parties are making—and (b) should then be given a copy not just of their transcript but of the complete case to review. Witnesses should be instructed to pay attention to the exhibits, particularly the relevant collective bargaining provisions and any grievance forms, in addition to those exhibits referenced in their own testimony. This will assist witnesses in responding to cross-examination questions. They should be aware that some exhibits, while not be specifically referenced in a given witness's transcript, may be helpful to that witness nonetheless in understanding the case well enough to respond correctly when being cross-examined. As well, some exhibits may not be referenced in any witness's transcript but it may nonetheless be important for all witnesses to review them in order to be as fully briefed as possible.

A note of caution: Although the casebook provides witnesses with scripts of questions and answers during direct examination, cross-examination will be spontaneous. The witnesses will therefore have to come up with answers to questions on subjects that are not dealt with in any transcript, e.g., processes or practices they may not be familiar with. However, witnesses subjected to cross-examination may often be able to answer specific questions in an appropriate manner based on their general knowledge of the facts of the case gained through careful preparation and life experiences in general.

In this regard, some stretching of the facts should be allowed. Witnesses should not, however, give answers that are not based on any facts or at least on fair inferences from the broad outlines of the case. Otherwise, the scale would be tipped too heavily to one side. Conservative embellishment of the facts is permissible, but not overexaggeration.

If a witness is unable to respond sufficiently to cross-examination in a particular instance, the student advocate who conducted the witness's direct examination should be allowed to assist in providing a response. Since student advocates presumably have a better grasp of the facts, answers generated by them should be more realistic than what witnesses may be able to offer. In preparing cross-examinations, student advocates should themselves be sensitive to the need not to stretch the facts too far.

Student advocates also can use the pre-arbitration meeting to fill perceived holes in the fact pattern. Occasional intervention by the professor, either at the pre-arbitration meeting or during cross-examination, may be called for to maintain a balance in the development of the overall fact pattern and to referee disputes between the advocates over the "rules of the game."

## Opening and Closing Statements

In addition to conducting direct and cross-examinations, student advocates are required to prepare and present opening and closing statements and a post-hearing brief.

- The opening statement is usually brief. It provides a road map of where the advocate is attempting to go. It sets forth the basic facts, the issue, what the advocate will attempt to prove, and the relief requested. The advocates may wish to submit a written opening statement; this is the process in some industries. It is read out loud with additional comments by the advocate. If a post-hearing brief is not going to be submitted, a written opening statement would have the advantage of providing the student arbitrator with a written document to work from in preparing the award. It also allows the student arbitrator to avoid having to take extensive notes during the case. In actual arbitrations, where there are written opening statements, the subsequent brief often is simply an elaboration of the opening statement.

- The closing statement is a summary of the proof presented, emphasizing both the strengths of the advocate's position and the weaknesses in the opponent's position, and summarizes the reasons why the issue presented and relief requested should be resolved in favor of the advocate's position.

Sample opening and closing statements are found in Appendixes E through H. An extensive discussion of the opening statement and the closing statement is found in the companion textbook LABOR ARBITRATION: A PRACTICAL GUIDE FOR ADVOCATES.

In actual arbitrations, the closing statement is usually short or left out if a post-hearing brief is to be filed; in a closing statement in such a situation, the advocate may cite statements in arbitration treatises and prior arbitration cases for the reasoning in them that supports the advocate's position. In the simulations, however, it is recommended that oral closing statements be required even if a brief is required, for several reasons.

- First, this helps students hone their advocacy skills.

- Second, it provides a satisfying climax to the exercise. Moreover, if the student arbitrator is called upon to render at least a preliminary "bench decision," closing statements are critical to the arbitrator making an informed decision.

- Third, closings provide a reference for the professor to work from after each presentation (if there is to be a class discussion) of the strengths and weaknesses of the facts for each side, the general arbitral principles involved, and of the advocates' arguments.

- Fourth, there are time constraints should the student arbitrator be required to provide a written award. In actual arbitrations, post-hearing briefs usually are filed 15 to 30 days after the arbitration hearing and the written award is due 30 to 60 days after simultaneous receipt of briefs. For class purposes, the due date for submission of the post-hearing briefs and the arbitration award is usually identical. Thus, the student arbitrator will not be privy to the contents of the post-hearing briefs. As a consequence, a student arbitrator must leave the hearing with all the information and materials necessary to write a decision. The closing statement should provide this information.

## Post-Hearing Briefs

The post-hearing brief contains in greater detail all the points presented in the closing statement. It also includes a discussion of supporting authorities with citations to arbitration cases and other authorities such as treatises. The structure of the arbitration brief is similar to that of briefs filed in appellate court. Arbitration briefs vary from the informal to the formal and from the fact-oriented to the law-oriented.

A sample brief is set forth in Appendix D. Discussion of the use of the brief is found in LABOR ARBITRATION: A PRACTICAL GUIDE FOR ADVOCATES (Part V). When students write briefs, they should be encouraged to cite to transcript pages using the numbers at the bottom of each page, following the style in the sample brief in Appendix D.

## Functioning as Arbitrator

Students may have an opportunity to serve as arbitrators during the mock proceedings. If the professor prefers, student arbitrators may be instructed to go into the arbitration "cold" (i.e., without having read the transcripts or reviewed the exhibits), to reproduce the experience of most arbitrators, and to reach decisions based solely upon what is presented by the advocates. This will in all likelihood require them to take notes and may require them to ask additional questions to clarify areas not clearly presented by the student advocates. Each student arbitrator can then be required to write an opinion setting forth the reasons for the decision, either being allowed to consult the written scripts or not, as the professor prefers. Student arbitrators should be allowed at a minimum to review exhibits, however, since those would be always available to a practicing arbitrator.

As mentioned above, student arbitrators, due to time constraints, are not likely to have the benefit of post-hearing briefs from the advocates when they write their decision. A professor can, however, direct student arbitrators to the classification systems for the myriad of arbitration awards in *Labor Arbitration Reports* (BNA) and *Labor Arbitration Decisions* (CCH), where many different styles of decisions and useful guidance on general lines of arbitrators' approaches to various issues can be found. Other useful overviews that may be recommended include the treatise HOW ARBITRATION WORKS, LABOR ARBITRATION DEVELOPMENT: A HANDBOOK, and the articles contained in volumes of the proceedings of the annual meetings of the National Academy of Arbitrators, all of which are published by BNA. In addition, selected sample arbitration awards are included in Appendix I.

## Additional Comments on Class Procedure

The procedure discussed above for making use of the materials in this casebook may obviously be altered to fit the preferences of the professor and the time available. The class can skip the step of following the script for direct examination, and advocates can conduct only cross-examination, provided witnesses have thoroughly familiarized themselves with the transcripts. Or the use of witnesses can be dispensed with altogether and student advocates can prepare only closing arguments before an arbitrator, referring to the transcript testimony; this is the equivalent of a summary jury trial described in Murray, Rau, and Sherman, PROCESSES OF DISPUTE RESOLUTION: THE ROLE OF LAWYERS, Second Edition (Foundation Press 1996). Written briefs and awards can still be required in such modified processes, to fulfill any writing or grading requirements.

It should be noted that there may be enough time during the semester for a student to be an advocate in one case and an arbitrator in another. This is particularly true if co-arbitrators are used, and there are co-advocates for each side. In such a situation, each of the several arbitrators and advocates could be assigned to write a post-hearing brief or award within several weeks of the hearing and then on the due date reassigned to a different role in a subsequent exercise. Whether additional written work is assigned would be left to the preference of the professor, or additional writing could be optional for the student.

The professor may wish to consider videotaping the oral proceedings, both to review performances and to allow the students the opportunity to screen their own performances with a view to improving their demeanor in a public forum. Such a practice also helps reinforce the formal nature of the exercise; also it may encourage students to give the best presentation they can and to stay focused on the activity at hand rather than "falling out of character." Requiring appropriate or authentic attire for all involved in the presentation of the case can also emphasize the seriousness of the activity.

Needless to say, the names of all companies and individuals involved in the original cases have been changed to protect the privacy of both the "guilty" and "innocent" (the categorization of which may depend on the eye of the beholder—or advocate). Names from both genders and from ethnic minorities have been used for individuals in all roles. Where there are male (or female) names for advocates, witnesses, or other roles, the names can be changed to suit the gender of the individuals in the class. Names of cities and states can be altered to reflect the locale of the class if the professor prefers.

Exhibits may be photocopied from the book so that advocates and witnesses can have them available during the examinations. Advocates should be aware that:

- It was not possible in this casebook to supply some exhibits, e.g., pieces of hair or photographs. Advocates will need to be creative in providing "props" to utilize where required. Such situations are noted in the case concerned.

- In some cases witnesses, during their testimony, point to and identify other prior or subsequent witnesses, or witnesses are brought back for additional testimony; such activities require proper "choreographing" and coordination among witnesses.

• As noted earlier, not all exhibits are referenced in transcripts; before doing anything else, advocates should examine the entire file, since the strength of arguments that can be made in a given case may be significantly affected by such unreferenced exhibits—particularly those involving the original grievance filed. The advocates may also "obtain" (i.e., develop) additional information and agree on stipulations during the pre-hearing arbitration proceeding, as discussed above.

In an effort to clarify the chronology of events, the authors have used a generic terminology for time sequence, i.e., "year 1" for events that occurred in the first year of the matter in question, "year 2" for events in the second year, and so on. In some cases, "year 1" is the year the individual was hired, not the year the controversy at issue began. In some cases, the designation appears in shorthand, for example, 3/21/01 for March 21, year 1. Students may substitute actual years in cases if they are more comfortable with this approach than with using "year 1, year 2," etc., but should be careful to coordinate so that all parties are using the same years for dates.

The order of presentation of cases reflects the fact that in actual arbitrations—i.e., in discipline and discharge cases the Company usually presents its case first. In contract interpretation cases the Union usually presents its case first.

## Remedies

In its opening and closing statements, the Union advocate generally indicates the remedy requested—and the issue if no joint stipulation has been made as to what the issue is.

• In a contract interpretation cases, the remedy requested usually is an interpretation of the contract in the Union's favor by the arbitrator and/or (depending on the circumstances) an order that the Company comply with the contract as so interpreted, with a make-whole award when an employee or employees and/or the Union have been damaged by the Company's (now found to be) improper interpretation of the contract.

• In a discipline or discharge case, the Union in its opening and closing statement requests that the arbitrator find the grievant was not discharged (or disciplined) for just cause. In a discharge case, the Union requests that the grievant be reinstated to his or her former position with back pay, full seniority, and all contractual benefits. In a discipline case, the Union requests that the grievant be made whole for the period of the suspension. Whether monies from other sources have been received by the grievant after the discharge, especially unemployment compensation, may be an issue.

Interest is not generally awarded in arbitration, even when requested, nor are punitive damages and attorney's fees usually awarded. However, for those cases which may be arbitrated under statutory theories in the emerging movement to arbitrate statutory claims, it may suit the professor's purpose to allow them to be requested and awarded. The professor might also require that an arbitrator write an opinion which provides the rationale for such an award.

The authors hope at some point to provide hidden agendas as teaching tools to be used by the instructor, detailing different unspoken goals to be sought by Union and management advocates, so that the exercises can be used as a basis for settlement negotiations or various ADR exercises other than arbitration. In the meantime, professors may wish to draw up their own hidden agendas and brief each side accordingly.

## Grading

In grading, the primary factors might include: the brief, the written decision, the presentation, and participation in general.

## Acknowledgments

The authors would like to acknowledge those who assisted in making this book possible, as noted below.

- *Institutions:* The University of Louisville, School of Law, and the ABA Section of Labor and Employment Law, particularly the members of the Committee on ADR in Labor and Employment Law.

- *Research Assistants:* Jean Swanson Carr, Robin Fletcher Duncan, Thomas Cecil, Sherry Dorner, Susan Meschler, Diana Myrick, Patricia Smith, and Catherine Ward.

- *Staff:* Donald Olson, Assistant Dean, The University of Louisville, School of Law.

- *Contributions:* Lawrence J. Casazza and D. Patton Pelfrey for providing a sample company opening and closing statement, respectively.

- *Publication assistance:* Camille Christie, Roger Long, and Timothy J. Darby. Special thanks are due to Tim for the considerable amount of editorial development time and effort invested in the manuscript.

WILLIAM F. DOLSON

CHRISTOPHER A. BARRECA

MAX ZIMNY

December 1996

# Contents

## Part 1 Discipline and Discharge

## Part 2 Seniority and Its Applications

## Part 3 Leave of Absence

## Part 4 Holidays

# Central State University

## Table of Contents

NOTES

# A. Caption

IN THE MATTER OF THE ARBITRATION BETWEEN:

CENTRAL STATE UNIVERSITY      )
OKLAHOMA      )
      )
AND      )      RE: SAM GREEN
      )         Discharge for Absenteeism
CUSTODIAL AND SERVICES      )
UNION NO. 1      )

Appearances:

For the Employer: Joe Thompson

For the Union: Sally Jones

Date: July 10, year 6

Place: Hortonville, Oklahoma

## B. Examination of Employer Witnesses

### 1. Frank Turner, Supervisor, Custodial Services Department

a. Direct Examination by Employer Advocate

*Mr. Thompson:*

**Q:** Mr. Turner, would you state your name for the record, please?

**A:** Frank Turner.

**Q:** Are you presently employed?

**A:** Yes, I am.

**Q:** Where?

**A:** Central State University.

**Q:** What position do you have at Central State University?

**A:** I am a front-line supervisor in the Custodial Services Department.

**Q:** How long have you held that position?

**A:** For one year and two months.

**Q:** Now, in connection with your employment, did you come to know one Sam Green?

**A:** Yes, I did.

**Q:** How did you know him?

**A:** He was assigned to me on second shift as one of my employees.

**Q:** So you knew him from the period of October year 4 through January year 5, is that correct?

**A:** Yes, I did.

**Q:** Were you involved in the incidents that led up to his discharge?

**A:** Yes, I was.

**Q:** Would you tell us what occurred on January 19th of year 5?

**A:** At approximately 3:15 p.m., when I reported for work early, the switchboard informed me that Sam Green had been trying to get hold of Morris Swift all day. I said, "I am on board, if Sam calls back and wants to talk to me instead, that is fine." About 3:45, Morris came into my office.

**Q:** Who is Morris?

**A:** Morris Swift is the Union president.

**Q:** Okay.

**A:** He came into my office and said that Sam had called him and he asked if I would talk to Sam on the phone. Morris gave me a summary of the problem—

**Q:** What did Morris say to you?

**A:** He said that Sam did not feel that he could come to work and he had a lot of legal problems. Morris told him that it was not up to him, Morris, whether Sam came to work or not. Then Morris told Sam that he should talk to me. So Morris gave me a phone number where I could reach Sam.

I called the number and a lady answered the phone. I told her who I was, and she said it would be a few minutes because Sam was in the bathroom. So, I waited approximately five to seven minutes, and I could hear her keep telling him in the background that I was on the phone waiting. I could hear him responding to her, but I could not hear exactly what he was saying. He finally picked up another extension and started to speak.

**Q:** What did he say to you?

**A:** He said, "Frank?" and I said, "Yes, Sam, what is the problem?" He commenced to tell me that he had been with attorneys all day. He told me that he had all these legal problems. He just wanted time to think about them, did not feel he could come to work, that Mexican authorities were involved in this, with his children and wife.

I told Sam that I was three people short due to a funeral. He kept going on and on about these legal problems. He said, "I also need February 12th off." I said, "Well, Sam, why don't you come on into work and we will discuss the February 12th date. I don't feel you have a legitimate reason to take the night off and I really cannot authorize it. I don't feel I should authorize it according to what you have told me."

**Q:** Did you ask him any questions about what he needed to do on that night that he needed to be off?

**A:** I did ask him if he was still going to have more meetings with his attorneys that day.

**Q:** What did he say?

**A:** He said, no, he had been meeting with them all day and he had legal documents to prove it. At that point I said, "I think you should come to work."

**Q:** Then what happened?

**A:** At that time he said that the University was going to have a lot of legal problems also because this is hooked in with Mexican authorities. I said that I did not think he should be threatening people—threatening me. He said, "I don't want to get you in trouble, but you'll be involved." I told him that he should not threaten me and that he should come to work. Then he said, "You'll be hearing from the Mexican authorities" and hung up the phone.

**Q:** Then what did you do?

**A:** I briefly discussed it with Morris, saying that I did all I could do. I said that I had to have Sam here. I didn't feel he had a legitimate reason to be off. Morris said that he understood.

Then the phone rang again. Sam had called back wanting to talk to Morris. Morris took the phone and talked to Sam approximately one-half hour.

**Q:** Were you present during the conversation?

**A:** Yes, I was. I think Morris did a lot of listening, as I did when I talked to Sam. Morris did offer Sam some very good advice.

**Q:** Was this a conversation that was going on while you were in the room?

**A:** Yes.

**Q:** What did he tell Sam, that you heard him say?

**A:** He said that Sam should not jeopardize his job, that I had told him to come to work, and that he should come to work.

**Q:** Anything else that you want to report that you can recall about this conversation that you overheard?

**A:** No.

**Q:** What happened next?

**A:** The next thing I did was call my director, Moses Abraham, and inform him of the problem I was having. Moses said to document it and pull Sam's card; when he comes in tomorrow at 4:30 p.m., suspend him, send him home, and direct him to be in Moses's office on the 25th for a hearing.

I did document everything. I did pull the card and attach it to the documentation. The following day, when I reported to work, I had a slip from the switchboard that Sam had called in sick and had made the statement that he just did not need the hassling. That was also passed on to Moses Abraham.

**Q:** What happened next in the Green case?

**A:** The next thing was the suspension and the hearing set up by Moses to investigate whether Sam could substantiate his reason for not coming to work.

**Q:** Well, at the time of suspension, did you actually talk to Mr. Green yourself?

**A:** No, I did not.

**Q:** How did that occur then and how do you know it occurred?

**A:** I am trying to look back on dates.

**Q:** For the record, he was suspended on January 21st?

**A:** January 21st, correct, January 21st I met Sam at Moore Hall. He came in and I informed him that he was being suspended without pay until there was an investigative hearing held.

**Q:** Did you attend that hearing?

**A:** Yes, I did.

**Q:** Who conducted that hearing on behalf of the University?

**A:** Moses Abraham.

**Q:** Do you recall when the hearing was?

**A:** January 25th.

**Q:** And do you recall who said what to whom?

**A:** Moses addressed Sam. He asked Sam if he could give his reasons for not reporting to work as instructed.

**Q:** Do you recall if Mr. Green responded or what he did? What happened?

**A:** Basically, he gave similar reasons to the ones he gave me on the phone.

**Q:** Do you recall anything else about that meeting?

**A:** Not much, other than Sam really did not come up with any good strong reason for not coming to work.

**Q:** What happened after the meeting was over?

**A:** Moses and I discussed it and discussed Sam's excessive absenteeism. We talked about the insubordinate attitude. We felt that it was in the best interests of Central State University that he be discharged.

### b. Cross-Examination by Union Advocate

*Ms. Jones:*
[to be supplied by student]

## 2. Morris Swift, Union President (called as an adverse witness)

### a. Direct Examination by Employer Advocate

*Mr. Thompson:*
Q:   Would you please state your name and current place of employment?
A:   Morris Swift, Central State University.
Q:   And what position do you have there?
A:   Painter's position.
Q:   Are you a member of the Custodial and Services Union?
A:   Yes, I am.
Q:   Do you have any Union office?
A:   I am President at the present time.
Q:   In January of year 5, did you hold a Union office?
A:   Yes, I did.
Q:   What Union office did you hold then?
A:   I was Chief Steward at the time.
Q:   On or about January 19th, did you receive a call from Sam Green?
A:   Yes, I did.
Q:   I want to talk about the first call you received first. What did Mr. Green tell you during that telephone call?
A:   He just told me that he needed time off from work for legal matters, that he wanted me to talk to his supervisor.
Q:   What did you tell him?
A:   I told him I would talk to Frank Turner.
Q:   Did you do that?
A:   Yes.
Q:   And Frank Turner was his supervisor?
A:   Yes.
Q:   Did you tell Mr. Green that he should call his supervisor, that you could not give him time off?
A:   Yes, I did.
Q:   Fair enough. Did you ask Mr. Turner to give Mr. Green a call?
A:   Yes.

Q:   And Mr. Turner gave Mr. Green a call?
A:   Yes.
Q:   Were you present while Mr. Turner talked to Mr. Green?
A:   Yes, I was.
Q:   You heard Mr. Turner testify here today about what he said to Mr. Green, is that correct?
A:   I did.
Q:   And do you recall at that time hearing Mr. Turner telling Mr. Green that he should report to work?
A:   He told him he should come into work.
Q:   After that telephone call was completed, did you receive a call from Mr. Green?
A:   Yes.
Q:   And you also gave Mr. Green the advice that he should not put his job in jeopardy, that he should come to work, did you not?
A:   No, I did not. I did not say it that way.
Q:   You did not say it quite that way, is that what you are saying?
A:   I did not say it that way at all. I mean—
Q:   What did you say then? Let's not have any mysteries here.
A:   I told him there would be possible discipline, from what Frank had told me, if Green did not come into work.
Q:   That's fair enough. Now, I will direct your attention to Thanksgiving of this year. This case was first scheduled to be heard by the Arbitrator on December 2nd. Do you recall that?
A:   Yes, I do.
Q:   And on behalf of the Union, did you attempt to get hold of Mr. Green?
A:   Yes.
Q:   How did you do that?

Q:   That is all I have.

A: I went to his house because he does not have a phone.

Q: How many times did you do that?

A: Three, to my knowledge.

Q: Did Mr. Green answer his door at any of those times?

A: No, he did not.

Q: Did you subsequently learn that Mr. Green was home and was there and could have answered the door?

A: Yes, I did.

Q: No further questions.

### b. Cross-Examination by Union Advocate

*Ms. Jones:*
[to be supplied by student]

## 3. Moses Abraham, Assistant Director for Building Services

### a. Direct Examination by Employer Advocate

*Mr. Thompson:*

Q: Would you state your name and current place of employment for the record?

A: Moses Abraham, Central State University.

Q: And what position do you have at Central State University?

A: Assistant Director for Building Services with the Facilities Management Department.

Q: How long have you held that position?

A: About 12½ years.

Q: In connection with your employment, did you come to know one Sam Green?

A: Yes.

Q: Did you in fact terminate his employment?

A: Yes, sir.

Q: Can you tell me what transpired in the months of December year 4 and January year 5 which led you to that decision?

A: We began to experience some severe absenteeism problems with Sam. He was being insubordinate as well as absent—unapproved absences.

Q: First, what does Mr. Green's absenteeism record look like as compared to other employees in the department?

A: Sam's absenteeism record is the worst that we have in Building Services by far, and we have approximately 112 employees in that service.

Q: Is Joint Exhibit 7 a record of Sam's absenteeism?

A: Yes.

Q: In the 12 years you have been there, have you ever discharged anybody else for absenteeism?

A: No.

Q: Has anyone else ever had an absenteeism record like Mr. Green's?

A: No, sir.

Q: Other than in December year 4 and January of year 5, have you and representatives of your staff counseled Mr. Green regarding the fact that he needed to be at work?

A: Yes.

Q: On more than one occasion?

A: Yes, sir.

Q: Did you personally counsel him on more than one occasion?

A: I have personally counseled Sam on more than one occasion.

Q: Is Joint Exhibit 6 a copy of a verbal warning you gave Sam?

A: Yes.

Q: As a matter of fact, did you ever recommend to him that he consider taking a leave of absence in order to protect his job?

A: One period in time, I believe it was in year 3, when Sam came in and was experiencing problems with absenteeism, I even encouraged him to consider a leave of absence to protect his job because at that time he was out of available approved time—vacation or personal time. There was just nothing left.

I told him we could not continue to experience this type of absenteeism, and that I would like him to consider taking a leave of absence. I said I would approve it. Hopefully, he could get his life back together, because he kept experiencing problems with divorce and children and custody. So we have tried to work with him repeatedly, encouraged him to do things, and to no avail. It was just fruitless efforts.

**Q:** For the Arbitrator's information, you said you have 112 employees. Does the University have a lot of extra employees so that if somebody is absent, you can just move people all around to fill in the needs?

**A:** No, we do not have available a lot of relief employees to plug in at any time. When someone is absent we try to do the best we can with our limited manpower.

**Q:** Okay. Have there been any budget restraints on your department over the last four or five years with respect to employees?

**A:** We have really experienced some budget crunches. Over the last six years we have lost some positions because of budget problems. We had at one time 126 custodians. Now we are down to approximately 112.

**Q:** Have you subcontracted out a lot of work to take the place of those 14 or so custodians that you have had to eliminate from the work force?

**A:** No, we have had to redistribute the work force. That is why it is very important that custodians come to work when they are scheduled. Otherwise we have nobody in there.

**Q:** Tell us what happened with the December year 4 incident and what role you played in that, Mr. Abraham.

**A:** At that point, Sam called me. Generally, I will not take calls from employees. We refer them to the supervisors. In the case of second and third shift, I get a few of these calls because the supervisor is not on campus.

Sam called, wanted some vacation time—a day, because he said the following day he had an appointment in Texas with his attorney. I asked Sam what time that appointment was. He said 10 a.m. I explained to Sam that we were really short on help right now and that we could not afford to let him go. We referenced the fact that he continued to have absenteeism problems, and I told him that I wanted him to come to work. He said that he could not come in because he had to be in Texas. After some more discussion, I agreed that if he came in for the first four hours of the shift, that would be okay. He said he would come in.

**Q:** This was December 9th, correct?

**A:** Yes. However, within a few minutes one of the ladies on the switchboard came in and informed me that Sam had called and said that he would not be in at all. In fact, he never showed up for work, even after he agreed to come in for four hours.

**Q:** What happened next?

**A:** I considered this not only a continuation of his absenteeism, but a bit of insubordination. He was told to come in, he agreed to do so, and he did not do it. We talked to Sam at a hearing where we suspended him for three days. In the suspension letter, we indicated that we would not continue to accept insubordination and absenteeism and that further infractions could lead to discharge.

**Q:** So, that is part of Joint Exhibit 5, your letter to Mr. Green, dated December 18, year 4, correct?

**A:** Yes.

**Q:** Did that letter come after an investigative meeting on December 14th?

**A:** Yes.

**Q:** Was the Union present at the meeting?

**A:** Yes.

**Q:** Did the Union ever grieve this discipline that was issued to Sam Green?

**A:** Not to the best of my knowledge.

**Q:** Turn your attention to January year 5. What happened in January of that year that caused you to reach the decision to discharge Sam Green from employment with Central State?

**A:** Well, I received a call at home one evening from my first-line supervisor, Mr. Turner. Evidently, Sam had called Morris Swift requesting time off. Mr. Swift contacted Frank Turner. And, while I am only paraphrasing the discussion, Mr. Turner told Sam that it was incumbent on him to come to work, that no time off would be approved. Sam said that Frank would have to deal with the Mexican authorities, which Frank took to be a threat of some sort. Of course, Sam never showed up to work that night.

**Q:** During that day, did Mr. Green ever contact you and tell you he was going to be off?

**A:** No.

**Q:** Are you sure about that?

**A:** I am positive. I would not forget a thing like that.

**Q:** All right. What happened on January 20th, that night? Did he come to work?

**A:** January 20th—that night I instructed Frank to write up what had happened. Sam did not show up on the 20th. He called the switchboard and indicated that the switchboard should notify Mr. Turner that he did not need any further hassles and would not be in to work that night, that they should just mark him for sick time.

**Q:** Then what happened?

**A:** Well, Frank and I communicated the next morning when I came into the office. We discussed the call from Sam, his stating that he did not need the hassle and the fact that he had said if Frank wanted to speak with him he should send him a telegram. We considered this a continuation of the insubordinate conduct—not showing up for work, absenteeism, it was becoming a pattern.

Frank and I decided to initiate a suspension with Sam. I told Frank to pull Sam's time card the next day and to meet Sam whenever he came back to work. Frank was to tell Sam that he was suspended pending the outcome of a hearing to be held the following week.

**Q:** Did you have the hearing?

**A:** Yes, we did.

**Q:** What took place at the hearing?

**A:** At the hearing, I told Sam that it was a hearing to decide whether we should continue his suspension. I told him that we wanted him to provide us with some hard evidence that his absenteeism was caused by legal formalities that required his absence.

Also, I informed Morris Swift before the meeting that he should tell Sam that if Sam had anything in writing that would shed light on the matter, he should bring it in.

During the hearing, Sam offered absolutely nothing. He was, in fact, very silent during the hearing. He offered no justification for his absenteeism.

**Q:** What did you do after the meeting?

**A:** Frank Turner and I talked after the meeting. There was no hard evidence or anything signed by lawyers that Sam's absence was required. We had nothing to substantiate any reconsideration of the matter. In the interest of the University, weighing the burden to be undertaken to replace Sam against his lack of dependability, we decided to terminate him based on his past record.

**Q:** Did his insubordination have anything to do with that termination?

**A:** It had a whole lot to do with it. It was basically due to his absenteeism, but the insubordination was taken into consideration. We need these employees to be at work when they are supposed to be there.

**Q:** In terms of employee absenteeism, other than Mr. Green, have you ever had a problem like this?

**A:** We had one other employee recently who asked for vacation time, and although his vacation was not granted, he took it upon himself to take a vacation anyway. We suspended that man for three days.

**Q:** Has anybody ever done that to you twice like Mr. Green did?

**A:** No.

**Q:** Nothing further.

### b. Cross-Examination by Union Advocate

*Ms. Jones:*
[to be supplied by student]

# C. Examination of Union Witnesses

## 1. Morris Swift, Union President

### a. Direct Examination by Union Advocate

*Ms. Jones:*

Q:	How long have you worked for the University, Morris?

A:	Almost six years.

Q:	And you gave testimony that you have been a member of the Union for that six years, is that correct?

A:	Right.

Q:	And you have held positions in the Union?

A:	Ever since the Union won bargaining rights, in year 1.

Q:	Give me a brief description of what those positions were since the time you worked there.

A:	I have been a Steward on the Executive board, Chief Steward, and now President.

Q:	Through the whole six years?

A:	All but maybe the first year.

Q:	Are you familiar with the lost-time policy here at the University?

A:	Yes, basically.

Q:	Would you explain to the Arbitrator what lost time is?

A:	To the best of my understanding, lost time is provided when you run out of paid sick time, personal time, or extended sick leave.

Q:	Does lost time have to be approved?

A:	Sometimes yes, sometimes no.

Q:	Give an example of when it is approved.

A:	If they call in and ask for time off for a long period.

Q:	Maybe I don't need to get into this with you, Morris, but have you ever dealt with a grievance over discharge or discipline in any matter dealing with use of lost time?

A:	No.

Q:	Is lost time commonly given at the University, to the best of your knowledge?

A:	Yes.

Q:	Does an employee receive pay when he or she is off on lost time?

A:	No.

Q:	From your personal experience in the use of lost time, does an employee generally request lost time?

A:	Yes. I used it myself. Once I was sick and I ran out of sick time. I asked for lost time and was granted it.

Q:	That is all I have for this witness.

### b. Cross-Examination by Employer Advocate

*Mr. Thompson:*
[to be supplied by student]

## 2. Sam Green, Grievant

### a. Direct Examination by Union Advocate

*Ms. Jones:*

Q:	Sam, would you state your full name and the date of your seniority with the University?

A:	Sam Green.

Q:	Sam, how long have you worked for the University?

A:	Twenty-five years. I received a 25-year pin last year.

Q:	Is November 7th, year 1, your seniority date?

A:	Oh, well, yes, it is. We do not receive seniority for the years we worked before this place was organized in year 1.

**Q:** What did you do for the University?
**A:** I was a custodian for physical plant.
**Q:** What shift did you work?
**A:** Second shift.
**Q:** You have heard the testimony concerning your absenteeism, and as I hand you Joint Exhibit 7, have you seen that document before, Mr. Green?
**A:** Not until today.
**Q:** You have had an opportunity to review it, correct?
**A:** That is true.
**Q:** Can you recall the times on this document that you were in the hospital?
**A:** Three times.
**Q:** Why were you in the hospital?
**A:** Severe depression.
**Q:** And have you been under a doctor's care since year 3?
**A:** Yes.
**Q:** What was that for?
**A:** Depression.
**Q:** Have you talked to Mr. Abraham on occasion about your problem?
**A:** Yes, I have. I have talked to him.
**Q:** Is he aware that you were under a doctor's care?
**A:** I would say, yes, because I had to have my doctor excuses to come back to work.
**Q:** Have you provided these doctor's excuses to the employer?
**A:** Yes.
**Q:** Did you at any time request that you be granted lost time?
**A:** No.
**Q:** How did you get lost time, do you know?
**A:** They gave it to me, I guess.
**Q:** Were you at any time disciplined for the use of lost time?
**A:** No.
**Q:** Looking at Joint Exhibit 7, where it says sick or personal, were you paid for all that time?
**A:** Yes.
**Q:** Did you know that you were violating any rule or regulation established by the employer by using lost time?
**A:** No. I was not being paid for lost time, only personal or sick time.
**Q:** Did anyone tell you that you were, by using lost time, violating a rule?

**A:** No.
**Q:** Did anyone at any time tell you that you would be disciplined if you continued to use lost time?
**A:** No.
**Q:** On January 19th, when you called in and talked with Mr. Turner, did he tell you that you would be disciplined if you did not return to work?
**A:** No.
**Q:** You did talk to Mr. Swift?
**A:** Yes, I did.
**Q:** Did he indicate that you might possibly be disciplined if you did not come in to work?
**A:** I believe so.
**Q:** Did Mr. Abraham tell you that if you did not come to work, you *would* be disciplined?
**A:** No.
**Q:** Sam, have you recently resolved your legal and personal problems?
**A:** Yes, finally after all these years.
**Q:** Are you currently under the care of a doctor for depression?
**A:** No.
**Q:** During this period of time that you were depressed, were you on any kind of medication at any point in time?
**A:** Yes, I was.
**Q:** Are you a little confused today about things that have happened in the past?
**A:** That is for sure.
**Q:** What do you mean by that?
**A:** At first, I was taking a drug for a year that caused bad side effects. I also did not improve very much. I was still depressed. Then they came along with a new drug that had fewer side effects, but the doctor had trouble finding the right dose. Sometimes I was high, sometimes low. But now I'm OK.
**Q:** Have your supervisors ever criticized your work?
**A:** No.
**Q:** If you were reinstated, would you be a reliable worker?
**A:** Yes.
**Q:** Did you have psychotherapy?
**A:** No.
**Q:** Why not?
**A:** The company insurance does not cover it. I went to the company insurance director, but she said my general practitioner would have to help me in that area.

**Q:** Does your general practitioner have a specialty in psychology or psychiatry?

**A:** No. His specialty is orthopedics.

**Q:** Despite all of this—your wife leaving you with the children—and your severe bout with depression—do you now have your life under control?

**A:** Yes, but if I don't get back to work I will not be able to afford the new drug and who knows what will happen.

**Q:** Do you believe your bosses knew you had this medical problem when you were accumulating all the absences?

**A:** Certainly. I discussed it with them—Mr. Abraham and Mr. Swift. They said don't worry, snap out of it, do your best.

**Q:** Did you feel that they were going to string along with you for a while, until you got on your feet medically?

**A:** Absolutely. I have been an asset to the University for years. Why should they abandon me now?

**Q:** That is all.

### b. Cross-Examination by Employer Advocate

*Mr. Thompson:*
[to be supplied by student]

# D. Exhibits

### *JOINT EXHIBIT NO. 1*

CENTRAL STATE UNIVERSITY
EMPLOYEE GRIEVANCE

Employee:  Sam Green

Work Location:  Physical Plant    Seniority Date:  11/07/01

STEP I.   IMMEDIATE SUPERVISOR (ORAL)

Meeting held with ____Frank Turner____ on ____1/29/05____
                    immediate supervisor        date

Oral answer received ____1/29/05____ or no answer received
                         date

STEP II.   ADMINISTRATIVE LEVEL (WRITTEN)

A.   The provision or provisions of agreement alleged to have been violated:  Discharge or Discipline   Pages 22 & 23

     Rules and Regulations Page 67

     and all other provisions of this agreement which may apply

B.   The facts which are known which are alleged to pertain to the matter:
     I was discharged from the employ of CSU because of excessive absenteeism:  I feel that this section has been improperly imposed and without just cause.

C.   The remedy desired:  That I be reinstated with all back benefits lost to me.  Make me whole.


Received 2/2/05

/s/ _Mary Potter___      /s/ _Morris Swift__      2/2/year 5
     Acting Asst. VP     /s/ _Sam Green___

*JOINT EXHIBIT NO. 2*

CENTRAL STATE UNIVERSITY

Personnel Office

March 29, year 5

Mr. Morris Swift, President
Custodial and Services Union

Re: Step 3 answer regarding Sam Green

Dear Mr. Swift:

We met with the Union on March 17, year 5, to discuss the termination of Mr. Green. Mr. Green was terminated on January 28, year 5, due to excessive absenteeism. The Union grievance contends that the discharge was improperly imposed and without just cause; however, the Union offered no argument to that effect in the March 17 meeting. The Union indicated they felt that Mr. Green's personal situation has changed so that he is better able to meet his obligations as an employee. The Union requests that he be given another chance and be returned to work without backpay.

While we can certainly empathize with the difficulties Mr. Green has experienced, we do not feel we can reverse our decision in this case. Because of the difficulties Mr. Green was experiencing, the supervisor attempted to assist Mr. Green during this time, but Mr. Green was not at all communicative or cooperative. While his personal situation may have changed, neither Mr. Green nor the Union provided us with any assurance or proof that Mr. Green has changed and is now better able to cope or accept the responsibility of communicating and resolving his attendance problems.

The termination of Mr. Green stands.

Sincerely,


/s/ Mary Potter
Acting Asst. Vice President

*JOINT EXHIBIT NO. 3*

April 13, year 5

Ms. Mary Potter
Human Resources
Central State University

Dear Ms. Potter:

The Union finds the third step answer dated March 29, year 5, to
a grievance filed by Sam Green on February 16, year 5,
unacceptable.

Therefore, the Union is requesting arbitration on this matter
according to the agreement between the Union and Central State
University, under section 13-13.

                              Respectfully,


                         /s/ Morris Swift,_____
                             President, Custodial and Services Union

*JOINT EXHIBIT NO. 4*

January 28, year 5

Mr. Sam Green
Physical Plant Building
Central State University

SUBJECT:  Discharge from CSU

Mr. Green:

You are being discharged from the employ of Central State University because of excessive absenteeism.

Your most recent refusal to report to work as directed by your supervisor was Tuesday, January 19, year 5.  On this date you called the Physical Plant switchboard and asked for Morris Swift, Chief Union Steward, to call you.  You then informed Mr. Swift you wanted time off and you asked him to get in contact with your supervisor.  Mr. Swift contacted Frank Turner at 3:45 p.m. and relayed your request and also requested Mr. Turner call you by phone.

Mr. Turner called you by phone and asked what the problem was. You stated you could make it hard on him and the University if you didn't have time off.  Mr. Turner informed you that you needed to schedule time off in advance and, at such late notice, he could not arrange to cover your area.  He further stated to you that you were to report to work.  You then stated that Mr. Turner and the University would be dealing with the Mexican authorities and hung up the phone.

On Wednesday, January 20, you called the Physical Plant switchboard and informed the operator to tell your supervisor you called in sick, that you did not need a hassle.

When you did report to work on Thursday, January 21, at 4:30 p.m., Mr. Turner informed you that you were being suspended and asked you to surrender your keys, which you did.  He also directed you to attend a disciplinary hearing in the Physical Plant Conference Room on Monday, January 25, year 5, at 2:30 p.m.

The investigative hearing was attended by you, the Union President, Chief Steward, 2nd shift Custodial Supervisor, and myself.

When asked by me why you could not come to work, you refused to answer other than to say you have had legal problems in dealing with a divorce.  You could not produce any documentation which would substantiate the necessity of your absence, nor would you provide a specific reason for your absence.

We have tried to work with you to correct your attendance problems by giving you repeated warnings, but you have been uncooperative. Since progressive discipline has failed, we have no other alternative but to terminate your employment.  The effective date of your discharge is Thursday, January 21, year 5.


  /s/  Moses Abraham
       Superintendent
       Assistant Director for Building Services
                    14

*JOINT EXHIBIT NO. 5*

December 18, year 4

Sam Green
Physical Plant
Central State University

Subject: Disciplinary Suspension

Mr. Green:

You are being given a written reprimand and three-day disciplinary suspension without pay for failure to report to work as directed by me on December 9, year 4. You were given a verbal warning on February 26, year 4, for failure to report to work.

When you phoned me on December 9, you stated your attorney required you to be in Texas by 9 a.m., December 10, and you would not be in for work. Due to your many absences, I instructed you to report for the first four hours of your shift, but would allow you the last four hours as vacation time. This would allow you to leave work at 8:30 p.m. You agreed this arrangement would work out to accommodate your needs. A few minutes later you phoned the Physical Plant switchboard and told the operator you would not be in at all this day.

We held an investigative meeting on December 14, year 4, with you, the Union President, your supervisor, and myself present. At that time, you did not give any reason to justify your changing our arrangement and in fact expressed no remorse over your behavior.

Because of your insubordination and continued absenteeism you will be suspended without pay on Thursday, December 10, Friday, December 11, and Monday, December 14.

Should we continue to experience problems with your attendance, further disciplinary action may be taken, including possible discharge. Should you have questions, feel free to contact me.

/s/ Moses Abraham
Assistant Director for
Building Services

## *JOINT EXHIBIT NO. 6*

(Handwritten)

2/26/04

Mr. Sam Green
Custodian
Physical Plant Department
Central State University

Subject:  Verbal Warning

Dear Mr. Green:

You are hereby given a verbal warning for not reporting your absence from work on February 25, year 4.  If this behavior continues, further disciplinary action will be taken.  It is your responsibility to report to work at your prescribed time.  This verbal is being given to you on the above date, before your Union Steward, your supervisor, and myself.


                                    /s/ Moses Abraham

## *JOINT EXHIBIT NO. 7*

### Absence Record - Sam Green
(vacation and holidays not shown)

Year 3

| | |
|---|---|
| June | 16, 17, 18, 19, 20 - sick |
| July | 11 - sick |
| July | 20 - personal |
| August | 13, 14, 15, 16 - sick |
| August | 19, 20, 21, 22, 23 - sick |
| October | 3 - personal |
| October | 23 - 2 1/2 hours lost time |
| October | 24 - 1 hour lost time |
| November | 11, 12, 13, 14 - sick |

Year 4

| | |
|---|---|
| January | 26 - 4 hours sick |
| January | 27 - sick |
| February | 19 - 4 hours personal |
| February | 20 - personal |
| February | 25 - 2 hours lost time |
| February | 26 - disciplinary verbal warning |
| April | 6 - sick |
| April | 15 - 1 hour lost time |
| May | 20, 21 - sick |
| May | 28, 29 - sick |
| June | 1 - 4 hours lost time |
| June | 2, 3, 4, 5 - lost time |
| June | 10, 11, 12 - lost time |
| June | 15 thru 17 - sick |
| July | 24 - sick |
| July | 31 - personal |
| August | 12 - lost time |
| August | 13 - sick |
| August | 14 - 2 hours sick, 6 hours lost time |
| September | 15 - personal |
| September | 25 - 2 hours personal |
| October | 23 - 6 hours personal, 2 hours lost time |
| November | 16, 17, 18 - sick |
| November | 19 - 4 hours sick |
| December | 9, 10, 11 - lost time |
| December | 14 - lost time |
| December | 18, 21 & 22 - disciplinary suspension and final warning |

Year 5

| | |
|---|---|
| January | 19, 20 - lost time |
| January | 21 thru 27 - disciplinary suspension |
| January | 28 - DISCHARGED |

*JOINT EXHIBIT NO. 8*

COLLECTIVE BARGAINING AGREEMENT

BETWEEN

CUSTODIAL AND SERVICES UNION NO. 1

AND

CENTRAL STATE UNIVERSITY

OKLAHOMA (1/1/04-1/1/07)

. . .

## Article X - DISCHARGES

1. No employee shall be discharged except for just cause, and whenever an employee is discharged the Company shall give written notice to the Union within one (1) work day giving the reason for such discharge.

2. Whenever the Union desires to question the discharge of an employee other than a probationary employee, the same shall be taken up as a grievance written three (3) work days of such discharge.

. . .

## Article XI - STATUTORY CLAIMS

Statutory claims of employees arising out of their employment shall be subject to the grievance/arbitration procedure.

# Home Health Center

### Table of Contents

**Table of Contents contd.**

**NOTES**

# A. Caption

IN THE MATTER IN ARBITRATION BETWEEN

| | | |
|---|---|---|
| HOME HEALTH CENTER CASEY, PENNSYLVANIA | ) ) ) | |
| AND | ) ) | RE: MAY BRADY DEE MILLS Discharges for Absenteeism |
| UNIVERSAL UNION OF SERVICE WORKERS, LOCAL 22 | ) ) ) ) | |

Appearances:

For the Company: Roberto Sanchez

For the Union: Mel Golden

Date: October 11, year 4

Place: Casey, Pennsylvania

# B. Examination of Company Witnesses

## 1. Greta Nice, Director, Nursing Services

### a. Direct Examination by Company Advocate

*Mr. Sanchez:*

**Q:** Would you state your full name, please, for the record?

**A:** Greta Nice.

**Q:** What is your job, Ms. Nice?

**A:** I am Director of Nursing Services, Home Health Center.

**Q:** How long have you been Director?

**A:** Since the 1st of September, year 3.

**Q:** Who was your predecessor?

**A:** Nita Thomas.

**Q:** What are the responsibilities and duties of the Director of Nursing Services?

**A:** I coordinate all nursing services for patient care.

**Q:** Okay. How many nurses and aides do you have on your staff?

**A:** Let me think here a minute.

**Q:** That is, an approximation.

**A:** Probably about 35.

**Q:** Do you do the hiring of new personnel for your staff?

**A:** Yes.

**Q:** Do you also handle discipline and discharge of staff members?

**A:** Yes, I do.

**Q:** What has been your employment history? At what point in time were you first hired at Home Health Center?

**A:** July 9th, year 3, as the Assistant Director.

**Q:** Had you been a nurse elsewhere prior to coming to Home Health?

**A:** Yes.

**Q:** Where was that?

**A:** Pennsylvania University Hospitals.

**Q:** How long had you been employed there?

**A:** About four and a half years.

**Q:** Are you familiar with May Brady and Dee Mills?

**A:** Yes, I am.

**Q:** Were they members of your staff?

**A:** Yes, they were.

**Q:** What was their job?

**A:** They were nursing attendants.

**Q:** Both of them were?

**A:** Yes.

**Q:** Were they on the staff at the time you were hired at Home Health Center?

**A:** Yes, they were.

**Q:** Were you also responsible for scheduling of employees?

**A:** Yes, I was.

**Q:** You sat down and worked up what work schedules would be utilized, is that correct?

**A:** Yes.

**Q:** Was absenteeism a problem at Home Health Center?

**A:** Yes, it was.

**Q:** Was it a topic of discussion with you and your employees and also with your boss?

**A:** Yes.

**Q:** What efforts were undertaken by the management at the Center with respect to this absenteeism problem?

**A:** Okay. We made a guideline pamphlet as to things that we expected of people—that is, absenteeism, time policies, any of our policies, unexcused absences—and what would be done about them. We also met with the aides. I and my assistant met with the attendants around the first week or the second week in September.

**Q:** Of what year?

**A:** Year 3. And we talked with them about absenteeism and the scheduling and these types of things, and then after the meeting I did talk with several of the people that had— if they had three write-ups, they were subject to dismissal, so those people that had one or two write-ups, I counseled.

**Q:** So the first step of your policy, then, was to communicate it to the employees, is that right?

**A:** Yes.

**Q:** Were employees receptive to your discussion about the problems?

**A:** I felt they were.

**Q:** Handing you relevant parts of the guideline pamphlet marked as Company

Exhibit 1, would you take a moment to look at that and then identify it for the record, please?

(Witness examines pamphlet.)

**Q:** Now, did you help to put together this particular pamphlet?

**A:** Yes, I did.

**Q:** What was the purpose of putting this together?

**A:** I was striving for a bit more organization and for everybody to realize what the policies were so everybody would have the same policies in mind.

**Q:** Okay. Was this distributed to employees?

**A:** Yes, it was.

**Q:** To every employee?

**A:** Yes.

**Q:** How was it distributed?

**A:** It was distributed when they received their paychecks and there were also some left at each nursing station.

**Q:** Okay. You indicate that it was distributed with paychecks. What would—what month—if you remember, what month was it distributed?

**A:** It was distributed in September.

**Q:** Okay. Do you remember the exact date or not?

**A:** I don't remember the exact date, but it was shortly after I took over on the first of September, so it was probably toward the end of September.

**Q:** Okay.

**A:** The last week.

**Q:** Looking at Company Exhibit 1, are there provisions dealing with absenteeism?

**A:** Yes, there are.

**Q:** What ones do you feel deal with absenteeism?

**A:** Numbers 6 and 16.

**Q:** You indicate that this pamphlet was distributed to employees and was posted.

**A:** Yes, there were several copies, ten or twenty, in each unit.

**Q:** Was this Company Exhibit 1 distributed before or after you indicated that you began having meetings with individual employees?

**A:** This was after.

**Q:** This was after. Okay. Now, turning our thoughts to the meeting with employees, did you meet with each employee during the month of September?

**A:** No, not separately.

**Q:** Okay. Did you meet with all the employees collectively?

**A:** I met with the attendants at a meeting and the nurses at a meeting.

**Q:** Okay. Was absenteeism the topic of your meeting with the attendants?

**A:** Yes. As I said, following one of the meetings I had a list of those people that had one or two write-ups, and I talked with them at that time and reminded them that they had one or two write-ups.

**Q:** Did you specifically notify the attendants at these individual meetings that a third absenteeism without authorization was grounds for discharge?

**A:** Yes.

**Q:** You specifically told them that?

**A:** Those that I talked to, yes.

**Q:** Okay. Do you remember if you also said that at the group meeting?

**A:** I can't recall.

**Q:** Turning your attention now to the events beginning on Monday, October 1, could you recount for the Arbitrator to the best of your memory any conversation that you had either with Ms. Brady or Ms. Mills with respect to their leaving their jobs?

**A:** Ms. Brady and Ms. Mills both came into my office in the morning after Ms. Brady had received word that her brother had died, and Ms. Brady said she wanted permission to leave to go to the funeral. Dee Mills was going to go with her.

**Q:** Are Ms. Brady and Ms. Mills related?

**A:** Not to my knowledge.

**Q:** Okay.

**A:** And I did grant them permission to go to the funeral.

**Q:** What time of day was this?

**A:** This was in the morning.

**Q:** What shift do Ms. Mills and Ms. Brady work?

**A:** 7 a.m. to 3:30 p.m.

**Q:** Okay. When you granted them permission to go, did you indicate how long they were granted permission to leave?

**A:** I asked that when they got there that they should call me.

**Q:** Okay. When they got "there," where does that refer to?

**A:** I believe they were going to West Virginia.

**Q:** The state of West Virginia?

**A:** Yes.

**Q:** Do you specifically recall directing Ms. Mills or Ms. Brady to call when they got there?

**A:** I asked that someone call when they got there.

**Q:** Did you tell them why you wanted them to call?

**A:** To let us know what the situation was and when they would be back.

**Q:** Now, was that on Monday, October 1?

**A:** Yes.

**Q:** What was your next conversation with either Ms. Brady or Ms. Mills?

**A:** It was on Friday of that week.

**Q:** And that is October 5?

**A:** Yes. Ms. Brady called me.

**Q:** Were you here at work?

**A:** Yes, I was.

**Q:** What time of day was that call received?

**A:** It was around noon.

**Q:** Okay. What did Ms. Brady say to you during that conversation, to the best of your memory?

**A:** That the funeral was that day.

**Q:** Friday?

**A:** Yes, and that they would be back sometime Sunday. She did not indicate a time.

**Q:** The immediately following Sunday?

**A:** Yes.

**Q:** Two days rather than nine days away?

**A:** Yes.

**Q:** Do you distinctly remember her telling you that?

**A:** Yes, I do.

**Q:** Did you talk to Ms. Mills at the same time?

**A:** No, I didn't.

**Q:** Did you understand Ms. Brady to be speaking for both herself and Ms. Mills?

**A:** Yes, I did.

**Q:** Okay. Do you recall any other topics of that particular conversation?

**A:** Yes, they gave me a telephone number, or Ms. Brady gave me a telephone number, to give to Kate Care to call them in regard to Kate picking up their paychecks.

**Q:** Friday morning or October 5th, the date that you are having this conversation, is that normally payday here at Home Health?

**A:** It was payday, yes.

**Q:** Did Ms. Brady say anything to you during that conversation that would lead you to believe that they couldn't return without their paychecks?

**A:** No.

**Q:** Was there anything else discussed that you can recall during that telephone conversation on Friday, October 5th?

**A:** No.

**Q:** Do you remember where you were when you took the telephone call?

**A:** Yes, I was at the front office.

**Q:** Okay. After concluding that telephone conversation, did you in fact get in touch with Kate Care?

**A:** Yes, I did.

**Q:** What did you tell her?

**A:** I gave her the number that she was to call.

**Q:** Okay. Again, what was your understanding as to Ms. Care's duties or responsibilities?

**A:** That she was going to pick up their paychecks.

**Q:** Okay. In fact, do you know if the checks of Ms. Brady and Ms. Mills were delivered to Kate Care on Friday, October 5th?

**A:** I don't know that, no.

**Q:** Do you know whether Ms. Brady and Ms. Mills knew when they were next scheduled to return to work?

**A:** We were running on a master work schedule at that time.

**Q:** Okay.

**A:** And that is posted and we use the same one all the time. Like every four weeks we just repeat it.

**Q:** So they could compute when they were scheduled to work and when they were scheduled to be off?

**A:** Yes.

**Q:** Handing you what has been marked as Company Exhibit 2, will you look at that and identify it for the record, please?

**A:** This is the work schedule of Ms. Mills and Ms. Brady, October 1 through October 11.

**Q:** Just to put it in a frame of reference, October 1 was a Monday?

**A:** Yes.

**Q:** So October 8 was also a Monday, right?

**A:** Yes.

**Q:** Now, is this one part of the master work schedule that you have referred to?

**A:** Yes.

**Q:** And that pattern just repeats and repeats, is that correct?

**A:** It's a four-week pattern. This is not the entire year.

**Q:** You received the phone call from Ms. Brady on October 5th, according to your testimony.

**A:** Yes.

**Q:** You were told that they would return to Casey on Sunday, October 7th?

**A:** Yes.

**Q:** Were both Ms. Brady and Ms. Mills scheduled for work on Monday, October 8th?

**A:** Yes, they were.

**Q:** Were both scheduled for work on Tuesday, October 9th?

**A:** No, just Ms. Mills.

**Q:** Ms. Mills was. How about Wednesday, October 10th?

**A:** They were both scheduled.

**Q:** And Thursday, October 11th?

**A:** Both of them.

**Q:** Were scheduled?

**A:** Yes.

**Q:** After receiving the telephone call on Friday, October 5th, did either Ms. Mills or Ms. Brady appear for work on Monday, October 8th?

**A:** No, they did not.

**Q:** Did you receive a telephone call from either of them on Monday, October 8th?

**A:** No, I did not.

**Q:** You didn't hear anything?

**A:** No.

**Q:** How about Tuesday, October 9th?

**A:** Nothing.

**Q:** How about Wednesday, October 10th?

**A:** No.

**Q:** How about Thursday, October 11th?

**A:** Yes, I did. Ms. Mills called me.

**Q:** Ms. Mills called you?

**A:** Ms. Mills called me, yes.

**Q:** What time of day did you receive a call from Ms. Mills?

**A:** I believe it was around 11 a.m.

**Q:** What time were they scheduled to report to work?

**A:** 7 a.m.

**Q:** So on the morning of Thursday, October 11th, they didn't report to work?

**A:** No.

**Q:** And at the time they were scheduled to report to work you had not yet received a phone call with respect to their whereabouts?

**A:** That's correct.

**Q:** What was the status of the work staff during these particular days, Monday through Thursday, October 8 through the 11th?

**A:** Very poor.

**Q:** When you say "very poor," in what way?

**A:** Well, we usually carry approximately fourteen attendants, twelve to fourteen attendants on a day shift.

**Q:** On the day shift?

**A:** Yes, and we were running at approximately seven.

**Q:** Why were you so low? Do you recall?

**A:** There was illness at the time and we were hiring at the time.

**Q:** What was the attitude of the seven employees who were trying to cover the work of fourteen?

**A:** Very put upon. Very upset.

**Q:** Were they aware of the actions of Ms. Brady and Ms. Mills?

**A:** Very much so.

**Q:** Did they know why they were gone?

**A:** Yes, they did.

**Q:** Were there any comments made to you about their absence?

**A:** Yes, they questioned why they were gone so long, especially to a funeral, and they seemed to know that Ms. Mills was not related to the deceased and they were just very upset that they were so shorthanded.

**Q:** Did you have to go out and hire temporary help during this time?

**A:** Yes, I did. I used temporary help from Medtemp and my assistant worked on the floor and a woman from the laundry came up and worked on the floor.

**Q:** What action was taken when you received the phone call from Ms. Mills on Thursday, October 11th?

**A:** Okay. Thursday, October 11th, I felt that there was more than adequate unexcused absence for them. The morale just was getting very bad since they had been gone so long. I had not heard from them, so as much as I hated to do it, I did write them a letter at that time telling them that they were terminated. When Ms. Mills called, I expressed to her this fact.

**Q:** Okay. Did you write that termination letter, then, before Ms. Mills called on Thursday, October 11th?

**A:** Probably about an hour before she called, yes.

**Q:** So you wrote it after you found out that neither of them reported to work at 7 a.m. on Thursday?

**A:** That's correct.

**Q:** Had there, in fact, been at least three separate unexcused absences before you wrote that letter?

**A:** Yes.

**Q:** Looking at that schedule, recount again the days of unexcused absences.

**A:** Okay. Ms. Mills would have been out Monday, Tuesday, Wednesday, and Thursday.

**Q:** So that is four days for her, is that correct?

**A:** Yes, sir, and Ms. Brady was out Monday and Wednesday and Thursday.

**Q:** Do you regard the preceding week, the week of October 8th, as being excused absences?

**A:** I did, yes.

**Q:** After you issued the termination letter, did either employee or any Union representative request an immediate hearing of any kind with you?

**A:** No.

**Q:** Was the next thing that you received an employee grievance?

**A:** Yes.

**Q:** With respect to prior work records of the two subject employees, had there been an absentee problem with either employee?

**A:** Ms. Brady.

**Q:** Does Home Health Center maintain individual files on each employee?

**A:** Yes, we do.

**Q:** What kind of paperwork goes into those files?

**A:** Any disciplinary type of write-up that would occur, a physical history, an application, any doctor's excuses that are

brought in, any kind of correspondence that goes on with that member at all.

**Q:** And is it the normal procedure to keep such records in the personnel files?

**A:** Yes.

**Q:** Ms. Nice, you have been handed Company Exhibits 3 through 13. Could you take a moment to review those and then identify them for the record? You might identify them individually and state, if you can, whether or not they are copies of records taken from the personnel file of Ms. Brady. Now, do these records contain previous write-ups for absentee problems with respect to Ms. Brady?

**A:** Yes, they do.

**Q:** Do the records show that Ms. Brady had been warned about her continuing absentee problem?

**A:** Yes.

**Q:** Do the records that I have handed you contain the write-ups that you prepared with respect to the three days of absence, namely, October 8, 10, and 11?

**A:** Yes, they do.

**Q:** Did you prepare those particular write-ups? Those last three?

**A:** Yes, I did.

**Q:** Now, with respect to the decision to discharge Ms. Brady, did you make that decision?

**A:** Yes, sir, I did.

**Q:** Did you consult with anybody before you made it?

**A:** I spoke with my administrator.

**Q:** Who was that?

**A:** Mr. Ed Toll.

**Q:** Okay. Did you need to get authorization from him before you undertook the action to discharge Ms. Brady?

**A:** On most discharges I consult with him.

**Q:** Did you recommend discharge?

**A:** Yes.

**Q:** Did Mr. Toll agree?

**A:** Yes, he did.

**Q:** Do you recall whether you met individually with Ms. Mills during the month of September, year 3, to discuss the absenteeism problem?

**A:** I don't believe I did.

**Q:** Okay. But you did meet with her as part of a group to the best of your memory?

**A:** Yes.

**Q:** Ms. Nice, I am handing you what has been marked for identification Company Exhibits 14 through 17. Would you take a moment and identify those for the record, please?

**A:** These are the unexcused absence reports for Ms. Dee Mills.

**Q:** Who prepared those reports?

**A:** I did.

**Q:** And for what dates did you prepare them?

**A:** For October 8, 9, 10, and 11 of year 3.

**Q:** No further questions.

### b. Cross-Examination by Union Advocate

*Mr. Golden:*
[to be supplied by student]

## 2. Edwin Toll, Acting Administrator

### a. Direct Examination by Company Advocate

*Mr. Sanchez:*

**Q:** Would you state your full name for the record, please?

**A:** Edwin Toll.

**Q:** And what is your present employment?

**A:** I am Acting Administrator for Home Health Center.

**Q:** Will you recount, if you would please, what your tenure is at Home Health Center? When were you first hired by Home Health and how long have you served in that capacity?

**A:** I was hired by Home Health Centers on February the 8th, year 1, as Assistant Administrator for a 315-bed nursing home in Patterson, Virginia. I stayed at Patterson until March the 19th of year 3, at which time I was transferred to Casey, Pennsylvania, to try to straighten out the problems that we had here.

**Q:** Okay. From March year 3 until what date were you the full-time Acting Administrator at the facility here in Casey, Pennsylvania?

**A:** Well, as of the 16th of January, year 4, is when I terminated my employment.

**Q:** Okay. You were the only administrator during the months of September and October, year 3?

**A:** Yes, I was.

**Q:** You were the only administrator at this facility during that period of time?

**A:** Yes, I was.

**Q:** Okay. Now, when you came to Home Health Center in March of year 3, do you happen to know offhand how long this facility had been open?

**A:** Approximately two and a half years.

**Q:** And were there difficulties here?

**A:** Very much so.

**Q:** Recount the difficulties, if you would.

**A:** Well, in December of year 2, Home Health Center was informed by the state that they were considering closing this home because of poor patient care and complete lack of cooperation. At that time, Mr. Long, who was the vice president for the Company, talked to me about coming to Casey, and I told him that I would come.

**Q:** Is Home Health Center a corporate entity which encompasses lots of individual facilities?

**A:** Yes, we have twenty nursing homes and also an accounting service that acts for 4,000 nursing home beds, so we are quite large in the industry.

**Q:** Okay. Upon your arriving here in Casey, did you assess that it was a problem, or—I'm sorry—that absenteeism was a problem?

**A:** We—yes, this was a great problem here, and Mr. Long briefed me on productivity before I came to work here. He showed me records which showed that for the last several months people were only showing up half the time. There was 50 percent attendance. I was sitting there looking at those figures and I assessed that this was the greatest problem for patient care. You can't take care of anybody if there is nobody here. At the time I came we had approximately 140 patients. From my observation the staff was very poor throughout the nursing home. That includes supervisors along with the aides and the housekeepers and the kitchen personnel.

**Q:** Was there a substantial turnover of personnel—management personnel?

**A:** Yes, there was. I believe this home was under four or five other managers before I came here and I think this contributed to some of the problems, because they couldn't get any continuity.

**Q:** What were some of the measures that you took to deal with this problem of absenteeism?

**A:** Well, first of all I met with Union representatives and we discussed absenteeism and they—Mr. Call—fully recognized that this was a tremendous problem. Now, it was not so much a problem on our 3 p.m. to 11 p.m. or 11 p.m. to 7 a.m. shifts. It was basically that the day shift personnel came and went as they pleased.

**Q:** Approximately what point in time did you meet with Mr. Call?

**A:** I believe it was two days after I arrived, so it was the week of the 19th. Probably the 21st was our first meeting with Mr. Long. We all went to lunch. We discussed problems in the office and then had lunch afterwards.

**Q:** This is in March of year 3?

**A:** Right.

**Q:** During that meeting did Mr. Call understand that absenteeism was a problem?

**A:** Yes, he was very much aware that absenteeism was a problem at this facility and he was also aware that our day shift was giving us the most problems.

**Q:** Was there any conclusion reached from that meeting?

**A:** Well, basically, he said the Union contract says write them up, so write them up and terminate accordingly.

**Q:** Was it necessary to terminate any employees for absenteeism then, beginning with, let's say, early April up through September, year 3?

**A:** I believe since July we have terminated approximately 30 persons from the staff and I would say about ten of the terminations would be for absenteeism—not calling the office and getting excused. Most of those terminated were aides.

**Q:** Okay. Do you believe then that most of the employees here at Home Health were aware of the fact that the Company was dealing with this absentee problem?

**A:** Yes. I do. They were very well aware of what we were doing and how we were going about it.

**Q:** How did they find out?

**A:** Well, we started pulling time cards. We fired one worker because she had another person punch in for her and she was late—came in the building two hours late, failed to notify a supervisor, and we asked her about it. She said she just forgot. You know, she just forgot to take the time out to get her time card signed. This was my first case. I think this was about four days after I got here, but there were people punching for other people coming in late and we started keeping some tally sheets.

**Q:** Did you ever have communications with employees that would reveal to them the fact that the Company was, in fact, going to begin cracking down on absenteeism?

**A:** Yes, I had meetings the second week in every department.

**Q:** But you did have meetings with the aides, for example?

**A:** Yes, we did.

**Q:** Was one of the topics of discussion at that meeting the absentee problem?

**A:** Yes, it was.

**Q:** Okay. There had been some testimony here that there was a change in policy with respect to the issuance of checks during the weeks of October. Do you have any recollection as to what that was? Was there a change?

**A:** When I came up here the Company policy was to give out checks between the hours of 12 noon and 5 p.m. on Friday afternoon.

**Q:** Every Friday?

**A:** Every other Friday. After I came here I decided that the checks, which were received on Thursday, would be disbursed on Thursday.

**Q:** Where do you receive the checks from?

**A:** From our central office. They print all the checks and mail them to us. Prior to the first week in September I was notified by our comptroller, Mr. Ward, that I was breaking Company policy by handing out the checks ahead of time, because they were being cashed. We were supposed to hold them so they would not be cashed until Friday at 2:00, but they were being cashed immediately and going through the bank. I was told to cease this operation. The week of October 1st I posted a bulletin stating that checks would be handed out Friday according to Company policy.

**Q:** So to the best of your knowledge, the week of October 1, checks were not disbursed until Friday the 5th?

**A:** That's correct.

**Q:** Okay. Now, do you have any knowledge as to how the checks of Ms. Brady and Ms. Mills were handled on Friday, October 5th?

**A:** My secretary gave them to Ms. Care at 12 noon. I know that because she signed a register at 12 noon when she picked them up. She picked up all three checks and signed for each of them.

**Q:** Okay. Do you know what Ms. Care did with the checks of Ms. Brady and Ms. Mills?

**A:** I talked with Ms. Care afterwards, about a week after the incident. I asked her exactly what the problem was with the checks. She said to me that first of all she went down to the bank and tried to have them cashed.

**Q:** You are talking about here in Casey?

**A:** Right. She went downtown to Pennsylvania Federal.

**Q:** You are recounting what Ms. Care told you that she did with the checks after she received them on October 5th?

**A:** Right. After I received the grievances. She tried to get them cashed at the bank, but the bank would not cash them because she didn't have sufficient funds to cover them in case they bounced.

**Q:** You mean she was trying to cash Ms. Brady's and Ms. Mills' checks?

**A:** Right.

**Q:** How could she do that?

**A:** I don't know.

**Q:** She tried to cash them, though?

**A:** Right.

**Q:** What else did she tell you with respect to the checks?

**A:** She tried to get a money order for the checks at the post office and they wouldn't accept them, either, and it worked out where she just mailed them, from what she told me. She mailed them Saturday, at 5 p.m.

**Q:** That was on Saturday, October 6th?

**A:** Right.

**Q:** Did you personally have any conversation with either Ms. Brady or Ms. Mills anytime between Monday, October 1, and Thursday, October 11?

**A:** None whatsoever.

**Q:** Okay. So any conversation that either employee had with management personnel at the Home was with Ms. Nice?

**A:** Right.

**Q:** Did you have any contact with either of the grievants on Thursday or Friday, the 11th or 12th?

**A:** I had no contact with them. Mr. Call did phone and he asked me about the discharges. I told Mr. Call that they were discharged in accordance with our policies. They had not shown up. He was notified that week how short we were because I phoned him myself, because we had four or five people sick. Another aide, Charles Less, went with these two ladies to West Virginia for the ten-day stay.

**Q:** Was Mr. Less related to the deceased?

**A:** I believe he is a brother, too. I mean a brother or brother-in-law.

**Q:** So three of your aides were down in West Virginia attending the funeral?

**A:** Yes, they were. I also sent a letter to the aide in question asking him when he would be back, because he failed to notify us when he would be back to work. It was just like it was an open leave of absence and we can't grant that.

**Q:** When was the first contact you had with respect to the discharges? The first contact you had with the employees or their representative was on what?

**A:** On October 11th Mr. Call saw me in the afternoon.

**Q:** The same day that the employees were discharged?

**A:** Yes.

**Q:** Did he indicate at that time that he would file a grievance or that grievances would be filed?

**A:** No, he just said "Thank you very much" after I told him about the terminations, and that was the end of our conversation.

**Q:** That was to get information, right?

**A:** Right.

**Q:** What did you tell him was the reason for the discharges?

**A:** Because of unexcused absenteeism. I also noted that Ms. Brady had a record. It was not just this offense.

**Q:** Thank you.

### b. Cross-Examination by Union Advocate

*Mr. Golden:*
[to be supplied by student]

# C. Examination of Union Witnesses

## 1. May Brady, Grievant

### a. Direct Examination by Union Advocate

*Mr. Golden:*

**Q:** State your name and address, please.

**A:** May Brady, 208 Maryland Drive.

**Q:** Where were you employed prior to October the 11th, year 3?

**A:** Home Health Center.

**Q:** What was your classification?

**A:** Nursing Assistant.

**Q:** How long had you been employed?

**A:** Since April the 7th, year 2.

**Q:** During that period of time, from April of year 2 until October 11, year 3, had you ever been suspended by the Company for any period of time?

**A:** No, I hadn't.

**Q:** Had you ever filed a grievance?

**A:** No.

**Q:** All right. Now, on October the 1st, year 3, would you tell the Arbitrator what happened on that morning when you reported for work?

**A:** On October the 1st, year 3, I received a long-distance phone call from my sister in Morton, West Virginia. It was about 7:15 or 7:30 in the morning.

**Q:** What was the call about?

**A:** The call was about my brother, who passed away early that morning.

**Q:** Who was the charge nurse on duty?

**A:** Ms. Peek was the charge nurse on duty that morning.

**Q:** Did you talk to her about the phone call?

**A:** Not really, because I didn't completely, you know, finish taking the message. Ms. Care took the phone and she told Ms. Peek what was happening. Ms. Peek suggested that I leave that morning. Ms. Mills and Ms. Care took me home.

**Q:** All right. Now is Ms. Mills also a grievant in this case?

**A:** Yes, she is.

**Q:** Is Ms. Mills in any way related to you?

**A:** Yes, she is my niece by marriage.

**Q:** Is Ms. Care related to you?

**A:** No, she is not.

**Q:** So Ms. Care and Ms. Mills took you home on the morning of October 1st?

**A:** Yes.

**Q:** Did you subsequently return to the nursing home?

**A:** Yes, I did.

**Q:** What time?

**A:** About 8:30 that morning Ms. Mills and I returned to the nursing home. We went into Ms. Nice's office.

**Q:** Is Ms. Nice the one who testified?

**A:** Right. I explained to her that my brother died and that I would like permission for Ms.

Mills and me to leave and she granted us the leave. I also explained to her—she asked if we knew when the funeral was going to be. I told her no, but I would let her know when I found out the date of the funeral. I also told her that we would have to have our checks to get back to Casey.

Q:  How did you get to West Virginia?

A:  I borrowed the money from Ms. Care.

Q:  By what method of transportation did you get there?

A:  We went down by bus.

Q:  Both you and Ms. Mills?

A:  Yes.

Q:  So now you told Ms. Nice what you have just related?

A:  Yes.

Q:  And what did she tell you with respect to your need for money?

A:  She said okay, and then I asked how would we go about Ms. Care getting the checks and sending them to us, and then Ms. McDoe came into the office.

Q:  Who is Ms. McDoe?

A:  Mr. Toll's secretary. Ms. Nice asked Ms. McDoe, and Ms. McDoe suggested that we go to the front office and sign our names and write out a statement saying that it would be okay if Ms. Care picked our checks up and signed the register so she could mail them to us.

Q:  Did you do that?

A:  Yes, we did.

Q:  Who prepared the form for you?

A:  Sue Broskowski. She is the receptionist.

Q:  Is she also the person who normally hands out paychecks?

A:  Yes.

Q:  What was your understanding on the 1st of October about when checks were to be distributed?

A:  They were to be distributed on Thursday, as they always have been, except if Mr. Toll decided at the last minute that he didn't want to give them out on Thursday. Then he would give them out on Friday. But normally he would pass them out on Thursday.

Q:  You were in the hearing room when Mr. Toll testified, were you not?

A:  Yes, I was.

Q:  You heard him testify about posting a bulletin stating that on the week of October

1st checks would be handed out on that Friday? You heard him testify to that?

A:  Yes, I did.

Q:  Now, was that bulletin posted to your knowledge at the time you talked to Ms. Nice about 8:30 or 8:40 or whenever it was the morning of October 1st?

A:  No.

Q:  Did Ms. Broskowski or Ms. McDoe or Ms. Nice tell you the checks would be handed out on Thursday or Friday or did they say anything about that?

A:  They didn't say.

Q:  I don't recall—did you tell Ms. Nice how you were going to get money to go down to West Virginia?

A:  No.

Q:  Now, after you prepared the forms that you got from Ms. Broskowski, what did you do next?

A:  I talked to Ms. Care and told her that it was okay, that we had signed the forms and that it would be okay if she picked the checks up.

Q:  Was Ms. Care working at the time?

A:  Yes, she had gone back to work.

Q:  She was working here at the nursing home?

A:  Right.

Q:  Then what did you do after your talk with Ms. Care?

A:  We then left the building and went home and proceeded to pack.

Q:  Okay. Now, prior to leaving the building, did you have any other talk with Ms. Nice other than the one that you have testified to?

A:  No.

Q:  You say you traveled by bus to Morton, West Virginia?

A:  Yes.

Q:  How did you get the fare now, both of you?

A:  Well, Dee borrowed the fare from her sister's boyfriend.

Q:  Do you know that of your own personal knowledge?

A:  Right. I borrowed the money from Ms. Care.

Q:  What time did the bus leave for Morton?

A:  6:20 p.m.

Q:  On the 1st of October?

A:  Yes.

**Q:** At the time you left for Morton on Monday, did you give the nursing home a telephone number where you could be reached?

**A:** No, I didn't.

**Q:** Where were you going to stay in Morton?

**A:** With my mother, and she doesn't have a phone.

**Q:** All right. When did the bus bring you to Morton?

**A:** We got in about 10 or 10:30 a.m., Tuesday morning.

**Q:** Where did you go from the bus station?

**A:** We went directly to my mother's home.

**Q:** Did both you and Ms. Mills stay at your mother's?

**A:** Yes.

**Q:** At the time you arrived on Tuesday morning, had funeral arrangements been made?

**A:** No, they hadn't.

**Q:** When were funeral arrangements decided upon?

**A:** It was decided upon late Wednesday night that they were going to prepare the body and bring the body home that Thursday and the burial would be Friday.

**Q:** That would be October the 5th?

**A:** Right.

**Q:** When did you call the nursing home to tell them about the funeral?

**A:** I called—as a matter of fact, I called that Friday, twice. The first time I called, I called to speak to Ms. Care to see if she had sent the checks out. Ms. Care wasn't there. The next time I called, I called Ms. Nice. First I talked to Melody Tunne.

**Q:** Who is Melody Tunne?

**A:** She's part-time receptionist.

**Q:** Do you recall the time of the day?

**A:** It was early in the morning. It was before 11 a.m., I think, or around 11.

**Q:** Did you have any conversation with Melody?

**A:** Yes. I asked Melody if Ms. Care had picked the checks up on that Thursday. She stated no, that Mr. Toll had decided that he wasn't going to release the checks until Friday at 12 noon. Then I asked her if Ms. Nice was in the building and she said yes, so I asked if I could speak with Ms. Nice.

**Q:** And you did speak to her?

**A:** Yes, I did.

**Q:** And you recognized that it was Ms. Nice to whom you were speaking?

**A:** Yes.

**Q:** And what did you say to Ms. Nice? And what did she say to you?

**A:** I told Ms. Nice that my brother's funeral was that evening. I also told her that I was waiting for Ms. Care to send the money so we could return back to Casey, and she stated that I said that we would be back Monday, which I didn't, because I didn't know if Ms. Care had gotten the checks. I didn't know when the checks were going to be arriving.

**Q:** Did you tell Ms. Nice on Friday, the 5th of October, that you would be back in Casey on Sunday?

**A:** No.

**Q:** You told Ms. Nice that you were waiting for the money to be sent by Ms. Care, is that correct?

**A:** Right.

**Q:** What did she say?

**A:** She said okay, and she would see us when we got back.

**Q:** Did she say anything to you about not having been called prior to Friday morning?

**A:** No, she didn't.

**Q:** Did you give her a telephone number to give to Ms. Care?

**A:** Yes, I did.

**Q:** Whose telephone number was that?

**A:** That was my aunt's.

**Q:** Where is her home in relation to where you were staying?

**A:** It was not too far from where I was staying. Well within walking distance.

**Q:** Your mother didn't have a telephone?

**A:** No.

**Q:** After you talked to Ms. Nice at about 11 in the morning on Friday, October 5th, did you at any time on that day talk to Ms. Care?

**A:** No, I didn't. I tried to reach Ms. Care and she wasn't home.

**Q:** Where did you call her?

**A:** At her home.

**Q:** How many times did you call, if you can remember?

**A:** Two, maybe three, maybe four.

**Q:** Did Ms. Care call Morton on the day of October the 5th?

**A:** Yes, she called.

**Q:** Were you home?

**A:** No, I wasn't there. She left a message that she was unable to get the checks cashed. Western Union would not cash the checks so she could wire the money, so she had to wait until Saturday and mail them special delivery.

**Q:** With whom did Ms. Care leave this message?

**A:** With my aunt.

**Q:** Whose name is what?

**A:** Lillie Parks.

**Q:** Lillie Parks?

**A:** Uh-huh.

**Q:** Did you talk to Ms. Care on Saturday, the 6th?

**A:** No, I didn't.

**Q:** Did you ever talk to Ms. Care from West Virginia?

**A:** No, I wasn't able to get in contact with her, but my brother did.

**Q:** Your brother is who?

**A:** Mr. Charles Less.

**Q:** Charles is employed at the nursing home as an aide?

**A:** Yes.

**Q:** He was with you in Morton for the funeral?

**A:** Yes.

**Q:** Do you know if Ms. Mills talked with Ms. Care from West Virginia?

**A:** No, she didn't.

**Q:** Ms. Brady, I will hand you what has been marked Union Exhibit No. 1 and I will ask you what that is, please?

**A:** This is a list of telephone calls that I made from Morton back to Casey.

**Q:** First of all, tell me what is the document? What are those—there are three pieces of paper, correct?

**A:** Right.

**Q:** Would you tell us first what that is?

**A:** Okay. The first page is just the notice of the telephone bill.

**Q:** Who is Betty Wontley?

**A:** That is my aunt's daughter, who also lived with my aunt. The phone is in her name.

**Q:** Would the phone have been in Betty's house?

**A:** Yes.

**Q:** To make things easier, is this the telephone bill of Betty?

**A:** Yes.

**Q:** And is that the phone you were using to make your calls?

**A:** Yes. I called from 304-555-4200.

**Q:** Now, directing your attention to the date of October 5, do you see that on the exhibit?

**A:** Yes, I do.

**Q:** And I note three calls at number 304-555-4076. Do you know whose number that is?

**A:** That 4076 is Ms. Care's.

**Q:** What is 555-4948?

**A:** That is the nursing home.

**Q:** So that, as I understand it, October the 5th there were three calls from Morton, West Virginia, to Ms. Care and one call to the nursing home?

**A:** Yes.

**Q:** How did you come into possession of that document that has been marked as Union Exhibit 1?

**A:** Well, after we got back it was said that we hadn't called in, that Mr. Toll didn't know where we were or anything about us leaving or anything, and that we hadn't called in from West Virginia to tell them anything. So I called my aunt and asked if she would send a copy of the phone bill to prove that we did call, so she sent them to us.

**Q:** You got this in the mail?

**A:** Right.

**Q:** Now, when did you and Ms. Mills receive your paychecks?

**A:** We received our paychecks on Tuesday.

**Q:** October 9th would be Tuesday?

**A:** October 9th, Tuesday.

**Q:** Was October the 8th a holiday?

**A:** Yes, it was.

**Q:** What holiday was that?

**A:** Columbus Day.

**Q:** Were the post offices open?

**A:** No.

**Q:** So on October 9th, Tuesday, you received your paycheck in the mail?

**A:** Right.

**Q:** What time did you get it?

**A:** It was after 2 p.m. because the mails were just misdelivered.

**Q:** Are you saying that the envelope did not come directly to your mother's house?

**A:** No, it didn't.

**Q:** Where did it go?

**A:** It went to my cousin's house, and she called my aunt and we went over to pick the checks up.

**Q:** What time did you go to your cousin's house to pick up the checks?

**A:** It was about 2:30, maybe quarter to 3. Maybe 3 p.m.

**Q:** How far is your cousin from your aunt?

**A:** Maybe a mile.

**Q:** What is your cousin's name?

**A:** Kathryn Scott.

**Q:** So you went to the Scott house to pick up your checks?

**A:** Right.

**Q:** What did you do after you picked up the checks?

**A:** Then we tried to find a place to have them cashed and because they were out-of-town checks and everything, a lot of stores didn't want to cash them, so finally my aunt found a filling station, service station or whatever, that knew her husband and he cashed them for us.

**Q:** About what time of day was this on Tuesday, the 9th of October?

**A:** It was about 5:30, maybe even 6 p.m. It was late in the afternoon.

**Q:** Why didn't you catch a bus that night, October the 9th?

**A:** Number one is because being so far from the bus station to my home, you know, it's really a long way.

**Q:** How far is long?

**A:** About eight, maybe nine miles. Everybody down there worked late in the evening. Therefore, it was hard for us to get transportation from my mother's home to the bus station, so that is the reason why we didn't catch the bus out that night.

**Q:** All right. On Wednesday, the 10th of October, when was the first available bus from Morton back to Casey?

**A:** 6:20 p.m.

**Q:** Did you take that bus?

**A:** Yes, we did.

**Q:** What time did you arrive back in Casey?

**A:** It was about 10 a.m. Thursday.

**Q:** October the 11th?

**A:** Yes.

**Q:** All right. Did you or Ms. Mills call the nursing home when you got back into Casey at the bus station?

**A:** Ms. Mills called when we returned.

**Q:** How were you advised on the 11th that you had been terminated?

**A:** Ms. Mills came back over to my house. She told me that she had talked to Ms. Nice and Ms. Nice told her as of the 11th that we had been terminated, so we went to see Mr. Call.

**Q:** All right. Mr. Call is the Union Business Agent?

**A:** Right.

**Q:** You didn't call the Company October 8th, 9th, or 10th, did you?

**A:** No, I didn't.

**Q:** Why didn't you call and tell Mr. Toll or tell Ms. Nice the problems you were having getting the checks and everything else that you have already testified to?

**A:** After I had called Ms. Nice on Friday and explained that we were waiting on Ms. Care to send the checks, she said everything was okay, she would see us when we got back. So I didn't see any reason to call them because I thought that Ms. Nice knew that we would return as soon as we got the money.

**Q:** Now, Ms. Brady, I am going to hand you what has been marked as Company Exhibits 3, 4, and 5. Would you take a look at these exhibits, and after you do, I am going to ask you some questions. All right. Now, having looked at these three exhibits, Ms. Brady, were you notified sometime around the 3rd of March of year 3 that Ms. Thomas, the director of nursing, had recommended your termination?

**A:** Yes, I came in to talk to Ms. Thomas. I had called in on the day before to let them know why I hadn't been to work.

**Q:** Are those the days that you set out on Company Exhibit 3?

**A:** Yes.

**Q:** Those dates in February?

**A:** To the best of my knowledge, yes.

**Q:** And it's your testimony that you called in on those dates?

**A:** Yes.

**Q:** What was the problem? Why were you absent on those days?

A:    Well, at the time I was pregnant and I was having a lot of difficulties with it.

Q:    Did you have a meeting with the Company officials and Mr. Call concerning this recommendation for termination?

A:    Yes, I did.

Q:    You were not, in fact, terminated?

A:    No.

Q:    Were you suspended for any period of time?

A:    No.

Q:    As a result of this letter of March 3rd?

A:    No, I wasn't suspended. I brought a doctor's statement in.

Q:    You never filed a grievance as a result of this, did you? If you can recall.

A:    I don't remember.

Q:    You went back to work?

A:    Right.

Q:    I notice in here that on Company Exhibit 5 it states at the bottom, ''Ms. Brady was informed she would be assigned to station C.'' Was that a different station than you had been previously working?

A:    Yes, it was a different station.

Q:    Is there some significance to this new assignment that you know of?

A:    No.

Q:    Had nothing to do with the write-up?

A:    No.

Q:    Going back to your termination, did you attend any meetings after the 11th of October with Mr. Toll or Ms. Nice concerning your discharge?

A:    No. The only contact that I came into with Mr. Toll was one evening I came over to pick my brother up from work. Mr. Toll then asked me if I had a reason for being on the premises and I explained to him that I came to get my brother. He then asked me if I wouldn't come on the premises anymore because he didn't want me on the premises. I don't think he went into detail why or anything like that, but I know that was his statement, for me not to come on the premises anymore.

Q:    Prior to that conversation with Mr. Toll, had he called you to find out your story about why you were absent?

A:    No.

Q:    Ms. Nice didn't either?

A:    No.

Q:    No further questions.

### b. Cross-Examination by Company Advocate

*Mr. Sanchez:*
[to be supplied by student]

## 2. Dee Mills, Grievant

### a. Direct Examination by Union Advocate

*Mr. Golden:*

Q:    State your name and residence address.

A:    Dee Mills. I reside at 120 Kentucky Drive.

Q:    Prior to October the 11th of year 3, where were you employed?

A:    Home Health Center.

Q:    What classification?

A:    Nursing attendant.

Q:    How long had you been so employed?

A:    Twenty-three months.

Q:    During that twenty-three-month period, had you ever received a suspension from the Company because of discipline?

A:    No.

Q:    Had you ever been written up?

A:    One time.

Q:    For what?

A:    Tardiness. I was written up for being eighteen minutes late reporting on the floor. I arrived at work before 7 a.m., but I didn't report on the floor until eighteen minutes after 7.

**Q:** Did you file a grievance with respect to that?

**A:** No. The Union wasn't here then.

**Q:** The contract which has been marked as Joint Exhibit 1 which is dated effective January 24, year 3—was that the first labor contract which covers the employees at the nursing home?

**A:** To the best of my knowledge, yes.

**Q:** And since the contract became effective, it is your testimony that you have not been disciplined to your knowledge?

**A:** No, I haven't, until the 11th.

**Q:** The 11th of October, and on that date you were terminated?

**A:** Yes.

**Q:** On October the 1st, year 3, Ms. Mills, were you at the nursing home when Ms. Brady received the call about her brother's death?

**A:** Yes, I was.

**Q:** And you are related to Ms. Brady?

**A:** By marriage, yes.

**Q:** And how is that?

**A:** Her brother is my stepfather. Charlie Less is married to my mother.

**Q:** Do you recall when that phone call was received at the nursing home?

**A:** To the best of my recollection it was between 7:15 and 8 a.m.

**Q:** Did you accompany Ms. Brady home after the telephone call?

**A:** Yes, I did. I took her home.

**Q:** Did you also return with her subsequently and go to see Ms. Nice?

**A:** Yes, I did.

**Q:** Could you tell us when that was?

**A:** Oh, it was, to the best of my recollection, 8:30, 8:45. Somewhere along in there. I don't remember the time actually.

**Q:** Tell the Arbitrator the discussions that occurred with Ms. Nice upon your return to the nursing home.

**A:** We told Ms. Nice of Ms. Brady's brother's death and we said that we would be leaving, you know. We asked for permission to leave to attend the funeral. She asked us if we had any idea when we would return and Ms. Brady told her no, she had no idea of the funeral, you know, when the arrangements were or when the funeral would be, and Ms. Nice said to call when we found out about the

arrangements. Then we asked her—by that time, excuse me, Ms. McDoe came in the office and we were inquiring about provisions to have Ms. Care send us our checks.

**Q:** All right. What is your understanding with respect to whether or not Ms. Nice knew that you needed the checks for transportation?

**A:** You mean for transportation to get back or transportation to get down there?

**Q:** Either way. Whatever.

**A:** Well, I assumed that she would figure that we'd have to have the checks to get back because we asked for the information to have the checks sent out.

**Q:** Who told you how to make these arrangements?

**A:** Ms. McDoe advised us to go to the front desk and have Ms. Broskowski give us paper to write out a written permission to have Ms. Care retrieve the checks for us.

**Q:** And you did that?

**A:** Yes, we did.

**Q:** Did you, subsequent to that time, have a conversation with Ms. Care?

**A:** After we wrote out the permission and signed the slips and everything, then we notified Ms. Care about the provisions having been made for her to send our checks to us.

**Q:** Then you left the nursing home?

**A:** Yes, we did.

**Q:** You only had one conversation with Ms. Nice on the morning of October the 1st?

**A:** Yes.

**Q:** Did Ms. Nice ask you where you could be found in Morton?

**A:** To the best of my recollection, no.

**Q:** Did you know the telephone number of the residence where you were going to be staying?

**A:** No, I did not.

**Q:** Did you know where you were going to be staying before you got there?

**A:** Yes. With Ms. Brady's mother.

**Q:** All right. Then I assume you went to Morton by bus, arriving on Tuesday, is that correct?

**A:** That's correct.

**Q:** How did you obtain your bus fare?

**A:** I borrowed my bus fare from my sister's boyfriend.

**Q:** When you got to Morton on Tuesday morning, did you know when the funeral was going to take place?

**A:** No, I did not.

**Q:** When did you learn when it was to be held?

**A:** I learned late Wednesday evening.

**Q:** Did you make any telephone calls to the nursing home yourself?

**A:** No, I did not.

**Q:** Were you standing by when Ms. Brady made the call to Ms. Nice?

**A:** No, I was not present.

**Q:** All right. So you have no personal knowledge of what was discussed between Ms. Nice and Ms. Brady the morning of October the 5th?

**A:** No, I have not.

**Q:** When did you first learn that Ms. Care had called West Virginia?

**A:** I learned that she had called on Friday about 7:30 that evening. I went down to Ms. Brady's aunt's house and the message was given to me that Ms. Care had called. I went back and gave the message to Ms. Brady and her sister, and in turn we went back and they tried to call and they were unable to reach her.

**Q:** Who gave you the message?

**A:** Betty Wontley, the person the telephone bill is made out to.

**Q:** What was the message?

**A:** Kate Care was unable to send the checks off Friday and that she would have to send them off Saturday.

**Q:** On Saturday, the 6th of October, did you talk to Ms. Care?

**A:** No, I did not.

**Q:** From October the 8th until October the 11th, did you at anytime call the nursing home?

**A:** I called the nursing home upon my return October the 11th at approximately 11 a.m. Ms. Nice advised me that as of October the 11th Ms. Brady and I had letters of termination in the mail stating that we were terminated.

**Q:** Did you notify Ms. Brady of this?

**A:** Yes. I went over to her house where we were staying at that time and I told her.

**Q:** Do you recall when your paychecks were received in Morton by you?

**A:** Yes. They were received approximately 2:15, 2:30, somewhere along in there on

Tuesday morning—Tuesday afternoon, excuse me.

**Q:** And you heard Ms. Brady testify as to the misdirection of the envelope and where you went to receive the checks?

**A:** Yes.

**Q:** If you were asked those questions, would you have given the same replies?

**A:** Yes.

**Q:** Is there anything you can add to that part of her testimony?

**A:** No, I agree with her testimony.

**Q:** What happened? Would you describe your attempts to cash the checks after you received them Tuesday afternoon?

**A:** It was hard, but we finally cashed our checks at a filling station where the husband of Ms. Brady's aunt knew the manager.

**Q:** Why didn't you borrow the money from someone down there and come back sooner?

**A:** No one had it to my recollection. That is why we were waiting on our checks.

**Q:** And it was not until sometime after 6 p.m. on Wednesday the 10th when you caught a bus for Casey?

**A:** Yes.

**Q:** Why didn't you leave for home earlier in the day on the 10th or after you finally cashed your checks on the 9th?

**A:** Well, we had problems. Tuesday, we had problems like I said cashing the checks. It was later on in the evening, early evening, and we did finally get the checks cashed and by that time we, you know, had problems getting to town to the bus station. As far as an earlier bus on Wednesday, we had no knowledge of a bus leaving earlier than the 6 p.m. Wednesday departure.

**Q:** Why didn't you call Ms. Nice or Mr. Toll on Monday, Tuesday, or Wednesday, to tell them specifically of the problems you were having in getting the checks and advising them when you were going to return to work?

**A:** Well, Ms. Brady told me of her conversation with Ms. Nice. She told me Ms. Nice said that she would see us when we got back, so I assumed that we didn't have to call Monday, Tuesday, or Wednesday.

**Q:** Are you aware of the Company's call-in policy?

**A:** Yes.

**Q:** That policy is what? To call in when you are not going to show up for work?
**A:** Yes.
**Q:** Knowing the policy, you still didn't call in to tell them?

**A:** Because of Ms. Brady's telephone conversation with Ms. Nice on Friday.

**Q:** No further questions.

### b. Cross-Examination by Company Advocate

*Mr. Sanchez:*
[to be supplied by student]

## 3. Kate Care, Nursing Assistant

### a. Direct Examination by Union Advocate

*Mr. Golden:*
**Q:** What is your name, please, and where do you live?
**A:** Kate Care. I live at 804 Hurle Avenue.
**Q:** Where are you employed?
**A:** Home Health Center.
**Q:** What is your capacity?
**A:** Nursing assistant.
**Q:** How long have you been so employed?
**A:** About a year.
**Q:** Now, Ms. Care, calling your attention to October the 1st, were you with Ms. Brady and Ms. Mills when Ms. Brady was advised of a death in the family?
**A:** Yes, I answered the phone.
**Q:** You answered the phone here at the nursing home?
**A:** Yes.
**Q:** What did you do after that?
**A:** I notified Ms. Brady and Ms. Mills and Charles Less of the death.
**Q:** Did you have any conversation that day, October the 1st, either with Ms. Mills or Ms. Brady relating to picking up their paychecks?
**A:** Yes. We discussed getting the money. That I would receive the checks, pick up the checks, and send the checks to them by Western Union, which we thought was the quickest way to get the money there.
**Q:** Do you remember what time of day this was that you had this talk with them?
**A:** It was still the early part of the morning, I would say.
**Q:** Were you with Ms. Brady and Ms. Mills when they talked to Ms. Nice?

**A:** No, sir, I wasn't. I was on the floor.
**Q:** All right. Your conversation with the two women about the checks was on the floor.
**A:** Right.
**Q:** What else was discussed that has any relevancy to what we are doing here, other than picking up the checks?
**A:** Nothing else.
**Q:** Did they tell you where they were going to be staying?
**A:** Yes.
**Q:** Did they give you an address?
**A:** I was given an address where I could contact them.
**Q:** Did they give you a telephone number?
**A:** No, not at that time.
**Q:** And when were the checks to be distributed that week?
**A:** We were getting paid at that time on Thursday, so it would have been Thursday of that week.
**Q:** Did you get the paychecks on Thursday?
**A:** No, sir, I didn't, because I was informed that the payday had been changed to Friday between 12 noon to 5 p.m. That's when we could pick up our checks.
**Q:** October the 5th would be Friday?
**A:** Yes.
**Q:** And you picked up their checks on the 5th?
**A:** Yes, sir. I picked up mine and three other checks.
**Q:** Whose checks did you pick up?
**A:** Checks for Mr. Less, Ms. Brady, and Ms. Mills.

**Q:** Mr. Less is Brady's brother?

**A:** Yes.

**Q:** He also works at the nursing home?

**A:** Yes.

**Q:** When did your shift end on the 5th of October?

**A:** 3:30 p.m.

**Q:** What did you do after work with respect to the checks?

**A:** After I left the nursing home, I went straight to the downtown Western Union office.

**Q:** What happened at the Western Union office?

**A:** After filling out the slips, and, you know, getting ready to give the lady the checks, she informed me that she couldn't receive checks. It had to be the cash money.

**Q:** Did you have sufficient cash to send?

**A:** No, sir, I didn't.

**Q:** What did you do next?

**A:** I left there and went to the main office of the Pennsylvania Federal Bank, where I had an account, to see if I could either get the checks cashed or deposited or something in my account.

**Q:** That is some distance from downtown?

**A:** Quite a bit, yes.

**Q:** Were you traveling by car or bus?

**A:** Bus.

**Q:** What time would it have been that you arrived at the Pennsylvania Federal Bank?

**A:** It was approximately 5 or 5:15 p.m. when I got to the bank.

**Q:** What happened at the bank?

**A:** I was informed by one of the managers that because I didn't have sufficient funds and the checks hadn't been signed by any of them, that I could not get them cashed. Nor could I put them in my bank account because I didn't have sufficient money to cover them.

**Q:** What did you then do?

**A:** I then left there and went home because the post office closed around 5 or 5:30 p.m. It was then going on 5:30, close to 5:30.

**Q:** At any time after you got home on the 5th of October, did you call Morton, West Virginia?

**A:** Yes, I did.

**Q:** How did you get the number so that you knew where to call?

**A:** It was either one of the receptionists or somebody. I can't remember who the person was that actually gave me the number, but I did receive a number here at work. It was to return a call to Ms. Brady.

**Q:** Do you know whether it was Ms. Nice who gave you the number?

**A:** It may have been, sir.

**Q:** You can't remember?

**A:** I'm not sure.

**Q:** So you got home sometime on the evening of October 5th and your testimony is that you called Morton?

**A:** Yes, I did.

**Q:** To whom did you speak?

**A:** I spoke to a lady that identified herself as a relative of Ms. Brady and Mr. Less.

**Q:** Neither Ms. Mills nor Ms. Brady were there when you called?

**A:** No, they weren't even staying at the house, from what she said.

**Q:** Was Mr. Less there?

**A:** No, he wasn't.

**Q:** Did you leave a message for them?

**A:** Yes, I did. I left a message telling them that because we had gotten paid the following day instead of the time when we thought we were getting paid, I was having difficulty in sending the money. And just as soon as I could, I would send the money.

**Q:** Do you know whether Ms. Brady or Ms. Mills called back that night, October the 5th?

**A:** On October the 5th Ms. Brady did call, and at the time I don't think I was home. I think my mom gave me the message that I did have a call and later on my brother-in-law also gave me a message that someone had called for me.

**Q:** But you only called once down there that day?

**A:** Yes.

**Q:** What did you do with respect to the checks on the following day, Saturday, October the 5th?

**A:** The following morning I came to work and I talked to my charge nurse and asked her if I could go out and have the checks mailed and she told me yes. So on my break at 9:15 I went to the post office and asked them which was the quickest way that I could get to mail the money, and the people informed me that it was special delivery or something like that, so that's the way I sent it, three in one envelope, the three checks.

**Q:** On that Saturday did you talk with any of the three?

**A:** Yes, I talked to Mr. Less after I had returned from the post office. There was a call for me and he was on the phone.

**Q:** What did you tell Mr. Less?

**A:** That I had just come back from sending the money to them.

**Q:** To your knowledge that is the first time that Ms. Brady and Ms. Mills knew what had happened and what had been going on here?

**A:** Yes, as far as the money.

**Q:** So far as you are concerned?

**A:** Yes.

**Q:** Now, did you have any other talks with them after the 6th of October until they returned on the 11th?

**A:** No, sir, I didn't.

**Q:** When is the first time you talked to Mr. Toll about this whole incident? Was it after the 11th of October?

**A:** I think it was. The 11th was on—

**Q:** Thursday.

**A:** Yes.

**Q:** So you talked to him after that?

**A:** Yes.

**Q:** Did Ms. Nice talk to you at any time after the 5th or 6th of October about the checks or about anything concerning the whereabouts of Ms. Brady and Ms. Mills?

**A:** No, sir.

**Q:** Do you know whether, prior to the morning of Thursday, October 11th, Ms. Nice had consulted you with respect to what you have just testified to here today?

**A:** No, sir, not at all.

**Q:** Has she ever talked to you about it?

**A:** No.

**Q:** No further questions.

### b. Cross-Examination by Company Advocate

*Mr. Sanchez:*
[to be supplied by student]

## 4. Bob Call, Union Business Agent

### a. Direct Examination by Union Advocate

*Mr. Golden:*

**Q:** State your name and residence address, please.

**A:** Bob Call, home address, 2040 Cross Drive.

**Q:** What is your occupation, Mr. Call?

**A:** Business Representative for Local 22.

**Q:** That is the local Union that negotiated the contract which has been marked as Joint Exhibit 1?

**A:** Yes sir, it is.

**Q:** Is this contract the first contract which the Union has had with the Company?

**A:** Yes, it is.

**Q:** Now, you were here when Mr. Toll testified, were you not?

**A:** Part of it.

**Q:** You heard Mr. Toll testify concerning a conversation with you about problems with absenteeism at the nursing home?

**A:** Yes.

**Q:** Did you have knowledge that there was a problem with absenteeism?

**A:** Sure.

**Q:** Did you and Mr. Toll work out a policy that the Company could follow with respect to its problems of absenteeism?

**A:** Well, Mr. Toll and I have talked more than one time about the absentee problem that he is having, but it's a problem in all of the nursing home industry. All the homes in the nursing industry are having this problem. He did talk to me about the situation, yes, more than once, and there were a number of things that we talked about, particularly the three-day absence requiring a doctor's certificate.

**Q:** All right. Mr. Call, had you been consulted about the Company's promulgating Company Exhibit 1, the Nursing Service Guidelines?

**A:** No, not at all.

**Q:** Did the Union have any hand in drafting the Nursing Service Guidelines?

**A:** No, sir.

**Q:** Does the Company have the right to promulgate rules of conduct?

**A:** Article VI, section 6-2 says yes, as long as they coincide with the contract.

**Q:** Now there is language following item 16 under "Rules of Conduct" in The Guidelines, Company Exhibit 1 which states that: "All offenses will result in a disciplinary action report. Three within six months will result in immediate dismissal." Had Mr. Toll discussed with you the Company policy regarding the interpretation of that language?

**A:** No, not on that basis. We did have a conversation. In fact, we had more than one conversation when he was having these problems. He said he was having problems with the first shift on absenteeism. I told him I was willing to work with him, but not on the basis of the terminations. The contract states that, you know, you have three warnings and dismissal. As far as the three days mentioned in the guidelines, that is not part of the contract. In the contract negotiations we talked about the need for a doctor's certificate upon returning, if an employee were off for three consecutive days. Now, as I understand it, the Company's position is that with three consecutive days' absence, for each day missed there will be a write-up. I didn't agree to that, no, sir.

**Q:** The discussion between the Union and Company that you are talking about is that if you miss three days, you must bring a doctor's certificate?

**A:** That's correct.

**Q:** That is not in the contract, though?

**A:** No, but we talked about this in negotiations.

**Q:** You were here when Ms. Nice was asked about treating each day of absence as a separate occurrence?

**A:** Right.

**Q:** And you heard her testify that it was her interpretation of the Guidelines that each day is a separate offense?

**A:** I did.

**Q:** Did you discuss this interpretation of the Guidelines with anyone representing the Company?

**A:** I did not.

**Q:** Did you at any time feel that the Union would not object to this interpretation?

**A:** No. Absolutely not.

**Q:** To your knowledge, have there been employees who have had three unexcused absences and who are still working with the Company?

**A:** It is my understanding there are. I have heard it. I have no proof of it. I have heard it.

**Q:** Did Mr. Toll call you on the 11th of October or did you call him?

**A:** I called him.

**Q:** At that time did you know that the two women had been fired?

**A:** Yes. That is what I called him for.

**Q:** Did Mr. Toll state he would like a meeting with you and the women to find out their position and their reason for being absent?

**A:** We discussed it on the phone and I don't remember if it was on that particular day whether I met with Mr. Toll or not, but we did talk about it on the phone.

**Q:** He had not tried to get you prior to the time the women were fired?

**A:** Honestly, I don't remember. If he did, he did not call me and talk to me about Ms. Brady, I don't believe, and Ms. Mills as such, I don't believe. I don't really remember.

**Q:** Are there any supplemental Agreements to Joint Exhibit 1?

**A:** No, there are not.

**Q:** Is that the Agreement?

**A:** That is the entire Agreement, yes, sir.

**Q:** No further questions.

### b. Cross-Examination by Company Advocate

*Mr. Sanchez:*
[to be supplied by student]


## 5. *Charles Less, Nursing Attendant*

### a. Direct Examination by Union Advocate

*Mr. Golden:*
Q:   What is your name and your address?
A:   My name is Charles Less and my address is 285 Montrose Park.
Q:   Where are you employed, Mr. Less?
A:   Home Health.
Q:   As what classification?
A:   Nursing Attendant.
Q:   How long have you been so employed?
A:   About seventeen months.
Q:   Are you related to May Brady?
A:   She's my sister.
Q:   How about Dee Mills?
A:   She's my stepdaughter.
Q:   Were you working for the Company on October the 1st, year 3?
A:   Yes, but I was on a sick leave at the time.
Q:   When were you to return to work?
A:   It was sometime in October.
Q:   So that you were not working at the nursing home, on the premises—
A:   No.
Q:   —on October the 1st?
A:   No.
Q:   Now, it is true that you accompanied May and Dee to Morton, West Virginia?
A:   Yes, I did.
Q:   Now, on Friday that week, October the 5th, did you at any time talk with the nursing home, Ms. Nice, Mr. Toll, or Ms. Care?
A:   I talked to Ms. Care Friday night.
Q:   Friday night?
A:   Yes, about 8:30 p.m.
Q:   What did she say?
A:   Well, I didn't get—I called Ms. Care's home and I asked her mother could I speak to Ms. Care. Earlier that night Ms. Brady had called and Ms. Care's father told her that Ms. Care wasn't home, so my sister called around to other places where she thought Ms. Care would be, so we would know about the checks and things.
     I called Ms. Care later on and her mother told me that she was in bed and she was not going to wake her up, so I told her mother all I wanted to know was when Ms. Care was going to send the checks. Her mother told me, "Well, Kate tried to send your checks earlier today, but she couldn't because Western Union wouldn't cash the checks," and she went on with all of this, so I just said okay and hung up.
Q:   All right. Did you ever, while you were in Morton, talk to Ms. Care?
A:   Yes, I called her back Saturday morning and she said she had just come from the post office and she had sent the checks air mail special delivery. She said that the people told her down at the post office that we would get the checks on Sunday. Well, in West Virginia, you know, they don't have trucks to come around and deliver your mail when you get special delivery down there, so with Monday being a holiday and all, we didn't get the checks until Tuesday. My mother's box number had been changed, so they took our mail to my cousin's store, and in turn he called us later that day and told us that we had a special delivery letter over there, so we went over to the store and got the mail. We had trouble getting the checks cashed because they were out-of-town checks and we were from out of town and all, so finally my aunt knew somebody and took us to the service station and they cashed our checks.
Q:   So that you had talked to Ms. Care once and that was on Saturday?
A:   Right.
Q:   Thank you. No further questions.

### b. Cross-Examination by Company Advocate

*Mr. Sanchez:*
[to be supplied by student]

# D. Exhibits

*JOINT EXHIBIT NO. 1*

B A R G A I N I N G   A G R E E M E N T

Between

HOME HEALTH CENTER

and

Universal Union of Service Workers

Local 22 (1/1/02-1/1/05)

. . .

**ARTICLE VI**

MANAGEMENT RIGHTS

Section 6.1.    Except as expressly and specifically limited by the provisions of this Agreement, the Employer has and shall retain the full right of managing its work force.  Such right of management includes, among other things, but is not limited to: the maintenance of discipline and efficiency of employees; the right to hire, layoff, assign, transfer, promote, and to determine the qualifications of employees; the right to increase, decrease, discontinue, or relocate its operation; the right to assign work and duties in accordance with its determination of the needs of the business; the right to subcontract subject to the condition that present employees are not thereby displaced; the right to disseminate, change, modify, and enforce work rules; the right to impose discipline up to and including discharge upon employees for just cause, provided that an employee so disciplined may avail himself of the grievance procedure.  The Employer shall be the exclusive judge of all matters pertaining to the work to be done and the services to be performed, the schedules of the working time, and the methods, processes, means and supplies to be used.

Section 6.2.    The management rights as set forth above are not all-inclusive but merely indicate the type of matters or rights which belong to and are inherent in management.  All rights which the Employer has had in the past and those which are inherent in the Employer and which have not been explicitly contracted away by the specific terms of this Agreement are retained solely by the Employer.

The Employer's failure to exercise any right hereby reserved to it or its exercising any right in a particular way shall not be deemed a waiver of any such right or preclude the Employer from exercising the same in some other way not in conflict with the express terms of this Agreement.

. . .

## ARTICLE XII

<u>DISCIPLINE</u>

<u>Section 12.1.</u>  The Employer shall have the right to discharge, suspend, or otherwise discipline any employee for just cause, which shall include but not be limited to proven dishonesty, insubordination, insobriety, incompetence, willful negligence, failure to perform work as reasonably required, or proven patient abuse.
.  .  .

## ARTICLE XV

<u>MISCELLANEOUS BENEFITS</u>

<u>Section 15.5.</u>  Bereavement Pay — Funeral leave of up to three (3) days shall be granted to employees in case of death of an employee's spouse, child, parent, sister or brother, or mother or father of living current spouse.  Payment for scheduled workdays which would have been worked but for the funeral shall be paid for the day before, the day of, and the day after the funeral.
.  .  .

## ARTICLE XVII

<u>SENIORITY</u>

<u>Section 17.2.</u>  The employment relationship, including an employee's seniority, shall be terminated for any of, but not limited to, the following reasons:
   (a)  If an employee quits or retires;
   (b)  If an employee is discharged for just cause;
   (c)  If an employee does not return to work on the next scheduled workday following the expiration of vacation or approved leave of absence unless he or she gives prior notice and is excused by the Employer;
   (d)  If an employee fails to report to work within three scheduled workdays after being notified by telegram to his last known address to do so, unless excused by the Employer.

*JOINT EXHIBIT NO. 2*

# G R I E V A N C E   R E P O R T*

Name: ___May Brady___                Date: ___October 11, year 3___

Address: _75 Hampton Court___        Phone: _____

Company: __Home Health Center___   How long employed:_1 yr., 6 mo.___

Did you contact Steward? __yes___   Steward's name: __Charles Less___

Are you in good standing with the Union? ___Yes___

Explain as fully as possible the nature of the grievance.  If
necessary, use other side. ___I, May Brady, had a death in my___
_family (my brother).  I confronted Ms. Nice of my leaving on___
_Monday, October 1, year 3, and it was okay with her.  I was___
_waiting for Mrs. Kate Care to send our checks.  The checks were___
_delayed by Mr. Toll.  So, Mrs. Care was late mailing the money.___
_But I also talked to Ms. Nice on Friday, October 5, and I___
_explained about the funeral being on Friday and that we were___
_waiting for our money.  Ms. Nice gave me the okay.  Then, when we___
_returned on October 11, we were told we had been fired.  I told___
_Ms. Nice that we had to leave suddenly and we had to wait for___
_Mrs. Care to mail the money.  Monday was a holiday and the___
_postman didn't deliver mail on Monday.  So we received the money___
_on Tuesday and we left on Wednesday, because on Tuesday, by the___
_time we had gotten the money, there weren't any buses leaving___
_Morton.  When Mrs. Mills reported to work, she was told our___
_termination papers were in the mail___

                              /s/ _May Brady_____
                                  October 11, year 3

_____
*Dee Mills filed a similar report

*JOINT EXHIBIT NO. 2 (continued)*

Steward's Report:   I state that these facts are true.

Charlie Less  October 11, year 3

Give full details of the disposition:  As these facts are true,

we demand that Ms. May Brady be rehired with all lost pay.

Universal Union of Service Workers     Date Completed: 10-11-03
Local No. 22
210 East 1st Street
Casey, PA                              Business Agent: /s/   Bob Care
555-0995

_COMPANY EXHIBIT NO. 1_

## NURSING SERVICE GUIDELINES

Management recognizes the necessity for maintaining a two-way channel of communication and intends to do its best to be receptive to the desires and needs of the employees of the Home Health Center.

. . .

### Telephone Calls

No personal phone calls may be made or received during working hours. Should there be an emergency, inform your friends or relatives to notify the office, who will in turn notify the message to you.

. . .

### Rules of Conduct

Home Health Center expects every employee to observe basic rules of good conduct. Most of these are common-sense rules which require fair play with department heads and co-workers and most of all, the patients for whose care we are responsible. As a member of the Home Health Center Team, it is important that all employees understand these rules and the penalties involved in breaking them. The following may result in discharge or disciplinary action:

   . . .

   3. Insubordination

   . . .

   Failure to notify the supervisor of absence and reason for absence.

   . . .

   16. Unauthorized absence from assigned work area.

   . . .

All offenses will result in a disciplinary action report. Three within six months will result in immediate dismissal.

. . .

## Tardiness, Absenteeism, and Ill Calls

Employees shall be subjected to a disciplinary report if late more than 15 minutes. Three reports in a week for tardiness shall be grounds for dismissal. If you see that you will be late, call and notify the nursing station. If you ride the bus and arrive here late then you must make up the time at the end of the shift. Babysitter problems are considered an unexcused absence. In case of illness,

- On a 7-3 shift, call before 6 a.m.
- On a 3-11 shift, call before 12 p.m.
- On a 11-7 shift, call before 8 p.m.

These calls should go directly to your station. If nursing service is not notified by these times, sick pay will not be granted.

If an employee does not notify nursing service of absenteeism he or she will be issued a disciplinary action report. Three reports are grounds for dismissal.

If ill on any day of a scheduled weekend, you are to make up the time on the following weekend. If an employee is ill three or more days in a row, a doctor's slip must be presented when returning to work.

. . .

### *COMPANY EXHIBIT NO. 2*

### WORK SCHEDULE

| OCTOBER | MON 1 | TUE 2 | WED 3 | THU 4 | FRI 5 | SAT 6 | SUN 7 | MON 8 | TUE 9 | WED 10 | THU 11 |
|---|---|---|---|---|---|---|---|---|---|---|---|
| Ms. Mills | on | off | on | on | on | off | off | on | on | on | on |
| Ms. Brady | on | on | on | off | on | on | on | on | off | on | on |

*COMPANY EXHIBIT NO. 3*

**HOME HEALTH CENTER**
600 S. Arnold Rd. * Casey, Pennsylvania * Ph. (717) 555-4948

TO WHOM IT MAY CONCERN:

RE:  MS. MAY BRADY, NURSING ASSISTANT

DATE:   MARCH 3, YEAR 3

Work schedule for February, year 3 and March, year 3:

```
Late on February 5, year 3
Absent on February 10, year 3
Late on February 15, year 3
Absent on February 18, year 3   No notification or doctor's permit
Absent on February 23, year 3           "                    "
Absent on February 27, year 3           "                    "
Absent on February 28, year 3           "                    "
Absent on March 1, year 3               "                    "
Absent on March 3, year 3               "                    "
```

The Nursing Office had tried to contact Ms. Brady regarding absenteeism.  However, she has no telephone.

The Nursing Office was not informed of the causes of the frequent absenteeism.  It was never able to schedule relief persons to give adequate nursing care to the patients.

Ms. Brady came into the Nursing Office on Saturday, March 3, year 3, when she was scheduled on duty and with no physician's permit, to explain her reasons for being absent.

Ms. Brady was insubordinate and slammed the door twice on her way out.

The recommendation is that Ms. Brady be terminated as of March 3, year 3.

/s/ Nita Thomas, R.N.
Director, Nursing Services

<u>*COMPANY EXHIBIT NO. 4*</u>

**HOME HEALTH CENTER**

600 S. Arnold Rd. * Casey, Pennsylvania * Ph. (717) 555-4948

RE:    Ms. May Brady, Nursing Assistant

SUBJECT:   Recommended termination

DATE:    March 5, year 3

At 3:00 p.m. a meeting was held in the office of the Administrator.  Those present were as follows:  Mr. Dan Hill, Administrator; Mr. Bob Call, Union Representative; Ms. May Brady, Nursing Assistant; Ms. Addie Weller, Nursing Assistant and Union Steward; Ms. Nita Thomas, R.N., Director of Nursing Services; Ms. Donna Biggs, Nursing Secretary.

Group discussion centered on the written record of lateness, repeated absenteeism, and insubordination of Ms. May Brady, Nursing Assistant, assigned to Station B.

After considerable evaluation of the facts presented, the decision arrived at by Mr. Hill, Administrator. Ms. Thomas, Director of Nursing Services; and Mr. Bob Call, Union Representative, was:

That upon receipt of the physician's record which would verify Ms. May Brady's illness, she be allowed to continue as an employee of Home Health Center.

This decision was based on the following facts:

1.  That Ms. Brady stated she had called in ill to B Station, relative to her absence from duty.

2.  That there was no apparent way for Nursing Services to verify, on the pertinent Information Sheets, whether or not Ms. Brady had actually called in relative to absence from duty.

3.  That Ms. Brady had not been verbally warned regarding the proper procedure to follow relative to lateness and absenteeism, although she had been an employee since 4/7/02. The insubordination, apparently, was not a factor in the decision reached.

/s/ <u>Nita Thomas, R.N.</u>
Director, Nursing Services
Home Health Center

## *COMPANY EXHIBIT NO. 5*

### HOME HEALTH CENTER

600 S. Arnold Rd. * Casey, Pennsylvania * Ph. (717) 555-4948

RE:         Ms. May Brady, Nursing Assistant

SUBJECT:   Employment

DATE:      March 16, year 3

On March 12, year 3, Charles Less, brother of May Brady, presented a physician's certificate of illness relative to Ms. Brady's extended absenteeism.

It was requested that Ms. Brady call the Nursing Office regarding the date she would return.

On March 13, year 3, Ms. Brady notified the Nursing Office that she would be on duty Monday, March 19, year 3.

/s/ <u>Nita Thomas</u>
Director, Nursing Services

NT/db

3/19/03

## COMPANY EXHIBIT NO. 6

EMPLOYEE REPORT FORM

NAME: __M. Brady__          DEPT. __Nursing__   DATE: __3/23/03__

REPORT: ____Tardy--1/2 hour late, didn't call in_____

_____

PERSON MAKING REPORT: ___Nita Thomas_____

EMPLOYEE SIGNATURE: _____ DATE: _____

## COMPANY EXHIBIT NO. 7

EMPLOYEE REPORT FORM

NAME: __M. Brady__          DEPT. __Nursing__   DATE: __8/27/03__

REPORT: ____Tardy--on following dates:  7/1, (28 min.), 7/10__
__(46 min.), 7/15 (52 min.), 7/23 (13 min.), 8/11 (12 min.)__

PERSON MAKING REPORT: ___G. Nice, R.N._____

EMPLOYEE SIGNATURE: ___(refused to sign)_____ DATE: _____

## COMPANY EXHIBIT NO. 8

EMPLOYEE REPORT FORM

NAME: __M. Brady__          DEPT. __Nursing__   DATE: __9/21/03__

REPORT: ____Will not be in tomorrow, 7:00 to 3:30 shift_____
_Her brother Charles is going in the hospital and May is going_
with him._____

PERSON MAKING REPORT: ___E. Burke, L.P.N._____

EMPLOYEE SIGNATURE: _____ DATE: _____

## COMPANY EXHIBIT NO. 9

EMPLOYEE REPORT FORM

NAME: __M. Brady__          DEPT. __Nursing__   DATE: __10/1/03__

REPORT: ____May rec'd long distance phone call; brother in West_
Virginia had died; May went home.  C. Less and D. Mills went___
with May._____

PERSON MAKING REPORT: ___F. Hicks_____

EMPLOYEE SIGNATURE: ___(refused to sign)_____ DATE: _____

### *COMPANY EXHIBIT NO. 10*

EMPLOYEE REPORT FORM

NAME: __M. Brady__       DEPT. __Nursing__    DATE: __9/5/03__

REPORT: _____ Ms. Brady has been notified of her disciplinary action forms and has been warned._____

PERSON MAKING REPORT: ___Z. Barr_____

EMPLOYEE SIGNATURE: _____ DATE: _____

### *COMPANY EXHIBIT NO. 11*

EMPLOYEE REPORT FORM

NAME: __M. Brady__       DEPT. __Nursing__    DATE: __10/8/03__

REPORT: _____ unexcused absence_____

PERSON MAKING REPORT: ___G. Nice, R.N._____

EMPLOYEE SIGNATURE: _____ DATE: _____

### *COMPANY EXHIBIT NO. 12*

EMPLOYEE REPORT FORM

NAME: __M. Brady__       DEPT. __Nursing__    DATE: __10/10/03__

REPORT: ___unexcused absence_____

PERSON MAKING REPORT: ___G. Nice, R.N._____

EMPLOYEE SIGNATURE: _____ DATE: _____

### *COMPANY EXHIBIT NO. 13*

EMPLOYEE REPORT FORM

NAME: __M. Brady__       DEPT. __Nursing__    DATE: __10/11/03__

REPORT: _____unexcused absence_____

PERSON MAKING REPORT: ___G. Nice, R.N._____

EMPLOYEE SIGNATURE: _____ DATE: _____

*COMPANY EXHIBIT NO. 14*

EMPLOYEE REPORT FORM

NAME: D. Mills          DEPT. Nursing     DAT 10/8/03

REPORT:      unexcused absence _____

_____

_____

PERSON MAKING REPORT:      G. Nice, R.N. _____

EMPLOYEE SIGNATURE: _____ DATE: _____

*COMPANY EXHIBIT NO. 15*

EMPLOYEE REPORT FORM

NAME: D. Mills          DEPT. Nursing     DATE: 10/9/03

REPORT:      unexcused absence _____

_____

PERSON MAKING REPORT:      G. Nice, R.N. _____

EMPLOYEE SIGNATURE: _____ DATE: _____

*COMPANY EXHIBIT NO. 16*

EMPLOYEE REPORT FORM

NAME: D. Mills          DEPT. Nursing     DATE:10/10/03

REPORT:      unexcused absence _____

_____

_____

PERSON MAKING REPORT:      G. Nice, R.N. _____

EMPLOYEE SIGNATURE: _____ DATE: _____

*COMPANY EXHIBIT NO. 17*

EMPLOYEE REPORT FORM

NAME: D. Mills          DEPT. Nursing     DATE: 10/11/03

REPORT:      unexcused absence _____

_____

_____

PERSON MAKING REPORT:      G. Nice, R.N. _____

EMPLOYEE SIGNATURE: _____ DATE: _____

## _UNION EXHIBIT NO.1_

West Virginia Telegraph & Telephone Company
Post Office Box 98765
Morton, West Virginia

                        N O T I C E

Our records indicate that payment of your telephone bill as shown
below has not been received.  If remittance in full has been
made, please call our business office, as this account is subject
to suspension on October 30, year 3 with an applicable charge of
$25.00 for reconnection.  This reminder should be considered as
final notice.

Betty Wontley
P.O. Box 4321
Morton, West Virginia
304-555-4200


Long Distance Service

                        (ABRIDGED)

| DATE | CITY CALLED | NUMBER CALLED | CHARGE |
|------|-------------|---------------|--------|
| 10/1 | Glass, NY | 607 555-6138 | $2.25 |
| 10/1 | Oakdale, IL | 312 555-6234 | 1.50 |
| 10/5 | Casey, PA | 717 555-4948 | .50 |
| 10/5 | Casey, PA | 717 555-4948 | .50 |
| 10/5 | Casey, PA | 717 555-4076 | .50 |
| 10/5 | Casey, PA | 717 555-4948 | 1.10 |
| 10/5 | Oakdale, IL | 312 555-6234 | .75 |
| 10/5 | Casey, PA | 717 555-4076 | .50 |
| 10/5 | Casey, PA | 717 555-4076 | 1.10 |
| 10/5 | Glass, NY | 607 555-6138 | 2.15 |

# Archway Metals

## Table of Contents

**Table of Contents contd.**

**NOTES**

# A. Caption

## IN THE MATTER OF ARBITRATION BETWEEN:

ARCHWAY METALS )
HENLEY, KENTUCKY )
)
AND )
)
METAL, BRICK, AND GLASS )
WORKERS INTERNATIONAL UNION )
AFL-CIO, )
LOCAL 123 )

RE: DAN FOWLER
Discharge for Absenteeism Under
the No-Fault Absenteeism Policy

Appearances:

For the Company: Joseph Thomas

For the Union: Todd McMann

Date: September 18, year 6

Place: Henley, Kentucky

## B. Examination of Company Witnesses

### 1. Shirley Gardner, Employee Relations Specialist

a. Direct Examination by Company Advocate

*Mr. Thomas:*

**Q:** Would you state your name for the record?

**A:** Shirley Gardner.

**Q:** How long have you been employed at Archway Metals?

**A:** Twelve years.

**Q:** What positions have you held during that time?

**A:** Currently, I hold the position of Employee Relations Specialist, which I have held for six years. Prior to that I was secretary to the Employee Relations Manager.

**Q:** What responsibilities do you have in this position?

**A:** My responsibilities include assisting the Employee Relations Representatives in the department. I am involved in salaried administration, training and development, and labor relations. I also work on research assignments and projects including researching absenteeism.

**Q:** As part of your duties do you have access to Company records?

**A:** Yes, I do.

**Q:** Do you also have access to employee or personnel records?

**A:** Yes.

**Q:** Are you familiar with the grievance being discussed today?

**A:** Yes, I am.

**Q:** Have you seen it before?

**A:** Yes.

**Q:** Prior to the implementation of the No-Fault Absenteeism Policy, what was the grievant Dan Fowler's work record like?

**A:** Prior to the implementation of that policy he had received six reprimands over a thirty-five month period.

**Q:** Were any of those reprimands grieved and taken to arbitration?

**A:** Yes. I found that some were grieved but none were submitted to arbitration.

**Q:** How long has the grievant been actively employed since his date of hire?

**A:** He was hired five years ago but has only worked thirty-five months during his time of employment.

**Q:** You stated that as part of your assignment you worked on absenteeism in the plant?

**A:** Yes.

**Q:** What was the plant average for absenteeism two years ago?

**A:** The plant average was 1.2 percent, or three absences per employee per year.

**Q:** What was the plant average for absenteeism last year?

**A:** It was 1.7 percent, and again that's around three absences per employee per year.

**Q:** What was the grievant's absence rate last year?

**A:** He only worked four months of that year and during that time he had eight absences, not including sick leave.

**Q:** How are you calculating the percentage of absences?

**A:** I use the absence formula provided by the Bureau of Labor Statistics.

**Q:** What kind of absences are we talking about?

**A:** We're talking about casual absences.

**Q:** What is a casual absence?

**A:** Casual absences are absences that are noncontractual; they're intermittent periodic absences.

**Q:** Would these cover such areas as injuries due to Workers' Compensation or sick leave, or vacation?

**A:** No.

**Q:** Was there anything else that your research on absenteeism showed?

**A:** Yes. For year 4, it showed twenty percent of our employees had perfect attendance.

**Q:** How about year 5?

**A:** I did not compute attendance because in that year our people did not work a full twelve-month period. They only worked nine months due to a strike.

**Q:** Are you familiar with the absentee policy in effect prior to the adoption and implementation of the No-Fault Absenteeism Policy in February year 6?

**A:** Yes, I am.

**Q:** How was that prior policy handled?

**A:** It was handled on a case-by-case basis.

**Q:** Was it a written policy?

**A:** Yes, it was written.

**Q:** Did the policy state what excessive absenteeism was?

**A:** It defined what excused and unexcused absences were.

**Q:** Did it specifically state what excessive absenteeism was?

**A:** No.

**Q:** As part of your job, have you ever sat in on any grievance meetings?

**A:** Yes, I have.

**Q:** Have you heard any complaints about the previous absenteeism policy?

**A:** Yes, there were considerable complaints over it.

**Q:** What were they?

**A:** Under the previous policy, which again was case-by-case review, we did have a lot of complaints from our employees and a lot of grievances about the application of the policy in that they felt it was unfair. The employees felt that they were treated differently, or inconsistently, and they sometimes felt that the way they were treated was based on who they worked for. The Union also had complaints about it. The Union had been asking us for some period of time to look at a more fair and equal policy.

**Q:** Are these complaints in a sense what led to the introduction of the no-fault absence policy on February 20th, year 6?

**A:** Yes, in order to resolve that issue we did implement the no-fault policy, and it emphasizes the number of absences rather than looking at the reasons for absences, which is why it's called a no-fault policy.

**Q:** I have no further questions at this time.

<hr>

### b. Cross-Examination by Union Advocate

*Mr. McMann:*
[to be supplied by student]

## 2. Joseph Thomas, Vice President for Labor Relations

### a. Testimony by Company Advocate

*Mr. Thomas:* Mr. Arbitrator, my name is Joseph Thomas. I am Vice President for Labor Relations. I know that advocates usually do not testify in cases they are presenting. But I humbly have to say that no person knows the No-Fault Absenteeism Policy better than I do. I wrote it. I will now attempt to give you highlights of what our absence policy entails. I offer Company Exhibit 1, which contains the policy.

As Ms. Gardner testified, we previously had a policy based on excused and unexcused absences. It did not work. We then designed an up-front absence policy that was consistently administered throughout the plant—the No-Fault Absenteeism Policy. The emphasis in the new policy, highlighted in Section I, is the number of absences, rather than the reasons for absences. This policy was created to prevent bickering so everybody knew exactly where they stood. It was discussed with the Union, but the Union did not respond.

Prior to our implementing this policy it was explained to each worker. They were given two copies, one for them to take home and one for them to sign. Also, prior to our implementing this policy, all employees were given clean records. The purpose of the policy, again, was to develop good attendance habits by all employees. To accomplish this objective, a systematic review was put into effect. Employees with unsatisfactory attendance are reminded of their responsibility for good attendance as well as the consequence of failing to satisfy that requirement. In situations where unsatisfactory attendance persists, application of corrective discipline occurs. We feel that to run a business properly, one of the biggest assets is manpower and it's a must for people to be at work.

Section II pertains to the responsibility of each employee. Each employee was given the responsibility to call the Security Officer at the plant at least one hour prior to the start of their scheduled shift if he or she is going to be late or absent. The employees call the Security Officer, and the Security Officer only. We wanted to have a central clearinghouse so that all absences and lates were reported to one location. We also stated to the employees that if they wanted to speak to their foreman they could, but to make sure they made that phone call to the Security Officer, reporting their reason for absence before speaking to the foreman.

An employee calling in is requested to supply their number, name, clock number, supervisor, and reason for absence. When employees call in, we give each one a separate call-in number. The reason we do this is to avoid any arguments or bickering as to whether the employee actually called in. All we do is match up the call-in numbers with the call-in sheet.

The policy is designed to curb casual or intermittent absence. It was not designed to jeopardize people with bona fide injuries or illnesses or bona fide reasons for being away from work. Because of that, we set up a listing for nonchargeable absences—those that are recognized by the Labor Agreement, that is, the collective bargaining agreement, or by federal or state statute. In essence, nonchargeable absences are industrial injuries, vacations, jury duty, military leave, Union business, bereavement, and hospitalization or sick leaves.

On the second page, per our Labor Agreement, there is a provision for medical leaves. Anyone going on a medical leave in our plan after being injured was eligible for medical leave the very first day. He or she was not assessed points under the absence policy.

What we essentially did in terms of assessing points in the Policy was to classify lates and absences into three different areas. We determined that if people would call in one hour before their shift started we could properly function by securing overtime people, etc., so the points were lower the first hour. Under the Policy, anyone who called in to be off work one hour before the shift starts receives one point. Anyone who calls less than one hour before and up to two hours after the shift starts receives two points. The call-in time is noted on the call-in sheet. Anyone who calls in more than two hours after the shift starts or doesn't call at all receives four points for an absence. Thus, if an employee is going to be late and for some reason that lateness turns into an absence, the employee still has to call in an absence.

One more thing I think I should point out. If someone came in to work and had to leave early, they're assessed three-quarters of a point. Also, an unpaid leave of absence is one point. If employees obtain a leave of absence of one day, five consecutive days, or five consecutive weeks, they only are assessed one point, not one point for each day absent. So an entire leave of absence would only be one point.

In addition, we have set up a progressive disciplinary system. As it clearly states, a Written Warning would occur at eight points within the most recent twelve months worked. A Special Written Warning would occur with ten points within the most recent twelve months worked. A copy of such a warning is given to the employee when one is issued, as required under the Labor Agreement. At twelve points within the most recent twelve months worked, the employee would be discharged. This was designed with a twelve-month roll-off period, meaning whatever points accrue come off thirteen months later. As part of our Policy, our payroll system is programmed to track points. We send out a weekly computer printout to each department's superintendent. The points of every individual in that department are conveyed to that department. We put up postings in the plant to the employees telling them to check their points. We've also set up a hotline in the plant to answer any questions the employees may have regarding this absence policy. If somebody asks a question, it's answered and posted on the bulletin boards in the plant.

I think I've highlighted for the most part what the program entails. Company Exhibit 2 shows that the grievant was given the opportunity to ask any questions regarding the Policy. We designed a policy where everyone knew exactly where they stood and we gave feedback weekly. If there are any questions concerning the assessment of points, those questions are handled individually.

I think that there is one thing we should bring out. Our policy is not meant to jeopardize people with bona fide injury or illness. We have at least two people at the plant who have cancer. They go to the hospital for treatment on a regular basis without incurring points. With such types of prior notification and approval, we have made some very few exceptions or exemptions from this Policy. We recognize that individuals with chronic illness requiring leave for treatment would have been terminated otherwise under the Policy. I understand there would be those rare exceptions, but they have to be documented and approved.

I would now like to outline the grievant's particular situation. On April 10, year 6, after working a midnight shift, Mr. Fowler came to my office and stated to me that he had four points under the attendance program and that he liked his job, that he did not want to lose his job, and that he was experiencing some problems with his wife. He had told me that he had some marital problems and that he felt he may have been the person that caused her seizures. We talked about this for a little bit and then I asked Mr. Fowler what he wanted to do. I asked Dan if he wanted to take a leave of absence while his wife got through this critical period. He told me that he didn't want to miss work. After we got into the discussion a little bit more he began to tell me that she had some problems. I responded by saying, "Dan, why don't you do this: why don't you go see your foreman and make a request for a non-chargeable medical leave of absence provided for under III.B of the Policy." Mr. Fowler showed good faith that he wanted to continue working. I made it clear to Mr. Fowler that this type of leave could not last indefinitely. As a guideline I said it will last the next seven to ten days. This was

explained to Mr. Fowler very clearly. He agreed with what I said. As we were about to end the conversation, he said to me, "Oh, by the way, I'm not coming into work tonight." I stated to him, "What do you mean you're not coming in to work tonight?" He stated that he had to take his wife somewhere after completing his midnight shift and it was his turn to be forced to work overtime. I had some discussion with him, saying that was no reason not to come to work at all, that I would make arrangements for him so that he could work the overtime the next day and that he should come to work that night and work his regular shift. To this he responded—he was a very concerned employee—thank you, and he left my office. We talked approximately twenty or thirty minutes.

Following this conversation I attempted to contact Rob Stevens, the third shift Supervisor, by leaving several phone calls at his home. I did not get hold of him until ten o'clock that night. I talked to Rob, telling him that Mr. Fowler has some problems and let's work something out. In addition, I said that if and when he comes in tonight, he would not be assigned overtime and he'd pick it up at a later date. Rob then said, "Joe, I'm on a special assignment so I'm not coming in tonight, I'm coming in tomorrow during the day. Ted Raymond's handling the third shift tonight." I then telephoned the plant and talked to Security and Ted. I told Ted what was going on and that Mr. Fowler was not to work overtime tonight—this being the night of April 11. Ted Raymond said to me, it's too late, Joe, he's already called in absent.

On April 30, I got a phone call from Rob Stevens. He told me, "Are you aware that Mr. Fowler has got eleven and three-quarters points under the absence policy?" I said no, not really. "Are you also aware that there's a rumor being spread around the plant that you told Mr. Fowler he could miss as many days as he wanted?" I said no. I immediately arranged a meeting with Mr. Fowler, Mr. Stevens, and myself. It was a nondisciplinary meeting. There was no need for Union representation. When I walked in there I told Mr. Fowler about the rumor that I had heard and asked him if there was any truth to it. He responded, you told me I could miss as many days as I wanted. My response to him was,

"You know fully well I didn't say that to you." Mr. Fowler responded, "I don't care what the Company policy is, I'm going to take time off whenever I need it, my family comes first, you do what you have to do and I'll do what I have to do." After that, I left the foreman's office.

I realized that this employee already had eleven and three-quarters points on his record; by going home early that night, he could very easily be terminated. I felt it was my obligation to give him the opportunity to go through the Employee Assistance Program. I didn't know what type of personal problems he was experiencing. I went to find Mr. Stevens and together we approached Mr. Fowler. I asked him if he'd like to seek Employee Assistance. He stopped and looked at me for about ten or fifteen seconds and said yes. We went to the foreman's office. I called

our contact person, Dr. Kalm, and told him that the employee could possibly have some problems at home. Because this program is confidential, I then left the office to let the employee speak with Dr. Kalm alone.

Several days later, I was called into Mr. Storm's office along with Darnell and Fowler and we discussed Fowler's situation. Fowler stated to me, "I didn't realize the four-point A.W.O.L. broke the camel's back when I called in absent." He also stated to me "I didn't know what I was doing." He repeated that I told him he could miss as many days as he wanted. In response to that I said, "Dan, you're questioning the managerial authority to deal with absenteeism. You have misrepresented what I stated to you and what the Security Officer put on the call-in slip." Dan just shrugged his shoulders.

I have no further testimony.

### b. Cross-Examination by Union Advocate

*Mr. McMann:*
[to be supplied by student]

## 3. David Rich, Security Officer

### a. Direct Examination by Company Advocate

*Mr. Thomas:*
**Q:** For the record, what is your name?
**A:** David Rich.
**Q:** How long have you been employed at Archway Metals?
**A:** Approximately eleven and one-half years.
**Q:** What have been your areas of responsibility?
**A:** Security Officer for the last ten years. My duties include emergencies, fire protection, plant protection, checking employees in and out of the gate, vendors, and handling call-ins.
**Q:** Are you familiar with the grievance being discussed here today?
**A:** Yes, I am.
**Q:** What was your involvement with the grievance?
**A:** On April 29, at about 2:30 or 2:35 p.m., I took a call from Dan Fowler.
**Q:** Is this a copy of that call-in? Company Exhibit 7?

**A:** Yes.

**Q:** Can you explain for the Arbitrator what happened when you received this call-in?

**A:** When Mr. Fowler called, I stamped the call-in and proceeded to take down the information as he gave it to me. He gave me his name and his clock number, and I put that down with the date and my initials. Dan told me he was at the airport in Lexington waiting on Flight 238. He said his brother was coming in from California and the flight was running a few minutes late, and he stated that he would be possibly one-half hour late. I said, Dan, if you see you're going to be more than one hour late, you should call back and let your foreman know or let us know so that he can possibly hold someone over, especially if you're not coming in at all. He thanked me and said that he would.

**Q:** How were you instructed to take call-ins?

A: We're instructed to take down the person's name, the clock number, social security number, and exactly what they state as their reason for calling in lateness or absence.

Q: Did he call in and say he'd be absent?

A: No.

Q: Did you treat this call-in differently than any other call-in that you handled before?

A: No.

Q: I notice on the bottom it says "never called back." Do you know who put that there?

A: Yes. That was put there by the officer on the next shift, John Tinker.

Q: No further questions.

## b. Cross-Examination by Union Advocate

*Mr. McMann:*
[to be supplied by student]

## 4. Jim Phelps, Process Foreman

### a. Direct Examination by Company Advocate

*Mr. Thomas:*

Q: For the record, what is your name?

A: Jim Phelps.

Q: How long have you been employed by Archway Metals?

A: Approximately eleven years.

Q: What positions have you held?

A: I worked in the bargaining unit for a while, Process Technician, now a Process Foreman.

Q: Did the grievant appear on your time sheet in your work area at that time?

A: Yes, he did.

Q: Are you familiar with the grievance being discussed today?

A: Yes, I am.

Q: What involvement do you have with this particular grievance?

A: I issued the Written Warning and the Special Written Warning.

Q: Who was present when this letter, the Written Warning, was issued?

A: C.D. Wilson, Dan Fowler, Clyde Hall, another foreman, and myself.

Q: What are the numbers on the bottom for?

A: Those are the days missed and points assessed.

Q: Could you read the letter to the Arbitrator please? This is Company Exhibit 4.

A: "You have exceeded the established guidelines for acceptable attendance under the Absence Policy. Your absence from work has created manpower scheduling problems and overburdened your coemployees to work harder, all of which lead to inefficient operations and increased costs. For the above reasons you are being issued a written warning as disciplinary action to remind you to correct your absence problem. Please be reminded that failure to correct will lead to further disciplinary action up to and including discharge. I am available in my office to discuss the matter further if you desire."

Q: Why did you administer the Written Warning?

A: He had received eight points, actually more than that within twelve months.

Q: Were any other warnings issued?

A: Yes, I issued a Special Written Warning.

Q: Why was that issued?

A: He had reached at least ten points within twelve months.

Q: Can you read to the Arbitrator what that letter says? This is Company Exhibit 5.

A: "You were previously given a written warning on May 2, year 6 for exceeding the guidelines for acceptable attendance. Since that date, you have continued to be away from work. Once again, your absence has led to scheduling problems and overburdening others to cover for your absence, all leading to inefficient operations and added expense. The

Company will make efforts to work with you to correct your attendance problem. Available is an Employee Assistance Program to help you deal with any personal or family problems you may be encountering. Be reminded that failure to correct your attendance problem will lead to further disciplinary action up to and including dismissal. I am in my office to discuss this matter further if you desire.''

**Q:** Jim, in your own words, what is the Employee Assistance Program?

**A:** It's a tool to help people that have problems: family, personal, alcohol, or drugs.

**Q:** In both of these cases, was a copy given to Mr. Fowler?

**A:** Yes.

**Q:** Did you have any other involvement with the grievant?

**A:** I handled the termination on May 9.

**Q:** Is Company Exhibit 6 a copy of the termination letter?

**A:** Yes.

**Q:** Would you read this letter please?

**A:** ''The Company has previously issued a written warning on May 2, year 6, and a special written warning on May 2, year 6, to correct your attendance problem. You were given a copy of the attendance policy and warned of the consequences of exceeding it. You have been given the opportunity to explain your problem and the Company has tried to work with you to correct the problem, yet you have continued to be absent. The Company has met its obligation and under the attendance guidelines, it must terminate your employment on this date.''

**Q:** Who was present when this discharge letter was administered?

**A:** C.D. Wilson, Mr. Fowler, Rob Stevens, Shirley Gardner, and myself.

**Q:** Why was the employee terminated on May 9?

**A:** For overall absences reaching twelve points within twelve months.

**Q:** During your process of issuing the reprimands and the discharge, did the grievant at any time state that he didn't understand the absence policy?

**A:** No.

**Q:** Did he at any time state that he was denied a leave of absence?

**A:** No.

**Q:** I have no further questions.

### b. Cross-Examination by Union Advocate

*Mr. McMann:*
[to be supplied by student]

## C. Examination of Union Witnesses

### 1. Ronald Nagle, Union Local President

#### a. Direct Examination by Union Advocate

*Mr. McMann:*

**Q:** Would you state your full name for the record?

**A:** Ronald Nagle.

**Q:** Are you an employee of Archway?

**A:** Yes, I am.

**Q:** How long have you been an employee of Archway Metals?

**A:** About twelve years.

**Q:** Were you present when the first labor contract was negotiated?

**A:** Yes, I was.

**Q:** Have you held a Union office in the past twelve years other than the position you hold right now?

**A:** Yes, I have.

**Q:** Could you explain for the Arbitrator what these positions have been?

8

**A:** I have held the position of Shop Steward and Vice President, and presently Local President.

**Q:** How many years have you been an officer or an agent of the Local Union?

**A:** Approximately ten years, I would say.

**Q:** How long have you been President of the Local Union?

**A:** Approximately three years.

**Q:** Is part of your functions handling the grievance procedure for the Local Union?

**A:** Yes, it is.

**Q:** Are you familiar with the Dan Fowler case before the Arbitrator today?

**A:** Yes.

**Q:** Ron, were you also familiar with the previous absentee control system that the Company had prior to the one implemented on February 20th, year 6?

**A:** Yes.

**Q:** Could you explain the Union's position concerning the previous absentee control system?

**A:** We felt like a lot of employees were handled unjustly. We contested it on numerous occasions, both through the grievance procedure and verbally.

**Q:** Were all employees treated the same under the previous program?

**A:** No.

**Q:** Ron, could you explain the Union's position on the new No-Fault Absenteeism Policy?

**A:** Well, the Union's position on it is that it's unreasonable and unfair on a lot of occasions.

**Q:** Would you explain that for the Arbitrator, what you mean by that?

**A:** Well, it doesn't have any way that anyone can be absent unless they're assessed a point.

**Q:** Has the Union contested this program from the onset?

**A:** Yes, we have.

**Q:** Has the Union ever attempted to negotiate with the Company concerning this program?

**A:** What do you mean?

**Q:** Has the Union ever sat down to a bargaining session and had input as far as changing rules in that Policy?

**A:** We have questioned the fairness of it, if I'm understanding you right.

**Q:** But the Union did not negotiate with the Company over the policy?

**A:** Definitely not, no.

**Q:** I have no further questions.

## b. Cross-Examination by Company Advocate

*Mr. Thomas:*
[to be supplied by student]

## 2. Daniel Fowler, Grievant

### a. Direct Examination by Union Advocate

*Mr. McMann:*

**Q:** State your full name for the record.

**A:** Dan Fowler.

**Q:** Could you give the Arbitrator your present address, Mr. Fowler?

**A:** Yes, it's 300 North Fifth Avenue, Alma, Michigan.

**Q:** Are you currently employed?

**A:** Yes, I am.

**Q:** By whom?

**A:** Alma Boatworks.

**Q:** Mr. Fowler, you were an employee of Archway when you were terminated last May, year 6, is that correct?

**A:** That's true, yes.

**Q:** How long did you work at Archway Metals?

**A:** About six years.

**Q:** What was your position with Archway at the time you were terminated?

**A:** I worked there as a material handler.

**Q:** Where did you live at that time?

**A:** In Henley, Kentucky.

**Q:** Mr. Fowler, are you familiar with the Company Exhibit 1, the No-Fault Absenteeism Policy that was established February 2nd, year 6?

**A:** Yes, I have seen this.

**Q:** Would you turn to the last page of that document? Is that your signature on that document?

**A:** Yes, it is.

**Q:** Were you in a meeting with other employees when that program was explained?

**A:** There were two other employees present when it was briefly run over, yes.

**Q:** Who explained the program to you?

**A:** That was . . . I'm sorry, I can't recall his name.

**Q:** It was one of the company supervisors?

**A:** It was a foreman, yes. That was Steve Given. I think he was a technician at the time.

**Q:** Mr. Fowler, the record shows that your first absence under the new absentee no-fault system was March 20th, year 6, is that correct?

**A:** I believe that's correct, yes, sir.

**Q:** And what was the reason that you reported off that day?

**A:** That was personal business.

**Q:** The record also shows that you were absent on April 2, year 6. Do you recall why you called off that day?

**A:** That was also personal business.

**Q:** At that point you had received two points, is that correct?

**A:** That's correct.

**Q:** On April 7, year 6, you reported you would be off work on April 8, year 6, on the 12 to 8 a.m. shift, is that correct?

**A:** That is correct.

**Q:** Why did you call?

**A:** My wife had a seizure earlier, that was on Saturday, April 7, and I had to take her to the Suburban Hospital Emergency Room and stayed there until approximately 11 p.m. that night. She was allowed to go home, with orders from the doctor for me to keep a close watch on her and to awaken her several times during the night.

**Q:** When did your wife's seizure occur?

**A:** At approximately four o'clock Saturday afternoon.

**Q:** What happened?

**A:** I received a phone call from her place of employment—she's the manager at this store. An employee of hers called and told me that my wife Carolyn had had a seizure or a spell of some kind. The employee said that she looked like she was in pretty bad shape and she was in a very confused state and did not want to go to the hospital. So she called me to come get Carolyn and take her.

**Q:** Did you go pick her up?

**A:** Yes, I did.

**Q:** About what time did you pick her up?

**A:** Approximately five.

**Q:** Around five o'clock that afternoon. Did you take her to the hospital?

**A:** Yes, I did. I took her to the emergency room.

**Q:** What was her condition as far as you could observe?

**A:** She seemed very confused. Her speech was not slurred, but her words were transposed, and she couldn't say what she wanted to say. She had a trembling in her right hand, intense headache, nausea, she couldn't stand bright light, and she had various other symptoms.

**Q:** What time did you arrive at the hospital?

**A:** I'm not exactly sure of the check-in time but it was between 5:30 and 6 o'clock.

**Q:** Did the doctor on duty examine your wife?

**A:** Yes, he did. After a brief examination he felt that a specialist should be called in, so he called Dr. Jones, who is a neurosurgeon.

**Q:** Did Dr. Jones examine your wife?

**A:** Yes, he did.

**Q:** What were his findings?

**A:** Well, he examined her and took me into the hall and asked me several questions. He seemed to feel that he had narrowed the diagnosis but further tests should be run. The hospital's C.T. Scan Machine was broken down and there was nothing he could do at the moment. She seemed to be much better. He was afraid that the worst possibility could be a brain tumor and the second possibility would be an epileptic-type seizure, but he told me that he definitely pinpointed it to the front or lower area of the brain or what he called a grand mal seizure.

**Q:** Had your wife experienced any kind of a seizure of this nature before?

**A:** No, sir.

**Q:** You mentioned a C.T. Machine. What's a C.T. Machine?

**A:** I think it's commonly referred to as a CAT scan; it's an apparatus similar to an X-ray machine that gets a reading of the brain or takes pictures of the brain.

**Q:** So he wasn't able to perform a CAT scan at that time?

**A:** That's correct.

**Q:** Did he leave you with instructions on how to handle your wife or what you should do with her?

**A:** Yes. He mentioned the possibility of a stroke. He said the symptoms, when they're in that area of the brain, are hard to pinpoint. He said the best way to make a diagnosis is if she had the attack again to get her to the hospital immediately, that she needed close observation, and to awaken her several times during the night.

**Q:** Did he then tell you to take your wife home?

**A:** Yes, he did.

**Q:** Did you take her home?

**A:** Yes, I did.

**Q:** Approximately what time was that?

**A:** I think we left the hospital at approximately 11:15 p.m. on April 7.

**Q:** Now your shift was to start at twelve o'clock midnight, April 8, in other words, that same night, is that correct?

**A:** Yes, sir.

**Q:** Did you call in?

**A:** Yes, I did. I called from the hospital.

**Q:** Was this from a pay phone?

**A:** Yes.

**Q:** Okay, the record shows that you also missed work on Monday April 9, year 6, and that you properly called the plant on April 8 at 9 p.m. to report off on April 9, for the midnight to eight a.m. shift. Is that correct?

**A:** Yes sir, that's true.

**Q:** Why did you report off on that day?

**A:** Because of my wife's unspecified illness. I had the doctor's instructions to keep a close eye on her and that this thing could occur at any time. It would have been uncaring and unnecessary to go to work at the time, and I felt that I should be with my wife per the doctor's instructions.

**Q:** Dan, would you identify this document for the Arbitrator? This Union Exhibit No. 1.

**A:** Yes sir, this is a bill for the emergency services.

**Q:** And what date was that billing for?

**A:** April 7, year 6.

**Q:** Mr. Fowler, did your wife have tests run also on April 9?

**A:** Yes, she did.

**Q:** Do you know what those tests were?

**A:** Yes. She had a full physical and also an EEG, a brain wave test.

**Q:** Was this also performed by Dr. Jones?

**A:** Yes, sir.

**Q:** And could you identify this document, Union Exhibit 2, and the dates at the bottom for the Arbitrator?

**A:** Yes. This is a health insurance claim form for emergency service on April 7, and also for the comprehensive re-exam and EEG on April 9.

**Q:** Now, on April 9 your wife had tests run, which shows up in Union Exhibit 2. Approximately what time of the day did she have those tests run?

**A:** I think we arrived at the medical center about 11 a.m.

**Q:** Dan, why didn't you go to work that day for the midnight to eight a.m. shift?

**A:** Because my wife had a serious incident with her health and I had no idea what it was. She was very frightened and in a strange frame of mind. I'm her husband and I needed to be there to support her.

**Q:** Did the doctor tell you to be there with her?

**A:** Yes, he did. Could I add something, please?

**Q:** Yes.

**A:** The EEG test consisted of injecting—I'm not exactly sure of the drug, but it's to put her into a light sleep before the EEG test. Naturally, she could not drive herself home from the test, and we don't have any relatives nearby.

**Q:** Did the doctor feel it was imperative for you to be present with her?

**A:** Yes, he said that she should be under a low-stress environment and that she needed all the support I could give her.

**Q:** Again, would she have been able to drive herself home after the tests were run?

**A:** No.

**Q:** Okay, Dan, the next day, Tuesday, April 10, did you work that day?

**A:** Yes, I did.

**Q:** Did you work eight hours that day?

**A:** Yes, I did.

**Q:** Did you talk with Mr. Thomas that day?

**A:** Yes, sir, I did.

**Q:** Would you explain the conversation that you had with Mr. Thomas?

**A:** Yes, I went into his office and asked for a few moments of his time to explain the situation, that I was afraid it would cause problems with my job. I was concerned about my job. I realized I already had a couple of points due to absenteeism, and that with the nature of my wife's serious illness I wanted to make the Company fully aware that I would be taking time off for the various tests being run and to stay with my wife if necessary during this serious period in her life.

**Q:** Is this the same Mr. Thomas sitting as the Company advocate today?

**A:** Yes, it is.

**Q:** Did Mr. Thomas discuss with you the possibility of taking a leave of absence at that time?

**A:** Yes, he did. He said that I could have leave of absence in a consecutive period. In other words I could have a week, two weeks off, whatever I needed. I told him that under the circumstances I would like to work as much as possible because the tests were intermittent. I tried to explain to him that I felt a consecutive leave of absence would be more harmful than good.

**Q:** Did the doctor explain to you or at any time give you an idea of when a reoccurrence of this same nature that happened on April 7 could occur?

**A:** Yes, he said depending on the exact nature of her illness that it could occur at any time.

**Q:** Was he conclusive about a period of time like two weeks, or anything that you could put a finger on for a leave of absence?

**A:** No, he told me we'd have to ride this thing out and watch her closely and see what happens.

**Q:** So at that time did you feel a two-week leave of absence would cover the situation?

**A:** Not at all.

**Q:** On Wednesday, April 11, the record shows that you reported off because your wife was having a brain scan test?

**A:** Yes.

**Q:** Did the doctor inform you that it would be necessary for you to be with your wife during those tests?

**A:** Yes, he did.

**Q:** When did you take your wife in for those tests, approximately?

**A:** Approximately 10:30 in the morning.

**Q:** How long did they last?

**A:** The entire duration of the stay at the hospital was approximately three and a half to four hours.

**Q:** Was your wife coherent enough to drive home after those tests?

**A:** No.

**Q:** Was it necessary as part of those tests to inject any kind of dye?

**A:** Yes.

**Q:** Did the doctor inform you of the seriousness of injecting blood dyes into the system?

**A:** Yes, he did.

**Q:** How many hours did you work that day, that is on the midnight to 8 a.m. shift on April 12?

**A:** I worked sixteen hours on back-to-back shifts that day.

**Q:** Did you work on the midnight to 8:00 a.m. shift on April 13?

**A:** I worked eight hours, and then they let me go home before I put in all my extra forced overtime hours.

**Q:** Dan, would you identify Union Exhibit No. 3 for the Arbitrator?

**A:** This is the medical bill for the CAT scan.

**Q:** Would you now explain what a "force" is?

**A:** Force relates to a policy whereby if not enough people volunteer for a shift, then a man who is up for a "force" is forced to stay an extra eight-hour shift.

**Q:** And on April 13 it was your day to be forced over, is that correct?

**A:** Yes.

**Q:** However, you were allowed to go home without being forced to work?

**A:** Yes, I had notified the proper people.

**Q:** Why did you want to go home that day?

**A:** Because Carolyn had another exam scheduled for that day.

**Q:** On April 17, year 6, the record shows that you were absent again. That was a Tuesday and you were to be on the 8 a.m. to 4 p.m. shift, is that correct?

**A:** I think that's correct, yes.

**Q:** And the record also shows that you were staying home with your wife?

**A:** Yes.

**Q:** Why did you stay home with your wife?

**A:** Because she had a reoccurrence of the symptoms like the day she went to the emergency room, including a strange taste in her mouth and hypersensitivity to bright lights.

**Q:** As of April 17 you had received six points, is that correct?

**A:** Up to that time I had no idea how many points I had. No one had told me I had six points, although I knew I had some due to my wife's illness and the tests. My foreman and Mr. Thomas were aware of the tests, but no one said anything about the points. As a matter of fact, in my conversation with Mr. Thomas he said that we would try to work something out and that he was uncertain as to exactly what we would work out. As he was aware of the situation due to the seriousness of it, I didn't question it.

**Q:** The absences of April 9, 11, and 17 had all occurred because of your wife's illness, is that correct?

**A:** Yes.

**Q:** And up to this time you didn't realize that you had points assessed for every one of those illnesses?

**A:** That's true.

**Q:** The record shows that on April 21, year 6, that you reported off work again, that your wife was sick and you were going to take her to the doctor.

**A:** Yes.

**Q:** This was on the 8 a.m. to 4 p.m. shift?

**A:** I believe that's right.

**Q:** Why did you report off? Was the reason that you were going to take her to the doctor?

**A:** It was a reoccurrence of the same symptoms. You have to understand that even at this time the neurosurgeon could not pinpoint what was wrong with my wife. Of course, the anxiety of not knowing what's wrong and the seriousness of what had happened was unnerving to her. She seemed to lose her sense of reality. To be honest with you, she could not function to take care of our two children.

**Q:** Did you take her to the doctor that day?

**A:** No, I didn't.

**Q:** Why didn't you?

**A:** The main reason I wanted to take her was because of the intense headache she had. I gave her some Tylenol and codeine tablets and put some blankets over the windows to shut out the light. After a couple of hours the headache seemed to ease up and she did not want to go through the trauma of going to the hospital. She seemed to feel better, so I let her stay home.

**Q:** Did you work the following day, April 22, year 6?

**A:** Yes, I did.

**Q:** How many hours did you work that day?

**A:** I worked sixteen hours that day, back-to-back shifts.

**Q:** How do you recall April 22?

**A:** Because I myself was sick at the time, and it was hard to get through the shift, to be honest with you.

**Q:** Did you volunteer to work over that day or did you get forced over that day?

**A:** It was a force.

**Q:** The record shows that you received three-quarters of a point on the next day, April 23, because you left work early?

**A:** This is true, yes.

**Q:** And that was on a Monday on the eight a.m. to four p.m. shift?

**A:** Yes.

**Q:** Why did you leave work early that day?

**A:** Because I was very sick, much sicker than the day before when I worked sixteen hours. With the problems I had already I did not want to miss any work, and I thought I could do it. I got progressively worse, especially my breathing. The dust inside bothered me. I had acute tonsillitis, as it turned out. I felt very bad and did not think I could perform the job, so I asked the foreman if I could have an early out. This was about 1 p.m.

**Q:** Did the Company doctor tell you that you were too ill to work?

**A:** Yes, he did. He said, for a reason he wasn't very clear about, that he couldn't treat me at the plant site but that I needed to get out of there and get a shot as soon as possible.

**Q:** Who was the doctor?

**A:** It was Dr. James Trent.

**Q:** Did he tell you what doctor you should go to?

**A:** He asked if I had a personal physician and I told him, no, that I did not have a personal physician. He then told me to meet him at his office at 3 p.m.

**Q:** Where was his office located?

**A:** Lexington, Kentucky.

**Q:** Did you inform your supervisor that you were sick?

**A:** Yes, I did.

**Q:** And that you needed to go home?

**A:** Yes.

**Q:** What was his response?

**A:** He told me I would be assessed three-quarters of a point. Then he said he didn't think I could afford it.

**Q:** Prior to this conversation with Mr. Stevens, had you ever been forewarned that you were getting into trouble due to absenteeism?

**A:** Once before, yes. As a matter of fact, the first time I was aware that the dates I had taken off for the tests and my wife's illnesses were assessed against me was when a supervisor, Clyde Hall, told me that I reached seven and three-quarters. This was oral, you know, just a discussion.

**Q:** When Mr. Stevens told you that you would be assessed three-quarters of a point if you went home, what was your response?

**A:** Distressed. I tried to get through the day. I felt really bad. I had a severe headache. I could hardly speak. Under the circumstances, at that point I valued my job, I wanted to keep it, so I decided to hang with it and told him I'd stay.

**Q:** And did you go back to work?

**A:** For a short time, yes.

**Q:** Did you eventually go home early that day?

**A:** Yes, I did.

**Q:** Why couldn't you hang with the job?

**A:** Just the way I felt. It was really bad. I had to go up on a catwalk and come back down in all that heat. I almost passed out. I stumbled down the stairs and into the bathroom where I rested for a while and

decided it was not worth it; I needed to go home.

**Q:** Where are the catwalks located in the plant?

**A:** They're the small areas of passage between the smelting pots.

**Q:** And the smelting pots, do they have hot metal in them?

**A:** Yes, they do.

**Q:** Molten aluminum?

**A:** Yes.

**Q:** Is the heat intense in that area?

**A:** Quite intense.

**Q:** Did you then request a pass to go home again?

**A:** Yes, I did.

**Q:** Did you receive a pass?

**A:** Yes.

**Q:** From whom?

**A:** From Rob Stevens.

**Q:** Do you recall about what time that was?

**A:** It was approximately one o'clock. I'm not exactly sure of the time because I was quite ill and distressed about my job. I really don't remember what time it was.

**Q:** Did you leave the plant at that time?

**A:** Yes.

**Q:** And did you go home?

**A:** Yes. I did not go straight home. I went to the doctor's office in Lexington, Kentucky.

**Q:** Were you treated by Dr. Trent that day for acute tonsillitis?

**A:** Yes.

**Q:** Would you identify this for the Arbitrator? This is Union Exhibit 4.

**A:** Yes, this is the bill from Dr. Trent for the office visit and for an injection of bicillin on April 23, year 6.

**Q:** Were you then assessed three-quarters of a point for leaving early?

**A:** Yes, I was.

**Q:** Is Company Exhibit 3 the grievance that you filed?

**A:** Yes, it is.

**Q:** And does it concern that three-quarters of a point?

**A:** Yes, it does.

**Q:** Dan, you said that a supervisor, Clyde Hall, had talked to you briefly concerning the approximately seven and three-quarters points you had at that time or that you were getting into trouble with your absences?

**A:**  Yes.

**Q:**  Did this alarm you at the time?

**A:**  Yes, it did. I was confused about the discussion I had with Mr. Thomas. I couldn't believe that they were assessing me points all those days over the same problem relating to my wife's illness, and until that time I didn't know that points would be assessed for those days.

**Q:**  Did you understand that you would receive points for absences for the personal business?

**A:**  Yes, I did for the personal business.

**Q:**  Were you aware that for April 23 that you would receive points for leaving work early for being sick?

**A:**  Yes, my supervisor, Rob Stevens, told me that I would be assessed three-quarters of a point for leaving early.

**Q:**  So you understood the Absenteeism Policy?

**A:**  I understood the Policy, you know, as they intended to implement it. It doesn't mean that I agreed with it.

**Q:**  You felt that there was an exception made in your case by Mr. Thomas?

**A:**  Absolutely, yes.

**Q:**  Did you then work on April 27, year 6, on Friday? Did you have a discussion with Mr. Thomas and Mr. Stevens on that day?

**A:**  Yes, sir, I believe that's the day that they pulled me off the job. I was cleaning out the back aisle, and they asked me to follow them to the office.

**Q:**  What was your first response to that?

**A:**  The first response I had was, what was it about and could I get a Union representative?

**Q:**  Did you ask for a Union Steward?

**A:**  Yes, I did.

**Q:**  What were you told?

**A:**  They told me that this was informal, that I didn't need Union representation.

**Q:**  Did you not get a Union Steward at that time?

**A:**  No, I didn't.

**Q:**  What was the context of this discussion?

**A:**  Mr. Thomas told me that I had a problem, that there was an Employee Assistance Program available to me and

that . . . he didn't ask me but insisted that I talk to a Dr. Kalm in Lexington.

**Q:**  Who is Dr. Kalm?

**A:**  I have no idea. I assumed he was somehow involved in the Employee Assistance Program.

**Q:**  What did the Employee Assistance Program mean to you at the time you were told about it?

**A:**  All I had heard about it was that the program was available to people who had emotional problems, drug or alcohol problems, etc.

**Q:**  And what was your problem?

**A:**  As far as I knew I had no problem; my wife was sick.

**Q:**  Was Mr. Thomas forceful in that meeting that you must talk to Dr. Kalm, or were you asked whether you should or could talk to Dr. Kalm?

**A:**  No, as a matter of fact, he was quite agitated and abusive and insisted on it. He even dialed the phone and handed it to me. Then he left the room and so I talked to the doctor.

**Q:**  Did you talk to Dr. Kalm?

**A:**  Yes, I did.

**Q:**  What was the discussion you had with him?

**A:**  He identified himself to me over the phone as Dr. Kalm with the—I think I remember correctly—Comprehensive Mental Health Clinic, something like that. He asked what the problem was, and I didn't know even where to start. I said, well, you can only start at the beginning, so I briefly explained my problems with Employee Relations at the plant. He knew about my wife's illness. He asked questions about that, how serious it was, etc., and I told him the doctor's name. Then he said that he didn't see any way he could be of assistance, it sounded like an internal problem, and he suggested that I go around Joe Thomas and talk to Bill Storm.

**Q:**  Who is Bill Storm?

**A:**  The Plant Manager.

**Q:**  After your discussion with Dr. Kalm, did you have any further discussion with Mr. Thomas and Mr. Stevens?

**A:**  There were . . . I can't remember, to be honest with you, what exactly transpired.

There was no lengthy discussion or more comments made, etc., that was it.

**Q:** Did you bring to Mr. Thomas's attention your wife's illness and indicate that you understood that there would be some leeway in that you wouldn't be assessed points?

**A:** No, at that time he didn't give me an opportunity to talk to him. Like I said, it was more of an aggressive and abusive type of thing. He said . . . I don't think I can quote exactly what he said, something like "I went out on a limb for you on this thing and you rubbed my face in it."

**Q:** Did you ask him what he meant by that?

**A:** Yes, I did.

**Q:** What was his response?

**A:** Excuse the language. He said, "You know damn well what I'm talking about."

**Q:** Did he ever make it clear to you what he was talking about?

**A:** No, he didn't.

**Q:** After the discussion with Dr. Kalm, did you have a lengthy or short discussion with Mr. Thomas?

**A:** I wouldn't call it lengthy, it was long enough for me to explain the situation, no more than seven or ten minutes.

**Q:** Did you work the following day, April 28, year 6?

**A:** Yes, I did.

**Q:** Did you work more than eight hours that day?

**A:** Yes, I did.

**Q:** Did you work overtime that night into the morning of the 29th?

**A:** It's difficult to remember, but I think you're correct, yes.

**Q:** You worked sixteen hours?

**A:** Yes.

**Q:** So you worked from four p.m. to midnight and then worked an additional eight hours over and got off at eight a.m. on the morning of the 29th.

**A:** Yes.

**Q:** On April 29, year 6, the record shows, Dan, that you received four points. With these points you had accumulated eleven and three-quarters points under the Company's Policy. Can you explain why you missed work that day?

**A:** Yes, my brother was discharged from the Air Force and was flying in from California to the Lexington Airport. The time of arrival was 2:20 p.m., and I was scheduled in that afternoon for the four-to-midnight shift, which would give me plenty of time to pick him up at the airport and be dropped off at work, which is what I intended to do. When I arrived at the airport, I was informed that the flight was grounded in St. Louis because of fog and that it would be approximately two hours late. At that time I didn't have any choice but to call the plant and inform them of the situation.

**Q:** Who did you talk to at the plant?

**A:** I talked to the security guard who answered the phone.

**Q:** What time did you call the plant and report off?

**A:** I think it was about 2:30 p.m., something like that. I'm not exactly sure.

**Q:** It was within the proper time frame of reporting off?

**A:** Yes, it was.

**Q:** What time did the flight eventually arrive?

**A:** Approximately 5 p.m.

**Q:** When you reported off to the plant, you talked with security officer David Rich?

**A:** That's true, yes.

**Q:** Could you explain how you reported off?

**A:** Yes, I called in and first said I would be late. During the conversation I gave him the information on my whereabouts. I gave the number of the flight and told him that I would be two hours late, and in doing so I realized that nobody gets in the gate after two hours. So I thought if it was any later than that, by the time I drove from Lexington to Henley there would be no way to work my shift, so I told him to go ahead and report me off, that I wouldn't be in. I also said if the plane should arrive, if it gets here any sooner, I will call you back and tell you I'm coming in.

**Q:** Did you, based on the discussion you had with Dr. Kalm, have a meeting on or about April 30, with Mr. Storm, the Plant Manager?

**A:** Very briefly, yes.

**Q:** Who was present in that meeting?

**A:** Myself, Dennis Darnell. . . .

**Q:** Who is Dennis Darnell?

**A:** Shop Steward.

**Q:** Did you discuss with Mr. Storm at that time the phone conversation you had with Dr. Kalm?

**A:** Yes, I did.

**Q:** What was Mr. Storm's reaction?

**A:** Mr. Storm's reaction was sympathetic, but he stated that he did not want to get involved and that I would have to talk to Joe Thomas about this.

**Q:** Did Mr. Storm have any further discussion with you concerning it?

**A:** No, he didn't. He went next door to where Mr. Thomas was and brought him in.

**Q:** Did Mr. Storm stay there when Mr. Thomas arrived?

**A:** Very briefly, for a few moments, and then he left.

**Q:** And was Mr. Thomas there with you?

**A:** Yes, he was.

**Q:** Did you have a Union Steward present at that time?

**A:** Yes, Dennis Darnell was there with me.

**Q:** What was Mr. Thomas discussing at that time?

**A:** Well, initially Dennis asked him exactly, you know, what was going on, what seemed to be the problem, that there was a misunderstanding, and that I was quite upset. Frankly, it seemed like they were out to get me. I couldn't believe the four points for calling in and on top of the personal problems that I had made them aware of, I just assumed that there had to be another reason. Of course, I was not going to speak to him again without Union representation. I had been burned with that once, so Dennis did most of the talking and asked him if some of the points could not be negotiated, that there were very serious reasons and that he thought that Mr. Thomas should give this consideration.

**Q:** What did Mr. Thomas say?

**A:** He said he'd think about it.

**Q:** On May 2, year 6, you received a Written Warning and a Special Written Warning, both at the same time, for attendance from Mr. Phelps, is that correct?

**A:** Yes, that's correct.

**Q:** Who was present in that meeting, or do you remember?

**A:** Myself, Union Steward Wilson, Mr. Phelps, and Clyde Hall.

**Q:** Who is Clyde Hall?

**A:** He is a line foreman.

**Q:** He's one of the other foremen that you work under besides Mr. Phelps?

**A:** Yes.

**Q:** And sometimes you work under Mr. Raymond?

**A:** That's true, yes.

**Q:** That's the same Mr. Hall that briefly spoke with you concerning the fact you were getting pretty close to an eight-point written warning level?

**A:** That's true, yes.

**Q:** And at that time they gave you two written warnings in one day, is that correct?

**A:** Simultaneously, yes.

**Q:** At this point you were made aware that you were at eleven and three-quarters points?

**A:** At the time of the written warnings, yes, they informed me.

**Q:** Now, on May 7, year 6, the record shows you left work early and received three-quarters of a point for that. Did you work your midnight to 8 a.m. shift that day?

**A:** Yes, I did.

**Q:** Did you work overtime that day?

**A:** Yes, I did, but I didn't complete that shift.

**Q:** You left early on the overtime shift?

**A:** Yes.

**Q:** Why did you leave early that day?

**A:** I received a phone call from my sister-in-law, who was staying at my house at the time. She said that my wife seemed to be having an attack again, that she was asking for me, and that I should come home.

**Q:** Did she explain the symptoms of the attack she was having?

**A:** Yes.

**Q:** Were they the same as those she had on April 7?

**A:** Precisely the same.

**Q:** Did you ask for a pass to go home that day?

**A:** Yes, I did.

**Q:** Do you recall which supervisor gave you the pass?

**A:** To the best of my recollection, it was Bob Weeks.

**Q:** Who was your supervisor on the midnight-to-8 shift that day?

**A:** Mr. Stevens.

17

**Q:** Was he still at the plant or still in the area whenever it was that you asked for a pass to go home, or do you recall that?

**A:** There were still several foremen in the office. I do not recall precisely if Mr. Stevens was there.

**Q:** So you obtained a pass and went home?

**A:** Yes.

**Q:** You returned again on May 9, year 6. That was the 8 a.m. shift again, is that correct?

**A:** That's true, yes.

**Q:** Upon entering the plant, what took place?

**A:** Well, I did not enter the plant site, I was stopped at the security guard shack and was told to go to the conference room and to wait there.

**Q:** Did anybody else come into that room?

**A:** I was there for a long time and then C.D. Wilson, the Shop Steward, came in.

**Q:** Did anybody else come into the room?

**A:** Later Shirley Gardner arrived, as did Jim Phelps and Rob Stevens.

**Q:** And what was the discussion that you had with them at that time?

**A:** No conversation with Rob Stevens in particular. Shirley Gardner was handling the termination, as I found out. She gave me a copy of the termination procedure, read it out loud, and then said that I was terminated.

**Q:** For what reason?

**A:** Because I had attained the twelve-point limit.

**Q:** Did you at that time attempt to explain to Ms. Gardner the condition of your wife or some of the problems you had encountered?

**A:** Yes, I did.

**Q:** What was Ms. Gardner's response to that?

**A:** Her response was that I had reached the twelve-point limit and that my employment at Archway was terminated.

**Q:** You subsequently filed a grievance on the Written Warnings, the Special Written Warning, and your final termination?

**A:** Yes, I did.

**Q:** I want to clear up one point, regarding the forced overtime. When you're asked to work an overtime shift, which results in you working sixteen straight hours, do they accept any excuses relieving you from working the overtime shift?

**A:** Yes. There have been numerous occasions where people for one reason or another have been released from forced overtime.

**Q:** One earlier time it happened to you and you were excused, is that right?

**A:** That's correct.

**Q:** I have no further questions.

### b. Cross-Examination by Company Advocate

*Mr. Thomas:*
[to be supplied by student]

## 3. Dennis Darnell, Employee and Former Union Vice President

### a. Direct Examination by Union Advocate

*Mr. McMann:*

**Q:** Are you an employee of Archway Metals?

**A:** Yes, I am.

**Q:** How long have you worked there?

**A:** Approximately eight years.

**Q:** Do you presently hold a position with the Local Union?

**A:** No, I don't.

**Q:** Have you ever held a position with the Local Union?

**A:** Yes, I have.

**Q:** What were those positions?

**A:** I held the position of Shop Steward, Trustee, Vice President, various Union committees, and Acting President.

**Q:** There was testimony concerning an incident in which Daniel Fowler had to leave work early on or about April 23, year 6. Were you working that day?

**A:** Yes, I was.

**Q:** Were you working the same shift that Dan was working?

**A:** Yes, I was.

**Q:** Did you have a conversation with Dan that morning?

**A:** Yes, I did.

**Q:** Could you explain what the conversation was?

**A:** Dan came to me and explained the situation about being really sick and told me that he would get three-quarters of a point if he left and asked me what he should do. At that time, I was under the impression that he didn't have as many points as what he had, that this three-quarters of a point would put him at seven and three-quarters, so I advised him that if at all possible that he should remain working at that. . . .

**Q:** And what was his response to you?

**A:** He said, okay, I'll give it a shot, I'll go back to work and see if I can make it.

**Q:** About what time of day was that?

**A:** Approximately 10:30.

**Q:** Were you at this time holding any Union position?

**A:** Yes, I was Vice President. I get my dates wrong, but I might have been acting as President in Ron's absence.

**Q:** So at that time you were advising him as an official of the Local Union?

**A:** Absolutely.

**Q:** And to your knowledge he did attempt to go back to work?

**A:** Yes, he did.

**Q:** However, he didn't work the shift?

**A:** That's correct.

**Q:** On or about April 30, year 6, do you recall a meeting with Mr. Bill Storm?

**A:** Yes, I do.

**Q:** What was that meeting about?

**A:** Basically, it was about Mr. Fowler's so-called absenteeism problem. I guess Dan had been told by Dr. Kalm to contact Mr. Storm. He really didn't know Mr. Storm and asked me if I knew him. I said Mr. Storm was the Plant Manager and I have worked often with him, so I went with Dan to Bill Storm's office for a discussion.

**Q:** Did Mr. Fowler attempt to explain to Mr. Storm at that time the reason for his absences concerning his wife's illness?

**A:** Yes, to some extent. He mainly told Mr. Storm what Dr. Kalm had said, that Dan was to go talk to him instead of going to talk to Mr. Thomas.

**Q:** Was Mr. Fowler trying to protect himself from termination?

**A:** Absolutely.

**Q:** What was Mr. Storm's response?

**A:** Mr. Storm's response was quite negative. He felt that it wasn't his responsibility, I guess, and he didn't want to get involved. He told us we'd have to talk to Mr. Thomas about it.

**Q:** Did you then talk with Mr. Thomas?

**A:** Yes. He called Mr. Thomas into the office and stayed briefly and then left.

**Q:** What was the extent of the conversation you had with Mr. Thomas?

**A:** We discussed the problems that were going on with Mr. Fowler. All of this happened in such a short period of time that a lot of the information I had was by word of mouth, and I wanted to know exactly what was going on. Both Mr. Thomas and Mr. Fowler tried to explain some of the things that went on.

**Q:** Did Mr. Thomas appear to be trying to compromise in any manner?

**A:** Not at this time.

**Q:** I have no further questions.

### b. Cross-Examination by Company Advocate

*Mr. Thomas:*
[to be supplied by student]

## 4. C.D. Wilson, Employee and Former Shop Steward

### a. Direct Examination by Union Advocate

*Mr. McMann:*

**Q:** Would you state your full name for the record?

**A:** Charles D. Wilson.

**Q:** Are you better known as C.D.?

**A:** Yes.

**Q:** Are you an employee of Archway Metals?

**A:** Yes.

**Q:** How long have you worked there?

**A:** About eleven years.

**Q:** Have you ever held the position of Shop Steward?

**A:** Yes, briefly.

**Q:** Were you the Shop Steward who is referred to in the grievance being heard today?

**A:** Yes.

**Q:** On or about April 23, year 6, Mr. Fowler had become ill and saw the Company doctor. The doctor evidently advised him that he needed to go home and he informed his supervisor of that. Were you aware of this incident?

**A:** Yes.

**Q:** Were you present during any of the discussion between the employee and Supervisor Stevens?

**A:** Yes.

**Q:** Could you explain to what extent you have knowledge of that discussion?

**A:** Well, I went with Dan to see Mr. Stevens to ask him why, if the Company doctor ordered him to go home, why he was going to be charged three-quarters of a point, being as sick as he was. Mr. Stevens said it was just the system, that there's no way around it, charging three-quarters of a point, Company doctor or no Company doctor. We argued about that for a long time.

**Q:** There was no change in the supervisor's position?

**A:** No change at all.

**Q:** On or about May 2, year 6, Mr. Fowler received two written warnings on the same day, Company Exhibit 3 and Company Exhibit 4. Can you identify those?

**A:** Yes, I can.

**Q:** Were you present when those written warnings were issued?

**A:** Yes.

**Q:** Did Mr. Fowler or yourself bring up at that time the problems concerning Mr. Fowler's wife and some of the problems that he had had as far as points assessed towards him?

**A:** Yes, we did.

**Q:** Did he explain that after his discussion with Mr. Thomas he felt he wouldn't be assessed the points attributable to the illnesses of his wife?

**A:** That's what Dan had told me and that's what I based my arguments on.

**Q:** That the Company did know?

**A:** Yes.

**Q:** What was Mr. Phelps's response?

**A:** Well, he said he was just doing it because of the number of points accumulated by Dan, and it was his obligation to give him these warnings.

**Q:** Was Supervisor Clyde Hall in that meeting?

**A:** Yes, I believe he was.

**Q:** Do you recall Mr. Hall at any time sympathizing with Mr. Fowler's situation during the discussion?

**A:** Well, I can't remember word for word or anything, but they always talk about the problems and say we'll work something out with the Employee Assistance Program or something like that. Dan had already tried that route.

**Q:** Did the Employee Asssistance Program come up in that discussion?

**A:** Not that I can remember.

**Q:** Company Exhibit 5 is the final termination notice of Mr. Fowler, dated May 9, year 6. Were you present in that meeting?

**A:** Yes.

**Q:** Could you explain the extent of the discussion that you had with Ms. Gardner, Mr. Phelps, and the other supervisor? Who was present in that meeting?

**A:** Gardner, Stevens, Phelps, Dan, and myself.

**Q:** So you were there to represent Mr. Fowler?

**A:** Yes, I was.

**Q:** Did you try to explain to the Company at that time that you felt the point system was unfair to Mr. Fowler?

**A:** Yes, I did.

**Q:** Did you inform the Company that you had filed grievances on the other write-up of three-quarters of a point?

**A:** Yes, I did.

**Q:** What was the Company's attitude towards assessment of the points at that time?

**A:** He had accumulated twelve points or better, so that was it, no matter what.

**Q:** Didn't it matter what they were for?

**A:** Didn't matter what the reasons were. Twelve points and you got it; that's how the No-Fault Absenteeism Policy is intended to work.

**Q:** And Mr. Fowler was then escorted out of the plant after that meeting?

**A:** Yes.

**Q:** Then did you file a grievance concerning his termination?

**A:** No, Ron Nagle did that. That's out of my hands.

**Q:** I just have a few more questions. How long have you worked in the potline area?

**A:** For about the whole time I've been working there.

**Q:** What are the conditions where Mr. Fowler was working on April 23, when he went home early?

**A:** Up where he was on the catwalk, it's hot. There is molten metal below.

**Q:** Is it dusty?

**A:** Oh, yes, it's always dusty, and it's hard to catch your breath in a lot of places, because of that and the heat.

**Q:** Are employees furnished any equipment to alleviate the situation?

**A:** No, it's too hot to wear any kind of mask.

**Q:** I have no further questions.

---

### b. Cross-Examination by Company Advocate

*Mr. Thomas:*
[to be supplied by student]

# D. Exhibits

### *JOINT EXHIBIT NO. 1*

COLLECTIVE BARGAINING AGREEMENT

BETWEEN

ARCHWAY METALS

AND

LOCAL 123

METAL, BRICK AND GLASS WORKERS INTERNATIONAL UNION

AFL-CIO (1/1/04-1/1/07)

.   .   .

ARTICLE 21

Discipline and Discharge

The Company retains the right to discipline and discharge employees for just cause.

Section 1: If the Union protests the discipline or discharge of an employee by the Company, it must within ten (10) calendar days after the Company's action submit its protest in writing, setting forth the grounds therefor.

Section 2: Upon receipt by the Company of such written protest, the discipline or discharge shall be processed as a grievance under the grievance and arbitration provisions of this Agreement, according to the time limits therein set forth. A discharge grievance shall commence with the second step of the Grievance Procedure.

Section 3: If the Union fails to protest the Company's action in writing within the time as set forth above, the Company's action shall be deemed final and binding and shall not be subject to said grievance and arbitration provisions of this Agreement.

Section 4: An employee will receive a copy of any verbal warning or written reprimand placed in his personnel file.

*COMPANY EXHIBIT NO. 1*

ARCHWAY METALS PLANT

NO-FAULT ABSENTEEISM CONTROL PROGRAM

I.    Purpose

The purpose of the Policy is to encourage and develop good attendance habits by all employees at the Archway Metals Plant. To accomplish this objective, a systemic review of employee attendance records will occur; and where problems are identified, those employees with unsatisfactory attendance records will be reminded of their responsibility for good attendance, as well as the consequence of failing to satisfy this basic job requirement. In those cases where unsatisfactory attendance persists, the application of a corrective discipline will occur.

Regular attendance and punctuality by all employees is a "must" for efficient operations, and both are considered a condition of your employment.

II.   Responsibility of the Employee

Each employee is responsible to report to work when scheduled. If an employee is going to be late or absent from work, then he/she must report it to the Security Officer at least one (1) hour prior to his/her scheduled starting time. When reporting late or absent, an employee must give the Security Officer the following information:

1.    Name and Social Security Number
2.    Clock Number
3.    Supervisor, Department, and Shift Assigned
4.    Reason for absence and additional information
      concerning the absence as requested by Security.

Upon reporting an absence or later arrival, each employee will be assigned a call-in number. This number serves as verification to the employee that he/she reported off work. The telephone number for reporting absence or lateness to the Security Officer is (808) 555-5555.

III.  Non-chargeable Absences

A.    A non-chargeable absence is any absence, lateness, or
      leaving work early which is recognized by the Labor
      Agreement or Federal or State statute (with the
      exception of a voluntary leave of absence) provided the
      Company has been properly notified and the reason has
      been properly substantiated, verified, and authorized.

B. Medical Leave of Absence for the purpose of this section of the program, a substantiated medical leave may begin only when the Medical Department or Employee Relations Department has received verification from the medical doctor in charge of an employee's case of the reason for his/her inability to work. In medical cases of a serious nature, which require hospitalization and recovery time, an employee's medical leave may begin on his/her first day of admission to a hospital.

IV. <u>Chargeable Absences</u>

Each day of any absence, lateness, or leaving work early that does not qualify as a non-chargeable absence.

<u>Charging of Absences</u>

Absence (when proper notification has been given)..... 1 Point

Written Leave of Absence (one (1) day or more)....... 1 Point

Leaving Work Early.................................. 3/4 Point

Lateness (without proper notification
prior to start of shift)........................... 3/4 Point

Lateness (less than one (1) hour, with notification
to the Company at least one (1) hour prior to
the start of the shift)............................ 1/2 Point
Late Call-In*...................................... 2 Points

A.W.O.L.**......................................... 4 Points

* Late Call-In - Any notification for an <u>absence</u> (entire shift) received by the Security Officer after the employee's scheduled starting time, but not later than two (2) hours after the start of the shift.

** A.W.O.L. - Any absence or lateness not reported to the Security Officer by an employee within two (2) hours after the start of his/her starting time.

V. <u>Progressive Disciplinary Procedure</u>

Written Warning - Eight (8) points within the most recent twelve (12) months worked.

Special Written Warning - Ten (10) points within the most recent twelve (12) months worked.

Discharge - Twelve (12) points within the most recent twelve (12) months worked.

1. The twelve (12) month period referred to above excludes layoff time due to cutbacks or work stoppages, and medical leaves in excess of five (5) scheduled work days.

2. An employee who is absent for five (5) consecutive scheduled work days and who has not substantiated his/her absences by the medical doctor in charge of his/her case before the start of his/her sixth (6th) scheduled work day will be subject to discharge.

3. An employee who receives two (2) warnings during his/her first twenty-four (24) months of active employment will be subject to discharge. (Active employment excludes layoff time, time off due to work stoppages, and medical leaves in excess of five (5) scheduled work days.)

4. An employee who receives three (3) Special Written Warnings within the most recent thirty-six (36) months worked will be subject to discharge.

## MEDICAL LEAVE OF ABSENCE

If it is medically necessary to miss work other than for casual illness, all hourly employees must comply with the following procedure:

1. A. Reported non-hospitalized absence because of disability or illness of three (3) or more consecutive work days must be substantiated by a doctor to qualify as a medical leave.

   B. Medical leave will commence only upon the employee's request.

2. Any employee requesting a medical leave of absence is required to submit a diagnosis including an estimated return to work date from the doctor in charge of the case to the Medical Department.

3. Any employee returning from a medical absence of more than three (3) consecutive working days due to an injury or illness must provide documentation from a physician stating his/her ability to return to work. Only upon presenting this release will they be allowed to return to work.

4. All employees who are returning to work from medical leave must contact the Medical Department, provide a physician's statement, and receive an authorization to return to work.

5. All absences for illness or injury which do not qualify for medical leave will be counted as separate absences for each day off of work.

## COMPANY EXHIBIT NO. 2

EMPLOYEE ACKNOWLEDGEMENT OF KNOWLEDGE
OF NO-FAULT ABSENTEEISM POLICY

On this date the Archway Metals No-Fault Absenteeism Policy,
revised February 14, year 6, was explained to me and I had the
opportunity to ask any questions concerning this policy.

/s/ Dan Fowler
Name

Feb. 17, year 6
Date

## COMPANY EXHIBIT NO. 3

GRIEVANCE FORM

PLANT: ARCHWAY      GRIEVANCE NO.: 3025   DATE: APRIL 27, year 6

DEPARTMENT: POTLINES           FOREMAN: JIM PHELPS

GRIEVANCE: On April 23, year 6, Unjust No-Fault Absenteeism
Policy.  Employee was given 3/4 of a point for being sick on the
job and having to go home early.  On Company doctor's advice,
employee was told to go home and receive treatment for sickness.

REQUEST FOR SETTLEMENT: That the 3/4 of point be removed from
employee work record.

STEWARD: C.D. Wilson                    EMPLOYEE: Dan Fowler
DATE RECEIVED BY FOREMAN: April 27, year 6    FOREMAN: Jim Phelps

---

FIRST STEP ANSWER: The 3/4 of a point was issued in accordance
with attendance policy.

DATE ANSWERED: May 25, year 6 SUPERINTENDENT: Rob Stevens for D.F.

---

APPEALED TO SECOND STEP:          GRIEVANCE COMMITTEEMAN:
SECOND STEP ANSWER:

DATE ANSWERED:                    EMPLOYEE RELATIONS:

---

Case Expedited to Arbitration

per contract.

---

## _COMPANY EXHIBIT NO. 4_

DATE: May 2, year 6

SUBJECT: Written Warning for Attendance

FROM: Jim Phelps, Process Foreman
TO: Dan Fowler

    You have exceeded the established guidelines for acceptable attendance under Article V of the absence policy.  Your absence from work has created manpower scheduling problems and over-burdened your co-employees to work harder, all of which lead to inefficient operations and increased costs.

    For the above reasons, you are being issued a written warning as disciplinary action to remind you to correct your absence problem.  Please be reminded that failure to correct will lead to further disciplinary action up to and including dismissal.

    I am available in my office to discuss the matter further if you desire.


                                          /s/  Jim Phelps
                                             Foreman

| Days of Absence | | Dates Home Early | |
|---|---|---|---|
| 3/20 | 1 pt | 4/23 | 3/4 pt |
| 4/02 | 1 pt | | |
| 4/08 | 1 pt | | |
| 4/09 | 1 pt | | |
| 4/11 | 1 pt | | |
| 4/17 | 1 pt | | |
| 4/21 | 1 pt | | |
| 4/29 | 4 pts | | |

### COMPANY EXHIBIT NO. 5

DATE: May 2, year 6

SUBJECT: Special Written Warning for Attendance

FROM: Jim Phelps, Process Foreman
TO: Dan Fowler

You were previously given a written warning on May 2, year 6 for exceeding the guidelines for acceptable attendance. Since that date, you have continued to be away from work. Once again, your absence has led to scheduling problems and over-burdening others to cover for your absence - all leading to inefficient operations and added expense.

The Company will make efforts to work with you to correct your attendance problem. Available is an Employee Assistance Program to help you deal with any personal or family problems you may be encountering.

Be reminded that failure to correct your attendance problem will lead to further disciplinary action up to and including dismissal.

I am in my office to discuss this matter further if you desire.

　　　　　　　　　　　　　　　　　　　/s/　Jim Phelps
　　　　　　　　　　　　　　　　　　　　　　Foreman

| Days of Absence | | Dates Home Early | |
|---|---|---|---|
| 3/20 | 1 pt | 4/23 | 3/4 pt |
| 4/02 | 1 pt | | |
| 4/08 | 1 pt | | |
| 4/09 | 1 pt | | |
| 4/11 | 1 pt | | |
| 4/17 | 1 pt | | |
| 4/21 | 1 pt | | |
| 4/29 | 4 pts | | |

## *COMPANY EXHIBIT NO. 6*

DATE: May 9, year 6

SUBJECT: Discharge - Absenteeism

FROM: Jim Phelps and Shirley Gardner
TO: Dan Fowler

    The Company has previously issued a written warning on May 2, year 6 and a Special Written Warning on May 2, year 6, to correct your attendance problem.  You were given a copy of the attendance policy and warned of the consequences of exceeding it. You have been given the opportunity to explain your problem and the Company has tried to work with you to correct the problem, yet you have continued to be absent.

    The Company has met its obligation and under the attendance guidelines, it must terminate your employment on this date.


        /s/ Jim Phelps
          Foreman


        /s/ Shirley Gardner
          Director, Employee Relations


| Days of Absence | | Dates Home Early | |
|---|---|---|---|
| 3/20 | 1 pt | 04/23 | 3/4 pt |
| 4/02 | 1 pt | 05/07 | 3/4 pt |
| 4/08 | 1 pt | | |
| 4/09 | 1 pt | | |
| 4/11 | 1 pt | | |
| 4/17 | 1 pt | | |
| 4/21 | 1 pt | | |
| 4/29 | 4 pts | | |

*COMPANY EXHIBIT NO. 7*

ATTENDANCE RECORD CHANGE FORM
To be completed by Employee Relations

Call Number     879

Date Absent     4/29/06          Time of Call-in     14:30

Absence Code     99

1. Employee Name -     Dan Fowler


2. Reason / Comments

        At airport in Lexington. Waiting on Flight 238. Brother
coming in from Calif.  May be 1/2 to 1 hour late - If longer,
will call back.
Dan Fowler
1600 to 2400 shift
Potline Department
Rob Stevens, Sup.

5. Person completing form -     David Rich
Never called back.
                            Form completed at 21:25.
_____
KEY
Attendance type code
01 Excused Absence
02 Unexcused Absence
03 Late Call In
04 Leave Early
05 AWOL

Reason Codes and Reason Names
00 No reason given
01 Personal Illness, injury with valid doctor's statement
02 Personal Illness, injury without valid doctor's statement
03 Family Illness, injury with verification
04 Family Illness, injury without verification
05 Occupational illness/injury
06 Vacation
07 Vacation shutdown
08 Jury duty with verification
09 Jury duty without verification
10 Court appearance, witness with verification
11 Court appearance, witness without verification
12 Court appearance, personal with verification
13 Court appearance, personal without verification

SEE NEXT PAGE FOR FURTHER CODES AND REASONS

```
14 Union business
15 Funeral leave, immediate family with verification
16 Funeral leave, immediate family without verification
17 Funeral leave, other with verification
18 Funeral leave, other without verification
19 Holiday
20 Leave of absence, military
21 Leave of absence, personal illness/injury
22 Leave of absence, personal illness, maternity
23 Leave of absence, family related
24 Leave of absence, personal
25 Leave of absence, other
26 Plant layoff
27 Disciplinary layoff
28 Prior permission from supervisor
29 Weather
30 Transportation
31 Traffic obstruction, with verification
32 Traffic obstruction, without verification
33 Serious accident with verification
34 Serious accident without verification
35 Emergency situation, other
36 Work related training/education
37 Nonwork related training/education
38 Walked off job
39 Lockout
40 Strike
41 Wildcat strike
42 Overslept
43 No phone/ phone out of service
44 Utility power failure, with verification
45 Utility power failure, without verification
46 Babysitter, no show
47 Personal, with verification
48 Personal, without verification
49 Sent home by medical department
50 Disaster
51 Death, work related
52 Death, on Company property, non-job related
53 Death, away from job
99 Other
```

```
APPROVED BY        DATE
S. Gardner         4/30/06
```

## _UNION EXHIBIT NO. 1_

SUBURBAN HOSPITAL

Carolyn Fowler                          ADMISSION NO. 9-36513
627 Southside Ave.          DISCHARGE 11:00 p.m. 04/07/06
Henley, Ky.

| DATE | DESCRIPTION CODE | SERVICE DESCRIPTION | PRICE |
|------|------------------|---------------------|-------|
| 04/07 | *** 17<br>4003-4 | EMERGENCY SERVICES<br>CLASS III EMERGEN. SERV. | $   64.00 |
| 04/07 | *** 22<br>0153-9 | LAB DIAGNOSTIC<br>GLUCOSE BLOOD | 10.50 |
| 04/07 | 0162-3 | BLOOD UREA NITROGEN | 10.75 |
| 04/07 | 0172-5 | SODIUM | 10.25 |
| 04/07 | 0187-8 | POTASSIUM | 10.25 |
| 04/07 | 0186-7 | CHLORIDE | 10.25 |
| 04/07 | 0202-4 | BICARBONATE | 10.25 |
| 04/07 | 1021-2 | CRC WITH DIFFERENTIAL | 13.25 |
|  |  | BALANCE DUE | $139.50 |

## *UNION EXHIBIT NO. 2*

HEALTH INSURANCE CLAIM FORM

| 1. Patient's Name<br><br>Fowler, Carolyn | 2. Insured's name<br><br>Fowler, Daniel | 3. Insured's I.D. No.<br><br>12345 |
|---|---|---|

| 4. Patient's Address<br><br>627 Southside Ave.<br>Henley, Ky | 5. Health Insurance Coverage<br><br>Archway Metals Co. |
|---|---|

6. Name of facility and address where services rendered

Suburban Hospital, Henley, Ky.

7. Diagnosis

1. 780.3 Convulsions
2. 345.7 Epilepsy Partial Continua
3.
4.

| 8. Date of Service | Description of Procedure | Diagnosis Code | Charges | |
|---|---|---|---|---|
| April 7 | EM SRV INTERMD HP W DI-TR PROG | 780.3 | $41.00 | |
| April 7 | CONSULT REQ COMPREHEN HIST/EX | | $80.00 | |
| April 9 | COMPREHENSIVE RE-EXAM / RE-EVALU | 345.7 | $46.00 | |
| April 9 | PHOTIC STIM/EEG RECORDING | | $109.50 | |

| 9. Total Charge<br><br>$276.50 | 10. Amount Paid<br><br>$ 0 | 11. Balance Due<br><br>$276.50 |
|---|---|---|

_**UNION EXHIBIT NO. 3**_

SUBURBAN HOSPITAL

Carolyn Fowler                    ADMISSION NO. 9-36834
627 Southside Ave.               DISCHARGE DATE 04/11/06
Henley, Ky. 42415

| DATE | DESCRIPTION CODE | SERVICE DESCRIPTION | PRICE |
|------|------------------|---------------------|-------|
| 04/11 | 5325-5 | HEAD SCAN WITH CONTRAST | $203.50 |
|       |        | BALANCE DUE | $203.50 |

_**UNION EXHIBIT NO. 4**_

James Trent, M.D.
Box 246
415 East Main Street
Lexington, Ky.

PATIENT:  Dan Fowler
          627 Southside Ave.
          Henley, Ky

| April 23 | Office visit; Acute tonsillitis | $15.00 |
| April 23 | Injection; bicillin | 5.00 |
|          | Balance Due | $20.00 |

# Sechamp Corporation

## Table of Contents

**NOTES**

# A. Caption

### IN THE MATTER OF AN ARBITRATION BETWEEN:

| | | |
|---|---|---|
| SECHAMP CORP. | ) | |
| COLUMBIA, WASHINGTON | ) | |
| | ) | RE: BO DILL |
| AND | ) | Discharge for |
| | ) | Selling Drugs |
| ELECTRICAL WORKERS | ) | |
| OF THE WORLD | ) | |
| LOCAL 2 | ) | |

Appearances:

For the Company: Joan White

For the Union: James Carter

Date: March 18, year 2

Location: Columbia, Washington

## B. Examination of Company Witnesses

### 1. John Orr, Supervisor, Plant Security

<u>a. Direct Examination by Company Advocate</u>

*Ms. White:*

**Q:** John, would you state your full name and spell your last name, please?

**A:** John Orr, O-R-R.

**Q:** What is your position with Sechamp?

**A:** Supervisor of Plant Security.

**Q:** How long have you held that position?

**A:** Approximately fifteen months.

**Q:** What was your experience prior to that position?

**A:** I was a First Lieutenant in the United States Army, Military Police, for three years.

**Q:** Were you Supervisor of Plant Security for Sechamp in September of year 1?

**A:** Yes, I was.

**Q:** In that capacity were you involved in events leading to the termination of Bo Dill, the grievant in this case?

**A:** Yes, I was.

**Q:** What action did you take, with respect to the grievant, prior to his termination?

**A:** I initiated a surveillance of the grievant.

**Q:** Did you participate in the surveillance of the grievant?

**A:** Yes.

**Q:** Where were you located during this surveillance?

**A:** On the roof of the plant, primarily using a skylight and exhaust fan for observation.

**Q:** All right. I am showing you Company Exhibit 1, a photograph. Can you identify this photograph?

**A:** This is a picture taken from the aisle in the plant to the skylight window in which I was positioned.

**Q:** Would you take this red fiber pencil and circle the skylight window where you indicated you were positioned?

**A:** (The witness did so.)

**Q:** Were you present when this photograph was taken?

**A:** Yes, I was.

**Q:** Was this photograph taken under my instructions?

**A:** Yes.

**Q:** I show you another photograph, Company Exhibit 2. Can you identify what this photograph shows?

**A:** Yes. This is the view from the skylight to the interior of the plant. It is in the exact opposite direction from the picture previously marked.

**Q:** Were you present when this photograph was taken?

**A:** Yes, I was.

**Q:** Was this photograph also taken at my instructions?

**A:** Yes.

**Q:** Now, with regard to the grievant in this case, what did you personally see from your observation post at the skylight that is circled in red on the first photograph, and when did you make the observation?

**A:** On September 21, year 1, at approximately 10:20 p.m. I observed the grievant, on a fork lift truck, stop in the aisle, get off the truck, remove something from his right sock. He had over-the-calf socks, and he removed a four-inch by two-inch manila envelope and handed it to an unidentified male who was partially obscured by a machine and had his back turned to me.

The unidentified male took the envelope. There was a sum of money passed to the grievant by him. The grievant folded it, placed it in his pocket, got back on his truck, and left the area.

**Q:** How far were you from the grievant when you saw this transaction?

**A:** Approximately 50 feet.

**Q:** Did you view this transaction with your naked eye?

**A:** No, I did not.

**Q:** How did you observe it?

**A:** I was using field glasses.

**Q:** Are those field glasses present in the hearing?

**A:** Yes, they are.

**Q:** Are these the binoculars that were used by you on the evening of September 21st?

**A:** Yes.

**Q:** Now, do you recall what the grievant was wearing that evening?

**A:** Yes, he had a red or maroon-colored sweat shirt and a pair of dark-green-colored pants on.

**Q:** What happened the next day?

**A:** On September 22nd at approximately 4 p.m. Captain Stovall, Mr. Mattingly, and Mr. Lewis from Wills Detective Agency, and I positioned ourselves near the 16th Street gate, which is the entrance to our plant, where we could observe the parking lot.

We saw the grievant come into the lot, park his car, and cross 16th Street and come through the 16th Street gate, at which time Mr. Mattingly approached the grievant and there was a conversation.

Mr. Mattingly and the grievant then left and proceeded to the Union Relations Conference Room, at which time Mr. Lewis, Captain Stovall, and I followed.

**Q:** What happened next?

**A:** There was a conversation between Mr. Mattingly and the grievant that resulted in our going to the grievant's locker.

**Q:** Did you accompany Mr. Mattingly and the grievant to the grievant's locker?

**A:** Yes, I did.

**Q:** Did the grievant open his own locker?

**A:** Yes.

**Q:** Would you tell the Arbitrator what was found in the locker?

**A:** On the top shelf we found a Styrofoam coffee cup with approximately $19 in assorted bills and silver. There were two packages of book matches and an envelope—excuse me— a notebook. On the floor of the locker was a pair of green work pants and a red sweat shirt. These were identical to the clothes I had seen the grievant wearing the night before. There were a pair of old work shoes. There was a top to a shoe box, underneath which we found two packages of cigarette papers. In the right rear pocket of the green work pants we found two manila coin envelopes, approximately four by two, which were identical to the type I had seen passed the night before, and also a piece of folded piece of brown paper in which we found a quantity of crushed green plant particles.

**Q:** I show you Company Exhibit 3, a notebook containing a list of names and amounts of money and telephone numbers. Is this the notebook found in the locker on September 22, year 1?

**A:** Yes, it is.

**Q:** Now, I show you Company Exhibit 4, two packets of cigarette paper. Are these the cigarette papers found in the locker on September 22nd?

**A:** Yes.

**Q:** I show you Company Exhibit 5, another photograph. Can you identify what this particular picture shows?

**A:** Yes. The top is the notebook and on the left-hand side are two books of matches and the two cigarette paper packages. At the top right are the two manila coin envelopes, and at the center is the folded brown paper containing the crushed green plant particles we found in the pants. On the extreme right is the Styrofoam cup containing the money.

**Q:** Were you present when this picture was taken?

**A:** Yes, I took it.

**Q:** John, what happened to the two sealed manila coin envelopes and the piece of folded brown paper containing the crushed particles found in the right rear pocket of the green pants in the locker?

**A:** On September 23rd I turned them over to Bill Sputman, Special Agent from the Washington Bureau of Investigation, Narcotics.

**Q:** Did you receive a receipt for this material?

**A:** Yes, I did.

**Q:** I show you a document. Can you describe this document?

**A:** Yes, sir. This is the receipt given to me by Special Agent Sputman and has his signature on it.

**Q:** Did you subsequently receive a lab report identifying the particles?

**A:** Yes, I did.

**Q:** What did the lab report say?

**A:** The particles were identified as marijuana.

**Q:** Mr. Arbitrator, the parties have stipulated that this is what the lab report says.

**Q:** That is all.

### b. Cross-Examination by Union Advocate

*Mr. Carter:*
[to be supplied by student]

## 2. Dennis Mattingly, Manager, Investigation Dept., Wills Detective Agency

### a. Direct Examination by Company Advocate

*Ms. White:*
**Q:** Would you state your full name and spell your last name?
**A:** Dennis Mattingly, M-A-T-T-I-N-G-L-Y.
**Q:** What is your position?
**A:** Manager of the Investigation Department for Wills Detective.
**Q:** How long have you held that position?
**A:** Approximately five years.
**Q:** What was your prior experience?
**A:** City of Seattle Police Department.
**Q:** Were you in that position that you described, as Manager of the Wills Investigation Department, in September of year 1?
**A:** Yes, I was.
**Q:** Were you called to the Sechamp Plant on September 22, year 1?
**A:** That is correct.
**Q:** Would you briefly tell the Arbitrator what happened that day, to the extent that the grievant in this case was directly involved?
**A:** We received a call—when I say "we," Mr. Al Lewis and myself—received a call from Mr. John Orr of Sechamp, to meet him at the plant, that he had a problem. The particular problem was there was evidence or a rumor that an employee was dealing in marijuana on the premises.
**Q:** So, what did you do then?
**A:** We proceeded over there, to Sechamp, and went into the Executive Offices, where we were briefed by Mr. Orr and other members of Sechamp as to what procedure they wanted us to adhere to. Namely, we were to accost or to meet an employee whose name, as later I found out, was the grievant, Bo Dill, and to talk with him and bring him into the Executive Offices and more or less interrogate him as to his participation in the sale of marijuana at Sechamp.
**Q:** So, what did you do?

**A:** About 4 p.m. we saw Mr. Dill park his car over at the employees' parking lot. Al Lewis and I walked over to him, told him we would like to talk with him, asked him to come into the offices of Sechamp with us. He voluntarily complied with our request.

We sat down with Mr. Dill and explained what the circumstances were.
**Q:** State what you told the grievant on that occasion, to the best of your recollection.
**A:** We told the grievant that we were security agents of the Sechamp Corporation and as a result we were called over to talk to him in reference to marijuana, the sale of marijuana on the Sechamp premises. Captain Stovall, Al Lewis, and myself, with Mr. Dill's permission, then walked over to Dill's locker.
**Q:** Did he lead the way to the locker?
**A:** Yes, he did. Mr. Dill led the way to the locker, I think it was Locker No. 867, and "Miller, Jr." was on the locker with a piece of tape. That is the name on Locker 867.
**Q:** Who opened the locker?
**A:** Mr. Dill.
**Q:** The name "Miller, Jr." was on the locker. Was Mr. Dill's name on the same piece of tape that "Miller, Jr." appeared on?
**A:** I do not believe so. It was a small piece of tape. So, we began to open the locker, take out the contents, namely, a couple of packs of cigarette paper, old trousers—bluish green—a maroon faded sweat shirt; some old shoes; part of a shoe box; a piece of brown paper; and a Styrofoam cup with approximately $19 in currency and change in it.
**Q:** Was there any question as to the ownership of those trousers raised at that time?
**A:** Yes. We asked him to get his belongings out. The trousers and the sweat shirt Mr. Dill said were his, and the old shoes and the $19

4

in currency found in the Styrofoam cup on the shelf.

**Q:** Then what happened?

**A:** Then we proceeded back to the Executive Offices of Sechamp, where we examined this brown paper, which had some brownish-green dry material in it, and we asked him, did he know anything about it. He said, "No." So, we proceeded to ask him, "Well, are these your belongings?"

**Q:** Mr. Mattingly, did you examine the contents of the rolled-up brown piece of paper?

**A:** Yes, I did.

**Q:** Did you have any experience in the past—in the course of your profession—have you ever been exposed to marijuana?

**A:** Yes, I have.

**Q:** What was your prior experience?

**A:** Four years with the Seattle Police Crime Lab, four years in the narcotic detail, approximately three years vice and prostitution, and temporary Sergeant in the Chicago Crime Lab.

**Q:** Did you have an opinion of what the contents were on the day in question?

**A:** It smelled like pot, or marijuana.

**Q:** Then what happened, Mr. Mattingly?

**A:** We confronted Mr. Dill with this, asked him did he know anything about it. He said it was not his. So I said, "Well, you admit this was your locker?" He said, "Yes, this is my locker, but I have not been in the locker." If I am not mistaken, Miller, Jr., and Mr. Dill had the locker, but he had not seen Miller, Jr., for about a month. Since this time, during this month, he was the only occupant of the locker.

**Q:** Did he tell you whether or not anyone else had shared that locker with him for any specific period of time?

**A:** The only person was Miller, Jr.

**Q:** Did he tell you how long it had been since Miller, Jr., according to his statement, had been sharing a locker with him? What did he tell you concerning Miller, Jr.'s occupation of the locker with him?

**A:** To my recollection, Miller, Jr., worked in Department 8. Mr. Dill stated that he had not seen him for a month. He did not say he had not used the locker in the month. He said he had not seen him for a month.

**Q:** Then what happened in that situation?

**A:** We went back to the Executive Offices and I took a statement from Mr. Dill with reference to his involvement, which he denied.

**Q:** What else happened?

**A:** Someone from Sechamp, after we finished interrogating Mr. Dill, told him under the circumstances and due to what we had found in the locker, he was under suspension and to get all his belongings out of the locker and anything else he had, and for Captain Stovall and myself to escort him off the premises, which we did.

**Q:** Did you accompany him back to the locker?

**A:** Yes.

**Q:** What did he remove as belongings from the locker?

**A:** A pair of shoes, the trousers and sweat shirt.

**Q:** The trousers he removed were the same trousers from which you previously had removed two envelopes and the crushed brown paper?

**A:** Yes, they were.

**Q:** Nothing further.

### b. Cross-Examination by Union Advocate

*Mr. Carter:*
[to be supplied by student]

## 3. Lynn Riley, Manager, Union Relations

### a. Direct Examination by Company Advocate

*Ms. White:*

**Q:** Lynn, would you state your full name for the recorder, please?

**A:** Lynn Riley, R-I-L-E-Y.

**Q:** What is your position with Sechamp?

**A:** Manager of Union Relations.

**Q:** How long have you held that position?

**A:** Present position about three-and-a-half years.

**Q:** Who is responsible for the overall administration of the Sechamp disciplinary procedure?

**A:** I am.

**Q:** What is the Sechamp procedure for disciplinary action where employees are suspended, as happened in this case?

**A:** Well, we conduct an investigation to determine what action should be taken, and this investigation includes giving the employee an opportunity to state his side of what occurred. It includes a review of the employee's work record. It includes a review of the total situation that occurred. And then, of course, there is an evaluation of what is the appropriate discipline that should be taken or may be taken.

**Q:** All right. Did you review the evidence in this case as you have described, as far as the Company procedure is concerned?

**A:** Yes, I did.

**Q:** And was the grievant—after he was suspended on September 22nd and before the decision was made as to the disposition of his case—was he given an opportunity to tell his side of the story?

**A:** Yes, he was.

**Q:** Did anything come up as a result of his being given this opportunity which caused you to conduct further investigation?

**A:** Yes. He claimed in this interview that someone named Miller, Jr., first name unknown, was in the locker. He thought he was from 8, had worked in 8.

**Q:** Would you, for the Arbitrator, describe what "8" means in this context?

**A:** We have various plants, and Plant 8 is one of them. Mr. Dill worked in Plant 2.

**Q:** What did you do as a result of this contention by the grievant that he shared the locker involved in this situation with a Miller, Jr.?

**A:** The first thing I did, and I did it personally, was check the personnel records and file on active employees to see if there was any Miller, Jr. listed in Plant 8, which he made reference to. I found no Miller, Jr.'s on the payroll at all. I did find that there were three employees with the last name of Miller presently working in Plant 8.

I then personally contacted the foreman of each of the Millers indicated—they worked in three different departments—and asked each foreman if he personally would go out and ask the employee under his supervision if they had a locker in Plant 2 or if they ever had a locker in Plant 2. Each foreman called me back personally and said that each employee denied ever having a locker in Plant 2, and in fact had never even worked in Plant 2.

**Q:** Did you review the records which showed the assignment of this particular locker?

**A:** Yes, I was just going to say that Mr. Dill in his interview had indicated that this locker was assigned to Miller, Jr., first name unknown, by the foreman, Phil Jenkins, so I then personally went out to see Mr. Jenkins, who is a second shift foreman in the components area, and asked him if he had any knowledge. I asked him what information he had concerning this locker of which Mr. Dill had possession. He brought out a list which indicated that locker had been assigned to Mr. Dill some time ago. In fact, he volunteered the information to me that Mr. Dill worked for him years ago and was given that locker at that time and had never changed it. He said he had no—

**Q:** Let me interrupt you here just a second. The records that you reviewed, did they show that locker being assigned to anyone other than Mr. Dill?

**A:** No, they did not. It was just assigned to Mr. Dill.

**Q:** Now, with respect to the identification of Miller, the alleged Miller, Jr. in this situation, were you ever able to locate or identify anyone that would fill that description?

**A:** No, I was not.

**Q:** I believe you testified earlier that your normal procedure also included a review of other similar cases. Did you so testify earlier?

**A:** I did not say that exactly, Ms. White. I said we conduct an investigation and that would include a review.

**Q:** One of the items would be a review?

**A:** Yes.

**Q:** Did you make such a review in this case?

**A:** Yes, I did.

**Q:** First of all, what did your review reveal as to the past practice in this situation?

**A:** Well, for example, five years ago, we had a situation where two employees in Plant 1 were discharged following suspension and investigation for possession of marijuana in their locker.

**Q:** They were discharged or suspended?

**A:** They were suspended and subsequently discharged for possession of marijuana in their lockers on Company property.

**Q:** Do you recall any other cases?

**A:** There were four employees three years ago who also were involved in a similar situation and were subsequently discharged for possession of marijuana on Company property, again in their lockers.

**Q:** Do you know of any case where the Company has had evidence that an employee had possession of narcotics on Company property where he was not discharged?

**A:** Not to my knowledge.

**Q:** Now, you also indicated that the normal procedure, in terms of responsibility, was for evaluation to be made as to the appropriate discipline. Did you come to a conclusion in this case as to the appropriate discipline?

**A:** Yes, I did.

**Q:** That conclusion, according to the record, was what?

**A:** Discharge.

**Q:** I have nothing further at this time.

## b. Cross-Examination by Union Advocate

*Mr. Carter:*
[to be supplied by student]

# C. Examination of Union Witnesses

## 1. Albert Bly, Employee

### a. Direct Examination by Union Advocate

*Mr. Carter:*

**Q:** Will you state your name, sir?

**A:** Albert Bly.

**Q:** Your address?

**A:** 1 Senator Avenue.

**Q:** Mr. Bly, Al Bly, are you employed?

**A:** Yes, by the Sechamp Corp.

**Q:** How long have you been so employed?

**A:** For four years.

**Q:** During the course of your employment at Sechamp, what plant were you working out of?

**A:** Plant 8.

**Q:** During the course of your employment at Sechamp, did you ever have the occasion to encounter or meet one Bo Dill?

**A:** Yes, sir, but I did not know what his last name was. I knew his name was Bo.

**Q:** Do you recall when you first saw Mr. Dill?

**A:** Just about a year ago, I guess.

**Q:** Are you familiar, sir, or have you learned during the course of your employment on the Sechamp premises whether or not certain

7

individuals make loans of money to other employees?

**A:** Yes, sir.

**Q:** And what is the arrangement that is made in reference to these loans?

**A:** Well, if you borrow money, you got to pay interest on the money that you borrow.

**Q:** And what form of interest?

**A:** 25 cents on the dollar.

**Q:** In other words, if I borrow a dollar from you on the Company premises, I repay to you $1.25?

**A:** Yes, sir.

**Q:** Do you recall ever having obtained such a loan from Bo Dill upon the Company premises?

**A:** Yes, sir.

**Q:** Do you recall when this was?

**A:** Well, I guess it was about right after vacation time.

**Q:** Of year 1?

**A:** Yes, sir.

**Q:** Mr. Bly, I am going to ask you to look at Exhibit 1, the notebook produced by the Company. Are you listed there anywhere?

**A:** Yes, sir.

**Q:** Did you at any time owe Bo Dill the sum of $18?

**A:** With the interest, yes, sir.

**Q:** I have completed my examination.

### b. Cross-Examination by Company Advocate

*Ms. White:*
[to be supplied by student]

## 2. Charles Brown, Employee

### a. Direct Examination by Union Advocate

*Mr. Carter:*

**Q:** Will you state your name and address, please?

**A:** Charles Brown, Columbia.

**Q:** By whom are you employed?

**A:** Sechamp Corp. I have been there for three years.

**Q:** During the time that you have been employed at Sechamp, did you have the occasion to know one Bo Dill?

**A:** Yes, sir.

**Q:** Where is your locker, sir?

**A:** Three lockers from his, three doors from his.

**Q:** How long have you used that particular locker?

**A:** Two years.

**Q:** How many lockers are in that area?

**A:** Six.

**Q:** How many people are assigned to each locker at this time, and how many were assigned back in September?

**A:** Well, there are two to a locker. There is only one for mine.

**Q:** Why, sir?

**A:** Because my other locker, I did not have the key to it, so I put my own lock on this vacant locker.

**Q:** So, in other words, you were assigned a locker by the Company?

**A:** Yes.

**Q:** And that locker was not functioning correctly, so you took another locker.

**A:** I took another lock and put it on the locker that I have, which is not the same locker I had before.

**Q:** Did you at any time in the past have another locker mate?

**A:** No.

**Q:** Have you ever had a locker mate at Sechamp?

**A:** Yes.

**Q:** Would you be able to indicate to the Arbitrator who that was?

**A:** His name was Hill.

**Q:** Is he still employed by the Company?

**A:** No, he left.

**Q:** Directing your attention to the last summer, do you recall when the vacation period of Sechamp took place?

**A:** August.

**Q:** What, if any, procedure is followed at the start of the vacation period at Sechamp in reference to the contents of the locker of each employee?

**A:** You are to remove anything you have in the locker.

**Q:** What procedure was followed or given by Sechamp in reference to the labeling of lockers as to occupants?

**A:** Well, we were told to place our name on our locker.

**Q:** How did the Company tell you this?

**A:** They left a note up on the lockers.

**Q:** What did you do in reference to your locker?

**A:** I placed my name up there on tape.

**Q:** Did you ever have occasion to observe the locker of Mr. Dill?

**A:** Yes, I walk right by it.

**Q:** What did you observe in reference to a name or names on the locker of Mr. Dill?

**A:** Well, there were two names on the front of it, Bo Dill and Miller, Jr.

**Q:** Do you remember when you first saw these two names on the locker?

**A:** Yes, it was right after they left the slips up there to place your name up there. Everybody placed their name, individually.

**Q:** How were the names placed?

**A:** Well, we put them up there on paper tape.

**Q:** Do you know Miller, Jr.?

**A:** Well, I saw a guy that I assume was Miller, Jr. I have not seen him in some time, but I can recall him going to the locker and opening the locker that belonged to Bo Dill and Miller, Jr.

**Q:** What does he look like?

**A:** He is dark, five-eleven.

**Q:** How many times did you see him?

**A:** Twice.

**Q:** When did you last see him on the Company premises?

**A:** It was September or August of year 1, I cannot remember the date.

**Q:** Did you at any time see Bo Dill in the same locker?

**A:** Yes, I saw him changing clothes.

**Q:** Did you work at the same times as Mr. Dill?

**A:** Yes, basically.

**Q:** What area would he work in?

**A:** Well, he drove a lift truck and he basically was all over.

**Q:** Did you see him every day?

**A:** Yes.

**Q:** Did you ever see him selling soda pop?

**A:** Yes, he sold it every day.

**Q:** During working time?

**A:** Yes.

**Q:** What type of clothing did you see Mr. Dill wearing during the course of his employment?

**A:** All I saw him wear was brown pants and a red shirt. Maybe sometimes in the summer he wore a T-shirt.

**Q:** Did you at any time see him with a pair of trousers that were not brown?

**A:** No.

**Q:** Did you ever borrow any money from Bo Dill?

**A:** Yes, about eight or nine months ago. I borrowed five dollars and I repaid him six and a quarter.

**Q:** Nothing further.

## b. Cross-Examination by Company Advocate

*Ms. White:*
[to be supplied by student]

## 3. Ken Bandy, Shop Steward

### a. Direct Examination by Union Advocate

*Mr. Carter:*

**Q:** Will you state your name and place of employment?

**A:** Ken Bandy. I am a factory worker at Sechamp.

**Q:** What association do you have with Local 2?

**A:** I am a Shop Steward.

**Q:** Do you know Bo Dill?

**A:** Yes, he was within my representation group. That is him right there. (gesturing)

**Q:** How long prior to September of year 1 did you represent Mr. Dill?

**A:** A year and a half.

**Q:** What type of work did you do?

**A:** I am a punch press operator.

**Q:** Is your punch press located in an area that Mr. Dill would service in the operation of his lift truck?

**A:** Yes, sir.

**Q:** Do you have any recollection of the type and color of clothing that Mr. Dill would wear in his employment?

**A:** He wore a pair of brown pants and a red sweat shirt regularly.

**Q:** Do you have any knowledge as to whether Mr. Dill would sell soda pop on Company premises?

**A:** Yes, he sold it during the meal break, around 8 p.m. I used to buy it from him every day.

**Q:** Where would he get the soda pop that he sold?

**A:** It came off of one of the catering trucks, I am not sure which.

**Q:** So, he bought the soda pop outside, from a caterer?

**A:** Yes.

**Q:** Where did he sell it from?

**A:** He sold it from his lift truck, every day.

**Q:** What type of container was on the lift truck holding the pop?

**A:** It was a metal container, which I would say was about two feet high and maybe two-and-one-half feet long.

**Q:** Was there anything else besides soda pop inside the container?

**A:** Ice was in there to keep it cold.

**Q:** Were there supervisors in the area where he would be servicing?

**A:** Yes.

**Q:** Did you at any time ever see supervisors purchase soda pop from Mr. Dill?

**A:** Yes, sir, every day.

**Q:** Now, when did you first receive knowledge regarding the suspension and discharge of Mr. Dill?

**A:** It was about two days after it happened.

**Q:** How did you first learn of it?

**A:** Through the foreman named John.

**Q:** Please indicate the circumstances under which you learned of the suspension.

**A:** Well, John approached me and told me that he had word that Bo Dill had been suspended for possession of narcotics.

**Q:** Mr. Bundy, you have known Mr. Dill for some time prior to the 22nd of September, year 1?

**A:** Oh, yes, we were hired in together, that is, at pretty close to the same time.

**Q:** Would you say you are a close friend with Mr. Dill?

**A:** At work, yes.

**Q:** To your knowledge, did he ever lend money upon the Company premises?

**A:** Yes.

**Q:** How would the money be repaid, do you know?

**A:** I heard a fellow say once on the day shift that there was interest of a quarter on the dollar.

**Q:** I gather that you never personally borrowed money from Mr. Dill?

**A:** No, I did not.

**Q:** Without naming names, are there other individuals on the Company premises who to your knowledge make these types of loans?

**A:** Yes, there are several fellows that do it. There are at least two or three that I know of.

**Q:** Do you know what that interest rate would have been?

**A:** No, I do not know that.

**Q:** Did you at any time ever know of Mr. Dill ever selling, possessing, or disposing in

10

any way of any narcotics on the Company premises?

**A:** No, sir.

**Q:** The first knowledge you had of this was when the foreman advised you of the circumstances of the suspension of Mr. Dill?

**A:** Right.

**Q:** I am going to ask again. Did you ever see Mr. Dill wear anything but the brown pants on the Company premises?

**A:** No, he wore them every day. He must have had two pairs. It really caught my attention, you know, the same doggone pants every day.

**Q:** Can you recall what other individuals who work with you wore in your area during their employment?

**A:** There are only two fellows that I work right with, and they usually wear a kind of uniform of green khakis.

**Q:** What calls your attention to that clothing?

**A:** I wear the same thing—green khakis.

**Q:** What called your attention to the type of clothing that Bo Dill wore?

**A:** The color.

**Q:** Nothing further.

## b. Cross-Examination by Company Advocate

*Ms. White:*
[to be supplied by student]

# 4. Bill Huddleston, Polygraph Examiner

## a. Direct Examination by Union Advocate

*Mr. Carter:*

**Q:** Mr. Arbitrator, the parties have stipulated that the next witness may testify on the results of his polygraph examination of Mr. Dill, using his records to refresh his memory if necessary. However, the Company reserves the right to object to the admissibility of the polygraph results or alternatively to the weight given to the results.

**Q:** State your name for the record, sir.

**A:** Bill Huddleston.

**Q:** What educational specialty background do you have?

**A:** I went to polygraph school.

**Q:** What is your employment background?

**A:** Well, I worked for a national security agency in intelligence. Then I worked with the Bismarck Police Department in North Dakota. Finally I came here and began to work for a polygraph firm.

**Q:** What was the highest capacity that you reached with the police department in Bismarck?

**A:** I was Chief of Detectives.

**Q:** So, how long have you been engaged in the business of polygraph examinations?

**A:** Since I came here, it has been my sole occupation for the past 21 years. I have had extensive training in all aspects of polygraph examination, administration, and interpretation.

**Q:** What is your professional assessment of the degree of accuracy that a polygraph examination can render?

**A:** I would say that a qualified polygraph examiner can give a test and get the same degree of accuracy in a polygraph examination as you would find in fingerprint analysis or other identification along the same line.

**Q:** Did you have occasion to examine Bo Dill, at my request?

**A:** Yes.

**Q:** Did you ask Bo Dill about his income from sources other than his salary?

**A:** Yes. I asked question 1: "Do you have any income other than from your wages," and he answered in the negative. I pointed out to him that his answer appeared deceptive and that he did not tell me the truth about his outside income. Then he explained to me he had another job where he worked as a bartender and had other sources of income, all outside of his salary, but legitimate sources.

11

**Q:** Is that where the deception appeared?

**A:** Yes.

**Q:** Was he then telling—in your opinion—telling the truth about the outside income with this explanation?

**A:** Yes.

**Q:** Did I submit a letter to you?

**A:** Yes, sir, I have it here.

**Q:** Right. A copy of that letter is Union Exhibit 1. In that letter I suggested some five questions that you could ask, one of which you have already alluded to.

**A:** Yes.

**Q:** By the way, have you performed these examinations for me in the past?

**A:** I seem to recall two prior occasions.

**Q:** Did you have a degree of nonbelief when you began your examination?

**A:** When I first saw Mr. Dill, I had nothing but to look at him. Subjectively I thought he was a wise guy and I wouldn't have believed him for all the tea in China. I tried desperately for two hours to prove him a liar and I finally had to go with my instrument, which said the man is not lying.

**Q:** Now, I gather you did ask him these questions I propounded to you.

**A:** Yes, I asked question 2: "Did you at any time sell or buy narcotics on the premises of the Sechamp Corp.?" There was no reaction to indicate any deception. He answered negatively and the instrument said that he was telling the truth.

Then I asked question 3: "Did you at any time have narcotics in your locker at Sechamp, which belonged to you?" He again answered in the negative, and in my opinion that was the truth.

I asked question 4: "Did you know on September 22, year 1, that there were narcotics in your locker prior to the time it was opened in response to a request by the security officer?" He again answered in the negative and again I opined that he was telling the truth.

I asked him the other questions about whether the green trousers were his, or whether he knew there were narcotics in the trousers, or if he ever removed narcotics from the green trousers. He answered in the negative to all these questions, and I opined that he was telling the truth.

I asked him question 5: "Prior to September 22, year 1, did you share a locker with Miller, Jr.? and he answered, "Yes." In my opinion he was again telling the truth.

**Q:** Did you restrict your investigation to the events which occurred on the Company premises as I suggested in my letter to you?

**A:** To tell you the truth, I never even read your letter, beyond using your questions. I knew this guy was supposed to be in narcotics and I was going to get at it. I covered this man's entire 26 years of life, because he came to me as a challenge. I did not believe him, but he convinced me that he was telling the truth. I specifically asked him—and these are my exact words—if he ever "used or sold marijuana," and he answered in the negative. While I found it hard to believe subjectively, objectively I just had to believe the man. In my opinion he never used marijuana.

**Q:** And you asked question 2, "Did you at any time sell or buy narcotics on the Sechamp property?"

**A:** Yes, I did, and like I said, the answer was, "No." Again, in my opinion the man was telling the truth when he answered that question.

**Q:** So, based upon the experience you have had in the field and the procedure you have followed and with, if I may, your own somewhat antagonistic attitude because of the appearance Bo Dill portrayed to you, did you effectively pursue this line of questioning, whether or not Bo Dill was receptive to this line of examination?

**A:** I did, because at first I was convinced that this man was a junkie who would steal nickels off a dead person's eyes. I was hoping for some deception. I was wrong, though. He was telling the truth in every one of his responses to those questions.

**Q:** Thank you, that is all.

12

## b. Cross-Examination by Company Advocate

*Ms. White:*
[to be supplied by student]

# 5. Bo Dill, Grievant

## a. Direct Examination by Union Advocate

*Mr. Carter:*

**Q:** State your name and address, please.

**A:** Bo Dill, 1111 South Norton.

**Q:** Are you currently employed?

**A:** No.

**Q:** Have you ever in the past been employed by Sechamp?

**A:** Yes, sir.

**Q:** When did you begin your employment with Sechamp?

**A:** January 17, ten years ago.

**Q:** Have you been active in the Union?

**A:** Yes, I was one of the employees who brought the Union to Sechamp. I have been the Local Union Treasurer for ten years. I was a strike captain during a 10-month strike five years ago.

**Q:** Regarding your work duties, what position have you been in?

**A:** I worked in the Ring Department, hanging rings and driving a fork lift truck.

**Q:** I direct your attention to immediately before summer vacation of year 1. What type of work were you doing then?

**A:** I was a fork lift operator.

**Q:** How long had you been a fork lift truck operator?

**A:** For about fifteen months—a year or so.

**Q:** What shift were you on prior to September of year 1?

**A:** Second shift.

**Q:** How long had you been on second shift?

**A:** Since September 12, four years ago.

**Q:** When did the second shift begin and end, time-wise?

**A:** It started at 4 p.m. and ended at 12:30 a.m.

**Q:** Were there other starting times for shifts in the area in which you worked?

**A:** Yes, sir.

**Q:** What were these changes as compared to yours?

**A:** Well, they had one from 3:30 to midnight, and that is the only other shift I know, besides the third shift, which started at 10:15 p.m.

**Q:** Just exactly what did you do in the performance of your duties?

**A:** Well, my job was hauling scrap.

**Q:** What type of scrap?

**A:** Excess material that comes off the dies in the punch presses that the guys use to cut panels out of sheet metal. They throw the excess in a big scrap barrel, and I take it over to the scrap pile and they bale it up and make squares of it.

I also was supplying the men that operate the machines with the metal sheets so they can punch them out on punch presses.

**Q:** I see. So, your operation and performance of your duties was really twofold. It involved the removal of the scrap and the supplying of materials so the employees could function, correct?

**A:** Yes, sir, it is.

**Q:** During the working day, would you be able to indicate the general area that you would service?

**A:** Well, it was really a wide area.

**Q:** During the course of your employment what, if any, association did you have with the selling of any type of soda pop on the Company premises?

**A:** Well, I sold the soda pop daily from ten minutes to 8 to 8:30 p.m. My meal break comes at 8 o'clock, and people come up to my fork lift truck and purchase two or three cans of soda pop, sometimes only one. I sold about 100 cans of soda pop a day.

**Q:** Where did you get the soda pop?

**A:** Out of a hot truck that came around and sold hot sandwiches.

**Q:** Did you purchase the soda pop off Company premises?

**A:** Yes, sir, right outside the plant.

**Q:** Would you go to this truck more than once during your working time?

**A:** Yes, sir.

**Q:** Would you drive your truck over there?

**A:** I would drive my truck up to the gate, and then I would walk outside the gate and put soda pop in a metal container and bring it back in on my truck.

**Q:** What else did you have in the metal container besides the pop?

**A:** Ice.

**Q:** Where did you keep that metal container?

**A:** On my fork lift truck.

**Q:** Well, there is a front and a back. Can you be a little more precise about where you put it?

**A:** I could either put it down at the side of me or behind me on the back.

**Q:** I see. Could you indicate the size of the container of this soda pop?

**A:** I'd say about two feet long and about twelve to eighteen inches high.

**Q:** How many cans of soda pop did this container hold?

**A:** About 80 to 100 cans of soda pop.

**Q:** Did you sell that many during the course of a night?

**A:** This was between ten minutes to 8 and 8:30 that I would sell 100 cans of soda pop.

**Q:** Now, how much did you pay for the soda pop and how much did you sell it for?

**A:** The pop is regularly 50 cents a can, but I had to make a profit, so I added a dime and sold it for 60 cents a can.

**Q:** How long before September 22, year 1, did you sell the soda pop like this?

**A:** It was about eight months.

**Q:** Did you at any time ever sell this soda pop to supervisors?

**A:** Yes, sir.

**Q:** How many times?

**A:** Just about every day or twice a day.

**Q:** Did any supervisor ever make an objection to you selling the soda pop?

**A:** No, sir.

**Q:** How many supervisors did you sell soda pop to?

**A:** Four or so.

**Q:** Do you have a recollection now of how many cans these individual supervisors would purchase?

**A:** Well, they each purchased one or two soda pops a day. One guy asked me to just drop one off on his desk and he would pay me later.

**Q:** Did you ever go back to the hot truck a second time?

**A:** Yes, sir. I would meet the fellow on the hot truck down by the employment office at 8:15, because it only took about 20 minutes to sell the soda pop I had at the first time, and later I would go out and give him the money and keep my profit separated from his money and I would give him the money from the first run. Then I would fill up a small box, which held about 30 cans of soda pop. I would return to the plant and during the break I would start selling soda pop again.

The money that I got the second time, I just put in a cup and left it in my locker in the back, every night, and then the next day I gave the fellow on the hot truck the money from the cup.

**Q:** Mr. Dill, you indicated that you kept the money separated. How was that done?

**A:** Well, I had these bell bottoms that I wear, because holes were in the pockets of my pants, because when I first got them I put money in them, and it eventually wore holes. So, I thought of an idea. I just rolled my pants leg up and put the money in my socks. You know, the baggy socks I wear that come up to my knees. The dime that I get on every can would go in my left sock, and the fifty cents would go in the right sock.

**Q:** Did everybody who purchased soda pop have even change?

**A:** No, sir.

**Q:** About how many times a night did you have to make change?

**A:** Several times. I would say about twenty times. It made me kind of mad at times, because I did not have enough change some of the time. If I could not break a big bill, I told them to come back the next day with the correct change. I would note this in my book. Then, I would have to tell the man outside that I am short that day.

**Q:** Where did you keep the dollar bills?

**A:** In the baggy knee socks I wore under my pants.

**Q:** I am going to show you a pair of brown trousers. Are these the type of trousers that you wore?

**A:** Yes, sir.

**Q:** How many pairs of those trousers did you have?

**A:** Two.

**Q:** Are these your work trousers that you wore on the Company premises?

**A:** Yes, sir.

**Q:** Why did you put the change in your socks?

**A:** Well, 100 cans of soda pop, 60 cents a can, that is a lot of change. I would lose quite a bit of money from the pockets of pants like these, but *my* way I would not lose any.

**Q:** Did you carry anything in your pockets?

**A:** No, sir, nothing at all. Like I told you, I had holes in the pockets, so anything I'd put in them could just fall out.

**Q:** Where did you carry your belongings?

**A:** My locker key, I put in my shoe, my left shoe all the time, and my cigarettes were in my left pants leg, as were the matches. My money, the dime that I get, would go in my socks.

**Q:** How about the bills?

**A:** They would also go in there. When I got finished selling the soda pop, I would straighten the money out and take the change and put it with the paper money and ball it up to take out to the guy at the truck.

**Q:** How long have you had those particular trousers?

**A:** About a year.

**Q:** During the time that you had these trousers, did you have any trousers comparable to those?

**A:** Yes, sir, a pair exactly the same color, but they did not have any pockets in the back. Exactly the same color, and bell bottoms also.

**Q:** They have no pockets in the back?

**A:** No.

**Q:** When you began selling soda pop, did you learn whether or not there was any other employee who had a job comparable to yours who also had sold soda pop?

**A:** Yes, sir, Butch Burton.

**Q:** What type of job did he have?

**A:** He was also a fork lift operator.

**Q:** Is he still in the Company?

**A:** When I left he was.

**Q:** Now, Mr. Dill, would you describe the area where you had your locker on the Company premises.

**A:** It was in Plant 2, back by the railroad tracks, where trains came in.

**Q:** Do you recall how many lockers were in the area?

**A:** About six, I would say.

**Q:** Do you know who occupied the other five lockers prior to September of year 1?

**A:** A few of them. There was Charles Owens for one, and a guy that worked days named José.

**Q:** When you were assigned this particular locker, Mr. Dill, who gave you that assignment?

**A:** Frank Janacek, the foreman on the second shift.

**Q:** What were the circumstances of that assignment?

**A:** Well, I did not have a locker when I came there. I used to ask him every day about getting me a locker, because I wanted to change my clothes. Eventually he got me a locker.

**Q:** Do you remember when that was?

**A:** It was three years ago.

**Q:** From the time you first acquired it up until the time of your separation from employment in September of year 1, did you have the same locker all during this period?

**A:** Yes, sir.

**Q:** When you were first assigned the locker, was there anybody else that you had as a locker mate?

**A:** Not at the time.

**Q:** Did you ever forget your key?

**A:** Yes.

**Q:** What would happen?

**A:** I would go to Foreman Phil Jenkins and have him open the locker for me. He would open it up and tell me the locker was open and that I could go and change. Then the locker would stay open until the next day when I came in with the key.

**Q:** Can you indicate how many times this occurred during the course of your employment?

**A:** Over eight times, I would say.

**Q:** Could you explain that once again for me, just to straighten it out?

**A:** Well, I would ask Jenkins to open the locker. I would begin working in my street clothes with an apron in front of me. No later than one-half hour after I began working he would have the locker open. Then, I would go and change clothes. The locker would stay open during the shift. After the shift I changed clothes again and then the locker would have to stay open all night until I came in the next day.

**Q:** How many keys were available to that locker?

**A:** I do not know, sir.

**Q:** During your employment with Sechamp, have you had occasion to lend fellow employees money?

**A:** Yes, sir.

**Q:** Under what circumstances?

**A:** Well, I got a quarter on an even dollar. Then, likewise, if I was short and had to borrow five dollars from somebody else, I would have to pay them the same interest—on five dollars I would have to pay six and a quarter too.

**Q:** Is that type of transaction a frequent occurrence on the Company premises, to your knowledge?

**A:** Yes, sir.

**Q:** Directing your attention to the 21st of September, year 1, do you remember working that particular night?

**A:** Well, it's the same thing every night when I come to work.

**Q:** Do you remember the gentleman who testified, John Orr, on behalf of the Company?

**A:** Yes, sir.

**Q:** Do you recall that he had indicated that he had spy glasses and, looking out of the skylight, he saw you at a particular location shown in the photograph?

**A:** Yes, sir.

**Q:** Here is the photograph—Company Exhibit 1. Looking at that photograph, do you recognize that area?

**A:** No, sir.

**Q:** Would you be able to locate or tell me where that particular area is upon the Sechamp premises?

**A:** No, sir.

**Q:** Would you look at this second photograph produced by the Company and tell me whether or not you can identify the location of that photograph?

**A:** I see these rings in there that I used to work with. I do not know where the particular machine is.

**Q:** Do both of these photographs portray what could be any of a number of areas on the Company premises?

**A:** Yes, sir.

**Q:** You recognize this as being a general working area of Sechamp, correct?

**A:** Only because I see the rings that I used to work with.

**Q:** Now, do you have a recollection—at any time on the 21st day of September, year 1, in the operation of your fork lift—of stopping in an aisle and giving an envelope to a fellow employee?

**A:** No, sir.

**Q:** Did you at any time, on any day, ever deliver or hand to an employee an envelope?

**A:** No, sir.

**Q:** Did you ever have an envelope such as was described, approximately two inches by four inches, in your personal possession?

**A:** No, sir.

**Q:** Where did you say that you carried your cigarettes?

**A:** In my socks.

**Q:** Do you have a pack of cigarettes with you?

**A:** Yes.

**Q:** Indicate for the record approximately how big the pack is.

**A:** About two inches this way, and two-and-a-half inches that way.

**Q:** During the time that you were operating your truck, did any employee ever borrow or ask you for a cigarette?

**A:** Yes, sir.

**Q:** What would you do?

**A:** I would just reach in my sock and hand him the pack and let him get a cigarette.

**Q:** Did you do that very often?

**A:** Yes, sir, every day.

**Q:** Did you ever get money in return for the cigarettes?

**A:** No, sir.

**Q:** Did you, at any time while on the Company premises, hand to another employee an envelope of the type indicated and have the employee hand you back money?

A: No, sir.

Q: Do you recall the investigator saying that an employee in a black sweat shirt approached you and you stopped your lift truck and got off the lift truck and handed something to the employee, and he handed you something back?

A: Yes.

Q: Was that factual testimony?

A: Well, if the investigator saw me handing anything, it was this pack of cigarettes.

Q: Did you ever exchange anything for money on the Company premises other than the soda pop?

A: No, sir.

Q: How about the lending of money, where did that take place?

A: Anywhere they would stop me at.

Q: Did you ever keep notations of this?

A: Yes, sir.

Q: Mr. Dill, I show you the notebook produced by the Company. Do you recognize that particular page from the notebook?

A: Yes, sir.

Q: Is that your handwriting?

A: Yes, sir.

Q: Can you identify the meaning of the names with the amounts alongside of them?

A: Yes, sir.

Q: What were they for?

A: This was the money that I would receive in interest—a quarter on the dollar or names of people who owed me money for soda pop because I could not make change.

Q: Now, who is Butch?

A: Butch Burton; he is a truck driver. These are all nicknames of people who work at Sechamp. The numbers represent what I would lend them. Some of the numbers were simply phone numbers.

Q: Have you ever possessed, sold, or purchased dope or anything of a narcotic nature on the Company premises?

A: No, sir.

Q: Did you ever have anything of that nature on your person on the premises?

A: No, sir.

Q: What happened when you came to work on the 22nd of September, year 1?

A: Well, Mr. Mattingly, whom I had never seen before, approached me as I came through the gate and asked me if I was Bo Dill. They took me to a room and told me to sit down. There was another guy who says he was from the Washington State Bureau of Investigation there also. I did not know why we were there at the time. They asked me a lot of questions. There were six or seven guys in that room. They asked me what was in the locker and I identified what was in there.

Q: Did any of the other men indicate their capacity with the Company or their purpose in being there?

A: No, sir. I thought maybe I was going to get an upgrading or something. I did not know—I thought maybe I was getting a better job.

Q: What else happened?

A: They kept asking about what was in the locker. I identified all the things that I owned in the locker. They asked if there was anything else in the locker, and I told them that there was a pair of pants in the locker that did not belong to me; they belong to Miller, Jr. They asked me who he was, but I did not know, he just used the locker.

Q: What type of pants were those?

A: They were green. They were rolled up in the bottom of the locker in the corner. They had been in the locker since right after vacation in August and this was September.

Q: Who is Miller, Jr.?

A: I do not know, I just saw him use my locker.

Q: When did you first see him on the Company premises?

A: After vacation in year 1.

Q: Describe your first meeting with Miller, Jr.

A: He was at my locker and it was open. There was a key in the door, which he took with him. I walked up to the door and he was changing clothes. He said he was my locker mate and I said fine.

Q: Did you ever see the man at the locker after that?

A: No, sir, but I did see him walking through Plant 8.

Q: Did you know what shift he worked or what type of work he did?

A: No, sir.

**Q:** What did Miller, Jr. look like?

**A:** Well, he had long blond hair.

**Q:** What, if anything, did you do concerning names on the locker?

**A:** We were told to put our names on the locker that we used, so I used a piece of tape and put "B. Dill" on the locker.

**Q:** Were there any other names on your locker?

**A:** Yes. Miller, Jr. was on the locker. I don't know how it got there.

**Q:** Going back to the day of the conference, were you asked about Miller, Jr.?

**A:** Yes, they asked me who he was and I told them what I just told you. Then we went to my locker.

**Q:** When you went to the locker, what happened?

**A:** Well, I opened the locker without any objection at all. I did not understand what was going on. I stuck the key in and opened it, then I stepped back.

**Q:** Did they ask you at that time, before you went to the locker, whether or not you had sold narcotics on the Company premises?

**A:** No, sir.

**Q:** So what else occurred at the locker?

**A:** Well, we all went to the locker, me and some of the same guys who were in the room with me. One of the men went into the locker and took out the green pants, and I repeated many times that they were not my pants. They picked up the pants, unrolled them, and took something out of the back pocket. I did not know what it was and they did not show it to me. Then there was the other stuff that was mine in the locker; my brown pants, my sweat shirts, my cup of money, and my pair of Stetson shoes.

**Q:** Where were your clothes in the locker?

**A:** Well, there were hangers on the sides and my clothes were hung on the right side of the locker.

**Q:** These green trousers were where?

**A:** They were rolled up on the floor of the locker.

**Q:** Were they asking you who these things belonged to?

**A:** Yes, in the room and at the locker. They did not ask me about my pants and sweat shirt. They just kept asking me about the green pants, which was the first thing they went for in the locker.

**Q:** How did they search the green pants?

**A:** They just unrolled them and went straight to the back pocket and pulled something out. Then we all went back to the office and they started asking a lot of questions of me. They asked me if this stuff was mine. I said, "What stuff?" and they put it on the table for me to look at.

**Q:** How long were you in the conference room?

**A:** The first time for about an hour, and the second time I was in there for about twenty minutes.

**Q:** So, what went on from there?

**A:** They kept asking me a lot of questions, but this time it was about narcotics. They showed me what they said was marijuana. They asked me if I knew what it was, and I said yes. Then they wanted to know how I knew, and I said, "Because you just told me it was marijuana."

**Q:** Had you ever seen marijuana before this time?

**A:** No, sir.

**Q:** What did it look like?

**A:** It looked like green tobacco. They put two envelopes of it on the table. Then they told me they were going to put me in jail. They were going to lock me up and take my car. I just sat there and kept telling them that it was not mine. One of them said that if I would just stay with him that we could make some kind of a deal. He asked me if I wanted to call anybody, and I said no, just maybe my mother.

**Q:** Bo, were the contents of those envelopes ever in your possession?

**A:** No, sir. Prior to that day, I was totally unaware the envelopes were in my locker.

**Q:** Were those envelopes ever handed to you or did you know the contents of them?

**A:** No, sir.

**Q:** Then what happened?

**A:** Well, this bigger guy came in—he must have been some big guy at Sechamp—he came in and told them to escort me back to the locker and to escort me off the Company premises after I cleaned my locker out. So I went to my locker with these two guys and cleaned out the locker.

**Q:** Do you know what happened to the green trousers or the material that was taken from them?

**A:** No, sir.

**Q:** So, what transpired next?

**A:** Well, that big guy told me that if I came back on Company premises before I was called that I would be automatically fired. Then he told me that I could go on home.

**Q:** Was there ever a statement taken from you?

**A:** Yes, one of them was taking my statement. After I got finished telling them what was and was not mine out of the locker, then I signed it. They kept the statement.

**Q:** How were you escorted out?

**A:** Well, we went to the back gate and they told me to leave. There were some people looking as we walked through the plant and I was embarrassed, but I really wasn't paying much attention because I was trying to figure it all out.

**Q:** What was the next notice that you got from the Company?

**A:** Well, this was all on a Tuesday. On Friday or Saturday they called me, telling me to come to work Monday morning. I showed up early Monday at Personnel because I wanted to find out what was going on. I received a telegram saying I was discharged, but they also wanted me to show up on the Monday morning. So I went in on Monday and gave my statement of what went on that Tuesday to another man, after which I signed the statement. So after we finished he said that he would be back in a few minutes and left the office. I stood up to get a drink of water and after I took a couple of steps, two guys grabbed me and kicked my legs out from under me. They said, "We got a warrant for your arrest. Are you Bo Dill?" I said, "Yes, sir." This was all inside the Personnel Office. So, they handcuffed me behind my back and sat me in a chair.

While I was sitting there I asked the man who had taken my statement whether I could get my check while I was there. He said yes and got it for me. They took my Sechamp card from me and then unhandcuffed me.

**Q:** Do you know who these men that arrested you worked for?

**A:** They worked for the State Police—at least, that is what they told me.

**Q:** Did you deny to these individuals that you were involved in the charge that was placed against you, Bo?

**A:** Yes, sir.

**Q:** At any conference you had with any representative of Sechamp, what reference, if any, was made about your taking a lie detector test?

**A:** At the time they stopped me at the gate and took me into the office and asked me about the stuff they found in the locker, they asked me would I take a lie detector test. I said yes.

**Q:** How many times did they ask you?

**A:** Oh, it was several times.

**Q:** Did you ever refuse to take the test at that meeting in the conference room?

**A:** No, sir. I expected that they were going to give it to me then.

**Q:** Okay, that is all.

## b. Cross-Examination by Company Advocate

*Ms. White:*
[to be supplied by student]

# D. Exhibits

## *JOINT EXHIBIT NO. 1*

COLLECTIVE BARGAINING AGREEMENT
BETWEEN
SECHAMP CORP.
AND
LOCAL 2
ELECTRICAL WORKERS OF THE WORLD (1/1/01-1/1/03)

. . .

ARTICLE IV

Discrimination and Coercion

1.  The Company agrees that it will not coerce, intimidate, or discriminate against any employee because of age, race, color, creed, sex, national origin, or Union membership or because an employee is acting as a representative of the Union.

ARTICLE XXV

General

. . .

2.  No employee shall be discharged without just cause.

## *JOINT EXHIBIT NO. 2*

Grievance, Local 2, E.W.W.

**Step 3**

**Request:** The Union protests the discharge of Bo Dill, who has been an employee for ten years and an active Union member. The Company violated Articles IV and XXV of the contract when it removed him from the work premises and then later discharged him.

**Remedy:** Bo Dill should be reinstated to his former position with full seniority and back pay including interest.

**Company Answer**

The Company has reasonable grounds to remove the grievant from the premises. He constituted a danger to the workplace including supervision and employees. His discharge was for just cause. The Company did not violate Article IV or XXV. Grievance denied.

## COMPANY EXHIBIT NO. 1

Photograph of skylight from inside plant

[The Company advocate should supply a dummy prop.]


## COMPANY EXHIBIT NO. 2

Photograph of inside of plant from skylight

[The Company advocate should supply a dummy prop.]


## COMPANY EXHIBIT NO. 3

Notebook with list of names and amounts of money
and telephone numbers

[The Company advocate should supply a dummy prop.]


## COMPANY EXHIBIT NO. 4

Two packets of cigarette paper

[The Company advocate should supply a dummy prop.]


## COMPANY EXHIBIT NO. 5

Photograph of notebook, two books of matches and two cigarette
paper packages, two manila coin envelopes, folded brown paper
containing crushed green plants

[The Company advocate should supply a dummy prop.]

_UNION EXHIBIT NO. 1_

January 15, Year 2

Bill Huddleston
Examiner
Truth to Tell
1234 South St.
Columbia, WA

Dear Mr. Huddleston:

As discussed over the phone, you are hereby directed to conduct a polygraph examination of Bo Dill. The following are the questions I wish you to ask:

1.  Do you have any income other than from your wages?
2.  Did you at any time sell or buy narcotics on the premises of the Sechamp Corp.?
3.  Did you at any time have narcotics in your locker at Sechamp, which belonged to you?
4.  Did you know on September 22, year 1, that there were narcotics in your locker prior to the time it was opened in response to a request by the security officer?
5.  Prior to September 22, Year 1, did you share a locker with Miller, Jr.?

Please contact me by phone with preliminary results within a day or two of completion of the examination, and forward a written report in a timely fashion thereafter.

You should restrict your investigation to events which occurred on the Company premises, in order to avoid raising any issues concerning invasion of privacy or off-duty conduct.

Sincerely,

/s/ James Carter

Electrical Workers of the World

# Builders Supply Company

## Table of Contents

**NOTES**

# A. Caption

IN THE MATTER IN ARBITRATION BETWEEN:

BUILDERS SUPPLY COMPANY          )
LANESVILLE, TENNESSEE            )
                                 )          RE: HAROLD (HARRY) DENT
AND                              )              Discharge for Fighting
                                 )
UNIVERSAL UNION OF DRIVERS       )
AND ASSISTANTS                   )
LOCAL UNION NO. 9880             )

Appearances:

For the Company: Donald Gipp

For the Union: Alice Lake

Date: January 15, year 2

Place: Lanesville, Tennessee

# B. Examination of Company Witnesses

## 1. Larry Blunt, Yardman

### a. Direct Examination by Company Advocate

*Mr. Gipp:*

**Q:** State your full name and address.

**A:** Larry Blunt, Lanesville, Tennessee.

**Q:** How old are you?

**A:** Thirty-five.

**Q:** Where do you work?

**A:** Builders Supply Company at the Fourth Street plant.

**Q:** How long have you worked at Builders Supply?

**A:** Seven years.

**Q:** What is your present job?

**A:** To keep the yard clean.

**Q:** And that is the job that you had on the day of October 25, year 1, when this incident happened with Harold Dent?

**A:** Yes, sir.

**Q:** Yardman. That is your job title?

**A:** Yardman.

**Q:** Had you known Dent prior to this, to October 25?

**A:** Only at work.

**Q:** Had you ever had a run-in of any kind with him at work or anyplace else prior to that day?

**A:** No, sir.

**Q:** Had you ever exchanged words or anything of that kind with him?

**A:** No, sir.

**Q:** Tell us what happened on this day.

**A:** I was cleaning the wash rack and I had just taken a load of material up on the hill in my payloader and as I was coming back down I looked behind me and Dent was going behind me. He drove his concrete truck on down and got out and started reversing his cylinder. As a result, the concrete that was left in the cylinder was dumped on the driveway. I asked him not to put the concrete there, to put it on the wash rack, but he went ahead and dumped concrete on the driveway.

**Q:** Is dumping concrete on the driveway the normal practice?

**A:** No. They usually wash out the cylinder on the wash rack.

**Q:** What happens with the material that is washed out?

**A:** It's usually cleaned up and put into another pit up on the hill.

**Q:** That is what you had been doing prior to this, is this correct?

**A:** Yes.

**Q:** What happens if it is dropped in the driveway?

**A:** It has to be cleaned up.

**Q:** And rather than it all being gathered in the one place in the pit, in the wash rack, you have to go around and pick it up before it hardens, is that it?

**A:** Yes.

**Q:** So when you saw Dent dumping his material in the driveway, what did you do?

**A:** I pulled my payloader up beside his truck and I asked him to drive his truck over on the wash rack, not to put the concrete there.

**Q:** As best you can recall, what exactly did you say to him?

**A:** I said, "Don't put the concrete there, put it over on the wash rack."

**Q:** Did you curse at him?

**A:** No.

**Q:** All right. What was his response?

**A:** He went ahead and washed his truck cylinder out on the driveway.

**Q:** All right, then what happened?

**A:** After he finished, he pulled his truck on up in line and I pulled the payloader over next to him. I got off the payloader and walked over to his truck and I said, "Why did you wash the concrete out there? I asked you to put it on the wash rack. Don't ever wash it out in the yard again." When I said that he opened the door of his truck, got out, and hit me.

**Q:** Where did he hit you?

**A:** Across the nose.

**Q:** What damage did it do?

A: My nose bled and my head hurt for about a week.

Q: Did he knock you down?

A: Not completely.

Q: What did you do at that point?

A: I immediately got up and went over to the telephone and called the office.

Q: Why didn't you go back for him?

A: I have always heard if you fight on the job you are automatically fired.

Q: Is that what kept you from going back at him?

A: Yes.

Q: So you reported this to the office?

A: Yes.

Q: When you went up to his truck the second time, did you strike him in any way?

A: No, sir.

Q: Did you curse him in any way?

A: No.

Q: Do you have any explanation for why he hit you?

A: No, sir.

Q: Now, did you have to go see any physician as a result of his striking you?

A: In about a week, I did.

Q: What for?

A: Well, I was having headaches.

Q: Okay. Now, did you attend a meeting down at the Union Hall or someplace with Don Folz, the Union Business Agent, and Dent concerning this incident?

A: They came out to the plant and talked to me.

Q: All right. Now at that time did Dent say anything about you allegedly striking him before he hit you?

A: I think that he said I hit him on the arm.

Q: Was it at that time or at a grievance meeting?

A: I believe it was at the grievance meeting.

Q: But at this first meeting did Dent mention it?

A: I don't think so.

Q: How long after this happened was it that Folz and Dent came out to see you?

A: About a week, I think.

Q: Now, at that time did Dent say anything to you about it being a mistake or it being wrong or something like that, about his striking you?

A: I asked him if he had the right to hit me for what I said and he said no, he was in the wrong.

Q: Did he attempt to offer you some explanation of why he had done it?

A: I think he said his wife had been sick and he was worried about her.

Q: How was that supposed to explain why he had struck you?

A: I don't know.

Q: No further questions.

---

### b. Cross-Examination by Union Advocate

*Ms. Lake:*
[to be supplied by student]

## 2. James Lenz, Director, Concrete Production

### a. Direct Examination by Company Advocate

*Mr. Gipp:*

Q: State your name and address, please, sir.

A: Jim Lenz, Sunnydale, Tennessee.

Q: Where are you employed, Mr. Lenz?

A: Builders Supply Company.

Q: In what capacity?

A: Director of Concrete Production.

Q: How long have you been with the Company?

A: Six years.

Q: Did you, in your capacity, handle a grievance meeting concerning this case?

A: The final grievance meeting.

Q: Who was present at that meeting?

**A:** Henry Brass, Elton Horn, Larry Blunt, Don Folz, and Harold Dent.

**Q:** At that meeting, was anything said about Blunt having struck Dent first?

**A:** No.

**Q:** What is the rule in the plant concerning fighting?

**A:** There's no written rule. It is just a general understanding that fighting results in immediate discharge.

**Q:** Why is that?

**A:** We have some hundred and twenty employees and we have some rough fellows. This is a tough business, but it is the type of business where fighting is just not allowed. There is no way to conduct a business if one employee is allowed to hit another employee.

**Q:** Do you try to strictly control situations, such as fighting, that might cause some problems?

**A:** Absolutely.

**Q:** For example, do you have a written rule on weapons?

**A:** No.

**Q:** Do you discipline employees for bringing weapons onto the plant?

**A:** Yes, we do.

**Q:** Have you recently fired someone for that?

**A:** Last week we fired an employee for bringing a pistol on the property.

**Q:** No further questions.

### b. Cross-Examination by Union Advocate

*Ms. Lake:*
[to be supplied by student]

## 3. Carl Wasson, Assistant Manager, Concrete Production

### a. Direct Examination by Company Advocate

*Mr. Gipp:*

**Q:** State your name and address, please, sir.

**A:** Carl Wasson, Thorp, Tennessee.

**Q:** Where are you employed, Mr. Wasson?

**A:** Builders Supply Company.

**Q:** In what capacity?

**A:** As the Assistant Manager of Concrete Production.

**Q:** How long have you been with Builders Supply?

**A:** Fifteen years.

**Q:** When did you first learn of the incident between Dent and Blunt?

**A:** Elton Horn called me on the telephone and asked me to come to the plant right away.

**Q:** Who is Mr. Horn?

**A:** He is the Production Manager, my boss. He related the incident to me when I got to the plant. He is presently in the hospital undergoing surgery.

**Q:** What did Horn tell you to do?

**A:** He told me to go to the office and pick up Harold Dent's check and give it to him.

**Q:** And to fire him?

**A:** Right.

**Q:** What has been the situation at the Company concerning any fighting on the job by employees?

**A:** It was always understood that you didn't fight on the Company property; if you did, you were dismissed—subject to dismissal.

**Q:** Did you go to Dent and give him his check?

**A:** Yes, I did, that afternoon.

**Q:** What did you say to him?

**A:** I handed him the check and told him that he was being dismissed. He replied, "Why?" I said, "I think you know why," and he said, "Okay." That was all the conversation that we had.

**Q:** Nothing further.

4

b. Cross-Examination by Union Advocate

*Ms. Lake*
[to be supplied by student]

## 4. Henry Brass, President, Builders Supply Company

### a. Direct Examination by Company Advocate

*Mr. Gipp:*
**Q:** State your name and address please, sir.
**A:** Henry Brass, Lanesville, Tennessee.
**Q:** And in what capacity are you connected with Builders Supply Company?
**A:** I am President.
**Q:** How long have you been connected with this Company?
**A:** Seventeen years.
**Q:** Mr. Brass, what is the Company policy concerning the fighting of employees on the job?
**A:** It is the Company policy that fighting is not allowed. I will not allow, nor tolerate, violence of any nature.
**Q:** In light of Harold Dent's record and the situation in which he was involved, would you rehire Dent?
**A:** I would not.
**Q:** Tell us why.

**A:** Well, we really don't know why he did it but he did hit Blunt. If everyone were entitled to one hit, with some hundred fifty to two hundred people we would have chaos. A few years ago we had a murder and suicide on the Company property. A man was instructed to carry out some order; he went home, got a gun, and came back and murdered his supervisor and killed himself. I am opposed to violence and I think if we allow any fighting to go on at the plant, the supervisors that work for me will lose all control over the workers.
**Q:** Why?
**A:** I think the supervisors would always be a little hesitant to give workers the orders that must be carried out to run a business. If you tell a man to do something, you are always going to be a little bit nervous. Maybe he is not going to like it. Maybe he will react violently.
**Q:** Thank you.

### b. Cross-Examination by Union Advocate

*Ms. Lake:*
[to be supplied by student]

## 5. Cal French, Driver

### a. Direct Examination by Company Advocate

*Mr. Gipp:*
**Q:** State your name.
**A:** Cal French.
**Q:** Do you live in Lanesville?
**A:** Yes, sir.
**Q:** Where are you employed?
**A:** At Builders Supply Company.
**Q:** You have been a driver for them?
**A:** Yes, sir.

**Q:** Were you working on the day that Harold Dent and Larry Blunt were involved in an incident?
**A:** I sure was.
**Q:** What did you see?
**A:** I was under the mixer getting a load and I saw Harold jump out of his truck and hit Larry.
**Q:** Did you see Blunt hit Dent before?

A:   No.
Q:   You ever get in any fights down there?
A:   No, sir. Well, I am pretty easy to get along with, so long as they don't start messing with me. I tell you, the Company has been real good to me.

Q:   What would happen to you if you were fighting on the job?
A:   If I was fighting?
Q:   Yes.
A:   I would get fired.
Q:   Nothing more.

### b. Cross-Examination by Union Advocate

*Ms. Lake:*
[to be supplied by student]

## 6. Ben Keller, Dispatcher

### a. Direct Examination by Company Advocate

*Mr. Gipp:*
Q:   State your name, please.
A:   Ben Keller.
Q:   Where do you live?
A:   South Lanesville, Tennessee.
Q:   Where are you employed?
A:   Builders Supply Company.
Q:   What's your job?
A:   Dispatcher.
Q:   Which yard?
A:   Jackson Street.
Q:   Were you working as dispatcher on October 25 when this incident occurred between Harold Dent and Larry Blunt?
A:   Yes, sir.
Q:   Did you see any part of it?
A:   Yes, sir.
Q:   Tell us what you saw.
A:   Well, at the time I was going to the pit and Dent drove by me. Blunt was getting off the payloader or backing the payloader and he walked past me. A little later I turned around and saw a conversation going on between

Blunt and Dent. I couldn't hear it because of the plant noise and the truck noise.
Q:   Where was Blunt?
A:   He was standing next to Dent's truck.
Q:   Where was Dent?
A:   In the truck.
Q:   So you saw them engaged in a conversation, which you could not hear?
A:   Right.
Q:   What happened?
A:   A minute, maybe less, maybe a little more, and Dent came out of the truck and hit Blunt, causing him to back up two or three steps. Blunt then immediately turned and walked away to the telephone to call up to the office—I assume that is what he was going to do.
Q:   Did Blunt strike Dent in any way before Dent came out of the truck?
A:   No, sir.
Q:   Did Blunt strike Dent in any way after Dent came out of the truck?
A:   No, sir.
Q:   That's all.

### b. Cross-Examination by Union Advocate

*Ms. Lake:*
[to be supplied by student]

## C. Examination of Union Witnesses

### 1. Harold (Harry) Dent, Grievant

#### a. Direct Examination by Union Advocate

*Ms. Lake:*

**Q:** Give your name and address.

**A:** Harold Dent. They also call me Harry.

**Q:** Where do you live?

**A:** Gordny, Tennessee.

**Q:** Did you work for Builders Supply Company?

**A:** Yes, almost twelve-and-a-half years.

**Q:** And what was your job there?

**A:** Driver. I drove truck 777.

**Q:** All right Harold let's go to the 25th day of October. Do you recall the incident?

**A:** Yes, I do.

**Q:** Well, would you describe to the Arbitrator just what happened that led up to this?

**A:** Well, I had been on a job at a construction site. After I finished it, got unloaded, I had put about thirty-five or forty gallons of water in the cylinder and washed it out real good in the open field there at Hamburg Lane. Upon arrival at the Fourth Street plant, I was told to put my truck under, but there was a truck there being loaded at the time.

**Q:** What does "put under" mean?

**A:** To go under the hopper and get a load.

**Q:** Under what?

**A:** The chute from the hopper, which is a giant concrete mixing machine. So you have to circle around because they have a big conveyer belt and everything and while I was driving around there, the dispatcher asked me if I had anything on, meaning concrete, and I said no, but that I might have a little bit of water in the cylinder. He said to get rid of the water, because a little water could ruin a good load.

So, as I circled around, Larry Blunt came backing down the hill in the payloader and he almost hit my truck in the side, but he slid to a halt to keep from hitting my truck, so I pulled on down. He backed down. I got out on the right side of my truck where the controls are. I walked to the back of it, where the controls are, and he backed the payloader down near me and he said, "Hey, don't you ever do that again." It is not so much what he said, it was the tone of voice that he was using. So, I said, "What's that?" And he said, "I almost got you in the side," and I said, "You had better not do that, you will lose your driver's bonus." See, if you drive a hundred and twenty hours a month without having an accident, you get a little bonus, which laborers, like Larry, don't get. So, I was just kidding him. Anyway, while we were talking I had put the cylinder in reverse, in other words, to discharge it, because I knew all I had was only just a gallon or maybe two of water in it.

**Q:** Were you in a hold position before you went under to get your load?

**A:** Yes, I was right in front of the wash-out rack. So, anyway, while we were talking, this water hit the chute and, well, like I said, a handful, maybe a couple of handfuls of gravel came out of the cylinder. But there wasn't any danger of it setting up, because I had already washed out on the job. So when the water hit the chute he said, "Hey, what are you doing?" I said, "I'm getting rid of this water." He said, "Get rid of it over there," meaning the wash-out rack. So, while we were talking I hit the throttle, it made the cylinder speed up and that one gush of water is what I had, so I reversed it. I ignored him, got in my truck, moved on down eight, ten, twelve feet to get closer to where I would get loaded, and he parks the payloader into the wash-out rack. I am in my truck. He jumps off the payloader, comes over, he's looking up at me and pointing his finger at me.

**Q:** Did Blunt ask you why you discharged the water?

**A:** Yes. He then said, "Hey, did you hear what I said?" and I said, "Yeah." He said, "Why did you do it?" and I said, "Larry, the water had already hit the cylinder chute, it was too late then." He said, "Let me tell you something, whenever you are out here, don't you ever dare to do that again.'' All I said was, ''Damn.'' He immediately hit my hand, or back of the wrist there, my arm, so I got out of the truck and I hit him.

**Q:** All right. What happened after that?

**A:** Well, I get back in my truck, I am waiting for this other truck to leave . . . and Larry went over to the telephone. After that other truck left, then I pulled down. The dispatcher, his name is Bill Schulz, came over, and I got out of my truck. He says, ''What happened?'' so I was trying to tell him and about that time Elton Horn was coming up.

**Q:** Who is Elton?

**A:** Well, he is the supervisor over the production plant, I suppose.

**Q:** He's the fellow that fired you eventually?

**A:** Yes.

**Q:** Go ahead.

**A:** And Bill Schulz said, ''There is something I have to take care of,'' and by that time Elton was there. So, Horn said, ''What happened?'' So, I was telling him; Blunt was on the left of Horn and Schulz was on the right of him, and after I talked to Horn a little while, well, he said, ''Okay, if anything like this happens again, somebody won't be here.'' Now, he didn't mention any names, but I automatically took it to mean me. So, we discussed it a little bit further and then Horn said, ''Okay,'' and then he said, ''The Company cannot tolerate things like this. If it happens again, somebody won't be here.''

**Q:** Did Larry say anything or was there anything discussed about what had taken place while Horn and Schulz were there?

**A:** Larry said, ''You are a liar. I am in charge of the yard. It is my duty to clean the yard.'' I told Larry, ''I won't do anything on purpose to cause any extra work.'' So, I believe that is when Horn said, ''Okay, the Company cannot tolerate this and if it happens again, somebody won't be here.'' They all left.

**Q:** Did Horn ask you whether you had heard Blunt say, ''Why did you discharge the water?''

**A:** Yes, Horn asked me, ''Did you hear what Larry said,'' and I said? ''Yes.'' He then asked, ''Why did you do it?'' And I said, ''The water had already hit the chute and the

damage was done.'' I said, ''You can look up there, it didn't make that much difference.'' From where we were standing you could see where I had been parked. After they left I got a load of concrete. Larry then came up to me and said, ''What's the matter with you, when you come out here you won't talk to me or anything?'' I turned around to him and said, ''Okay, Larry,'' I said, ''I'm sorry, I apologize.'' He walked away and I got in my truck.

**Q:** Did he say anything when you said you apologized?

**A:** He said okay.

**Q:** Then what happened?

**A:** I got back in my truck and made another delivery. After I returned to the plant, I washed out the cylinder and punched out. As I was going to my car, Carl Wasson handed me an envelope and a couple of checks. The envelope had a letter in it telling me I had been discharged. Carl said, ''Elton wants me to give you this,'' and he turned around and started walking off. I said, ''Wait, Carl, what is this for?'' and he said, ''I think you know,'' and he just kept going. He wouldn't even talk to me. I had filed a grievance against Carl about five months previous and since then he doesn't talk to me. I could meet him face to face and he wouldn't talk to me. So, I couldn't go to him for anything.

**Q:** Well, did you and the Union Business Agent, Don Folz, talk to Larry about this incident?

**A:** Yes.

**Q:** Would you tell us about that?

**A:** Well, Don and I went out and we talked to Larry Blunt. I had already told my version of it to Mr. Folz, and he said, ''Well, let's go see Larry, I want to hear his side of it.'' The three of us talked and Larry told his version. I repeated mine and Mr. Folz asked Larry, ''Would you like to see this boy get fired?'' and he said, ''No.'' I don't remember now all that was said.

**Q:** Now, you said that Carl Wasson wouldn't talk to you because you had filed a grievance five months earlier. When exactly was that and what was it all about?

**A:** Well, I don't remember the exact date, but one afternoon, I pulled into the plant and a couple of the guys were discussing something.

I could tell that they were bugged about it, so I asked them what was the matter. They were in the process of telling me when Ben Keller, who was another dispatcher, said, "Well, I don't guess I have to tell you, they've already done it," and I said, "Tell me what?" and he said, "That from now on you will grease the rollers." One of the other boys asked him to call Ted Wills, the Union Steward, but instead of calling the Union Steward, Keller called Carl Wasson. While this was going on I was in the process of washing out and I am pulling away from the rack. Ben came up and jumped on the running board and said, "From now on you will grease the rollers." I said, "Ben, it is not our job." He replied, "Carl Wasson told me you will either do it or else you will be fired." And I said, "Okay, Ben, I will do it tonight, but I am going to file a grievance."

**Q:** And I take it you did file a grievance and that it's been disposed of?

**A:** Yes, I did.

**Q:** All right. There is talk about some disturbance you caused over the checkoff of Union dues. Explain what happened.

**A:** One time there was this mistake in my check regarding the deduction for Union dues, so I called up Brenda Morris in the Payroll Department and called her attention to it. She said, "Boy, I am so glad you called and brought it to my attention." She was apologetic.

I identified another payroll deduction error a month later. I was asked by a couple of the drivers to check on a $2.85 deduction in our wages for uniforms. I went to the main office and I asked to see Mr. Lenz. While I was in Lenz's office, I was told that the other drivers and I should be reimbursed for the $2.85 because uniforms were to be furnished free, according to the Collective Bargaining Agreement.

**Q:** While you were in Lenz's office, did you talk to Mr. Lenz about how you were going to be more cooperative and not take on the problems of all the other people?

**A:** I realized Lenz was not too happy about being reminded of errors by payroll. I said, "From now on I am just going to look out for number one and forget about my brothers. I'll leave it up to the Union Business Agent to bring problems to the attention of management." Lenz replied that I should have left it alone a long time ago.

**Q:** Did you go through some discussions with the management personnel and Mr. Folz about your discharge?

**A:** Yes.

**Q:** Did they ask you to give the details of the incident?

**A:** Not really. Folz kept on telling me to wait to explain my side at the arbitration hearing. I told Folz that Blunt was a troublemaker, but Folz refused to hear me out.

**Q:** And was there a meeting on November 3?

**A:** Yes.

**Q:** Who was present?

**A:** Mr. Brass, Larry Blunt, Elton Horn, and Ted Wills, who Mr. Lenz failed to mention a while ago.

**Q:** As a result of that meeting, was any resolution of this discharge made or any decision made at that time?

**A:** No, we just discussed a few things and then asked Larry if he wanted to see me fired and he said, "No."

**Q:** Was that at this meeting?

**A:** Yes.

**Q:** All right. Go ahead.

**A:** Mr. Folz asked Mr. Horn if he made the remark that, "Okay, but if anything like this happens again, somebody won't be here." Elton kind of denied it at first, and later he said, "Why, I may have."

**Q:** I might have asked you this earlier but just to make sure, have you ever been disciplined in your twelve years with the company?

**A:** Never. In fact, when I reached ten years of service, Mr. Brass gave me a good conduct pin.

**Q:** Nothing further.

## b. Cross-Examination by Company Advocate

*Mr. Gipp:*
[to be supplied by student]


## 2. Marvin Mills, Driver

### a. Direct Examination by Union Advocate

*Ms. Lake:*
**Q:** What is your name and address?
**A:** Marvin Mills, Lanesville, Tennessee.
**Q:** Do you work for Builders Supply Company?
**A:** Yes.
**Q:** And what is your job there?
**A:** Truck driver.
**Q:** How long have you worked for Builders Supply?
**A:** About seven and a half years.
**Q:** Do you know Larry Blunt?
**A:** Yes. He's the Yardman.
**Q:** Would you describe to the Arbitrator an incident that took place between you and Larry and when it happened?
**A:** Well, it was about two days before this happened between him and Dent.
**Q:** You mean two days before October 25?
**A:** Yes. I was going under the hopper, sitting there waiting to get loaded and Larry came over and got on the running board of my truck and was talking to me about something. I don't remember what we were talking about, but he turned the mirror around and I told him not to do that. I said, "These are knock-away mirrors, they are harder to adjust than the others are," and he said, "You are just hard to get along with." He said, "You have a bad temper. How does your wife get along with you?" And I said, "I don't say anything to her and she doesn't say anything to me." He then reached in and grabbed me.
**Q:** He just reached in the window and grabbed you?
**A:** Yes.
**Q:** What did he grab?
**A:** My jacket.
**Q:** Well, did you hit him?
**A:** No. If he had made me mad at the time, though, I would have hit him.
**Q:** No further questions.

### b. Cross-Examination by Company Advocate

*Mr. Gipp:*
[to be supplied by student]


## 3. Don Folz, Business Agent

### a. Direct Examination by Union Advocate

*Ms. Lake:*
**Q:** Your name and address?
**A:** Don Folz, Holly, Tennessee.
**Q:** What is your position with the Union?
**A:** Business Agent for Local 9880.
**Q:** And in that capacity have you processed this grievance of Mr. Dent concerning his discharge?
**A:** To the best of my ability.
**Q:** When did you first hear of it?
**A:** Well, I heard about it the next morning after the incident occurred.
**Q:** That would be the 26th of October?
**A:** Twenty-sixth, yes. Dent talked to me that morning. This is the usual way we do things, to be sure you don't file a bad grievance.

10

There is no use filing one if there is no merit to it.

**Q:** What did you do after it was filed?

**A:** I talked to Dent and he told me what had happened and I told him I would want to talk to the other man involved, but if he felt like he had a grievance at this time we would get hold of the Steward and make out a grievance. I asked him first if he had talked to his immediate supervisor. He said he tried to but the supervisor, Carl Wasson, walked away from him.

So, as I said, I advised him to have the Steward call me and the Steward did call me. He called me and told me that he was going to turn in a grievance sometime the next day and try to set up a meeting. The Steward called me back after the meeting he had with Elton Horn and Dent and told me he had tentatively set up a meeting for a few days later, on a Friday.

**Q:** All right. Did you have the meeting?

**A:** We did.

**Q:** Meanwhile, had you talked to Mr. Blunt or did you talk to him that morning?

**A:** Yes, I came down to see Mr. Blunt and heard his side of the story and I made it very clear to him that I didn't want him to tell any lies or anything. I think he will back me up. All I wanted was facts and truth from every side.

I did ask him, ''You don't want to see Dent fired, do you?'' and he said, ''Certainly not''; he didn't want to see that happen to anybody.

**Q:** I now show you Joint Exhibit 6, a petition with twenty-nine signatures. Who are some of these people on this petition and can you explain it to us?

**A:** Well, the petition was due to a conversation I had with Mr. Brass over the phone. He said that the people working with Dent didn't want him to come back and I said, ''I have talked to quite a few of the drivers and I just can't believe it.'' I talked to Dent and he talked to some of the drivers and they decided to sign this petition.

**Q:** No further questions.

## b. Cross-Examination by Company Advocate

*Mr. Gipp:*
[to be supplied by student]

## D. Exhibits

### *JOINT EXHIBIT NO. 1*

COLLECTIVE BARGAINING AGREEMENT

BETWEEN

BUILDERS SUPPLY COMPANY

AND

UNIVERSAL UNION OF DRIVERS AND ASSISTANTS

LOCAL NO. 9880 (1/1/01-1/1/03)

**Article 3**   The Company shall have the right to discipline and discharge employees for just cause. An employee may file a grievance when discharged or disciplined pursuant to the grievance/arbitration procedure in Article 15.

### *JOINT EXHIBIT NO. 2*

**GRIEVANCE**
**LOCAL 9880, U.U.D.A.**

**Step 3**                                          **Grievance No. 2244**

I was wrongfully discharged for hitting Larry Blunt.  I request reinstatement with seniority, back pay, and interest.


November, Year 1                          /s/ Harold Dent

---

**Step 3**          **Company Answer**          **Grievance No. 2244**

The grievance is denied


/s/ Henry Brass
President

*JOINT EXHIBIT NO. 3*

Builders Supply Company                                    JUNE 1, Year 1

Lanesville, Tennessee

Dear Sir,

    Would you please see to it that the driver of your cement truck Number 777 on June 1st, receives this check. There is the ten dollars he loaned me and ten dollars for his kindness towards my children at Arby's. He has left me an idea of how wonderful Tennessee people can be. Your company is indeed fortunate to have such a man.

                                            Gratefully yours,

                              /s/ <u>Veronica M. Stowe</u>
                                 Lompoc, Iowa

*JOINT EXHIBIT NO. 4*

BUILDERS SUPPLY COMPANY
INCORPORATED
LANESVILLE, TENNESSEE

June 3, Year 1


Mr. Harold Dent
c/o Concrete Division

Dear Harold,

It is indeed a pleasure for me to forward to you the enclosed note and check from Mrs. Stowe, of Lompoc, Iowa. Your small act of kindness was apparently greatly appreciated as evidenced by the fact that Mrs. Stowe has gone to the trouble of returning your favor and making sure that I was aware of it.

I, too, appreciate what you have done and commend you for it. Although Mrs. Stowe is not a local resident and we are not likely to hear from her again, I am confident that with employees who can show consideration to strangers, our relationship with our friends and customers will continue to grow and prosper.

Again, let me say thank you.

Very truly yours,


/s/ Henry Brass
    President

HDB:ss

cc: Mr. Don Folz, Business Agent, Local 9880
    Mr. Elton Horn, Mgr., Concrete Division

*JOINT EXHIBIT NO. 5*

**SAFE DRIVER CERTIFICATE**


PRESENTED TO **HAROLD DENT**

as an expression of appreciation

of his ability in driving 4 years

without accident.


BUILDERS SUPPLY COMPANY


Date July 1, Year 1                    /s/ Henry Brass, President

*JOINT EXHIBIT NO. 6*

**PETITION**

NOVEMBER 15, YEAR 1


TO WHOM IT MAY CONCERN:

WE THE UNDERSIGNED DRIVERS WOULD LIKE TO SEE HAROLD DENT GET HIS PLACE BACK ON THE SENIORITY LIST AND BE WITH US AGAIN.


/s/ Bob Brown                    /s/ Mike Garcia

/s/ Arthur Smith                 /s/ Joe Rich

/s/ Alice Mays                   /s/ Alice Smith

/s/ Jerry White                  /s/ Eunice Marvell

/s/ Tawanna Reese                /s/ John McRail

/s/ José Rodriquez               /s/ Hal Orrick

/s/ Susan Chen                   /s/ Johnny Ray Osgood

/s/ Michael O'Rourke             /s/ Billy John Osgood

/s/ Horace Douglas               /s/ Ricky Marciano

/s/ Walter MacNeice              /s/ Tim Reilly

/s/ Albert Jones                 /s/ Bert Coats

/s/ Maurice Dueber               /s/ Beretta Ildefonso

/s/ Reynaldo Montoya             /s/ Sam Wu

/s/ Wilfred Mann                 /s/ Lincoln Steffins

/s/ Jerry LaMonte

# McTiny Kitchens, Inc.

**Table of Contents**

**Table of Contents contd.**

**NOTES**

# A. Caption

## IN THE MATTER OF ARBITRATION BETWEEN:

| | | |
|---|---|---|
| McTINY KITCHENS, INC.<br>HOT SPRINGS, ALASKA | ) ) ) ) ) | |
| AND | ) ) ) ) | RE: SUSAN NORMAN<br>Discharge for Fighting |
| WOODWORKERS UNIVERSAL UNION<br>LOCAL NO. 5140 | ) ) | |

Appearances:

For the Company: Joan Kasten

For the Union: Thomas Webb

Date: April 26, year 2

Place: Hot Springs, Alaska

## B. Examination of Company Witnesses

### 1. Linda Ross, Supervisor

a. Direct Examination by Company Advocate

*Ms. Kasten:*

Q: Will you state your name, please?

A: Linda Ross.

Q: Where do you reside?

A: Henryville.

Q: How long have you been employed at McTiny Kitchens?

A: Five years.

Q: What is your present position?

A: Supervisor.

Q: How long have you been a supervisor?

A: A year this month.

Q: How long have you been acquainted with Susan Norman?

A: Since she was employed at McTiny Kitchens. I don't know when she came there. I knew her family prior to that.

Q: What was your relationship with Susan prior to this incident?

A: Susan and I talked about every day. My husband is from her hometown. If she got any news, she always related it to me.

Q: What hometown was that?

A: Oneida, Alaska.

Q: How would you describe your relationship with her prior to this incident?

A: I thought I had a good relationship with Susan. I never had any trouble, really, out of Susan.

Q: Had you ever assisted Susan in filing any grievances?

A: Yes, I advised her while I was supervisor. I told her that she would have to find some provision in the contract that had been violated by the Company and explain what restitution she wanted the Company to make. That's the information I gave to Susan. I believe Diane was there at the time.

Q: Had you ever had one word of trouble with Susan Norman prior to September 15, year 1?

A: No, I did not.

Q: All right. I'd like for you to go back to September 15, year 1, and recount the events of that day. First of all, what time did you come to work?

A: Oh, I came to work about 20 minutes of 7. We start at 7 in the morning.

Q: And when did you first observe Susan?

A: At 7 o'clock. But Susan didn't start work at that time. She was just griping that they had this grievance meeting the night before on her grievance against Frank Lyle, the Personnel Manager, and she was not happy. She felt the Union hadn't done its part, that she had to apologize to Lyle and I think Lyle in turn maybe apologized to Susan. Susan wasn't satisfied with what had taken place and she was standing around griping about it and would not start to work.

Q: And what, if anything, did you do?

A: I asked her if she would start to work.

Q: And what was her attitude?

A: Everything that she did on her job was just like real slow, exaggerated moves.

Q: Would you continue then with the results or the events of the rest of the morning?

A: Lois, the front line supervisor in charge of the next department, told me that some of the nailing from my employees looked bad. So I got the inspection report and I showed it to the girls and Susan's initials appeared quite a few times. I told them if you see your initials on it, watch what you are doing and correct it. Every time Susan saw her initials, she said "Huh-uh" and it seemed to agitate her that I had even showed her that report. I started watching the cabinets on the line after I had shown the women their report to see if the cabinets were coming through any better than they had. Susan had sent two cabinets down the line. On the two she sent down she had missed the shelves completely with the staples that fasten them in, and left a row of 5-inch staples through the back wall of the cabinet. You shoot the cabinet from the back. You are shooting from the back of the cabinet and hitting a shelf. A guide is used, but Susan had missed the shelves. She didn't even bother to pull the nails out, so I carried the two cabinets back and I gave them to Susan and I said, "Susan, you're missing your shelves. Would you pull your staples out?"

So the next time another of her cabinets came down I found she had missed a hang rail. If a hang rail is missed the proper procedure is to correct it right then, but Susan didn't do this and she left an inch-and-a-quarter nail sticking out on the inside. I took the cabinet to Susan and I asked her if she would correct it. Just then Lois, the supervisor, returned another cabinet in which Susan had missed the shelf. It had five-eighth inch nails and the staples sticking right out through the front of the cabinet backing. All Susan did was get mad because she was getting the cabinets returned to her.

**Q:** After you had had your conversation with Susan about the quality of her work, what further events occurred?

**A:** While I was in the front office, Paula Norris, the Shop Steward, was in there and she told me that she had an argument with Susan in the ladies' restroom. When I returned to my department the line was backed up as it is on occasion. No cabinets had been moved out. All the cabinets were still in my department and the girls were stacking them three high. That meant there were 20 girls in the paint shop standing around waiting for cabinets. I borrowed help to fill nail holes and I filled some nail holes myself.

**Q:** Did you have any comment with anyone about your working?

**A:** Yes, I said that I would help if they had no objection and they said they didn't see any problem.

**Q:** Did you then proceed to fill some holes?

**A:** I had filled holes in three cabinets and I was turning the cabinets in the direction of the paint shop where they are painted after leaving my department.

**Q:** What then happened?

**A:** Diane Johnson, one of the Union Committee members, came and said that was I working and I asked her if somebody was objecting and she said Susan Norman and Joyce Hall were objecting. I looked up and Joyce had her head down in the cabinet just nailing to beat the dickens and Susan was standing there laughing at me with her hands

on her hips. Susan came up and I asked her "Do you want to do this job?" And Susan answered, "I don't give a damn what I do." By that time I had put five girls on the job and the line had cleared up. I told the girls, "Well, the line is unjammed, now you can go back to your jobs." And Susan just kept on standing.

**Q:** Had Susan done anything during this period of time?

**A:** No, she was just standing there from the time that we first started trying to get the line unjammed. Susan just stood there and I told Susan three times that the line was cleared up and to go back and nail. I told Susan, "You go back and nail," and she moved toward me and my finger touched her face. She then hauled off and hit me in the face. She hit me at least twice in the face. She hit me on the right side of my face and I had a place that was cut under my right eye and my mouth and on the right side of my nose. She reached up and she jerked my wig off and threw it on the floor. As I stepped back and stooped over to pick the wig up, she just grabbed me by the hair. She was pulling it all. I was going where my head and hair was going and we moved, I would say, approximately 8 or 10—at least 8 feet up the aisle with Susan pulling my hair. I thought the way she was acting, if she gets hold of one of the wood pieces nearby she's liable to kill me. I finally reached around and got her arm. I was going up the aisle with her pulling my head and me hanging onto her arm. Finally I heard somebody, and I believe it was Paula, telling Susan to stop it. Diane had been screaming "Stop it," all along but it was, I think, Paula that I heard and I don't know which one of the girls got Susan off of me.

**Q:** At what point in time did you discharge her?

**A:** I discharged her when she pulled my wig off and threw it on the floor.

**Q:** After she pulled your wig off, what did you say to her?

**A:** I said, "Susan, you are fired. Get your things and get out of here." That's when she grabbed me by the hair.

**Q:** At this time I'd like to ask you if you can identify the contents of the envelope labeled "Ross's Hair" and marked Company Exhibit 3?

**A:** That is my hair.

**Q:** And where did it come from?

**A:** From my head.

**Q:** On that date?

**A:** On that date, I just reached up and that hair was all out.

**Q:** No further questions.

### b. Cross-Examination by Union Advocate

*Mr. Webb:*
[to be supplied by student]

## 2. Frank Lyle, Personnel Manager

### a. Direct Examination by Company Advocate

*Ms. Kasten:*

**Q:** State your name, please.

**A:** Frank Lyle.

**Q:** By whom are you employed?

**A:** McTiny Kitchens.

**Q:** What is your position?

**A:** Personnel Manager.

**Q:** How long have you been so employed?

**A:** Since June of year 1.

**Q:** I'll hand you what has been marked as Joint Exhibit 3, which purports to be a letter dated September 15, year 1 discharging Susan Morris. Is that your signature?

**A:** Yes.

**Q:** And did you send that letter?

**A:** Yes.

**Q:** I'll hand you what has been marked as Joint Exhibit 4, which purports to be a letter dated September 22. Did you send that letter?

**A:** That letter was to advise the Union that I had received the grievance and that I would like to set up a meeting.

**Q:** And did you, in fact set up a meeting?

**A:** Yes, we did. Monty Erb and I marked on the bottom of the letter that we were to meet on October 4th.

**Q:** And did you, in fact, meet on October 4th?

**A:** Yes, we did.

**Q:** I'll hand you what has been marked as Joint Exhibit 5 and will ask you if that is your signature?

**A:** Yes, it is.

**Q:** And how did that letter come about?

**A:** It was the Company's answer to the grievance.

**Q:** And is it true that you, in effect, disallowed the grievance?

**A:** I certainly did.

**Q:** I'll hand you what has been admitted as Joint Exhibit 6 and ask you if you mailed that letter?

**A:** Yes, I did.

**Q:** Prior to your mailing that letter, had there ever been a written demand made for arbitration?

**A:** No.

**Q:** What has been the policy of the Company either under this contract or the old contract regarding written demands for arbitration?

**A:** Under the old contract, I can't tell you too much. On my pre-employment, I was told there had never been a personnel manager and now they were creating a job and the sole purpose was to deal with the 42 grievances the Union claimed we lost by time limitations.

**Q:** What do you mean "lost by time limitations"?

**A:** The Union evidently had taken the position that the Company should lose the 42 grievances if they had not made timely response according to the procedure outlined in the contract. My job was then to adhere to the contract and adhere to the time limitations.

**Q:** Now, with reference to your letter of October 30, did you, either by a letter or by word of mouth, at any time indicate to the Union or the Union representative that you

4

were waiving the contract requirement that written demand be made within ten days for arbitration?

A: No, I did not.

Q: Did your letter refer to this requirement in the contract?

A: Yes, it did.

Q: Following your letter of October 30, in which you express a willingness to arbitrate without waiving the time limitation, did you have any further correspondence or meetings with the Union regarding this particular grievance?

A: Yes, in selecting an arbitrator and in selecting a hearing and a time.

Q: Was there a delay in selecting the arbitrator?

A: I believe there was.

Q: And how did that come about?

A: Basically, it's a matter of communication or lack of it. I have made phone calls to the Union hall asking that we get together and select an arbitrator from a list provided by the Federal Mediation and Conciliation Service (FMCS). It takes time to respond to my calls.

Q: And did you make such phone calls in this instance?

A: Yes, I did.

Q: And did that meet with any success?

A: No, it did not.

Q: And did you therefore write the letters of January 17, year 2, and January 26, year 2?—Joint Exhibits 7 and 8?

A: Yes.

Q: What was the purpose of those letters?

A: Well, the January 17th letter had several purposes.

Q: With reference to this specific case then?

A: I advised the Union that I still had the pending arbitration for Susan Norman, that I wished to make a selection of an arbitrator and set an early hearing, and asked that they cooperate and prompt attention be given to the matter.

Q: All right. Now let's go back in time. Where were you when you first learned that there had been some type of altercation between Susan Norman and Linda Ross?

A: In my office.

Q: And after you learned this, what did you do?

A: I was called by the plant manager to come to the cafeteria.

Q: And did you do that?

A: Yes, I did.

Q: What did you find when you arrived?

A: On going to the cafeteria I took with me Mr. Earl Wall, who is Vice President of Manufacturing. I found Mr. Forest, our Plant Manager; the chief steward, Mr. Baxter; Diane Johnson, Union committee woman, I believe at this time; Paula Norris, a shop steward; Susan Norman; and our supervisor, Linda Ross.

Q: What did you observe about Linda?

A: When I walked in, she was in tears, her face was red, her right eye was cut. The right side of her nose was swollen and looked like there was a little cut on it and her mouth was cut on the right side. I believe it was her upper lip that was bleeding. She was standing there with a wig in one hand and hair in the other hand.

Q: Did you observe any other hair in the cafeteria or anywhere else later that morning?

A: Well, at the time that Linda was talking to me, both in the cafeteria and my office where she came later, she was trying to smooth her hair down and hair was flying all over. There was a lot left on my floor and my desk and the chair when she left the office.

Q: Was there any conversation in the cafeteria with Susan Norman?

A: Most of the talking was done by Diane Johnson and Linda Ross. However, I did ask Susan if she had hit Linda, at which she admitted she had, and I also asked Susan if Linda had hit her, to which she had replied "No, but she pointed her finger in my face." I was going to then tell her she was discharged, at which time Paula Norris, who is a Shop Steward, came between me and Susan and said that I should not say anything to her because there had been a problem earlier with her that morning and no one could talk to her, including the Union. At that time I said, "Susan, would you please leave? I'll get with your Steward and then inform you."

Q: Now, did you interrogate the employees that morning to find out what had happened?

A: I did not interrogate the employees, no. I asked Mr. Forest to see if he could find out what went on. He did obtain a statement from Kathy Stewart. I later asked to see two of the people involved, which was Diane Johnson and Paula Norris. I did talk to Diane, but not Paula.

**Q:** You have heard testimony that Susan had filed a prior grievance against you, is that true?

**A:** Yes, that's true.

**Q:** Is that the grievance in Company Exhibit 2?

**A:** Yes, it is.

**Q:** And what was the nature of that grievance?

**A:** The nature of the grievance was that I had more or less harassed her and been nasty to her in my office.

**Q:** And was that grievance resolved?

**A:** Supposedly, yes.

**Q:** When?

**A:** I'm not sure of the date. I don't have the grievance in front of me—wait a minute.

**Q:** With reference to September 15?

**A:** It was prior to that.

**Q:** The night before the fight had there been a meeting attended by you and Norman?

**A:** Yes.

**Q:** All right. And is it true that there was a mutual apology by you and Norman at that meeting the night before?

**A:** Yes.

**Q:** Could you relate your encounters with Susan Norman before the grievance filed by her against you?

**A:** Not long after I arrived at work I received a telephone call from Susan about her vacation pay, at which time I explained to her we were not putting through the vacation check while the strike was in progress. She had a few comments about the strike, that she didn't know what it was for and she didn't like the Union, et cetera, hoping, I guess, that I would give her the vacation check, at which time I told her I would not but if it changed, I would get back with her. I received several phone calls from her. She also came into my office when I was very busy.

The day after the strike was settled, on Monday, July 31, I received a phone call from Susan stating that she was coming in after her check. I then told Susan that the check would have to go through normal payroll procedure, and it would be in the office that Thursday, which is the earliest we get our payroll from

Central Trust. She informed me that I could write a handwritten check for her vacation pay. I then told her that we were not permitted by the auditor to write handwritten checks and that she could have it Thursday. She hung up in my ear. I informed my secretary that when Susan came in Thursday, that I wanted to talk to her.

Susan then called me Thursday and told me who she was and that she was coming in for her vacation check, and I said I looked forward to meeting her. She says, "You'll have the opportunity in a few minutes," and clunk in my ear again. So she came in and I said, "So you're the lady that's been hanging up in my ear." Her response was kind of shocking, like, "I did." She got her vacation pay, and it ended sort of pleasant and mutual. That was the first encounter.

The next encounter was a phone conversation—with the Shop Steward, Paula Norris, on June 27th. She said Susan's son was hospitalized and could I get her covered under Blue Cross-Blue Shield. She did not have the coverage. I told Paula I'd do all I could; I'd send the letter. I called Blue Cross immediately, explained I was new to the Company and there were a lot of errors in the records and could we have an open enrollment. Then I told them the situation with Susan's son. They requested I send the letter, which I did. I did get her Blue Cross even though her son was already hospitalized. However, it took a long time because of the strike and the plan change. So there were a lot of delays in Susan getting her coverage, but she was covered. I told her this. She made several visits to my office about the delay in insurance coverage, which I explained. In the meantime I had been told by supervisors that Susan had been telling people on the production line that I wasn't getting her insurance coverage.

When Susan visited me on August 30, I asked her if she had made those statements about me. She claimed she did not and wanted to know where I heard them. I said it was not important, but I didn't appreciate those statements because I was doing all I could and I had explained to her the reasons for all the delays. She then said her son may be hospitalized again that evening and she needed to get coverage. While she was in the office I called the local Blue Cross-Blue Shield and asked why Susan had no coverage number. They called back to my office after quitting time and gave me an insurance contract number for Susan. I had my secretary call Susan at home to advise her of the number although we did not have the card.

The next day, August 31, Linda Ross called me and explained to me that Susan was complaining to the people downstairs that she was going to have my job, she was going to have me fired. She asked, ''what was it about?'' I said, ''No need you getting into it; send Susan to my office.'' She came to my office with Paula Norman, the Union Steward. I asked Susan what the problem was. Susan said she had no problem. I said, ''Evidently there is a problem. What is the problem? I want to get it resolved, get you to work and to stop this attitude.'' Susan had very little to say. Paula was in the meeting all the way through, and it ended that I apologized to Susan for getting upset with her, but I said I was trying and we would have her insurance contract as soon as possible.

From that point on, Susan did not drop it. She evidently had discussed it with numerous people in the plant. I had a visit from three Union officials—Mr. Baxter, Miss Norris, and Miss Johnson—who didn't know what to do with Susan because she filed a grievance on me. I told them I had already apologized.

On September 14, the grievance was settled by mutual apologies. I explained to Mr. Baxter the next morning that I felt Susan was still not satisfied. He informed me that evidently she was not because there was a run-in that morning with Paula Norris and Susan Norman in the restroom concerning the grievance settlement the day before.

**Q:** No further questions.

## b. Cross-Examination by Union Advocate

*Mr. Webb:*
[to be supplied by student]

## 3. Diane Johnson, Union Committee Member

### a. Direct Examination by Company Advocate

*Ms. Kasten:*

**Q:** Will you state your name, please?

**A:** Diane Johnson.

**Q:** Where do you live?

**A:** Morrisville.

**Q:** By whom were you employed on September 14, year 1?

**A:** McTiny Kitchens.

**Q:** During what period of time did you work for McTiny Kitchens?

**A:** One year.

**Q:** Calling your attention to September 15, year 1, did you hold any official position with the Union at that time?

**A:** I was a Union Committee member.

**Q:** Were you working on September 15?

**A:** Yes.

**Q:** All right. Did you have occasion to observe an altercation between Linda Ross and Susan Norman on that date?

**A:** Yes.

**Q:** Would you just tell us what happened in your own words?

**A:** That was the day that Linda Ross was on the line cleaning and countersinking the cabinets, and the girls were back in nailing working, and all of them were kind of complaining because the foreman was not supposed to touch the cabinets, only to instruct and train. So I went down and I told Linda. I said, ''The girls are complaining and they want to file a grievance.'' And Linda said, ''Who?'' And I said, ''Joyce Hall and Susan Norman.'' She hollered, ''Joyce, Susan, come down here.'' Then she said, ''Susan, come down here!'' Susan came down there, and she said, ''Susan, do you want to get over and countersink those cabinets?'' Susan said, ''I don't care what I do.'' Linda took her finger and shook it at Susan. She said, ''You get back up there and nail those cabinets: you've been talking all day; I want to see the cabinets nailed.'' Susan said, ''You make me.'' Linda's finger then touched Susan's nose and Susan hit Linda with her hand and there was a struggle. Paula finally separated the two girls.

**Q:** And did you at any time see Linda Ross strike Susan Norman?

**A:** Not that I remember, except for her finger touching Susan's nose. They were so entangled.

**Q:** But you did see Susan Norman strike Linda Ross?

**A:** Yes.

**Q:** No further questions.

### b. Cross-Examination by Union Advocate

*Mr. Webb:*
[to be supplied by student]


# C. Examination of Union Witnesses


## 1. Susan Norman, Grievant

### a. Direct Examination by Union Advocate

*Mr. Webb:*

**Q:** Would you give us your full name and address.

**A:** Susan Norman, Hot Springs. My name was Morris when I was hired by McTiny. I married Sam Norman while working at McTiny.

**Q:** How long were you employed at McTiny Kitchens prior to your discharge?

**A:** The following June I would have been there two years.

**Q:** I see. And what was your job at the time of your termination?

**A:** Nailing.

**Q:** Nailing Department?

**A:** Yes, sir.

**Q:** I direct your attention to September 15, year 1. Did you have any meeting, discussion, or any words with Paula Norris on that morning?

**A:** We discussed it but we never had words, no.

**Q:** Where did this discussion take place?

**A:** In the restroom.

**Q:** And could you tell me what the subject of the discussion was?

**A:** When we were in the meeting that night over the grievance against Mr. Lyle, everything that was said, well, Lyle and Forest would laugh and, of course, Paula would grin, too, so that's the reason I asked her if she was laughing at me and she said, ''No, if I had something to say about you, I would come and tell you.'' That's it.

**Q:** Well, now, how did that meeting between you and Paula Norris end up?

**A:** As friends, like we were before.

**Q:** Were either of you mad at each other when you walked out of the restroom?

**A:** No; no, sir.

**Q:** That same morning, what work, if any, did you observe Linda Ross performing that you thought was Union work?

**A:** She was countersinking and pushing the cabinets through the line.

**Q:** Is that work that's normally performed by the Union employees?

**A:** Yes, it is.

**Q:** What, if anything, did you do about it personally?

**A:** Nothing personally. It went around the line and everybody was complaining. I was one of them.

**Q:** Did you personally say anything to Linda about it?

**A:** No, sir, I did not.

**Q:** Who did you complain to?

**A:** Nobody in particular. We all just were talking among ourselves.

**Q:** Well, now, what prompted Diane Johnson to go up to Linda that morning?

**A:** Because we all were complaining about it and she knew that Linda wasn't supposed to work.

**Q:** Did you observe Diane go up and talk to Linda?

**A:** No, sir, I did not.

**Q:** Well, what happened?

**A:** Well, the next thing I knew she was hollering, "Come here, Susan!"

**Q:** Who was that?

**A:** Linda.

**Q:** What were you doing at the time when she hollered?

**A:** I was working.

**Q:** Do you recall at any time standing up with your hands on your hips with a smirk on your face?

**A:** No, sir, I do not.

**Q:** Now, tell me again; what did Linda say to you?

**A:** "Come here, Susan," with a real ill-sounding voice.

**Q:** Was it loud?

**A:** Yes, sir, it was. It had to be pretty loud because I was down next to the end of the line.

**Q:** All right. Now, what, if anything, did you do next?

**A:** I just dropped everything and went up to where she was at and I said, "What do you want?"

**Q:** When you dropped what you were doing and you started walking up to where Linda was, at that particular moment, were you mad at Linda about something?

**A:** No, because I didn't know what she wanted.

**Q:** Had anything occurred prior to that time between you and Linda that day that you would have been mad about?

**A:** No, sir.

**Q:** Did you at any time after she called your name put your hands on your hips and put a smirk on your face?

**A:** No, sir, I did not.

**Q:** So you walked up to where Linda was standing, and—tell me in your own words then what happened.

**A:** Well, she asked me if I was complaining. She said Diane said that I was complaining and I said, yes, I was complaining just like the other girls. Then I turned and I asked Diane, I said, "Why did you just say that I was complaining?" Diane started to name others who were complaining too. Then Linda started screaming and telling me to get back to my table. I started to turn around until she repeated herself a little louder and her finger poked my nose, and the next thing I knew, well, I guess I hit her.

**Q:** All right. Could you stand up for a minute? I want you to describe where you were standing and how close Linda was standing to you. How close was she?

**A:** I would say about a foot and she screamed and her finger poked my nose. I started to turn and go back until she repeated herself, screaming a little louder.

**Q:** What was she saying?

**A:** "Get back to your table and get to work" and she didn't mean maybe.

**Q:** All right. Sit down. You don't deny that you struck Linda?

**A:** That's right, I did. I momentarily lost my cool. That has never happened before. I am sorry it happened.

**Q:** All right. Did she strike you at any time during the fight?

**A:** She scratched my arm bad enough that I had to go to the doctor with it.

**Q:** What did she do immediately after you struck her?

**A:** Well, we just tangled. I was trying to protect myself. She scratched my arm and Paula jumped over the line and separated us and we had no more, there was nothing else between us then, it was all over with right there.

**Q:** You say you went to the doctor as a result of the scratches on your arm?

**A:** I did, yes.

**Q:** Which arm were they on?

**A:** My left one.

**Q:** And what did your doctor do for you as a result of the scratches?

**A:** He gave me some medicine to go on it.

**Q:** Prior to that incident, had you had any trouble with Linda?

**A:** No, sir, I have not.

**Q:** Other than her poking her finger into your face and yelling, is there anything else that prompted you at that particular moment to strike out?

**A:** No, sir.

**Q:** Have you had any difficulty with any other employees in the department that you work with?

**A:** No, sir, I have not.

**Q:** Have you ever had any previous fights in the plant?

**A:** No, never.

**Q:** Ever had any previous fights anywhere?

**A:** No. I am a religious woman and my religion condemns the use of violence.

**Q:** Have you ever been reprimanded or disciplined by the Company for any previous action?

**A:** No, sir.

**Q:** That same morning, did you complain to Linda about anything prior to the time this fight occurred?

**A:** No, sir, I had not.

**Q:** Did you complain to her about the grievance settlement that you had the previous day?

**A:** Not to my recollection, no, I did not.

**Q:** Do you recall Linda saying anything to you that morning about your slowing down or not working?

**A:** No, sir, I did not.

**Q:** What has been your attitude in the past, if someone found something wrong with your work and asked you to do it over?

**A:** I did it over because I felt like if I didn't do it right the first time, it was my place to make it right.

**Q:** Do you recall making a statement to Linda to the effect that when she said get back to your work station you said, "You make me"?

**A:** Yes, I did.

**Q:** You did make that statement?

**A:** I did when she screamed the second time, I did.

**Q:** Do you remember that morning getting any cabinets back or having complaints about cabinets that you were working on?

**A:** Yes, I do.

**Q:** Could you tell me what happened as you recall?

**A:** Well, I remember this girl at the next table asked me to look at a cabinet she was working on. Rose was her name. We both looked at it and we couldn't find anything wrong with it. We set it back on the line and it went through again, so there must not have been that much wrong with it.

**Q:** Was Linda the one who was inspecting at the time?

**A:** Yes, she was working on them.

**Q:** How did she happen to put this particular cabinet back or how did it get back to you?

**A:** I can't remember whether she brought it or I went to get it. I told Linda it was Rose's cabinet but she ignored me.

**Q:** Was it part of your duties to inspect the cabinets?

**A:** No.

**Q:** Was it part of Linda's duties to inspect cabinets?

**A:** No. She wasn't even supposed to touch them, that was not part of her job. We have an inspector who is a member of the Union.

**Q:** Did you grab Linda by the hair and pull her approximately 10 feet down the line as she described?

**A:** No, sir, I did not. I would never think of doing such a thing!

**Q:** Do you recall the meeting in the lunchroom after this occurred?

**A:** Yes, sir, I do.

**Q:** Do you recall Mr. Lyle being there?

**A:** Yes, sir.

**Q:** Who else was there on behalf of the Company?

**A:** Dan Forest.

**Q:** Did you make any statement to Mr. Lyle to your recollection that Linda didn't hit you?

**A:** No, sir, I did not.

**Q:** You say you had a red spot on your face that came from the struggle?

**A:** Yes, sir.

**Q:** During this fight, did you bump up against anything with your face?

**A:** No, sir, I couldn't have.

**Q:** Did you fall to the floor?

**A:** No, sir.

**Q:** With respect to this incident over your vacation check, you heard the testimony of Mr. Lyle on that subject?

**A:** Yes, sir.

**Q:** Is it true that your vacation just happened to occur during the time when the strike took place?

**A:** Yes, sir.

**Q:** Did you get your check during or after your vacation?

**A:** The last day of my vacation, I got my check.

**Q:** Had you tried to get the check prior to that time?

**A:** Yes, sir.

**Q:** Did you ever threaten Mr. Lyle over your check?

**A:** No, sir.

**Q:** Were you upset when you came to the plant and your check wasn't ready?

**A:** Not that—no.

**Q:** When you came to pick up your check, what happened?

**A:** Well, Mr. Lyle had it but I had come in on Thursday to get my check and the girl at the desk said, well, Mr. Lyle took it to lunch with him because he wanted to see me and wanted to give it to me.

**Q:** Did you leave the plant at that time?

**A:** Yes, I went back home.

**Q:** Did you have to come back to get your check?

**A:** I did.

**Q:** And you did get the check that same day or next day from Mr. Lyle?

**A:** Next day. I called and asked him if it would be there, if I could get it.

**Q:** Do you recall abruptly hanging up on him on any of the occasions you called him?

**A:** I hung up. I don't know if it hurt his ear or not. I hung up as I usually do.

**Q:** Now, on this other item, the grievance that you filed, that was over a statement that you allegedly were to have made about Mr. Lyle. Someone informed Mr. Lyle of that statement?

**A:** Yes.

**Q:** Did you make a statement about Mr. Lyle?

**A:** No, sir, I did not.

**Q:** The purpose of your grievance was to find out who was responsible for making the false statement to Mr. Lyle?

**A:** Yes. I wanted the truth known.

**Q:** Now, that grievance was settled by both of you apologizing to each other; is that correct?

**A:** Yes.

**Q:** How far were you from Linda Ross when she hollered for you to come here?

**A:** Well, I would say 50 feet, because I was all the way down at the end of the nailing line.

**Q:** Do you know of any reason why she picked you out rather than any of the other girls?

**A:** No, sir, I don't. I surely didn't deserve such treatment from her.

**Q:** No further questions.

### b. Cross-Examination by Company Advocate

*Ms. Kasten:*
[to be supplied by student]

## 2. Paula Norris, Production Employee and Shop Steward

### a. Direct Examination by Union Advocate

*Mr. Webb:*

**Q:** What is your name and address?

**A:** Paula Norris, Crow River.

**Q:** How long have you worked at McTiny Kitchens?

**A:** Approximately two-and-a-half years.

**Q:** How long have you been employed in the Nailing Department?

**A:** Six months, somewhere thereabouts.

**Q:** Were you working in the Nailing Department at the time of the fight between Susan Norman and Linda Ross?

**A:** Yes, I was.

**Q:** All right. Do you hold any office in the Union?

**A:** I'm Day Steward.

**Q:** Were you Day Steward back in September of year 1?

**A:** Yes, I was.

**Q:** The morning of September 15, year 1, did you have a conversation with Susan in the restroom about her grievance the day before?

**A:** Yes, I did.

**Q:** Could you just tell us briefly what that was about?

**A:** Well, Susan just came right out and asked me if I was laughing at her the preceding night after the grievance settlement meeting. I said, "Susan, if I was laughing at you, I'd tell you to your face, I wouldn't go behind your back."

**Q:** Is that the end of it?

**A:** That was primarily the end of it. She did make the remark that she thought that I was laughing at her.

**Q:** Well, was she mad when she left the restroom at that time?

**A:** No, she seemed like there was a great load off her mind.

**Q:** Was anything said between you and her about that at any time after?

**A:** Well, we had went back to work, and I was back getting hang rails or something to that order because I was in the hang rail room and had to come back and Susan said, "I had heard that you were laughing at me." I said, "I don't do that." I said, "If I am going to do that, I'll do it to your face, I won't go behind your back and do it," and that was it.

**Q:** After this fight started, did you have any part in breaking it up?

**A:** Yeah, you might say I intervened.

**Q:** All right. At the time you intervened, what, if anything, were the parties doing at that particular moment?

**A:** Well, when I stepped in between I laid my hand on Susan's arm, and she pulled her left arm back and I proceeded to grab that arm and I seen Linda's hand come over my shoulder, for what purpose I don't know.

**Q:** Did you get the impression that they were trying to get at each other at that point?

**A:** Well, it seemed that way to me.

**Q:** Did you observe any marks or any other indications on Susan with respect to this fight?

**A:** Susan had a red mark on her face and I presume scratches on her arm, that's what they looked like to me.

**Q:** How long have you known Susan?

**A:** I've known her since I went to work there.

**Q:** How would you describe her personality since you've known her?

**A:** I really never did have any trouble with her, and to the best of my knowledge none of the rest of us did. Nobody said anything to me about her and usually I'm the one that knows about it.

**Q:** Would you call her a friendly person?

**A:** Almost always she had a smile on her face and seemed happy. She never had a bad word for anyone.

**Q:** Since you've been a Steward, do you know of any incidents where she's had any trouble with any other employees?

**A:** Not to my knowledge. She did ask me one time to call Mr. Lyle about her insurance and I proceeded to do so. When I came back and told her that Lyle hadn't found out anything yet, she said that she needed insurance coverage for her son. She seemed to be down after I gave her the news.

**Q:** But I mean as far as any other employees, did she have any fights or any other trouble with any other employees?

**A:** No. She seemed to get along with everyone.

**Q:** No further questions.

### b. Cross-Examination by Company Advocate

*Ms. Kasten:*
[to be supplied by student]

## 3. Kathy Stewart, Production Employee

### a. Direct Examination by Union Advocate

*Mr. Webb:*

Q: Would you give us your full name and address?

A: Kathy Stewart, Big Bow.

Q: And are you presently employed at McTiny Kitchens?

A: Yes.

Q: And how long have you worked there?

A: It was a year November 2nd.

Q: And you were at work on September 15, year 1?

A: Yes.

Q: And you were employed in the same department as Susan Norman?

A: Yes.

Q: And do you recall a fight that took place that same morning between Susan and Linda Ross?

A: Yes, sir.

Q: Prior to the time the fight started, were you present when Diane Johnson came up to speak with Linda?

A: Yes, sir.

Q: Could you relate to us what you heard Diane say to Linda, if anything?

A: Well, she said, "Linda, some of the girls are complaining because you're working." Linda asked her who was complaining, and she said, "Joyce and Susan."

Q: What happened at that point?

A: Well, Linda hollered at Susan and Susan didn't hear her and then she hollered at her again and she motioned for her to come up to the line.

Q: What was Susan doing at the time she hollered the first time?

A: Well, she was nailing with her head inside a cabinet.

Q: Now, after Linda hollered the second time, first of all, would you describe what was the volume of Linda's voice when she hollered?

A: Well, with all the noise that there is there at that particular spot, in order to speak to anybody at the other end of the line, you know, you have to holler, but first time she hollered, you know, it wasn't so loud, but the second time was louder when she motioned for her.

Q: How did she motion for her?

A: Just her arm, straight out, waving her hand.

Q: Now, what did Susan do then, the second time when Linda hollered?

A: Well, I wasn't looking directly at Susan, you know, I was watching Linda and then, the next time I looked back, Susan was coming towards the front of the line.

Q: Did you get any indication from observing Linda how she felt at that particular moment?

A: She looked angry.

Q: Is this while Susan was walking up?

A: No, that was before.

Q: All right. Then did you observe Susan strike Linda?

A: Yes. Just once with an open hand.

Q: And what did you observe after that as to what Linda or Susan did?

A: Well, I heard what was said up to the point when Susan struck Linda and then they had a hold of each other.

Q: And then they were just wrestling around at that time?

A: Yes, sir.

Q: Prior to the time that Susan slapped Linda, did you observe the two of them talking together?

A: Yes, sir.

Q: And can you tell us from your recollection how close the two of them were standing and the position they were in when they were standing?

A: They were very close.

Q: How close would you estimate?

A: Oh, I would say probably 2 feet.

Q: All right. And when—did you observe Linda shake her finger at Susan?

A: Yes, when she told her to go back there and nail some cabinets.

Q: Did Linda's finger hit Susan?

A: It brushed her nose.

Q: Did you hear Linda's tone of voice at that time when she was talking with Susan?

**A:** Yes.

**Q:** And could you describe her tone of voice?

**A:** Well, she became upset, she became angry, and she was speaking louder than I had heard her before.

**Q:** Well, other than her voice, how could you tell she was angry?

**A:** Mostly by the loudness of her voice and the shrillness of it, and her face was red.

**Q:** After the fight was over, did you observe any marks on Susan?

**A:** Yes, sir.

**Q:** Where, if any, on her body did you note any marks?

**A:** Well, she was scratched on her left arm and I noticed the blood running down towards her elbow and she did have a red spot on her face.

**Q:** Did you at any time observe Susan Norman drag Linda Ross down the line by her hair?

**A:** No, sir.

**Q:** How long have you known Susan?

**A:** Ever since she came into the Nailing Department, which was a year ago.

**Q:** Since Susan came into the Nailing Department, do you know of any trouble she's had with any of the other girls in the department?

**A:** No, we always got along good together.

**Q:** How would you describe Susan's personality?

**A:** I think she's happy-go-lucky. She's easy to get along with, always seemed happy.

**Q:** Anything else about her personality?

**A:** She is very religious. I know she felt bad about hitting Linda.

**Q:** Did you have some kind of a party at your home the day after this incident occurred?

**A:** Yes, sir.

**Q:** What kind?

**A:** Tupperware party.

**Q:** Was Linda Ross at any time present at that get-together?

**A:** Yes, sir. I was sweeping my front porch and sidewalk and she pulled up out in front of the house. She saw me outside and she stopped.

**Q:** Did you hear her make any remark to the those present with respect to the incident the day before?

**A:** Yes. She pointed to her black eye and said, "Look what my husband's highschool sweetheart, Susan Norman, did to me."

**Q:** What was the response of those present?

**A:** Some laughed. Others, said they could not believe Susan could do such a thing.

**Q:** No further questions.

### b. Cross-Examination by Company Advocate

*Ms. Kasten:*
[to be supplied by student]

# D. Exhibits

***JOINT EXHIBIT NO. 1***

COLLECTIVE BARGAINING AGREEMENT BETWEEN

McTINY KITCHENS, INC.

AND

LOCAL NO. 5140

WOODWORKERS UNIVERSAL UNION (4/11/01-4/11/05)

. . .

### SCHEDULE "B"

**COMPANY RULES AND REGULATIONS WITH PENALTIES FOR VIOLATIONS**

**A.** The Union agrees to the rules and regulations and penalties for violations set forth in Sections B and C below. The Company agrees that written notice of changes in such rules and regulations or penalties for violations shall be posted on the Company Bulletin Board.

**B.** The conduct specified below is prohibited by Company rules and regulations and any Employee who engages in such conduct will be discharged.
1. Proven dishonesty or proven theft.
2. Willful destruction of Company property or property of another Employee.
3. Insubordination.
4. Reporting to work under the influence of alcohol.
5. Sabotage of plant or equipment.
6. Bringing alcoholic beverages into the plant.
7. Fisticuffs with Supervisor or another Employee.
8. Possession of weapons, ammunition, or explosives on Company property at any time.
9. Driving Company vehicle under the influence of alcohol.
10. Failure to report accident while operating Company vehicle.
11. Threatening or intimidating Supervisor.
12. Permitting wages to be subject to garnishment for more than one indebtedness.
13. Habitual tardiness or absenteeism.
14. Walking off the job.

(more)

C. The conduct specified below is also prohibited by Company rules and regulations and any Employee who engages in such conduct shall for each violation (but not necessarily committed on different occasions nor necessarily a violation of the same kind) be subject to a warning notice for the first offense, suspension without pay for 3 days for the second offense, suspension without pay for 5 days for the third offense, and discharge for any subsequent offenses. In considering previous offenses under this section, the Company shall go back no further than 1 year from the date of the most recent offense.

1. Engaging in horseplay or disorderly conduct.
2. Engaging in immoral conduct other than dishonesty.
3. Ringing in and out for another Employee.
4. Repeated negligence resulting in scrap, inferior work, tool breaking, or excessive waste.
5. Reading newspaper on Company time.
6. Poor performance or non-performance of duties.
7. Taking unauthorized breaks.
8. Smoking in prohibited areas.
9. Playing radio in the Shop (providing uniformly applied).
10. Repeatedly leaving regular work area on unauthorized visiting.
11. Unauthorized driving or abuse of Company vehicle or vehicle of another Employee.
12. Failure to report citation received while operating Company vehicle.
13. Making unauthorized phone calls or leaving the premises during assigned shift without notifying Supervisor.
14. Violation of safety rules.
15. Loafing or sleeping on the job.
16. Failure to report to the Personnel Office upon leaving or returning from leave of absence.

*JOINT EXHIBIT NO. 2*

LOCAL NO. ___5140___

OF

WOODWORKERS UNIVERSAL UNION


AGGRIEVED EMPLOYEE: ___Susan Norman_____
ADDRESS: ___425 E. King Ave., Hot Springs, Alaska_____

DEPARTMENT: _Nailing__ CLASSIFICATION __Nailer_ WAGE RATE $6.00_

NAME OF COMPANY:_____McTiny Kitchens_____
DATE GRIEVANCE OCCURRED:_____9/15/01_____

NATURE OF GRIEVANCE:_____Discharge_____

__I believe I was unjustly discharged 9/15/01 because of a_
disagreement with my supervisor because she was working in_
violation of Contract Article XXII Sec. 5. Therefore, I want my
job back and pay for all time lost plus interest due to action
taken by Co. which is also in violation of Contract Schedule "B"
Sec. B.

The undersigned aggrieved employee having processed this grievance in accordance with Article XVI, Grievance Procedure, does hereby appeal this grievance and assigns to Local No. _5140_, this grievance for final agreement and/or disposition.

/s/Susan Norman_____


/s/Paula Norris_____
WITNESS: DEPT STEWARD

DATE: ___9/22/1_____

File in 4 copies

*JOINT EXHIBIT NO. 3*

McTINY KITCHENS

September 15, Year 1

Mrs. Susan Norman
425 E. King Ave.
Hot Springs, Alaska

Dear Mrs. Norman:

In accordance with Company and Union Contract, Article XXI, Section 1, Management Prerogatives, and Schedule "B", B3, 7 and 11 you are discharged effective September 15, year 1, at 10:45 a.m.

Enclosed is your final pay check.

Sincerely,


/s/ Frank Lyle
    Personnel Manager

FL:nc

cc: M. Erb
    D. Baxter

```
RECEIPT FOR CERTIFIED MAIL -- 30¢ (plus postage)

Sent to:  Mrs. Susan Norman

Street & No.:  425 E. King Ave.

P.O., State and Zip Code:

          Hot Springs, Alaska
     NO INSURANCE COVERAGE PROVIDED
       NOT FOR INTERNATIONAL MAIL
```

## *JOINT EXHIBIT NO. 4*

September 22, year 1

McTINY KITCHENS

Local No. 5140
Woodworkers Universal Union
1228 Walnut Street
Alaska City, Alaska

Attn:  Mr. Monty Erb,
Business Manager, W.U.U.

Dear Mr. Erb:

     I am in receipt of the below listed grievance dated 9/22/01.
I would like to meet at your earliest convenience to discuss it.

     Grievance of Susan Norman 9/22/01

     Sincerely,

/s/  Frank Lyle
     Personnel Manager

FL:nc

Enc.

cc: D. Baxter

Meeting scheduled October 4.

                    M.E
                    F.L.

*JOINT EXHIBIT NO. 5*

McTINY KITCHENS

October 5, Year 1

GRIEVANCE

AGGRIEVED EMPLOYEE:   Susan Norman

DATE - 9/22/year 1

COMPANY'S POSITION

The fact that Susan Norman's supervisor was in technical violation of the Agreement does not justify Susan not being discharged under Schedule "B" of the Collective Bargaining Agreement, subsections B.3., B.7., and B.11. If the employee felt the Supervisor had violated any article of our Agreement, she should have exercised her prerogatives under the Agreement.

Susan Norman is undesirable to the Company, has proven an undesirable Union member, and her actions indicate this was not a mere disagreement. She does not control her physical and mental faculties, and has not only fisticuffed, threatened, and been insubordinate with her immediate Supervisor but has intimidated other Company members. She seems unstable and allows her emotions to control. The Company will not reconsider her for reemployment.

GRIEVANCE DENIED.

/s/ Frank Lyle
     Personnel Manager

cc: M. Erb
    C. Baxter

*JOINT EXHIBIT NO. 6A*

McTINY KITCHENS

October 30, year 1

Local Union No. 5140
Woodworkers Universal Union
2 Page Street
Alaska City, Alaska

Attn: Mr. Monty Erb,
Business Manager, W.U.U.

Dear Mr. Erb:

Pertinent to our phone conversation of October 30, year 1, I feel
I should notify you of the Company's position on the grievances
you notified me you wished to take to arbitration.

Grievance - Susan Norman - 9/22/01 - Discharge

A meeting was held on the above on 10/4/01 and our reply was
given in the letter of 10/5/01.  Today you informed me you intend
to submit this case into arbitration.  We do not deny your
procedural right to arbitration; however, along with the
Company's position as stated in the letter of 10/5/01, we will
stress as one of our defenses your failure to comply with the
grievance procedure in the Agreement. We received no written
notice of your intent to arbitrate within 10 days and this case
should be considered settled under the grievance procedure. A
failure to comply with this time limitation constitutes a waiver
of the Union's right to arbitrate the grievance.


/s/ Frank Lyle
    Personnel Manager

## *JOINT EXHIBIT NO. 6B*

November 2, year 1

To: Frank Lyle, Personnel Manager
    McTiny Kitchens, Inc.
    Hot Springs, Alaska

From: Monty Erb
      Business Manager, W.U.U.
Re: Susan Norman Grievance

Realizing you have not been with McTiny very long, I should
inform you that in the past both parties have strictly adhered to
the time limitations set forth in the grievance and arbitration
procedure. Your reliance on a time limitation is a first. We have
always, in the past, resolved grievances on their merits.


## *JOINT EXHIBIT NO. 7*

McTINY KITCHENS

January 17, year 2

Local Union No. 5140
Woodworkers Universal Union
2 Page Street
Alaska City, Alaska

Attn: Monty Erb,
Business Manager, W.U.U.

Dear Monty:

I find pending arbitrations for Susan Norman and the 11
grievances concerning classification pay. I wish to make our
selection on arbitrators and notify for early hearing.

Your prompt attention to all matters listed will be greatly
appreciated.

        Very truly yours,


/s/ Frank Lyle
        Personnel Manager

*JOINT EXHIBIT NO. 8*

McTINY KITCHENS

January 26, year 2

Local Union No. 5140
Woodworkers Universal Union
2 Page Street
Alaska City, Alaska

Attn: Monty Erb,
Business Manager, W.U.U.

Dear Mr. Erb:

On several occasions I have advised you of my willingness to select an arbitrator for the below listed grievances:

Grievance 1 thru 11 - Classification Pay

Grievance 12 - Discriminatory Discharge

I have, at this point, been unable to arrange with you a selection. I remind you that the grievance procedure requires we cooperate to establish an early hearing date. Failure on the part of the Union to cooperate in selecting an arbitrator may cause the Company to suffer damages in a possible back pay order. Therefore, the Company intends to raise the delay issue at the arbitration hearing and request that if any back pay is awarded, the Union be obligated to pay its portion due to the delay in selecting an arbitrator.

I suggest you contact me within three (3) days after receipt of this letter.

Sincerely,

/s/ Frank Lyle
     Personnel Manager

*JOINT EXHIBIT NO. 9*

**Article X—Discharges**

Section 1. No employee will be discharged except for just cause, and whenever an employee is discharged the Company shall give written notice to the Union within one (1) workday, giving the reason for such discharge.

Section 2. Whenever the Union desires to question the discharge of an employee other than a probationary employee, the same shall be taken up as a grievance within three (3) workdays of such discharge.

**_COMPANY EXHIBIT NO. 1_**

INSPECTION REPORT

*Sept. 15 (Fri.)*

| | | |
|---|---|---|
| W4218 | Nail through side | S.M. 11 |
| W4824 | No brace | W |
| B36 | Loose toe kick brace | Deb 1 |
| B36 | No blocks | Deb |
| W4218 | Broken hang rail | S.M. |
| W3024 | Sand top | Laura |
| W2730 | Nails under shelf | Diane |
| W4218 | Sand top | S.M. 11 |
| CB48 | No shelf brace | Linda 1 |
| W2130 | Chip casing | Laura |
| W2430 | Chip side | Linda |
| W2430 | Sand top | Linda |
| B24 | Chip side | " |
| W3315 | Chip side | Laura |
| | Loose top | " |
| W2430 | Nail in hang rail | Diane |
| W3618 | Tape shelf | " |
| W3018 | Bad hang rail | Diane |
| W2430 | Loose back | Kathy |
| B18 | Chip side 11 | Linda |
| W3019 | Sand top | Linda<br>" |
| W2430 | Nail in hang rail | Kathy |
| W3030 | Nail in hang rail | Kathy |
| B36 | Loose bottom | Nora |
| B36 | Chip side | Nora |

*COMPANY EXHIBIT NO. 2*

LOCAL NO. ___5140___

OF

WOODWORKERS UNIVERSAL UNION


AGGRIEVED EMPLOYEE: ____Susan Norman_____

ADDRESS:___425 E. King Ave., Hot Springs, Alaska_____

DEPARTMENT: __109__ CLASSIFICATION __Nailing_ WAGE RATE __$6.00__

NAME OF COMPANY:_____McTiny Kitchens_____

DATE GRIEVANCE OCCURRED:____Aug. 30-31, year 01_____

NATURE OF GRIEVANCE:__harassment, slander, falsely accusing me__

of talking about Mr. Lyle.  I want to know the person's name

that told him that I was supposed to have talked about him.

_____

_____


    The undersigned aggrieved employee having processed this
grievance in accordance with Article _XVI_, Grievance Procedure,
does hereby appeal this grievance and assigns to Local No. _5140_,
this grievance for final agreement and/or disposition.


                              /s/Susan Norman_____

/s/ Paula Norris_____
     WITNESS: DEPT STEWARD

DATE: ___9/11/01_____

File in 4 copies

PLANT MANAGER'S ANSWER ____Both parties apologized and grievance_
is settled as of 9/14/01_____

_____


                    _____  __9/14/01_
                         SIGNATURE            DATE

<u>*COMPANY EXHIBIT NO. 3*</u>

[Students are urged to supply a sample of hair in an envelope]

# Purity Food Company

## Table of Contents

NOTES

# A. Caption

## IN THE MATTER OF A CONTROVERSY BETWEEN:

PURITY FOOD COMPANY            )
SAN BRUNO, CALIFORNIA       )
                                   )
AND                                )       RE: DAVID WHITE
                                   )              Discharge for Sexual
GROCERY WORKERS UNION,     )              Harassment
LOCAL 32                           )
                                   )

Appearances:

For the Company: Frank Green

For the Union: Louis Tanner

Date: February 9, year 4

Place: San Bruno, California

# B. Examination of Company Witnesses

## 1. Sandy McCrae, Employee Complainant

### a. Direct Examination by Company Advocate

*Mr. Green:*

**Q:** You work at Purity Food Company, correct?

**A:** Yes, I do.

**Q:** And how many years have you been with the Company?

**A:** For fourteen years.

**Q:** Could you tell the Arbitrator something of your educational background? For example, did you go to high school?

**A:** Yes, I went to high school and graduated. I also went to college. I am a mother of three children and I have three grandchildren. I am from a family of eight.

**Q:** Before going to work at Purity, did you have some other work experiences?

**A:** I worked for the Union in different warehouses—Heavenly Foods, two warehouses, and then I went to Purity.

**Q:** Now, did you also work as a teacher before working in warehouses?

**A:** Yes, I did. For approximately ten years I was a substitute teacher for a classroom of students who had emotional problems.

**Q:** That's fine. Now, at Purity, the work you do is that of a packer, is that right?

**A:** Packer operator.

**Q:** And on what team, what do you call that?

**A:** I think it is a 13-ounce team.

**Q:** What does that mean?

**A:** That is the size of the cans of food on the line that we are responsible for running and maintaining. I package them.

**Q:** Could you describe briefly what the job entails?

**A:** Basically, it is a line where I have control over the overcaps, seeing that the cans are not greasy, that there are no scratches, that type of thing, before it reaches the packer portion of the line. And then it is cased and it leaves the room and goes out to the unit load-former, which palletizes the cases so that they are able to go into the stacks or be sent out on the trucks.

**Q:** Now, do you remember when David White joined the team, approximately?

**A:** Yes.

**Q:** Did he join your team?

**A:** Yes.

**Q:** Did you have anything to do with training him?

**A:** I trained David on the packer. That was my first meeting with him.

**Q:** Sandy, I want to ask you, did David White ever do anything to you that you found offensive?

**A:** Yes.

**Q:** Could you describe the first incident that comes to your mind?

**A:** The first incident that we had was verbal—verbal exchanges, derogatory remarks he made in the lunchroom.

**Q:** Why don't you just explain what happened.

**A:** I was at the snack bar purchasing some sweets, which is one of my bad habits.

**Q:** Is the snack bar a room within the plant?

**A:** Yes, it is in the lunchroom. I was going to buy something sweet. He came into the lunchroom and he made a remark about me already being fat, that I really did not need that. I told him I had dieted all week and I deserved some sweets.

**Q:** Did he say anything else at that point in time?

**A:** He said that my pants were already too tight, but I continued to try to purchase something out of the snack bar. And then what transpired was, well, he slapped me across my buns and ran out of the lunchroom.

David was closer to the door, because there are three snack machines together and the one that I was purchasing from is in the center. After he did that, I used some colloquial language; I cursed. I pursued him, and there was some more derogatory exchange.

**Q:** Did you tell him anything about whether you approved or disapproved of him touching you?

**A:** I made it very clear that I did not approve of his behavior. And I do have a bad habit of scolding people like they are my children but—

**Q:** How did that incident make you feel? What were your feelings about it?

**A:** I felt very upset about it to the point of really wanting to hit him, to be quite frank about it.

**Q:** Did you mention this incident to any Union Shop Steward?

**A:** Yes, the Union Shop Steward that I first approached was Tony Sands. Generally if I have a disagreement or something like that, I go to Tony because he is not in our room and so he would be nonbiased. He works for the mechanics.

**Q:** Did you talk to Tony about this incident?

**A:** Yes, I spoke to Tony and then I spoke to Ben Silver. Tony was coming in from lunch and another Shop Steward was with him.

**Q:** What was their reaction?

**A:** To me, it was not very supportive, let me put it that way.

**Q:** Do you remember anything specific that any of the Shop Stewards said?

**A:** They said I had been there long enough to have handled situations like that, and it was more or less left to me to decide to pursue it or to handle it if it occurred again. I got the impression, like, it was not their problem, so it did not matter.

**Q:** What do you mean, it was not their problem?

**A:** I mean it was not their own person that was being abused or whatever, or their family, so it really did not upset them the way it upset me.

**Q:** Now, do you remember any other incident or any other time when David White did anything to you that you found offensive in any way?

**A:** The other time there was a load of coffee cans that had dumped at the unit load-former, which is outside the packing area of the warehouse. It is just before you get to the stacks. There was another colleague who I had asked to help. I did not know that she was not working at the QC—Quality Control—table

and she was complaining rather loudly, saying "That's not my job."

All I wanted to do was get the coffee cans up, because you had to go through them because some had been damaged. I wanted to get them up so they would be shippable and the workers could wrap them and put them away, because the floor was rather crowded that day.

I did yell for some help and I asked her to come and help me. David White intervened and came outside to speak to me about it, as far as to say that I was always yelling and giving orders with my "little old bitty self," and what could I do?

He, in turn, came around the table. There was a table there, by the other colleague who I was having the discussion with about moving everything. At one point he came around the table at me and he made a remark like I wanted to give orders but I wasn't big enough to be giving a lot of orders and yelling at people and making demands, more or less. That is what he implied.

At that point, I told him to—

**Q:** Rather than telling me the remarks of the moment, tell me, what did he do?

**A:** It was at that point after the argument ensued, about me giving the orders, that he came around the table and he scooped me up. When he grabbed me, his arm was up under me like you would scoop up a baby and then with the force that he scooped me up in, that is when my feet and everything left the ground.

**Q:** Lifted you up, huh?

**A:** Yes.

**Q:** And he held you in that position?

**A:** Yes. He swept me up this way and my feet and all were off the ground and I was struggling with him. Then Rob Moss, one of the mechanics working at the scale weight, told him to put me down or something like that. Then David put me down, and I went into the packing room.

**Q:** So after he put you down, you went into the packing room?

**A:** Yes.

**Q:** Was any comment made after that?

**A:** I remember cursing him at that time. You know, like, "You're not wrapped too tight," among some other things. I was not feeling good that day. I left, went into the room, and that was right at break time.

Then on our break we went up to the coffee room. It was at that time in the coffee room that I heard him tell a colleague or mention the fact about how heavy I was when he picked me up. They made a derogatory exchange about my weight, more or less.

**Q:** Now, when he held you up and lifted you, how did that make you feel?

**A:** I was very upset, I was very hurt by it. And at that particular time when David made the remarks in the coffee room—I remember I had gone in to get me a cup of coffee and I had sat down—and I just walked out of the lunchroom and went into the ladies' lounge.

**Q:** Do you recall any other incident in which David acted in a manner that was offensive or intimidating to you in any way?

**A:** There was a time when I was cleaning the packer. We were out of water and they had just filled it up. He and one of my colleagues came by.

I was cleaning the packer, and in order to reach the brew heads on the inside, I either have to step up or go under—crawl under the machine, more or less, to get to the brew heads on the far side. So to save time, most of the time I will step up on it. Well, that does put me in a bent-over position, like, I am bent over at the waist. I am on a part of the packer for leverage. So he comes by with Tessie and they were bringing some cups—no they had not gotten the cups yet.

I remarked to them, "Why don't you do something useful," after David said something about my pants being tight and I was just asking for it. At that time I weighed about 145 pounds, and that does make my clothes rather tight fitting, but that is neither here nor there.

**Q:** So, David White made a remark about your pants being too tight?

**A:** Yes, about my pants and that I was asking for it in this position, but I was minding my business doing my work. And then he laughed and so did Tessie. They walked over to the water cooler. I remember saying, "Why don't you get some cups to make yourself useful, find something to do. Don't hassle me," that kind of thing. Then he got the cups.

I went to get some water and he had the cups in his hand. I went to get one and he put the two cups on his chest. I did not think anything about it, but Tessie said, "Oh gosh, she's slow."

He also laughed at that time because I didn't catch on.

**Q:** Was he shaking the styrofoam cups on his chest?

**A:** Yes, David had the styrofoam cups in the plastic and he had them on his chest and was shaking them.

**Q:** Is that all that transpired at that time?

**A:** Yes.

**Q:** Now, do you remember a confrontation that involved the Quality Control lab?

**A:** We got into a disagreement in the QC lab on the graveyard shift one night. First of all, it was break time. I was in there having my break and listening to the radio.

**Q:** Is the QC room within the plant?

**A:** It is a room within the packing area that they use for the testing of cans to see if they leak and things of that nature.

**Q:** Is there a door that you enter?

**A:** One door, and the room's about the size of an average walk-in closet.

**Q:** Well, what happened?

**A:** I had my back to the door and the first person to walk in was a subteam coordinator on another line, Sammy Cutler, and then he went over to do his testing. He had some cans from off the line.

Then Polly Bird walked in and she sat on the counter. Then Tessie came in, David came in, and Thelma Blossom also came in. Thelma was standing by the door.

At the time, we got into a discussion about me not wanting to help out the team and do the nighttime clean-up, which pertained to the seamers. Now, I am a classified packer operator. I have not cleaned seamers in about three years—at that time, in March, it would have been about three years. The last time I cleaned a seamer was during the time that Mary was the QC person in the packing room.

I told them that I was kind of outdated for cleaning that thing, because there are certain things you have to know about or you can lose a finger. I just did not have much experience with the new additions to the seamers. Well, we got into an argument, and I said that if they wanted me to do it they could call a supervisor down there. I said, "You can have Hy Stein or any supervisor or some other Shop Steward." There were two Shop Stewards there, but I did not want them to deal with it.

**Q:** When you say "we," who are you talking about?

**A:** Well, the whole crew was kind of upset with the idea and felt that I did not want to work. I said, "My goodness, what do you think I've been doing for all these years?" But anyway, I told them I did not mind cleaning, but I could not clean the seamer that night until I was retrained on it. I felt that I would need at least a week's training before I could actually clean a seamer.

They did not want to hear that. David came over from where he was sitting and got in my face and started yelling and screaming in a threatening way that implied—

**Q:** We do not want to know what he implied, only what you know as the facts, okay?

**A:** Well, he was in my face and yelling and screaming at me and he told me I was going to do my part and this and that kind of thing. I was very upset. I reached for my bag, and when I did that, he told me that he was going to whip my tail and my husband's tail if I drew anything.

**Q:** What happened then?

**A:** That is when Sammy turned around and told David that was enough. Tessie and Thelma ushered David out of the room at that time.

Then we went on to discuss my reasons for not wanting to do the work. So, Sammy decided that I would get some training again so that I would be ready to clean the seamers.

**Q:** So, when David got in your face, what was your feeling?

**A:** I was scared, to be honest about it, because if a person comes from a sitting position and starts yelling and screaming at me like that, I felt that the next thing would be physical abuse. *That* I was not going to tolerate. There was no supervisor there, and there have been incidents where there have been physical situations on the job. I was far enough from the door to feel that in order to

get out of that room, I was going to have to go through somebody.

**Q:** Did you go to management after each of these incidents?

**A:** No, I did not.

**Q:** Why not?

**A:** As a rule, we try to handle things, even really bad things, without management's knowledge. Everyone seems to frown on going to management as ratting.

There had been other incidents where people had gone to management, and then had their houses vandalized—they had their cars with candy bars in the gas tank, paint thrown on the houses, that kind of thing. So, from past experience, I was a bit apprehensive about seeking help and I tried to take care of it myself.

**Q:** You finally did go to management, though?

**A:** Yes.

**Q:** What finally caused you to do that?

**A:** It was another time on graveyard where my team and I had a disagreement about the same thing. I was going to come join the team on the seamer, but I was working on the depalletizer at the time and had to clean it up first. I was taking my time and everything. David came out to ask me to come in and start on the seamer. He was working on QC that night.

Anyway, earlier that evening, I had been asked to relieve the 39-ounce people, which we do so that we can work through lunch and breaks. I did that. The next morning I was called in by the Shop Steward and they had a conference, more or less off the record, near the seamer line about me not being willing to cooperate with the team as far as cleaning. I was accused of telling one of my colleagues to screw off, that I was not going to do anything or help relieve or anything.

I explained to him that he knew me well enough, and that if I had said "screw off," I would have stood flat-footed and told him again.

**Q:** So what finally caused you to go to management?

**A:** I just realized that it was not getting any better, it was getting worse. They were using one thing after the other to cause me to have a real uncomfortable time working with the group.

**Q:** What about David White in particular?

**A:** The conversation with him was always derogatory. It was always heated and forceful. So, at that time I told him, "I don't want to hear anything from you, don't tell me anything."

**Q:** Who did you go to talk to?

**A:** I went to talk to a supervisor at the time—Marty Monk.

**Q:** These other incidents came out in the course of your talking to Marty about the situation that had just happened?

**A:** Yes.

**Q:** That is all.

### b. Cross-Examination by Union Advocate

*Mr. Tanner:*

[to be supplied by student]

## 2. Max Brown, Plant Manager

### a. Direct Examination by Company Advocate

*Mr. Green:*

**Q:** Would you state your position with the company?

**A:** I am the plant manager of the Purity Food plant.

**Q:** How long have you held that position?

**A:** I have been in that position since September 1 of year 1. I began training for the position in July of that year.

**Q:** And when did you first join the Company?

**A:** Nineteen years ago.

**Q:** Had you served as plant manager previously?

**A:** Yes, prior to coming to Purity, I was the plant manager of another company.

**Q:** What is your educational background?

**A:** I have a Bachelor of Science degree. The degree was engineering in management with a minor in mechanical engineering.

**Q:** So, your entire work history has been with this company?

**A:** Yes, except for five years at the company I mentioned.

**Q:** Now, you made the decision to terminate David White's employment at Purity, correct?

**A:** Correct.

**Q:** Would you explain the basis for your decision?

**A:** The basis was the information that was provided me by our two representatives from Corporate Security Division and the facts that they shared with me about David's ongoing harassment of another employee, Sandy McCrae—both sexual harassment and verbal and physical harassment.

**Q:** What was it about the conduct in question that caused you to conclude that termination was appropriate?

**A:** The ongoing nature of the conduct, the conduct resulting in Sandy McCrae feeling physically threatened at work, just the wrongness of the individual incidents, but more the ongoing nature of the incidents.

**Q:** What were the incidents as you understood them?

**A:** The members of the Security Division really reported three incidents to me. The first incident took place in the break area at work, during a break in which David had made sexually explicit comments about Sandy's tight-fitting pants and had patted her on her buns. She made it obvious to him that she did not appreciate that kind of behavior.

The second incident security reported to me involved Sandy cleaning up or inspecting cans. She was soliciting some help. David came out and made comments that she should not be telling other people what to do, because she was not big enough to be doing that kind of stuff. He grabbed her and picked her up off the ground and physically lifted her up and showed force. I interpreted this as his way of showing that he was bigger and stronger than she was, a form of control.

6

The third incident involved an argument in the Quality Control lab. During the course of the argument David got in Sandy's face and was very intimidating and threatening to her. He told her that he would kick her rear. That altercation had to be broken up by other employees in the same room.

**Q:** From whom did you first hear that there was any kind of a problem involving this situation?

**A:** I first heard a report of some of these kinds of things relative to David and Sandy from one of my supervisors—actually, two of them. One had responsibility for the team that David and Sandy were on, and the other is a department supervisor responsible for that area.

**Q:** When did they report these things to you?

**A:** I can tell you exactly. It was January 17th of year 3, the year just passed. They reported some of these kinds of things that might be going on that they had heard about.

**Q:** And you testified that you had corporate security people come out and investigate this matter further, correct?

**A:** Yes.

**Q:** What was the reason for bringing those people in?

**A:** Over about a six-month period, there had been a large number of reports coming to my attention about potentially inappropriate activity at the plant, either illegal or against company policy—reports about theft, drug usage, harassment, and sleeping on the job. I had been gradually getting a number of reports from employees.

I had actually received two anonymous letters at the plant, talking about some of the things, making accusations, saying, "Do something." In February, I got an anonymous phone call from someone making accusations of drug usage at the plant.

Specifically, during January and when things came to a head midmonth, there had been sexually harassing and racially harassing phone calls made to the plant and left on the voice mail of my supervisors. I got this in particular from the plant supervisor on January

17th or 18th and I went on vacation the next week.

During this time, we were undergoing the second week of internal controls audits. The auditors uncovered what they thought was some potential mismanagement of Company funds and reported those. But the icing on the cake was that a truckload of finished product was stolen off the lot while I was gone.

When I returned from vacation I had all these things to deal with, the reports and everything, and I decided to get some help to let me see what was going on at my plant.

I called in the security people because they are professionals at handling things of this nature, in hopes that we could get to the bottom of all these disruptive incidents and get back to running our business.

**Q:** And one of the things you asked them to look into was the allegation involving David White?

**A:** I did not mention any names when I called them. I just mentioned the types of allegations and asked them to look into those kinds of allegations.

**Q:** When they came on site, did you inform them specifically of the allegations concerning David White?

**A:** They interviewed me as one of the first people on site. I shared all of the specific allegations that had been made to me and asked them to follow up on those and any other allegations made to them throughout the course of their investigation.

**Q:** After receiving the information from the investigators, did you consider a lesser form of discipline for David White, short of termination?

**A:** Very briefly. When I looked at the type of harassment that had taken place and its ongoing nature, my starting point was what we call step 5—that is termination. Then I asked myself whether there were any extenuating circumstances that would cause me to back off of step 5. Still, when I looked into it, considering the seriousness of the threats to an employee's well-being, I determined that termination was the appropriate decision.

**Q:** Okay, that's all.

*Mr. Tanner:*
[to be supplied by student]

# C. Examination of Union Witnesses

## 1. Jim Wilson, Personnel Manager (called as an adverse witness)

### a. Direct Examination by Union Advocate

*Mr. Tanner:*

**Q:** I call Jim Wilson as an adverse witness. Mr. Wilson, it is my understanding that you were the individual who actually delivered the news about the discharge to Mr. White, correct?

**A:** Yes, both myself and David's department manager.

**Q:** And is this letter, Union Exhibit 1, dated March 11th, year 3, the one you referred to in Union Exhibit 2 as being the letter that was given to David with the details of why he was being terminated?

**A:** Yes, it is.

**Q:** There was no other letter given?

**A:** No.

**Q:** It is my understanding from this memo that you wrote to the file that when David came to the meeting you indicated to him that he was going to be terminated, correct?

**A:** I indicated to David that it was our intention to terminate him and asked him if he had any information to share which might change our minds.

**Q:** You put the burden on him to change your mind, correct?

**A:** Yes.

**Q:** Had you ever talked to him about any of the alleged incidents before?

**A:** No, I had not.

**Q:** And the only detail you gave him about what specifically was alleged to have occurred between Sandy McCrae and himself was that which is contained in the letter marked Union Exhibit 1?

**A:** That is correct.

**Q:** And that just says that he violated posted house rules which prohibit harassment of employees or behavior which would be offensive, etc., etc., correct?

**A:** It points to the specific house rule.

**Q:** Did you go over with him the specific incidents he was alleged to have committed?

**A:** No, I did not.

**Q:** So there would not have been any way for him to have pointed out witnesses who could deny or support his denial, would there?

**A:** I guess you could conclude that.

**Q:** Was David a party to, or was he allowed to see, the results of the security investigation?

**A:** No, he was not allowed to do that.

**Q:** Is it true that the Union Rep, who accompanied David—I believe it was Victor Borg—asked you to specify and explain what specific charges were being made against David and you declined to do so other than what was listed in Union Exhibit 1?

**A:** That's right. Victor did ask that and I declined to answer that.

**Q:** Did you have any concern whatsoever for David White's feelings or his well-being or his job future?

**A:** David did not express any concerns about his safety or well-being to me at that time.

**Q:** What I asked you is whether *you* had any concerns about David White's life?

**A:** Well, I had a great concern about David, like I do about all the employees. I felt we used a very thorough process to evaluate the data at hand, to be thorough in our investigation, to protect and follow through with our concerns about all our employees, including David.

**Q:** Nothing further.

## b. Cross-Examination by Company Advocate

*Mr. Green:*
[to be supplied by student]


# 2. *Jack Johnson, Past Coordinator for 13-Ounce Line Team*

## a. Direct Examination by Union Advocate

*Mr. Tanner:*
**Q:** Mr. Johnson, where are you employed?
**A:** I am employed at Purity Food Company.
**Q:** And how long have you been employed there?
**A:** For twenty-three years.
**Q:** At your work, are the production employees organized into production teams?
**A:** Yes, we are in teams.
**Q:** Can you explain how the teams work or what the organization is?
**A:** We have line teams. The 13-ounce line team, and the 39, and the 26. There are also subteams within the whole team structure.
**Q:** Are you saying that each sort or processing line has its own team?
**A:** Yes, each line has a team, and that team is broken down into three different groups: days, swing, and graveyard.
**Q:** So when you talk about rotating, you are talking about the subteams rotating shifts?
**A:** Subteams moving from a shift, yes.
**Q:** What particular team were you assigned to, and what team are you assigned to now?
**A:** Well, now I work with all the teams, but I was previously the team coordinator for the overall 13-ounce team. In other industries I would be called a "leadman."
**Q:** Were Sandy McCrae and David White on that team?
**A:** They were part of one of the subteams.
**Q:** What period of time were you the overall coordinator for the 13-ounce team?
**A:** For approximately one-and-one-half to two years.
**Q:** When did you stop?
**A:** Four months ago.
**Q:** So, what were your responsibilities as the overall team leader or coordinator?
**A:** My responsibilities were to see that the production schedules were met, see that the needs of the team were met, and communicate with other departments and so forth for that particular team.
**Q:** Did your responsibilities also include resolving any difficulties between people who worked on the various teams?
**A:** Yes, it was not my responsibility only, but that was the way the team was structured. The team handled things the best way they could before moving outside the team. Under this, there was what we called a conflict resolution, and I was the person who wrote it.
**Q:** What was the conflict resolution?
**A:** It was whenever a conflict occurred between individuals. The first step that we would try is for the individuals to work it out between themselves, and if that was unsuccessful, then the team would get involved. If the team could not solve it, then they could ask the team coordinator to become involved. And anywhere along the line we could have the Union involved.
**Q:** Who instituted the team program? Was it the employees or management?
**A:** Oh, this came from management. Years ago, after taking a survey of the pulse of the plant, it was decided that there was a need for a change from the type of operation that we had. Throughout Purity's plant, team structures were developed.
**Q:** Were there any meetings that were part of this team structure?
**A:** Top management conducted numerous meetings throughout the plant.
**Q:** What kind of meetings were held?
**A:** There were on-site meetings to inform the people of management's intentions and the ideas behind the teams and what they were, and to get input. The team system is somewhat similar to the "quality circle" concept which has been adopted worldwide.

**Q:** Once the team system was put into effect, were there things called team meetings or subteam meetings?

**A:** Once the team system went into effect, there were, and also we had placed them in the last negotiated contract. There would be 30-minute meetings before each team went into operation. Also, whenever there was a necessity for the team to get together, they would get together and talk.

**Q:** Now, does this mean that every time somebody came to work before their shift began there was a full team or a subteam meeting?

**A:** There would always be a subteam meeting for that particular shift operation.

**Q:** Who would preside at a subteam meeting?

**A:** The subteam coordinators. And if it was the shift that I was on, usually I did it as team coordinator.

**Q:** Does the subteam coordinator have the same responsibility for his or her subteam that you have for the whole team?

**A:** Yes. And each member also shares responsibility for team effort.

**Q:** And that includes resolving problems between the employees?

**A:** Yes, it does.

**Q:** Now, at these meetings, can you describe what these subteam meetings are like, what is discussed?

**A:** What we always did first at the meetings was to take care of all of the necessary business. We discussed what had taken place the previous shift, how the machines were running, and all the information that was necessary to help the team meet the required production. Then we would deal with whatever problems the individual members had.

**Q:** Were any of these team meetings ever heated meetings or involving arguments?

**A:** Lots of them were. The way we operated was that we wanted to make sure that whatever problem somebody had, it was vented there and finished, so that when we got it on the floor, we would have nothing standing in our way as far as production was concerned.

**Q:** Did people ever raise their voices at team meetings?

**A:** Oh, yes.

**Q:** Did they argue with each other at team meetings?

**A:** Yes, they argued. We felt that once we finished getting the information out as far as what we needed to do for production, then nobody should keep anything pent up. They should speak their piece.

**Q:** Was this system—involving employee input in making production decisions and resolving personnel matters—approved by management? Was management aware that it was going on in the team meetings?

**A:** Yes. It condoned and encouraged it.

**Q:** Were management personnel, for example supervisors, members of the teams?

**A:** Yes. But each supervisor was just another member of the team, until lately, that is. Boy, has there been a change in attitude by management.

**Q:** Who was on the subteam with David White?

**A:** At one time there were Polly Bird, Tessie Bondy, David White, Sandy McCrae. And at another time Jack Lipper was also part of it.

**Q:** Was Sammy Cutler ever on David White's subteam?

**A:** No, Sammy Cutler may have worked on that subteam periodically, but Sammy was a subteam coordinator of another subteam.

**Q:** During the time that you were a team leader, were there any problems with the subteam that Sandy McCrae and David White were on, any recurring problems that came up?

**A:** Yes, there were.

**Q:** Can you describe those for us?

**A:** One of the main problems was that the subteam could never get Sandy McCrae to help in the cleaning. The only thing that she was cleaning was the thing that she was assigned to. If that meant that she was working on the depalletizer, she would stay there and clean only that depalletizer all night.

If it meant that she was working with the packers, she would stay and clean only that packer all night and never assist the individuals in all of the other cleaning that was necessary.

**Q:** How much other cleaning was necessary?

**A:** Oh, there was quite a bit more. If you are running the 13-ounce line, you have two seamers. You have a depalletizer. You have the magnets that have to be cleaned. You have these numerous things to clean. And just cleaning the seamer alone is a major job. That takes some time.

**Q:** Is that one of the more difficult tasks?

**A:** It is one of the more difficult tasks because of the dirtiness and nastiness of it, yes.

**Q:** Well, were there any other problems with Sandy McCrae, about her operating machinery or anything like that?

**A:** Her operating machinery had been a problem not only with the people that she worked with, but also the mechanics that were there on the line. The line she worked on was constantly stopping. On some occasions, we had problems where a new machine was brought in, the Douglas case packer, and she just did not keep the machine going. I don't know why.

**Q:** Was there anything that she did in particular with that machine that made it not operate properly any way that she ran it?

**A:** Yes. Sandy always had her own system and nobody was allowed to question her system.

**Q:** Do you know what Sandy's system is?

**A:** Sandy's system was running anything the way Sandy wanted and that is it. Don't question Sandy.

**Q:** Did the things that she worked on appear to break down more frequently than the things others worked on?

**A:** Yes, they did, constantly. If they broke down, Sandy would take and put on the light for the mechanic. Even if it was something very simple, she never would think of repairing that.

There were occasions where we were given tool boxes, so that if there were a minor adjustment to be made, we would make those repairs—small repairs, tighten a screw here, remove a bolt here, bend a wire here, or whatever. That was part of the job.

I got keys to the tool boxes for all of the members of the team, and I gave them to all of the operators. I tried to present one to Sandy, and she said, "Honey, you keep that. I won't need it. If something needs to be done, I'll get one of the mechanics there. I don't need it." That sort of thing made the line stay

down longer than it necessarily should be down.

**Q:** Did Sandy's behavior or ability to operate the line hold the team back in any way?

**A:** I felt that it did. I even went to the other subteams to decide if it was possible to move Sandy, but the other subteams said they did not want any disruptions. So I talked with David and I talked with Tessie and told them, "Just try to do the best thing that you possibly can do to keep things going in spite of Sandy."

**Q:** Did Sandy have any particular machines that she agreed to work on, any other machines that she would not work on?

**A:** Sandy would not work on the packer. I left it open that anyone who wished to have any training on anything, there were people that would train them—on any one of the machines that were under our control. Sandy never stepped forward to learn any of those. The Douglas case packer was the only one that she agreed to train on, that I know of. And that was one that she just got attached to.

**Q:** What were the machines that she would work on?

**A:** The Douglas case packer and the depalletizer. They were the only two.

**Q:** Was there ever a particular incident with Sandy McCrae over the Douglas case packer?

**A:** Yes, there were two. The first one, we were having visitors from Cincinnati. One of the Company engineers was coming to look at the Douglas case packer to see if it was something that they would like to put on one of the other lines, the 39-ounce line.

We were told about that, and our feelings were that we would like to have this machine running to the best that it could possibly be run. They told us that he would be there around 2:30 p.m.

Sandy was running the Douglas case packer and it was down close to 2:30. I tried to stay over there to help her as much as possible, but I had to leave. When I came back, the packer was down and she could not get it running.

I asked her what the problem was and she said, "Maybe the cardboard"—packing materials cardboard, that is. So, I said, "Sandy, the guy will be coming through very shortly and we want the thing running, because a lot depends on this." She said, "Well, I am doing the best I can." I told her that we had to do something else. We both knew that Tessie is very good, really an expert, so I said, "I am going to ask Tessie if she can come over and help us."

I went over to speak with Tessie, and she said, "Jack, you know how Sandy is. I don't want a problem with her, so you get her to move away from there first and then I will come over."

So, I arranged it that Sandy could run the depalletizer. I told her she would have to go to the depalletizer so that we could get this thing running again, because we needed to make a good showing. She really started talking nasty, but she took off.

**Q:** When you say she talked nasty, what did she say?

**A:** Sandy is pretty good at profanity.

**Q:** You need to be very specific.

**A:** Well, Sandy said, "Damn, Tessie, you know, what the hell? I can run this goddamned packer." I said, "Please, we have to get this thing running," and she took off.

**Q:** Where did she go?

**A:** She went to work the depalletizer. So when she went to work the depalletizer, Tessie came over. Within a period of about three or four minutes, Tessie had found the problem. She showed me what it was. It was one of the gears that moved. And she told me to get a mechanic. I got a mechanic over and within a few minutes Tessie had the case packer running smooth as silk. She ran the packer until the 2:30 break. The guy came along and he checked the line out. When the 2:30 break came, we went to our break.

After we returned, I had to get some samples. I have to take a Meade jar test. I came back from the Meade jar test and Sandy was on the machine, the Douglas case packer.

**Q:** What had happened at that point?

**A:** I asked Tessie what had happened and she told me that Sandy told her that she could go on back now, that she had it. I told her that was using Tessie and was not right. So I told Sandy, "You are out of line. It was the team's decision that we make this change as we did. You were not to take and just use Tessie to get things going and then move back, and

move Tessie out." I said, "That's wrong," which I always used to tell her when she was out of line. She said, "Well, I can run it now." So, I basically stayed away from Sandy for the rest of the year.

**Q:** Did you have any problems with her either that day or the next day about the Douglas case packer?

**A:** Yes, we were getting to the four-day holiday, which was within that same week—starting the next day, more than likely. Sandy came in and started running the Douglas case packer, started it up to run it.

All that morning it was up, down, up, down. We did everything possible to try to help her, but she did not understand that much about the equipment. I could see that. She kept telling me, "It's the cardboard." I told her that it was not, because we used the same cardboard every day.

She would push one of the buttons and the cans would get all messed up inside. I had helped her to remove about seven or eight cases of cans. I told her we just cannot go through this, because we have this weekend coming up, and processing has already told me about the amount of food that they have on hand they need to use up. We had to get that machine going so we could get all the product out.

She would say, "Well, I will have it in a few minutes. I can do it." I told her that it was getting close to noon and we could not wait any longer, so I was going to change it again. She said, "No, I can get it going." I told her that she had been unable to get it going all morning and that I was going to ask the others if they would change so that we could get this machine operating. So, I talked to Tessie and she said, "Jack, I am not going over there, you see how I got screwed yesterday." I told her that regardless, she had to do it. She said that she would do it, but I had to get Sandy out of there first.

So, I arranged it and when I told Sandy that she was going to have to go back to the depalletizer, she just exchanged some looks with me and started raising her voice. So I said, "Go ahead, run it, let's see you run it." She could not get it to move so I told her to go on over to the depalletizer, and she took off to one of the bathrooms. Tessie came over and got the thing running, but nobody was on the depalletizer.

So, I went out to the depalletizer and I began to run the depalletizer, thinking that she would be back, but she did not come back. After a few minutes the line was stopped down and a supervisor came along and told me that she had to send Sandy home. She said Sandy had come over and was crying and was just all out of it, saying that I was abusive to her and said all kinds of things to her.

I explained to the supervisor what took place. She said she was glad that I did change things around because we did not have any place to put all of that product. The supervisor said that we would talk about this the next week, and I went back and ran the depalletizer for the rest of the day.

**Q:** Did you ever observe how Sandy treated other members of the team?

**A:** Yes, I observed instances between Sandy, Tessie, and David, since they were there on the team together. Most people totally avoided Sandy. That is, on our team as well as the other teams. She treated David like her kid, a little boy or something, not really like her kid, but like a boy. She even called him "boy" a lot. David was always saying that he was a man and nobody's boy.

Most other members of the teams would say they did not want her over with them because they did not want any type of trouble with Sandy.

**Q:** During some time, either the spring or summer or fall of year 2, did you go on vacation at any point and ask David White to be the subteam coordinator?

**A:** Yes. You see the coordinator's role included rotating within the subteam. David and Tessie had both done it a lot. David's turn was coming around and we talked about it. He told me that he had to try to find some way to get Sandy to help them to clean up, that they could not do it by themselves. I agreed and told him that I would talk to Sandy as well. So I had Sandy come in with David and Tessie and we talked about it.

**Q:** What was said?

**A:** Sandy agreed. She first said that she had not been properly trained. I told her that they had agreed to take care of the safety factors, to put the machine wherever it was necessary

to be placed and lock out the machine, after pulling the disconnect, and she just had to help them clean the machine wherever it was. It seemed like everything calmed down at that point; she agreed to help them clean.

**Q:** What does it mean that they would place the machine and lock it out?

**A:** Once you pull the disconnect and place a lock where the disconnect cannot be moved, all electricity that goes to that machine is gone. There is no possible way that this machine can move—no way.

**Q:** So, there is no safety risk if it is unplugged?

**A:** None whatsoever.

**Q:** So, at various times, had Sandy had the opportunity to be trained on the seamer or any piece of equipment she wanted?

**A:** At various times, the whole team, Sandy included, had been given the opportunity to have training anywhere that the team had responsibility.

**Q:** Did their team, except for Sandy, rotate positions around all of the machines?

**A:** All of them did. David and Tessie would work in different places. Polly would be in different places at all times. But Sandy stayed in the same spot.

**Q:** Where was it that she stayed?

**A:** Either the packer or the depalletizer, wherever she was placed. To keep the monotony down, sometimes each would operate two hours here and two hours there.

**Q:** David was the newest member of the team, correct?

**A:** Yes.

**Q:** What kind of worker was he?

**A:** I always told David that he made my job easy. He was an exceptional worker. There was not one thing that I ever asked David to help with that he would not do, straight time or overtime.

David took care of all the team's computer responsibility. He was the one that taught us the programs to use on our computer line. He got all of us started and he had to communicate with everybody to do that.

**Q:** Did he appear to have any communication problems with anyone besides Sandy McCrae?

**A:** I never heard it.

**Q:** Did you ever hear that there was a problem with the team or an argument between David and Sandy while you were on vacation?

**A:** Yes, I even got the news on vacation. I got a phone call that there was a big problem, an argument, loud yelling, and so forth.

**Q:** Who told you that?

**A:** Tessie called me at home.

**Q:** Did you do anything about it when you got back to work?

**A:** I asked what happened, because we had the agreement Sandy would help clean. They told me that she refused to help. So I came in the next morning. They were on graveyard and they were very upset because there they were, cleaning, and covered in grease and product. They had been trying to get her to help and it was wrong that she would not. It is goddamned wrong that she would not help them out.

**Q:** Who are you referring to by "they"?

**A:** David and Tessie.

**Q:** And who are you referring to by "she"?

**A:** Sandy McCrae.

**Q:** What did you do about their complaints?

**A:** I told them that they were exactly right and that it was time that we did something about it other than with the team, so I went over to the head Steward, Ben Silver. I asked him to come over because we had a problem, and I asked him to ask Sandy to come over also.

**Q:** Did he do that?

**A:** Yes. He went over and told Sandy and we waited for about ten minutes and then finally she came over.

**Q:** What happened when Sandy came over?

**A:** I began to tell her that she had to help clean and she said that she was cleaning her machines. I told her that she had been on the depalletizer all night long and that she was supposed to help these people clean the rest of the line. She said that she was not properly trained and that she was not going to do anything until she was. I told her that we had talked about that and that we did not need to do that.

So, I told the Head Steward, Ben Silver, that he could see that we had a problem and that we needed to do something about it. Ben tried to talk to her but she would have nothing

to do with it. After she walked off, I told Ben that he was going to have to get the Business Agent.

**Q:** Was an appointment set up with the Business Agent?

**A:** An appointment was set up for the Business Agent to come out and we would all meet at 6 a.m. the next morning.

**Q:** Did Sandy know about the appointment?

**A:** Yes, she did, but Sandy left at 5 a.m. or around there.

**Q:** She did not show up for the appointment?

**A:** No, she did not. Everybody else was there, though.

**Q:** Has Sandy ever accused you of something that you know you did not do?

**A:** Well, someone said that I pushed somebody against a wall, and that is the furthest thing from the truth. I keep my hands to myself.

**Q:** Who told you that?

**A:** I was told this by the investigative group sent by management. That was one of the questions: "Didn't you push somebody against the wall?"

**Q:** Do you know for a fact whether Sandy McCrae accused you of pushing her against the wall or not?

**A:** I do not know if it was her, but she was the only one I had any type of words with.

**Q:** Did you ever hear Sandy McCrae talk about voodoo?

**A:** Yes, on many occasions.

**Q:** What did she say about voodoo?

**A:** That she would take a flight to Louisiana and she would come back and she could take care of any problem that there is.

**Q:** Did she mention any specific names of problems that she wanted to take care of?

**A:** Well, she was referring to the quarrels and arguments that she had with the people in the room, the ones which I had heard.

**Q:** And what are you referring to?

**A:** The conflicts she felt she had with David.

**Q:** Did you ever hear Sandy McCrae talk about her husband?

**A:** Yes, I have.

**Q:** At the time that you were the team leader or coordinator, did Sandy ever refer to her husband?

A: Yes, she did. According to Sandy he was a police officer. According to her, he was always off on different trips and she was going to the airport to pick him up and they were going to their place in Half Moon Bay or to be together somewhere. Also, she was not going to allow any of her kids around them, because the kids were always interrupting. You know, Tony goes off on these long trips and when he gets back, she just wants to be there alone with Tony.

Q: I would like to ask one thing further. Did management in any manner ever talk to you or question you about any problems between David White and Sandy McCrae?

A: Not one time.

Q: Did they ever talk to you about the meeting where David and Sandy were supposed to have had their argument?

A: Not one time.

Q: Nothing further.

## b. Cross-Examination by Company Advocate

*Mr. Green:*
[to be supplied by student]

## 3. Rob Moss, Mechanic

### a. Direct Examination by Union Advocate

*Mr. Tanner:*
Q: Mr. Moss, where do you work?
A: Purity Food.
Q: How long have you worked there?
A: Thirteen years.
Q: And what is your position there?
A: Mechanic.
Q: Have you had any occasion while working at Purity Food to work near or with Sandy McCrae?
A: Yes, many times.
Q: Did you ever observe David White pick Sandy McCrae up and lift her up off her feet?
A: No.
Q: Did you ever indicate to Sandy McCrae that you had observed that and shake your head and walk off?

A: No.
Q: Did anyone from management ever ask you whether you had observed any incident like that?
A: No.
Q: If you had observed that, would you have done something about it?
A: Oh, yes. I would have up and seen the Steward. I mean, I would talk to a few mechanics, you know, a guy is crazy doing something like that, you know. I do not care who it is or who he picks up or anything, you know, it is not right. I would not want to work around a guy like that. He may do it to you next. People would want to know if I had seen it. And believe me—
Q: That is all.

## b. Cross-Examination by Company Advocate

*Mr. Green:*
[to be supplied by student]

## *4. Polly Bird, 13-Ounce Line Team Member*

### a. Direct Examination by Union Advocate

*Mr. Tanner:*

**Q:** Ms. Bird, where do you work and how long have you worked there?

**A:** I have worked at Purity Food for two years.

**Q:** Are you assigned to a particular team or subteam?

**A:** I am on a 13-ounce line subteam.

**Q:** At the time David White was terminated, who was on your subteam with you?

**A:** David White, Tessie Bondy, and Sandy McCrae.

**Q:** Who was the subteam coordinator?

**A:** At first, Sandy. Later, David.

**Q:** Were there any recurring problems that you had on your team with regard to Sandy McCrae?

**A:** Yes.

**Q:** And what were those problems?

**A:** A couple having to do with the work itself. Sandy did not want to participate in her share of helping to keep the line clean.

**Q:** Can you explain that a little bit further? What was she not willing to clean?

**A:** She was not willing to clean the seamers or the scale. She was willing to clean the packer.

**Q:** Did she give you a reason for not being willing to clean?

**A:** She said at one point she had not been trained to clean it.

**Q:** Did you or anyone else offer to train her?

**A:** Yes, everyone on the team had offered at one point or another.

**Q:** Did you personally offer?

**A:** Yes, I did.

**Q:** What was the other problem that you had with Sandy McCrae or that the team had with her?

**A:** She was often condescending towards us, calling us children or treating us like children.

**Q:** Did you ever have a particular, direct run-in with her about it?

**A:** Yes, she and I at one point got in an argument over that, and I told her that I had two children of my own and that I was capable of holding my own job and had a mother and did not need another one.

**Q:** What was it that she said to you that caused you to react that way to her?

**A:** She called me ''baby'' or ''honey'' or something when we were talking while running the line.

**Q:** Had you already indicated to her that you did not like to be called that?

**A:** Yes.

**Q:** Had you done that more than once?

**A:** Yes.

**Q:** Was Sandy an easy person to communicate with?

**A:** No.

**Q:** Why do you say that?

**A:** Whenever she was having problems and we would come over to help, she would push me out of the way and say that she had it and then take over. When you tried to raise such problems in the team meeting, she would just be unresponsive most of the time. She would not talk.

**Q:** Now, you mentioned team meetings. Can you describe what went on in team meetings or what they were like?

**A:** When we talk about running the line, we talk about what was needed to run the line, you know. Or if we were running or cleaning, we'd talk about whatever the needs were of the shift and problems or training. Sometimes there would be disagreements and sometimes there would not.

**Q:** When there were disagreements, did people raise their voices and argue with each other?

**A:** Yes, sometimes. People were mostly pretty comfortable with each other and so we felt free to express ourselves in our disagreements. So, sometimes we raised our voices, yes.

**Q:** Did that happen with some frequency at the meetings?

**A:** It was not a daily occurrence, but yes, it happened.

**Q:** Did you ever observe how Sandy treated David?

**A:** Yes.

16

**Q:** How was that?

**A:** She was very condescending toward him. She called him a boy. She would compare him to her son in terms of his being a child.

**Q:** Was this done in a motherly fashion, or what manner was it done in?

**A:** It was just talking down to him, treating him as if he were not equal.

**Q:** Did you have occasion to be at a team meeting or an impromptu team meeting where there was an argument between David White and Sandy McCrae during the summer of year 2 or sometime around then?

**A:** Yes.

**Q:** Can you tell us what happened at the meeting? How did you get called into the meeting?

**A:** Well, we had several discussions in team meetings about the problem of cleaning the line and so this was another one of those. We were in the QC lab in the packing department and David said he wanted to talk—to try again to resolve it. He talked first. He said to Sandy that we needed her to help the line; it was not fair that the rest of us should have to do all this and that she would just be able to refuse.

**Q:** What was his voice like, or what was his manner like, when he started the meeting?

**A:** He was just talking in a regular voice.

**Q:** What was Sandy's response?

**A:** She refused and she said that she was not trained. He said that this was not a problem, because we could train her. She said that we were not qualified, that there was not anybody qualified to train her, and that we could not make her do something that she did not want to do.

**Q:** What was Sandy's tone like when she said that?

**A:** It was angry.

**Q:** What happened after that?

**A:** It went like that back and forth a little bit and the voices got louder and David stood up and Tessie stood up and said that we were not getting anywhere and we should go. Tessie and Thelma were outside the room, but—

**Q:** Finish your sentences, please, so the reporter can take down what you mean.

**A:** Tessie and Thelma took David out of the room. And at that point it pretty much ended.

**Q:** Did you at any point feel that Sandy McCrae was being threatened by David?

**A:** No.

**Q:** Did David ever threaten to kick Sandy's ass?

**A:** No.

**Q:** Did he ever threaten to kick Sandy's husband's ass?

**A:** No.

**Q:** Did he ever threaten to kick anyone's ass?

**A:** No.

**Q:** Did he ever say anything to her about pulling out a knife?

**A:** Nothing that I heard.

**Q:** Do you remember any specific comments that they threw back and forth?

**A:** Not any specifics. I mean, they were just arguing over it. "You need to do this." "No, I don't want to. You can't make me." They said things like that.

**Q:** Did you help to sort of stop the argument?

**A:** Well, I said something to the same effect that Tessie said, "This is not working; just stop."

**Q:** Why did you do that?

**A:** We were not getting anywhere. It just was not going to be resolved.

**Q:** Did anyone from management or Purity Food ever talk to you about what you observed at this meeting?

**A:** No.

**Q:** Was the heated exchange between David and Sandy in that meeting any different than what went on at other meetings?

**A:** No, just in a smaller room.

**Q:** How did David treat you?

**A:** He was always very nice to me and respectful. I mean, when we had disagreements, which we had, it was always done on the basis of what the issue was.

**Q:** I am going to show you Union Exhibit 3. Do you recognize this document, Polly?

**A:** Yes, it is a petition that I passed around to my coworkers.

**Q:** And why did you pass this around to your coworkers?

**A:** For two reasons: I felt that David had been unfairly fired and I wanted to show some kind of support to him. And because at a plant meeting that followed his being fired, the plant manager guaranteed the anonymity of anyone who came forward with information, and I did not want my name to be associated because of the situation. I wanted to be separated from the whole affair.

**Q:** Was David well liked as an employee by his team members?

**A:** Yes.

**Q:** How about Sandy?

**A:** No.

**Q:** Was Sandy known to carry a knife?

**A:** I heard her say that she did. I never saw it.

**Q:** No further questions.

### b. Cross-Examination by Company Advocate

*Mr. Green:*
[to be supplied by student]

## 5. Thelma Dorf, 39-Ounce Line Team Member

### a. Direct Examination by Union Advocate

*Mr. Tanner:*

**Q:** Ms. Dorf, where do you work and how long have you worked there?

**A:** I have worked at Purity Food Company for fourteen years.

**Q:** What team or subteam are you assigned to?

**A:** I am assigned to a 39-ounce subteam.

**Q:** And is that the overall team that David White and Sandy McCrae were on?

**A:** No, David and Sandy were on a 13-ounce line team.

**Q:** But did you have occasion to work the same shift that they did?

**A:** Yes, I did. We rotated together from first, to second, to third—when 13-ounce was running a third shift.

**Q:** Where is it that you work? On the 39-ounce line, correct?

**A:** Basically, I do QC and just generally run the equipment.

**Q:** And does your job take you in proximity to the people working on the 13-ounce line?

**A:** Yes, I have to interface with the 13-ounce line throughout the night.

**Q:** So you have had occasion to work with Sandy McCrae and David White?

**A:** Yes, I have.

**Q:** During your breaks, when you take breaks, do you ever play cards?

**A:** Yes, we do.

**Q:** And who is the "we" that plays cards?

**A:** Basically, the four of us. Helen and myself are partners. Tessie and David were partners. The four of us played together.

**Q:** Before David played cards, did Sandy McCrae play cards with you?

**A:** Yes, she did.

**Q:** And when David came, did he take Sandy McCrae's place?

**A:** No, he did not. She started to come in to play only sometimes. Some breaks she would come and some breaks she would not. And when she showed up, whenever she wanted to, she expected David, namely, to let her have her seat. She stated, "This is my seat. I play here." She expected her seat back.

**Q:** Did David give up his seat to her?

**A:** No. We told him he did not have to because if she wanted to be a steady partner, she had to be there at all times, not whenever she felt it was okay for her to be there.

**Q:** Was there any preference in playing with David over Sandy or anything like that?

**A:** We preferred playing with David, yes.

**Q:** Why was that?

**A:** We liked his conversation better.

**Q:** Did Sandy McCrae ever talk about voodoo when you would play?

**A:** Yes, I heard her mention it.

**Q:** What did she say about voodoo?

**A:** On occasion I would hear her say she had to fly off to Louisiana to get whatever she needed to practice whatever she had to do.

**Q:** Was it ever in conjunction with any other people or taking care of any business?
**A:** Yes, she said if she ran into any unusual problems or things she could not handle, then she would resort to her voodoo magic to help her out.
**Q:** Did she ever talk about having been a teacher?
**A:** Yes, she did.
**Q:** Prior to coming to work at Purity, did you ever work in the San Francisco School District in some capacity as a teacher's aide?
**A:** Yes, I worked for the San Francisco Unified School District as a teacher's aide for four years.
**Q:** During what period of time?
**A:** Oh, it was from between sixteen and nineteen years ago.
**Q:** And did you know Sandy McCrae from that period of time?
**A:** Yes, I met Sandy McCrae around fifteen years ago. I am not sure of the year, but I met her in the hiring hall for teacher aides.
**Q:** Did you ever have any discussions about being teacher's aides together?
**A:** Yes, we talked about the schools where we worked, because I told her where I was employed part-time, and she talked about where she was working—the school was District 2.
**Q:** And did you know anyone who worked at the school with her?
**A:** Yes, I knew a person that worked with her personally. My sister-in-law worked with Sandy as a teacher's aide also at District 2.
**Q:** What was Sandy's position at District 2?
**A:** She was a teacher's aide.

**Q:** As a teacher's aide, are you required to have a Bachelor of Arts degree?
**A:** No, you are not.
**Q:** Do you know whether or not you are required to have a Bachelor of Arts to be a teacher?
**A:** Yes, you do.
**Q:** I would like to show what has been marked as Union Exhibit 3. Have you seen this piece of paper before?
**A:** Yes, I have.
**Q:** When did you see it or under what circumstances?
**A:** I saw this piece of paper at the plant, Purity.
**Q:** And was there anyone in particular who was showing it to you or giving it to you?
**A:** Yes, Polly Bird. She started this petition.
**Q:** Did you sign that paper?
**A:** Yes, I did, because I felt that David White had done no wrong to Sandy McCrae.
**Q:** How did David White treat you while you worked with him at Purity?
**A:** With respect.
**Q:** Was he ever disrespectful to you in any way?
**A:** No.
**Q:** During any of your conversations with Sandy or interactions with her, did she ever tell you that David White had sexually harassed her?
**A:** No.
**Q:** Did she ever mention that he had harassed her in any way, shape, or form?
**A:** No.
**Q:** I have no further questions.

### b. Cross-Examination by Company Advocate

*Mr. Green:*
[to be supplied by student]

## 6. David White, Grievant

### a. Direct Examination by Union Advocate

*Mr. Tanner:*

**Q:** David, prior to your discharge, how long had you worked at Purity Food?

**A:** It was approximately a year and a half.

**Q:** And did you have any problem in qualifying for a place on a subteam and obtaining seniority after a probationary period?

**A:** No, I had no problems whatsoever.

**Q:** What line did you work on during your probationary period?

**A:** All of them to some extent.

**Q:** Did you have any trouble learning any of the machines or anything like that?

**A:** No, I had no problems learning any of the machines or even getting along with the majority of the workers in the plant. It was a really pleasant place to work and I enjoyed it. You know, I was hoping all along that I would make it.

**Q:** And you were a member of a subteam?

**A:** Yes, I was.

**Q:** I want to show you Union Exhibit 4. Can you identify this document for me?

**A:** Yes, I can. This is a copy that was made from one of my assessments on qualifying during my probationary period.

**Q:** And the date on this is December 4th, year 1, correct?

**A:** December 4th.

**Q:** Okay. And it was about a month after you started working at the plant?

**A:** That is correct.

**Q:** And is this something that was shown to you previously by someone from the Company?

**A:** It was not shown to me by someone. When I was evaluated by supervisors and they wrote their assessments, I asked for a copy because I wanted one for my own personal records.

**Q:** And this was a copy of the report that was given to you, correct?

**A:** Yes.

**Q:** David, what team and subteam were you assigned to?

**A:** I was assigned to the 13-ounce team. The subteam that I was assigned to was the one consisting of Tessie Bondy, Polly Bird, myself, and Sandy McCrae.

**Q:** Was that actually your first choice of the team to work on?

**A:** No, it was not. My first pick was packing materials team, but I was under the impression that there were no openings. When there were, you usually got your first choice. So I went to my second choice, which was 13-ounce.

**Q:** So, I take it that you were assigned to this team. You did not ask to be placed on this team, correct?

**A:** Correct.

**Q:** While you were on the subteam, were there any particular recurring problems with Sandy McCrae?

**A:** Yes, there were. There were a few altercations between Sandy and myself, and between Sandy and other team members as well. When I expressed my concerns about some of the problems that we were having concerning her work, about her helping out the team and the cleaning capacity of the team, and just her overall cooperation with the subteam, I was approached by other members of the Union on my subteam. They told me to just kind of let Sandy stay over there at her packer and not get involved in that because it is really deeper than you can see.

So, at first, we just kind of left her alone. I just did not want any altercations. But at the same time, while I was starting to move into my role as coordinator, I wanted as much cooperation as I was giving.

**Q:** Did Sandy ever show you how to run the packing machine that she worked on regularly?

**A:** Yes, she did. And it was only because I wanted to learn. It was not that it was a requirement. During my probationary period I had finished with my assessments on the 13-ounce scale. I was due to end my probationary period within the next week. I asked the team coordinator, Jack Johnson, if there would be a problem with me training on the packer because if I was going to be assigned on the 13-ounce line, I wanted to know how to run the entire line. This would be a good opportunity for me, since I had been learning everything else, to spend a week on the packer. So, yes, Sandy did train me.

**Q:** Were there any problems with the way that she trained you how to use or how to operate the packer?

**A:** Well, yes, there was. After first working on the 39-ounce line and then transferring to the 13-ounce line, the operation of the machines were similar and there was no problem. It was just that Sandy expected me to run it the way that she ran it. But I had input from all team members about the correct procedure in running the machine. So, when I questioned Sandy about it, there was always a problem. She said that I should ''just listen to me, and follow my directions and everything will be all right." It got to the point that I was not doing anything right according to her and then there was a problem.

I asked Johnson if I could go work somewhere else, because I could see that there was going to be a problem working with her this last week and I wanted to qualify and obtain seniority. So, I was taken off the packer and put back on the scale to train with someone else.

**Q:** How was it that Sandy told you to operate the packing machine?

**A:** Well, Sandy was really concerned about body positions, how you stand so you can look at the line and tell if there is something going wrong with the switches. She was telling me that a lot of times the machine acts up so you want to set it in the hand-operated position so that if the photo eye does not catch, a certain mechanism does not click, the machine runs anyway.

That was not what I had heard from other people who run the machines. They said doing that does not do anything but tear the machine up. It causes a lot more problems for the mechanics to fix and the machine would be down more often.

**Q:** Did other people on the team tell you not to follow Sandy's instruction?

**A:** Yes, even the mechanics. They said you do not want to run it in the hand-operated position at the same time you are running it in automatic because it has a cycle that it runs through. And when the cycle is broken, then the machine starts to tear down.

**Q:** How did Sandy address you when she spoke to you?

**A:** With Sandy there really was not any type of address besides the fact that she would really refer to me as "boy." And because I was still a probationary employee, I really did not want any problems.

It was the rumor around the plant that if you crossed anybody during your three months of probation that somebody could say the words to the manager—the employee, that is, could say the words, that this guy does this or this person does that, and it is a possibility that they would not qualify. So I did not want to cause any waves. I just dealt with it.

After I qualified, it just increased. You know, "You're just my son. You're as young as my son. And I am just going to call you Junior." So, in the team meeting I was Junior. I was "boy." I was everything but David White. When I expressed my concerns about how she addressed me, there was still really nothing to gain from this. She continued and it got to the point where I just avoided her at all costs.

**Q:** Did you ever say to her that you did not want to be called "boy" or "Junior"?

**A:** Yes, I did. As a matter of fact, it was at a team meeting with my teammates, Tessie Bondy and Polly Bird. Jack was there also. I had asked her to please call me by my name, and if she could not call me by my given name, to not say anything, I would just prefer it that way.

**Q:** You said there were specific problems with Sandy not cooperating with the rest of the team. Was one of those problems that the rest of the team rotated machines and that Sandy did not rotate machines?

**A:** Yes, that was a problem. There were four positions on one line—quality control, the depalletizer, the scale, and the packer. And for each machine you needed a person to run it.

So the job would not get monotonous, the team decided that—the majority of the team decided—that we wanted to rotate once a week, that we give a person long enough to run each machine and also keep everybody familiar with their skills on their machines.

When we addressed Sandy with it, she said that she was comfortable on her packer and she did not want to do anything else but stay on the packer even after we expressed that we all needed to run the packer too. You have to kind of give and take a little. The only other place she could go was the depalletizer.

So, it got to the point where we would say, "Well, Sandy, you have to work on the depalletizer this week because everybody else wants to rotate." And there was a problem. She would come into the team room silent and would not say anything to anybody, would not talk, would just ignore us. That is the way it got.

**Q:** Was there a problem over her helping to clean the machinery?

**A:** Yes, there were a lot of problems that arose out of the cleaning. I was verbal, quite verbal to Jack Johnson as to how uncomfortable I was with that.

Every time we were on the third shift, you would usually have to take the whole entire shift to clean the line well so it can run for the next day's production. And when I say "clean the line," you have really got to get the product and grease out of the seamers and get the product from the scales so it does not mess up the balance of the weights going in the cans.

There are a lot of things that need to be done for sanitary reasons as well as just running the production on a normal day. Two people just cannot clean that machine as well as it should be cleaned in eight hours.

We needed a third person, whether it was just cleaning a minor—you know, we wanted Sandy to help clean the scale, the seamers, but we were satisfied with having her clean other things, but she was not willing to do anything.

**Q:** Let me ask you, are we talking about the third, the graveyard shift?

**A:** Yes, that is the graveyard shift. Later, we stopped running three shifts. We used to do a lot of cleaning on the graveyard shift because it was the least productive of the three shifts.

**Q:** So, it was only when you were on the graveyard shift that you would have the problems over cleaning the line with Sandy, correct?

**A:** Yes.

**Q:** How often did you do a graveyard shift?

**A:** I have to break it down to how often we rotated shifts, every three weeks. So, it was three weeks at a time we stayed on graveyard, and the same for first and second.

**Q:** You mentioned that two people could not do the cleaning, but I thought there were four people on your subteam. Was there a problem with that?

**A:** Yes, there was a problem. We had four people on the subteam, but to run the 39-ounce line through lunch and breaks our subteam usually sent a person over there from the graveyard shift to help run that line during the first or the second shifts through lunches and breaks. So that only left three people on the 13-ounce line in the graveyard shift.

And Sandy never wanted to break her rotation schedule, so she always went to third and wouldn't provide relief on the first or second shift. Whenever my subteam went to third shift, she was usually there, because she never broke any pattern. She never was willing to help or to realign her schedule to help the needs of the team. And of course when she *was* on the third shift she wouldn't clean the seamers, which left just two of us to do it.

**Q:** Are you talking about the needs of the overall team?

**A:** Correct, not just the subteam.

**Q:** So, whenever you would go on third shift, the graveyard, one of your people would stay on either second or first shift to fill in as a break reliever, correct?

**A:** Correct.

**Q:** Was there ever any personal tension between you and Sandy over any other issue besides your name or participating in the cleaning of the seamers?

**A:** I never felt like it was personal. I never felt like there was anything worse, where I could mention it to a certain degree. I did not want to go far enough to get anybody in trouble. I just wanted her to realize the severity of what was needed from her.

And no matter how you went about it or who you asked to talk to her, you never got results.

**Q:** Did you play cards on your break when you worked at Purity?

**A:** Yes, I played cards on my breaks and lunch.

**Q:** Who did you play cards with?

**A:** I played cards with Thelma, Polly, and Tessie.

**Q:** Prior to when you started to play cards with them, did Sandy McCrae sit in to play cards with them to your knowledge?

**A:** Well, it's like this. When I was a probationary employee, I was rotating with that subteam. I was actually training on the 39-ounce line, but it was still the same subteam rotation.

One time I went up into the break room and saw that they played cards. I told them that whenever they had an opening that I would like to play. So, they said, "Well, fine. Do you know how to play?" I said, "Yes," and a couple days later when Sandy did not come in the room, I played instead. We had a good time and they asked me to play with them, if I did not mind, because Sandy did not really know the game, and they preferred to play with me. I told them that I did not mind playing when I come up.

Q: Was there ever an instance where Sandy tried to muscle into the game to play instead of you?

A: Yes, there were times where Sandy would leave the line before the scheduled break and Tessie, the subteam coordinator, would ask Sandy what was going on or Sandy would say, "I have to go to the bathroom." This would cause the line to shut down ten minutes or more before break time.

When we would arrive at the break room, Sandy was sitting there at the usual table where they played cards and she would tell me, "Well, I will play now, and you can play at lunch." It was not a problem for me. It was a problem for the ladies, because they did not really want to play with Sandy. But I did not want any controversy, so I just backed off. I said, "Fine."

Q: I take it that you attended team meetings, correct?

A: Yes, I did.

Q: Did team meetings ever get heated? Do people ever argue in them?

A: Yes, they did. This was even so in other teams when I was rotating. There were times that I worked 39-ounce and times I worked 13-ounce. All the team meetings that I participated in there was always some type of heated discussion about something or other.

Q: Did you feel free and did the other employees apparently feel free to express their feelings?

A: Definitely.

Q: Did people sometimes get angry?

A: Yes, there were times that people even left the room because they were so upset. They would leave to try to maintain their composure.

Q: Was there a time some time last year during the summer when Jack Johnson asked you to be the team coordinator while he was on vacation?

A: Yes, I remember that incident. Tessie was on another rotation schedule because of

something about baby-sitting needs and she could not work that particular shift, which was the swing shift. We were actually on a graveyard, but we were kind of flexing some hours so we could kind of get out early because of the holiday that was coming up.

Q: What does it mean to "flex hours"?

A: Well, we come in four hours earlier. If it was the third shift and we normally came in at 11:00 and the team decided to come in early, we would all come in and help run the lines through lunches and breaks and do spot cleaning. That way, when the line went down at 12:00, we would only need two hours to clean.

Q: During the time when Jack asked you to be the team coordinator in his absence, did you say that you would do it upon any conditions?

A: Yes. I expressed to Jack that it would be difficult for two people to clean the line under any circumstances and that we needed participation from Sandy to keep getting out early. I said the only way that I would accept the coordinator's role was if, before he left, he got an understanding that she was going to help out in any way that was necessary. I knew Sandy would question my appointment to team coordinator, especially since she had more seniority than I did. So did Tessie, our subteam coordinator.

Q: And did he get that understanding?

A: Yes, quite clearly.

Q: Were you at the meeting where she said that she would participate?

A: Yes, I was.

Q: How did it come up? What was said?

A: Well, Jack, Tessie, Polly, Sandy, and I were all at the meeting. After Jack brought up all the daily business, I brought up the fact that we needed Sandy's participation on third shift to help clean because it was going to be a skeleton crew. She responded that she would do whatever was necessary. Jack Johnson stated that it was a good thing that we could come and talk about something that was a problem and deal with it. I remember it quite vividly.

Q: Did Sandy keep to her agreement while Jack was gone?

A: No. We came in the next week to start cleanup, and since Sandy was so cooperative in the team meeting the previous week, I asked her specifically what she wanted to start on, and told her that later we would all kind of gather in the middle and do the hard parts.

She specifically told me that she was not going to do anything. She said Tessie should have been named as team coordinator instead of me. Then she said, "Why did Jack ask you of all people, to take his place?" She was going to do what she wanted to do and nothing that I wanted her to do, and I was puzzled. By that time it was break time, and we were supposed to help run 39-ounce through lunches and breaks, so I had to help coordinate that. I had to leave. When we all came back from break, I asked everybody if they would come in the team room for a meeting. Sandy would not go to the team room, so we just moved into the QC room and we all went in and sat down.

**Q:** Why wouldn't she go to the team room?

**A:** I do not know. I never asked. Sammy Cutler and Tessie were the Union reps, and I asked them if they would go ask her to come to the team room. Tessie Bondy came back and asked me why we did not just go in the QC room. So, the subteam went in there to talk about it. After everybody got settled in, we were all in the room and I expressed my concerns and told them that I was under the impression from Sandy that she was not going to help. I said that we needed to resolve this because last week she told me that she was going to help. While I was talking, Sandy was saying, "I did not say that. I did not say that."

So, I asked her what she did say. She said that she was not going to clean up on any machine that she had not been trained on. And then everybody agreed that whatever she needed training on we would give it to her. We said we just needed her help and asked her to please help.

At that time she said, "Well, I'm not doing anything, and who in the hell are you to tell me what to do?" Then nobody was saying anything. I asked Sandy why she lied, and she said, "I'm not a damned liar; you're a damned liar."

At that time, I was totally frustrated. I felt that if we did not get the work done, it was going to be a reflection of my capabilities of handling the team coordinator role. I did not

know what to do. I was totally frustrated. Nobody had any suggestions or was saying anything. I stood up and said, "You are a damned liar. You know what you said. Jack knows what you said, and everybody in this room knows what you said."

So, at that time when I stood up, you know, and I called her a damned liar, she looked at me and she started reaching towards her bag. I looked at her and I said, "So, what, you going to grab a knife and cut me?" She said, "Well, whatever it takes." By that time Tessie and Thelma said, "David, this is not worth it. We're not getting anywhere. Let's just go." We all left, and the only people that were left in the room were Sammy Cutler and Sandy.

**Q:** Why did you make that comment to her about, "Are you going to cut me now?"

**A:** Because from the time that I first arrived at Purity and after I made seniority, I had always heard that Sandy kept a sharp knife or a putty knife or a utility knife on her person or in her utility bag for occasions such as either defending herself or if somebody crossed her, and that she would cut them. There was even a rumor that she had cut her ex-husband or something like that.

**Q:** Was there a rumor around the plant that she had actually used the knife on somebody who had sexually harassed her?

**A:** I do not remember that particular rumor, but there were quite a few rumors about her and her knives.

**Q:** When you were in the meeting arguing with Sandy, were you ever going to hit her?

**A:** No, I would never hit a woman. I do not know what else to say to convince anybody that I would not physically threaten anybody. I felt that we had an understanding where, if something was on your chest, we could all talk about it and get some kind of understanding. That is the way I approached it.

I never had any malice toward her and never made any threatening moves or threatening motions towards Sandy. I do not even understand how she could even conceive of that. I always tried to treat everybody with respect, the same amount of respect that I felt that I received from others. I just was not getting that from Sandy.

**Q:** Did you ever threaten to kick her ass or her husband's ass?

**A:** No, not at any time.

**Q:** Did you ever threaten her in any way in that meeting?

**A:** No.

**Q:** Did you ever threaten her in any way at any other meeting?

**A:** No, I did not.

**Q:** Did you ever threaten her at any time?

**A:** No.

**Q:** You heard Sandy's testimony this morning about four separate incidents of harassment having to do with sexual connotations. She testified that there was a time when you were in the lunchroom and there was a verbal exchange in which you commented on her pants being too tight and she cursed you and then you slapped her buns. Did that happen?

**A:** No, that never happened. I never touched any woman at Purity in any sexual way. I have never touched Sandy McCrae. The only relationship that we ever had was a working relationship and that was not as smooth as it should have been. I do not understand why she would accuse me of anything like that, but it never did happen.

**Q:** You heard her testify this morning about your having scooped her up and lifted her up in your arms. Did you ever do that?

**A:** No, I did not. I remember that incident because at the time Tessie, Polly, Sandy, and I were all at that station discussing production reports for the prior week. I did not pick her up. I did not touch her. I always tried to make Sandy feel like I was the type of person that she could work with.

**Q:** Sandy also testified about an incident where you supposedly held some cups on your chest in a sexually suggestive manner. Did you ever do that?

**A:** No, and I do not think there is anybody else at that plant who would say that I acted any other way but professionally at the plant.

**Q:** Sandy also testified this morning that there was an incident where you asked her to work on the seamer again and that Ben Silver was called in to participate. Do you remember that occurring?

**A:** Yes, I remember that occurring, and I was not a part of the confrontation as it was

made. It seems like Tessie and I were cleaning the seamer at the time and the conversation with Jack Johnson and Sandy was right near the seamer. So, when they were talking, he asked us if Sandy said she was not going to clean. We said, yes. That was my only involvement with Sandy's stance on cleaning the seamer.

**Q:** I would like to turn your attention to the day that you were terminated. Who was it who told you that you were terminated?

**A:** Jim Wilson, the personnel manager, told me that I was being terminated.

**Q:** Did he give you any reasons for your termination?

**A:** The only reason that he gave me was that he said I broke the house rule and there was a brief section in the statement saying harassing or any type of racial, sexual—

**Q:** I am showing you what has been marked as Union Exhibit 1. Is that the statement that he gave you?

**A:** Yes, it is.

**Q:** Did Mr. Wilson give you any further details about what your alleged conduct was?

**A:** No, and I remember that specifically because I asked, "Well, what is it?" He told me that I would have a chance to grieve it and find out what I was being charged with exactly.

**Q:** When you began to talk to him, what was the first thing he told you?

**A:** That I was being terminated for breaking the house rule. I cannot remember exactly how he worded it, but he said for breaking a house rule and because of another incident, regarding my conduct toward Sandy.

**Q:** Did he tell you that you were going to be terminated before he asked you whether you had anything to say?

**A:** Yes, he told me that I was going to be terminated and did I have anything to say to convince him otherwise.

**Q:** What did you say?

**A:** I told him, there is no way I could say anything if I do not know what I am being charged with.

**Q:** Did you ever talk to any investigators from corporate headquarters?

**A:** Yes, I did.

**Q:** When was it that you talked to them?

**A:** I cannot remember the specific date. I think it was at the beginning of the year.

**Q:** When you talked to them, did they indicate to you that there were any charges or allegations against you?

**A:** Not the first time. The first time they talked to me, they were asking me in a witness type of role. They asked if I had noticed any racial harassments or sexual harassments. Did I notice any drug abuse in the plant? Did I notice anybody being slammed against a wall? Did I notice anybody picking anybody up or any stealing in the plant? I had nothing to say because I did not know of any of these incidents.

**Q:** What happened at the second interview that you had?

**A:** At the second interview, it was more like an interrogation. They sat me in a corner with one investigator directly in front of me and another at my side, and the first one directed the questioning face-to-face while the other guy watched me. They asked me, "Well, we've got some conflicting reports. You say that you don't know anything about what's going on in the plant. And we have witnesses who say that you have harassed people and that you are an intimidating factor in the plant. What do you have to say about this?"

**Q:** What did you say in response?

**A:** I told them that I did not know who told them what they heard, but it was all untrue. They kept asking, "Are you sure? How do you expect us to believe you, Mr. White?" I told them that they would have to take my word for it, because I did not know any other way to inform them that I was not a part of any of these incidents of harrassment and intimidation.

**Q:** At any time did they give you details of alleged incidents that you were supposed to have participated in?

**A:** No, they did not give any details. They just said that they had witnesses to state that I was harassing people, that I was intimidating people here at the workplace.

**Q:** I have nothing further.

### b. Cross-Examination by Company Advocate

*Mr. Green:*
[to be supplied by student]

# D. Exhibits

## *JOINT EXHIBIT NO. 1*

COLLECTIVE BARGAINING AGREEMENT

BETWEEN

PURITY FOOD COMPANY

AND

LOCAL 32

GROCERY WORKERS UNION (5/10/01-5/10/04)

. . .

Section 20.   Discharge

   20.1 Right of Discharge

   The Employer shall have the right to discharge any employee for dishonesty, insubordination, drunkenness, incompetence, willful negligence, failure to perform work as required or to observe Employer's house rules, or for engaging in strikes, individual or group slowdowns or work stoppages, or refusal to accept overtime without good and sufficient reason involving a conflicting obligation on the part of the employee, or for violating or ordering the violation of this Agreement.

   20.2 Appeals in Discharge Cases

   The Employer shall not discriminate against any employee because of Union membership or activities. If an employee feels he has been unjustly discharged, the employee shall have the right to appeal the case to Arbitration. Such appeal must be filed in writing by the Union within ten (10) calendar days from date of discharge and unless so filed the right of appeal is lost. In case the discharge is found to be without just cause by the Arbitrator, the Arbitrator shall order the employee's reinstatement with or without back pay.

   Any discharged employee shall, upon request, be furnished the reason for his or her discharge in writing.

   All complaints regarding discharges shall be given preference over any other matters pending between the parties, and a written arbitration decision shall be given within ten (10) days.

. . .

*JOINT EXHIBIT NO. 2*

HOUSE RULES

<u>Objective Statement</u>:   The purpose of these rules is to provide consistent understanding of safety, sanitation, attendance, and work performance.   Violation of these rules can result in disciplinary action up to and including discharge.

.  .  .

9.   The use of abusive or threatening language, gestures, or slurs. This includes harassment of employees, or behavior in a way which would be offensive to any person of any race, ethnic group, national origin, religion or sex.

10.   Possession of firearms or other dangerous weapons while on company premises.

.  .  .

*JOINT EXHIBIT NO. 3*

PURITY FOOD COMPANY                    GROCERY WORKERS UNION, LOCAL 32

**GRIEVANCE**

<u>Complaint</u>:   The Grievant was discharged without cause.
<u>Request</u>: Reinstatement and to be made whole.
<u>THIRD STEP ANSWER</u>: Grievance denied.

*UNION EXHIBIT NO. 1*

Purity Food Company
March 11, year 3

Mr. David White

Dear Mr. White:
     Your employment with the Purity Food Company was terminated on March 11, year 3, pursuant to Section 20.1 of the Agreement for violation of posted House Rule No. 9 which prohibits harassment of employees or behavior which would be offensive to any person of any race, ethnic group, national origin, religion or sex; plus the warning letter issued to you on October 1, year 2. You are entitled to appeal your discharge pursuant to Section 20.2 of the House Rules.

/s/ <u>Jim Wilson</u>
Personnel Manager

cc:   Local 32

**_UNION EXHIBIT NO. 2_**

Re:  David White   3/12/03

     This is a file memo for David White's personnel file from Jim
Wilson and Joe Boise that documents a discussion with him on March
11.  Jim Wilson and Joe Boise met with David White today to discuss
the results of last week's security investigation at the Plant by
Corporate Security personnel.  Victor Borg was also in this meeting
as a Steward.

     Joe shared with David that upon review of the data collected
last week, the Purity Food Company intended to terminate him for
violation of House Rule No. 9, which we allowed David to read.  Joe
gave him a letter which gave all the specifics for which we
intended to terminate him.  Joe asked David if he had any
information to share which would convince us not to terminate him.
David denied he did anything and had no more information to share.

     Victor asked what did David specifically do, what was he being
terminated for.  Joe said for violation of House Rule No. 9 and
Section 20.1 of the Agreement, and that we were not at liberty to
share anything more specific.  Jim said that David knows what he
did and did not do, and can determine that for himself.

                    /s/ Joe Boise      /s/ Jim Wilson


**_UNION EXHIBIT NO. 3_**

PETITION

                                        March 19, year 3


The undersigned female employees of Purity Food Company's plant
freely state that we have neither witnessed nor experienced
sexual harassment/misconduct on the part of David White and would
not like our names to be associated with any such charges against
him.

| | | |
|---|---|---|
| /s/ Polly Bird | /s/ Dolores Hart | /s/ Julia Choate |
| /s/ Tessie Bondy | /s/ Davita Hayes | /s/ Sylvia Reyes |
| /s/ Thelma Dorf | /s/ Marla MacInnes | /s/ Jane Ten Bears |
| /s/ Joyce Chen | /s/ Susan Seagraves | |
| /s/ May Valentine | /s/ Nancy Smith | |

## *UNION EXHIBIT NO. 4*

PROBATIONARY EMPLOYEE ASSESSMENT UPDATE

DATE:    12/4/01
Name:  David White
Date of Employment 11/13/01

| STRONG | | | ACCEPTABLE | | | WEAK |
|---|---|---|---|---|---|---|
| 7 | 6 | 5 | 4 | 3 | 2 | 1 |

A.  Striving to Do Work Well:  This rating 6

Learned to reset container coder on his own.  Spent a lot of time on overtime to train with others in order to get different perspectives.  Has absolutely no qualms about doing any other kinds of work—hand stacking, etc.  He aced the evaluation, knew everything extremely well.

B.  Working Well With Others:  This rating 7

Works very well with others, the team really likes him.  He has voluntarily spent extra time assisting less capable probationary employees. He credited Helen for his good training. He speaks up freely in the team mtgs, and has a positive way of letting people know just how far they can go with him.

C.  Learning and Adapting:  This rating 6

He learned the packer the first night he trained on it ...

SUMMARY COMMENTS:

David seems to be a very well rounded candidate. He is intelligent and has the technical ability, people skills, and willingness to work hard that would make him an ideal teammate and possibly a leader in the future. Next evaluation, look at weight control/number work.  Explore the scale technology more.

In summary, David should qualify at the end of his probationary period if he continues to demonstrate the above-described traits.

cc: David White                          /s/ Bob Smith
Union Steward                             Training Manager

# Auto Dealers, Inc.

## Table of Contents

NOTES

# A. Caption

IN THE MATTER IN ARBITRATION BETWEEN:

AUTO DEALERS, INC.                     )
KORNVILLE, IOWA                        )
                                       )
AND                                    )        RE: RAY BOND
                                       )            Discharge for Theft
UNIVERSAL ASSOCIATION OF               )
MACHINE WORKERS                        )
LODGE 7171                             )

Appearances:

For the Company: James Mason

For the Union: Harry Yost

Date: November 19, year 1

Place: Kornville, Iowa

# B. Examination of Company Witnesses

## 1. Don Behr, Assistant Service Manager

### a. Direct Examination by Company Advocate

*Mr. Mason:*

**Q:** Will you state your name and address and present occupation?

**A:** Don Behr, 101 Oak Street, Kornville. Right now I am a part-time student at Kornville Community College, and I work part-time at Kornville Auto Leasing.

**Q:** And were you employed on July 15, year 1?

**A:** Yes, I was.

**Q:** Where?

**A:** At Auto Dealers as Assistant Service Manager.

**Q:** What were your duties as an Assistant Service Manager?

**A:** My duties were to act as a service writer during normal working hours, and on the evening in question I had duties of the Service Manager because our Service Manager, Mr. Peters, was not in at the time.

**Q:** Were you on the premises of Auto Dealers at about 8 o'clock that night?

**A:** Yes, I was.

**Q:** Did you have occasion to see Ray Bond over the course of that day?

**A:** Yes, I did.

**Q:** Was he at work that day?

**A:** Yes, he was.

**Q:** What activity was he involved in at 8 p.m. Why was he there?

**A:** Because of our excess of cars that had not been pre-serviced for delivery, we asked our mechanics if they could come back one night that week to help out with the servicing. Ray Bond was one of the mechanics that came back. He was pre-delivering cars.

**Q:** Can you tell us what occurred at about 8 p.m., where you were and where Mr. Bond was and what you saw just starting about that time?

**A:** I was walking out the back door, which leads to the alley. Upon entering the alley I looked before crossing the alley and noticed Ray Bond was standing outside of a new car parked by a lot on the other side of the alley from the garage. We had rented that lot for the purpose of storing new cars. At that time he was rolling a tire away from the new car, which he was pre-delivering at the time, and rolled it onto the new car lot. I walked down there to see what was happening, and I asked Ray what he was doing. He avoided the question about the tire and stated that he was trying to repair the automatic trunk opener on the new car he was pre-delivering. I then proceeded to walk onto the lot which we had rented to look for the tire which I had seen Ray roll onto that lot. I found it underneath the back of one of the new cars we had stored on that lot. Later in the day I asked Ray one more time what he had been doing with the tire, and once again he avoided the question. He didn't answer it.

**Q:** What type of vehicle was Mr. Bond servicing on that night?

**A:** It was a new Zenith.

**Q:** Where was the Zenith parked when you came out of the door?

**A:** In relation to the rental lot where we stored the new cars, it was almost directly in front of the lot, in the alley.

**Q:** Was it pointing north or south?

**A:** It was facing north.

**Q:** The cars that were in the rented lot were facing which direction?

**A:** West, facing the alley and across it from the back of the garage.

**Q:** Were all the cars parked facing the back of the garage?

**A:** Yes.

**Q:** And the rears to the east?

**A:** Correct.

**Q:** And they were in a straight line?

**A:** Yes.

**Q:** How far were you standing from the car in the alley?

**A:** Anywhere, I would say, from 40 to 80 feet. I couldn't say for sure. It just took me a couple of seconds to walk down there from the back door of the garage.

Q: What type of lighting is there?

A: It was 8 o'clock in the evening in the summertime and there was fairly good light.

Q: Was the sun still up?

A: Yes.

Q: Did you see Mr. Bond rolling the tire?

A: From what I could see he was rolling the tire toward the new car lot after he got it out of the trunk.

Q: What was the distance from the Zenith's trunk to the place where you found the tire? Fifteen feet? Twenty feet?

A: Fifteen to twenty feet, I would say, at least.

Q: Did you ask Mr. Bond what he was doing with the tire?

A: I asked him twice, and he avoided the question about the tire. He said he was working on the trunk-opening mechanism of the car he was working on.

Q: Now, that alley you were in, I assume that is a public alley?

A: Right.

Q: The lot where you found the tire and where the cars were parked was a rental lot?

A: Yes.

Q: Auto Dealers did not own it?

A: No.

Q: Was the tire visible from the alley?

A: No.

Q: It was concealed from view?

A: Yes. It was under the rear of one of the cars parked in the new car lot which faced the alley.

Q: You sent an employee, Tom Connell, down to pick up the tire?

A: Yes, I sent Tom Connell to pick up the tire.

Q: What did he do with the tire?

A: He put it in the Parts Department, and I immediately locked the Parts Department.

Q: How big a tire is this?

A: 195-15, which is a wagon tire and wheel.

Q: Was it inflated and rimmed?

A: Yes, it was.

Q: Do you have any idea what that tire weighs inflated and rimmed?

A: I would say 50 pounds. It is probably more than that.

Q: Was anyone with Mr. Bond on this job?

A: Yes. Another one of our mechanics, Rod Last, was inside the new car parked in the alley, which Ray was pre-delivering. It was being road tested as part of the pre-delivery work.

Q: Did you have any conversation with Mr. Last about this?

A: At the time I couldn't see any need for it because I was more interested in what Ray was doing than what Rod was doing.

Q: Did you have any further conversation with Mr. Bond after you closed your shop?

A: No, I didn't. He seemed to be avoiding me, as a matter of fact, for the rest of the evening.

Q: When Mr. Bond was working on the latch, where was he, physically, in relation to the trunk he was working on? Inside or leaning over it?

A: Leaning over from the outside of the car.

Q: He was not inside the trunk?

A: No, not that I saw.

Q: Have you ever worked on a trunk of a vehicle?

A: Yes, I have.

Q: Have you ever had to take the spare tire out or an extra spare out?

A: No.

Q: You said later in the evening you called Mr. Peters?

A: Yes, I did.

Q: Did you and Mr. Peters come to any conclusions as to what could be done?

A: Not that evening, no. The time I called him was around midnight. I called him about the unusual circumstances. I thought he should be informed.

Q: As long as you have been associated with Auto Dealers has it been the normal procedure to put a car that has something wrong with it, like this latch, on the new car lot?

A: Occasionally it is if we are pressed for time and the circumstances make it necessary. We do make notes of what has to be repaired.

Q: At the time you went down the alley were all the stalls inside filled, do you remember?

A: I don't know.

Q: If the stalls were all filled, is there still room in your garage for this car to sit and be worked on inside?

**A:**  In the aisleway itself there is room for four or five cars to be parked in the front drive and rear drive.

**Q:**  Was there room available that night?

**A:**  Yes.

**Q:**  I don't suppose you would recall what specifically was wrong with this electric latch?

**A:**  Not specifically. All I know is that Ray Bond told me he was working on the trunk-opener mechanism.

**Q:**  Ray told you that?

**A:**  Ray told me that.

**Q:**  When?

**A:**  When I went down to ask him about the tire.

**Q:**  No further questions.

### b. Cross-Examination by Union Advocate

*Mr. Yost:*
[to be supplied by student]

## 2. Tom Connell, Part-Time Helper

### a. Direct Examination by Company Advocate

*Mr. Mason:*

**Q:**  Give your name, address, and occupation.

**A:**  Tom Connell, 60 Howell Street, Kornville, part-time Lot Man.

**Q:**  Were you employed by Auto Dealers on or about July 15, year 1?

**A:**  Yes, as a part-time helper.

**Q:**  Are you familiar with the vehicle that we are talking about, the one that was being worked on?

**A:**  Yes. A new Zenith four-door sedan.

**Q:**  Did you have occasion to drive the car?

**A:**  Yes.

**Q:**  Why, and where, and when?

**A:**  I drove the car over to Randle Brothers Gas Station because, when we pre-deliver new cars, it is a practice to put five gallons of gasoline in the car. I took it over to put five gallons of gasoline in it. I had previously taken over a tire off of a wagon to be fixed. The man at Randle Brothers station told me the tire was ready. I figured as long as I was there with the Zenith I would put the tire in the trunk and bring it back.

**Q:**  And did he put the tire in the trunk or did you?

**A:**  Yes, I did.

**Q:**  When you got back to Auto Dealers the tire was in the trunk?

**A:**  Yes.

**Q:**  What day was this, do you recall?

**A:**  July 15, that evening.

**Q:**  What time did you go pick up the tire?

**A:**  I would say 7:45 in the evening.

**Q:**  When you got back, what did you do with the car?

**A:**  I drove it in the front door.

**Q:**  Where is the front door of the garage?

**A:**  It is off East State Street. I drove it in the front door, and I either parked it in front of the service desk or in one of the stalls we have.

**Q:**  Did you see Mr. Bond and Mr. Last move the car?

**A:**  Yes.

**Q:**  Did Don Behr ask you later to pick up the spare tire from the new car lot used by Auto Dealers to store new cars?

**A:**  Yes.

**Q:**  How did you do it?

**A:**  I walked out of the back door of the building, crossed the alley to the new car lot, walked between parked cars, and looked for the tire. I found it underneath a two-door Star. I pulled it from underneath the Star and rolled it back through the service department and locked it up in the Parts Department.

**Q:**  Was it the same tire which was picked up earlier from Randle?

**A:**  Yes.

**Q:**  Was the tire that you picked up under the station wagon?

**A:** No.

**Q:** Didn't you say earlier that the tire belonged to a wagon?

**A:** Yes.

**Q:** But the wagon was nowhere near where Ray Bond rolled the tire?

**A:** No, it was not.

**Q:** How far is the new car lot in question down the alley from the back of the garage?

**A:** About thirty feet.

**Q:** Was the tire visible from the alley way when you were in front of the lot?

**A:** No.

**Q:** It was concealed from the alley vantage point?

**A:** Yes. I had to go onto the lot and search for it.

**Q:** Did Bond know you picked up the tire?

**A:** I believe he did. When I walked across the alley, Bond was getting into the new Zenith he was pre-delivering. I asked him what he was doing with the tire I was sent to get. He did not reply. He then got into the car with Last and drove off.

**Q:** Was the tire visible from the alley?

**A:** No.

### b. Cross-Examination by Union Advocate

*Mr. Yost:*
[to be supplied by student]

## 3. Dave Peters, Service Manager

### a. Direct Examination by Company Advocate

*Mr. Mason:*

**Q:** State your name and address.

**A:** Dave Peters, 720 Jefferson Avenue, Kornville.

**Q:** What is your position at Auto Dealers?

**A:** Service Manager.

**Q:** How long have you been Service Manager?

**A:** Approximately two years.

**Q:** Then you were employed as Service Manager on July 15, year 1?

**A:** Yes.

**Q:** At about 8 o'clock that night you were not at the shop?

**A:** No.

**Q:** Don Behr testified you had other plans for the evening and he was in charge?

**A:** Yes.

**Q:** Did Don call you either that night or early in the morning of the 16th of July?

**A:** Yes, he called me sometime right after midnight.

**Q:** What did he tell you?

**A:** He told me what he had observed— seeing Ray rolling a tire onto the rented lot where it was found under a car—and wanted to know what should be done. I told him it was too late at night to do anything that night; we would discuss it in the morning and get more details of what was going on.

**Q:** So at that time you made no decision as to what to do?

**A:** No, none whatsoever. I wanted to wait until the next day so that we could do a proper investigation and get all the facts before taking any action.

**Q:** Where was John Behr, the General Manager, at that time?

**A:** John was on vacation, I believe, at the time.

**Q:** He wasn't there on the 15th?

**A:** No.

**Q:** Or the 16th?

**A:** No.

**Q:** In your position would you have been able to do something on your own without discussing it with John?

**A:** Yes.

**Q:** But you decided to wait until morning?

**A:** Right.

**Q:** What did you do the next morning?

**A:** The next morning, July 16th, I talked to Don about it, and he explained the story and what he had seen and stuff. Then I talked to

Bob Early about it, about what he thought we should do. Bob is my superior.

**Q:** Did you have occasion to speak to Harold Madden that day?

**A:** Yes, out at the shop.

**Q:** Can you tell me who Harold Madden is?

**A:** He is President of the Local Union and has quite a bit to do with it, and I felt I should go and discuss with him what should be done.

**Q:** Where did you have this conversation?

**A:** At Harold's place of employment.

**Q:** E-Z Body Shop?

**A:** Yes.

**Q:** What did you tell Mr. Madden and what did he tell you?

**A:** I told him what happened. First off he said, ''You should fire the man.''

**Q:** Did you mention the man's name?

**A:** No, not at that time. We stood there and talked about some things and decided to leave and he said, ''Who is the guy?'' Finally I told him who it was, Bond, and then he kind of changed his mind. He said Bond was an official in the Union and it would look kind of bad if we fired a man that had a position in the Union like that. He felt the best thing then would probably be to have a conference with the Union and discuss it, and maybe we could reach some agreement without firing him.

**Q:** When did you have your discussion with Mr. Early, before or after you talked to Mr. Madden?

**A:** I had one before and one after.

**Q:** After you talked to Bob Early what did you do?

**A:** Talked to Mr. Charles Behr, the President.

**Q:** Were you in the shop on the day of July 15th?

**A:** The 15th, yes, but I left at 5:30 p.m.

**Q:** Was Charles Behr in at all that day?

**A:** No, he was on vacation, too, and he was due to be back any time. He got back later that night, I think, on the 15th.

**Q:** Are you in the shop every day?

**A:** Yes.

**Q:** How often in the course of a day do you see Charles Behr in the shop?

**A:** In the shop? I see him probably once or twice a week, that's all. He may be in more often, but as far as my seeing him—he may come in the front door and in the office, not back where I am.

**Q:** Does he get involved in any management as far as employees are concerned?

**A:** Not too often. The only reason we called him in was because John was gone and we were at a loss to know what to do.

**Q:** During the time you have been in your position have you had to call Charles Behr on other matters?

**A:** No.

**Q:** Nothing serious had come up?

**A:** No.

**Q:** Have you had any theft problems in the shop the last six months to a year prior to this incident?

**A:** Well, there are mysterious disappearances of tools. They are shop tools and are kept in a tool bin and they are supposed to be put back. If they are missing they could be mislaid, lost, or taken home.

**Q:** Are you familiar with the tire we are talking about?

**A:** Yes.

**Q:** Can you tell me what it would cost to buy that tire from you?

**A:** I believe with the tire and rim $75 to $80, maybe even a little more.

**Q:** Are you familiar with the trunk and latches on this car, this new Zenith?

**A:** Right.

**Q:** Where is the catch latch?

**A:** The catch, itself, is in the trunk lid. It has a solenoid which activates the automatic trunk opener which bolts to the bottom part of the trunk lid there in the lower deck panel.

**Q:** Were you familiar with the problems of this particular car?

**A:** No, I didn't know it had any kind of problem. It was just being pre-delivered, and they check all the accessories on it and if they find one that is not working, they fix it.

**Q:** How do you repair a latch?

**A:** First off you start by checking it out. It could be a bad wire, an unplugged wire, bad solenoid, bad lock. It could be a number of things. It could be just misalignment.

**Q:** How do you go about checking one out physically?

**A:** Well, to start with you probably check to see if it is plugged in. You might take a test light to make sure it had electricity going to it. If it did, you would probably have somebody push the bottom and work it while you were examining the lock to see what was happening. If nothing was happening, you figure you have a bad lock or broken wire, or whatever.

**Q:** How large is the trunk of this car?

**A:** It's good sized, one of the largest around.

**Q:** Can you fit in it?

**A:** I never tried but I imagine I could very easily and I'm 5'11" and weigh 200 lbs.

**Q:** Is it necessary to get in the trunk to fix the latch?

**A:** No. No reason at all to get in the trunk. The latch is right at the back of the trunk, and two bolts hold the solenoid and three hold the latch assembly. You can get right at it with the trunk open standing at the back of the car just by reaching over.

**Q:** When you are pre-delivering, is this one of the things you always check, this latch?

**A:** Yes. You are supposed to check them.

**Q:** Where do you usually check it?

**A:** Usually in the garage. It is usually all checked before it gets road tested. There should be no reason to check one in the alley.

**Q:** What time did you go home the night of July 15th?

**A:** That night probably about 5:30.

**Q:** Have you ever been a mechanic?

**A:** Oh, yes.

**Q:** Have you ever had to remove a spare?

**A:** Yes.

**Q:** Where do you normally put it?

**A:** I lean it on the car itself.

**Q:** The car?

**A:** Yes. The rubber tire does not scratch the car.

**Q:** Is this the normal practice in your shop?

**A:** Yes, if it is to be taken out. But most people would go out of their way to keep from taking a tire out of a trunk because it is time-consuming.

**Q:** It is unusual for there to be two spares in the trunk?

**A:** Right.

**Q:** This tire was there because Tom Connell had gone to pick it up from Randles where it had been repaired?

**A:** Right.

**Q:** Have you ever had a situation where you have had a car come in for repairs on the trunk and either the regular spare has been laying in the trunk or there were two?

**A:** I have had it where there were three in the trunk. A lot of people carry their snow tires in the trunk. It is not too often, but you still find some people put their snow tires in the trunk and leave them there besides the regular spare.

**Q:** If you had to work on the trunk, you would have to take these out?

**A:** To get in to fix a water leak, yes, but not anything like the repair of a latch.

**Q:** If you did take them out, the practice would be to leave them there next to the car?

**A:** Stack them against the car or lay them next to the car—not over five feet away from the car at the most.

**Q:** Not over five feet away?

**A:** Yes.

**Q:** After Bob Early called Charles Behr, did he come down?

**A:** Yes.

**Q:** Were you present when he and Mr. Bond had their conversation?

**A:** Yes.

**Q:** You were there?

**A:** Yes.

**Q:** Who else was present?

**A:** Bob Early.

**Q:** Do you recall any of the conversation between Charles Behr and Ray Bond?

**A:** Yes.

**Q:** Do you recall how long this encounter took?

**A:** I would say we were in there for probably about 15 to 20 minutes.

**Q:** Did Mr. Bond at any time admit to taking the tire?

**A:** Well, he kind of—I can't think of the exact words he said, but to me my idea of the thing was he did say that he had taken the tire. He said it was the first time he had ever done this.

**Q:** When you left were you satisfied from what he said that he had taken the tire?

**A:** Yes.

**Q:** Did Bond at any time request that a Union official or other person represent him at this meeting?

**A:** No.

**Q:** Was Bond dismissed while you were present?

**A:** Yes.

**Q:** What was Bond's reaction?

**A:** He asked to talk to Mr. Charles Behr in private.

**Q:** That's all.

## b. Cross-Examination by Union Advocate

*Mr. Yost:*
[to be supplied by student]

## 4. Bob Early, Sales Manager

### a. Direct Examination by Company Advocate

*Mr. Mason:*

**Q:** State your name, address, and occupation.

**A:** My name is Bob Early. I live at 70 Station Prairie in Kornville. I am a Sales Manager at Auto Dealers.

**Q:** Were you so employed on the 15th of July, year 1?

**A:** Yes, I was.

**Q:** Were you involved in any of this activity that occurred on the 15th of July?

**A:** I was involved only in the fact that it was reported to me. I was tied up in two or three sales at that time and it was getting late in the evening. It was just reported to me, and no other action was taken.

**Q:** Who reported it to you?

**A:** Don Behr, the Assistant Service Manager then, called me out of a meeting and told me.

**Q:** Did you during the course of the day have any connection with this vehicle Mr. Bond was working on?

**A:** None whatsoever.

**Q:** The following day you and Dave Peters decided to call Charles Behr, the President, is that correct?

**A:** Correct.

**Q:** You and Dave agreed to call Charles the next day?

**A:** Right.

**Q:** And ask him to come down?

**A:** Yes.

**Q:** Did he come down immediately?

**A:** It couldn't have been more than 10 to 15 minutes when he arrived.

**Q:** Did you have a chance to talk to Charles when he got there?

**A:** Yes.

**Q:** What did you tell him?

**A:** I told him exactly what Don Behr told me the night before, that Mr. Bond had been seen rolling a tire onto the rented lot and Tom Connell was instructed to bring it back from where it was found under the Star. I just completely described what was described to me.

**Q:** Who called Mr. Bond in to meet with Dave, Mr. Behr, and you?

**A:** I believe Dave was instructed to have Mr. Bond come to the office.

**Q:** Were you there during the conversation?

**A:** Yes.

**Q:** Did you feel at any time while Mr. Bond and Charles Behr were talking that Bond was either guilty or not guilty?

**A:** Absolutely.

**Q:** What did you feel?

**A:** I felt he was guilty.

**Q:** Did he admit it?

**A:** He said, "Now that I have done this I suppose I am going to be blamed for everything else around here,"— quote, unquote.

**Q:** Do you recall him denying what he did?

**A:** No. He never denied it.

**Q:** And then—how long, can you tell me, did this conversation take place?

**A:** From the time all four of us were in the office—Mr. Behr talked for a while—I would say, approximately 15 minutes.

**Q:** And then you and Dave left?

**A:** We left.

**Q:** Then did you and Dave and Mr. Bond get back together again?

**A:** No. Before I left, Mr. Bond was instructed he was released from duty.

**Q:** You didn't go back in for any further conversation?

**A:** No.

**Q:** Did you have any discussion with Charles as to Mr. Bond's relationship to the Union that morning?

**A:** No. I simply called Mr. Behr and told him what was described to me. We had a busy evening the evening before and it was a busy morning. I felt an officer of the company should come down.

**Q:** I take it you work every day?

**A:** Yes.

**Q:** During the time you have been Sales Manager has anyone else been fired for theft, do you know?

**A:** I can't recall anyone else that has been fired for theft. There might have been but I can't recall.

**Q:** How often does Charles Behr usually come to the shop?

**A:** Usually a few times a week.

**Q:** Does he take any active control in hiring and firing?

**A:** No, but in Bond's case he had to, because John Behr was out of town.

### b. Cross-Examination by Union Advocate

*Mr. Yost:*

[to be supplied by student]

## 5. Charles Behr, President

### a. Direct Examination by Company Advocate

*Mr. Mason:*

**Q:** State your name, please.

**A:** Charles Behr.

**Q:** Your address and occupation?

**A:** 101 Oak Street. Car sales and real estate.

**Q:** Are you President of Auto Dealers?

**A:** Yes.

**Q:** How much were you involved in the day-to-day operations of Auto Dealers in the last year prior to this incident?

**A:** I am in there once or twice a week, but I check in by telephone if not every day, at least every other day. The operation we have is controlled in our corporate office, all our operations. When I say our operations, I mean all the dealerships in this area my brother Elston and I own.

**Q:** Did you take any part in the hiring and firing of mechanics or the work schedule?

**A:** No. We have men that are assigned to that job. It is their responsibility.

**Q:** Who was primarily responsible for hiring and firing and work schedules at Auto Dealers?

**A:** My oldest son, John, is the principal manager, and he might instruct someone else under him. This is his choice, but he has to answer to us—to Elston and me.

**Q:** You were on vacation in July of this year, were you not?

**A:** Yes, I returned the night of the 15th.

**Q:** Can you tell us what happened on the morning of the 16th as best you can remember?

**A:** I was at our corporate office and I got a call from Bob Early, who in John's absence is manager of the garage, and he mentioned the situation, and I immediately said that I would be right down. The corporate office is only two blocks away. This was approximately 10 o'clock in the morning. Upon my arrival at the office I called Bob Early and Dave Peters in, who in turn related the story to me. I mentioned that if I hadn't been there that due process would be to do exactly what I am going to do, and that is to release the man from employment if the story is true. I asked Dave Peters to call Ray Bond in.

**Q:** Ray was at work that day on the 16th?

**A:** Yes, he was. He immediately came in.

**Q:** Who conducted this meeting and conversation?

**A:** I did.

9

**Q:** Can you tell me what you said? I assume you opened the conversation?

**A:** I did, yes.

**Q:** Can you tell me what you said to Mr. Bond?

**A:** I immediately asked what had happened. I also said anybody that was stealing from any of our garages would have to be released from employment. At the same time I asked Bond why he did it. Bond sat there with his chin in his fist and he said, ''I don't know. I don't know.'' I told him he would be released after he continued to say ''I don't know. I don't know why'' in answer to my accusations that he stole the tire. I asked Dave Peters what Ray Bond was working on, and I instructed him to get somebody else to complete the job because Ray was done as of this moment, that we couldn't tolerate this. This, of course, took 10 or 15 minutes time. All the time he said, ''I don't know why. I don't know why.''

**Q:** Did he at any time make a statement concerning being blamed for everything else?

**A:** Yes, he said, ''Now that I have done this, I suppose I will be accused of all the other things that have been missing around this garage.'' This was not new to me. I was aware that wrenches and tools were missing constantly. You can't say it is from theft. It is disappearance. Often cars are serviced and some tools are left in the car. I think everybody has had this experience. I said, ''No, not unless somebody can prove you are the one that did it.'' About that same time he asked for me to excuse the two other people; he wanted to talk to me alone.

**Q:** Did you know Mr. Bond and his family?

**A:** I knew his dad Bob better than I knew him. His dad worked for us many years ago. We belonged to the same church. This is a small community. As for Ray, I wouldn't have known him from the other employees. I am not in the shop that much.

**Q:** Were you aware of the fact he had some relationship with the Union other than being a member?

**A:** Yes, I am sure he was a Union Steward. I believe he was a Shop Steward because I think he was at some of our profit-sharing meetings.

**Q:** Have you ever fired a man for stealing prior to this?

**A:** I can recall one that stole a lot of license money from us, and the day we caught it, he was discharged.

**Q:** Catching an employee stealing, you will fire him?

**A:** Yes, you don't have any other choice.

**Q:** What did you base your firing of Bond on?

**A:** The evidence that was presented at our little session that morning. I said, ''Why did you do it?'' He said, ''I don't know why. I don't know why.'' He said the same thing when he and I were in the office alone.

**Q:** What else did he say when you two were alone?

**A:** He wanted to make restitution for the tire.

**Q:** Were you at that time familiar with any of his activities as Union Steward in the shop?

**A:** No.

**Q:** Did you have a discussion with Don Behr about it?

**A:** Never talked to him about it.

**Q:** The first you knew of it was when Bob Early called?

**A:** Yes. Unfortunately, Don, my youngest son, came home after I was in bed and left before I got up. Don still lives at home with us. He had a responsibility to answer to somebody else, and I tried to keep it that way. He works under somebody else's supervision.

**Q:** Did you know whether Mr. Bond's work performance was good or bad?

**A:** I have no idea. I had his paycheck in front of me. I think it was $247. I am not familiar with what work he did.

**Q:** Your sole reason for firing Mr. Bond was this incident?

**A:** Yes.

**Q:** You implied earlier that if you caught somebody stealing, you would fire them?

**A:** That is right.

**Q:** Even today?

**A:** Yes, sir, even today. In any of our operations. I would expect the Manager to discharge a man for stealing. That is part of our operating policies.

**Q:** Did you fire Bond when he walked in or did you talk to him?

**A:** Certainly I talked to him first.

**Q:** Then you told him?

A: I told him he was done as of now. We let him leave his tools in the office for a day or two.

Q: But you did have this conversation before you let him go?

A: Yes, definitely.

Q: You testified you did not talk to Don prior to the dismissal?

A: Correct.

Q: How did you learn what happened regarding the tire?

A: From Bob Early and Dave Peters in a private meeting prior to calling Bond in.

Q: What did Peters say?

A: He told the story about contacting the President of the Union and what the remarks were. I asked what they felt should be done, and they said they felt the man should be discharged, and I said, "That is what I am here for."

Q: Early also reported his story?

A: Yes.

Q: You asked them what should be done, and what were their answers?

A: Not Dave Peters; I asked Bob Early and he said, "As far as I am concerned, if you were not here I would discharge him."

Q: No further questions.

## b. Cross-Examination by Union Advocate

*Mr. Yost:*
[to be supplied by student]

## 6. John Behr, General Manager

### a. Direct Examination by Company Advocate

*Mr. Mason:*

Q: State your name, address, and present occupation.

A: John Behr, 1103 Buttermilk, Kornville, General Manager of Auto Dealers.

Q: Were you General Manager on July 15, year 1?

A: Yes, sir.

Q: You were out of town at that time?

A: Yes, sir.

Q: There seems to be some question about pressing criminal charges against Bond. I wish you would explain it because I think it was partially your decision.

A: On Saturday, July 24th, Larry Wilks, the Chief Shop Steward, came in the shop and wanted to know what had transpired. I got the people involved in the thing to come into the office. A remark was made to the effect that we wouldn't want to press criminal charges against this guy because of our past relationship as far as the family is concerned, but that in order, if there were a grievance, to substantiate our case, we would of necessity have to go to the State Attorney's Office, and that is the reason that we went there.

Q: Anything else?

A: Monday, the next Monday I believe, Larry presented me with the grievance dated the 24th. That very same day I went to the State's Attorney's Office and made a statement. Dave Peters and Bob Early also made a statement. Don Behr was not able to make a statement because he was out of town. Upon hearing all the verbiage from all the other people, the State's Attorney decided to wait to file a complaint until they heard Don's story. Don returned on a weekend, and that Monday he made a statement to the State's Attorney's Office. Shortly after Don's return we had our first grievance meeting in a hotel. We suggested to the State's Attorney that he could probably find Bond at this meeting. So they served him with the warrant or summons for theft as he left the grievance meeting held in the hotel. The timing of the two events was just coincidence.

Q: Did you at any time discuss Mr. Bond's activities as a Shop Steward with Charles Behr or anyone in management?

A: No.

**Q:** Was this relationship with Ray as the Union man, was it a particularly discomforting thing to you?

**A:** There was always the labor-management consideration. Ray had a point of view, and we had a point of view, which was not always the same. Many times we were in agreement and at other times in disagreement.

**Q:** Did you ever criticize and harass Ray because of his Union activities?

**A:** No.

**Q:** Isn't it true that you were informed that the State's Attorney's Office will not take a criminal complaint without an eyewitness?

**A:** Yes.

**Q:** That is the procedure, isn't it?

**A:** Yes.

**Q:** Are you familiar with a grievance meeting at Auto Dealers' other garage, the one managed by Kent Behr?

**A:** No, I have no idea.

**Q:** I have no further questions for this witness.

### b. Cross-Examination by Union Advocate

*Mr. Yost:*
[to be supplied by student]

## C. Examination of Union Witnesses

## *1. Ray Bond, Grievant*

### a. Direct Examination by Union Advocate

*Mr. Yost:*
**Q:** Ray, will you state your name and address?

**A:** Ray Bond, Rural Route #1, Kornville.

**Q:** Where are you now employed?

**A:** At the Kornville Country Club.

**Q:** How long were you employed at Auto Dealers?

**A:** Approximately two-and-one-half years.

**Q:** When were you discharged?

**A:** July 16th of year 1.

**Q:** What type of work did you do at Auto Dealers?

**A:** I was a mechanic. I did all front-end alignment, most of the air-conditioning work, and most of the rear-end jobs, and other miscellaneous work.

**Q:** While working there did you receive any awards?

**A:** Yes, I received two craftsman awards.

**Q:** How do you go about receiving those?

**A:** The car manufacturers prescribe a test, and you take a test and if your average is high enough you get an award.

**Q:** Ray, did you have any other duties besides being an employee of Auto Dealers while you were there?

**A:** I was the Shop Steward.

**Q:** How long were you the Shop Steward?

**A:** Almost two years.

**Q:** What does a Shop Steward do?

**A:** Well, he is supposed to keep track of any infractions of the labor contract by either the employee or the management.

**Q:** During this period of time did you have occasion to file any grievances?

**A:** Yes, I did.

**Q:** Would you tell us approximately how many during this two-year period?

**A:** I think five or six, something like that.

**Q:** Were these written grievances?

**A:** Yes.

**Q:** Did you have other grievances that resulted in Auto Dealers having to pay money?

**A:** Yes, I did.

**Q:** All of the written grievances required Auto Dealers to pay more money?

**A:** Yes.

**Q:** Would you explain to us what these grievances were about?

**A:** Two of them involved people fired for unjust cause, and they had to pay them back pay and vacation pay.

**Q:** What did this amount to?

**A:** It was over $300 on each one.

**Q:** Did you have any other grievances?

**A:** Yes, there was one by Rod Last and me over incentive oil filters installed.

**Q:** Your names were on the grievance?

**A:** Yes.

**Q:** What did this amount to?

**A:** Approximately $250.

**Q:** Between you?

**A:** Between the both of us.

**Q:** That right there adds up to a total of $850 on just 3 grievances, doesn't it?

**A:** Yes, I suppose.

**Q:** What were some of the grievances that weren't written up?

**A:** The grease rack would fall about one foot and needed oil, but the Company didn't check it. Also, the paint on the floor was ordinary paint, and you would have a tendency to slip on it.

**Q:** Is there a nonskid paint?

**A:** Yes. Part of the shop was painted with it.

**Q:** Any other grievances?

**A:** A grinder didn't have a shield on it.

**Q:** These were the type of grievances you would bring to the attention of the manager?

**A:** Yes, the Service Manager, Dave Peters.

**Q:** Ray, on the night that led up to your discharge, will you tell us in your own words, as near as you can, what happened?

**A:** Well, at approximately 8 p.m. we had just got done having a break, and Rod Last and myself went out in this new Zenith 4-door sedan to road test it.

**Q:** Will you tell us what road testing requires?

**A:** Completely checking the car to make sure everything on it works properly.

**Q:** Does this entail driving the car off the Company premises?

**A:** Yes, to check for squeaks and rattles and wind and water leaks.

**Q:** You say you and Rod road tested this car?

**A:** Yes.

**Q:** Is this the new Zenith that the other witnesses have been talking about?

**A:** Yes, it is.

**Q:** Will you tell us what you did when you road tested it? How far did you drive it?

**A:** We went approximately three miles altogether, out around the State Prison and turned around and came back.

**Q:** Is three miles the average distance of a road test?

**A:** It depends, but on the average, three miles would be pretty close.

**Q:** Did you see anything malfunctioning on the car?

**A:** One thing. We found the remote trunk opener wouldn't work.

**Q:** What did you do after you had driven two or three miles?

**A:** We turned around and came back and stopped in the alley next to the new car lot which is rented by Auto Dealers.

**Q:** Why did you stop in the alley?

**A:** Because we couldn't pull it into the garage because all the stalls were full.

**Q:** Is it normal procedure to work on a car in the alley?

**A:** No, but since this was probably an electronic problem I just wanted to check and see if it was a loose wire or something that could be fixed right there.

**Q:** Did you have the proper parts to fix this latch?

**A:** No, but then they more than likely didn't have the right parts in the shop either; they very seldom have the parts for the new cars.

**Q:** You were next to company property?

**A:** Yes, the new car lot across the alley is rented by Auto Dealers.

**Q:** Will you tell us what happened when you stopped there?

**A:** Well, I got the key for the trunk and I got out and opened the trunk up to see if I could see what was wrong with it, and I found an extra spare tire in the car.

**Q:** We are talking about a tire mounted on a wheel?

**A:** Yes.

**Q:** Did you have knowledge that this extra tire and wheel was in the car before you opened the trunk?

**A:** No, I did not.

**Q:** When you opened the trunk, did you observe anybody in the alley?
**A:** I saw Don Behr standing in the alley by the doorway to the garage.
**Q:** Did you see him when you got out of the car?
**A:** Just about the time I got out of the car I saw him.
**Q:** Was he in the alley when you opened the trunk?
**A:** Yes, he was.
**Q:** What happened when you opened the trunk and saw the extra mounted tire?
**A:** I tried to find out what was wrong with the latch and couldn't see. I took the tire out from the trunk and rolled it over to the new car lot next to the alley and gave it a little shove and it rolled to the back of one of the new cars. I shoved it underneath the car so that somebody wouldn't fall over it.
**Q:** What did you do then?
**A:** I walked down to the Zenith and started working on the trunk lock.
**Q:** Did Don watch you roll the tire over to the car on the new car lot?
**A:** As far as I know he did.
**Q:** You knew he was in the alley?
**A:** Yes, I did.
**Q:** Incidentally, how tall are you?
**A:** 6'4".
**Q:** How much do you weigh?
**A:** 275.
**Q:** You say you had difficulty seeing in the trunk. Did you have to lean into the trunk to do the work?
**A:** Yes, I did.
**Q:** You didn't get into the trunk or attempt to?
**A:** No, I just leaned in.
**Q:** Is it necessary to get into the trunk to work on it?
**A:** Sometimes you might have to.
**Q:** How long did you work on the trunk lock?
**A:** Approximately five to ten minutes.
**Q:** Incidentally, where is this lock located in the trunk?
**A:** The part I was working on is on the bottom body panel or the back body panel.
**Q:** Were you able to determine what was wrong with the lock?
**A:** No, I wasn't.

**Q:** What did you then do?
**A:** I closed the deck lid down without putting the tire back in.
**Q:** Why did you close the deck lid down without putting the tire back in?
**A:** Because I forgot I took the tire out.
**Q:** Were you in a hurry that evening?
**A:** Yes, we were trying to get as many cars serviced as we could.
**Q:** Were you interested in going home?
**A:** Yes. The other employees really didn't want to work that night but I persuaded everybody to keep working.
**Q:** Was Don Behr in the area when you got in the car and drove away?
**A:** Yes, he was standing by the new cars.
**Q:** Did Don say anything to you while you were in the alley?
**A:** No, he did not.
**Q:** You're sure he didn't ask you any questions or talk to you?
**A:** No, he didn't.
**Q:** Didn't he ask you what you were doing with the tire?
**A:** No, sir, he did not.
**Q:** When you prepared to get into the car and leave, did you see Tom Connell in the alley or hear him say something to you?
**A:** No, sir, I did not.
**Q:** You say you drove the car out of the alley. Where did you go to?
**A:** Rod Last was driving the car. He drove it to another new car lot and parked it.
**Q:** How far would that be away?
**A:** A little over a block away altogether.
**Q:** Did you do anything more to the car after you got out?
**A:** Rod got out and looked at it, too, and couldn't find what was wrong with it, so we walked back into the shop.
**Q:** How long was it from the time you drove out of the alley until you got back in the shop?
**A:** Approximately five to seven minutes.
**Q:** After you got back into the shop what did you do?
**A:** I think there were three more cars in the stalls when we got back. We finished pre-delivering them and went home.
**Q:** Pre-delivering? What is that?
**A:** Finishing up whatever wasn't done on them, and then we went home.

**Q:** Did you report something was wrong with the car in the lot?
**A:** Yes.
**Q:** Who did you report it to?
**A:** I didn't myself. Rod Last reported it to Don Behr.
**Q:** Was anything said to you up to this time about you having left a tire in the alley?
**A:** No, sir.
**Q:** Do you know whether they had to order parts for the lock or not?
**A:** No, sir.
**Q:** You say you pre-tested—pre-delivered—two or three more cars. What did you do then?
**A:** We punched out and Jack Gast gave me a ride home.
**Q:** Do you remember what time this was you punched out?
**A:** It was approximately quarter to 9.
**Q:** Was it still light?
**A:** Well, it was just starting to get dark then.
**Q:** Where was Gast's car located?
**A:** Sitting over on the street next to the railroad tracks.
**Q:** Why didn't you have your car that night?
**A:** Because we were asked to work over, Gast drove to work that day. I left my car at home so I shared a ride with Gast.
**Q:** How far do you live from there?
**A:** Approximately 12 miles.
**Q:** You live out in the country?
**A:** At the time I lived 12 or 14 miles out of town.
**Q:** Did you at any time—after you left the premises of Auto Dealers—did you at any time return to the alley?
**A:** No, I had no means of returning.
**Q:** You didn't go to the vicinity of the new car lot around the alley?
**A:** No. As I said, I didn't drive that day, Jack Gast did.
**Q:** Did you return to town on that night, to Kornville?
**A:** No, I stayed home the rest of the night.
**Q:** Will you tell us what you did the next morning when you reported to work?
**A:** I reported to work at the regular time, about a quarter till 8, and I worked up till approximately 10 o'clock when Dave Peters told me Charles Behr wanted to talk to me in his office.

**Q:** What did you do then?
**A:** I followed Mr. Peters into the office.
**Q:** Who was present in the office?
**A:** Mr. Charles Behr, Bob Early, Dave Peters, and me.
**Q:** What was said to you at the meeting?
**A:** Charles Behr told me to sit down, and I sat down, and Mr. Behr said we had a problem. I asked him what it was. He told me that I had stolen a wheel and tire from them the night before.
**Q:** Had you thought of this wheel and tire before this statement was made to you?
**A:** No, sir, I did not. I forgot that I was supposed to put it back in the car.
**Q:** Did they tell you the tire and wheel were stolen?
**A:** They just said I stole the wheel and tire. I told them I had no idea if somebody else had taken it or what happened to it.
**Q:** You did eventually remember that you left it out of the car?
**A:** Yes, I was negligent in that.
**Q:** What else was said to you?
**A:** Mr. Behr asked why I did something like that, and I told him again I hadn't stolen any wheel and tire. He told me again that I did and as of right then I was through and any work I had started somebody else would finish.
**Q:** What happened then?
**A:** Well, then he told me that I violated the labor contract and since I helped write it I should know what was in it.
**Q:** Did you understand what he meant?
**A:** No, sir, I did not.
**Q:** What did you do after this?
**A:** Well, he said I was through then and I asked if I could speak to him alone.
**Q:** Were you able to speak to him alone?
**A:** Yes, after Bob Early and Dave Peters left the room.
**Q:** Will you tell us what you said to Mr. Behr then?
**A:** Well, Mr. Behr asked me how many children I had, and I told him I had two children in school and my wife was expecting another one.
**Q:** What else was said?
**A:** He asked me why I took the wheel and tire with a family like that, and I told him I did not take any wheel and tire. He said I was

through and there was nothing I could do. I asked him if there was some kind of restitution I could make because I needed a job with my wife being pregnant again, and with two kids.

Q: Is that why you offered to make restitution?

A: I had been in trouble before, and then they brought this up. I didn't want to cause my wife and family any more troubles or publicity.

Q: Did you feel some responsibility because you forgot you had left the wheel and tire in the new car lot?

A: Yes, I knew I had left the tire outside. I was actually responsible for it.

Q: Did you know they had recovered the tire?

A: No. Not until a week later. After the investigation by the Union, Larry Wilks told me they had recovered the tire.

Q: What did you do after you offered restitution?

A: Mr. Behr said it didn't make any difference, that I was through, and I got up and walked out of the office.

Q: Did you go immediately to see the Union about filing a grievance?

A: No, sir, I did not.

Q: When did you approach the Union?

A: It was approximately four days later.

Q: Who did you go to see?

A: I went to see the Union President, Harold Madden.

Q: What did Harold tell you?

A: Harold asked me all about it, and I explained the situation to him, and he said it was up to me. If I wanted to fight it the Union would fight it, and if not, the matter would be dropped.

Q: Did he say anything about the Union investigating it?

A: Yes, he said he would send Larry Wilks out to investigate.

Q: You wouldn't know what took place as far as the investigation?

A: No, sir, I would not.

Q: When you had the conversation with Behr, Early, and Peters, did you make a statement to the effect, "Now that I have done this I will be blamed for everything else?"

A: No, sir.

Q: What did you say?

A: I said, "Now that this has happened I will be blamed for everything else." When I said that I was referring to my negligence in forgetting about the tire left in the new car lot.

Q: Do you remember a grievance meeting held at another Auto Dealer garage or location?

A: Yes.

Q: When did that occur?

A: A few weeks prior to July 15.

Q: What did management say to you at the meeting?

A: Charles Behr said I didn't belong there, because I wasn't a steward at that location.

Q: What happened?

A: Harold Madden told me to stay and let him do the talking.

Q: From the road test, could you have pulled the Zenith inside on the night of July 15?

A: Not without blocking the doorway. All the stalls had cars in them.

Q: Were there other cars coming in?

A: There were a couple of cars parked by the front door.

Q: Ready to go in?

A: Yes.

Q: I have no further question of this witness.

## b. Cross-Examination by Company Advocate

*Mr. Mason:*
[to be supplied by student]

## 2. *Harold Madden, Union Local President*

### a. Direct Examination by Union Advocate

*Mr. Yost:*

**Q:** Will you state your name and address?

**A:** Harold Madden, 200 Southland Drive, Kornville.

**Q:** Where are you employed?

**A:** EZ Body Shop.

**Q:** How long have you been employed there?

**A:** It will be six years in April.

**Q:** What is your classification of work?

**A:** Journeyman automobile painter.

**Q:** You work in a body shop?

**A:** Right.

**Q:** Do you hold a position with the Union?

**A:** I have been the Local President for the last three years.

**Q:** What were you prior to that?

**A:** I have been Shop Steward for a number of years. Before that I was Recording Secretary, the first one they ever had in the Local.

**Q:** You have been active in the Union ever since you have belonged?

**A:** Quite a bit.

**Q:** Will you tell us what happened when you first became aware there was a discharge involved?

**A:** Before the discharge was when I first got into it. Dave Peters came to talk to me.

**Q:** Was this the morning of July 16th?

**A:** Right. Dave Peters, who was Service Manager at Auto Dealers, approached me at the shop where I was working and asked if he could speak with me a few minutes. I said, "Yes, you can." I asked him what he needed or what he wanted to know. The first thing he asked was a straight question, "Harold, what do you do with a man when you catch him stealing?" I said, "Just fire him. That is all there is to it. Just fire him." He said, "Well, there are circumstances surrounding this that I would like to explain to you before we do that." I said, "All right, what are they?" He explained to me they had two men that were pre-delivering a new car. He said during the time they were pre-delivering this car, they stopped in the alley to repair a lock on a deck lid and that Don Behr had observed one of them rolling a mounted tire down the alley onto a new car lot a half a block from the garage. And he told me the employee put this tire underneath a car in the lot—that he hid it underneath the car on the lot. This is how it was explained to me. We got to talking about it and I asked him if he had actually seen the guy steal the tire and wheel. He said, "No, not really." He said Don, while standing in a doorway, had seen the employee roll it down the alley and place it underneath the car. But in my mind, knowing the Auto Dealers' setup and the alley and this lot, I thought he meant on a lot across the railroad tracks some distance away. This is what I thought when he told me the story.

**Q:** How far from the alley was that particular lot you had in mind?

**A:** It would have been about two blocks.

**Q:** Did you ask for further details?

**A:** I asked him if they actually took the wheel and tire and put it in a car and tried to get away with it. Did they really take it? He said, "No." In fact, a helper had gone down and retrieved the tire and brought it back to the shop. I said, "Who are you talking about?" and he said, "Ray Bond and Rod Last." I said, "It is getting sticky. These two people filed a grievance a week or two before this." We got to talking about it more and I asked if this wheel and tire was actually on the Auto Dealers' property or where their cars were. He said, "Yes, it was," and I told him then and there, "If you are going to fire a man for theft you better make sure he stole something. If you see a man put Company property in his car, then you can fire him." But after I found out it was Ray Bond and Rod Last that were involved in this and that the helper had gotten the tire and rolled it back to the garage, I felt that no theft had taken place.

**Q:** Did you tell Peters that?

**A:** Before he left I told him the thing to do with Bond if you think he is trying to get away with it, is to call him into the office and talk to him and maybe you can do some good. I told him Bond is a good mechanic and can make you some money, and he is an officer in the Union.

**Q:** When did you learn what happened with Bond?

**A:** I hadn't heard anything for a few days and then Ray walked in the shop one day and we started talking about the incident. After quizzing him and feeling him out and based on the answers he gave me, I didn't feel as though they were right in firing him for stealing a wheel and tire that had never actually been stolen. I asked him if he wanted to file a grievance and warned him that he would probably have to go through a lot of heartaches and headaches and explained what it would entail. He felt at the time he was unjustly discharged; he had no intention whatsoever of stealing that wheel and tire. He also made a remark to me that he was willing at that time to take a lie detector test. He convinced me that he was innocent. So Ray decided to get in touch with Larry Wilks and have Larry investigate the incident.

**Q:** In your part of the investigation, did you discuss getting together with the Executive Board of the Union?

**A:** After Larry, who is the Chief Shop Steward, investigated the matter and brought his findings back to our Executive Committee we sat down and went over the whole thing. We had heard that John Behr told Larry Wilks if we persisted in this case and filed a grievance he would have Bond arrested. The Committee took this into consideration, along with the fact that Ray wanted to clear his name and was willing to file the grievance.

**Q:** Did the Executive Committee make any recommendation?

**A:** One hundred percent voted to take the grievance to arbitration.

**Q:** Did they make any recommendation to the whole membership?

**A:** We took it before the membership at the next meeting and explained the situation, and they gave us the O.K. to take this to arbitration.

**Q:** Has your Local Union ever had an arbitration case?

**A:** This is our first arbitration case.

**Q:** Do you have a large union?

**A:** Two hundred members, who work at various dealerships in the vicinity of Kornville. Auto Dealers' three dealerships were organized two years ago.

**Q:** Have you had any other grievances at Auto Dealers?

**A:** Yes. It was a grievance over oil filters concerning Ray Bond and Rod Last.

**Q:** Did the company pay?

**A:** Bond and Last were paid something.

**Q:** Do you remember how much?

**A:** It was a prorated deal. They never paid the full amount.

**Q:** I want to cover the third-step grievance meeting over this dismissal, held at the Kornville Hotel. Do you remember Charles Behr making a statement that he had a witness who heard Bond say, ''Now that I have taken this I will be blamed for everything''?

**A:** No. The thing that Mr. Behr stated in that meeting was the fact that Ray admitted stealing the tire and wheel and he had proof of the fact that Ray said he stole the tire and wheel, and he said Bob Early was in on the meeting. I turned to Early and asked him, ''Is this what you heard Bond say?'' Bob said, ''No, the thing I heard him say was 'Since this has happened I will probably be blamed for every damned thing that is stolen around this place.' ''

**Q:** I have no further questions for this witness.

### b. Cross-Examination by Company Advocate

*Mr. Mason:*
[to be supplied by student]

## 3. Larry Wilks, Chief Shop Steward

### a. Direct Examination by Union Advocate

*Mr. Yost:*

Q: Give your name and address.
A: Larry Wilks, Route #4, Kornville.
Q: Where are you employed?
A: Major Body Shop.
Q: What is your classification of work?
A: Body and paint.
Q: Besides this, do you have any office in the Union?
A: Yes, I am Chief Steward.
Q: What are the duties of Chief Steward?
A: Well, if the steward in the particular shop can't solve a problem, he calls me and I go in to see if I can do anything with it.
Q: Are you involved in the writing of grievances?
A: Occasionally.
Q: Do you investigate serious grievances?
A: Yes, sir, I do.
Q: Even if the shop steward has come up with a solution, do you go ahead and investigate?
A: Yes, I investigate both sides.
Q: When did you first hear about Ray Bond being discharged?
A: Harold Madden called me, I believe, the Friday night after it happened and asked if I had heard anything. I told him no. He told me what he heard. I asked him if he wanted me to call Bond. He said, "No, let him call us, if he is guilty we won't hear from him." I dropped it and didn't hear anything until a week later when Harold called me and told me to contact Bond and set up a meeting with Ray. Bond wanted to talk to me. I set up a meeting with Ray after work on Friday afternoon and quizzed him about what happened.
Q: Was this on Saturday afternoon?
A: No, on Friday. With a dismissal you automatically go to the third step of the grievance procedure, which is to put it in writing, which I did. And I went down the following morning to Auto Dealers to investigate the whole thing.
Q: What did you do in your investigation?
A: I talked to Dave Peters and asked him to tell me as much as he knew about what happened. He took me to the lot where the wheel and tire were supposed to have been put and I looked the situation over. We went back to the office and John Behr, Charles Behr, and Bob Early were all in the office. I told them what I was there for and that I wanted to hear their side of the story.
Q: Did they say anything about Don Behr having a discussion with Bond in the alley?
A: No, sir, they didn't.
Q: Did they say anything about Tom Connell speaking to him?
A: No. They said Don had seen him down there, and Ray had looked up and seen Don. I asked if I could talk to Don Behr, and they said he was out of town.
Q: Was Bond an aggressive Union Steward?
A: Yes, sir, he was.
Q: Do you consider him as being fair?
A: Yes, sir.
Q: Was there any statement made by Auto Dealers' management that if we persisted with the grievance, they would have Bond arrested?
A: The statement was that if we fought it they would have him arrested. I told them I would take my recommendations back to the Executive Committee.
Q: But you did file a grievance that day?
A: Yes, sir, because that is the way it should be handled.
Q: Was there anything said at the third-step grievance meeting held at the Kornville Hotel about Ray being arrested?
A: Yes, sir there was. John Behr made the statement that there was a Deputy Sheriff standing out in the hall to arrest Ray for stealing the wheel and tire if we persisted with the whole thing.
Q: Was anything served on Ray?
A: I found out after the meeting he was served with a summons at the hotel.
Q: When did this happen?
A: When he stepped outside for a drink of water he was served with a summons for petty theft.
Q: Is this case still pending?
A: Yes, sir, it is.
Q: I have no further questions for this witness.

b. Cross-Examination by Company Advocate

*Mr. Mason:*
[to be supplied by student]

# D. Exhibits

## *JOINT EXHIBIT NO. 1*

COLLECTIVE BARGAINING AGREEMENT

BETWEEN

AUTO DEALERS, INC.

AND

LODGE 7171

UNIVERSAL ASSOCIATION OF MACHINE WORKERS (3/08/01-3/08/04)


Article XXX. Discipline and Discharge

The Company shall not discipline or discharge an employee save for just cause. An employee may grieve his or her discipline or discharge pursuant to the grievance procedure, article XXXI.


## *JOINT EXHIBIT NO. 2*

Lodge 7171
Grievance No. 202

The discharge of Ray Bond violated Article XXX of the Collective Bargaining Agreement, which requires just cause for discharge.

The relief requested is reinstatement to his former position with back pay, full seniority, and all contractual benefits.

/s/ Ray Bond

COMPANY ANSWER - STEP 3

The Grievance is denied.

/s/ John Behr
General Manager

# Olde Towne Envelope Company

## Table of Contents

**Table of Contents contd.**

**NOTES**

# A. Caption

## IN THE MATTER OF ARBITRATION BETWEEN:

| | | |
|---|---|---|
| OLDE TOWNE ENVELOPE CO.<br>MEMPHIS, TENNESSEE<br><br>AND<br><br>UNITED PAPERWORKERS UNION,<br>LOCAL 2618 | )<br>)<br>)<br>)<br>)<br>)<br>) | RE: GEORGE WILLIS<br>Discharge for Poor Job<br>Performance |

Appearances:

For the Company: Martin Spiegal

For the Union: Alan Bright

Date: December 4, year 7

Place: Memphis, Tennessee

## B. Examination of Company Witnesses

## 1. Frank Everett, Foreman of the Cutting Department

### a. Direct Examination by Company Advocate

*Mr. Spiegal:*
Q:  Would you state your name for the record?
A:  Frank Everett.
Q:  What is your place of employment and job title?
A:  I have been a foreman in the Cutting Department at Olde Towne Envelope Company for ten years.
Q:  As foreman of the Cutting Department, were you the supervisor of the grievant?
A:  Yes, I was.
Q:  Were you supervisor at the time of his discharge?
A:  Yes.
Q:  Are you familiar with the grievance?
A:  Yes, I am.
Q:  Did you share in the decision to discharge the grievant?
A:  Yes, I did.
Q:  Would you tell the Arbitrator the reason the grievant was discharged?
A:  The reason for the discharge on that particular Monday was the production in the Cutting Department had been running low and consistently week after week. I determined at that time, with the supervisor of the company, that we had to get the cutters together and make a decision regarding what the problem was and what we could do. On that Monday we started out with the various cutters in that department and we laid down the situation according to their respective cutting productions. With George Willis, at that time he was called upon for his fourth step, which was dismissal.
Q:  You had supervised the grievant for some time, had you not?
A:  Yes.
Q:  Frank, I'm going to give you what has been marked as Company Exhibits 1A through 1D, consisting of four sheets. Are you familiar with these?
A:  Yes, I am.

Q:  The first letter, Company Exhibit 1A, is a verbal reprimand, is it not?
A:  Yes, it is.
Q:  It's dated by foreman Scott Garrett, is that right?
A:  Yes, it is.
Q:  The second page, Company Exhibit 1B, is a written warning, is it not?
A:  Yes, it is.
Q:  The second step is reduced to writing, and you did sign this?
A:  Yes, I did.
Q:  What was the nature of that situation?
A:  Well, the low production continued, which required a second step to be a written warning and, of course, it was also done to distinguish from the first step, where tardiness was included. That charge was excluded at the second step because his tardiness had picked up satisfactorily. But low production continued.
Q:  Did you talk to the grievant about his production at that time?
A:  Yes, I did.
Q:  Did you tell him it would have to be raised satisfactorily?
A:  Yes, I did.
Q:  On the third page, Company Exhibit 1C, this is a letter written by you?
A:  Yes.
Q:  You gave the grievant a three-day layoff, is that correct?
A:  Yes.
Q:  Was his production still down?
A:  His production continued to be down and he was given the reprimand and the discipline of a three-day layoff. At the time it was explained to him why his production continued to be low, which included horseplay and walking away from his die press too much and lengthy breaks.
Q:  Were you having trouble keeping the grievant on his machine?
A:  Yes, I would say quite a lot.

2

**Q:** Was he causing you more trouble than the average employee?

**A:** I would say more than the average. Each employee had his or her own respective problems, but George Willis was exceptional, as far as a slowdown, which included breaks, which were too often and too long.

**Q:** Had any other supervisors talked to you about him being away from his machine and problems with him?

**A:** Yes, they had.

**Q:** Who specifically?

**A:** Mr. Rhodes, the Shop Superintendent.

**Q:** On page three, Company Exhibit 1C, you say if improvement is not made, the next and final step will be dismissal. Was the grievant told this, to your knowledge, and given a copy of this letter?

**A:** Yes. At the meeting, it was explained verbally to him, and he was given a copy of the letter.

**Q:** To your knowledge, was the written warning on the second page given to him also?

**A:** Yes, all the steps were.

**Q:** Frank, do you keep a daily production record on each employee?

**A:** Yes, I do.

**Q:** Did you do so on Willis?

**A:** Yes, I did.

**Q:** Did you pull those records for the month of April?

**A:** Yes, I did.

**Q:** Was there anything else involved, any personality problems between you and the grievant?

**A:** None that I know of.

**Q:** Are you familiar with the efficiency percentage charts that exist at the plant such as are shown in Company Exhibit 5A?

**A:** Yes.

**Q:** Is that a weighted percentage, that is, does it account for easy and hard jobs?

**A:** Yes, it does.

**Q:** And you have a percentage applicable overall, is that correct?

**A:** Yes.

**Q:** Am I correct that the objective is 100% or more on this chart for the employees?

**A:** Yes, it was.

**Q:** The 100% doesn't mean being perfect, but just the way the chart is drawn up to reflect "making quota," correct?

**A:** That's right.

**Q:** At any time did you meet with the people in the Cutting Department regarding this low production?

**A:** Yes, I have met with each individual.

**Q:** Did you tell the grievant prior to his discharge that you expected 100% from him?

**A:** At various times, yes.

**Q:** Frank, Company Exhibit 2A comprises production sheets for each day beginning with the last day of March through the fifth day of April. Is this your handwriting and do you keep these?

**A:** Yes, I do.

**Q:** Would you explain this sheet, Company Exhibit 2A?

**A:** This sheet is the start of a daily and weekly production record in the Cutting Department. The 3/31 represented that Monday, where I have each cutter listed and the hours of the day which pertain to his eight-hour shift, and then in the next column at the end of the day his production is totaled and put in that column. The next column is late and absent, if there were any hours out, how long, etc. At the end of the day, the amounts are totaled.

**Q:** Then your totals for the those six days were 7,633,935?

**A:** That's right.

**Q:** Is it a fair statement to say you can just follow the line and you can tell how many units he did?

**A:** Yes.

**Q:** Looking at March 31 on Company Exhibit 2C, Willis produced 90%?

**A:** That's right.

**Q:** On April 2 it was 82%?

**A:** Right.

**Q:** On April 3, he dropped down to 58%?

**A:** Yes.

**Q:** On the daily cutting sheets, Company Exhibit 2B, do those show the number of cuts and number of units?

**A:** The first column shows the order number of the particular job he was assigned to cut, and the second column marked "Sheets" is the sheets required for that order. The third column is the number of cuts of correctly sized paper for folding—pieces—you get out of that particular sheet. The fourth column represents the weight of that individual order. The fifth column is the total quantity that you receive out of the number of sheets times the number of pieces cut out. And then the "Remarks" indicate whether the order is completed or partially finished or started one day and may be completed the next or so-and-so cut so much a day and then was taken off the order and started something else.

**Q:** In your opinion, is 100% difficult to make?

**A:** No, it isn't.

**Q:** If on one day I cut 150% and the next day I cut 75%, so my average is over 100%, does this fluctuation greatly affect the operation of the plant?

**A:** Very much so. Our production for each cutter reflects back on the folding machines, some of which are operated at fast speeds, others at slow speeds. Product from the cutters moves directly to the folding machines. So taking the individual cutting totals for each day and combining them with all the cutters for that department, the result must total the same or more than what the Folding Department is capable of folding. If one individual's production is low for a day and the rest of the cutters' totals might be fairly low or even at 100% average or a little above on the same day, we would still be below the daily 100% total production that the Folding Department needs to run their machines at full shift.

**Q:** Which would cause a lag in the operation?

**A:** Yes. There would be a slowdown of machines, people standing around idle, machines down, etc.

**Q:** This sheet in front of you now, Company Exhibit 3A, is another week, from April 7 to April 11, is that correct?

**A:** Yes.

**Q:** And the chart reads the same and you diagnose it the same, is that correct?

**A:** Yes.

**Q:** I notice on this one you have dropped from a weekly cutting total of 7,633,935 to one of 7,253,534?

**A:** That's correct.

**Q:** Were you happy with this production?

**A:** No, it showed a decline in weekly and individual production.

**Q:** Did you tell your crew about it, that is, talk to them about your unhappiness with this situation?

**A:** To individuals, yes.

**Q:** Is there any question in your mind that the grievant knew that you were having production problems or were unhappy with the cutting production?

**A:** No, I don't think there was any doubt in his mind at all as far as the grievant George Willis's production being up and down, being inconsistent.

**Q:** Turning to Company Exhibit 3C, I notice that on April 9 Willis made 75%, correct?

**A:** Yes.

**Q:** On April 10, he jumps to 91%?

**A:** Yes.

**Q:** On April 11, back to 75%?

**A:** Yes.

**Q:** On April 7 and April 8, he produced 135% and 110% respectively?

**A:** Yes.

**Q:** Are these all weighted based on the complexity of the job? Can anyone say "I made that because it was an easy job that day"?

**A:** In a sense, no, because in this instance on April 7, there were approximately 15 different jobs that were his individual cuts on that particular day, and all the changes mean it wasn't an easy day.

**Q:** The daily cutting report for April 7 in Company Exhibit 3B shows approximately 15 jobs?

**A:** As an example, he cut a total of about 183,905 on April 7 and was at 135%. On April 9, he cut only 75%, but his production for that day amounted to even more— 224,855. So there was an increase in quantity, yet the production with the higher total was only 75% while the production with the lower total equaled 135%.

**Q:** Did you object or have reservations regarding the fluctuation in the performance of Willis?

**A:** Yes, I did.

**Q:** The 135% indicating that he could do the job?

**A:** That's correct.

**Q:** Do you regard the 75% as unsatisfactory?

**A:** Yes.

**Q:** Company Exhibit 4A contains the production numbers for April 14 to 18, correct?

**A:** Yes.

**Q:** I notice that the cutting totals have now fallen to 6,992,353. Is that right?

**A:** Yes.

**Q:** Did the supervisor of the factory production, Mr. Rhodes, let you know he was unhappy with the totals?

**A:** Yes, at the end of the week of April 14, Mr. Rhodes talked to me about the consistent decline in production and said that something had to be done.

**Q:** Did you talk to the grievant about the situation?

**A:** Yes, I did.

**Q:** I think you testified to this before, but did you tell the grievant that 100% was what you were trying to get him to produce?

**A:** Yes, especially with the fact that his production was falling off on some days and then was well above 100% on other days. Company Exhibit 4C indicates that Monday, 4/14, he had 73.8%, Tuesday 79%, Wednesday 91%, then on Thursday he fell to 76%. Finally on Friday he was back up to 112%. Even though over three months his average was 98%, we couldn't have these drastic variations.

**Q:** Then on Monday you and Mr. Rhodes determined that something had to be done and that is when you disciplined the four employees?

**A:** Yes.

**Q:** Is it correct to say that this individual was the one who suffered discipline in the form of discharge because he had three other situations pertaining to production in his file?

**A:** That's right.

**Q:** No further questions.

<hr>

### b. Cross-Examination by Union Advocate

*Mr. Bright:*
[to be supplied by student]

## 2. William Rhodes, Plant Superintendent

### a. Direct Examination by Company Advocate

*Mr. Spiegal:*

**Q:** Will you state your name for the record please?

**A:** William Rhodes.

**Q:** Would you give your job title and your place of employment?

**A:** I am Plant Superintendent at Olde Towne Envelope Company.

**Q:** I will ask you the same question I asked Mr. Everett. Are you familiar with the grievance and circumstances surrounding this case?

**A:** Yes, I am.

**Q:** Taking you back to April year 5, is it correct to say that you were having severe problems in the business?

**A:** Yes, that's correct.

**Q:** Were you also having production problems?

**A:** I most certainly was.

**Q:** What problems were you having?

**A:** Well, we weren't getting enough paper cut to enable our machines to fold enough envelopes to fill our customers' orders on time. I was experiencing down time from twenty to thirty or forty hours a week in the Folding Department waiting on paper because there was no paper cut to run those machines.

**Q:** What do the employees do when that happens?

**A:** There have been a few occasions when we have sent the operators home, but that has been very few. The operators just hang around in case we do get some paper and then, when we do, we start the machine back up. So it's a loss of production, a loss of on-time delivery dates to our customers, and a loss of time on our folding equipment.

**Q:** What if anything did you do about this loss of equipment?

**A:** Well, I went through a period of time from the beginning of April until the time Mr. Willis was fired, averaging several hours a week down time. Each day I would go to Frank Everett, the foreman of the Cutting Department, and I would go over with him the problems I had in not getting paper. This went on for some weeks. I became very upset about the fact that we could not get our orders finished for our customers. Finally, I had to tell Frank we had to do something to correct our problem and get back into the business market.

**Q:** Do you know the grievant?

**A:** Yes, I do.

**Q:** Did you have any occasion personally to observe his work habits or did you know anything about him prior to the discharge?

**A:** I certainly did. George was the type of individual that when Frank or the supervisor would leave, he would make frequent visits to the other employees in that Department, take time to go upstairs to the mezzanine to have a smoke, or walk out the back door. He liked to be away from his press when no one was there.

**Q:** Have you personally observed him away from his press?

**A:** I have and I have brought it to the attention of his supervisor.

**Q:** More than once?

**A:** Definitely, yes.

**Q:** Many times?

**A:** Yes.

**Q:** The loss of production, going from 7.6 million the first week of April down to about 7 million by April 18—does that represent the same thing it does to me, that you had a direct loss of units of production?

**A:** It represented, in the week of April 5, 38.75 hours of down time in the Folding Department. Some of those machines run 30 million units an hour. So 30 million an hour times the number of hours down would equal the loss of units that we absorbed that week. But not every machine can run that fast. Some run 12 thousand, some run 10 thousand, but we did experience a number of hours down that week.

**Q:** Let's go to the Friday before the grievant was discharged. Were you aware of the production figure for that week?

**A:** Yes.

**Q:** Were you aware of it when you left the plant that weekend?

**A:** Yes, because I checked the production on Friday up to what our total output was for first shift and it was lower than normal.

**Q:** As Plant Superintendent, were you responsible for the discharge of the grievant?

**A:** Yes, I discussed this with Frank Everett and we disciplined all the other cutting individuals who were cutting on the hand press, based on their percentage, and we gave each of them a reprimand. The grievant had already had three and we had talked to him several times between each reprimand and asked him to pick up his production and keep it at a consistent level. We don't want to have to walk over here every day to tell them to stay at their presses because this is causing us down time. But this didn't help. And I suffered almost forty hours down time in my Folding Department the week of April 5 just waiting on the paper.

**Q:** You said the grievant had three previous reprimands including a disciplinary layoff, is that right?

**A:** Yes, and on the fourth, discharge is customary.

**Q:** As I recall, that would be a negotiated item and not outside the contract?

**A:** That is standard procedure throughout the Union and the Company that we have used as long as I have been there and before.

**Q:** Were the other people who were doing similar jobs to the grievants, were they disciplined too with reprimands?

**A:** Yes, they were.

**Q:** If they had had previous violations in their files, would they have been discharged too?

**A:** They would have, because before we go to the next step of disciplinary action we always go in between each step and talk to the individual, ask him to get his job done, do a better job so we don't have to take that fourth step. So actually there is free warning in there that we don't have to do.

**Q:** You don't take into consideration any reprimand beyond a year back, do you?

**A:** No.

**Q:** Are you familiar with the production percentage chart?

**A:** Yes, I am.

**Q:** 100%—is that optimum or is that what you want to strive for?

**A:** 100% is an average level which can be reached very easily. If a person wants to work a little more or stay at his job and stay at a steady pace, he can obtain figures as high as 150%. So this doesn't mean that 100% is perfect, as we've been taught in school. It means 100% compared to our chart for computing the percentages of workers that have cut that particular order in the required amount of time set by the Company.

**Q:** Is 100% hard to do?

**A:** No, it's not. I have been a paper cutter myself. There have been times when Frank could not get other employees to cut paper. As Plant Superintendent, I have gone—and so have other foremen—to the Cutting Department after the shift ended because they couldn't get anyone to stay and cut on overtime, and we've cut more in two hours than these individuals cut in eight hours. And if they think I'm padding it, they can take one half of what I was doing and it still reaches 100%.

**Q:** At any time has the Company to your knowledge ever accepted a figure of 85%?

**A:** To my knowledge, no. It wouldn't be smart to put out a chart to say that this is the amount of time that we want you to do it in and then say if you do it 85% of the time then that is acceptable. That's not good business.

**Q:** Is it a fair statement to say that what you actually were requiring or would like to have is 100% or more?

**A:** That is correct.

**Q:** How about these fluctuations that I spoke to Frank about, do they hurt you? In other words, if I produce 75% one day and 125% the next. . . .

**A:** It certainly does hurt our operation and our building is not such that we can store a week or more of production surplus. We can't run more than a day or two ahead of time from the cutting to the folding. So we can't cut a lot of surplus envelopes ahead. When an individual drops down to 50% or 75%, that means that day or the next day that particular

machine that he was cutting for is going to suffer.

**Q:** This production percentage chart, which is Company Exhibit 5A, would you explain to the Arbitrator what it shows?

**A:** Using the examples on this sheet, when the ticket comes out for an order, it already has broken down the number of sheets. By this chart it would be 8,500 sheets. You divide that by a standard board or flat that is specified—in this chart, a board of 340 sheets per board. That gives you 25 boards to that order. Then you look on the table for 25 boards and it gives you the amount of time that is set aside to cut each board. You multiply the amount of time set aside to cut each board times the total number of boards, giving you the number of hours required to cut an order. There is also time set aside to read your order and get your die. There is allowance made for an order when you have trouble with it—if you have to have springs put in there to make the paper cut better, for combination cutting, for small orders where you only cut 800 sheets or 1,000 sheets. This chart does not say that is as many as you can cut. This is merely an amount set aside to cut. So with different weights in paper, the number of sheets will fluctuate. Company Exhibit 5B gives you the standard hours per board for die cutting.

**Q:** Have you as Plant Superintendent indicated to Frank Everett and the rest of the foremen that you wanted them to make the 100% rate or more?

**A:** Yes. I emphasized very much, especially this month, that I was having problems getting the paper for the Folding Department. We have to maintain the 100% because it doesn't look good, and it doesn't make sense, to go out and hire another cutter when the individuals you have are not producing what they are supposed to be.

**Q:** If you were cutting 100%, would that keep the folding operation going?

**A:** Not necessarily. That means if they are cutting 100% and the Folding Department is still without paper, then I need to get another employee to do cutting. Because I can speed my production up and I may need a little more paper cut. Then we can take into consideration whether we need another cutter.

**Q:** At any time did you advise Mr. Everett or any other superintendent to treat the grievant any differently than any other employee?

**A:** No.

**Q:** Was the sole reason that the employee was discharged because of this lack of production?

**A:** It was.

**Q:** After the discharge and discipline of these four employees did your production pick up?

**A:** Yes, it did. The week after his discharge our down time dropped to 24 hours. The week ending May 23 we had only ten hours down time in the Folding Department.

**Q:** Are you telling the Arbitrator that all these hours are attributed to lack of production in the Cutting Department?

**A:** No, I have them broken down. I have different numbers that represent different reasons for being down.

**Q:** These numbers that you're giving us are directly related to lack of production in the Cutting Department?

**A:** They certainly are.

**Q:** Let's go through the numbers, which are in Company Exhibit 7. For the week ending April 5, there were 38.75 hours attributable to down time waiting for paper alone?

**A:** Yes. And for the weeks ending April 12, 26.25 hours; the week of April 19, 28.5 hours; the week of April 26, 24.5 hours; the week of May 3, 10.25 hours, and the week of May 10, 1.24 hours of down time waiting for paper. The second shift also had down time, but I don't have that with me.

**Q:** You just looked at the down time in the Folding Department and you were able to see how much of that is attributable to lack of production in the Cutting Department?

**A:** That's right.

**Q:** I have no further questions.

---

### b. Cross-Examination by Union Advocate

*Mr. Bright:*
[to be supplied by student]

---

## C. Examination of Union Witnesses

## *1. George Willis, Grievant*

### a. Direct Examination by Union Advocate

*Mr. Bright:*

**Q:** Would you give your name please?

**A:** George Willis.

**Q:** Have you ever been an employee of Olde Towne?

**A:** Yes, until April 21.

**Q:** How long had you been with the Company?

**A:** About five years.

**Q:** Why did you leave the employment of Olde Towne?

**A:** I was discharged.

**Q:** What was the reason that the Company gave you?

**A:** Low production.

**Q:** Were you aware at the time you were discharged that your production rate was not up to standards that the Company required?

**A:** No.

**Q:** What were the production standards that the Company had given you that you should meet?

**A:** Well, they said if we would get 85% average or better that would be satisfactory.

**Q:** You received a three-day suspension. From the time that you received your suspension had anybody ever counselled you

8

or talked to you about your production, whether it was good, bad, or satisfactory?

**A:** On Friday, April 18, I met with my foreman, Frank Everett, and asked him about my production, because I had seen some production papers laying on the desk. He said, ''I have two weeks' production in here where you have cut a 98% and an 87%.'' He said if I cut like that I won't have any problems around there at all. Nobody ever came to me during the period between that meeting and my discharge to warn me that my production was unsatisfactory.

**Q:** You mean April 18 is the only time that they ever talked to you about your production from the time you received a three-day suspension?

**A:** Yes.

**Q:** When did you first hear that the Company was going to require a 100% production rate?

**A:** I didn't hear they required 100% until the day I was discharged in the meeting in the office.

**Q:** Who gave you the 85% figure that the Company would require?

**A:** I was given it from Frank Everett, Scott Garrett, and William Rhodes.

**Q:** What was Scott Garrett's position?

**A:** He used to be the foreman of the Cutting Department.

**Q:** Did the Company post the weekly production percentages for the employees?

**A:** They used to have a chart posted on the bulletin board above the foreman's desk. Then they took that down and didn't put up any more figures. They would just bring the percentages out of the office. They would bring three or four of them out at a time or sometimes they would go a month or two without bringing any percentages out.

**Q:** You had no way of knowing, then, how you were producing?

**A:** No.

**Q:** Did you ever understand the formula that was explained to the Arbitrator today?

**A:** No.

**Q:** Did anyone ever take the time to try to explain it to you?

**A:** No.

**Q:** Getting back to the meeting on Friday, April 18, prior to your discharge on April 21,

what time did Mr. Everett talk to you on that day?

**A:** I talked to him approximately 2:25 p.m. It was after the first bell.

**Q:** What is your normal quitting time?

**A:** 2:24. We have three minutes until the second bell at 2:27 and then we punch out at 2:30.

**Q:** You had a conversation with him. Did you work the Saturday and Sunday after that?

**A:** No.

**Q:** Mr. Everett informed you on this Friday that your work was satisfactory?

**A:** Yes.

**Q:** And that you wouldn't have any problems if you kept these kind of percentages up?

**A:** That's right.

**Q:** He gave you the indication that everything was satisfactory?

**A:** Yes, he never said anything was wrong.

**Q:** When did the Company call you in and discharge you?

**A:** It was approximately between 8:00 and 8:30 the next Monday morning, April 21.

**Q:** How long had you been at work?

**A:** I was at work at 6:30.

**Q:** Within an hour or two the Company decided to fire you?

**A:** That's right, out of the clear blue they just up and fired me.

**Q:** And the reason they gave?

**A:** My low production, whatever that's supposed to mean.

**Q:** Did you point out to Frank at the meeting that you had just talked with him on Friday and you were told everything was satisfactory?

**A:** Yes, I did. I looked him right in the eyes and said it.

**Q:** Had your production improved since you received that three-day suspension?

**A:** Yes, it definitely did.

**Q:** At the time you received the suspension did anybody talk to you about percentages?

**A:** When I received the three-day suspension, Mr. Rhodes and Frank Everett took me into the office to give me that step. They didn't just tell me what my percentages were, they just said we can't have you cutting 45% and 50%. Then they gave me the suspension. They said if I didn't improve I will go to my fourth and final step, discharge. But they never said specifically what my production should be.

**Q:** They didn't say that you had to go to 100% or 85% or anything else, is that right?

**A:** They said I had to improve, but from what percentage to what percentage, I didn't know.

**Q:** Are you sure that at no time did they ever talk to you about percentages except that 40% or 50% wouldn't be tolerated?

**A:** Yes, that's all they said.

**Q:** Are there any reasons why production might vary greatly from one day to the next?

**A:** Sure, there are plenty of reasons.

**Q:** State some of those reasons.

**A:** There are several times during the day when we will have to have our die filed and have the die filer come over when the paper cuts too small at the bottom of the stack and too big at the top sheet. There are several times we have to go away from our press to find empty skids to put blanks on; a lot of times we have to take our full scrapings container back to the baling room and bring out an empty one and sometimes even wait for one to be emptied. Pulling our own paper in and out of our machines, going to the flat stock area, and moving paper up to our press all take time, and we have to take time out waxing our dies.

**Q:** Are there times that you do have stock passers that take care of the stock for you?

**A:** There are times when there is a stock passer but I would say most of the time we do most of the stock passer's work ourselves; we're kind of a jack-of-all-trades at Olde Towne.

**Q:** Were you ever told that when you have down time that you should turn it in with your daily report?

**A:** No, they know the reasons, so I guess they never bothered to have us turn it in.

**Q:** Well, could this be one reason that down time doesn't show up on your daily record?

**A:** Sure, they know how to make it look bad for an honest group if they want to.

**Q:** Were you ever directed by your supervisor to pull other employees'—other cutters'—loads?

**A:** Yes, come to think of it, I did get dumped on at times.

**Q:** Could you give us an example?

**A:** One time after I came back from my suspension there was another cutter who refused to pull his own skids of paper out. The supervisor, Frank Everett, asked me to go over and pull this other employee's paper out because he was too stubborn to pull it out himself. So I did. Frank never did anything to him though.

**Q:** Did you do this at various times?

**A:** Yes, I did, many times.

**Q:** On various days?

**A:** Yes, I did.

**Q:** Did you ever turn this in on your report?

**A:** No, I didn't. They never asked or told us to.

**Q:** But Frank Everett knew that you did this?

**A:** Yes, he most certainly did. He told me to do the other employees' work.

**Q:** You only did it when he directed you to?

**A:** That's right.

**Q:** We've been through four hearings now, with the first three similar to what you are here for today—the fourth-step grievance meeting, two unemployment hearings—one fact-finding and one company appeal hearing—and the arbitration today. You've heard the Union ask the Company for figures?

**A:** Yes, I did.

**Q:** How many sets of figures has the Company come up with for your last three months at Olde Towne?

**A:** Four different sets. There are always changes. They know how to play with the numbers.

**Q:** Are you saying that every time we have a hearing, their figures are different?

**A:** Yes, they change just like the weather around here.

**Q:** Did you apply for unemployment?

**A:** Yes, I did.

**Q:** What happened when you applied?

**A:** The first time I applied I went down and opened up an account and I was refused my unemployment. I got a letter in the mail saying I wasn't eligible until I had six weeks of unemployment or earned $360.00 or more. I went down and filed a protest against that and I was turned down again for the same reason. The third appeal I made, which was a fact-finding interview, I had you represent me. That decision came back in my favor.

**Q:** After that interview, what happened?

**A:** I got to collect my unemployment.

**Q:** Would you look at the document marked Union Exhibit 1? Is this the document where they advised you that you would receive unemployment benefits?

**A:** Yes.

**Q:** After the unemployment benefits were allowed, what happened then?

**A:** I received another letter in the mail. I can't remember exactly what date it was, but the Company had filed a protest against my unemployment rights. We had a second hearing. It turned out the same way, in my favor and I got another letter telling me that. They never quit going after me.

**Q:** At each one of those hearings you went through the same kind of questions and ordeal that you are more or less going through today, is that true?

**A:** Yes.

**Q:** Would you please read the first paragraph in that last letter, Union Exhibit 2?

**A:** "By a decision on reconsideration, mailed August 1, year 5, the Administrator held that the Claimant was discharged by Olde Towne Envelope Co. without just cause in connection with his work, imposing no disqualifications for benefit rights, increased the total amount chargeable to the Employer from zero to $2,300.00, and allowed the first claim for week ending May 3. On August 13, year 5, the Company appealed. The appeal hearing date was set for October 30, year 5." It then says who was notified of the date, hour, and place of the hearing.

**Q:** What was the finding of the facts?

**A:** It says "Claimant filed an application for determination of benefits rights on April 28, year 5, with respect to a benefits year beginning April 27, year 5. He filed his first claim for benefits for the week ending May 3, year 5, on the basis of total unemployment. Prior to filing said claim, Claimant was last employed by the Olde Towne Envelope Co. in Memphis, Tennessee, from October year 1 until his discharge on April 21, year 5, as a machine operator. Claimant was discharged on April 21, year 5 for low production. This Employer claims that Claimant's weekly production averaged less than 100% for the week's work. The Claimant was under the impression that 85% was acceptable and was never told or informed that he was expected to produce 100%.

"The Claimant received a three-day disciplinary layoff in December of year 4 for inconsistent production and was warned at this time that further violations could possibly result in his dismissal. He was also informed that he would have to make a substantial improvement. Between the time of layoff and the time of his discharge the Claimant averaged 94% production. The Employer considered the Claimant to have made a substantial improvement subsequent to his layoff in December and was informed by his foreman on April 18, year 5 that his percentages were acceptable."

**Q:** That's far enough, I think. I want to refer to the 94%. This was the figure that the Company provided at its appeal hearing, that you averaged 94% for the last three months of your employment?

**A:** Yes.

**Q:** What was the percentage for the last three months mentioned today?

**A:** 98%.

**Q:** At the first hearing what was the figure that the Company produced?

**A:** You mean the fourth-step grievance meeting at the plant?

**Q:** Yes.

**A:** 101%.

**Q:** No further questions.

## b. Cross-Examination by Company Advocate

*Mr. Spiegal:*
[to be supplied by student]

## 2. *Russell Mattingly, Shop Steward*

### a. Direct Examination by Union Advocate

*Mr. Bright:*

**Q:** Would you state your name for the record?

**A:** Russell Mattingly.

**Q:** How long have you been with the Company?

**A:** Almost six years.

**Q:** What is your job classification?

**A:** I am classified as an automatic cutting press operator.

**Q:** Do you do the same type of work that the grievant performed?

**A:** It's the same department, but I operate a different machine.

**Q:** Have you worked under the same sets of standards that have been indicated?

**A:** Yes.

**Q:** When did you first become aware that the Company was going to require 100% production?

**A:** On Willis's discharge date, April 21.

**Q:** What figure were you aware of before the 100% figure came out?

**A:** I knew that 85% and above was acceptable.

**Q:** Who gave you this figure?

**A:** Scott Garrett and Frank Everett, my cutting foremen.

**Q:** Do you hold a title with the Union?

**A:** Yes, I am Shop Steward.

**Q:** Were you present at the fourth-step grievance meeting?

**A:** Yes, I was.

**Q:** What percentage did the Company come up with about the grievant, that is, what was his three-month figure?

**A:** They gave us the figures and we computed it at 101%.

**Q:** And the Company didn't agree with these figures at the meeting, did they?

**A:** No.

**Q:** In the last three months prior to the grievant's discharge, how many meetings did you attend where management discussed Cutters' production?

**A:** One.

**Q:** And that was the meeting where Frank Everett and Scott Garrett were present?

**A:** That's right.

**Q:** Was Mr. Rhodes present at that meeting?

**A:** I think he was, yes.

**Q:** At any time was the 100% discussed?

**A:** No.

**Q:** No further questions.

### b. Cross-Examination by Company Advocate

*Mr. Spiegal:*
[to be supplied by student]

# D. Exhibits

## *JOINT EXHIBIT NO. 1*

COLLECTIVE BARGAINING AGREEMENT

BETWEEN

OLD TOWNE ENVELOPE CO.

AND

LOCAL 2618

UNITED PAPERWORKERS UNION (6/10/03-6/10/08)

. . .

Article XXX. Discipline and Discharge

The Company shall not discipline or discharge an employee save for just cause.  An employee may grieve his or her discipline or discharge pursuant to the grievance procedure, Article XXXI.

. . .

## *JOINT EXHIBIT NO. 2*

OLD TOWNE ENVELOPE COMPANY            UNITED PAPERWORKERS UNION, LOCAL 2618

GRIEVANCE

Complaint: Grievant was discharged without cause.

Request: Reinstatement and to be made whole.

THIRD STEP ANSWER: Grievance denied.

### COMPANY EXHIBIT NO. 1A

Olde Towne Envelope Company
Interdepartmental Letter

Date: August 13, year 4
Subject: Disciplinary Action, First Step (Verbal Warning)
Attention: Local 2618


George Willis was given his first step towards dismissal because of his low production and tardiness.  He has been cutting less than one half of what he is supposed to be cutting, and has been averaging two days of tardiness per week.


/s/ Scott Garrett


PRESENT WHEN WARNED
Russell Mattingly
George Willis
William Rhodes
Scott Garrett


### COMPANY EXHIBIT NO. 1B

Olde Towne Envelope Company
Interdepartmental Letter


Date: August 30, year 4
Subject: Disciplinary Action, Second Step (Written Warning)
Attention: George Willis


George Willis was given a second step towards dismissal August 30, YR04, for low production and taking too long breaks.


/s/ Frank Everett
Cutting Foreman


Union Witness: Russell Mattingly
Company Witness: William Rhodes


14

### *COMPANY EXHIBIT NO. 1C*

Olde Towne Envelope Company
Interdepartmental Letter


Date: December 13, year 4
Subject: Disciplinary Action, Third Step (Suspension with Written
        Report)
Attention: George Willis


     Being that George Willis's record of low production and too
much lost time (breaks, horseplay) away from his die press had
not improved, the third step, a three-day layoff will be in
effect Monday, December 16, Tuesday, December 17, and Wednesday,
December 18, year 4.
     If improvement is not made, the next and final step will be
dismissal.


           /s/ Frank Everett


Union Witness: Russell Mattingly
Company Witness: William Rhodes


### *COMPANY EXHIBIT NO. 1D*

Olde Towne Envelope Company
Interdepartmental Letter


Date: April 21, year 5
Subject: Disciplinary Action, Fourth Step (Discharge)
Attention: George Willis

     On December 13, year 4, George Willis was given a three-day
suspension. Since that date Mr. Willis's cutting production has
not been satisfactory. Therefore, effective Monday April 21,
year 5, George Willis is discharged.


/s/ William Rhodes
     Plant Superintendent
     Olde Towne Envelope Co.


     Copies to:
     George Willis
     Local 2618
     Frank Everett
     File

     Union Witnesses: Russell Mattingly, P. Cole
     Company Witnesses: Frank Everett, William Rhodes

### COMPANY EXHIBIT NO. 2A

| CUTTERS | 3/31 HRS. | 90%* DAILY PROD. | LATE/ ABSENT | 4/1 HRS. | 112%* DAILY PROD. | LATE/ ABSENT |
|---|---|---|---|---|---|---|
| W. Ross | 8 | 385,250 | | 8 | 445,016 | |
| S. Mattingly | 8 | 312,000 | | 8 | 344,000 | |
| D. Turner | 8 | 211,968 | | 8 | 305,464 | |
| G. Willis | 8 | 265,532* | | 8 | 188,500 | |
| V. Jenner | 8 | 126,400 | | 8 | 132,348 | |
| M. Blake | | VACATION | | 8 | 24,550 | |
| D. Hyatt | 8 | BOX SHOP | | called in | | 8 |
| F. Mercer | 8 | Night Shift Sheeter | | 8 | Janitor | |
| H. Lawson | 8 | Baler | | 8 | Baler | |
| Daily Total | | 1,301,150 | | | 1,439,878 | |

| CUTTERS | 4/2 HRS. | 82%* DAILY PROD. | LATE/ ABSENT | 4/3 HRS. | 58%* DAILY PROD. | LATE/ ABSENT |
|---|---|---|---|---|---|---|
| W. Ross | 8 | 288,000 | | 8 | 449,000 | |
| S. Mattingly | 8 | 128,000/3hr knife | | 8 | 103,260 | |
| D. Turner | 8 | 300,300 | | 8 | 201,458 | |
| G. Willis | 8 | 200,400 | | 8 | 185,500 | |
| V. Jenner | 8 | 215,698 | | 8 | 162,000 | |
| M. Blake | 8 | 36,000/5hr filing | | 8 | 40,000/5hr fil. | |
| D. Hyatt | 8 | 175,802 | | 8 | 244,006 | |
| F. Mercer | 8 | Janitor/Baler | | 8 | Janitor/Baler | |
| H. Lawson | 8 | 102,000/3hr filing | | 8 | 80,000/3hr Baler | |
| Daily Total | | 1,446,200 | | | 1,465,224 | |

| CUTTERS | 4/4 HRS. | 110%* DAILY PROD. | LATE/ ABSENT | 4/5 HRS. | 74%* DAILY PROD. | LATE/ ABSENT |
|---|---|---|---|---|---|---|
| W. Ross | 8 | 272,000 | | 5 | 281,000 | |
| S. Mattingly | 8 | 141,000 | | 5 | 158,550 | |
| D. Turner | 8 | 220,000 | | 5 | 154,040 | |
| G. Willis | 8 | 177,600 | | 4.3 | 107,960 | |
| V. Jenner | 8 | 179,960 | | | didn't work | |
| M. Blake | 8 | 6,000/Die Filing | | | didn't work | |
| D. Hyatt | 8 | 170,860 | | 5 | 105,690 | 8 |
| F. Mercer | 8 | 6,823 Janitor | | | didn't work | |
| H. Lawson | 8 | Baler | | 5 | Baler | |
| Daily Total | | 1,174,243 | | | 807,240 | |

Weekly Cutting Total = 7,633,935

*Daily Cutting Percent for G. Willis; see Company Exhibit No. 2C.

## COMPANY EXHIBIT NO. 2B

DAILY CUTTING REPORT

OPERATOR  WILLIS                                      NO.  Die Press
HRS. WORKED ___8___     DATE  3-31-05

| ORDER NO. | SHEETS | CUTS OUT | WEIGHT | PRODUCTION | REMARKS |
|---|---|---|---|---|---|
| 2368-1 | 6,627 | 16 | 24 | 106,032 | Complete |
| 2485-1 | 2,125 | 12 | 20 | 25,500 | " |
| 861-8 | 15,000 | 8 | 24 | 120,000 | Partial |
| 2383-4 | 7,000 | 2 | 28 | 14,000 | " |
| Daily Cutting Total | | | | 265,532 | |

DAILY CUTTING REPORT

OPERATOR  WILLIS                                      NO.  Die Press
HRS. WORKED ___8___     DATE 4-1-05

| ORDER NO. | SHEETS | CUTS OUT | WEIGHT | PRODUCTION | REMARKS |
|---|---|---|---|---|---|
| 2383-5 | 8,500 | 2 | 28 | 17,000 | Complete |
| 2383-4 | 2,250 | 2 | 28 | 4,500 | Partial |
| 861-19 | 4,500 | 4 | 24 | 18,000 | Complete |
| 861-45 | 4,500 | 4 | 24 | 18,000 | " |
| 861-25 | 5,500 | 2 | 24 | 11,000 | " |
| 861-48 | 5,500 | 2 | 24 | 11,000 | " |
| 861-35 | 5,500 | 2 | 24 | 11,000 | " |
| 861-38 | 9,500 | 1 | 24 | 9,500 | " |
| 861-11 | 9,500 | 1 | 24 | 9,500 | " |
| 861-32 | 9,500 | 1 | 24 | 9,500 | " |
| 861-28 | 5,500 | 2 | 24 | | " |
|  | 9,500 | 5 | | | |
| 2383-1 | 750 | 2 | 28 | 1,500 | " |
| 2383-2 | 4,750 | 2 | 28 | 9,500 | Partial |
| Daily Cutting Total | | | | 188,500 | |

58,500

DAILY CUTTING REPORT

OPERATOR  <u>WILLIS</u>                                    NO.  <u>Die Press</u>
HRS. WORKED ___<u>8</u>___          DATE <u>4-2-05</u>

| ORDER NO. | SHEETS | CUTS OUT | WEIGHT | PRODUCTION | REMARKS |
|---|---|---|---|---|---|
| 2451-1 | 1,500 | 10 | 80 | 15,000 | Partial |
| 861-29 | 19,000 | 8 | 24 | 152,000 | " |
| 2383-2 | 3,750 | 2 | 28 | 7,500 | " |
| 2675-1 | 1,300 | 1 | 28 | 1,300 | Complete |
| 248-1 | 3,300 | 2 | 80 | 6,600 | " |
| 2077-2 | 9,000 | 2 | 32 | 18,000 | " |

Daily Cutting Total                                      200,400


DAILY CUTTING REPORT

OPERATOR  <u>WILLIS</u>                                    NO.  <u>Die Press</u>
HRS. WORKED ___<u>8</u>___          DATE <u>4-3-05</u>

| ORDER NO. | SHEETS | CUTS OUT | WEIGHT | PRODUCTION | REMARKS |
|---|---|---|---|---|---|
| 861-29 | 2,000 | 8 | 24 | 16,000 | Partial |
| 2451-1 | 2,250 | 10 | 80 | 22,500 | " |
| 861- | 1,875 | 8 | 24 | 15,000 | " |
| 861-1 | 16,500 | 8 | 24 | 132,000 | Complete |

Daily Cutting Total                                      185,500


DAILY CUTTING REPORT

OPERATOR  <u>WILLIS</u>                                    NO.  <u>Die Press</u>
HRS. WORKED ___<u>8</u>___          DATE <u>4-4-05</u>

| ORDER NO. | SHEETS | CUTS OUT | WEIGHT | PRODUCTION | REMARKS |
|---|---|---|---|---|---|
| 861 | 5,500 | 2 | 24 | 24,000 | Partial |
| 861 | 5,500 | 2 | 24 | 21,000 | " |
| 861 | 5,550 | 2 | 24 | 21,000 | " |
| 861 | 5,550 | 2 | 24 | 21,000 | " |
| 2451 | 6,000 | 10 | 80 | 60,000 | " |
| 861 | 11,500 | 3 | 24 | 33,600 | " |

Daily Cutting Total                                      177,600

18

DAILY CUTTING REPORT

OPERATOR  WILLIS                                    NO.  Die Press
HRS. WORKED     4.3          DATE 4-5-05

| ORDER NO. | SHEETS | CUTS OUT | WEIGHT | PRODUCTION | REMARKS |
|---|---|---|---|---|---|
| 861-12 | 5,500 | 2 | 24 | 11,000 | Lithed-Partial |
| 861-15 | 5,500 | 2 | 24 | 11,000 | "          " |
| 861-6 | 5,550 | 2 | 24 | 11,000 | "          " |
| 861-20 | 5,550 | 2 | 24 | 11,000 | "          " |
| 2560 | 100 | 8 | 24 | 800 | Shortage |
| 2822 | 675 | 8 | 24 | 5,400 | Complete |
| 2790-5 | 3,282 | 8 | 24 | 26,256 | " |
| 2705 | 542 | 12 | 24 | 6,504 | " |
| 2792-3 | 1,100 | 10 | 24 | 11,000 | " |
| 2790-4 | 1,400 | 10 | 24 | 14,000 | Partial |

Daily Cutting Total                            107,960

**_COMPANY EXHIBIT NO. 2C_**

WILLIS

3/31
6627 ÷ 310 = 21 x .129 =  2.709 + .022
2125 ÷ 340 =  6 x .081 =   .486 + .022
15000 ÷ 310 = 48 x .060 = 2.880 + .005
7000 ÷ 283 = 24 x .029 =   .676 + .005
              7.5 hrs    6.751 + .054  = 6.815        90%

4/1
8500 ÷ 283 = 30 x .029 =  .870 + .022
2250 ÷ 283 =  8 x .029 =  .232 + .005
4500 ÷ 310 = 13 x .039 =  .507 + .022
4500 ÷ 310 = 13 x .039 =  .507 + .022
5500 ÷ 310 = 18 x .029 =  .522 + .022
5500 ÷ 310 = 18 x .029 =  .522 + .022
5500 ÷ 310 = 18 x .029 =  .522 + .022
9500 ÷ 310 = 30 x .023 =  .690 + .022
9500 ÷ 310 = 30 x .023 =  .690 + .022
9500 ÷ 310 = 30 x .023 =  .690 + .022
5500 ÷ 310 = 18 x .029 =  .522 + .022
9500 ÷ 310 = 30 x .044 = 1.320 + .022
 750 ÷ 283 =  3 x .029 =  .087 + .022
4750 ÷ 283 = 16 x .029 =  .464 + .005
             7.5 hrs.    8.145 + .274  = 8.419       112%

19

**COMPANY EXHIBIT NO. 2C (continued)**

```
4/2
1500 ÷ 253 =  6 x .071 =    .426 + .005
19000 ÷ 310 = 61 x .060 = 3.660 + .005
3750 ÷ 283 = 13 x .029 =    .377 + .005
1300 ÷ 283 =  4 x .023 =    .092 + .022
3300 ÷ 253 = 13 x .029 =    .377 + .022
9000 ÷ 253 = 35 x .029 =  1.015 + .022

         7.5 hrs.        4.326 + .037  =  6.128        82%

4/3
2000 ÷ 310 =  6 x .060 =    .360 + .005
2250 ÷ 253 =  6 x .071 =    .426 + .005
1875 ÷ 310 =  6 x .060 =    .360 + .005
16500 ÷ 310 = 53 x .060 = 3.180 + .022

         7.5 hrs.        4.326 + .037  =  4.363        58%

4/4
5500
5500
5550
5550               [Calculation missing but presumed accurate]
6000
11500
         8.0 hrs.                                     110%


4/5
5500
5500
5500
5500
100
675                [Calculation missing but presumed accurate]
3282
542
1100
1400
         4.3 hrs.                                      74%
```

INDIVIDUAL WEEKLY (6-day) AVERAGE - G. WILLIS = 87%

## COMPANY EXHIBIT NO. 3A

| CUTTERS | 4/7 HRS. | 135%* DAILY PROD. | LATE/ ABSENT | 4/8 HRS. | 110%* DAILY PROD. | LATE/ ABSENT |
|---|---|---|---|---|---|---|
| W. Ross | 8 | 440,800 | | 8 | 469,000 | |
| S. Mattingly | 8 | 107,000 | | 8 | 97,000 | |
| D. Turner | 8 | 179,204 | | 8 | 165,351 | |
| G. Willis | 8 | 183,905 | | 8 | 191,344 | |
| V. Jenner | 8 | 227,280 | | 8 | 233,958 | |
| M. Blake | 8 | 42,000 | | 8 | 42,000/Die flng | |
| D. Hyatt | 8 | 199,736 | | 8 | 215,689 | |
| F. Mercer | 8 | Janitor/Stock passer | | 8 | 27,000/Janitor | |
| H. Lawson | 8 | Baler | | 8 | Baler | |
| Daily Total | | 1,379,925 | | | 1,441,342 | |

| CUTTERS | 4/9 HRS. | 75%* DAILY PROD. | LATE/ ABSENT | 4/10 HRS. | 91%* DAILY PROD. | LATE/ ABSENT |
|---|---|---|---|---|---|---|
| W. Ross | 8 | 393,424 | | 7 | 378,896 | |
| S. Mattingly | 8 | 338,320 | | 8 | 244,056 | |
| D. Turner | 8 | 138,424 | | 8 | 180,240 | |
| G. Willis | 8 | 224,855 | | 8 | 275,885 | |
| V. Jenner | 8 | 197,425 | | 8 | 207,872 | |
| M. Blake | 8 | 27,000 | | 8 | Die flng/Knife | |
| D. Hyatt | 8 | 151,000 | | 8 | 175,988 | |
| F. Mercer | 8 | Janitor/Baler | | 8 | 55,012/Janitor | |
| H. Lawson | 8 | Baler | | 8 | Baler | |
| Daily Total | | 1,470,448 | | | 1,517,949 | |

| CUTTERS | 4/11 HRS. | 75%* DAILY PROD. | LATE/ ABSENT |
|---|---|---|---|
| W. Ross | 8 | 345,040 | |
| S. Mattingly | 8 | 258,260 | |
| D. Turner | 8 | 231,290 | |
| G. Willis | 8 | 191,448 | |
| V. Jenner | 8 | 256,561 | |
| M. Blake | 8 | Die flng./Knife | |
| D. Hyatt | 8 | 153,435 | |
| F. Mercer | 8 | 7,836/Janitor | |
| H. Lawson | 8 | Baler | |
| Daily Total | | 1,443,870 | |

Weekly Cutting Total = 7,253,534

*Daily Cutting Percent for G. Willis; see Company Exhibit No. 3C.

## COMPANY EXHIBIT NO. 3B

DAILY CUTTING REPORT

OPERATOR  WILLIS                                        NO.  Die Press
HRS. WORKED      8              DATE 4-7-05

| ORDER NO. | SHEETS | CUTS OUT | WEIGHT | PRODUCTION | REMARKS |
|---|---|---|---|---|---|
| 2511-4 | Used cut downs | 1 | 24 | 2,000 | Shortage |
| 2790-4 | 700 | 10 | 24 | 7,000 | Partial |
| 2982-1 | 1,143 | 7 | 24 | 8,001 | Complete |
| 2790-1 | 772 | 7 | 24 | 5,404 | " |
| 861-33 | 11,500 | 1 | 24 | 11,500 | " |
| 861-46 | 11,500 | 1 | 24 | 11,500 | " |
| 861-40 | 10,000 | 1 | 24 | 10,000 | " |
| 861-40 | 11,500 | 2 | 24 | 23,000 | " |
| 861-23 | 11,500 | 1 | 24 | 11,500 | " |
| 861-26 | 11,500 | 3 | 24 | 34,000 | Partial |
| 861-43 | 7,500 | 2 | 24 | 15,000 | Complete |
| 861-36 | 10,000 | 1 | 24 | 10,000 | " |
| 861-30 | 10,000 | 1 | 24 | 10,000 | " |
| 861-7 | 7,500 | 2 | 24 | 15,000 | " |
| 861-9 | 10,000 | 1 | 24 | 10,000 | " |

Daily Cutting Total                                    183,905


DAILY CUTTING REPORT

OPERATOR  WILLIS                                        NO.  Die Press
HRS. WORKED      8              DATE 4-8-05

| ORDER NO. | SHEETS | CUTS OUT | WEIGHT | PRODUCTION | REMARKS |
|---|---|---|---|---|---|
| 2896-1 | 675 | 8 | 80 | 5,400 | Complete |
| 861-44 | 6,250 | 3 | 24 | 18,750 | " |
| 861-31 | 6,250 | 1 | 24 | 6,250 | " |
| 861-10 | 11,500 | 1 | 24 | 11,500 | " |
| 861-21 | 11,500 | 2 | 24 | 23,000 | " |
| 861-24 | 11,500 | 1 | 24 | 11,500 | " |
| 861-27 | 11,500 / 6,250 | 3 / 4 | 24 | 59,500 | " |
| 861-47 | 11,500 | 1 | 24 | 11,500 | " |
| 2903-1 | 1,218 | 8 | 80 | 9,744 | " |
| 2714-1 | 3,800 | 9 | 20 | 34,200 | Shortage |

Daily Cutting Total                                    191,344

## DAILY CUTTING REPORT

OPERATOR __WILLIS_____ NO. __Die Press____
HRS. WORKED ___8_____ DATE_4-9-05_____

| ORDER NO. | SHEETS | CUTS OUT | WEIGHT | PRODUCTION | REMARKS |
|---|---|---|---|---|---|
| 2790-1 | 700 | 10 | 24 | 7,000 | Shortage |
| 2982-4 | Used cut downs | 1 | 24 | 2,500 | " |
| 2887-1 | 8,500 | 12 | 24 | 102,000 | Partial |
| 2939-1 | 8,760 | 8 | 70 | 70,080 | " |
| 2910-1 | 2,000 | 8 | 80 | 16,000 | Complete |
| 2486-1 | 2,600 | 8 | 20 | 20,800 | " |
| 3009-1 | 925 | 7 | 20 | 6,475 | " |

Daily Cutting Total                              224,855

## DAILY CUTTING REPORT

OPERATOR __WILLIS_____ NO. __Die Press____
HRS. WORKED ___8_____ DATE_4-10-05_____

| ORDER NO. | SHEETS | CUTS OUT | WEIGHT | PRODUCTION | REMARKS |
|---|---|---|---|---|---|
| 2922-5 | 2,750 | 4 | 24 | 11,000 | Partial |
| 2790-2 | Used cut downs | 1 | 24 | 4,000 | Shortage |
| 2796-1 | 267 | 6 | 28 | 1,602 | " |
| 2683-1 | 275 | 15 | 20 | 4,125 | " |
| 2780-1 | 2,289 | 7 | 24 | 16,023 | Complete |
| 2752-1 | 1,577 | 7 | 24 | 11,039 | " |
| 2796-1 | 879 | 8 | 28 | 7,032 | " |
| 2796-2 | 630 | 8 | 28 | 5,040 | " |
| 2796-3 | 753 | 8 | 28 | 6,024 | " |
| 2887-1 | 17,500 | 12 | 24 | 210,000 | Partial |

Daily Cutting Total                              275,885

DAILY CUTTING REPORT

OPERATOR  WILLIS _____  NO.  Die Press ____

HRS. WORKED ____8_____     DATE 4-11-05 _____

| ORDER NO. | SHEETS | CUTS OUT | WEIGHT | PRODUCTION | REMARKS |
|---|---|---|---|---|---|
| 2887-1 | 4,375 | 12 | 24 | 52,500 | Shortage |
| 2887-1 | 1,775 | 12 | 24 | 21,300 | " |
| 2922-5 | 575 | 4 | 24 | 2,300 | Partial |
| 2103-1 | 6,500 | 4 | 28 | 26,000 | Complete |
| 1930-2 | 12,000 | 4 | 28 | 48,000 | " |
| 1921-1 | 10,337 | 4 | 28 | 41,348 | Partial |

Daily Cutting Total                                191,448

### COMPANY EXHIBIT NO. 3C

#### WILLIS

4/7

$$2000 \div 310 = 6 \times .023 = .138 + .005$$
$$700 \div 310 = 2 \times .092 = .184 + .005$$
$$1143 \div 310 = 4 \times .055 = .220 + .022$$
$$772 \div 310 = 2 \times .071 = .142 + .022$$
$$11500 \div 310 = 37 \times .023 = .851 + .022$$
$$11500 \div 310 = 37 \times .023 = .851 + .022$$
$$10000 \div 310 = 32 \times .023 = .736 + .022$$
$$11500 \div 310 = 37 \times .029 = 1.073 + .022$$
$$11500 \div 310 = 37 \times .023 = .851 + .022$$
$$11500 \div 310 = 37 \times .034 = 1.258 + .005$$
$$7500 \div 310 = 24 \times .029 = .696 + .022$$
$$10000 \div 310 = 32 \times .023 = .736 + .022$$
$$10000 \div 310 = 32 \times .023 = .736 + .022$$
$$7500 \div 310 = 24 \times .029 = .696 + .022$$
$$10000 \div 310 = 32 \times .023 = .736 + .022$$

7.5 hrs.   9.904 + .279  =  135 %

4/8

$$675 \div 253 = 3 \times .078 = .234 + .022$$
$$6250 \div 310 = 20 \times .034 = .680 + .022$$
$$6250 \div 310 = 20 \times .023 = .460 + .022$$
$$11500 \div 310 = 37 \times .023 = .851 + .022$$
$$11500 \div 310 = 37 \times .029 = 1.073 + .022$$
$$11500 \div 310 = 37 \times .023 = .851 + .022$$
$$11500 \div 310 = 37 \times .034 = 1.258 + .022$$
$$6250 \div 310 = 20 \times .039 = .780 + .022$$
$$11500 \div 310 = 37 \times .023 = .851 + .022$$
$$1218 \div 253 = 5 \times .060 = .300 + .022$$
$$3800 \div 340 = 11 \times .066 = .726 + .005$$

7.5 hrs.   8.064 + .225  =  110%

*COMPANY EXHIBIT NO. 3C (continued)*

```
4/9
  700 ÷ 310 =  2  x .092 =     .184 + .005
 2500 ÷ 310 =  8  x .023 =     .184 + .005
 8500 ÷ 310 = 27  x .081 =  2.187 + .005
 8760 ÷ 283 = 31  x .060 =  1.860 + .005
 2000 ÷ 253 =  8  x .060 =     .480 + .022
 2600 ÷ 340 =  7  x .060 =     .420 + .022
  925 ÷ 340 =  3  x .071 =     .213 + .022

         7.5 hrs.     5.528 + .086  =  75%
4/10
 2750 ÷ 310 =  9  x .039 =     .351 + .005
 4000 ÷ 310 = 13  x .023 =     .299 + .005
  267 ÷ 267 =  1  x .063 =     .063 + .005
  275 ÷ 275 =  1  x .128 =     .128 + .005
 2289 ÷ 310 =  7  x .055 =     .385 + .022
 1577 ÷ 310 =  5  x .055 =     .275 + .022
  879 ÷ 283 =  3  x .078 =     .234 + .022
  630 ÷ 283 =  2  x .078 =     .156 + .022
  753 ÷ 283 =  3  x .078 =     .234 + .022
17500 ÷ 310 = 57  x .081 =  4.617 + .005

         7.5 hrs.     6.742 + .135  =  91%
4/11
 4375 ÷ 310 = 14  x .081 =  1.134 + .005
 1775 ÷ 310 =  5  x .081 =     .405 + .005
 4575 ÷ 310 =  2  x .049 =     .098 + .005
 6500 ÷ 283 = 23  x .039 =     .897 + .022
12000 ÷ 283 = 42  x .039 =  1.638 + .022
10337 ÷ 283 = 36  x .039 =  1.404 + .005

         7.5 hrs.     5.576 + .064  =  75%
```

INDIVIDUAL WEEKLY AVERAGE - G. WILLIS = 97 %

<u>*COMPANY EXHIBIT NO. 4A*</u>

| CUTTERS | 4/14 HRS. | 73.8%* DAILY PROD. | LATE/ ABSENT | 4/15 HRS. | 79%* DAILY PROD. | LATE/ ABSENT |
|---------|------|-------|-------------|------|-------|-------------|
| W. Ross | 8 | 287,512 | | 8 | 437,496 | |
| S. Mattingly | 8 | 116,000/union mtg | | 8 | 348,000 | |
| D. Turner | Vacation | | | Vacation | | |
| G. Willis | 8 | 141,652 | | 8 | 161,416 | |
| V. Jenner | 8 | 244,326 | | 8 | 160,206 | |
| M. Blake | 8 | 143,200 | | 8 | 52,845 | |
| D. Hyatt | 8 | 212,740/union mtg | | 8 | 263,063 | |
| F. Mercer | 8 | union mtg/janitor | | 7.5 | Janitor | |
| H. Lawson | 8 | Baler | | 8 | Baler | |
| Daily Total | | 1,145,430 | | | 1,423,026 | |

| CUTTERS | 4/16 HRS. | 91%* DAILY PROD. | LATE/ ABSENT | 4/17 HRS. | 76%* DAILY PROD. | LATE/ ABSENT |
|---------|------|-------|-------------|------|-------|-------------|
| W. Ross | 8 | 529,000 | | 8 | 450,000 | |
| S. Mattingly | 8 | 262,800/union mtg | | 8 | 348,000 | |
| D. Turner | Vacation | | | Vacation | | |
| G. Willis | 8 | 197,798 | | 7.8 | 130,500 | |
| V. Jenner | 8 | 231,504 | | 8 | 119,767 | |
| M. Blake | 8 | 54,420 | | 8 | 30,000 | |
| D. Hyatt | 8 | 250,160 | | 8 | 219,480 | |
| F. Mercer | 8 | Janitor | | 8 | Janitor | |
| H. Lawson | 8 | Baler | | 8 | Baler | |
| Daily Total | | 1,525,682 | | | 1,297,747 | |

| CUTTERS | 4/18 HRS. | 112%* DAILY PROD. | LATE/ ABSENT |
|---------|------|-------|-------------|
| W. Ross | 8 | 515,240 | |
| S. Mattingly | 8 | 484,000 | |
| D. Turner | Vacation | | |
| G. Willis | 8 | 155,584 | |
| V. Jenner | 8 | 218,590 | |
| M. Blake | 8 | 13,000 | |
| D. Hyatt | 8 | 214,054 | |
| F. Mercer | 8 | Janitor | |
| H. Lawson | 8 | Baler | |
| Daily Total | | 1,600,468 | |

Weekly Cutting Total = 6,992,353

*Daily Cutting Percent for G. Willis; see Company Exhibit No. 4C.

*COMPANY EXHIBIT NO. 4B*

DAILY CUTTING REPORT

OPERATOR  WILLIS                              NO.  Die Press
HRS. WORKED     8          DATE 4-14-05

| ORDER NO. | SHEETS | CUTS OUT | WEIGHT | PRODUCTION | REMARKS |
|---|---|---|---|---|---|
| 1921-1 | 24,663 | 4 | 28 | 98,652 | Partial |
| 3150-1 | 18,500 | 2 | 24 | 37,000 | Complete |
| 3015-1 | 650 | 2 | 24 | 1,300 | " |
| 2693-1 | 650 | 2 | 70 | 1,300 | " |
| 2856-2 | 1,700 | 2 | 70 | 3,400 | " |

Daily Cutting Total                           141,652

DAILY CUTTING REPORT

OPERATOR  WILLIS                              NO.  Die Press
HRS. WORKED     8          DATE 4-15-05

| ORDER NO. | SHEETS | CUTS OUT | WEIGHT | PRODUCTION | REMARKS |
|---|---|---|---|---|---|
| 1921-1 | 3,000 | 4 | 28 | 12,000 | Partial |
| 3221-3 | 2,667 | 6 | 24 | 16,002 | Complete |
| 2179-1 | 32,427 | 2 | 28 | 64,854 | " |
| 2807-2 | 1,375 | 8 | 20 | 11,000 | " |
| 3253-1 | 1,600 | 10 | 24 | 16,000 | " |
| 3149-1 | 1,313 | 8 | 70 | 10,504 | " |
| 3145-1 | 1,313 | 8 | 70 | 10,504 | " |
| 2949-1 | 2,569 | 8 | 80 | 20,552 | " |

Daily Cutting Total                           161,416

DAILY CUTTING REPORT

OPERATOR  WILLIS                              NO.  Die Press
HRS. WORKED     8          DATE 4-16-05

| ORDER NO. | SHEETS | CUTS OUT | WEIGHT | PRODUCTION | REMARKS |
|---|---|---|---|---|---|
| 3150-1 | 500 | 2 | 24 | 1,000 | Shortage |
| 3272-3 | 5,500 | 2 | 24 | 11,000 | Complete |
| 2193-1 | 22,000 | 2 | 24 | 44,000 | " |
| 3181-1 | 2,500 | 8 | 20 | 20,000 | " |
| 3143-1 | 7,000 | 8 | 20 | 56,000 | " |
| 2783-3 | 1,833 | 6 | 28 | 10,998 | " |
| 3102-1 | 400 | 7 | 70 | 2,800 | " |
| 3159-1 | 6,500 | 8 | 20 | 52,000 | " |

Daily Cutting Total                           197,798

DAILY CUTTING REPORT

OPERATOR  WILLIS _____  NO.  Die Press _____
HRS. WORKED _____8_____  DATE _4-17-05_____

| ORDER NO. | SHEETS | CUTS OUT | WEIGHT | PRODUCTION | REMARKS |
|-----------|--------|----------|--------|------------|---------|
| 2610-1 | 11,000 | 5 | 24 | 55,000 | Complete |
| 2693-1 | 150 | 2 | 70 | 300 | Shortage-O.E. |
| 3015-1 | 100 | 2 | 24 | 200 | "    O.E. |
| 3261-1 | 3,250 | 8 | 20 | 26,000 | Partial-Lithed |
| 2636-1 | 9,500 | 4 | 28 | 38,000 | Partial-O.E. |
| 3132-1 | Used cut downs | 1 | 24 | 3,000 | Shortage |
| 3246-19 | Used cut downs | 1 | 24 | 8,000 | Shortage |

Daily Cutting Total                    130,500

Die problems on str. fr. Cutting #3261-1

DAILY CUTTING REPORT

OPERATOR  WILLIS _____  NO.  Die Press _____
HRS. WORKED _____8_____  DATE _4-18-05_____

| ORDER NO. | SHEETS | CUTS OUT | WEIGHT | PRODUCTION | REMARKS |
|-----------|--------|----------|--------|------------|---------|
| 2636-1 | 1,500 | 4 | 28 | 6,000 | Partial-O.E. |
| 2192-1 | 14,762 | 2 | 24 | 29,524 | Complete-O.E. |
| 1917-1 | 20,400 | 4 | 28 | 81,600 | Partial-O.E. |
|  | 2,760/s-5 out |  |  |  |  |
| 2015-1 | 2,340/s-4 out |  | 28 | 38,460 | Complete-O.E. |
|  | 1,700/s-4 out |  |  |  |  |

Daily Cutting Total                    155,584

<u>WILLIS</u>

4/14
```
14663 ÷ 283 = 87 X .039 = 3.393 + .005
 8500 ÷ 310 = 59 X .029 = 1.711 + .022
  650 ÷ 310 =  2 X .035 =  .070 + .022
  650 ÷ 283 =  2 X .035 =  .070 + .022
  700 ÷ 283 =  6 X .029 =  .174 + .022
              7.5 hrs.    5.418 + .093 = 73.8 %
```

4/15
```
 3000 ÷ 283 =  10 x .039 =  .390 + .005
 2667 ÷ 310 =   8 x .050 =  .400 + .022
22427 ÷ 283 = 114 x .029 = 3.306 + .022
 1375 ÷ 340 =   4 x .060 =  .240 + .022
 1600 ÷ 310 =   5 x .071 =  .355 + .022
 1313 ÷ 283 =   4 x .060 =  .240 + .022
 1313 ÷ 283 =   4 x .060 =  .240 + .022
 2569 ÷ 253 =  10 x .060 =  .600 + .022
              7.5 hrs.   5.771 + .159 =  79%
```

4/16
```
  500 ÷ 310 =  2 x .035 =  .070 + .005
15500 ÷ 310 = 17 x .038 =  .646 + .022
22000 ÷ 310 = 70 x .038 = 2.660 + .022
 2500 ÷ 340 =  7 x .060 =  .420 + .022
 7000 ÷ 340 = 20 x .060 = 1.200 + .022
 1833 ÷ 283 =  7 x .050 =  .350 + .022
  400 ÷ 283 =  2 x .071 =  .143 + .022
 6500 ÷ 340 = 20 x .060 = 1.200 + .022
             7.5 hrs.   6.688 + .159 =  91%
```

4/17
```
11000 ÷ 310 = 35 x .044 = 1.540 + .022
  150 ÷ 150 =  1 x .038 =  .038 + .005
  100 ÷ 100 =  1 x .038 =  .038 + .005
 2250 ÷ 340 =  9 x .073 =  .657 + .005
 6500 ÷ 283 = 33 x .056 = 1.848 + .005
 3000 ÷ 310 =  9 x .023 =  .207 + .005
 7000 ÷ 310 = 25 x .023 =  .575 + .005
             7.5 hrs.   4.903 + .052 =  76%
```

4/18
```
 1500 ÷ 283 =  6 x .056 =  .336 + .005
14762 ÷ 310 = 48 x .038 = 1.824 + .022
20400 ÷ 283 = 72 x .056 = 4.032 + .005
 2760 ÷ 283 = 10 x .085 =  .850 + .022
 2340 ÷ 283 =  8 x .056 =  .448 + .022
 1700 ÷ 283 =  6 x .141 =  .846 + .022
             7.5 hrs.   8.336 + .098 = 112%
```

INDIVIDUAL WEEKLY AVERAGE - G. WILLIS = 86%

29

## COMPANY EXHIBIT NO. 5A

EFFICIENCY PERCENTAGES:

CUTTER EXAMPLES

51,000 envelopes. Cut 6 out of 20# Stock    No Spring
     51,000 ÷ 6 = 8,500 sheets

1. std. sheets/board = 340
     8,500 ÷ 340 = 25 bds (or look up in Table)

2. From chart   6 cuts out = 0.05 hrs/bd
     0.05 x 25 = 1.25 hrs

3. Standard order time = 0.022 hrs (1 ticket)

4. Add above 1.25 + 0.022 = 1.272

Divide by actual hours - if 1.272 were actual hours, then efficiency would be 100%.

If 2 hours were taken, efficiency would be 63.6%.

## *COMPANY EXHIBIT NO. 5B*

### DIE CUTTING EFFICIENCY: STANDARD HOURS PER BOARD

| CUTS OUT | REG.ORDERS − SPRING .001 | REG.ORDERS + SPRING .001 | COMB.CUTTING 3 BDS − SPRING .001 | COMB.CUTTING + SPRING .001 | SM. ORDERS − SPRING .001 | SM. ORDERS + SPRING .001 | HIGH QUAL WEDDS. − SPRING .001 | HIGH QUAL WEDDS. + SPRING .001 | D.E. − SPRING .001 | D.E. + SPRING .001 | LRG. DIES − SPRING .001 | LRG. DIES + SPRING .001 |
|---|---|---|---|---|---|---|---|---|---|---|---|---|
| 1 | .023 | .024 | .028 | .029 | .027 | .028 | | | | | .029 | .030 |
| 2 | .029 | .031 | .033 | .035 | .035 | .037 | | | | | .038 | .040 |
| 3 | .034 | .037 | .038 | .041 | .042 | .045 | | | .037 | .040 | .047 | .050 |
| 4 | .039 | .043 | .044 | .048 | .049 | .053 | .049 | .054 | .044 | .048 | .056 | .060 |
| 5 | .044 | .050 | .049 | .054 | .056 | .062 | .055 | .060 | .050 | .055 | | |
| 6 | .050 | .056 | .054 | .060 | .063 | .070 | .061 | .067 | .056 | .055 | | |
| 7 | .055 | .062 | .059 | .067 | .071 | .078 | .066 | .074 | .063 | .070 | | |
| 8 | .060 | .069 | .065 | .073 | .078 | .086 | .072 | .081 | .069 | .078 | | |
| 9 | .066 | .075 | .070 | .079 | .085 | .095 | .078 | .087 | .075 | .085 | | |
| 10 | .071 | .081 | .075 | .086 | .092 | .103 | .083 | .094 | .082 | .092 | | |
| 11 | .076 | .088 | .081 | .092 | .099 | .111 | .089 | .101 | .088 | .100 | | |
| 12 | .081 | .094 | .086 | .099 | .107 | .119 | .095 | .107 | .095 | .107 | | |
| 13 | .087 | .100 | .091 | .105 | .114 | .128 | .100 | .114 | | | | |
| 14 | .092 | .107 | .096 | .111 | .121 | .136 | .106 | .121 | | | | |
| 15 | .122 | .138 | .126 | .142 | .128 | .144 | .112 | .128 | | | | |
| 16 | .129 | .146 | .133 | .150 | .135 | .152 | | | | | | |
| 17 | .136 | .154 | .140 | .158 | .143 | .161 | | | | | | |
| 18 | .143 | .162 | .147 | .166 | .150 | .169 | | | | | | |
| 19 | .149 | .170 | .154 | .174 | .167 | .177 | | | | | | |
| 20 | .156 | .178 | .161 | .182 | .169 | .185 | | | | | | |
| 21 | .163 | .186 | .168 | .190 | .171 | .194 | | | | | | |
| 22 | .170 | .194 | .175 | .198 | .179 | .202 | | | | | | |
| 23 | .177 | .202 | .182 | .206 | .186 | .210 | | | | | | |
| 24 | .184 | .210 | .189 | .214 | .193 | .218 | | | | | | |
| 25 | .191 | .218 | | | .200 | .227 | | | | | | |
| 26 | .198 | .225 | | | .207 | .235 | | | | | | |
| 27 | .205 | .233 | | | .215 | .243 | | | | | | |
| 28 | .212 | .241 | | | .222 | .251 | | | | | | |
| 29 | .219 | .249 | | | .229 | .260 | | | | | | |
| 30 | .226 | .257 | | | .236 | .268 | | | | | | |
| 31 | .233 | .265 | | | .243 | .276 | | | | | | |
| 32 | .239 | .273 | | | .251 | .285 | | | | | | |
| 33 | .246 | .281 | | | .258 | .293 | | | | | | |
| 34 | .253 | .289 | | | .265 | .301 | | | | | | |
| 35 | .260 | .297 | | | .272 | .309 | | | | | | |
| 36 | .267 | .305 | | | .279 | .318 | | | | | | |
| 37 | .274 | .313 | | | .287 | .326 | | | | | | |
| 38 | .281 | .321 | | | .294 | .334 | | | | | | |
| 39 | | | | | .301 | .342 | | | | | | |
| 40 | | | | | .308 | .351 | | | | | | |
| 41 | | | | | .315 | .359 | | | | | | |
| 42 | | | | | .323 | .367 | | | | | | |
| 43 | | | | | .330 | .375 | | | | | | |
| 44 | | | | | .337 | .384 | | | | | | |
| 45 | | | | | .344 | .392 | | | | | | |
| 46 | | | | | .351 | .400 | | | | | | |
| 47 | | | | | .359 | .408 | | | | | | |
| 48 | | | | | .366 | .417 | | | | | | |
| 49 | | | | | .373 | .425 | | | | | | |
| 50 | | | | | .380 | .433 | | | | | | |
| 51 | | | | | .387 | .441 | | | | | | |
| 52 | | | | | .395 | .450 | | | | | | |
| 53 | | | | | .402 | .458 | | | | | | |
| 54 | | | | | .409 | .466 | | | | | | |
| 55 | | | | | .416 | .475 | | | | | | |
| 56 | | | | | .423 | .483 | | | | | | |
| 57 | | | | | .431 | .491 | | | | | | |
| 58 | | | | | .438 | .499 | | | | | | |
| 59 | | | | | .445 | .508 | | | | | | |
| 60 | | | | | .452 | .516 | | | | | | |

*COMPANY EXHIBIT NO. 5C*

STANDARD SHEETS PER BOARD FOR DIE CUTTING

| Substance Weight | No. Sheets Per Board for Std. Collar Dies | No. Sheets Per Board for Low Collar Dies | No. Sheets Per Board for Adjustable Dies |
|---|---|---|---|
| 13 | 390 | 320 | 287 |
| 16 | 367 | 301 | 270 |
| 20 | 340 | 279 | 250 |
| 24 | 310 | 254 | 227 |
| 28 | 283 | 232 | 208 |
| 32 | 253 | 208 | 187 |
| 36 | 227 | 186 | 167 |
| 40 | 198 | 163 | 145 |
| 46 | 170 | 149 | 125 |
| 70 | 283 | | |

|  | Sheets per Board |
|---|---|
| Window Die Cutting Sub. 20-24 | 150 |
| Printed Stock | 150 |
| Rag contents Bonds | 222 |
| (Sulphite Bonds take Regular Standard) | |
| Laid Finish - Sulphite Bonds | 283 |
| Mercury Air Mail (when cardboards are used) | 222 |
| Rough Fancy Finish (204, 218, 500 & similar papers) | 125125 |
| Warren's White Wove Antique | 250 |
| Cortlea #28 | 167 |
| Artemis #28 | 167 |
| Strathmore Bouquet | 167 |
| Jute (Ne'er Tear) | 167 |
| Strathmore Pastelle | 227 |
| Garbardine #24 | 283 |
| Garbardine #28 | 253 |
| Deckle Edge in 250 packages | 90 |
| Charmay (for artificial deckle) | 90 |
| Chroma #24 | 227 |
| Chroma #28 | 283 |
| Chroma #32 | 283 |
| Beau Brilliant #24 | 253 |
| Beau Brilliant #28 | 227 |
| Beau Brilliant #32 | 110 |
| Red Wallet | 253 |

| | Sheets per Board |
|---|---|
| All customers stock (except for large runs such as life orders) | 222 |
| Commercial Dies for Mch 35 | 253 |

*Low dies - 2-7/8 or under
Speeds for dextrine gums

| | | |
|---|---|---|
| Standard Wide Range | 18,000 | 300 RPM |
| RH | 42,000 | 700 RPM |
| Kit | 24,000 | 400 RPM |
| Window Machine | 15,000 | 250 RPM |

## *COMPANY EXHIBIT NO. 5C (continued)*

### Exceptions to above

| | | |
|---|---|---|
| Bulking - No bands | 13,000 | 218 RPM |
| Bulking - Handbanding (2 women) | 11,500 | 192 RPM |
| Flat Fold - Handbanding (2 women) | 12,500 | 208 RPM |
| Envelopes 5-3/4" - 6-1/4" inclusive height | 13,000 | 218 RPM |
| Envelopes over 6-1/4" height | 12,500 | 208 RPM |
| Open windows on regular wide range | 12,500 | 208 RPM |
| LO | 7,200 | 120 RPM |
| SO | 16,500 | 275 RPM |

### Machine Speed for Resin Gum

| | | |
|---|---|---|
| Standard Wide Range | 16,500 | 275 RPM |
| RH | 24,000 | 400 RPM |
| Kit | 21,000 | 350 RPM |

Runs under 25,000, (after change) best possible speed

### Procedure for Controlling Machine Speeds

The operator and adjuster will work together to attain the maximum speed applicable to the order being run; but if it is not possible to reach maximum speed, the adjuster will notify the foreman. At this point, the foreman and the adjuster may determine how much to reduce the speed or the foreman may want to have the head adjuster check into the problem to help in determining the best practical speed to run the order.

## *COMPANY EXHIBIT NO. 6*

December 5, year 2

Subject:  DISCIPLINARY STEPS

Attention:  All employees

This company agreed as a non-contractual matter to set forth in writing its policy concerning disciplinary steps involving members of the bargaining unit. The four steps are as follows:

(1)  A verbal warning by foreman or other supervisor, with a member of the Union committee as a witness;

(2)  A written warning to be delivered to the employee, with a copy to the Union;

(3)  A three-day suspension without pay, documented by a written report, with copy to the Union; and

(4)  Finally, dismissal. Reasons to be given to the employee in writing, with copy to the Union.

OLDE TOWNE ENVELOPE COMPANY

*COMPANY EXHIBIT NO. 7*

Down Time in the Folding Department

. . .

2. From Lack of Production in Cutting Department
Week ending April   5:  = 38.75 hours
    "       "      "    12:  = 26.25 hours
    "       "      "    19:  = 28.5 hours
    "       "      "    26:  = 24.5 hours
    "       "    May   3:  = 10.25 hours
    "       "      "    10:  =  1.24 hours

. . .

*UNION EXHIBIT NO. 1*

TENNESSEE BUREAU OF EMPLOYMENT SERVICES
ADMINISTRATOR'S RECONSIDERATION DECISION

Claimant:  George Willis   Soc. Sec. No. XXX-XX-XXXX
Employer's Name: Olde Towne Envelope Co.


ISSUE: Discharge
FACTS:      A determination dated May 21, year 5 held that claimant
was discharged by Olde Towne Envelope Co. for just cause in
connection with the work and suspended benefits until claimant worked
in six weeks of covered employment, earned $360.00 or more, and was
otherwise eligible.  Claim for week ending May 3, year 5, was
disallowed.

On May 23, year 5, claimant requested reconsideration on the grounds
that he was discharged under conditions that do not warrant a
disqualification.  He stated the contract contains no provisions as
to the amount of work that is required each day.  Claimant states
that at no time was he told the percentage of production he had to
meet was increased.

Information obtained during a fact-finding interview indicates that
claimant was not aware that the company had changed the cutting
percentage from 85% to 100%.  However, during the three weeks prior
to the date claimant was discharged, his average was 101%.

The employer discharged claimant because of unsatisfactory cutting
production.  This is a discharge under non-disqualifying conditions
because the employer has failed to establish that claimant's
inability to perform work to its satisfaction was the result of
negligence or misconduct on the part of claimant.

DECISION: Determination dated May 21, year 5, is amended.  Claimant
was discharged by Olde Towne Envelope Co. under non-disqualifying
conditions.  The suspension of benefits is removed.  Claim for week
ending May 3, year 5, is allowed.
Total amount charged to Olde Towne is increased from $0.00 to
$2,300.00.

*UNION EXHIBIT NO. 2*

TENNESSEE BUREAU OF EMPLOYMENT SERVICES
ADMINISTRATOR'S DECISION FOLLOWING EMPLOYER APPEAL
November 15, year 5
Claimant: George Willis    Soc. Sec. No. xxx-xx-xxxx
Employer's Name: Olde Towne Envelope Co.

ISSUE: Discharge

PRIOR DECISION: By a decision on reconsideration, mailed August 1, year 5, the Administrator held that the claimant was discharged by Olde Towne Envelope Co. without just cause in connection with his work, imposing no disqualifications for benefit rights, increased the total amount chargeable to the employer from zero to $2,300.00, and allowed the first claim for the week ending May 3. On August 13, year 5, the company appealed. The appeal hearing date was set for October 30, year 5. Parties notified of the date, hour, and place of the hearing: George Willis, Claimant; Martin Spiegal for Olde Towne Envelope Co.

FACTS: Claimant filed an application for determination of benefits rights on April 28, year 5, with respect to a benefits year beginning April 27, year 5. He filed his first claim for benefits for the week ending May 3, year 5, on the basis of total unemployment. Prior to filing said claim, Claimant was last employed by the Olde Towne Envelope Co. in Memphis, Tennessee, from October Year 1 until his discharge on April 21, year 5, as a machine operator. Claimant was discharged on April 21, year 5 for low production. This Employer claims that Claimant's weekly production averaged less than 100% for the week's work. The Claimant was under the impression that 85% was acceptable and was never told or informed that he was expected to produce 100%.

The Claimant received a three-day disciplinary layoff in December of Year 4 for inconsistent production and was warned at this time that further violations could possibly result in his dismissal. He was also informed that he would have to make a substantial improvement. Between the time of layoff and the time of his discharge the Claimant averaged 94% production. The Employer considered the Claimant to have made a substantial improvement subsequent to his layoff in December and the Claimant was informed by his foreman on April 18, year 5 that his percentages were acceptable.

The employer discharged claimant because of unsatisfactory cutting production. Information obtained during a fact-finding interview indicated that claimant was not aware that the company had changed the cutting percentage from 85% to 100%. This is a discharge under non-disqualifying conditions because the employer has failed to establish that claimant's inability to perform to work to its satisfaction was the result of negligence or misconduct on the part of claimant.

DECISION: Decision on reconsideration mailed August 1, year 5 is upheld. Claimant was discharged by Olde Towne Envelope Co. under non-disqualifying conditions.

# Elkorn Electric Company

## Table of Contents

NOTES

# A. Caption

IN THE MATTER OF ARBITRATION BETWEEN:

ELKORN ELECTRIC COMPANY )
ST. LOUIS, MISSOURI )
)
AND ) RE: DONNA HAND POLSON
) Bumping
INTERNATIONAL UNION OF ELECTRICAL, )
TELEVISION, AND MACHINE WORKERS )
LOCAL NO. 711

Appearances:

For the Union: Henry Powell

For the Company: Thomas Hamm

Date: April 26, year 2

Place: St. Louis, Missouri

## B. Examination of Union Witnesses

### 1. Donna Polson, Grievant

#### a. Direct Examination by Union Advocate

*Mr. Powell:*

Q: Will you state your name, please?

A: Donna Polson.

Q: How long have you been employed at Elkorn Electric?

A: Over three years.

Q: Will you describe what occurred on November 17, year 2, that led to this grievance?

A: My supervisor told me that I was going to be laid off as of Friday, November 19th, and that Nell Casey would talk to me later.

Q: What happened after that?

A: On the 18th, Nell Casey came up and called me and Edna Puckett in.

Q: Who else was there?

A: Bob Freeman, Jerry Frank, and the supervisor.

Q: Who is Jerry Frank?

A: He was our Union representative, a Chief Steward.

Q: Then what happened?

A: Edna and I asked if we could bump any probation people. The Company said that we could, but then changed the subject to the Wiring Department and they never gave us a chance to talk to the probation people.

Q: You asked for the right to bump these probationers, right?

A: Yes, we did.

Q: What happened next?

A: The next day I was talking to Dan Amos; Dan had also been laid off and he told me that he got to bump the probation people in the Paint Shop.

Q: Did Mr. Amos have more or less seniority than you?

A: A week less.

Q: What else happened?

A: We called Nell Casey to ask why he got to do this and we were told that we were being saved for the electrical jobs in Wiring, the TOW-2 operation.

Q: Did you have any more conversations with Miss Casey?

A: Several times. I found out that there was another probation person out in Stores. I heard that Red Snelling got to go out to Stores and bump one of the probation people. He also had less time than I did. I asked Nell why all of these people were getting to bump and not us? She said that there was nothing she could do about it. She said that there was a big layoff and that she was having meetings with Walter Still, the superintendent over in Wiring.

Q: Is that what you were waiting for, an appointment with Mr. Still?

A: Yes. I was also told to call Foreman Art Raven if I wanted a job in the Warehouse, but Raven told me that there wasn't any work out there.

Q: Nell Casey asked you to call him, yourself, and ask about the job?

A: Yes.

Q: This painting job that you were talking about, had you done any of this work earlier?

A: Yes, we were very low on work in Sheet Metal, and in order to keep us as long as they could they were taking us and putting us in the Paint Shop to perform their duties over there. When I worked at Electric Motor Company, I also did some painting work.

Q: Did you have more seniority than Red Snelling?

A: Yes, I think I had about a week on him.

Q: Did you finally get interviewed by Mr. Still?

A: Yes, the following week. We had an interview sometime during the week of the 22nd and then I got a call from Nell saying that I could do the Wiring job. She asked me whether I wanted the job or to be laid off. I took the job.

Q: And you came back to work December 1st?

A: Yes, sir.

**Q:** Did you have a chance to compare the pay rate of the Wiring job versus the job you didn't get in the Painting area?

**A:** I had no idea at the time what the Wiring job was going to pay, but I think I lost about sixty cents an hour.

**Q:** For what period of time?

**A:** Well, I was in Wiring for eight months before I got to bid on a higher paying job.

**Q:** You were aware that Dan Amos got the probation painter's job, weren't you?

**A:** Yes, I was.

**Q:** What was the purpose of filing this grievance?

**A:** I felt that a lot of people were out on the street—you're not only talking individuals, you're also talking families—and I didn't feel that the Company did it the right way. I felt like we were being set aside.

**Q:** Did you receive any unemployment when you were out?

**A:** No.

**Q:** Why not?

**A:** We received short-week contractual benefits, which kind of led us to believe that we were going to be back to work the next day.

**Q:** Donna, are you positive that in your meeting with Miss Casey that you requested the right to displace probationary employees?

**A:** Yes, I am.

**Q:** No further questions.

### b. Cross-Examination by Company Advocate

*Mr. Hamm:*
[to be supplied by student]

## 2. Edna Puckett, Employee

### a. Direct Examination by Union Advocate

*Mr. Powell:*

**Q:** State your name, please.

**A:** Edna Puckett.

**Q:** How long have you worked for Elkorn Electric?

**A:** Since May 12, year 1.

**Q:** Do you remember a meeting that you and the grievant were involved with on November 18, year 2?

**A:** Yes. It was the night that we were told that we were going to be laid off. In the group meeting with Sam Polson, Jerry Frank, and Bob Freeman, we discussed the placement of probationary people. Donna asked if we had any chance of taking the probationary people's jobs. Nell said yes, but that there were twenty openings in Walter Still's area and she was going to get us an interview with him.

**Q:** When was your last day of work?

**A:** The 19th.

**Q:** Did you have any conversations with Nell Casey after that?

**A:** Yes, sir. I called the Monday following our layoff, which would be the 22nd, and I talked to her again on the 24th and the 29th about the interviews with Walter Still and about the different people that were on probation and what bumping rights we had and so on.

**Q:** Were you aware of any people junior to you displacing probationaries?

**A:** None lower than myself, no.

**Q:** Were probationaries ever brought up at your discussions after that with Miss Casey?

**A:** She told me that there were some probationary people, but that we were going to have an interview with Mr. Still on the Wiring job.

**Q:** How long did you stay on layoff?

**A:** I believe I came back to work on December 2nd.

**Q:** No further questions.

## b. Cross-Examination by Company Advocate

*Mr. Hamm:*
[to be supplied by student]

## 3. Jerry Frank, Chief Steward

### a. Direct Examination by Union Advocate

*Mr. Powell:*

**Q:** Will you state your name, please?

**A:** Jerry Frank.

**Q:** How long have you worked at Elkorn Electric?

**A:** Approximately five-and-a-half years.

**Q:** Were you the Chief Steward during this grievance?

**A:** Yes.

**Q:** You remember a meeting which involved Donna Polson, Nell Casey, and several others?

**A:** Yes, it was on the 18th of November, year 2. The Company told me that there would be a layoff on the 17th and I called Nell and asked her if I could attend the meetings.

**Q:** What happened at that meeting?

**A:** Well, she called in people to let them know that they were to be laid off and that she would try to do everything she could to see that they could get a job immediately by checking the seniority lists.

**Q:** Were Ms. Polson and Ms. Puckett at that meeting?

**A:** Yes.

**Q:** Was there any discussion about probationaries at that time?

**A:** Yes, Donna brought it up. She asked if there were any probationaries that she could displace. Nell Casey said yes, but that there were going to be some openings in Wiring and that they were going to try to place as many people as they could.

**Q:** No further questions.

### b. Cross-Examination by Company Advocate

*Mr. Hamm:*
[to be supplied by the student]

## 4. Rick Golden, Union Local President

### a. Direct Examination by Union Advocate

*Mr. Powell:*

**Q:** Your name for the record, please?

**A:** Rick Golden.

**Q:** How long have you worked at Elkorn Electric?

**A:** For about thirty-seven years.

**Q:** You hold a Union position?

**A:** Yes, I am President of Local 711.

**Q:** Did you investigate this grievance?

**A:** Yes, I did.

**Q:** Can you explain what this is and where you received it? This is Union Exhibit 1.

**A:** This is a copy which I requested from the Personnel Department. It is a record of all the activities Donna Polson has done since she has been employed with Elkorn Electric.

**Q:** Does this page show her seniority?

**A:** It shows her seniority date as 2/16/01. It shows she went to Tube Assembler B on 8/23/02 and then did not have any more activity until 12/1/02, where she exercised her seniority.

**Q:** This Preliminary Assembler, 12/1/02, that is the Wiring area there?

**A:** Yes.

**Q:** Would you describe what this is? This is Union Exhibit 2.

**A:** This is the job record of Dan Amos.

**Q:** What is his seniority date?

**A:** Well, the date is 2/23/01. He had one week less seniority than Donna.

**Q:** Would you explain what this is? This is Union Exhibit 3.

**A:** This is a copy of the page showing that Amos exercised his seniority, gone from Sheet Metal Machine Working A to a Painter's C. It was issued 12/15, but the effective date was 11/22/02.

**Q:** So he was assigned to that job on 11/22 according to the Company's records, right?

**A:** That's correct.

**Q:** Please describe what this is; it's Union Exhibit 4.

**A:** This is the job record of Red Snelling.

**Q:** What is his seniority date?

**A:** 2/23/01.

**Q:** On 11/23/02, there is an abbreviation, SE, in the "shift" column. What does that mean?

**A:** Seniority Exercised.

**Q:** He displaced somebody or used his seniority to get to the Stores Clerk, Tool Stores position, is that right?

**A:** That's correct.

**Q:** Look at Union Exhibit 5 and explain to the Arbitrator what this is.

**A:** This is a page showing that Snelling exercised his seniority. The Company furnishes us with a copy of these. Again, it was issued on 12/15 and it shows the effect date of 11/23/02 and here, again, seniority exercised.

**Q:** Did Mr. Snelling have less seniority than the grievant?

**A:** Yes, he had one week less.

**Q:** Did you request time cards from the Company?

**A:** Yes, for Dan Amos.

**Q:** Is this a copy of the card that you received? This is Union Exhibit 6.

**A:** Yes. I requested three weeks, 11/21, 11/28, and 12/5. This is 11/21.

**Q:** This is Union Exhibit 7. Can you explain what this is?

**A:** This is week ending 11/28. It is Amos' time card which shows that he is assigned to station 2983 and worked 32 hours. The Personnel records show that he exercised his seniority on December 15 and went on to Painter's C, which is station 2983.

**Q:** This is Union Exhibit 8. Can you explain what this is?

**A:** This is the week ending 12/5. The station number was 2983, which is the Painting area, and it shows him working thirty-nine and six-tenths hours that week in that station.

**Q:** Looking at the calendar and going through the time cards, how many days are we talking about?

**A:** Eleven days altogether from the 19th, Polson's last day at work, until December 1st, the day that the Company placed her on the TOW-2 work.

**Q:** How many days were working days?

**A:** The working days would be the 22nd through the 26th, the 29th and 30th, and also the 27th and 28th, the overtime days.

**Q:** Your position is that the 27th and 28th were working days?

**A:** Yes.

**Q:** The 25th and 26th were holidays. Would you consider them as working days?

**A:** Yes, employees are paid for holidays. She was paid for them under another clause in the contract.

**Q:** No further questions.

b. Cross-Examination by Company Advocate

*Mr. Hamm:*
[to be supplied by the student]

# C. Examination of Company Witnesses

## 1. Nell Casey, Labor Relations Representative

### a. Direct Examination by Company Advocate

*Mr. Hamm:*

Q:   Would you give us your full name?

A:   Nell Casey.

Q:   By whom are you employed?

A:   Elkorn Electric Company.

Q:   What is your position?

A:   Labor Relations Representative.

Q:   How long have you occupied this position?

A:   Since I was hired, and I have been here about twenty-seven-and-a-half years.

Q:   What are your primary duties and responsibilities as a Labor Relations Representative?

A:   Contract interpretation, grievance investigations, handling layoff situations, and interviews.

Q:   How long have you have been handling layoffs at the Electronics and Space Division?

A:   As long as I have been here.

Q:   Currently, does anyone besides yourself handle layoffs?

A:   Joe Crown, my boss, helps me.

Q:   Who has the primary responsibility for doing all the work associated with layoffs and bumpings?

A:   Me.

Q:   Can you tell me what departments were affected by the November year 2 layoff?

A:   Machine Shop, Inspection, Plating, and Sheet Metal.

Q:   How many employees were affected?

A:   The original layoff involved 67 people, but a lot of them had bumping rights, so I don't really know the exact number.

Q:   Now, what is your duty with respect to a particular employee who has been affected by a layoff?

A:   Well, if they have more than five years, they bump within their occupational grouping first. After that, they can bump anybody in the plant with less seniority whose job they can immediately perform.

Q:   What about persons such as the grievant who had less than five years?

A:   She had to exhaust her occupational group first, and then she had the right to bump probationers or foreigners, or to take a job that was open to outside hires.

Q:   What is a foreigner?

A:   Another employee who is working outside of his occupational group.

Q:   What kind of qualification obligations would a bumping employee have?

A:   They would have to be able to go onto the job and immediately perform that job.

Q:   What about if they take a job that is open to new hires?

A:   They have up to two weeks to perform that job satisfactorily.

Q:   You visited the B shift employees on or about November 18?

A:   Yes.

Q:   Did you meet with them as a group or did you meet with them individually?

A:   There were three of them that I talked with individually later, but they knew that they were being laid off and they all came in at the same time, I believe.

Q:   You recall what you said to them as a group?

A:   The very first thing I said was that they had to exhaust their bumping rights in their occupational group first. There was no place for Donna and Edna to go in their group. I told them that they had a right under the contract to bump probationers or people who were working away from their occupational group. I said that we had somewhere between 15 and 20 openings in Electronic Assembly.

Q:   Did Ms. Polson ask you about probationers that she could bump at that time?

A:   Not at that time, no.

Q:   Anything else you can remember telling them at that time?

A:   Well, for the ones that expressed an interest in Electronic Assembly, I wrote out the RMA color code for them so they would know that when they went for their interviews.

**Q:** What is the RMA color code?

**A:** It is the universal wiring code. You order wire by the color codes.

**Q:** Did you ever meet individually with Ms. Polson?

**A:** I don't remember.

**Q:** Did she ever ask you if she could bump a probationary employee?

**A:** Yes. She mentioned it when I told her that she could replace a probationary employee.

**Q:** What happened then?

**A:** She asked where there were probationary employees, but I didn't have a list of the departments with me. I said I would check into it, but she didn't tell me what kind of job she was qualified to handle. She did not mention the Paint Shop whatsoever.

**Q:** Did she ever come back to you before she had made an election as to where she would go and to check for probationary employees?

**A:** No, she didn't. The first contact that I had was from Rick Golden, who asked why she couldn't bump into the job that Dan Amos had.

**Q:** In advising people that they are being laid off, do you review with them all the probationary employees?

**A:** No. I ask them where they think they might have qualifications where they could bump. If we have a probationary in that particular job, then I'd set up an interview with the foreman.

**Q:** Why don't you review all the probationary employees and all the jobs?

**A:** There isn't time. Currently, there are 1,463 employees at the Electronics and Space Division and there were more then.

**Q:** Approximately how many different job classifications were actively filled at that time?

**A:** Oh, 300, maybe 350.

**Q:** Involving a wide variety of skills?

**A:** Yes.

**Q:** How long have you used this particular system?

**A:** Since I have been with the Company.

**Q:** Was an award issued by Arbitrator Leon Brow concerning Roger Prim's grievance?

**A:** Yes.

**Q:** What was Mr. Prim's grievance?

**A:** He had been laid off; they reviewed his records and offered him a job that he had held before, in Inspection, and he said that he wouldn't take that job. There was another employee, less senior to him, in Inspection. They did not tell him about that other employee and that was his grievance.

**Q:** Was the grievance denied or sustained?

**A:** Denied.

**Q:** Since Arbitrator Brow's decision, have there been any grievances filed regarding the manner in which you approach employees and advise them of their bumping rights during layoff situations?

**A:** No.

**Q:** Did any of the employees affected by the layoff file a grievance?

**A:** Only Ms. Polson.

**Q:** Did you treat Ms. Polson any differently than you did any other employee?

**A:** No.

**Q:** If, in fact, Ms. Polson pursued with you the question of probationary employees and said that she wanted to move into the Paint Shop or wherever, would she have been entitled to bump?

**A:** Had she specified a particular department, yes, she would have been eligible for an interview.

**Q:** What happens if they don't mention it to you?

**A:** I don't say anything about it.

**Q:** You've got dozens of employees to be accommodated, you have a lot of interviews to set up, and you have only five days to do it, is that correct?

**A:** In some cases, I only have two.

**Q:** Do you recall any conversation you had with Ms. Polson concerning taking the job in the TOW-2 Electronic Assembly?

**A:** Yes, I told her that we had openings in there to outside hires and I asked her if she would like to have an interview; she said yes. I told her I would set it up and I got her phone number so that I could call to tell her what time the interview was set for.

**Q:** What was the first notice you had that Ms. Polson was dissatisfied with being transferred over to TOW-2?

**A:** I had a call from Mr. Golden and he asked me why I didn't offer her the job in the

Paint Shop. I told him that she didn't ask for it and that Dan Amos had bumped into the job. I told Golden that I would check and call him back. I did. Amos had already been bumped himself by Mr. Hammond, who had more seniority than Ms. Polson.

**Q:** When was Mr. Amos bumped by Mr. Hammond?

**A:** I believe Monday, the 22nd.

**Q:** And you told this to Mr. Golden?

**A:** Yes.

**Q:** When did Mr. Hammond actually step into the Painter's C job?

**A:** Mr. Hammond called me later and said that he still had four more days' vacation coming. Considering that the 25th and 26th were holidays, that would have meant that his first day on the job would have been December 1st. I notified the foreman that he wouldn't be reporting until December 1st, so the foreman went ahead and laid Amos off because there wasn't a lot of work out there. He notified Amos that he was being laid off effective the 26th, but the 24th was his last working day.

**Q:** Who had more seniority, Ms. Polson or Mr. Hammond?

**A:** Mr. Hammond.

**Q:** So if Ms. Polson had taken the Painter C job instead of Amos, she would have been bumped off that job in any event, anyway, correct?

**A:** Right.

**Q:** Mr. Snelling was in Stores around this time, right?

**A:** Yes.

**Q:** He had less seniority than Ms. Polson?

**A:** Yes.

**Q:** Did he bump someone to get that job in Stores?

**A:** No, he took an opening. It was open to outside hires.

**Q:** Would that have been available to Ms. Polson?

**A:** Yes.

**Q:** Did you mention the Stores job to her?

**A:** No, sir.

**Q:** Did she ask about other jobs?

**A:** Yes. I told her about three departments in which we had openings—Stores, Electronic Assembly, and maybe some in Electronic Test Ignitions.

**Q:** This was at the group meeting?

**A:** Yes.

**Q:** Did she pursue the Stores job?

**A:** No.

**Q:** Were there other probationary employees at the plant at the time this layoff occurred?

**A:** Yes.

**Q:** There were several probationary employees who were subject to bumping during this particular layoff?

**A:** Yes.

**Q:** Is the language of Article 7 the same or different from the language that existed at the time of the Brow arbitration award?

**A:** Identical.

**Q:** Do you recall any telephone calls from Ms. Polson during the period of her layoff?

**A:** I don't remember who all called; there were so many.

**Q:** Did you try to steer Ms. Polson away from the Paint Shop and into Electronic Assembly?

**A:** No, sir.

**Q:** Did you try to discourage Ms. Polson from exercising her seniority rights in any area?

**A:** No, sir.

**Q:** Did you try to talk her out of bumping probationary employees in any fashion?

**A:** No, sir.

**Q:** Did you place her within five working days?

**A:** Yes, sir.

**Q:** What are five working days?

**A:** Monday through Friday except for holidays.

**Q:** Is that the system you've always used?

**A:** Yes, sir.

**Q:** Have you ever counted holidays or weekend days?

**A:** No. I try not to work on those days myself if I can keep from it, number one. Number two is, you have to set up interviews with supervisors, and, basically, they are not here on those days to set up interviews with.

**Q:** In other words, it is practically impossible to go through this bumping procedure on a day that is not a regular workday?

**A:** That's right.

**Q:** Does the contract mention what workdays are?

**A:** Yes, sir. In Article 5, subparagraph a.

**Q:** And what does it define as workdays?

**A:** It calls it a work week, Monday through Friday.

**Q:** Has there ever been a Union grievance that you didn't place someone within five days, counting, perhaps, an intervening weekend or paid holiday?

**A:** No, sir.

**Q:** Employees who are laid off within a certain time period before a holiday receive holiday pay, correct?

**A:** The week preceding or the week in which the holiday falls. Even for a notification of a layoff, we don't count weekends or holidays; for example, if you are laid off on Friday and bump someone Friday, you don't go to the new job until Monday.

**Q:** Which days did Ms. Polson not get paid for?

**A:** The 22nd, 23rd, 24th, 29th, and 30th.

**Q:** Are you familiar with any prior claim by the Union to the effect that weekends or holidays ought to be counted as part of the five days involved in Section 7, subparagraph 'f'?

**A:** No, sir, never.

**Q:** In connection with this grievance, are you familiar with any claim stating that Ms. Polson had, in fact, asked to go to a probationary job and had been denied improperly?

**A:** No, sir.

**Q:** After employees make a choice as to whether or not they are going to bump a probationer or less senior person or move into a job that is posted for hire, can they change their minds and move into something else?

**A:** Yes, sir.

**Q:** And how do they go about doing that?

**A:** Simply contact me.

**Q:** What happened to Mr. Amos after Mr. Hammond bumped him?

**A:** He was laid off; he went onto the street.

**Q:** Is there a reason why he went to the street?

**A:** There was no place for him to go.

**Q:** No further questions.

---

### b. Cross-Examination by Union Advocate

*Mr. Powell:*

[to be supplied by student]

---

## 2. Joe Crown, Manager of Hourly Employees and Employee Relations

### a. Direct Examination by Company Advocate

*Mr. Hamm:*

**Q:** What is your name?

**A:** Joe Crown.

**Q:** What is your position at Elkorn Electric?

**A:** I am manager of hourly employees and labor relations.

**Q:** You are Ms. Casey's boss?

**A:** Yes, sir.

**Q:** Mr. Crown, were you involved in the handling of this particular grievance?

**A:** Yes, I was.

**Q:** Which grievance steps did you attend?

**A:** The Fifth Step Meeting in January of year 3.

**Q:** Who was present?

**A:** Myself, Bud Steele, Nell Casey, Ted Derren, and John Donald, President of the Company. The Union President, the Vice President, and the Plant Chairman were present for the Union.

**Q:** What was the nature of the grievance as it was explained to you by the Union at the meeting?

**A:** They felt it was unfair that the Company had allowed a person with less seniority than the grievant to work on a job during the time when she was not working.

**Q:** Similar to the grievance in the Leon Brow arbitration?

**A:** Yes.

9

Q: Was any claim made in the grievance, as required by the contract, that the Company had not placed Ms. Polson within five working days?

A: No.

Q: Was anything said at that time to the effect that Ms. Polson had requested in either specific or general terms that she be allowed to bump a probationer?
A: No, sir.
Q: No further questions

## b. Cross-Examination by Union Advocate

*Mr. Powell:*
[to be supplied by student]

## 3. Bud Steele, Director, Industrial Relations

### a. Direct Examination by Company Advocate

*Mr. Hamm:*
Q: Would you give us your full name?
A: Bud Steele.
Q: And what is your position at Elkorn?
A: Director, Industrial Relations.
Q: How long have you held that position?
A: A little over five years.
Q: Were you present at the Fifth Step Grievance Meeting on this grievance?
A: Yes, sir.
Q: What was the nature of the grievance, as you understood it?
A: Just as Mr. Crown testified.
Q: Did the Union raise any question as to whether or not Ms. Polson had been placed in a job in accordance with her seniority within five working days?
A: No, there was no question with regard to the five days.
Q: Has there ever been, in your time here at Elkorn, an issue raised by the Union as to the application of the five working days specified in Article 7, subparagraph f?
A: No, sir. The clear understanding is working days means Monday through Friday. The contract defines working day in Article 5, subparagraph a, I think.
Q: Do you count holidays?
A: No.
Q: At the Fifth Step, was there a claim that she had asked in specific terms to bump a

probationary employee and had not been allowed to do this?
A: There never was such a claim. The only thing we talked about was whether there were probationers and the answer was yes.
Q: Were there probationers other than in the Paint Department at that time?
A: Yes, sir, there were; there were probationers throughout the plant, some of which, of course, were occupying positions for which the grievant would not have had the qualifications.
Q: So, theoretically, the grievant might have had the seniority to displace a probationer?
A: But not the qualifications.
Q: Do you furnish seniority lists to the Union?
A: Yes.
Q: Why are the seniority lists furnished?
A: One of the contract provisions requires it.
Q: Other than the seniority lists, do you have any way to go back to construct who the probationers were?
A: We started per request of the Union and found that it would take well beyond this hearing date in order to reconstruct it. We would be able to do it, but it would be rather difficult.
Q: When were you asked to do this?
A: A couple of days ago.
Q: No further questions.

## b. Cross-Examination by Union Advocate

*Mr. Powell:*
[to be supplied by student]

# D. Exhibits

*JOINT EXHIBIT NO. 1*

COLLECTIVE BARGAINING AGREEMENT

BETWEEN

ELKORN ELECTRIC CO.

AND

LOCAL NO. 711

INTERNATIONAL UNION OF ELECTRICAL, TELEVISION, AND

MACHINE WORKERS (1/05/01-1/05/06)

. . .
ARTICLE 5
5A. WORK-WEEK
A five (5) day work-week shall be established as the basic work-week
for hourly-paid workers in the bargaining unit. The five (5) day
work-week shall be Monday through Friday inclusive. The work-week
shall begin at Midnight Sunday on the "C" shift, in which case,
through mutual agreement with the Company and the Union, the "C" shift
will revert to starting time of Monday night.

. . .
ARTICLE 7
7A. LAYOFFS: SENIORITY
Length of Continual Service shall be the determining factor in
effecting layoffs, provided, however, that ability and efficiency are
relatively equal.

. . .
ARTICLE 7
7D. REDUCTION IN FORCE
Employees with more than one (1) year, but less than five (5) years of
continual service shall be permitted to exercise their seniority
according to the seniority policy as defined in Article 7, 7A to
select their shift and occupation in their occupational group.

If work is not available for them in their occupational group, they
shall be permitted, in accordance with the seniority policy as defined
in Article 7, 7A to replace probationary employees in other
occupational groups or other employees who are away from their normal
occupational group. In so doing, they shall displace employees with
the shortest service possible to allow them to exercise this
privilege, normally displacing the employee with the least service in
the bargaining unit.

. . .
ARTICLE 7
7F TRANSFERS: ALLOWED TIME
If, during a force reduction, it is necessary for an employee to be
transferred to jobs outside his regular occupational group, the
Company will be permitted a maximum of five (5) working days in which
to make such a transfer.

12

*JOINT EXHIBIT NO. 2*

ELKORN ELECTRIC COMPANY      INTERNATIONAL UNION OF ELECTRICAL,
TELEVISION AND MACHINE WORKERS,
LOCAL 711

**GRIEVANCE**

Complaint: Improper application of bumping procedure.

Request: To be made whole.

ANSWER: Grievance denied.

*UNION EXHIBIT NO. 1*

NAME: Donna Polson
HIRE DATE: 2-16-01

# Elkorn Electric

| Date | Section | Job Class & Title | Shift |
|------|---------|-------------------|-------|
| 2-16-01 | 2980 | 98081 Tube Assembler B | B |
| | | 3-16-01 Merit Increase | |
| 3-30-01 | 2980 | 980-81 Tube Assembler B | C |
| | | 5-18-01 Merit Increase | |
| 6-22-01 | 2980 | 980-81  Tube Assembler B | B |
| | | 7-22-01 Merit Increase | |
| | | 8-3-01 General Rate Change | |
| | | 9-21-01 Merit Increase | |
| | | Sick Leave from 7-16 to 9-7-82 | |
| | | 8-2-02 General Rate Change | |
| 8-23-02 | 2980 | 980-81 Tube Assembler B | |
| 12-1-02 | | 956-01 Preliminary Assembly Elec | |
| 1-3-03 | | 956-01 Preliminary Assembly Elec | |
| | | 1-11-03 Merit Increase | |
| | | 3-14-03 Out of Step Increase | |
| 5-9-03 | 2949 | 949-50 Spare Parts Packing | A |
| 5-16-03 | 2949 | 949-50 Spare Parts Packing | A |
| | | (Written Request to Change Occ. Group) | |
| | | 6-13-03 Merit Increase | |
| | | 7-11-03 Merit Increase | |
| | | 8-1-03 General Rate Change | |
| | | 9-12-03 Merit Increase | |
| | | 9-7-03 Leave of Absence | |
| | | 1-9-04 Merit Increase | |
| 2-6-04 | 2642 | 464-51 Custodian | A |
| 2-20-04 | 2949 | 969-50 Spare Parts Packing | A |

*UNION EXHIBIT NO. 2*

NAME: Dan Amos
HIRE DATE: 2-23-01

# Elkorn Electric

| Date | Section | Job Class & Title | Shift |
|------|---------|-------------------|-------|
| 2-23-01 | 2980 | 98051 Sheet Metal Worker B | A |
| | | 3-23-01 Merit Increase | |
| | | 7-27-01 Merit Increase | |
| | | 8-1-01 General Rate Change | |
| | | 10-1-01 Laid Off | |
| 2-12-02 | 2980 | 980-15 Sheet Metal Worker B | A |
| 4-19-02 | 2980 | 980-50 Sheet Metal Worker A | B |
| | | 5-17-02 Merit Increase | |
| | | 6-21-02 Merit Increase | |
| | | 8-2-02 General Rate Change | |
| | | 8-23-02 Merit Increase | |
| | | 10-18-02 Merit Increase | |
| 11-22-02 | 2983 | 903-52 Painter C | B |
| | | 11-26-02 Laid Off | |
| 12-16-02 | 2930 | 930-03 Assembler C Electrical | B |
| 12-27-02 | 2930 | 981-51 Painter B (temp) | B |
| | | 1-31-03 Merit Increase | |
| | | 2-28-03 Merit Increase | |
| | | 4-25-03 Merit Increase | |
| 5-2-03 | 2930 | 930-03 Assembler C, Electrical | B |
| | | 5-16-03 Out of Step Increase | |
| | | 8-1-03 General Rate Change | |
| 9-26-03 | 755 | 950-88 Order Control Clerk | A |
| 10-4-03 | 755 | 950-88 Order Control Clerk | A |
| | | Written Request to Change Occ. Group | |
| | | 10-24-03 Merit Increase | |
| | | 12-19-03 Out of Step Increase | |

# Elkorn Electric

| Name & Address: | Dan Amos | |
|---|---|---|
| Section | 2980 | 2983 |
| Job Title | Sheet Metal Worker A | Painter C |
| Job Class/Rate | 980-5 / 8.055 | 903-52 / 6.93 |
| Shift | ( )A (x)B ( )C | |
| Occupational Group | 15 | |

| REASON FOR CHANGE | | EXPLANATION FOR TAKING THIS ACTION | |
|---|---|---|---|
| Efficiency | | | ISSUED |
| Transfer | | Seniority Exercise | 12/15/02 |
| ( ) Office to Factory | | | RECEIVED |
| ( ) Factory to Office | | | VC |
| | | | RECORDED |
| SEPARATIONS: | | | 1-3-03 |
| Resigned | | | |
| Laid Off | | | |
| Discharged | | | |
| Leave | Employee Work Record | | |

| | | EXC | GOOD | FAIR | POOR |
|---|---|---|---|---|---|
| 1. | QUALITY OF WORK | | | x | |
| 2. | QUANTITY OF WORK | | x | | |
| 3. | INTEREST IN WORK | | | x | |
| 4. | ATTENDANCE | | x | | |
| 5. | SUPERVISION | NONE( ) LITTLE(x) MUCH( ) | | | |

REHIRE    YES( )    NO( )

*UNION EXHIBIT NO. 4*

<u>NAME</u>: Red Snelling
<u>HIRE DATE</u>: 2-23-01

# Elkorn Electric

| Date | Section | Job Class & Title | Shift |
|------|---------|-------------------|-------|
| 2-23-01 | 2980 | Sheet Metal Worker A | C |
| | | 3-23-01 Merit Increase | |
| | | 5-25-01 Merit Increase | |
| 7-13-01 | 2976 | 976-51 Grinders B | B |
| | | 8-3-01 General Rate Change | |
| 8-17-01 | 2980 | Sheet Metal Worker A | B |
| | | 10-16-01 Laid Off | |
| 2-12-02 | 2980 | 980-50 Sheet Metal Worker A | A |
| | | 4-2-02 on occupational leave | |
| | | 4-27-02 removed from leave | |
| | | 6-14-02 Merit Increase | |
| | | 6-28-02 Military Leave till 7/9 | |
| | | 8-2-02 General Rate Change | |
| 11-23-02 | 2937 | 937-52 Stores Clerk  Tool Stores | B   SE |
| | | 12-27-02 Merit Increase | |
| | | 2-21-03  Merit Increase | |
| 6-20-03 | 2937 | 937-52 Stores Clerk Tool Stores | A |
| | | 6-27-03 Military Leave till 7/11 | |
| | | 8-1-03 General Rate Change | |
| | | Sick leave from 10-24 to 11/7 | |
| 11-1-03 | 2937 | Stores Clerk Tool Stores | A |
| 12-19-03 | 751 | Sheet Metal Worker A | A |
| 4-9-04 | 751 | Certified Welder A | A |
| | | 5-7-04 Merit Increase | |
| | | 6-23-04 Military Leave to 7-9 | |

# Elkorn Electric

| Name & Address: | Red Snelling | |
|---|---|---|
| Section | 2980 | 2937 |
| Job Title | Sheet Metal Worker A | Stores Clerk Tool Stores |
| Job Class/Rate | 980-50 / 8.13 | 937-52 / 7.035 |
| Shift | (x)A ( )B ( )C | |
| Occupational Group | 15/15/5 | |

| REASON FOR CHANGE | | EXPLANATION FOR TAKING THIS ACTION | | |
|---|---|---|---|---|
| Efficiency | | | | ISSUED |
| Transfer | | Seniority Exercise | | 12/15/02 |
| ( ) Office to Factory | | Effective 11/23/02 | | RECEIVED |
| ( ) Factory to Office | | | | 12/17/02 |
| | | | | RECORDED |
| SEPARATIONS: | | | | 12/22/02 |
| Resigned | | | | |
| Laid Off | | ======================================== | | |
| Discharged | | | | |
| Leave | Employee Work Record | | | |

| Military | | EXC | GOOD | FAIR | POOR |
|---|---|---|---|---|---|
| | 1. QUALITY OF WORK | | | x | |
| | 2. QUANTITY OF WORK | | | x | |
| | 3. INTEREST IN WORK | | | x | |
| | 4. ATTENDANCE | | | x | |
| | 5. SUPERVISION NONE( ) LITTLE(x) MUCH( ) | | | | |

| REHIRE | YES ( ) NO ( ) |
|---|---|

*UNION EXHIBIT NO. 6*

# ELKORN ELECTRIC
## Time Card

| WEEK OF 11-21-02 | | | |
|---|---|---|---|
| Name: Dan Amos | | | |
| XXX | Trans Code b 1 | | |
| | REG HOURS 40.00 | | |
| OTHER | TEMP | | RATE |
| TEMP HRS | REG WAGES | | |
| MAKE-UP WAGES | | | |
| TRANS CD B-2 | FUNERAL HRS | | |
| JURY PAY | | AVG RATE | |
| VACATION HRS | ADJ | | |
| SHIFT PREM | ADJ WAGES | | |
| IND. BONUS | | DIP BONUS | |
| STR. TIME | | | |

=====================================

### DAILY ATTENDANCE RECORD

| | | | | | | |
|---|---|---|---|---|---|---|
| | | | | | | |
| | | | | | | |
| | | | | | | |
| | | | | | | |
| | | | | | | |
| | | | | | | |
| | | | | | | |
| | | | | | | |
| 8 | 8 | 8 | 8 | 8 | | |
| | | | | | | |
| 1ST | 2ND | 3RD | 4TH | 5TH | 6TH | 7TH |

*UNION EXHIBIT NO. 7*

## ELKORN ELECTRIC
## Time Card

| WEEK OF 11-28-02 | Station 2983 | |
|---|---|---|

| Name: Dan Amos | | |
|---|---|---|
| 2983 | Trans Code | b | 1 | |
| | REG HOURS 32.00 | |
| OTHER 12.0 | TEMP 16.0 | RATE |
| TEMP HRS | REG WAGES | |
| MAKE-UP WAGES | | |
| TRANS CD   B-2 | FUNERAL HRS | |
| JURY PAY | AVG RATE | |
| VACATION HRS | ADJ | |
| SHIFT PREM | ADJ WAGES | |
| IND. BONUS | DIP BONUS | |
| STR. TIME | | |

===================================

### DAILY ATTENDANCE RECORD

| | | | | | | | |
|---|---|---|---|---|---|---|---|
| | | | | | | | |
| | | | | | | | |
| | | | | | | | |
| | | | | | | | |
| | | | | | | | |
| | | | | | | | |
| | | | | | | | |
| | | | | | | | |
| | | | | | | | |
| | | | | | | | |
| | | | | | | | |
| | | | | | | | |
| | | | | | | | |
| | 8 | 8 | | | 8 | 8 | |
| 1ST | 2ND | 3RD | 4TH | 5TH | 6TH | 7TH | |

*UNION EXHIBIT NO. 8*

# ELKORN ELECTRIC
## Time Card

| **WEEK OF** 12-05-02 **STATION** 2983 | | | | | | | |
|---|---|---|---|---|---|---|---|
| Name: Dan Amos | | | | | | | |
| XXX | Trans Code | b | 1 | | | | |
| | REG HOURS 39.60 | | | | | | |
| OTHER | | TEMP | | RATE | | | |
| TEMP HRS | | REG WAGES | | | | | |
| MAKE-UP WAGES | | | | | | | |
| TRANS CD  B-2 | FUNERAL HRS | | | | | | |
| JURY PAY | | AVG RATE | | | | | |
| VACATION HRS | | ADJ | | | | | |
| SHIFT PREM | | ADJ WAGES | | | | | |
| IND. BONUS | | DIP BONUS | | | | | |
| STR. TIME | | | | | | | |

===================================

**DAILY ATTENDANCE RECORD**

| | | | | | | | |
|---|---|---|---|---|---|---|---|
| | | | | | | | |
| | | | | | | | |
| | | | | | | | |
| | | | | | | | |
| | | | | | | | |
| | | | | | | | |
| | | | | | | | |
| | | | | | | | |
| | | | | | | | |
| | | | | | | | |
| | | | | | | | |
| | | | | | | | |
| | | | | | | | |
| | | | | | | | |
| 8 | 8 | 7.6 | 8 | 8 | | | |
| | | | | | | | |
| 1ST | 2ND | 3RD | 4TH | 5TH | 6TH | 7TH | |

# Good Manufacturing Company

## Table of Contents

**Table of Contents contd.**

**NOTES**

# A. Caption

IN THE MATTER OF ARBITRATION BETWEEN:

LOCAL UNION NO. 421,                    )
INTERNATIONAL MECHANICAL               )
WORKERS OF AMERICA,                    )
AFL-CIO                                )
                                       )
AND                                    )          RE: EVAN JARRETT
                                       )              Job Bid
GOOD MANUFACTURING CO.                 )
HARLAN, KENTUCKY                       )
                                       )

Appearances:

For the Company: Ronald White

For the Union: Stephanie Roberts

Date: September 30, year 21

Place: Harlan, Kentucky

# B. Examination of Company Witnesses

## 1. Larry Mailer, Manager, Employee Relations

<u>a. Direct Examination by Company Advocate</u>

*Mr. White:*

Q: Would you state your name please?

A: Larry Mailer.

Q: By whom are you employed and what is your position?

A: I work for Good Manufacturing and I am Manager of Employee Relations.

Q: Mr. Mailer, have you seen the job description for machine operator— horizontal boring mill—or HBM for short—which is Joint Exhibit 1?

A: Yes.

Q: Is that the description that was used for this job when it was posted in October year 19?

A: That's correct.

Q: Do you have a copy of Mr. Jarrett's employment application when he originally applied for employment at Good Manufacturing? That is Company Exhibit 1.

A: Yes.

Q: What is the date of that job application?

A: He signed this on July 19, year 13.

Q: And it's been stipulated that Mr. Jarrett's seniority date is January year 13.

A: That's also correct.

Q: Would you tell us what it shows his work experience was up to that time?

A: This is the part entitled ''Employment History.'' It shows that Mr. Jarrett worked for three years in an automotive warehouse where he filled orders. His next job was at Big House, Inc., where he was a warehouse worker who filled orders. Then he did some construction work where he formed and poured concrete. His next job was with Home Hunters, selling real estate. Then he worked for Murphy Miller in the sander room, sanding wooden parts.

Q: What does Murphy Miller do?

A: It makes furniture.

Q: Do any of those jobs qualify a person for the job of horizontal boring mill operator?

A: No.

Q: In general, what is a horizontal boring mill?

A: A horizontal boring mill is a precision machine as opposed to a production machine. It is a three-axis machine where we do a variety of work. Each one of those jobs more or less requires an independent individual setup as contrasted to a production type of machine, where you just set the part in there.

Q: Do you know whether Mr. Jarrett availed himself of any of the training programs here in town or at the County Vocational Technical School?

A: Yes, we have records that he did take some vocational courses when he was in high school. The records showed he took auto mechanics and auto body repair.

Q: Did that training qualify Mr. Jarrett for the job of horizontal boring mill operator?

A: No.

Q: Have you prepared a list of the jobs which Mr. Jarrett has held since his employment at Good Manufacturing?

A: Yes, we have.

Q: This is Company Exhibit 2, with the exception that the K rating of parts cleaner is now listed at K2. Now, Mr. Mailer, why is the mill, drill and tap job (K-10) not listed on Company Exhibit 2?

A: It's not listed on there because Mr. Jarrett was awarded that job after he filed the grievance.

Q: When was Mr. Jarrett awarded that job?

A: According to our records it was on October 25, year 19.

Q: And the day he was placed on the job was what?

A: December 3, year 19.

Q: Is this the job he's holding now?

A: No.

Q: Why not?

A: Because of reductions and layoffs.

Q: What did he do after that job?

**A:** After that we show that on January 7, year 20, Mr. Jarrett went on the mill, drill and tap job. He then went on the bore, turn and mill job on January 13, year 20.

**Q:** What is the pay rating for that job?

**A:** K8. About a week ago, however, he was bumped down to the keyway mill job.

**Q:** What is the rating on the keyway mill job?

**A:** K6.

**Q:** Now, Mr. Mailer, have you seen Joint Exhibits 2 through 8?

**A:** Yes.

**Q:** It has been suggested that these are jobs which Mr. Jarrett has held when he bid for the job, with the exception of the mill, drill and tap job. Is there any other job which he has not held?

**A:** Yes, there is. He has not held the machine operator—drills job (K6).

**Q:** Have you calculated the difference in wages from the time when he might have been awarded the HBM job in January, year 20, to the time period in October year 20 when he would have been laid off?

**A:** Yes.

**Q:** What is that amount?

**A:** Approximately $200.40.

**Q:** The HBM job was awarded to Ralph Topps, is that correct?

**A:** That's correct—on January 7, year 20.

**Q:** Is that when Mr. Jarrett was laid off?

**A:** Yes. At one point, Mr. Jarrett actually quit just before he was laid off, but he knew he was going to be laid off at that time.

**Q:** Are you able to tell us the difference in wages on an hourly basis which Mr. Jarrett would have received, according to your calculations?

**A:** Yes. Had Jarrett been awarded the HBM job on January 7, year 20, when he was a K10, in the normal progression of three months, on April 8, year 20, he would have gone to a K11. The difference at that time would have been the difference between $9.39 and $9.49, or roughly 10 cents an hour. In addition, on July 8, year 20, he would have gone to a K12, which would have been $9.61 an hour, and at that point he would have been entitled to a ten-percent night shift bonus.

**Q:** I have no further questions.

### b. Cross-Examination by Union Advocate

*Ms. Roberts*
[to be supplied by student]

## 2. David Peters, Production Specialist

### a. Direct Examination by Company Advocate

*Mr. White:*

**Q:** Would you state your name and employer for the record?

**A:** My name is David Peters and I work for Good Manufacturing.

**Q:** What is your position there?

**A:** My title is Production Specialist. In particular, I am involved with controlling production, doing some methods work, and working out problems with machine operators. On second shift, I'm really involved with any problem that comes up.

**Q:** Is that what some people would call a foreman?

**A:** Yes.

**Q:** How long have you been on this job?

**A:** Six years.

**Q:** Prior to that what did you do?

**A:** I was a machine operator with a K12 rating in the plant.

**Q:** How long did you do that?

**A:** Two or three years.

**Q:** Would you tell us your employment history from the beginning at the plant?

**A:** I was a vertical torrent lathe operator, K12, then a supervisor, and then a production specialist.

**Q:** Where did you work prior to that?

**A:** At the other Good Manufacturing plant in town. I worked in the Tube Department as a machine adjuster in the GRID Department and did machine maintenance in the GRID Department.

**Q:** Did you have any contact with Ralph Topps?

**A:** Yes, I did.

**Q:** What was that contact?

**A:** I was on third shift last year and he was an employee of mine.

**Q:** How long did he work under you on that shift?

**A:** Approximately nine months.

**Q:** Would you describe his performance on that job?

**A:** In my opinion he was an excellent operator.

**Q:** How much training did you have to give him when he started working under you?

**A:** When he came to my shift there was no further training given to him.

**Q:** Would you say whether or not he was familiar with the machine?

**A:** Yes. With my experience as a supervisor over the machine shop, I would say he was a fully satisfactory operator when he came to my shift.

**Q:** Have you had an opportunity to be acquainted with Mr. Evan Jarrett?

**A:** Yes.

**Q:** Has he worked for you?

**A:** Yes.

**Q:** How long has he worked for you, off and on?

**A:** I don't know for sure. Off and on he has worked in the machine shop on different jobs for maybe a couple of years.

**Q:** What sort of jobs has he done under you?

**A:** He has done bore, turn and mill and recently bore, turn and tap—but that was a job after this job posting was considered—and keyway mill, I think.

**Q:** And you had worked with him prior to the time he bid for the HBM job in October of year 19?

**A:** Yes.

**Q:** Based on your knowledge and experience of Mr. Jarrett, and your knowledge of these jobs in the machine shop, how long would it have taken him to train to do the HBM job?

**A:** I would say probably the normal training cycle, 10 to 12 weeks.

**Q:** Could Mr. Jarrett have given normal performance of the job at the time he applied for it?

**A:** I don't think so.

**Q:** No further questions.

---

### b. Cross-Examination by Union Advocate

*Ms. Roberts:*
[to be supplied by student]

## 3. Melvin Wilson, Production Specialist

### a. Direct Examination by Company Advocate

*Mr. White:*

**Q:** Would you state your name, please?

**A:** Melvin Wilson.

**Q:** Who are you employed by?

**A:** By Good Manufacturing Company in the small AC Motor Department.

**Q:** Are you a Production Specialist?

**A:** Yes, I am.

**Q:** What other position did you hold prior to being a Production Specialist?

**A:** I was the training coordinator administrator for the plant from the time the plant opened eleven years ago.

**Q:** Was that the job you held at the time Mr. Jarrett bid on this job?

**A:** Yes.

**Q:** Have you had any responsibilities with respect to the machine shop in your jobs?

**A:** Yes, I initially set up all the training for the machine shop during the plant start-up phases and have either trained, supervised, or coordinated the training of all employees.

Q: Have you done this type of training at any place besides Good Manufacturing?

A: Yes, I was a teacher in the vocational school system for about four and a half years, teaching machine shop.

Q: Did you continue to do that from time to time on a part-time basis after you were with Good Manufacturing?

A: Yes, I have taught classes at the vocational school occasionally as a substitute. I have also taught various classes that we have offered at Good Manufacturing in conjunction with the vocational school system as an advancement opportunity for our employees.

Q: What sort of classes have you taught?

A: For example, I've taught lathe operation, drill operation, basic machine shop, blueprint reading, math, basic measuring and gauging, basic machine operations, vertical torrent lathes, horizontal boring mills, etc.

Q: Did you ever train Evan Jarrett and/or observe his work?

A: Yes, his initial training when he came to work here was under my supervision. Some of his later training was either under my supervision or I did the training.

Q: When he came to Good, did he have any qualifications as a machine operator?

A: No.

Q: What kind of training did he receive here with respect to machine operation?

A: His initial training was for what we call a mill and drill job or burgomaster. It was a combination of three machines. They are production machines and the training is very basic. The machines are operated by NC controls or computers.

Q: Did he have some initial training in basic machine skills when he came here?

A: Yes, he also received training in basic blueprint reading, basic math, and basic measuring.

Q: Are you familiar with the HBM job?

A: Yes, I am.

Q: This is a description of the HBM job set out in Joint Exhibit 1. Can you tell the difference between the jobs which Mr. Jarrett had done up to the time he bid for the HBM operator position and the requirements of this job?

A: The HBM job, which is a K12 job, involves basically a low-volume occasional or semiproduction type of machine that we use for all kinds of machine operations. It requires multiple setups. There are a tremendous amount of different parts that go through the machine. The other jobs, the K8, bore, turn and mill, and the K6, keyway mill, are the types of jobs where the same kinds of parts go through those operations. Those setups are basically the same from part to part and those machines run at a high volume.

Q: I hand you Company Exhibit 4. First of all, what do the X marks and zeros stand for?

A: The X marks on this particular document indicate those basic entry-level skills that Mr. Jarrett has. The zeros indicate those basic entry-level skills that Mr. Jarrett does not have.

Q: Was this document used at the time he was considered for the job in question or was it prepared for arbitration?

A: This document is attached to each one of our job descriptions and has been for about the last seven or eight years. Also, the skills listed are not all-inclusive of the skill requirements for the job; they are only the entry-level skills for that job.

Q: Who filled out this form?

A: This is filled out by a manager of employee relations in conjunction with the person's supervisor, as well as, normally, myself or someone from manufacturing.

Q: That would be you and Mr. Mailer?

A: That's correct.

Q: Who was the supervisor?

A: I don't remember who may have been involved in this one.

Q: Could I ask you to compare Company Exhibit 4 with the ''Necessary Qualifications For Job Selection'' part of Joint Exhibit 1. On Company Exhibit 4, the first item is ''read and interpret work station instructions and schedules.'' What do you show with respect to Mr. Jarrett's ability to do that?

A: He could do that.

Q: The second one on Company Exhibit 4 is ''proficient in reading engineering drawings.'' What do you show as to Mr. Jarrett's ability to do that?

**A:** There was some reason to believe that Mr. Jarrett could do that, based on his experience.

**Q:** And the third one is "ability to complete a tally sheet."

**A:** That's correct.

**Q:** And you show he could do that?

**A:** Yes.

**Q:** The next one is "ability to add and subtract: decimals, fractions, and angles." And you show he could do decimals and fractions, but not angles. Is that correct?

**A:** Yes.

**Q:** The next item on Company Exhibit 4 is "trigonometry and geometry." Where is that on the job description in Joint Exhibit 1?

**A:** I would assume that's what they mean by the ability to make necessary required mathematical computations including decimals, fractions, and angles.

**Q:** Let me refer you to the first part of Joint Exhibit 1 under item three. Do you see a reference to trigonometry and geometry tables?

**A:** Yes.

**Q:** Is that what you are talking about, the ability to use tables?

**A:** To be able to use the tables as well as make the necessary mathematical computations involving these tables.

**Q:** What do you show as his ability to do that?

**A:** That he had had no exposure to this and couldn't do it.

**Q:** Now, on Company Exhibit 4, you have a list of things that starts out with the "ability to use," then a colon. How do these appear on the job description, Joint Exhibit 1?

**A:** These are under "Necessary Qualifications For Job Selection" where it lists the "degree of accuracy required" and it lists the various different measuring tools that are used on the job. But the job description only lists a few of the basic measuring tools.

**Q:** Rather than to take you through each one of these, I see that there are four abilities listed in Company Exhibit 4 which you say he could not do?

**A:** That is correct.

**Q:** Would you tell us which ones they are?

**A:** The 1 to 24 inch outside micrometers, the larger vernier calipers up to 48 inches, the

vernier calipers up to 24 inches, and the vernier depth rule.

**Q:** The next requirement on Company Exhibit 4 is "ability to calculate stock removal," and you show he could do that.

**A:** Yes.

**Q:** The next heading on Company Exhibit 4 is "ability to set up and operate HBM."

**A:** That's correct.

**Q:** And do you see each of these requirements listed there on Joint Exhibit 1, the job description under "Necessary Qualifications For Job Selection"?

**A:** Yes.

**Q:** You show Mr. Jarrett cannot do any of these?

**A:** That is correct.

**Q:** Can a person do this job if he or she is not able to set up and operate the machine, including selecting appropriate tooling, seating the part in the machine properly, selecting appropriate tools to verify the setup, selecting proper feeds and speeds, and measuring the completed parts to verify dimensions?

**A:** No, the person can't.

**Q:** Mr. Mailer has already described this HBM machine a little for us. Can you give us some additional details? How many different directional movements or pieces does it have?

**A:** The machine is commonly referred to as at least a three-axis machine. It can be even more than that when it's equipped with the various different work hauling devices that are placed on the machine.

**Q:** Which ways does it move?

**A:** Well, the work piece can be brought into the machine on the table or on the fixtures that are mounted on the table. The spindle or tool can be retracted and brought into the work piece, the tool can be moved up and down, the work piece can be moved horizontally as well as in and out to the tool, so it has many positions of that work piece in relationship to the tool. There are many different work-holding devices that are used on the machine to hold the part in place while it's being machined.

**Q:** Do any of the other jobs which Mr. Jarrett held prior to the time of posting for this job, that is, the mill and drill, parts cleaner, the bore-turn-mill, the hermetic rotor, and the keyway mill, have the complexity and impose the requirements of the HBM job?

A:   No.

Q:   Would you state in general why those jobs are not as complex or are easier to perform than the HBM job?

A:   They involve production equipment or standard machine shop pieces of equipment that have been converted to production operations. Those jobs do not have multiple setups. In contrast, the HBM has many uses and has many setups and operations.

Q:   Is there a normal progression that a person passes through in order to reach the HBM job?

A:   Yes. In our plant, there are many families of jobs that people can either normally progress through or, if they opt to, they can pick up additional training and education to help them progress into higher job rates. In this particular case, there is a family of mill jobs starting at the keyway mill, being a K6; bore, turn and mill, which is a K8; and miscellaneous mill parts, being a K10. This is the kind of progression it usually takes to get into the higher skilled jobs. It is also possible for a person to obtain education away from the plant that would help improve their entry level skills, such as through vocational school.

Q:   At the time Mr. Jarrett bid for this job, had he held all of these jobs in the normal progression?

A:   No.

Q:   Which jobs had he not held?

A:   The K10, miscellaneous parts machining.

Q:   Has there been any employee who has not gone through this normal progression but who has taken the HBM job?

A:   Yes, there have been some.

Q:   Why does that happen?

A:   Because at the time the decision was made, we had the flexibility to do the training, and there was no one in the area or within the plant who did have those minimum entry-level skills.

Q:   Do you offer courses to help your employees prepare for advancement in the area of machine shop jobs?

A:   Yes, we have on several occasions offered training opportunities to our employees as joint projects, as I mentioned earlier, between Good Manufacturing and the vocational school system. We have offered lathe operator and drill operator training. We have offered various levels of measuring, math, and blueprint reading courses. We have and still do coordinate with the vocational school system to make sure our employees have an opportunity to get additional training and skills that they need, specifically tailored to our plant and our operation.

Q:   Let me show you the plant employee newsletter, *The Prompter*. This particular issue is Company Exhibit 5. Is this involved in any way with the training which is offered for employees by the Company?

A:   In this particular issue we were trying to determine employee interest in some possible training programs and put in a small article requesting those who might be interested to let us know so that we could do what would be necessary.

Q:   This type of article is typical and not the only such *Prompter* issue advertising such training, is it?

A:   That's correct.

Q:   Did Mr. Jarrett ever sign up for any of these classes?

A:   No.

Q:   Does your company also have a tuition refund program connected with outside vocational training skills courses?

A:   Yes, we do.

Q:   Would you describe that program for us?

A:   That program will pay, under the new contract, up to $1,800 a semester for tuition and educational expenses associated with upgrading or improving skills in college, vocational school, or whatever it may be.

Q:   Has Mr. Jarrett ever taken advantage of this program?

A:   Not to my knowledge.

Q:   If he had done so, would there have been any courses through the program to provide training on machines like the HBM?

A:   Yes. The vocational school system offers a machine shop course consisting of 2,640 hours, of which I believe 600 or 800 hours is devoted to mill operations.

Q:   Were you involved in the decision about who would be assigned the HBM job?

A:   Yes.

Q:   In your opinion, was Mr. Jarrett qualified to perform this job?

**A:** No.

**Q:** Was it practical for him to be assigned this job in view of his qualifications and in view of the other alternatives available to the Company as a business?

**A:** No.

**Q:** Were you involved in the decision to place Mr. Topps in this position?

**A:** Yes.

**Q:** Did you review Mr. Topps' application, Company Exhibit 3, and have other contact with him?

**A:** Yes. I was part of the hiring teams. At that time, I operated what we called our pre-employment training program, so I had contact with him then.

**Q:** Before he was hired?

**A:** Yes.

**Q:** Would you tell us why Mr. Topps met the criteria for the HBM job and Mr. Jarrett did not?

**A:** Mr. Topps had actually operated horizontal boring mills. In addition, he had several years of training in the vocational school system in machine shop practices.

**Q:** What occurs during the pre-employment training?

**A:** Our pre-employment training consists of five days where we work with the new employee or train him, exposing him to Company practices, to our product, to safety, to math and blueprint reading, etc. During that time we have the opportunity to assess whether in fact the employee has the skills that he says he has. It became obvious to me after a day or two that Mr. Topps far exceeded the necessary entry-level skills into the job. In fact, we immediately went ahead and put him out on the job.

**Q:** Do you have an opinion as to how long it would have taken you to be able to put Mr. Jarrett to work on this machine—for him to be qualfied to do the job?

**A:** Based on my prior training experience with Mr. Jarrett, I would say that Mr. Jarrett would have gone at least the full training cycle, which would be 12 weeks.

**Q:** That's all the questions for now.

### b. Cross-Examination by Union Advocate

*Ms. Roberts:*
[to be supplied by student]

## C. Examination of Union Witnesses

## 1. Evan Jarrett, Grievant

### a. Direct Examination by Union Advocate

*Ms. Roberts:*
**Q:** Would you state your name and employer for the record?

**A:** Evan Jarrett, and I'm employed by Good Manufacturing Company.

**Q:** Prior to this dispute, had you had any disciplinary suspensions or written warnings?

**A:** No.

**Q:** I'm going to show you what's been marked as Joint Exhibit 7, which is a job description for machine operator—drills. Have you ever performed that job?

**A:** Yes.

**Q:** When did you perform that job?

**A:** When I was first hired by Good Manufacturing, I worked third shift. When I would come in, there would be an hour-and-a-half overlap in which there was already an operator on my machine, so they put me as a drill operator for an hour and a half each night.

**Q:** How long did this last?

**A:** I'd say approximately three to four months.

**Q:** Could you briefly tell me the order of the jobs that you have held while you were at Good?

**A:** I was hired on the mill and drill machine. I was there for approximately one year before I was laid off. Then I got a parts cleaner job and was there for about four months. I bid on and was awarded a bore, turn and mill job, which I held for about one year. I then bid on a hermetic rotary job. I was there for about one year, then I got laid off. When I went back and bumped into the bore, turn and drill job, I stayed there until I got laid off again six months later. Then I went back on the bore, turn and mill job, worked three weeks, and then was laid off again. When I was called back, I was given the keyway mill job, worked there about eight months, was laid off, called back, and given the bore, turn and mill job. After about four months, I bid on and was awarded the mill, drill and tap job. I was there for about nine months and got laid off. When I came back, I bumped into the bore, turn and mill job and stayed there about four months. I was then given a lack-of-work notice for the bore, turn and mill job and I'm presently at the keyway mill job.

**Q:** With respect to the bore, turn and mill job—Joint Exhibit 4—can you tell us what type of machine or machines you operate there and what the job involves?

**A:** That job involves two machines. One machine milled and drilled feet, the other bored the inside diameter of the frame.

**Q:** How would that compare to the boring of frames and drilling of feet that's done by the horizontal boring mill operator?

**A:** They are pretty similar except one is on a bigger scale than the other.

**Q:** Would you explain what you did as a hermetic rotary operator and what type of machine you worked on there? This is Joint Exhibit 5.

**A:** On that job, I ran drills, I ran keyway broach, a honing machine, a lathe, a bounce machine, and I used heat to straighten shafts.

**Q:** What, if any, rework would you have to do on that job?

**A:** Rework would have been basically the straightening out of the shafts.

**Q:** How do you do that?

**A:** You would set your shaft in V blocks, put a bell indicator on it, turn the shaft, and see where your high-low places were on your indicator. If you were high on one side, you would heat it to pull the shaft back around to where you could bring it back down to tolerance.

**Q:** Could you describe the mill, drill and tap job? This is Joint Exhibit 8.

**A:** On that machine we milled the frame and shield faces. We drilled and tapped the conduit box holes.

**Q:** In connection with the job you have now, have you ever assisted Mr. Wilson in preparation of training manuals for other employees to use?

**A:** Yes, my actual training on that job with Mr. Wilson was the writing of the training manual. I helped him to write the manual.

**Q:** Turn your attention to the section of Joint Exhibit 1 where it says ''ability to set up,'' etc. In the past and on other jobs, have you had to measure parts to verify their dimensions?

**A:** Yes.

**Q:** Can you give us an example?

**A:** On the bore, turn and mill job, I did the actual inside diameter finish to the frame, which I had to measure to verify that it was within specifications.

**Q:** How did you do that?

**A:** Used an inside micrometer, or a mic. Also on the hermetics job, on the outside rotor box, I had to use outside mics to cut the diameter down to specifications.

**Q:** On your other jobs, have you had to select tools in doing the setup?

**A:** Yes.

**Q:** Can you give an example?

**A:** On the mill and drill I would have to select tools, put them in the machine, do the tool touch-offs to make sure the tools wouldn't crash into the machine.

**Q:** Are you familiar with the difference between a vernier depth rule and a depth micrometer?

**A:** Yes.

**Q:** Describe for us the difference.

**A:** You can use both to measure depths. The difference is in how deep they can go. The vernier depth rule is one that you slide down by hand, then lock off, and take your reading.

You can use this to measure things as deep as 18 to 20 inches. The depth micrometer is a device you screw down to get the depth of a hole or something like that. You would do this for things that aren't very deep. Maybe 3 inches or less.

**Q:** No further questions.

### b. Cross-Examination by Company Advocate

*Mr. White:*
[to be supplied by student]

## 2. Harriett Albright, Horizontal Boring Mill Operator

### a. Direct Examination by Union Advocate

*Ms. Roberts:*
**Q:** Would you state your name for the record?
**A:** Harriett Albright.
**Q:** By whom are you employed and in what position?
**A:** I work for Good Manufacturing and I run a horizontal boring mill.
**Q:** And what job have you held for the last three or four years?
**A:** The horizontal boring mill job, referred to as "HBM" in the shop.
**Q:** And prior to that time what job did you have?
**A:** I was a shaft grinder.
**Q:** And do you know what the job rating was on the shaft grinder position?
**A:** It was a K12 also.
**Q:** Now, how many times during the years you have worked on the HBM job have you had to use trigonometry to do that job?
**A:** Never.
**Q:** How many times have you used geometry?
**A:** Never.
**Q:** How many times have you had to make computations of angles?
**A:** I never have to.
**Q:** During the time you have been an HBM operator, have you ever worked a flywheel?
**A:** No.
**Q:** Prior to today, have you ever heard of a part called a pillow block?
**A:** No.
**Q:** Did you get this job by bidding for it?
**A:** Yes.

**Q:** Did you have a training period after you were awarded the job?
**A:** Yes, I did.
**Q:** How long did that training period last?
**A:** I would say probably two to three months.
**Q:** I'm going to show you what is marked as Joint Exhibit 1, and in particular I want you to look at the listing underneath the heading "Ability to set up and operate manual HBM" and there are several items below that. Do you see them?
**A:** Yes, I do.
**Q:** Did you know how to do those things on the HBM before you had the job, or were you shown those during your training period?
**A:** The last one I knew how to do, the rest of them were shown to me during the training period. The last one was related to "measure completed parts. . ." to verify dimension. I knew how to do that before I took the job.
**Q:** What kind of work are you doing right now on the horizontal boring mill?
**A:** I am boring, milling, and drilling the feet of 500 frames.
**Q:** How long have you been doing that?
**A:** Well, continuously for about five or six months. I've switched back and forth between machines.
**Q:** When Mr. Topps was hired, how did that affect your shift assignment?
**A:** I switched to third shift so that someone could train him during the first shift.
**Q:** How long did you remain on third shift as a result of the training?

**A:** Five weeks at least. It might have been longer.

**Q:** No further questions.

### b. Cross-Examination by Company Advocate

*Mr. White:*
[to be supplied by student]

## 3. Allen Thomas, Drill Operator

### a. Direct Examination by Union Advocate

*Ms. Roberts:*

**Q:** Mr. Thomas, by whom are you employed and in what position?

**A:** I work for Good Manufacturing as a drill operator.

**Q:** How long have you held that position?

**A:** Seven and a half years.

**Q:** There has been some testimony today about the drilling of holes for flywheels. When that work came into the plant, to whom was it assigned?

**A:** It was assigned to the drill operators.

**Q:** And what rating do the drill operators have?

**A:** A K6.

**Q:** No further questions.

### b. Cross-Examination by Company Advocate

*Mr. White:*
[to be supplied by student]

## 4. John Arnett, Regional Director, International Mechanical Workers of America

### a. Direct Examination by Union Advocate

*Ms. Roberts:*

**Q:** Would you state your name, by whom you're employed, and in what capacity?

**A:** My name is John Arnett, and I'm employed as regional director by the International Union of Mechanical Workers.

**Q:** I'm going to show you what's been marked as Joint Exhibit 12, a letter to Fred Zimmer. Can you tell me if the Union ever agreed to the statement of the issue provided in that letter?

**A:** No, we did not.

**Q:** Did you have any discussion with the person who wrote that letter about the issue?

**A:** The only discussion I had with Mr. Hoffman was when he called my office and I was out of the city. He said he was getting ready to respond to our request for arbitration of the case. He said that he had never submitted for decision or responded to the question of arbitrability of the case over job descriptions and bidding and he indicated to me, he said to me, "I'm going to submit and phrase the submission." I said if the submission is the same as in the letter of agreement that appears in our contract, well, there's no problem. It was the same so there was no arbitrability issue presented.

**Q:** Mr. Arnett, how long have you been negotiating with Good Manufacturing with respect to this plant?

**A:** About eight years.

**Q:** And how long have you been negotiating with Good Manufacturing with regard to other facilities?

**A:** Probably thirty years or so.

**Q:**  Has the Union ever agreed to the job descriptions promulgated by the Company?

**A:**  No.

**Q:**  In your opinion was the grievant qualified for the HBM position?

**A:**  Yes.

**Q:**  No further questions.

### b. Cross-Examination by Company Advocate

*Mr. White:*
[to be supplied by student]

## 5. Elliott Irving, President, Local 421

### a. Direct Examination by Union Advocate

*Ms. Roberts:*

**Q:**  Please state your name, by whom you're employed, and in what position.

**A:**  My name is Elliott Irving, I work for Good Manufacturing, and I'm President of Local 421.

**Q:**  Mr. Irving, were you involved in the grievance meetings prior to arbitration of this case?

**A:**  Yes, I was.

**Q:**  Can you tell us whether or not there was discussion about job qualifications issues in those grievance meetings?

**A:**  Yes, there was quite a bit.

**Q:**  Did the Company provide you with the documentation they said they had used in determining the qualifications of the bidders?

**A:**  They did.

**Q:**  I'm going to show you what's been marked as Joint Exhibit 1. Can you identify this for me?

**A:**  Yes, I can. This is a job description for the HBM. It was given to us because we had considerable argument on the qualifications of Mr. Jarrett, as to whether he should have been awarded that job. They brought this document to us.

**Q:**  Who is "they"?

**A:**  The Company's industrial relations people; Mr. Mailer was one of the persons who presented this document to us.

**Q:**  This is Company Exhibit 4, the list of necessary qualifications for the HBM post. Can you tell whether the Union was ever provided with a copy of this document prior to today?

**A:**  No. This is the first time I've seen this document.

**Q:**  How many openings were posted for the HBM job?

**A:**  Originally they posted three openings.

**Q:**  How many did they fill?

**A:**  An employee, Scott got one, Topps—who came in off the street—got one, and they gave the other one to an employee by the name of Jacobs. Uh, I would like to make a correction; Jacobs got a vertical boring mill job, the other two got horizontal boring mill jobs.

**Q:**  Didn't Scott have more seniority than Evan Jarrett?

**A:**  That's correct.

**Q:**  And Mr. Scott had taken some vocational school courses?

**A:**  I believe he's had some vocational training, but not the courses. I think he took some vocational training before he came here.

**Q:**  No further questions.

### b. Cross-Examination by Company Advocate

*Mr. White:*
[to be supplied by student]

# D. Exhibits

## *JOINT EXHIBIT NO. 1*

GOOD MANUFACTURING COMMERCIAL & INDUSTRIAL MOTOR DEPARTMENT
HOURLY JOB DESCRIPTION

JOB TITLE:                              DATE REVIEWED:08-16-19 BY: LJD
Machine Operator—
HORIZONTAL BORING MILL (HBM)        SUPERSEDES:  02-06-16  BY: TWI

JOB CODE: 3-8138         JOB RATE:  K12

1. DESCRIBE THE OPERATION TO BE COMPLETED.  SUMMARIZE MAJOR DUTIES, PROCESSES, RESPONSIBILITIES, WORK FROM ORAL OR WRITTEN INSTRUCTIONS AS PROVIDED TO:

-Set up and operate HBMs to perform operations such as mill, bore, tap, drill and face various parts, such as frames, bases, etc.
-Layout frames and other motor and generator components as required for machining operations.
-Make necessary or required math calculations.

-CONFORM TO ALL SAFETY REQUIREMENTS AND PRACTICES
-PERFORM QUALITY CHECKS AS REQUIRED
-MAINTAIN DAILY PRODUCTION RECORDS AS REQUIRED
-MAINTAIN CLEAN WORK PLACE & FOLLOW GOOD HOUSEKEEPING PRACTICES

2. MACHINES OR STATIONS TO BE OPERATED ON PRIMARY BASIS:
WORK STATIONS -
T04, T70, S70

3. FACILITIES, MATERIALS, AND TOOLS USED:
Miscellaneous hand tools, cranes and hoists, variety of precision measuring tools (micrometers, depth micrometers, verniers, etc.) Trigonometry and geometry tables.

4. WORKING CONDITIONS:  (DESCRIBE CONDITIONS OF THIS JOB ENVIRONMENT)
_____ SITTING        _X_ STANDING

_X_ CLIMBING         _X_ STOOPING/BENDING

_X_ LIFTING--
    _X_ LIGHT(0-15#), _X_ MED.(15-35#), _X_ HEAVY (35# & OVER)

_X_ VARIOUS

COMMENTS:

Machine shop environment, chips, coolants, etc.

THE ABOVE STATEMENT REFLECTS THE GENERAL DETAIL NECESSARY TO DESCRIBE THE MAJOR FUNCTIONS OF THE OCCUPATION AND SHALL NOT BE CONSTRUED AS A DETAILED DESCRIPTION OF ALL THE MINOR WORK REQUIREMENTS.  INCUMBENT MAY INSTRUCT OTHERS.

*JOINT EXHIBIT NO. 1 (continued)*

NECESSARY QUALIFICATIONS FOR JOB SELECTION

JOB TITLE: <u>MACHINE OPERATOR—HORIZONTAL BORING MILL</u>

JOB CODE: <u>3-8138</u>       JOB RATE: <u>K12</u>
EDUCATION/SKILL/EXPERIENCE REQUIREMENTS:

Ability to read and interpret work station instructions and schedules
Proficiency in reading drawings.
Ability to complete a tally sheet.
Ability to add and subtract (decimals, fractions, and angles).
Ability to use variety of precision measuring and lay tools
accurately.*
Ability to calculate stock removal to obtain correct drawing
dimensions.
Ability to set up and operate manual horizontal boring mill to
perform operations:
     -Select appropriate tooling for setup.
     -Seat part in machine properly.
     -Select appropriate gages, indicators, etc., to verify setup.
     -Measure completed parts (not necessarily his own) to verify
       dimensions as compared to drawing.
Ability to make necessary or required mathematical computations,
including decimals, fractions, and angles.

*Degree of accuracy required: + or -

| | |
|---|---|
| -6" rule | 0.10 |
| -12" rule | 0.10 |
| -Steel tape | 1/32 |
| -0-1" outside micrometer | .001 |
| -1" to 24" outside micrometer | .001 |
| -Vernier calipers up to 48" | .005 |
| -Inside micrometer | .001 |
| | |
| -Dial calipers | .001 |
| -Vernier calipers 1-24" | .001 |
| -Vernier depth rules | .001 |
| -Depth micrometers | .001 |
| -Dial bore gages | .0005 |
| -Dial indicator | .0005 |

Go/No-Go Type Gages
-Thread

JOB EXPOSURES & WORKING CONDITIONS -REFER TO ITEM 4 ON JOB
DESCRIPTION
DATE <u>08/16/19</u>
SUPERSEDES DATE <u>03/11/16</u>

*JOINT EXHIBIT NO. 2*

GOOD MANUFACTURING COMMERCIAL & INDUSTRIAL MOTOR DEPARTMENT
HOURLY JOB DESCRIPTION

JOB TITLE:                      DATE REVIEWED:05-01-16 BY:TWI
Machine Operator—
KEYWAY MILL                     SUPERSEDES:01-05-15 BY:TWI

JOB CODE: 3006-8394      JOB RATE:    K6

1. DESCRIBE THE OPERATION TO BE COMPLETED. SUMMARIZE MAJOR DUTIES,
PROCESSES, RESPONSIBILITIES, WORK FROM ORAL OR WRITTEN INSTRUCTIONS
AS PROVIDED TO:

-Select and install correct tooling and setup
-Operate machine to cut keyways in shaft according to print
 specifications
-Measure parts to verify tolerances
-Make adjustments as needed


-CONFORM TO ALL SAFETY REQUIREMENTS AND PRACTICES
-PERFORM QUALITY CHECKS AS REQUIRED
-MAINTAIN DAILY PRODUCTION RECORDS AS REQUIRED
-MAINTAIN CLEAN WORK PLACE & FOLLOW GOOD HOUSEKEEPING PRACTICES

2. MACHINES OR STATIONS TO BE OPERATED ON PRIMARY BASIS:
WORK STATIONS -
R30, R32, R34, R36 Plus backup machines


3. FACILITIES, MATERIALS, AND TOOLS USED:
Hoists and cranes, miscellaneous hand tools, measuring devices such
as micrometers, verniers, solid gages, dial indicators, etc.


4. WORKING CONDITIONS:      (DESCRIBE CONDITIONS OF THIS JOB
ENVIRONMENT)
_____ SITTING               _X_ STANDING

_____ CLIMBING              _X_ STOOPING/BENDING

_X_ LIFTING--
    _X_ LIGHT(0-15#), _X_ MED.(15-35#), _X_ HEAVY (35# & OVER)

_X_ VARIOUS


COMMENTS:
Machine shop conditions, chips, coolants, etc.


THE ABOVE STATEMENT REFLECTS THE GENERAL DETAIL NECESSARY TO DESCRIBE
THE MAJOR FUNCTIONS OF THE OCCUPATION AND SHALL NOT BE CONSTRUED AS A
DETAILED DESCRIPTION OF ALL THE MINOR WORK REQUIREMENTS. INCUMBENT
MAY INSTRUCT OTHERS.

*JOINT EXHIBIT NO. 2 (continued)*

NECESSARY QUALIFICATIONS FOR JOB SELECTION

JOB TITLE: <u>MACHINE OPERATOR—KEYWAY MILL</u>

JOB CODE: <u>3006-8394</u>   JOB RATE: <u>K6</u>

EDUCATION/SKILL/EXPERIENCE REQUIREMENTS:

Ability to read and interpret work station instructions and engineering instructions for manufacturing.
Proficiency in reading engineering drawings.
Ability to add, subtract, and complete a tally sheet.
Ability to use variety of measuring tools accurately (rule, micrometers, dial indicators, etc.)*
Ability to calculate stock removal to obtain correct drawing dimensions.
Ability to set up manual or automatic horizontal knee-type or bed mills; perform operations such as straight, round end or woodruff keyways:
 -Set part in machine correctly.
 -Select appropriate tooling for setup.
 -Select appropriate gages, indicators, etc., to verify setup.
 -Select proper feed and speed settings.
 -Measure completed part (not necessarily his own) to verify dimensions as compared to drawing.

*Degree of accuracy required: + or -

| | |
|---|---|
| -6" rule | 1/32 |
| -12" rule | 1/32 |
| -Steel tape | 1/32 |
| -0-1" outside micrometer | .001 |
| -1" to 12" outside micrometer | .001 |

JOB EXPOSURES & WORKING CONDITIONS -REFER TO ITEM 4 ON JOB DESCRIPTION

DATE <u>03/11/19</u>
SUPERSEDES DATE _____

*JOINT EXHIBIT NO. 3*

GOOD MANUFACTURING COMMERCIAL & INDUSTRIAL MOTOR DEPARTMENT
HOURLY JOB DESCRIPTION

JOB TITLE:                    DATE REVIEWED:01-14-15 BY:TWI
Machine Operator—
MILL & DRILL                  SUPERSEDES:12-15-14    BY:TWI

JOB CODE:  3008-8136        JOB RATE:    K8
1. DESCRIBE THE OPERATION TO BE COMPLETED.  SUMMARIZE MAJOR DUTIES, PROCESSES, RESPONSIBILITIES, WORK FROM ORAL OR WRITTEN INSTRUCTIONS AS PROVIDED TO:

-Select and install proper tooling, mounting fixture, etc.
-Select and load correct tape.
-Make necessary adjustments.


-CONFORM TO ALL SAFETY REQUIREMENTS AND PRACTICES
-PERFORM QUALITY CHECKS AS REQUIRED
-MAINTAIN DAILY PRODUCTION RECORDS AS REQUIRED
-MAINTAIN CLEAN WORK PLACE & FOLLOW GOOD HOUSEKEEPING PRACTICES
2. MACHINES OR STATIONS TO BE OPERATED ON PRIMARY BASIS:
WORK STATIONS -
S90, T50      Burgomaster, N/C machining center, mill & drill station

3. FACILITIES, MATERIALS, AND TOOLS USED:
Miscellaneous hand tools, measuring tools such as micrometers, depth micrometers, verniers, gages, etc., cranes, hoists.

4. WORKING CONDITIONS:    (DESCRIBE CONDITIONS OF THIS JOB ENVIRONMENT)
_____ SITTING          _X_ STANDING

_X_ CLIMBING          _X_ STOOPING/BENDING

_X_ LIFTING--
      _X_ LIGHT(0-15#),  _X_ MED.(15-35#),  _X_ HEAVY (35# & OVER)

_X_ VARIOUS


COMMENTS:
Machine shop environment, chips, coolants, etc.


THE ABOVE STATEMENT REFLECTS THE GENERAL DETAIL NECESSARY TO DESCRIBE THE MAJOR FUNCTIONS OF THE OCCUPATION AND SHALL NOT BE CONSTRUED AS A DETAILED DESCRIPTION OF ALL THE MINOR WORK REQUIREMENTS.  INCUMBENT MAY INSTRUCT OTHERS.

*JOINT EXHIBIT NO. 3 (continued)*

NECESSARY QUALIFICATIONS FOR JOB SELECTION

JOB TITLE:  MACHINE OPERATOR—MILL & DRILL

JOB CODE:   3008-8136          JOB RATE:   K8

EDUCATION/SKILL/EXPERIENCE REQUIREMENTS:

Ability to read and interpret work station instructions and schedules.
Proficiency in reading engineering drawings.
Ability to add, subtract, and complete a tally sheet.
Ability to add and subtract decimals, fractions, and angles.
Ability to use variety of measuring tools accurately (rule, micrometers, dial indicators, bore gages, etc.)*
Ability to calculate stock removal to obtain correct drawing dimensions.
Ability to operate overhead cranes and hoists.
Ability to set up and operate mills and drills to mill, drill, and tap.
  -Select appropriate tooling as required to complete setup.
  -Seat part in machine properly.
  -Select appropriate gages, indicators, etc., to verify
   setup.
  -Measure completed part (not necessarily his own) to verify
   dimensions as compared to drawing.


*Degree of accuracy required: + or -

| | |
|---|---|
| -6" rule | .030 |
| -12" rule | .030 |
| -Steel tape | 1/32 |
| -0-1" outside micrometer | .001 |
| -1" to 24" outside micrometer | .001 |
| -Dial indicator | .001 |
| -Outside verniers 1" to 24" | .001 |

Go/No-Go Type Gage
-Thread



JOB EXPOSURES & WORKING CONDITIONS -REFER TO ITEM 4 ON JOB
DESCRIPTION



DATE    03/11/19
SUPERSEDES DATE

*JOINT EXHIBIT NO. 4*

GOOD MANUFACTURING COMMERCIAL & INDUSTRIAL MOTOR DEPARTMENT
HOURLY JOB DESCRIPTION

JOB TITLE:                              DATE REVIEWED:02-06-16 BY: TWI
Machine Operator
BORE, TURN & MILL           SUPERSEDES:   01-14-15  BY: TWI

JOB CODE: 3008-8139                   JOB RATE:  K8

1. DESCRIBE THE OPERATION TO BE COMPLETED.  SUMMARIZE MAJOR DUTIES,
PROCESSES, RESPONSIBILITIES, WORK FROM ORAL OR WRITTEN INSTRUCTIONS
AS PROVIDED TO:

-Set up and operate various equipment to perform operations such as
bore, turn, mill, drill, etc., on various size frames.

-CONFORM TO ALL SAFETY REQUIREMENTS AND PRACTICES
-PERFORM QUALITY CHECKS AS REQUIRED
-MAINTAIN DAILY PRODUCTION RECORDS AS REQUIRED
-MAINTAIN CLEAN WORK PLACE & FOLLOW GOOD HOUSEKEEPING PRACTICES

2. MACHINES OR STATIONS TO BE OPERATED ON PRIMARY BASIS:
WORK STATIONS -
T35, T50  Boring mill; mill & drill station

3. FACILITIES, MATERIALS, AND TOOLS USED:
Miscellaneous hand tools, cranes, and hoists, variety of precision
measuring tools (micrometers, verniers, dial indicators, etc.)

4. WORKING CONDITIONS:     (DESCRIBE CONDITIONS OF THIS JOB
ENVIRONMENT)
_____ SITTING          _X__ STANDING

_____ CLIMBING         _X__ STOOPING/BENDING

_X__ LIFTING--
      _X_ LIGHT(0-15#),  _X__ MED.(15-35#),  _X_ HEAVY (35# & OVER)

_X__ VARIOUS

COMMENTS:

Machine shop environment, chips, coolants, etc.

THE ABOVE STATEMENT REFLECTS THE GENERAL DETAIL NECESSARY TO DESCRIBE
THE MAJOR FUNCTIONS OF THE OCCUPATION AND SHALL NOT BE CONSTRUED AS A
DETAILED DESCRIPTION OF ALL THE MINOR WORK REQUIREMENTS.   INCUMBENT
MAY INSTRUCT OTHERS.

*JOINT EXHIBIT NO. 4 (continued)*

NECESSARY QUALIFICATIONS FOR JOB SELECTION

JOB TITLE: _MACHINE OPERATOR—BORE, TURN & MILL_____

JOB CODE: __3008-8139_____    JOB RATE: ___K8_____

EDUCATION/SKILL/EXPERIENCE REQUIREMENTS:

Ability to read and interpret work station instructions and schedules
Proficiency in reading engineering drawings.
Ability to add, subtract, and complete a tally sheet.
Ability to add and subtract decimals and fractions.
Ability to use variety of tools accurately (rule, micrometers,
verniers, dial indicators, bore gages, etc.).*
Ability to calculate stock removal to obtain correct drawing
dimensions.
Ability to operate overhead cranes and hoists.
Ability to set up and operate mills and drills to perform operations
such as bore, turn, mill, drill, tap, and chamfer.
  -Select appropriate tooling for setup.
  -Seat part in machine properly.
  -Select appropriate gages, indicators, etc., to verify setup.
  -Measure completed parts (not necessarily his own) to verify
   dimensions as compared to drawing.


*Degree of accuracy required: + or -

| | |
|---|---|
| -6" rule | 0.30 |
| -12" rule | 0.30 |
| -Steel tape | 1/32 |
| -1" to 24" outside micrometer | .001 |
| -Inside micrometer | .001 |
| -Vernier calipers | .001 |
| -Dial bore gages | .001 |
| -Dial indicators | .0005 |

Go/No-Go Type Gages
-Thread


JOB EXPOSURES & WORKING CONDITIONS -REFER TO ITEM 4 ON JOB
DESCRIPTION

DATE ___03/11/16_____
SUPERSEDES DATE _____

*JOINT EXHIBIT NO. 5*

GOOD MANUFACTURING COMMERCIAL & INDUSTRIAL MOTOR DEPARTMENT
HOURLY JOB DESCRIPTION

JOB TITLE:                          DATE REVIEWED:03-28-16 BY: TWI
Machine Operator—
HERMETIC ROTOR                      SUPERSEDES:01-14-15 BY: TWI

JOB CODE:  3010-8451        JOB RATE:  K10
1. DESCRIBE THE OPERATION TO BE COMPLETED.  SUMMARIZE MAJOR DUTIES,
PROCESSES, RESPONSIBILITIES, WORK FROM ORAL OR WRITTEN INSTRUCTIONS
AS PROVIDED TO:

-Set up and operate equipment to perform a variety of machining
 operations on hermetic rotor cores, such as broach, press quill,
 drill quill, turn, heat shock, assemble shaft to rotor, hone,
 balance, perform open bar tests, straighten shafts, etc.
-Repair or rework as required
-Perform quality checks

-CONFORM TO ALL SAFETY REQUIREMENTS AND PRACTICES
-PERFORM QUALITY CHECKS AS REQUIRED
-MAINTAIN DAILY PRODUCTION RECORDS AS REQUIRED
-MAINTAIN CLEAN WORK PLACE & FOLLOW GOOD HOUSEKEEPING PRACTICES
2. MACHINES OR STATIONS TO BE OPERATED ON PRIMARY BASIS:
WORK STATIONS -   Work Station B57, Various equipment: hone,
hydraulic & drill press, turning lathe, balance machine, bench
centers, hand torch, oven, broach, bar tester, etc.
3. FACILITIES, MATERIALS, AND TOOLS USED:  Miscellaneous hand and
power tools, cranes and hoists, variety of precision measuring tools
(dial bore gages, verniers, micrometers, comptor gages, etc.).

4. WORKING CONDITIONS:     (DESCRIBE CONDITIONS OF THIS JOB
ENVIRONMENT)
_____  SITTING          _X_  STANDING

_____  CLIMBING         _X_  STOOPING/BENDING

_X_  LIFTING--
     _X_  LIGHT(0-15#),  _X_  MED.(15-35#),  _X_  HEAVY (35# & OVER)

_X_  VARIOUS


COMMENTS:
Machine shop conditions, chips, coolants, etc.

THE ABOVE STATEMENT REFLECTS THE GENERAL DETAIL NECESSARY TO DESCRIBE
THE MAJOR FUNCTIONS OF THE OCCUPATION AND SHALL NOT BE CONSTRUED AS A
DETAILED DESCRIPTION OF ALL THE MINOR WORK REQUIREMENTS.   INCUMBENT
MAY INSTRUCT OTHERS.

*JOINT EXHIBIT NO. 5 (continued)*

NECESSARY QUALIFICATIONS FOR JOB SELECTION

JOB TITLE:  Machine Operator—HERMETIC ROTOR

JOB CODE:   3010-8451          JOB RATE:   K10

EDUCATION/SKILL/EXPERIENCE REQUIREMENTS:

Ability to read and interpret work station instructions and
schedules.
Proficiency in reading engineering drawings.
Ability to add, subtract, and complete a tally sheet.
Ability to use variety of measuring tools accurately (rule,
micrometers, dial indicators, dial snap gages, etc.).*
Ability to calculate stock removal to obtain correct drawing
dimensions.
Ability to operate overhead cranes and hoists.
Basic welding skills.
Ability to set up and operate a lathe to perform operations such
as turn, face, chamfer.
    -Select appropriate tooling for setup.
    -Seat part in machine correctly.
    -Select appropriate gages, indicators, etc., to verify
     setup.
    -Select proper tools as required.
    -Select proper feed and speed settings.
    -Measure completed part (not necessarily his own) to verify
     dimensions as compared to drawing.


*Degree of accuracy required: + or -

| | |
|---|---|
| -Steel tape | 1/16 |
| -1" to 24" outside micrometer | .001 |
| -Dial snap indicators | .001 |
| -Dial indicator | .001 |
| -1" to 6" outside micrometer | .001 |


JOB EXPOSURES & WORKING CONDITIONS -REFER TO ITEM 4 ON JOB
DESCRIPTION


DATE    10/1/16
SUPERSEDES DATE _____

*JOINT EXHIBIT NO. 6*

GOOD MANUFACTURING COMMERCIAL & INDUSTRIAL MOTOR DEPARTMENT
HOURLY JOB DESCRIPTION

JOB TITLE:            DATE REVIEWED:04-19-17 BY: LJD
Shop Service—
PARTS CLEANER         SUPERSEDES:01-14-15    BY: TWI

JOB CODE: 1-8135      JOB RATE:    K2

1. DESCRIBE THE OPERATION TO BE COMPLETED. SUMMARIZE MAJOR
DUTIES, PROCESSES, RESPONSIBILITIES, WORK FROM ORAL OR WRITTEN
INSTRUCTIONS AS PROVIDED TO:

-Operate cleaning station to de-burr and clean cast iron/aluminum
parts, such as frames, endshields, bearing caps, etc. Load and
unload pieces using conveyors, cranes, etc. Install sleeve
bearings. Assembly and disassembly of endshield split units.
Check and maintain cleaning solution as required. Primer paint
touchup. Operation of steam spray cleaner.

-CONFORM TO ALL SAFETY REQUIREMENTS AND PRACTICES
-PERFORM QUALITY CHECKS AS REQUIRED
-MAINTAIN DAILY PRODUCTION RECORDS AS REQUIRED
-MAINTAIN CLEAN WORK PLACE & FOLLOW GOOD HOUSEKEEPING PRACTICES

2. MACHINES OR STATIONS TO BE OPERATED ON PRIMARY BASIS:
WORK STATIONS -    S40

3. FACILITIES, MATERIALS, AND TOOLS USED:
Miscellaneous hand tools and power Burr Grinder, Calgon
detergent, temperature indicators, cranes and hoists, steam
cleaner, and related equipment.

4. WORKING CONDITIONS:    (DESCRIBE CONDITIONS OF THIS JOB
ENVIRONMENT)
____ SITTING           _X_ STANDING

____ CLIMBING         _X_ STOOPING/BENDING

_X_ LIFTING--
    _X_ LIGHT(0-15#), _X_ MED.(15-35#), _X_ HEAVY (35# &
OVER)

_X_ VARIOUS

COMMENTS:
Use protective equipment for splash protection, periodic exposure
to minor heat from solution.

THE ABOVE STATEMENT REFLECTS THE GENERAL DETAIL NECESSARY TO
DESCRIBE THE MAJOR FUNCTIONS OF THE OCCUPATION AND SHALL NOT BE
CONSTRUED AS A DETAILED DESCRIPTION OF ALL THE MINOR WORK
REQUIREMENTS. INCUMBENT MAY INSTRUCT OTHERS.

### _JOINT EXHIBIT NO. 6 (continued)_

NECESSARY QUALIFICATIONS FOR JOB SELECTION

JOB TITLE: SHOP SERVICE—PARTS CLEANER
JOB CODE:   1-8135              JOB RATE:    K2

EDUCATION/SKILL/EXPERIENCE REQUIREMENTS:

Ability to read and interpret work station instructions.
Ability to add, subtract, and complete a tally sheet.
Ability to read simple drawings.
Ability to operate overhead cranes and hoists.

JOB EXPOSURES & WORKING CONDITIONS -REFER TO ITEM 4 ON JOB
DESCRIPTION

DATE    04/19/17
SUPERSEDES DATE   03/11/16

*JOINT EXHIBIT NO. 7*

GOOD MANUFACTURING COMMERCIAL & INDUSTRIAL MOTOR DEPARTMENT
HOURLY JOB DESCRIPTION

| | |
|---|---|
| JOB TITLE: | DATE REVIEWED:10-12-20 BY: TWI |
| Machine Operator— | |
| DRILLS | SUPERSEDES: NEW BY: TWI |

JOB CODE: 3XXXD            JOB RATE: K6

1. DESCRIBE THE OPERATION TO BE COMPLETED. SUMMARIZE MAJOR DUTIES, PROCESSES, RESPONSIBILITIES, WORK FROM ORAL OR WRITTEN INSTRUCTIONS AS PROVIDED TO:

-Set up and operate various types of radial, single- and multi-spindle drills to produce quality parts.
-Perform various drilling, reaming, countersink, tapping, broaching, etc., operations on a variety of parts.
-Use drawings to make proper layouts and perform required operations.
-Provide parts as required by daily schedule.
-Machines to be operated on a secondary basis may include grinder/lapper, band  saw, baffle cutoff, balance machine, etc.
-CONFORM TO ALL SAFETY REQUIREMENTS AND PRACTICES
-PERFORM QUALITY CHECKS AS REQUIRED
-MAINTAIN DAILY PRODUCTION RECORDS AS REQUIRED
-MAINTAIN CLEAN WORK PLACE & FOLLOW GOOD HOUSEKEEPING PRACTICES

2. MACHINES OR STATIONS TO BE OPERATED ON PRIMARY BASIS:
WORK STATIONS -
S85, T10, P09R, P14

3. FACILITIES, MATERIALS, AND TOOLS USED: Hoists and cranes, miscellaneous hand tools, limited measuring tools or gaging (drill gages, scales, micrometers, verniers, etc.), sketches, prints, shop schedules.

4. WORKING CONDITIONS:    (DESCRIBE CONDITIONS OF THIS JOB ENVIRONMENT)
_____ SITTING          _X__ STANDING

_____ CLIMBING         _X__ STOOPING/BENDING

_X_ LIFTING--
      _X_ LIGHT(0-15#),  _X__ MED.(15-35#),  __X__ HEAVY (35# & OVER)


_X_ VARIOUS

COMMENTS:

Machine shop environment, chips, coolants, etc.

THE ABOVE STATEMENT REFLECTS THE GENERAL DETAIL NECESSARY TO DESCRIBE THE MAJOR FUNCTIONS OF THE OCCUPATION AND SHALL NOT BE CONSTRUED AS A DETAILED DESCRIPTION OF ALL THE MINOR WORK REQUIREMENTS.   INCUMBENT MAY INSTRUCT OTHERS.

*JOINT EXHIBIT NO. 7 (continued)*

NECESSARY QUALIFICATIONS FOR JOB SELECTION

JOB TITLE __MACHINE OPERATOR—DRILLS__

JOB CODE __3XXD__                    JOB RATE __K6__

EDUCATION/SKILL/EXPERIENCE REQUIREMENTS:

Ability to read and interpret work station instructions and
schedules
Proficiency in reading mechanical engineering drawings.
Ability to add and subtract decimals, fractions, and angles and
to complete a tally sheet.
Ability to use variety of tools accurately (rule, micrometers,
depth gage verniers, thread gages, etc.).*
Ability to operate overhead cranes and hoists.
Ability to set up and operate presses to perform operations such
as drilling and tapping.
        -Select appropriate tooling to complete setup.
        -Seat part in machine properly.
        -Select appropriate gages, indicators, etc., to verify
         setup.
        -Select proper tools as required.
        -Select proper feeds and speeds.
        -Measure completed parts (not necessarily his own) to
verify       dimensions as compared to drawing.


*Degree of accuracy required: + or -

| | |
|---|---|
| -6" rule | 0.30 |
| -12" rule | 0.30 |
| -Steel tape | 1/32 |
| -0-1" outside micrometer | .001 |
| -Vernier calipers 1" to 24" | .001 |
| -Depth gage | .005 |


Go/No-Go Type Gages
-Thread


JOB EXPOSURES & WORKING CONDITIONS -

DATE __10/11/20__
SUPERSEDES DATE _____

*JOINT EXHIBIT NO. 8*

GOOD MANUFACTURING COMMERCIAL & INDUSTRIAL MOTOR DEPARTMENT
HOURLY JOB DESCRIPTION

JOB TITLE:                          DATE REVIEWED: 02-24-18 BY: TWI
Machine Operator
MILL, DRILL & TAP          SUPERSEDES:  NEW          BY: TWI

JOB CODE: 3-813B                  JOB RATE:  K10
1. DESCRIBE THE OPERATION TO BE COMPLETED. SUMMARIZE MAJOR DUTIES,
PROCESSES, RESPONSIBILITIES, WORK FROM ORAL OR WRITTEN INSTRUCTIONS
AS PROVIDED TO:
-Set up and operate numerically controlled machining center to mill
 straight and     contour surfaces; drill, tap, and bore parts, such
 as frames and intermediates.
-Select and install proper tooling and mounting fixtures, etc.
-Select and load correct tape (use tape, memory or manual mode of
 operation).
-Set and adjust tool and part offsets as necessary.

-CONFORM TO ALL SAFETY REQUIREMENTS AND PRACTICES
-PERFORM QUALITY CHECKS AS REQUIRED
-MAINTAIN DAILY PRODUCTION RECORDS AS REQUIRED
-MAINTAIN CLEAN WORK PLACE & FOLLOW GOOD HOUSEKEEPING PRACTICES
2. MACHINES OR STATIONS TO BE OPERATED ON PRIMARY BASIS:
WORK STATIONS -
T90, N/C horizontal machining center with a GE1050 control.


3. FACILITIES, MATERIALS, AND TOOLS USED: 48-36-24-6" verniers
depth vernier, OD & ID mics, go/no go & thread gages, miscellaneous
wrenches (box & open end) and sockets, miscellaneous hand tools,
cranes & hoists, etc.


4. WORKING CONDITIONS:     (DESCRIBE CONDITIONS OF THIS JOB
ENVIRONMENT)
_____ SITTING          _X_ STANDING

_____ CLIMBING          _X_ STOOPING/BENDING

_X_ LIFTING--
     _X_ LIGHT(0-15#),  _X_ MED.(15-35#), _X_ HEAVY (35# & OVER)

_X_ VARIOUS

COMMENTS:

Machine shop environment, chips, coolants, etc.

THE ABOVE STATEMENT REFLECTS THE GENERAL DETAIL NECESSARY TO DESCRIBE
THE MAJOR FUNCTIONS OF THE OCCUPATION AND SHALL NOT BE CONSTRUED AS A
DETAILED DESCRIPTION OF ALL THE MINOR WORK REQUIREMENTS.  INCUMBENT
MAY INSTRUCT OTHERS.

*JOINT EXHIBIT NO. 8 (continued)*

NECESSARY QUALIFICATIONS FOR JOB SELECTION

JOB TITLE  <u>MACHINE OPERATOR—MILL, DRILL & TAP</u>

JOB CODE  <u>3-813B</u>          JOB RATE  <u>K10</u>

EDUCATION/SKILL/EXPERIENCE REQUIREMENTS:

Ability to read and interpret work station instructions and schedules.
Proficiency in reading engineering drawings.
Ability to add, subtract, and complete a tally sheet.
Ability to add and subtract decimals, and fractions; basic trigonometry.
Ability to use variety of tools accurately (rule, micrometers, verniers, dial indicators, bore gages, tap gages, thread gages, etc.).*
Ability to calculate stock removal to obtain correct drawing dimensions.
Ability to operate overhead cranes and hoists—use of proper lifting and sling devices.
Ability to set up and operate 2-axis (or more) N/C machines to perform boring, milling, drilling, and tapping operations.
    -Select proper tooling as required to complete setup.
    -Load and seat part in machine properly.
    -Select appropriate gages, indicators, etc., to verify setup
     and maintain quality parts.
    -Measure completed or semicompleted parts (not necessarily his
     own) to verify dimensions as compared to drawing.


*Degree of accuracy required: + or -

| | |
|---|---|
| -6" rule | 0.30 |
| -12" rule | 0.30 |
| -Steel tape | 1/32 |
| -0-1" out/inside micrometer | .001 |
| -1" to 24" out/inside micrometer | .001 |
| -Dial indicators | .001 |
| -Vernier 1" to 48" | .001 |


Go/No-Go Type Gages
-Thread


JOB EXPOSURES & WORKING CONDITIONS -REFER TO ITEM 4 ON JOB DESCRIPTION

DATE  <u>04/20/16</u>
SUPERSEDES DATE  <u>02/24/18</u>

GOOD MANUFACTURING CO.

JOB POSTING RESULTS

TO: Evan Jarrett

You recently signed Job Posting # __85-84__ for __Machine Operator—Horizontal Boring Mill (HBM)__ RATE: __K12__ Shift__1st__

_____ You have been awarded the job.

__X__ You do not have the necessary qualifications according to our records, and will not be considered further.

_____ You do not have enough seniority to be considered for this job at this time.

_____ You were not eligible to bid on this job because_____
_____.

_____ This opening has been cancelled.

_____ A more senior qualified person was awarded the position.


COMMENTS:




EMPLOYEE RELATIONS ___LARRY MAILER_____
DATE: ___10/16/19____

CHRONOLOGICAL DISPOSITION OF GRIEVANCE

Evan Jarrett _____          PAY NO. <u>12345</u>          DATE <u>2-7-20</u>

GRIEVANCE (12/19/19):

My grievance is the company was unfair about awarding the final 3rd
shift HBM job. They did not look at employee seniority or
qualifications close enough before they went to the outside to fill
this opening. Because if they had they would find that I am as
qualified as the employee that they awarded the other 3rd shift HBM
to. I demand to be made whole for any wages or benefits concerning
this grievance.

---

ANSWER at **STEP 1:**

Evan Jarrett did not meet the necessary qualifications of this job.
The candidate who was awarded the position has over six years of
machinist experience, which made him the most qualified person for
the job.

---

DISPOSITION AT **STEP 2:**

The job of HBM, third shift, was awarded in accordance with past
practice. This job award has been reviewed three times as a result of
prior requests from the grievant. Each review has confirmed that the
job award was correctly made, thus no relief is due.

                                   _____ 2/7/20 _____
                              Good Manufacturing Co., Harlan, KY

*JOINT EXHIBIT NO. 11*

GOOD MANUFACTURING CO.
Harlan, Kentucky

December 2, year 20

Mr. John Arnett
Director-Region IV
International Mechanical Workers
of America (AFL-CIO)
190 Main Street, Suite 10
Columbus, OH

Dear John:

The following are the Company responses following the Step 3 meeting held on November 11 and 12, year 20.

Case No. 1-85

Step 3

It is the Company position that the employee did not meet the necessary minimum qualifications required to perform the job in question.

Sincerely yours,

/s/ J. D. Hoffman
Manager
Production Employee Relations

JDH/mas/0479e

cc: Elliot Irving
L. Mailer

### JOINT EXHIBIT NO. 12

GOOD MANUFACTURING CO.

February 11, year 21


Mr. Fred Zimmer
Associate Director
Case Administration
American Arbitration Association


                                    RE: Grievance
                                    Local No. 421
                                    Harlan, Kentucky

Dear Mr. Zimmer:

The Good Mfg. Company and its Harlan Plant and the
International Union of Mechanical Workers have agreed to arbitrate
the above captioned docket in accordance with the submission below.
Please proceed with the administration of this case.

Contract arbitrators agreed to by the parties in the Current
Agreement include William F. Williams and Carl A. Wernson. This is
our first arbitration under this agreement.

The following submission is placed before the arbitrator:

"Did the grievant, Evan Jarrett, have the necessary
qualifications required under the provisions of Section
5 of Article VIII to be upgraded to the position of Machine
Operator-Horizontal Boring Mill (K12) in January, year 20?"

"If the Arbitrator determines that the grievant did
have the necessary qualifications required for such
upgrading, did the company violate Article VIII when
Ralph Topps was appointed to the position rather than
upgrading the grievant? If so, what shall the remedy be?"

Correspondence to the Union should be addressed to Mr. John
Arnett, Regional Director, International Mechanical Workers of
America (AFL-CIO), 190 Main Street, Suite 10, Columbus, OH.

Please send copies of all correspondence to Larry Mailer, Good
Mfg. Company, Harlan, KY.

                                    Very truly yours,


                                    /s/ J. D. Hoffman
                                    Manager

cc: John Arnett
    Larry Mailer

<u>*COMPANY EXHIBIT NO. 1*</u>

GOOD MANUFACTURING CO.
EMPLOYMENT APPLICATION

NAME ___Evan Jarrett_____ DATE __7-19-13____
ADDRESS__R.R. 1_____
_____Harlan, Ky_____
TELEPHONE_(616)555-1234_____ SOC. SEC. NO._____

<u>JOB INTEREST</u>
POSITION DESIRED _Factory Worker_____
OTHER POSITIONS FOR WHICH YOU ARE QUALIFIED _____
_____Machine Operator_____

DATE AVAILABLE FOR EMPLOYMENT _7-22-13_____

HAVE YOU EVER BEEN EMPLOYED BY GOOD MFG.? ____YES _X__NO
IF SO, WHERE AND WHEN_____

<u>EDUCATION AND TRAINING</u>
WHAT IS THE HIGHEST LEVEL
OF EDUCATION COMPLETED? __high school_____
                        NAME
1. GRADE SCHOOL _Taft Elementary_____
2. HIGH SCHOOL __Harlan Senior High_____
3. COLLEGE _____
4. GRADUATE SCHOOL _____
5. APPRENTICE, BUSINESS, TECHNICAL, MILITARY, OR
     VOCATIONAL SCHOOL Harlan Vocational School(machine shop)

OTHER TRAINING OR SKILLS(FACTORY OR OFFICE MACHINES OPERATED, SPECIAL
COURSES, MILTARY TRAINING) _Operated backknife lathes,_____
   _drill presses, bandsaws, and sanding machines_____

## COMPANY EXHIBIT NO. 1 (continued)

### EMPLOYMENT HISTORY

| EMPLOYER | MAJOR DUTIES | PERIOD OF EMPLOYMENT | POSITION |
|----------|--------------|----------------------|----------|
| Auto Warehouse | filling orders | 3 years | Laborer |
| Big House | filling orders | 2 years | Laborer |
| B & B Construction | pouring concrete | 2 years | Laborer |
| Home Hunters | selling real estate | 2 years | Sales representative |
| Murphy Miller | sanding furniture | 1 year | Sander |

## COMPANY EXHIBIT NO. 2

RE:   JARRETT, EVAN

### JOBS HELD BY JARRETT AT GOOD MANUFACTURING
### AS OF HIS BID ON HBM 10-16

| DATE | JOB TITLE | LABOR GRADE |
|------|-----------|-------------|
| 1-3-YR14 | Mill & Drill | K8 |
| 1-29-YR15 | Parts Cleaner | K2 |
| 9-1-YR15 | Bore, Turn & Mill | K8 |
| 12-15-YR15 | Hermetic Rotor | K10 |
| 8-8-YR15 | Keyway Mill | K6 |
| 10-8-YR19 | Bore, Turn & Mill | K8 |

_**COMPANY EXHIBIT NO. 3**_

GOOD MANUFACTURING CO.
EMPLOYMENT APPLICATION

NAME  Ralph Topps                                    DATE    11-21-19

ADDRESS     R.R. 2

            Harlan, Ky

TELEPHONE  (616)555-6626                  SOC. SEC. NO.

JOB INTEREST

POSITION DESIRED  Machinist

OTHER POSITIONS FOR WHICH YOU ARE QUALIFIED

DATE AVAILABLE FOR EMPLOYMENT  Anytime

HAVE YOU EVER BEEN EMPLOYED BY GOOD MFG.? ____YES  X  NO

IF SO, WHERE AND WHEN

EDUCATION AND TRAINING

WHAT IS THE HIGHEST LEVEL

OF EDUCATION COMPLETED?    2 yrs. technical school

                          NAME
1. GRADE SCHOOL  Owsley

2. HIGH SCHOOL    Bell County

3. COLLEGE

4. GRADUATE SCHOOL

5. APPRENTICE, BUSINESS, TECHNICAL, MILITARY, OR
      VOCATIONAL SCHOOL Harlan Vocational School(machine shop)

OTHER TRAINING OR SKILLS(FACTORY OR OFFICE MACHINES OPERATED, SPECIAL
COURSES, MILITARY TRAINING)

EMPLOYMENT HISTORY-List all employment starting with the most recent
employer, accounting for all periods including unemployment and
service with the Armed Forces.  Use additional sheet if necessary.

1. EMPLOYER  Ace Co.                          DATES MO. YEAR
   ADDRESS  Jenkins                           FROM:9-22-YR19
                                              TO:

**COMPANY EXHIBIT NO. 3** *(continued)*

JOB TITLE  Machinist
DESCRIBE MAJOR DUTIES  Running lathes, mills, grinder

DEPARTMENT
SUPERVISOR  Tom Stoll


2.  EMPLOYER  Select Brass Inc          | DATES MO. YEAR
    ADDRESS    Lexington                 | FROM: 9-19-YR15
                                         | TO:  9-22-YR19

    JOB TITLE      Machinist
    DESCRIBE MAJOR DUTIES  running lathes, mills, planer mill,
                           radial drill
    DEPARTMENT
    SUPERVISOR     Norman Brand


3.  EMPLOYER     Jones Machine          | DATES MO. YEAR
    ADDRESS      Lexington              | FROM: 9-4-YR19
                                        | TO:  9-19-YR19

    JOB TITLE     Machinist
    DESCRIBE MAJOR DUTIES  Lathes, mills (vertical, horizontal),
                           radial drill, boring mills, grinder
    DEPARTMENT
    SUPERVISOR     Joseph Albert

4.  EMPLOYER  _____   | DATES MO. YEAR
    ADDRESS   _____   | FROM:
                                        | TO:

    JOB TITLE  _____
    DESCRIBE MAJOR DUTIES  _____

    DEPARTMENT
    SUPERVISOR


I certify that the information that I have provided is true to the
best of my knowledge.

Applicant's Signature   /s/ Ralph Topps


Awarded MO-HBM job on January 7, YR20.


                            /s/ Larry Mailer

NECESSARY QUALIFICATIONS FOR HORIZONTAL BORING MILL

| EVALUATION CRITERIA | EMPLOYEE: EVAN JARRETT |
|---|---|
| Ability to read and interpret work station instructions and schedules. | X |
| Proficiency in reading engineering drawings. | X |
| Ability to add, subtract, compile tally sheet | X |
| Ability to add and subtract: | |
| Decimals | X |
| Fractions | X |
| Angles | 0 |
| Trigonometry & geometry | 0 |
| Ability to use: | |
| 6" rule | X |
| 12" rule | X |
| 0-1" outside micrometer | X |
| 1 to 24" outside micrometer | 0 |
| Vernier calipers up to 48" | 0 |
| Inside micrometers | X |
| Dial calipers | X |
| Vernier calipers 1-24" | 0 |
| Vernier depth rules | 0 |
| Depth micrometer | X |
| Dial bore gages | X |
| Dial indicator | X |
| Go/No-Go type gages | X |
| Ability to calculate stock removal | X |
| Ability to set up and operate HBM: | |
| Select appropriate tooling | 0 |
| Seat part in machine properly | 0 |
| Select appropriate tools to verify setup | 0 |
| Select proper feeds and speeds | 0 |
| Measure completed parts to verify dimensions | 0 |

*COMPANY EXHIBIT NO. 5*

THE PROMPTER

Good Manufacturing Co.      December 8, year 18

WHAT ABOUT TRAINING?

Training Interest Survey

We have had a number of inquiries about taking training for future openings.  Plans are being made to offer the following courses:

1. Basic Math and Blueprint Reading which will meet at OMP two (2) nights per week, three (3) hours each night, for six (6) weeks.  This course is tentatively scheduled to start in late January.  Class time, day, and instructor to be named later.

2. Basic Measuring Tools, which will meet at OMP two (2) nights per week, three (3) hours each night, for four (4) weeks.  This course will start immediately following the completion of the Basic Math and Blueprint Reading.

Both courses are designed for individuals with little or no training/experience.

Books and other supplies will be furnished by the Company.  There is no registration fee.

If there is more response than can be met, selection will be on the basis of seniority.

Effort will be made for supervisors to work with employees enrolled in the program to resolve any problems that might arise with regard to work schedules, overtime requirements, etc., while complying with contract requirements.

If you are interested in taking either or both of these courses, return the following information to receptionist Michele Hollis by December 16: Name,
Clock #, Seniority Date, and Supervisor.

*COMPANY EXHIBIT NO. 5 (continued)*

Note: A minimum number of participants is required before each course can be held.

IT'S COLD OUT THERE!

When walking between buildings 3 and 4, please use the main doors instead of the overhead doors to enter the buildings. The overhead doors let in a lot of extra cold air that is uncomfortable to employees working nearby. They thank you for your consideration.

DELAYED TUITION PLAN

Finance Manager Dave Price has negotiated a special delayed tuition program with 2 local colleges for employees. See him for further details!

*COMPANY EXHIBIT NO. 6*

NORMAL PROGRESSION OF JOBS

| JOB TITLE | RATE |
|---|---|
| Keyway Mill | K6 |
| Production Bore & Mill | K8 |
| Miscellaneous Parts Machining | K10 |
| Horizontal Boring Machine | K12 |

*COMPANY EXHIBIT NO. 7*

COUNTY STATE VOCATION-TECHNICAL SCHOOL

OFFICIAL TRANSCRIPT

STUDENT INFORMATION

| Last Name | First | Middle | Maiden | Date of Birth |
|-----------|-------|--------|--------|---------------|
| Jarrett | Evan | | | 8/16 |

| Sex | Social Security No. | Home Address: City State Zip Code |
|-----|---------------------|-----------------------------------|
| Male | | |

| Date Entered | Date completed/Withdrew | Date Re-entered/Completed |
|--------------|-------------------------|---------------------------|
| 8/15/13 | 5/15/14 | Auto Mechanics High School |
| 8/15/14 | 5/15/15 | Auto Body Repair High School |

| Attendance: | Excellent | Good | Fair | Poor | Days Absent |
|-------------|-----------|------|------|------|-------------|
| | ☐ | ☐ | ☐ | ☐ | _____ |

AUTO MECHANICS
AUTO BODY REPAIR

DEPARTMENT

CLASS RECORD

AUTO MECHANICS                                AUTO BODY REPAIR

| UNITS OF TRAINING | HOURS | RATING | UNITS OF TRAINING | HOURS | RATING |
|-------------------|-------|--------|-------------------|-------|--------|
| Fuel & Electrical System | | | Estimating | | |
| Lubrication & Cooling System | | | Body Aligning | | |
| Pistons, pins, rods, rings, crankshaft, main bearings | | | Sanding/Masking | | |
| Cylinder blocks | | | Spray Painting | | |
| Internal parts | | | Lacquer/Enamel | | |
| Exhaust | | | Straightening | | |
| Total clock Hours = | 506 | C | Plastic Filling | | |
| | | | Clock Hours Total | 474 | C |

COMMENTS: _____

_____

_____

Date _____ 5-30-15 _____     Principal _/s/ Ray Gillespie_

40

*UNION EXHIBIT NO. 1*

COLLECTIVE BARGAINING AGREEMENT
BETWEEN
GOOD MANUFACTURING COMPANY
AND
INTERNATIONAL MECHANICAL WORKERS OF AMERICA,
AFL-CIO LOCAL UNION NO. 421 (1/01/17-11/01/21)

. . .

ARTICLE VIII, § 5(A)

A Company will, to the extent practical, give first consideration for job openings and upgrades to present employees, when employees with the necessary qualifications are available.  In upgrading employees to higher-rated jobs, the Company will take into consideration as an important factor, the relative length of continuous service of the employees who it finds are qualified for such upgrading; providing, however, that in upgrading employees to job openings with job rates within the one-a-month progression schedule, the relative seniority of those employees found qualified for such upgrading shall be the controlling factor.

## *UNION EXHIBIT NO. 2*

HORIZONTAL BORING MILL
NECESSARY QUALIFICATIONS MET BY BIDDERS

| Ability to: | Scott | Jarrett | Jacobs | Haynes | Topps* |
|---|---|---|---|---|---|
| Read & interpret work station schedules & instructions | X | X | X | X | X |
| Be proficient in reading engineering drawings | X | X | X | | X |
| Add, subtract, & complete a tally sheet | X | X | X | X | X |
| Add & subtract decimals, fractions & angles; use trig. & geom. | X | | X | | X |
| Calculate stock removal to obtain correct drawing dimensions | X | X | X | X | X |
| Use variety of measuring tools accurately | X | | | | X |
| Operate overhead cranes and hoists | X | X | X | X | X |
| Set up & operate manual HBMs | | | | | * |
| Select proper tools as required to complete setup | | | | | * |
| Select appropriate gages, indicators, etc. to verify setup | | | | | * |
| Select proper feed & speed settings | | | | | * |
| Measure completed part (not nec. his own) to verify dimensions as compared to drawing | | | | | * |

*Topps has six years all-around machine experience with multiple milling experience & setup vertical/horizontal.

# American Electric Corporation

## Table of Contents

NOTES

# A. Caption

IN THE MATTER OF ARBITRATION BETWEEN:

| | |
|---|---|
| AMERICAN ELECTRIC CORPORATION VICKSBURG, MISSISSIPPI ) ) ) )  AND ) )  PAN AMERICAN UNION LOCAL 204 ) ) | RE: RECALL GRIEVANCE |

Appearances:

For the Union: Harry Katz

For the Company: Janette Cross

Date: December 10, year 6

Place: Vicksburg, Mississippi

## B. Examination of Union Witnesses

### 1. J. Thomas Byrd, Chief Steward, Local 204

#### a. Direct Examination by Union Advocate

*Mr. Katz:*

**Q:** Mr. Byrd, are you an employee of the American Electric Corporation in Vicksburg?

**A:** Yes, I am.

**Q:** And how long have you been employed by American Electric?

**A:** Fourteen years.

**Q:** And do you hold any office in Pan Am Local 204?

**A:** Yes, I do.

**Q:** Local 204 represents what employees?

**A:** Production, Maintenance, and Salary.

**Q:** Now, what office do you hold at present with Local 204?

**A:** Chief Steward.

**Q:** Is that called "Administrative Chief Steward"?

**A:** It is now.

**Q:** And how long have you held that office?

**A:** Eight years.

**Q:** Prior to that did you hold any other office with the Union?

**A:** Yes, I did.

**Q:** And what was that? And for how long, please?

**A:** I was Second and Third Shift Chief Steward for three years. Prior to that, I was an Executive Board member for two years.

**Q:** Now, what are your duties as Chief Steward, in general?

**A:** I am the chairman of any committee that would have local negotiations with the Company. I would be responsible for any grievance procedure to step three. I am responsible for ensuring that the National Agreement is carried out in Vicksburg.

**Q:** Okay, since year 1, you have been the Chief Steward. I think that was your testimony. As such, did you have occasion to enter into discussions with the Company in year 1? Did you have occasion to discuss with the Company the Local Supplement?

**A:** Yes, I did.

**Q:** I show you Joint Exhibit 2, the Local Supplement, and ask you two questions. First, was year 1 the year of national negotiations?

**A:** Yes, it was.

**Q:** And the second question is, did you engage in any discussion with the Company in year 1 with respect to the Supplement?

**A:** Yes, we did.

**Q:** And what did those discussions concern? What portions of the Local Supplement?

**A:** In September and October of year 1, I spoke with Robert Custis, the Company spokesman.

**Q:** What was Mr. Custis's title at that time?

**A:** He was Manager of Employee-Plant-Community Relations and Union Relations Manager.

**Q:** Now, would you tell us what the discussions were about?

**A:** At the initial meetings, in the first two or three weeks, Mr. Custis was proposing language changes in the Local Supplement dealing with Section A, 1(a) and 3.

**Q:** You mentioned 1(a). Could you tell us what the Company's statements were with respect to that provision?

**A:** Well, the Company was proposing changes in the language that appears A.1(a). The Company wanted language that would state that the Local Supplement, also called the "Local Layoff Agreement," would not apply to temporary layoffs of up to two weeks in any calendar year.

**Q:** If you could, try to give us the actual conversations, as opposed to the conclusions drawn in the conversations, O.K.?

**A:** Yes.

**Q:** Was there any discussion in connection with section A.3., which is the rehiring or recall provision?

**A:** No, there wasn't.

**Q:** Incidentally, the language of the recall provision—do you know how long that language has been in the Local Supplement?

2

**A:** It has been in the Local Supplement for nineteen years, without any changes.

**Q:** Now, you stated that you have been employed by the Company for 14 years. Up until February of year 4, were you aware of any layoffs for lack of work occurring in Vicksburg where people were bumped down into other jobs—or bumped upwards, either?

**A:** Yes.

**Q:** And I am confining you to years prior to year 4—was there a layoff in year 3?

**A:** Yes, there was.

**Q:** And are you familiar with that layoff?

**A:** Generally, yes.

**Q:** And was there a layoff the year before that?

**A:** Yes, there was.

**Q:** And in the year before that?

**A:** Yes.

**Q:** So you are acquainted with layoffs in years prior to year 4. In any of the other layoffs with which you are familiar, what was the reason for these layoffs?

**A:** A lack of work situation in a given area of classification, created by a lack of orders or business at that particular time.

**Q:** And were there recalls of employees after these layoffs?

**A:** Yes, there were.

**Q:** Please tell me the procedure used in recalling employees after these layoffs.

**A:** As the workload increased, and the necessity of adding employees to a given classification was created, persons that had previously come off of those classifications for lack of work were recalled to their former classifications.

**Q:** Now, let's jump ahead to February of year 4. I think we stipulated that in year 3 and in years prior, the layoffs generally took the form of employees being taken off their regular classification and bumped down or placed in other classifications. Now, in light of that, can you describe specifically what the procedure was on a recall of such employees when there was an increase in workload?

**A:** I thought I had stated that when work picked up and created the necessity of additional employees in a particular classification, those employees that had previously been removed from that specific classification for lack of work were recalled to

that classification. They were given first preference in going back to that classification and had the option to refuse to go back.

**Q:** Now, can you describe to us what, if any, practice there was with respect to employees who were not affected by a lack of work in their classification, doing work of employees who were either bumped down or placed in another job because of lack of work in the latter employees' classification?

**A:** There was no practice which permitted those employees to do work in the classification where others had been laid off. The only exception would be if an assignment took place on an incidental basis.

**Q:** What is an "incidental basis"?

**A:** A couple of hours in a given day on a particular assignment, one that the individual would not normally be assigned to.

**Q:** You said that there was no Company practice permitting that?

**A:** It just didn't occur, other than incidentally.

**Q:** Was there ever a time when the Company required more than "incidental work"?

**A:** Yes.

**Q:** What occurred then?

**A:** Well, in a classification where there had been a reduction in force and people were on a layoff, there would be a recall of employees on layoff in that classification. Additionally, a classification that had had a reduction in forces may still have had as many as 30 people left in that classification. After the reduction in force, the need to perform other than "incidental assignments" within that classification was handled with limited overtime being worked by those people left in that classification.

**Q:** What was the cutoff for current employees doing "incidental work"?

**A:** The cutoff would have occurred when the amount of work that was being performed by persons other than those persons so classified would have constituted a full-time assignment for a person or persons that previously had been removed from that classification for lack of work.

**Q:** How much "incidental work" time was ever actually regularly assigned to people from outside classifications?

**A:** A couple of hours, once or twice a week, and not continuing.

**Q:** Now, assuming that the Company needed more work than just a couple of hours once or twice a week?

**A:** They would use those people that remained in that classification—work them overtime or recall people from layoff.

**Q:** Even though they are recalled, those people who had been laid off previously from that classification were only required to perform three, four, five, or six hours of work? Day in and day out for 21 weeks?

**A:** They would recall someone. They would give that person an assignment that would encompass that work plus other regular assembly or pipe work.

**Q:** Let's get back to February, year 4. Did you prepare Joint Exhibit 4, a sheet containing the names of five employees—Nemore, Dean, Lane, Demary, and Barnard.

**A:** Yes, I had it prepared.

**Q:** And what was it prepared from?

**A:** From a document that was given to me by Mr. Custis and Mr. Letcher.

**Q:** What is Mr. Letcher's position?

**A:** At the time, he was the Personnel Manager who assisted Mr. Custis in his duties and attended grievance board meetings. The document was given to us during the discussion on the particular grievance.

**Q:** And what did the sheet indicate?

**A:** It listed five employees who were not then classified as Assemblers or Pipers. It showed the amount of time that each was assigned to do either assembly or pipe work for a 17- or 18-week period, during which we had had people laid off from the assembly and pipe classifications for a lack of work.

**Q:** Now, each of the five people listed who performed assembly or piping work came from what classifications?

**A:** They were from classifications other than assembly or pipe.

**Q:** Now, go to Mr. Nemore for the week ending April, year 4. How many hours did he work and at what rate?

**A:** He worked thirty-six hours on assembly. He was paid the R-18 Assembler rate, instead of the lower rate for the classification he was in.

**Q:** Was Nemore an Assembler or Piper?

**A:** No.

**Q:** Were any of the five?

**A:** No. All were in lower-rated (and lower-paid) positions.

**Q:** Did the other four also receive a higher rate when they were assigned to the Assembler or Piper classifications?

**A:** Yes, in accordance with Article XXII Section 1, of the National Agreement.

**Q:** Do you know what Nemore's job was as of the week ending March 12? His job classification?

**A:** He was a Stage Builder or Erector.

**Q:** And do you know how long he had been in that classification?

**A:** He had been there since the middle of year 1.

**Q:** Now, let's go to Mr. Lane, as of the week ending March 26. What was his job classification?

**A:** Pickle and Grind Pipe.

**Q:** Is that a piping classification such as those we have been talking about in assembly?

**A:** No, it is not. It is a process that deals with pieces of pipe.

**Q:** Do you know how long he had been in that classification?

**A:** I believe that it was mid-year 1.

**Q:** Let's go to Mr. Fred Demary. Do you know what his classification was down to May 14?

**A:** At that time he was classified as a Painter.

**Q:** And how long had he been in that classification?

**A:** I don't know exactly, but it had been a number of years.

**Q:** Joe Barnard—as of the week ending March 12—what was his regular classification?

**A:** Gasket maker, tool crib attendant, and balancing. Those were his duties. I'm not sure of the classification name.

**Q:** How long had he been in that classification?

**A:** I'm not sure about Mr. Barnard.

**Q:** Mr. Jay Dean—what was his classification as of the week ending March 19, or immediately prior?

**A:** Stage Builder or Erector. He'd been there a couple of years.

4

**Q:** While the basic sheet that you received from the Company starts with the week ending March 12, we have had some discussion about the layoff commencing in February. Did you receive any information from the Company as to the amount of hours these five people may have worked or did work in assembly and piping for the period February 13 to the week ending March 12?

**A:** I don't believe so.

**Q:** Mr. Byrd, since you have been an officer or an official or anything directly connected with the Union, what is the longest period of time where people remained on layoff whose work was performed by people from other classifications? In other words, prior to this incident, what is the longest period of time that the same conditions existed?

**A:** You mean consecutive weeks?

**Q:** Yes.

**A:** Never had it.

**Q:** Never had it before?

**A:** No.

**Q:** Now, if it never happened before, how did that past practice you described exist?

**A:** What I am saying didn't happen before is an individual or five individuals assigned for 30 to 40 hours a week over a week, let alone a ten-week period. Recalls were directed at an increase in the workload. Recalls did not depend on the Company making assignments of out-of-classification people.

**Q:** So, then, what is the longest time period in the past of the Company making assignments of out-of-classification people?

**A:** We have never had a situation like the one in February year 4.

**Q:** What is the longest period of time that you had incidental assignments on a per-day basis?

**A:** They aren't consecutive days necessarily. A couple of hours at a time, once or twice a week.

**Q:** Now, how did that continue while people were on a lack of work from a given situation?

**A:** I don't know.

**Q:** To the best of your recollection?

**A:** An incidental assignment on a per/day basis may happen one week and then not happen again for six months and then happen again in three weeks.

**Q:** Has it ever happened that these incidental assignments ran for consecutive weeks?

**A:** I don't believe it happened.

**Q:** My last question is whether there was any layoff for lack of work in the Painter Apparatus, the Stage Builder, or the Tool and Gauge classifications that same February?

**A:** No, there was not.

**Q:** No further questions

### b. Cross-Examination by Company Advocate

*Ms. Cross:*
[to be supplied by student]

## 2. Norman L. Kupian, Welder

### a. Direct Examination by Union Advocate

*Mr. Katz:*

**Q:** Mr. Kupian, are you employed by American Electric Corporation?

**A:** Yes, I am.

**Q:** When were you hired by the Company?

**A:** Twenty-eight years ago.

**Q:** Now, did you ever work as a Painter in the bay area?

**A:** Yes, I did.

**Q:** Would you tell us long you did that?

**A:** For six years.

**Q:** Prior to being a Painter, what was your job with American?

**A:** I operated a Blanchard grinder.

**Q:** How did you happen to become a Painter in the bay area?

5

**A:** There was a layoff and I was laid off from the grinders. So I bumped a man out of the paint booth.

**Q:** Who was your foreman when you became a painter in bay?

**A:** Mr. Bedford.

**Q:** Incidentally, the man you bumped out of the paint booth is dead, isn't he?

**A:** Yes, he is.

**Q:** When you began in the paint area, when you ran out of work, were you assigned to do other work?

**A:** For a while I was assigned to help the pipers.

**Q:** When you say "help the pipers," for how long a period of time each time were you assigned?

**A:** Oh, very briefly. I was the only painter that they had on all shifts. So, it was for very brief periods of time.

**Q:** How long is "very brief"?

**A:** Well, it may be part of a day.

**Q:** How many hours?

**A:** Probably four or five.

**Q:** Four or five hours a day?

**A:** Yes.

**Q:** For how many days a week?

**A:** Probably one day a week.

**Q:** Now, were these occasions that you were assigned to help the pipers frequent or rare?

**A:** Pretty rare.

**Q:** And that means?

**A:** I might run out of work one day a month and I might go a couple of months without it. There might be a time when I go two days without work, but I don't think it ever went beyond the two-day period.

**Q:** Now, when you ran out of work and were assigned to help others, did you ever work on assembly?

**A:** No.

**Q:** During this period of time, did you ever work on piping jobs when the regular pipers were laid off?

**A:** No.

**Q:** Did there come a time when you were no longer assigned to piping work?

**A:** Yes.

**Q:** Can you tell me about when that was?

**A:** I'd say about 18 or 19 years ago.

**Q:** Can you describe the circumstances with respect to your not being assigned piping work?

**A:** Well, when I would run out of work, Mr. Bedford would have me report to one of his piping leaders. This one was Joe Tioroni. He was to keep me busy. He was breaking me in on bending tubing and doing small tubing work.

**Q:** Which is pipe work?

**A:** Yes. When I got fairly adept at it, I asked Mr. Bedford for a special rate while I was doing that type of work. He refused and he told me he didn't want me to pick up a piping wrench after that, so I never did any more piping duties after that. Instead I cut gaskets, I cleaned up the area and stuff like that.

**Q:** As a painter, what was your rate at that time?

**A:** R-13.

**Q:** What special rate did you ask for?

**A:** I figured they would start me with what the Piper Class B would get, probably R-15, and I could work my way up to R-18.

**Q:** Did Mr. Bedford say anything when you asked him for the special rate, other than he didn't want you to do piping anymore?

**A:** That's all.

**Q:** Since then, have you ever done any piping work?

**A:** No.

**Q:** Did there come a time when you left the Painter's classification?

**A:** Yes, there was. I went to a welding school they set up and became a welder. That's what I have done ever since.

**Q:** When you say, "they set up," what do you mean?

**A:** The Company set it up. There was a layoff at the time and they couldn't get welders. They had welders in with lower service and some of the older guys were on the streets, so they set up this welding school to break in some of the older people so they could take over.

**Q:** While you were in welding school, were you under Foreman Bedford's supervision?

**A:** No, I wasn't.

**Q:** Did there come a time when you returned to Foreman Bedford's supervision?

A: Yes, I bumped into an opening. I believe it was six years before the incident we are arbitrating.

Q: What has been your occupation since then?

A: Welding.

Q: Have you done anything else?

A: No.

Q: Were you a painter any time since then?

A: No.

Q: From the time you became a welder, have you ever been assigned to work either on assembly or piping work?

A: No.

Q: Who was your foreman for that period?

A: Mr. Bedford was.

Q: No further questions.

### b. Cross-Examination by Company Advocate

*Ms. Cross:*
[to be supplied by student]

# C. Examination of Company Witnesses

## 1. David H. Bedford, Supervisor, Final Assembly Control

### a. Direct Examination by Company Advocate

*Ms. Cross:*

Q: Mr. Bedford, what is your present position with the American Electric Company?

A: Supervisor, Final Assembly Control.

Q: And how long have you been in that position?

A: Four years.

Q: And would you briefly review your prior work record with the American Electric Company for the Arbitrator?

A: I was hired 31 years ago, was made a supervisor 10 years later in the Bay, and was a supervisor until year 3.

Q: All right. Would you briefly describe the product or products that are manufactured in the Vicksburg plant?

A: We make steam turbine drives both for industrial, utility and for generator service for Maine. These are quite large machines. The average weight probably runs something around 18 tons. We require cranes for practically all assembly and erection of these units.

Q: You were the Assembly Foreman during the layoff that is in dispute, right?

A: Yes, sir.

Q: Were Mr. Nemore, Mr. Barnard, and Mr. Demary under your supervision?

A: Yes, they were. Two were Staging Erectors, and one was on the second shift.

Q: Now, what was Mr. Barnard's classification?

A: Dynamic Balance.

Q: Prior to the layoff of the Assemblers and Pipers, did you assign Mr. Barnard to work outside the Dynamic Balance?

A: Yes, sir.

Q: How often?

A: Regularly.

Q: And on what basis?

A: Because the Dynamic Balance as such wasn't a full-time occupation. Never has been.

Q: And what did you assign him to?

A: Assembly. I would say that Dynamic Balance wouldn't require more than three days in any one week, and this was a continual thing.

Q: So, week after week, prior to February of year 4, he did Dynamic Balance work for three days a week and Assembly work for two days a week?

A: Yes, sir.

7

**Q:**   At any time during that period prior to February, year 4, was he assigned as you just outlined, while any of the Assemblers were on layoff?

**A:**   Yes. In both years prior to this incident.

**Q:**   You had layoffs among Assemblers, and Mr. Barnard, who is a Dynamic Balancer, was still assigned two days a week to work as an Assembler?

**A:**   Yes, sir.

**Q:**   What was Mr. Demary's job classification?

**A:**   Apparatus Painter.

**Q:**   Prior to year 4, did you assign the Apparatus Painter to work outside of the painting classification?

**A:**   Yes, I frequently did. Maybe one or two days a week, every week.

**Q:**   To what other job was he assigned?

**A:**   Assembly.

**Q:**   Was he ever assigned to Assembly while Assemblers were on layoff?

**A:**   Yes, in the manner I just expressed.

**Q:**   And the others—the Staging Erector, the Dynamic Balancer, and the Apparatus Painter—did you assign them to work in your area while Assemblers were laid off, prior to year 4?

**A:**   Yes.

**Q:**   Was there ever a grievance filed by the Union concerning such assignments?

**A:**   Not to my knowledge.

**Q:**   We have been assuming that when the workload increased sufficient to employ another full-time Assembler, another full-time Assember is supposed to be recalled. Were Assemblers or anyone else under your jurisdiction when they were on layoff automatically recalled as a result of that increase in workload?

**A:**   No.

**Q:**   On what basis were recalls made?

**A:**   I would calculate the number of planned hours of Assembly work in the number of units and divide that by the available people and then try to sell my manager on the number of people required to meet the objective.

**Q:**   When that requirement was fulfilled, did you take into consideration the fact that employees not classified as Assemblers were regularly and consistently assigned to Assembly work?

**A:**   Yes, but with the decrease in work we still assigned, for instance, the Balancer to Assembly work.

**Q:**   For what period of time during the week?

**A:**   Probably two to four days.

**Q:**   Despite the fact that the workload had been decreased?

**A:**   Yes. I don't have the records handy to be sure, though.

**Q:**   Was there a contractual justification for that?

**A:**   I don't really know that.

**Q:**   Now, during the layoffs over the years, was there any practice prohibiting employees from being assigned work, including overtime work, in classifications from which an employee or employees were laid off?

**A:**   Not that I know of.

**Q:**   During the year 4 layoff, was there full-time work for the remaining Assemblers, day in and day out, in their classification?

**A:**   No, at times there wasn't.

**Q:**   And did you assign the Assemblers remaining some work outside of that classification to keep them fully employed in Assembly work during that period?

**A:**   Yes, we did.

**Q:**   How do you explain, then, also working overtime in that same area during that period?

**A:**   As we manufacture our product, emergencies arise—certainly not every day, but there would be times when overtime was necessary because of a breakdown, mechanically, or in testing.

**Q:**   And how did you justify this happening for 21 weeks?

**A:**   I don't think I made that assumption. I am sorry if I was misunderstood, but there was overtime work before the layoff, and I don't think that there was any more overtime worked during the layoff period than there was prior to the layoffs.

**Q:**   Could you clarify yourself? During the period of the layoff, were the situations when there was insufficient work for the remaining Assemblers extensive or limited?

**A:**   It was very limited, very limited.

**Q:**   No further questions.

b. Cross-Examination by Union Advocate

*Mr. Katz:*
[to be supplied by student]


## 2. Richard Santas, Foreman, Plumbers and Steamfitters

### a. Direct Examination by Company Advocate

*Ms. Cross:*
Q: Would you state your position with American Electric Company?
A: I am a foreman on the day shift in the Plumbers and Steamfitters.
Q: All right. How long have you been a foreman? Incidentally, is that the Piping area?
A: Yes, it's the Piping area. I have been a foreman in the Piping area since year 1.
Q: Now, would you briefly review your work history at the Company, prior to the time you became the foreman of the Piping area?
A: I was hired twenty-four years ago. After three years I was laid off and then again, three years later, I was recalled. I became a Union official. About two years before the layoff we are discussing I became a leader in Plumbing and Steamfitting.
Q: Was that still in the Bargaining Unit?
A: Yes. I was the leader for eighteen months up to the point of being made foreman in September of year 1.
Q: So you were the Piping Foreman during the layoff in year 4 of the Assemblers and Pipers involved in this grievance. Is that correct?
A: Yes.
Q: Were you in the Piping area during the layoff ten years prior to the layoff in year 2?
A: Yes.
Q: Was Mr. Kupian an Apparatus Painter during that layoff?
A: Yes, sir.
Q: During that layoff, was he assigned to any Piping work in the Piping area?
A: Yes, sir.
Q: Now, was Mr. Lane one of the employees under your supervision in the Piping area during the period when you were a foreman?
A: Yes.
Q: What was his classification at that time?

A: Cut, Grind, Pickle and Hydro.
Q: Now, did you assign Mr. Lane to work outside of the Make Gaskets, Cut-off Thread, and Pickle Pipe classification?
A: Yes.
Q: On what basis?
A: On the basis that when he had no work, I knew that he was an ex-Piper, so I would assign him to pipe work.
Q: How often?
A: Roughly two days a week, depending on the work.
Q: How many weeks a year?
A: Roughly half.
Q: During your years as the foreman in the Piping area and in your prior assignments as a leader or as a Piper, were employees who were laid off from their regular classifications ever automatically recalled as the workload increased in those areas? Up to and including the year 4 layoff?
A: No, sir.
Q: Now, at my request yesterday, did you review the payroll register that we had present in the hearing room?
A: Yes, sir.
Q: For what purpose did you review it at my request?
A: For the hours of overtime spent by Mr. Lane.
Q: During what period?
A: From February to July of year 4.
Q: Can you recall the nature of any of that overtime work?
A: The work that he did and the overtime hours were in his own classification.
Q: How do you know that?
A: He didn't work that much overtime, but at that time, we did have some turbines that were Navy turbines that by specification called

for Hydro testing of pipe. That's what any overtime was spent doing.

**Q:** But you testified a moment ago that, on the average, half his time or somewhat less than that was spent elsewhere?

**A:** During the forty-hour week.

**Q:** Was any of that spent on overtime?

**A:** No, sir.

**Q:** I take it, then, that the total amount of overtime we are referring to was solely to overtime in his own occupation?

**A:** That's right.

**Q:** Now, Mr. Santas, during the layoffs over the years up to the layoff in year 4, was there any practice that you are aware of prohibiting employees from being assigned work, including overtime, outside of their own classifications in classifications from which other employees were laid off?

**A:** No, sir.

**Q:** When you were a Piper, before you were a foreman, were you ever assigned to work in classifications from which other employees were on layoff during the period they were off?

**A:** Yes, sir.

**Q:** No further questions.

## b. Cross-Examination by Union Advocate

*Mr. Katz:*
[to be supplied by student]

## 3. Brendan Candle, Manager, Union Contract Administration

### a. Direct Examination by Company Advocate

*Ms. Cross:*

**Q:** Mr. Candle, what is your present position with American Electric Company?

**A:** I am Manager of Union Contract Administration, Corporate Headquarters.

**Q:** How long have you held that position?

**A:** For approximately three years.

**Q:** Would you briefly review your history with the Company?

**A:** I started thirty-eight years ago. I have been in Union relations for twenty-nine years. Most of that time was spent in the Bangor and San Jose plants. Then four years prior to the incident at issue, I moved to headquarters.

**Q:** What do the responsibilities of your present job encompass?

**A:** My group's responsibilities are to handle grievances at the third step of the grievance procedure, to handle requests for arbitration, and to schedule arbitrations.

**Q:** Did you make a review of the request for arbitration for this case?

**A:** Yes, I did.

**Q:** Based on this review, had the Union ever previously requested arbitration challenging the company's right to work some employees on overtime while other employees were laid off?

**A:** The answer is no.

**Q:** Has the Union ever requested arbitration of a grievance claiming that Article XI restricted when a reduction in force could be made or when a recall was required?

**A:** No.

**Q:** Now, has the Union ever made demands in national contract negotiations seeking to restrict management's right to schedule overtime while other employees were on layoff?

**A:** Yes, it has.

**Q:** Seven years before the present incident, did the Union submit a proposal to restrict overtime while employees were in layoff?

**A:** Yes, sir.

**Q:** Was the proposal rejected by the company?

**A:** Yes.

**Q:** In negotiations four years prior to the present incident, did the Union demand to restrict overtime while other employees are laid off?

**A:** Yes.

**Q:**   Was that proposal also rejected by the
Company?

**A:**   Yes.

**Q:**   No further questions.

b. Cross-Examination by Union Advocate

*Mr. Katz:*
[to be supplied by student]

# D. Exhibits

## *JOINT EXHIBIT NO.1*

NATIONAL
COLLECTIVE BARGAINING AGREEMENT
BETWEEN
AMERICAN ELECTRIC CORPORATION
AND
PAN AMERICAN UNION (12/1/02-12/1/05)

. . .

ARTICLE XI:   Reduction or Increase in Forces

Section 1.  Whenever there is a reduction in the working force, or employees are laid off from their regular jobs, total length of continuous service, applied on a plant, department, or other basis as negotiated locally, shall be the major factor determining the employees to be laid off or transferred (exclusive of upgrading or transfers to higher-rated jobs). However, ability will be given consideration.

Similarly in all cases of rehiring after layoff, total length of continuous service, applied on a plant, department, or other basis as negotiated locally, shall be the major factor covering such rehiring if the employee is able to do the available work in a satisfactory manner after a minimum amount of training.

Where employees have accumulated six months or more of service credits, but have not established continuity service, such service credits will be considered in the above cases rather than total length of continuous service.

Section 2.  Since the number of employees in the individual bargaining units covered under this Agreement varies from less than 50 to more than 10,000, each Local shall negotiate with local management a written Agreement covering the layoff and rehiring procedure for the employees represented by the Local....

ARTICLE XV: Grievance and Arbitration
. . .
Section 4.
. . .
   b. In the consideration and decision of any question involving arbitrability (including any application to a court for an order directing arbitration), it is the specific agreement of the parties that:
. . .
   (iv)  In the consideration of whether a matter is subject to arbitration as a matter of right, a fundamental principle shall be that the Company retains all its rights to manage the business, including (but not limited to) the right to determine the methods and means by which its operations are to be carried on to direct the work force and to conduct its operations in a safe and effective manner, subject only to the express

12

limitations set forth in this National Agreement, Local Seniority Supplements executed under the provisions of Article XI thereof, and Local Understandings executed in accordance with Section 3 of Article XXI thereof; and it is understood that the parties have not agreed to arbitrate demands which challenge action taken by the Company in the exercise of any such rights, except where such challenge is based upon a violation of any such express limitations (other than those set out in Section 7 below).

...

Section 6.

...

b. A request for arbitration, in order to be subject to arbitration as a matter of right under the provisions of subsection (a)(ii) and (a)(iii) above, must allege a direct violation of the express purpose of the contractual provision in question, rather than of an indirect or implied purpose. For example, a request which claims incorrect application of the method of computing overtime pay under the provisions of Section 2 of Article V would be arbitrable as a matter of right, whereas a request which questioned the right of the Company to require the performance of reasonable overtime work, on the claimed ground that Article V contains no implied limitation on that right, would be subject only to voluntary arbitration. A request that Article XI and the appropriate Local Seniority Supplement had been violated by the layoff of a senior employee in preference to a junior employee would be arbitrable as a matter of right, but a request that subcontracting of work in the plant while bargaining unit employees are on layoff violated a claimed implied limitation of Article XI and the applicable Local Seniority Supplement would be subject only to voluntary arbitration.

...

Section 7.
All requests for arbitration which are not subject to arbitration as a matter of right under the provisions of Section 6 above are subject only to voluntary arbitration. In particular, it is specifically agreed that arbitration requests shall be subject only to voluntary arbitration, by mutual agreement if they...

...

(c) Involve claims that an allegedly implied or assumed obligation of this National Agreement has been violated.

ARTICLE XXI:  Local Understanding
...

Section 3.
The existence of, or any alleged violation of, a local understanding shall not be the basis of any arbitration proceeding, unless such understanding is in writing and sighted by the Company and Union.

. . .

ARTICLE XXII: Overtime
Section 1. An employee assigned to a different classification shall receive the higher of the two rates, the rate for his or her classification and the rate for the classification to which he or she is assigned.

*JOINT EXHIBIT NO. 2*

LOCAL SUPPLEMENT TO
COLLECTIVE BARGAINING AGREEMENT
BETWEEN
AMERICAN ELECTRIC CORPORATION
AND
LOCAL 204
PAN AMERICAN UNION (12/1/02-12/1/05)

**Preamble**

This agreement is pursuant to Section 2 of Article XI of the National Agreement.

A. Lay-off and Rehiring Procedure

This section incorporates the provisions of Section 1, Article XI, of the National Agreement.

   1. (a)  The following procedure will apply in selecting employees for layoff (or transfer) whenever the working force is reduced or employees are laid off from their regular jobs due to lack of work.

   (b)  Lists shall be made up of those employees within the occupations affected, and employees selected for layoff (or transfer) shall be those with the shortest continuous service within the affected group, provided that those remaining can do the work available.

. . .

   3. Rehiring

In all cases of rehiring after layoff, total length of continuous service shall be the major factor covering such rehiring if the employee is able to do the available work in a satisfactory manner after a minimum amount of training. Likewise, rehiring after layoff will be done on a plant-wide basis for all jobs within the bargaining unit.

. . .

*JOINT EXHIBIT NO.3*

PAN-AMERICAN UNION, LOCAL 204

GRIEVANCE (7/10/04)

<u>Violation</u>: The Company violated Article XI of the National Agreement, The Local Supplement, and past practice by assigning certain out-of-classification employees on an overtime basis to do assembly and pipe work for extended periods while employees in The Assembly and Pipe classification were on layoff. The Assembly and Pipe classification employees on layoff should have been recalled to perform this work.

<u>Remedy</u>: The Assembly and Pipe employees at the time of said illegal assignment be made whole.

COMPANY'S GRIEVANCE ANSWERS (7/11/04, 7/15/04 and 7/20/04)

Step 1: The grievance is denied. Neither the Agreement nor past practice supports the grievance.

Steps 2 & 3: Grievance denied for reason indicated in step 1 answer.

*JOINT EXHIBIT NO. 4*

Time spent by workers from lower classifications doing assembly or pipe work at higher Assembly and Pipe work pay rate during layoff of assembly and pipe workers.

| Week Ending | Individual | | | | |
|---|---|---|---|---|---|
| | Barnard[1] | Dean[2] | Demary[3] | Lane[4] | Nemore[2] |
| 3/12/04 | 32 | 37 | 30 | 33 | 38 |
| 3/19/04 | 35 | 35 | 37 | 32 | 39 |
| 3/26/04 | 38 | 33 | 30 | 37 | 32 |
| 4/2/04 | 30 | 38 | 36 | 32 | 36 |
| 4/9/04 | 33 | 35 | 31 | 38 | 38 |
| 4/16/04 | 34 | 33 | 38 | 30 | 36 |
| 4/23/04 | 32 | 31 | 37 | 39 | 40 |
| 4/30/04 | 38 | 40 | 33 | 36 | 35 |
| 5/7/04 | 30 | 31 | 32 | 30 | 30 |
| 5/14/04 | 31 | 30 | 30 | 30 | 30 |
| 5/21/04 | 34 | 35 | 37 | 40 | 39 |
| 5/28/04 | 32 | 35 | 36 | 31 | 34 |
| 6/4/04 | 40 | 30 | 33 | 37 | 38 |
| 6/11/04 | 34 | 30 | 34 | 30 | 31 |
| 6/18/04 | 31 | 33 | 30 | 32 | 30 |
| 6/25/04 | 30 | 30 | 32 | 31 | 30 |
| 7/2/04 | 30 | 31 | 30 | 30 | 31 |

---

[1] Gasket Maker, Tool Crib Attendant, and Balancing.
[2] Stage Builder or Erector
[3] Painter
[4] Pickle and Grind Pipe

# Princeton Manufacturing Company

## Table of Contents

**Table of Contents contd.**

**NOTES**

# A. Caption

IN THE MATTER OF A CONTROVERSY BETWEEN:

<table>
<tr>
<td>

PRINCETON MANUFACTURING CO.<br>
ALITA, OHIO

AND

LOCAL 209, INTERNATIONAL UNION OF<br>
COMPUTER TECHNICIANS (I.U.C.T.)

</td>
<td>

)<br>
)<br>
)<br>
)<br>
)<br>
)<br>
)<br>
)

</td>
<td>

RE: DENIAL OF PAY<br>
    FOR APPEARANCE<br>
    BEFORE THE OHIO HUMAN<br>
    RIGHTS COMMISSION<br>
    PURSUANT TO SUBPOENA

</td>
</tr>
</table>

Appearances:

For the Union: Leroy Mandrake

For the Company: Nancy Brewer

Date: December 4, year 11

Place: Alita, Ohio

# B. Examination of Union Witnesses

## 1. Ned Haliday, President, Local 209

### a. Direct Examination by Union Advocate

*Mr. Mandrake:*

**Q:** May we have your full name for the record, please?

**A:** Ned Haliday.

**Q:** Ned, what is your position with the Company?

**A:** My position with the Company? I'm a Designer. Draftsman.

**Q:** And how long have you been employed by the Company?

**A:** Twenty-two, going on twenty-three years.

**Q:** What is your position with the Union?

**A:** At the present, I'm President of Local 209.

**Q:** How long have you been active in some capacity as an official of the Union?

**A:** As far as this location goes, I participated in Union activities, you might say, from the first day that I got here. I joined the Union and became the Steward—I don't know when, but shortly thereafter. I've been on various committees, including the negotiating committee, and Vice President of the Local before I became President.

**Q:** Were you involved in, or President of, the Local during the year 4 negotiations?

**A:** Yes, I was.

**Q:** Was Section 1, Article XVI in the previous Agreement, years 1–5?

**A:** Yes.

**Q:** What is your understanding, of Section 1, Article XVI, of the Agreement, the Jury Duty Clause? Look at Joint Exhibit 1.

**A:** Just talking strictly, Section 1 of Article XVI, that's payment for anybody who is called to serve on jury duty. As far as it relates to Local 209, people who are covered by the contract would receive full payment for the time they're out of work and serving on jury. If they happen to be out one day, they receive one day's pay. Plus, if the court gives them anything—like in the case of the County Court here, they call them for two weeks at a time—they usually receive two weeks' pay, totaling forty hours a week each week, plus

what the court sometimes gives them, and that used to be $18.00 a day plus traveling expenses if they live a great distance away from the court. This is in relationship to salaried employees only. The only other thing I could add to that—my personal experience is that I've been on jury duty two times for two-week sessions, for which I got full pay plus what the court gave me. No traveling time because I lived in the city. Two other times I was called for one-day sessions at the City Court, for which I received eight hours pay, or four hours, whatever time I came back. I forget, it was so long ago. And another time I was called, I didn't know what it was until I got down there. It was a Justice of the Peace, and they had some kind of a trial in his office. Four or five of us were picked as a jury to decide the case. It was an informal-type thing. It was in an office, and I was paid for that.

**Q:** Ned, in reference to Article XVI, Section 2, of the year 5–9 Agreement, on subpoenas, which was inserted into the Agreement following the strike of year 4, did you at any time remember negotiating this with local management? Here take a look at Joint Exhibit 1.

**A:** No. It was given to us when we were on strike, and sometimes we didn't meet, sometimes we did. But I think this was something that was given to us right near the end, if I recall it right, and we never discussed it. They said, "Here it is," and that's it. There was no discussion to clarify it. If there had been, maybe we wouldn't be here today. But that's why we're here today, because it was never clarified, and we feel that we're right, and that's why we filed the grievance.

**Q:** How do you interpret the language in Section 2?

**A:** It was intended to apply to administrative hearings as well as court proceedings. This had been the past practice for years.

**Q:** Ned, when the employees Sally Adams and Barry Newell received subpoenas from the

Ohio Human Rights Commission, did they discuss the matter with you?

**A:** Yes. They called me on it when they got it and they wanted to know if they should go, and I said, "Well, you've been subpoenaed. You better go, or you're going to end up in trouble, because according to the law you can end up going to court and getting fined for not showing up even if your are only disinterested witnesses and not parties to the action."

**Q:** Aside from the fine, what else can happen in regard to the—if you don't answer the subpoena?

**A:** What would happen? Like I said, you'd be pulled into court, and maybe subject to a fine or jail sentence. I actually don't know— probably just a fine. But also with that, if he—according to the contract, if he is pulled into court, I don't know whether the Company even bothers paying him for something like that, whether he's covered on personal time or not. Or maybe he could use his vacation time. But I don't know the Company's rules as far as an individual who refuses to honor a subpoena and gets called into court, what happens to his payment of lost time from work. Would the Company pay that personal time? I'd have to ask the other side. I know he could put in for vacation pay, but he wouldn't be paid under the provisions of Article XVI of the Agreement when subpoenaed.

**Q:** Ned, were you issued a subpoena to attend a hearing of the Ohio State Division of Human Rights, also referred to as the Human Rights Commission?

**A:** Yes.

**Q:** By whom?

**A:** By Princeton Manufacturing Company.

**Q:** Did you attend?

**A:** Yes, I attended the hearing.

**Q:** Did you receive payment for lost time to attend the meeting?

**A:** Yes, but I don't know how I was—under what, where they put it. I don't think they put it on the personal time, and I know they didn't charge it to my vacation time. Where they slotted it, I don't know. Probably under some kind of—if you look at the time voucher Princeton Manufacturing has, they have got Code 05 indicated on one of them, which pays you for going to different types of meetings,

whether it be business meetings or whatever, and under Code 02, which is jury duty, personal time, sick time.

**Q:** You were not advised that in order to be paid you had to use personal time or vacation time if you honored the subpoena?

**A:** I was told that I wouldn't have to use personal or vacation time to get paid. I would get paid because the Company subpoenaed me.

**Q:** What were employees Sally Adams and Barry Newell told by the Company?

**A:** They were given a choice. The Company told me that as far as the subpoenas to Sally Adams and Barry Newell were concerned, the Company wasn't going to pay them unless they used personal time or vacation time, and that's all. Otherwise they wouldn't get paid.

**Q:** And were you informed by the Company that you would get paid if you attended the hearing?

**A:** Yes. Like I said, it wasn't under the personal time or the vacation time.

**Q:** Ned, in reference to Barry Newell, did he lose actual time from work?

**A:** He lost time from actual working time, yes. As far as money goes, he was paid under the personal time code. They charged it under personal time for him so he wouldn't lose any money out of his paycheck.

**Q:** Of course, he was compelled to sacrifice one of his contracted personal days, or personal time, in order to get paid?

**A:** Yes.

**Q:** In reference to Sally Adams, did she receive any payment?

**A:** She has had a lot of sickness, which required her to use personal time—problems in the family where she was taking a lot of time off. She said that she refused to use her personal time or her vacation time. She wanted to save her personal time if illness struck again. So as far as she is concerned, she didn't receive payment for that time. She lost money.

**Q:** Ned, is the Union seeking actual payment of monies in reference to Barry Newell, or are you seeking to restore his personal time?

**A:** Both.

**Q:** What is the Union seeking in reference to Sally Adams?

**A:** Well, I'm going to have to say that Sally Adams was not reimbursed for any time lost. So in that case we're asking, basically, the same as Barry Newell plus the payment of lost time since she did not receive any money for that time.

**Q:** That's all I have of the witness.

### b. Cross-Examination by Company Advocate

*Ms. Brewer:*
[to be supplied by student]

# C. Examination of Company Witnesses

## 1. Vincent Spinner, Manager, Union Relations for Computer Systems Department

### a. Direct Examination by Company Advocate

*Ms. Brewer:*
**Q:** Would you state your name for the record, please?
**A:** Vincent Spinner.
**Q:** Vincent, what is your position with Princeton Manufacturing Company, currently?
**A:** I am the Manager of Union Relations for the Computer Systems Department.
**Q:** And how long have you been Manager of Union Relations?
**A:** Since April of year 8.
**Q:** And what position did you hold prior to this position as Manager of Union Relations?
**A:** I was Specialist, Union Relations, for the Computer Systems Department from January of year 1 to April of year 8.
**Q:** And how long have you been employed at Princeton Manufacturing Company?
**A:** In excess of twenty-four years.
**Q:** Has that all been in this plant?
**A:** Yes, it has.
**Q:** Now, what are your duties in your position as Manager of Union Relations?
**A:** To negotiate collective bargaining agreements with the Unions that represent our employees; to interpret and apply those agreements; to resolve grievances; to keep our management aware of the interpretation and application of those agreements; to participate in training programs for our supervisory personnel so that they're acquainted with the contents of the contracts; to keep supervisors aware of legislative decisions and arbitration decisions that have an effect on our relationships with the people that are represented by our Unions.

**Q:** All right. Now, Vincent, did you participate in the negotiations between Local 209 and the Princeton Manufacturing Company in year 4 leading to the year 5 to year 8 Collective Bargaining Agreement between the parties?
**A:** I did.
**Q:** And did Local 209 make any demands, locally, concerning the jury duty provisions in Article XVI?
**A:** They did not.
**Q:** And do you confirm Mr. Haliday's testimony that there was no discussion locally with respect to the provisions of Article XVI, Section 2, as they were subsequently included in the Collective Bargaining Agreement between the parties?
**A:** I do.
**Q:** Now, at any time during those negotiations did Local 209 indicate that it was involved in the Coordinated Bargaining Committee efforts in the national negotiations between Princeton and the International Union of Computer Technicians, I.U.C.T. and the I.A.E. Unions?
**A:** It did.
**Q:** In what way? How?

**A:** Local 209 acknowledged that it was a member of the Coordinated Bargaining Committee; that it had telecommunications hookups with the negotiations going on at the national level; that it had representatives at the national level, George Sams and Tony Myer; that there would be no settlement locally unless there was a settlement nationally; and in Local 209's written demands and in our discussions during negotiations, there were references to national demands.

**Q:** All right. Now, I show you Sections 1 and 2 of Article XVI of the year 5–9, Joint Agreement Exhibit 1. Where did the language come from?

**A:** Section 1 was in the prior contract and as for Section 2 that language was supplied to us by our corporate officials when they authorized us to make this benefit offer to Local 209.

**Q:** All right. Now, Vincent, between the time the year 5 to year 8 Collective Bargaining Agreement took effect and the time of the incident in May of year 9 which gave rise to this arbitration hearing, had the Company, to your knowledge, in the Computer Systems Department in Alita ever paid an employee under the provisions of Article XVI, Section 2, for attendance pursuant to a subpoena at a hearing of the Ohio State Division of Human Rights?

**A:** It did not.

**Q:** Or the Ohio Workman's Compensation Board?

**A:** It did not.

**Q:** Or any hearing of the National Labor Relations Board?

**A:** It did not.

**Q:** Or any other administrative hearings?

**A:** It did not.

**Q:** Or any arbitration hearings?

**A:** It did not.

**Q:** Now, during this same period and prior to—to this period in which this particular provision was included in the local Collective Bargaining Agreement at Alita, has the Company at the Alita plant paid the wages for time lost by employees to be witnesses on behalf of the Company at any administrative agency hearings or any arbitration hearings, or any court proceedings?

**A:** It has.

**Q:** And were they paid when they appeared as Company witnesses, whether they were subpoenaed or not?

**A:** They were.

**Q:** On what basis?

**A:** That was their work day for that day.

**Q:** Now, with specific regard to Mr. Haliday in the hearing before the State Division of Human Rights, were you present when he was asked to be a witness in that hearing?

**A:** I was.

**Q:** And was he—what was he told with respect to the method of payment?

**A:** He would be paid for attending that hearing because that would be his work for that day, and he would not be paid under any subpoena. If he was issued a subpoena, he would not be paid under the Jury Duty Article of that contract.

**Q:** Vincent, I would like you to look at Company Exhibit 1. Would you please describe the document to the Arbitrator?

**A:** Yes, this is a clock card for Mr. Haliday. It is for the week ending May 20, year 9.

**Q:** What is the entry for the absence on the day of the meeting?

**A:** It says "Princeton meeting."

**Q:** Was Mr. Haliday a witness at that meeting?

**A:** No.

**Q:** I show you Company Exhibit 2. Would you please describe this document, including the entry for any absence?

**A:** This is a clock card for Mr. Haliday for the week ending May 25, year 9. There is an entry for absence written as "Company business meeting."

**Q:** Was Mr. Haliday a witness at that meeting?

**A:** No.

**Q:** I show you Company Exhibit 3. Would you please describe this document for the Arbitrator, including any entry made for an absence?

**A:** This is a clock card for Mr. Haliday for the week of the third hearing. The entry on this says, "Company witness at Ohio State Equal Opportunity meeting—hearing."

**Q:** Was Mr. Haliday a witness at that meeting?

**A:** Yes.

**Q:** I have no further questions.

b. Cross-Examination by Union Advocate

*Mr. Mandrake:*
[to be supplied by student]

## 2. Nancy Barber, Manager, Union Contract Administration, Corporate Headquarters

a. Direct Examination by Company Advocate

*Ms. Brewer:*

**Q:** Would you state your name for the record, please?

**A:** Nancy Barber.

**Q:** Would you state what your position is with the Princeton Manufacturing Company, please?

**A:** I'm Manager, Union Contract Administration, at Corporate Headquarters.

**Q:** And what are the responsibilities of that position?

**A:** The Union Contract Administration Operation is responsible for handling grievances and arbitration cases under the I.U.C.T. and I.A.E. National Agreements, as well as giving advice and counsel to our plants around the country regarding contract interpretation for all Union contracts.

**Q:** Did you participate in the year 4 negotiations between I.U.C.T. and the Princeton Manufacturing Company leading to the year 5 to year 9 National Agreement between those parties?

**A:** Yes, I did.

**Q:** And in what capacity?

**A:** I was a member of the Company's Negotiating Committee and a member of the Contract Language Subcommittee.

**A:** All right. And were members of the so-called Coordinated Bargaining Committee of the AFL-CIO present in those negotiations as members of the I.U.C.T. Bargaining Committee?

**A:** Yes, they were.

**Q:** And were any officials of the International Association of Electronic Technicians, I.A.E., included in that group?

**A:** Yes.

**Q:** And do you recall who they were?

**A:** George Sams and a Mr. Carver.

**Q:** All right. I show you a document, Company Exhibit 5. Would you tell the Arbitrator what this document is?

**A:** This is a copy of the Contract Proposals made by the I.U.C.T. during our year 4 negotiations.

**Q:** Now, is there any proposal by the I.U.C.T. in this document concerning the issue in dispute here—witness duty?

**A:** Yes, there is.

**Q:** All right. What is the particular provision?

**A:** The new proposal that they made is Section 2 of Article XVI, which says, "Employees who are compelled to report to court under subpoena or any other court process shall be paid in the same manner during such time they are called to court as employees reporting for jury duty."

**Q:** Now, in the course of the year 4 negotiations, did the Company give the Union any information, statistical or otherwise, concerning the availability of this particular benefit in collective bargaining agreements, generally?

**A:** Yes, we did.

**Q:** I show you a document, Company Exhibit 6, entitled "Pay for Jury Duty." Would you tell the Arbitrator what this document is?

**A:** This is a copy of a slide that was used in the Company's presentation to the I.U.C.T. Negotiating Committee, indicating the number of contracts in our plant communities where make-up pay was paid for jury duty and where make-up pay was paid for witness duty.

**Q:** And what does it show with respect to witnesses, as to the availability of that particular benefit in collective bargaining agreements, generally?

**A:** About ninety percent of those contracts made no provision for pay for witness duty.

6

**Q:** Did the Company respond to the I.U.C.T. demand which is set forth in Company Exhibit 5?

**A:** Yes, we did.

**Q:** All right. I show you Company Exhibit 7A, dated October 7, year 4. Would you tell the Arbitrator what this document is?

**A:** This is a copy of the cover letter signed by Mr. Stan Stanford, President of Princeton Manufacturing, addressed to Mr. Collins, Chairman of the I.U.C.T., Princeton Conferences Board, enclosing proposals for contract language.

**Q:** And the second page, Company Exhibit 7B?

**A:** The second item is the proposal from the Company to the Union amending Article XVI, Jury Duty by adding Section 2. The proposed language, to be effective October 26, year 5, was, "Similar make-up pay as specified in Sections 1 and 2 will be granted to an employee who loses time from work because of an appearance in court pursuant to proper subpoena, except when he or she is either a Plaintiff, Defendant, or other party to the court proceeding."

**Q:** I show you a copy of a year 5 to year 8 Princeton–I.U.C.T. National Agreement. Would you refer the Arbitrator to the part of the contract concerning jury duty?

**A:** Article XXV.

**Q:** And the Section . . .

**A:** Section 3 . . .

**Q:** . . . concerning the dispute involved in this arbitration case—witness pay?

**A:** Section 2 became effective in the year 5 contract, using the language that I previously read in Company Exhibit 7.

**Q:** At any time during the negotiations leading to this year 5 contract, when this language in the Jury Duty Article was discussed in the negotiations at the national level, did the Union claim that this language applied to any situation other than a court proceeding?

**A:** No, they did not. As a matter of fact, all the discussion related to, if you will, an extension of the Section 1 language to cover people who were called to appear as witnesses in a court proceeding.

**Q:** In preparation for this hearing, did you make a survey of Union grievances at other Princeton Manufacturing Company plant locations with respect to the issue in dispute in this case?

**A:** Yes, I did.

**Q:** And did you find any grievances protesting the Company's refusal to pay for attendance at an administrative hearing pursuant to a subpoena on the basis that the Company did not—on the basis that the hearing, rather, did not constitute a court proceeding, other than the one which is the subject of this hearing today?

**A:** Yes, I did.

**Q:** I show you Company Exhibit 9, a document with the title "American Arbitration Association" at the head of it. Would you tell the Arbitrator what this document is?

**A:** This is a summary of the issue and award in a case decided by Arbitrator Jessup, AAA Case. Docket No. 23345, Princeton Manufacturing Company and I.U.C.T.

**Q:** And was the issue in that dispute similar to the one in the instant case?

**A:** Yes The stipulation reads, "Did the Company violate Article XVI of the Agreement for year 5 through year 8 Princeton–I.U.C.T. National Agreement when payment was denied W. Morris and A. Stevens when they appeared before the Ohio State Workmen's Compensation Board outside their normal working hours? If so, what shall the remedy be?"

**Q:** Now, Mr. Arbitrator, to save some time here, we've agreed to stipulate that the Arbitrator there—I guess you'd have to say he talks about the issue in dispute in that case, but then defines the grievance without reaching the resolution of that particular issue, specifically. All right. I show you another document, Company Exhibit 10. Would you tell the Arbitrator what this document is?

**A:** This is a letter written to Mr. Collins regarding AAA Docket No. 34456 as a result of the I.U.C.T. requesting arbitration of this case.

**Q:** What was the issue in dispute in that particular case?

**A:** The proposed submission was, "Did the Company violate Article XVI of the agreement for year 5 through 9? National Agreement when payment was denied Evelyn Campbell for her absences from work on September 14, year 8, to appear before the Ohio State Workmen's Compensation Board? If so, what shall the remedy be?''

**Q:**   And then I ask you whether that case ever went to arbitration?

**A:**   No, it did not.

**Q:**   And why did it not go to arbitration?

**A:**   The Union withdrew it from arbitration.

**Q:**   All right. I show you Company Exhibit 11—a document dated October 8, year 9. Would you tell the Arbitrator what this document is?

**A:**   That's Mr. Collins' letter withdrawing that grievance from arbitration.

**Q:**   All right. I show you another document, Company Exhibit 12, dated April 9, year 9. Would you tell the Arbitrator what this document is?

**A:**   This also is a letter to Mr. Collins from me proposing a submission for AAA Docket No. 34444 in which . . .

**Q:**   Was there an administrative agency involved in that particular submission?

**A:**   Yes. It concerned an employee who was subpoenaed to serve as an election officer in Clinton County, Ohio.

**Q:**   Now, did that case ever go to arbitration?

**A:**   No, it did not.

**Q:**   Why did it not go to arbitration?

**A:**   The Union withdrew.

**Q:**   All right. I show you Company Exhibit 13, dated October 8, year 9. Would you tell the Arbitrator what this document is?

**A:**   This is the Union's withdrawal from arbitration.

**Q:**   All right, Nancy. I show you a document, Company Exhibit 14, dated September 25, year 9. Would you tell the Arbitrator what this document is?

**A:**   This, again, is a proposed submission to arbitration, National Docket No. 45567, from the Jackson, Montana, Local.

**Q:**   And did that document involve an administrative agency? Did the submission, rather, involve an administrative agency?

**A:**   In this case it concerned fourteen employees who were attending a hearing of the Montana Commission Against Discrimination.

**Q:**   Did this case go to arbitration?

**A:**   No, it did not.

**Q:**   Why not?

**A:**   The Union withdrew it.

**Q:**   All right. I show you Company Exhibit 15, a document dated July 11, year 10. Would you tell the Arbitrator what this document is?

**A:**   This is a copy of the Union's withdrawal from arbitration on National Docket No. 45567.

**Q:**   All right. I show you Company Exhibit 16, a document dated March 6, year 10. Would you tell the Arbitrator what this document is?

**A:**   This is a proposed submission to arbitrate for National Docket No. 56678 from the Jackson, Montana, Local, concerning an employee who was absent to appear before the Industrial Accident Board.

**Q:**   Did that case ever go to arbitration?

**A:**   No, it did not.

**Q:**   Why not?

**A:**   The Union withdrew it.

**Q:**   All right. I show you Company Exhibit 17, a document dated July 14, year 10. Would you tell the Arbitrator what this document is?

**A:**   This is the Union's letter withdrawing that National Docket No. 56678 from arbitration.

**Q:**   Now, Nancy, other than those cases which we have just reviewed and the instant proceeding, are you aware of any request for arbitration at any other Company location concerning this issue?

**A:**   No, I am not.

**Q:**   In your capacity as Manager of Union Contract Administration for Princeton Manufacturing, are you aware of any situations across the country where a claim has been made to the National Labor Relations Board that the Company's refusal to pay wages for lost time due to compliance with a subpoena to appear before that particular agency was improper?

**A:**   Yes, I am.

**Q:**   And what Union did that involve?

**A:**   I believe it was I.A.E. in Dallas—our Dallas plant.

**Q:**   I show you Company Exhibit 18, a document dated July 10, year 9. Would you tell the Arbitrator what this document is?

**A:**   This is a copy of an N.L.R.B. charge transmitted to Princeton Manufacturing Company by the Regional Director.

**Q:** Now, Nancy, I show you Company Exhibit 19, dated October 1, year 9. Would you tell the Arbitrator what this document is?

**A:** This is a copy of a letter addressed to the I.A.E. Union.

**Q:** What plant did it concern?

**A:** This was the Dallas plant.

**Q:** All right. Is this in reference to the charge that was involved in the document in Company Exhibit 18?

**A:** The previous document, yes.

**Q:** Yes.

**A:** And this is a copy of the Acting Regional Director's letter refusing to issue a complaint, Company Exhibit 19.

**Q:** And what was the issue in dispute in that particular case?

**A:** Whether employees should be reimbursed for appearing before an administrative hearing.

**Q:** And would you refer the Arbitrator to the portion of the Regional Director's decision which relates to the issue in dispute in that case at that particular time?

**A:** That is the second paragraph.

**Q:** And would you read the first sentence in that paragraph?

**A:** "Rather, it appears that the employer was following past practice in interpreting the Collective Bargaining Agreement to reimburse employees who appear in 'court' but not administrative hearings."

**Q:** And the next sentence?

**A:** "The employer is not required to pay witnesses testifying on behalf of the Union, despite the fact that the employer may have reimbursed employees it subpoenaed."

**Q:** I have no further questions at this point, Mr. Arbitrator.

### b. Cross-Examination by Union Advocate

*Mr. Mandrake:*
[to be supplied by student]

# D. Exhibits

## *JOINT EXHIBIT NO. 1*

COLLECTIVE BARGAINING AGREEMENT

BETWEEN

PRINCETON MANUFACTURING COMPANY

AND

LOCAL #209

INTERNATIONAL UNION OF COMPUTER TECHNICIANS (12/1/05-12/1/09)

. . .

ARTICLE XVI

JURY DUTY

Section 1 - General
    When a salaried employee is called for service as a juror, he will continue to be paid his normal straight-time salary during the period of such service.

Section 2
    Similar payment as specified in Section 1 will be granted to an employee who loses time from work because of his appearance in court pursuant to proper subpoena, except when he is either plaintiff, defendant, or other part to the court proceeding.

. . .

## *JOINT EXHIBIT NO. 2A*

SUBPOENA

May 11, year 9

Sally Adams is hereby summoned to appear at a hearing before a duly designated Hearing Examiner of the Ohio State Division of Human Rights on May 14, year 9, at 10 a.m. to testify in a proceeding before said Hearing Examiner.

## *JOINT EXHIBIT NO. 2B*

SUBPOENA

May 11, year 9

Barry Newell is hereby summoned to appear at a hearing before a duly designated Hearing Examiner of the Ohio State Division of Human Rights on May 14, year 9, at 10 a.m. to testify in a proceeding before the said Hearing Examiner.

## *JOINT EXHIBIT NO. 3*

May 20, Year 9

President
Princeton Manufacturing Co.
Alita, Ohio

Dear Mr. President:

At this time, Local #209, pursuant to Step 2 Grievance procedures, lodges this protest of the Company failure to pay Grievants Sally Adams and Barry Newell for time lost from work due to proper subpoena under the provisions of Article XVI, Section 2. They were not parties in these cases, but rather disinterested wittnesses.

Sincerely,

/s/  Ned Haliday
President, Local #209

*JOINT EXHIBIT NO. 4*

Princeton Manufacturing Company
Alita, Ohio
June 20, year 9


Ned Haliday, President
Local 209
Alita, Ohio

Dear Mr. Haliday:

In answer to your grievance in the matter of the subpoenas served on Sally Adams and Barry Newell to appear at the Division of Human Rights administrative hearing, and in order to confirm our position on this matter, we are providing this written response.

The contract language in Section 2 of Article XVI of the current Agreement between the Company and the Union specifies that payment may be made for appearances in court following receipt of a subpoena, provided the individual is neither the plaintiff nor the defendant. The contract language clearly identifies that appearance is to be in court.

There are many different administrative hearings which may require the presence of individuals. Some of these involve matters of the Equal Employment Opportunity Act, Unemployment Insurance, the Occupation Safety and Health Act, and the State Commission on Human Rights, to name several.

We do not regard the hearing to which the above two employees were subpoenaed to attend as court. Therefore, payment for such time so spent is not approved.

It is further noted that the individuals concerned were told that they were excused for the day on May the 14th, year 9, because they would not be expected to participate on that date. Mr. Newell immediately returned to work, but Sally Adams elected voluntarily to spend the day at the hearing. She, too, could have returned to work.

Sincerely,



/s/ John Stanford
President
Princeton Manufacturing Co.

### *JOINT EXHIBIT NO. 5*

July 19, Year 9

President
Princeton Manufacturing Co.
Alita, Ohio

Dear Mr. President:

Pursuant to the Agreement, Article VI (Arbitration Article), Local #209 requests arbitration on the grievance regarding the Company failure to pay Grievants Sally Adams and Barry Newell for time lost from work due to proper subpoena, under the provisions of Article XVI, Section 2.

Sincerely,

/s/  Ned Haliday
President, Local #209

### *JOINT EXHIBIT NO. 6*

February 5, year 10

Issue for Arbitration:

Did the Company violate Article XVI, Section 2, of the year 5 through year 9 Agreement between the Company and the Union when payment under Article XVI, Section 2 was denied Sally Adams and Barry Newell when they appeared before a duly appointed Hearing Examiner of the Ohio State Division of Human Rights?  If so, what shall the remedy be?

### *UNION EXHIBIT NO. 1*

SUBPOENA

May 11, year 9

John Simmons is hereby summoned to appear at a hearing before a duly designated Hearing Examiner of the Ohio State Division of Human Rights on May 14, year 9, at 10 a.m. to testify in a proceeding before said Hearing Examiner.

### UNION EXHIBIT NO. 2

May 31, year 9

Ned Haliday, President
Local #209
Alita, Ohio

Dear Sir;

This is to notify you that Sally Adams was not excused from the administrative hearing held by the Division of Human Rights on May 14, year 9.

Sincerely,


/s/ George Zenta
          Hearing Examiner
          Ohio State Division of Human Rights

### COMPANY EXHIBIT NO. 1

"Clock Card":

Week of 5/16 - 5/20/09

Name:  Ned Haliday
May 16:  Reason for absence—"Princeton meeting"

### COMPANY EXHIBIT NO. 2

"Clock Card":

Week of 5/21 - 5/25/09

Name:  Ned Haliday
May 22:  Reason for absence—"Company business meeting"

### COMPANY EXHIBIT NO. 3

"Clock Card":

Week of 5/28 - 6/1/09

Name:  Ned Haliday

May 29: Reason for absence—"Company witness at Ohio State Equal Opportunity meeting—hearing"

_**COMPANY EXHIBIT NO. 4***_

COLLECTIVE BARGAINING AGREEMENT

BETWEEN

PRINCETON PURITY MANUFACTURING COMPANY

AND

LOCAL 209

INTERNATIONAL UNION OF COMPUTER TECHNICIANS


. . .

Article XVI

JURY DUTY


**SECTION 1 - General**
    When a salaried employee is called for service as a juror he
will continue to be paid his normal straight-time salary during
the period of such service.

**SECTION 2**
    Similar payment as specified in Section 1 will be granted to
an employee who loses time from work because of his appearance in
court pursuant to proper subpoena, except when he is either a
plaintiff, defendant, or other part to the court proceeding.

. . .

*Also submitted as Joint Exhibit No. 1


_**COMPANY EXHIBIT NO. 5**_


    Contract Language Demands: I.U.C.T. Contract Proposals year 4
                            Negotiations

Add to Article XVI, Section 2 as follows:

Employees who are compelled to report to court under subpoena or
any other court process shall be paid in the same manner during
such time they are called to court as employees reporting for
jury duty.

## *COMPANY EXHIBIT NO. 6*

Pay for Jury Duty

Nationwide Summary
Princeton Manufacturing Co. Contract Benefits

| Type of Benefit | Percent of Plant Communities with Benefit |
|---|---|
| Make-up pay paid for jury duty: | 100% |
| Make-up pay paid for witness duty: | 10% |

## *COMPANY EXHIBIT NO. 7A*

October 7, year 4

Mr. Collins, Chairman
I.U.C.T., Princeton Conferences Board
Alita, Ohio

Dear Mr. Collins:

Enclosed are the proposals for contract language submitted by
Princeton Manufacturing Company for the current year 4
negotiations for the contract between I.U.C.T. and Princeton
Manufacturing Company.
. . . .

/s/ Stan Stanford
President

## *COMPANY EXHIBIT NO. 7B*

Company Contract Proposals, Year 4 Negotations
. . .

ARTICLE XVI

JURY DUTY

Section 2: Effective October 26, year 5, similar make-up pay as
specified in Section 1 will be granted to an employee who loses
time from work because of his appearance in court pursuant to
proper subpoena, except when he is either a Plaintiff, Defendant,
or other party to the court proceeding.

## COMPANY EXHIBIT NO. 8

COLLECTIVE BARGAINING AGREEMENT

PRINCETON MANUFACTURING

AND

INTERNATIONAL UNION COMPUTER TECHNICIANS

Year 5 through 8 Agreement
Effective date:  January 1, year 6

. . .

Article XVI JURY DUTY

Section 2
Jury Duty:  Similar payment as specified in Section 1 will be
granted to an employee who loses time from work because of his
appearance in court pursuant to proper subpoena, except when he
is either a plaintiff, defendant, or other party to the court
proceeding.

. . .

## COMPANY EXHIBIT NO. 9

American Arbitration Association

Issue: AAA Case Docket No. 23345

Did the Company violate Article XVI of the Agreement for Year 5
through Year 9 Princeton-I.U.C.T. AAA Agreement when payment was
denied W. Morris and A. Stevens when they appeared before the
Ohio State Workmen's Compensation Board outside their normal
working hours?  If so, what shall the remedy be?

Award: Grievance denied.

/s/ Arbitrator Jessup
1/15/year 7

### *COMPANY EXHIBIT NO. 10*

July 1, year 9

Thomas Collins, Chairman
I.U.C.T., Princeton Conferences Board
Alita, Ohio

Re: AAA Docket No. 34456

Dear Mr. Collins:

The following issue submitted for arbitration by the I.U.C.T. has been assigned AAA Docket No. 34456.

Did the Company violate Article XVI of the contract for year 9 through year 9 Princeton Manufacturing-I.U.C.T. Agreement when payment was denied Evelyn Campbell for her absence from work on September 14, year 8, to appear before the Ohio State Workmen's Compensation Board?  If so, what shall the remedy be?

Sincerely,

/s/ Harvey Smith
American Arbitration Association

### *COMPANY EXHIBIT NO. 11*

October 8, year 9

Harvey Smith
American Arbitration Association

Dear Mr. Smith:

On behalf of the I.U.C.T., I respectfully request that AAA Docket No. 34456 be withdrawn from arbitration.

Thank you.

Sincerely,

/s/ Thomas Collins
Chairman
I.U.C.T., Princeton Conferences Bd.

<u>*COMPANY EXHIBIT NO. 12*</u>

Princeton Manufacturing Co.
Corporate Headquarters
April 9, year 9

Thomas Collins, Chairman
I.U.C.T., Princeton Conferences Board
Alita, Ohio

Re: AAA Docket No. 34444

Dear Mr. Collins:

    I propose the following issue be submitted for arbitration
as AAA Docket No. 34444.

Did the Company violate Article XVI of the year 9 through year 11
Princeton Manufacturing-I.U.C.T. National Agreement when payment
was denied Abigail Dowell for her absences from work on March 14,
year 9, to serve as an election officer in Clinton County, Ohio?
If so, what shall the remedy be?

                    Sincerely,

                    /s/ Nancy Barber
                    Manager
                    Union Contract Administration
                    Princeton Manufacturing Co.

<u>*COMPANY EXHIBIT NO. 13*</u>

October 8, year 9

Harvey Smith
American Arbitration Association

Dear Mr. Smith:

On behalf of the I.U.C.T., I respectfully request that AAA Docket
No. 34444 be withdrawn from arbitration.

Thank you.

                    Sincerely,

                    /s/ Thomas Collins
                    Chairman
                    I.U.C.T, Princeton Conferences Board

## COMPANY EXHIBIT NO. 14

September 25, year 9

Thomas Collins
I.U.C.T., Princeton Conferences Board
Alita, Ohio

Re:  National Docket No. 45567

Dear Mr. Collins:

The following issue submitted for arbitration by the I.U.C.T. has been assigned AAA Docket No. 45567.

Did the Company violate Article XVI of the year 9 through year 11 Princeton Manufacturing—I.U.C.T. National Agreement when payment was denied fourteen employees of Local #25 of the I.U.C.T. in Jackson, Montana, for absences from work to appear before the Montana Commission Against Discrimination. If so, what shall the remedy be?

Sincerely,

/s/ Harvey Smith
          American Arbitration Association

## COMPANY EXHIBIT NO. 15

July 11, year 10

Harvey Smith
American Arbitration Association

Dear Mr. Smith:

On behalf of the I.U.C.T., I respectfully request that AAA Docket No. 45567 be withdrawn from arbitration.

Thank you.

Sincerely,

/s/ Thomas Collins
          Chairman
          I.U.C.T., Princeton Conferences Board

<u>**COMPANY EXHIBIT NO. 16**</u>

March 6, year 10

Thomas Collins, Chairman
I.U.C.T., Princeton Conferences Board
Alita, Ohio

Re: AAA Docket No. 56678

Dear Mr. Collins:

The following issue submitted for arbitration by the I.U.C.T. has been assigned AAA Docket No. 56678.

Did the Company violate Article XVI of the year 5 through year 9 Princeton Manufacturing—I.U.C.T. National Agreement when payment was denied Michelle Mortimer, Local 25 of the I.U.C.T. in Jackson, Montana, for her absence from work on January 10, year 10, to appear before the Montana Industrial Accident Board? If so, what shall the remedy be?

Sincerely,

/s/ Harvey Smith
American Arbitration Association

<u>**COMPANY EXHIBIT NO. 17**</u>

July 14, year 10

Harvey Smith
American Arbitration Association

Dear Mr. Smith:

On behalf of the I.U.C.T., I respectfully request that AAA Docket No. 56678 be withdrawn from arbitration.

Thank you.

Sincerely,

/s/ Thomas Collins
Chairman
I.U.C.T., Princeton Conferences Board

COMPANY EXHIBIT NO. 18

July 10, year 9

Nancy Barber, Manager
Union Contract Administration
Princeton Manufacturing Company
Alita, Ohio

Dear Ms. Barber:

This is to inform you that a charge has been lodged by the
national office of the International Association of Electronics
Technicians (I.A.E.), Arlington, Texas.  Your plant has been
charged with improperly refusing to reimburse employees who
appeared under subpoena at an administrative meeting in violation
of the Collective Bargaining Agreement, Article XVI, Section 3.

The matter will be reviewed to determine whether a formal
complaint will be issued by the National Labor Relations Board
(N.L.R.B.).  You will be notified of our decision.

Sincerely,


/s/ George Thurmond
    Acting Regional Director
    National Labor Relations Board

<u>*COMPANY EXHIBIT NO. 19*</u>

October 1, Year 9

Sam Cole, President
International Association of Electronics Technicians (I.A.E.)
Arlington, Texas

Re: N.L.R.B. Charge- July 10, year 9

Dear Mr. Cole:

The National Labor Relations Board has reviewed the charge made by the I.A.E. on the issue of whether employees should be reimbursed for appearing before an administrative meeting. After reviewing the charge, we must decline to issue a complaint. The evidence shows that the employer has not violated the Collective Bargaining Agreement.

Rather, it appears that the employer was following past practice in interpreting the Collective Bargaining Agreement to reimburse employees who appear in "court" but not administrative hearings. The employer is not required to pay witnesses testifying on behalf of the Union, despite the fact that the employer may have reimbursed employees it subpoenaed.

Sincerely,

/s/ George Thurmond
Acting Regional Director
National Labor Relations Board

# Fine Products, Inc.

## Table of Contents

NOTES

## A. Caption

IN THE MATTER OF A CONTROVERSY BETWEEN:


FINE PRODUCTS, INC.                    )
MASON, GA.                             )
                                       )
AND                                    )          RE: HOLIDAY PAY
                                       )               GRIEVANCE
MECHANICS AND FABRICATORS              )
INTERNATIONAL UNION                    )
LOCAL NO. 2                            )
                                       )

Appearances:

For the Union: Jake Bivens

For the Company: Thomas Maxwell


Date: March 15, Year 26

Place: Mason, Georgia

# B. Examination of Union Witnesses

## 1. Wilbur Potts, President, Local 2

### a. Direct Examination by Union Advocate

*Mr. Bivens:*

**Q:** Would you state your name for the record, please?

**A:** Wilbur Potts, P-O-T-T-S.

**Q:** Are you employed by Fine Products Company at Mason, Georgia?

**A:** Yes, I am.

**Q:** How long have you been employed there?

**A:** I started there about 36 years ago.

**Q:** What is your current job title?

**A:** I am President of Local 2.

**Q:** I meant your job title at work.

**A:** Tool and die maker.

**Q:** Tell us, in your own words, what the practice has been on the day before the Christmas holiday as far as attendance during the day?

**A:** You have to understand the logistics of the operation. The main tool room was a separate department by itself away from the manufacturing area. The manufacturing personnel were allowed to have their holiday party food and beverages in the plant at the lunch break, and when they got out of hand they were told to go home or close the department down. In contrast, the tool room never had parties and we couldn't drink and eat on the premises and then leave for the holiday because of safety concerns about being around the equipment. So we would just leave early and not return.

The manager, the previous manager, got to realize that if he came down to the main tool room in the afternoon to shake the employees' hands and wish them a Merry Christmas and a Happy New Year, he found nobody there, or possibly one or two fellows sitting around doing nothing.

Many times on the day before Christmas holiday, I myself have left for lunch at noon and did not return. Practically all the tool and die makers did the same. There was a general understanding that you can leave, you did not have to get permission. Permission was a

given. The previous administrators or the supervisors understood that and came down at 9 a.m. or 10 a.m. to wish you a Merry Christmas because they knew nobody would be in the department after that.

The foreman eventually picked up the time cards and signed them and that is how it was until the new administrators came in and announced the new rule. But since then I have myself left for a long lunch—extended lunch periods—and never returned to the tool room to complete the day. There was no work after 11 a.m.

**Q:** Earlier you said something about distinguishing between the practices in manufacturing and in your department with regard to having a party the day before the Christmas holidays?

**A:** Yes. Well, the manufacturing personnel were allowed to have their lunch break with food and beverages and if it got out of hand— well, anything gets out of hand . . .

**Q:** What do you mean by "beverages"?

**A:** Alcoholic beverages. If the supervisors found that their employees could not perform or finish the day, they would close the department down. Manufacturing personnel are piece-workers.

**Q:** Piece-workers as distinguished from whom?

**A:** From us, the tool and die makers in their area.

**Q:** What do the tool and die makers do, in terms of their party?

**A:** We were not invited to their party nor were we allowed to have a party of our own, with drink and food; even at lunchtime.

**Q:** But the manufacturing personnel were?

**A:** Yes.

**Q:** And was this done in the plant?

**A:** Yes.

**Q:** Mr. Potts, Article VII, Section 2(a)(2), in Joint Exhibit 1, says "such employee" must work his last scheduled workday prior to a holiday to get paid for the holiday. You also know of a decision from 16 years ago in another plant, where the Arbitrator said that under a similar clause—I am not exactly sure what the clause said in that case—but the Arbitrator said it was not sufficient to qualify for pay if you only worked a portion of that work day. Now, I am going to ask you to read me the definition of the workday in the contract and tell me where you are reading from in Article V. Could you tell me what the workday is by definition of the contract, as shown in Joint Exhibit 1?

**A:** I am reading from Article V, Section 1 (a): "An employee's workday is the twenty-four hour period beginning with his regularly assigned starting time of his work shift, and his day of rest starts at the same point on the day or days he is not scheduled to work."

At Mason, the understanding in the tool room was a four-hour day was OK, as far as going out prior to a holiday or vacation. You were allowed and it was acceptable.

**Q:** And that is four hours before or after a holiday?
**A:** Right. In fact, some people have come back—
**Q:** Any four hours?
**A:** Yes. Some people come back at 11:00 a.m.
**Q:** What is the shift at Mason?
**A:** In this area it is 7 a.m. to 3:30 p.m. with a half-hour lunch.
**Q:** And that lunch is traditionally around 11 a.m. or thereafter?
**A:** Actually, it is usually at 12 noon.
**Q:** Now, let me ask you, in your experience, in your position as the head of a Local Union, how do you find management has interpreted their requirement to work the day before and the day after—as an eight-hour workday, a twenty-four-hour workday, or a four-hour work day?
**A:** Four-hour workday.
**Q:** That's it.

## b. Cross-Examination by Company Advocate

*Mr. Maxwell:*
[to be supplied by student]

## 2. Michael D. Morgan, Tool and Die Maker

### a. Direct Examination by Union Advocate

*Mr. Bivens:*
**Q:** Would you give your name for the record?
**A:** Michael D. Morgan.
**Q:** Do you work for the Fine Products Company at Mason?
**A:** Yes.
**Q:** And how long have you worked there?
**A:** This is my seventeenth year.
**Q:** Seventeen years. What is your present job title?
**A:** I am a tool and die maker.
**Q:** And has there ever been any question about your attendance?
**A:** No.
**Q:** You figure you worked at least 2,080 hours a year?
**A:** Right.

**Q:** Work some overtime?
**A:** Yes, I do.
**Q:** Do you feel that you more than pay for your holiday?
**A:** Yes, I do.
**Q:** Why don't you tell us, in your 17 years, what happens the day before a Christmas holiday, generally?
**A:** Well, generally, whoever is the boss usually comes down and shakes hands with everybody in the morning. Later on at some portion of the morning Mr. Gordon usually came around and said that if anyone wanted to go home early, that it was up to our own discretion because usually there was not much work done after 11 a.m., and most of the employees would punch out and go home.

3

**Q:** Now, on the day in question in year 1—I have forgotten the date, but whatever it was, the 23rd I guess—did you go out to lunch?

**A:** Right.

**Q:** And when you went out to lunch, was the foreman or anybody else in charge?

**A:** On that particular occasion Mr. Gordon and Mr. Schmidt were not there before we left for our lunch.

**Q:** I see. And who is Mr. Gordon?

**A:** Mr. Gordon is our supervisor.

**Q:** And the other gentleman you named?

**A:** Mr. Leon Schmidt is under Mr. Gordon. If Mr. Gordon is not there, Mr. Schmidt will give out work assignments or generally do the same job that Mr. Gordon does—only if Mr. Gordon is not in the plant.

**Q:** Okay. You say during the last seventeen years to your knowledge it has been customary for people—

**A:** Well, it has been customary, I feel, that the people have been leaving early because there have been parties in the plant and we do work with hazardous machinery. So it was the feeling that if someone did have a drink or, you know, came back from lunch hour and maybe had had a drink or something of this effect—instead of going back to work, working with the machinery, which, like I said, is dangerous, it is all open equipment—the understanding and the feeling was that this way if we were punched out and home, no one could get injured. And as far as I know since I have been there, we have had a perfect record as far as no one ever being hurt in the department bad enough for lost time, injury of this effect. When people have punched out and gone home, I have not heard of any type of an injury. This is the main reason, the safety.

**Q:** Did you have a drink at lunch that day?

**A:** Me, yes.

**Q:** What was the drink?

**A:** I don't remember now.

**Q:** Did you leave your area any time on that day and observe what was going on in the rest of the plant?

**A:** No, we are more or less by ourselves in the area.

**Q:** I see. But do you know that other employees left early and went home?

**A:** I do not know. I would think that probably some did. All I know is that when I returned from lunch I punched out and went home. That gave me four hours of work.

**Q:** That is all I have for you.

### b. Cross-Examination by Company Advocate

*Mr. Maxwell:*
[to be supplied by student]

## 3. Dick Blake, Prototype Developer

### a. Direct Examination by Union Advocate

*Mr. Bivens:*

**Q:** Please state your name for the record.

**A:** Dick Blake.

**Q:** How long have you worked for Fine Products Company?

**A:** Fourteen and one-half years.

**Q:** What is your current job title?

**A:** My current job title is Prototype Developer.

**Q:** Are you a Union member?

**A:** Yes.

**Q:** How is your attendance record?

**A:** Excellent.

**Q:** In your 14 1/2 years, what is your experience with people's attendance on the day before a Christmas holiday?

**A:** It was understood that if you worked a minimum of four hours, that it covered you for the next day, for the holiday.

**Q:** Now, on the 23rd of December, year 1, you went out for lunch with some of the other people.

**A:** Right.

**Q:** And did you return to the Company from lunch?

**A:** I did.

**Q:** What time did you come back?

**A:** 1:30 p.m.

**Q:** You heard Mr. Griffin testify that when you went out to lunch, there was nobody in authority on the job?

**A:** Right. When I went to my tool box at five minutes of noon to get my keys and to pick up my watch and take off my apron, I was going to inform Mr. Gordon that we might not be back from lunch because I know how these things get carried away, but there was nobody in the office at five minutes of noon.

**Q:** Do you know where the supervisors were?

**A:** Out of the plant.

**Q:** Out of the plant. Do you think they were having a party of their own?

**A:** I have no idea.

**Q:** When you came back, what did you do?

**A:** I met Mr. Schmidt in the hallway and we walked up the aisle together and discussed the lunch period that we had taken. I informed him that the guys were not coming back and that I was going to lock up some of the guys' tool boxes and I was leaving.

**Q:** Was that before or after lunch?

**A:** After lunch.

**Q:** But before the end of the shift?

**A:** 1:30 p.m.

**Q:** Now, we have had testimony that Mr. Schmidt was the person in charge when Mr. Gordon was not there.

**A:** Right.

**Q:** When you told him that the men were not coming back, what did he say?

**A:** He just said "fine," wished me a Merry Christmas, and I left. The reason I did not tell Mr. Gordon was that he was having a conference in the back room with a couple of people from another department, and I did not feel that it was that important that I should have to disturb his conference.

**Q:** When you spoke to Mr. Schmidt, were you asking permission for the employees?

**A:** No, I was not asking Mr. Schmidt's permission. I was informing Mr. Schmidt in the hopes that he would inform Mr. Gordon.

**Q:** The Union rests.

### b. Cross-Examination by Company Advocate

*Mr. Maxwell:*
[to be supplied by student]

## C. Examination of Company Witnesses

### 1. Charles Wallace, Manager, Union Contract Administration, Corporate Headquarters

#### a. Direct Examination by Company Advocate

*Mr. Maxwell:*

**Q:** Charles, would you state your full name for the record?

**A:** Charles Wallace.

**Q:** And what is your position with the Fine Products Company?

**A:** I am Manager of Union Contract Administration at corporate headquarters in Fargo.

**Q:** And what are the responsibilities of that position?

**A:** Our group administers the third step of the grievance procedure for the Local 2 and the Fine Products contracts, administers the processing of arbitrations, gives advice and counsel to our labor relations people around the country, and participates in National Negotiations.

**Q:** Have you had any particular responsibility in the National Negotiations?

**A:** On several occasions I have been the Chairman of the Company's Subcommittee on Contract Language.

**Q:** And how long have you been involved in Union relations for the Company at the corporate level?

**A:** Fifteen years.

**Q:** Now, at my request, did you review the negotiations history between the Company and the Union with respect to the question of holiday pay qualification?

**A:** Yes, I did.

**Q:** And how long has the requirement that an employee work the last scheduled work day before a holiday as a qualification for holiday pay been in the collective bargaining agreement between the parties?

**A:** Since the original agreement between the Fine Products Company and Local 2, which was twenty-six years ago.

**Q:** I show you a copy of the current agreement in Joint Exhibit 1 and ask you to locate the holiday pay proviso for the Arbitrator.

**A:** Article VII, Section 2(a).

**Q:** And what are the qualifications with respect to holiday pay?

**A:** Subsection (2) reads, "Such employee works his last scheduled workday prior to and the next scheduled workday after such holiday within the employee's scheduled workweeks"—is the phrase we are concerned with here.

**Q:** I now show you another document and ask you to identify it for the Arbitrator. This is Joint Exhibit 5.

**A:** This is just as it is titled, "Amendment Proposed by the MFIU to the Company at the National Negotiations," which the Union submitted to the Company in year 2. It was not accepted by the Company.

**Q:** Is there anything in that proposed amendment with respect to the holiday pay qualification that is in dispute in this case?

**A:** Yes. Specifically the amendment would make an important change regarding conditions attached to receiving holiday pay. The proposed amendment provided: "The above payment will be made to hourly paid employees who earn some wages during the week in which the holiday falls, or in any preceding week."

**Q:** And if that proposal had been accepted, would it have eliminated the requirement that the employee work the last scheduled workday before the holiday?

**A:** Sure it would.

**Q:** I ask counsel for the Union to stipulate as we agreed, that in each negotiation session following the expiration date of the first National Contract, 25 years ago, the Union proposed the amendment described by Mr. Wallace. (Union counsel so stipulated.)

**Q:** Now, during the National Negotiations between the Company and the Union, has the Union expressed a position on these so-called conditions with regard to the qualification of the last scheduled workday before the holiday?

**A:** Yes, they have.

**Q:** Then what has been—

**A:** In every negotiation that I have participated in, at least, it has basically been the Union's position that overall we have too many conditions for qualifying for holiday pay. Specifically the conditions that the employee work the day before and the day after were onerous, and the workers had often said to us that they should not be required to work a full day before or after, or in fact even work part of the day before or after, because they felt they already paid for that holiday.

**Q:** Thank you.

### b. Cross-Examination by Union Advocate

*Mr. Bivens:*
[to be supplied by student]

## 2. Mildred J. Stein, Manager, Plant Relations

### a. Direct Examination by Company Advocate

*Mr. Maxwell:*

Q: Would you state and spell your name for the record, please?

A: Mildred J. Stein, S-T-E-I-N.

Q: What is your position with the Fine Products Company?

A: I am Manager of Plant Relations.

Q: And what does that responsibility include?

A: I am responsible for Union relations, for personnel practices, wage administration, benefits, and safety.

Q: How long have you been involved in Union relations for the Mason plant?

A: Over thirty years.

Q: Did you hear the assertion of the Union witnesses that there is a practice in the Mason plant to the effect that employees are only required to work for four hours the day before a holiday to qualify for holiday pay?

A: Yes, I did.

Q: Are you aware of any such practice at the Mason plant?

A: No, I am not.

Q: Now, at my request, did you review the grievances at the Mason plant concerning an employee's leaving work early during his or her last scheduled workday before a listed holiday, as regards the question of eligibility for holiday pay?

A: Yes, I did. I went through some 60 to 70 Step 2 Grievances covering the last ten years.

Q: Were any of the grievances that you reviewed resolved in a way that is consistent with the Union's claimed practice?

A: No.

Q: I now show you a document marked Joint Exhibit 3 and ask you to identify it for the Arbitrator.

A: This is a July 4 holiday Grievance dated July 16, ten years ago.

Q: Would you tell the Arbitrator what this grievance is?

A: It's a copy of a Step 2 Grievance submitted by the Union dated 7/18 requesting holiday pay for an employee who had been denied holiday pay for July 4.

Q: Now, did you participate in the discussion of this grievance at any step of the grievance procedure?

A: Yes, I did at Step 2.

Q: Will you tell the Arbitrator what the position of the parties was on the issue of holiday pay qualification as far as the employee working his or her last scheduled workday before the holiday?

A: May I refer to the Company minutes, please? These are my notes and I don't have that good a memory.

Q: Yes. (The witness reviewed her notes.)

Q: What was the position of the parties?

A: The Union took the position that the employee should be paid for the holiday because the employee had received permission from his supervisor to leave early on that day, and we concluded the Union's position was incorrect and we were not going to pay.

Q: Did the Union claim in that case that the employee only had to work four hours on the last scheduled workday before the holiday to qualify for holiday pay?

A: Yes, it did. We said that management took the position that this employee did not get permission and therefore would not get paid. And one Mr. K. R. Langely, who at that time was the Union Vice President and a member of the Grievance Committee, said that the grievant had a sick mother and wanted to leave early. I said that people have been misinformed by someone that four hours constitutes a full day's work.

Mr. Langely then went on to say that four to five hours was enough to qualify for a day's work and that has been a practice at Mason for years, and I made it clear to him that I was not aware of any such practice. I indicated if the employee had asked the foreman for permission in advance and had been given that permission, then that employee would qualify.

Q: Ms. Stein, let me make sure that I have got this correct. The specific reason for denying the holiday pay in this case from the Company's point of view was that the employee in fact had not received permission to take time off on that day preceding the holiday.

A: That is correct.

Q: You are not testifying that even if he had worked the four hours and then received permission that he still would not have qualified for the holiday pay.

A: I am sorry, in this case this employee did work four hours.

Q: But the reason you denied the holiday pay was not that he had only worked four hours. As I understand it, it was that he had not received permission.

A: He had not received permission to leave after four hours, right. That is correct.

Q: Is there anything else you want to say with respect to that issue?

A: No.

Q: Did the Union pursue this grievance beyond Step 2 of the grievance procedure?

A: It did not.

Q: Let me ask you first, with respect to that last grievance, what was the year of the grievance in that case?

A: I thought it was ten years ago.

Q: Okay. That was a grievance concerning Fred Motely. Now I show you Joint Exhibit 4, a grievance concerning Larry Goodin. Would you tell the Arbitrator what the grievance was in this case?

A: This was submitted by the Union to Step 2. It involved an employee by the name of Larry Goodin. The Union claimed he had requested, and had been given permission, to leave at 11 a.m. and that he had been denied holiday pay; they were requesting payment for such holiday pay.

Q: What was the Company position?

A: That we would not pay the holiday pay.

Q: What was the basis of that? Did the Union in that case claim again anything with respect to this alleged four-hour practice?

A: Again, I will need to refer to my notes. (The witness did so.)

Q: What was the Union's claim?

A: The Union again maintained that the employee had permission to leave and on that basis was entitled to holiday pay. I said that this is similar to the misconception about four

hours work constituting a full day on the day before a holiday, and that actually permission was not granted and he could have and perhaps should have been disciplined for leaving. In any event, the employee's absence was not approved by his supervisor and therefore no holiday pay was justified.

Q: Ms. Stein, as you went through these grievances, did you find any inconsistency with respect to the question of discipline as contrasted with the question of denial of holiday pay?

A: Yes, there were some inconsistencies regarding the practice of disciplining.

Q: Was there any inconsistency with respect to the denial of the holiday pay in the grievances where the employee did not work the last scheduled workday before the holiday?

A: No, there was not.

Q: In any of the cases that you reviewed, did the Union process the case beyond Step 2 of the grievance procedure?

A: There was only one that I can recall that they went to the third step.

Q: And was the grievance granted on the third step on that one?

A: The grievance was denied at the third step.

Q: And did the Union pursue that case to arbitration?

A: It did not.

Q: Let me clarify your testimony, if I may. I did not understand you to testify that the holiday pay would have been denied because they had only worked four hours. It was denied because they had not received permission to take the rest of the day off.

A: In any case, if an employee asks permission to leave and is granted permission to leave, whether the employee has worked five minutes or five hours, the Company would stipulate that if it gave the employee permission to leave, the employee would be eligible for holiday pay. There was nothing magic about four hours.

Q: Did any of those 60 or 70 grievances you spoke of deal with a Christmas holiday dispute?

A: No, sir, they did not.

Q: That completes the Company case.

b. Cross-Examination by Union Advocate

*Mr. Bivens:*
[to be supplied by student]

# D. Examination of Union Rebuttal Witnesses

## 1. Michael D. Morgan, Tool and Die Maker (Recalled)

### a. Direct Examination by Union Advocate

*Mr. Bivens:*
**Q:** There is a question I forgot to ask you earlier. Does it ever happen that it was suggested by management that you go home early the day before the Christmas holiday?
**A:** Yes. Usually our boss, Mr. Gordon, not only for the Christmas holiday but any holiday, likes to get our time cards in. We are on estimated jobs, so he has to get our time cards in early so that he can go over whatever jobs we work on. He has suggested a number of times the earlier we go, the earlier he can go home on a holiday, too.
**Q:** Is that particularly true of Christmas?
**A:** Yes.
**Q:** That is all.

### b. Cross-Examination by Company Advocate

*Mr. Maxwell:*
[to be supplied by student]

## 2. Manny Finaldi, Tool and Die Maker

### a. Direct Examination by Union Advocate

*Mr. Bivens:*
**Q:** What is your position?
**A:** A Tool and Die Maker, for 25 years.
**Q:** Manny, in past years, if you recall, did you ever leave work the day before the Christmas holiday early without permission and get paid?
**A:** Yes, many times, prior to six years ago.
**Q:** You told me something I found interesting about the relationship in the Tool Shop in the tool and die group between the employees and the management people. Would you care to repeat that? Some others might find it interesting.
**A:** Yes. Management people, speaking of Mr. Gordon, who is our first superior, we have what I think is a really good rapport with him. Well, I have to say, all this mumbo-jumbo over here about difinitions and grievances—really, I have to take my hat off to him. It is terrific, although I don't understand most of it, but the rapport we have with Mr. Gordon is a very congenial and nice kind of a relationship. There are many things that I guess if you went by the book we are doing wrong, but in order to run a tool room and keep it going the way we have been all these years, because we don't get supported by anybody but ourselves, the rapport, that is, if we—I don't even remember ever asking for permission to leave. We just leave and the next day we are asked if we would like to have personal time or it is, like, if we call in and we say we are not coming in for a day, it is the next day we are asked if we want it as a personal day or a holiday. It is that kind of a whole general feeling that we have.

**Q:**  When you say holiday, you mean vacation, right?

**A:**  Vacation day, right. If we want it as a vacation day, it is so marked and it is just that kind of a rapport we have. And before we got the double holidays—before the holidays all fell on Friday and we had Saturday, Sunday, Monday, and Tuesday off, before all of that came—we had the day before Christmas, which was the 24th. And if you look my records up, I would say practically every day before that, for 25 years which I have been working there, I believe I have taken off half a day and I don't ever remember asking permission. It was that type of a thing. Secondly, the time card that Mr. Morgan spoke about is the time that we put in on the job numbers that we work on all week long and indirectly—if we write down on the time cards that we worked a 40-hour week and if it is really 35 hours—isn't that indirectly telling or asking permission that you are going to be leaving and not coming back? On the day in question I had no intention of coming back. I locked up my tool box. I never went partying, which has nothing to do with what they did after, but I had no intention of coming back and I just did as I always do, just lock the box and go, and went off. I never asked because I never thought that we had to ask. And again, you know, it is that kind of a working relationship that we have that I think is terrific. I think it is just nice.

Sure, you get high up, you got to get everything down in black and white, but when you are working with a group of men like we are, I think it is terrific the way it works.

**Q:**  Are you suggesting, Manny, that rapport does not extend to Mr. Gordon's supervisor?

**A:**  Yes, absolutely.

**Q:**  What is his name?

**A:**  Mr. Bixby. I have never had an occasion to deal with Mr. Bixby, so I don't really know.

**Q:**  Well, you have the occasion on the day before Christmas.

**A:**  Yes, that I do have, yes, I do have. He did go by the book and everything.

**Q:**  Okay, let's not get into that any further. The Union rests.

---

### b. Cross Examination by Company Advocate

*Mr. Maxwell:*
[to be supplied by student]

# E. Exhibits

## JOINT EXHIBIT NO. 1

COLLECTIVE BARGAINING AGREEMENT

BETWEEN

FINE PRODUCTS, INC.

AND

LOCAL UNION NO. 2

MECHANICS AND FABRICATORS INTERNATIONAL UNION (year 24-27)

. . .

**ARTICLE V**

1. (a) An employee's workday is the twenty-four hour period beginning with his regularly assigned starting time of his work shift, and his day of rest starts at the same point on the day or days he is not scheduled to work.

. . .

**ARTICLE VII**

Holidays

1. Listed Holidays

New Year's Day            Thanksgiving Day
Memorial Day              The day before Christmas Day
Independence Day
Election Day
Labor Day

2.  Hourly Rated Employees

     (a)  An hourly rated employee not on continuous operation will be paid for each of the above-listed holidays not worked, up to eight hours at his average straight-time hourly rate as taken from the last periodic statistics available at the time his holiday occurs (current rate for day workers), for a number of hours equal to his regular daily working schedule during such week, providing each of the following conditions are met:

          (1)  Such employee has been employed at least 30 days prior to any such holiday.

### *JOINT EXHIBIT NO. 1 (continued)*

(2)   Such employee works his last scheduled workday prior to and his next scheduled workday after such holiday within the employee's scheduled workweeks.  This condition shall not prevent payment of holiday pay to:

(i) an employee who has been absent from work because of verified personal illness for not more than three months prior to the week in which the holiday occurs and who reports for the Company's physical examination the next scheduled work day following the holiday; or. . .

*(ii) an employee who has been continuously absent from work for not more than two weeks prior to the week in which the holiday occurs and who is not at work on either or both such workdays due to approved absences for personal illness or emergency illness at home, death in his family, layoff, or Union activity; or

**(iv) an employee who is not at work on either or both such work-days solely due to military encampment or jury duty; or

(v) an employee who is absent from work on either the last scheduled workday prior to double consecutive holidays or his next scheduled workday after such double consecutive holidays. (In such case, the employee will be entitled to holiday pay only for the first of such double consecutive holidays if he works the last scheduled workday prior to that holiday, but not the next scheduled workday after the second holiday; and he will be entitled to holiday pay only for the second of such double consecutive holidays if he fails to work the last scheduled workday prior to the first of such double consecutive holidays but works the next scheduled workday after the second of such double consecutive holidays.)

. . .


*Effective January 1, year 2, subsections (ii) and (iii) were combined into subsection (ii) as shown.

** Subsection (iv) is effective July 1, year 2

*JOINT EXHIBIT NO. 1 (continued)*

**ARTICLE XXI**

3.   Any local understanding to be enforced through arbitration
must be in writing and signed by the Company and Union.
Section 4(b)(iii) This Agreement sets out expressly all the
restrictions and obligations assumed by the respective parties,
and no implied restrictions or obligations in this Agreement were
assumed by the parties in entering into this Agreement.

. . . .

5.   The powers of an Arbitrator shall include the authority to
render final and binding decision with respect to any dispute
brought before him or her, including the right to modify or
reduce or rescind any disciplinary action taken by the Company
but excluding the right to amend, modify, or alter the terms of
this Agreement, or any local understanding.

*JOINT EXHIBIT NO. 2*

**Grievance - Local No. 2, MFIU**                  January 1, year 26

Step 2

Request: The Tool and Die Makers were not paid for Christmas
holiday as they have been in the past under similar
circumstances. The Company violated Article VII of the Agreement
and Past Practice.

Remedy: The Tool and Die Makers as a class be paid for Christmas
Day holiday, year 2.

                                        /s/ Wilbur Potts
                                        Local 2, President

Company's Answer: The Tool and Die Makers did not have permission
to leave early the day before the Christmas Day holiday.

Grievance denied.

*JOINT EXHIBIT NO. 3*

**Grievance - Local No. 2, MFIU**                    July 16, year 18

Step 2:

Request: The Union requests holiday pay for Fred Motely an employee in the Manufacturing Department, who was denied holiday pay for the Independence Day holiday. The Company violated Article VII of the Agreement and Past Practice.


Remedy: Fred Motely be paid for July 4.



                                        /s/ Wilbur Potts
                                            Local 2, President




Company's Answer: Grievance denied.

Grievant did not receive permission to leave work after four hours on the day before the holiday.


                                        /s/ Mildred J. Stein
                                            Manager, Plant Relations

*JOINT EXHIBIT NO. 4*

**Grievance - Local No. 2, MFIU**                January 12, year 20

Step 2:

Request: The Union requests holiday pay for Larry Goodin, an
employee in the Manufacturing Department, who was denied holiday
pay for the New Year's Day holiday. The Company violated Article
VII of the Agreement and Past Practice.

Remedy: Larry Goodin be paid for the New Year's Day holiday.


                                        /s/ Wilbur Potts
                                            Local No. 2, President


Company's Answer: Grievance denied.

Grievant did not have permission to leave work early on the day
before the holiday.


                                        /s/ Mildred J. Stein
                                            Manager, Plant Relations

**_JOINT EXHIBIT NO. 5_**

Amendment Proposed by the
MFIU to the Company
at the National Negotiations

September 1, year 19

Article VII, Section 2(2) is amended to read "the above payment
will be made to hourly paid employees who earn some wages during
the week in which the holiday falls, or in any preceding week."

Rejected by Company, September 30, year 19.

# Superior Products, Inc.

## Table of Contents

# NOTES

# A. Caption

IN THE MATTER OF A CONTROVERSY BETWEEN:

SUPERIOR PRODUCTS, INC.              )
ELKHARD, CALIFORNIA               )
                                         )
AND                                 )         RE: Holiday Pay
                                           )
UNIVERSAL WORKERS AND         )
SPECIALTY UNION                 )
LOCAL 11                          )

Appearances:

For the Union: Mike Solly

For the Company: Susan George

Date: June 20, year 4

Place: Elkhard, California

## B. Examination of Union Witnesses

## 1. Moe Barsky, Business Agent

### a. Direct Examination by Union Advocate

*Mr. Solly*

**Q:** Your name and position?

**A:** Moe Barsky, Business Agent with Local 11.

**Q:** How long have you been a Local 11 Agent?

**A:** Approximately ten years.

**Q:** Describe your duties, generally.

**A:** Duties of a business agent are to negotiate contracts and enforce them.

**Q:** Are you responsible for negotiating and administering Local 11's agreement with Superior?

**A:** Yes.

**Q:** How long has Superior been part of your responsibilities?

**A:** A little over four years.

**Q:** Let me show you Joint Exhibit 1, which is a portion of the current Collective Bargaining Agreement, dated June 8, year 2. Were you involved in the negotiation of that Agreement?

**A:** Yes, I was.

**Q:** When did these negotiations take place?

**A:** In May and June of year 2.

**Q:** Were you involved in negotiating the previous agreement?

**A:** No, I was not.

**Q:** Let me direct your attention to Section 7.H. of the current Agreement in Joint Exhibit 1. There has been some reference to an agreement in year 2 regarding the implementation of 12-hour continuous shifts. Is that agreement reflected in Section 7.H.?

**A:** Yes.

**Q:** Was there a previous Letter of Understanding with substantially the same terms?

**A:** Yes. It was dated February 12, year 2.

**Q:** Let me ask you to identify Joint Exhibit 7. Is that the Letter of Understanding?

**A:** Yes.

**Q:** And you were involved in the negotiation of that?

**A:** Yes.

**Q:** When did the Company first propose modifying the Collective Bargaining Agreement to provide for a 12-hour continuous shift?

**A:** December 15, year 1.

**Q:** How did it come up?

**A:** I received a phone call in early December from Tom Jones, the Plant Manager, asking for a labor–management meeting, which we agreed to set up for December 15 of year 1. A couple of days prior to that, Tom asked me to meet with him on December 14th so he could explain what the Company's proposal was going to be on the 15th.

**Q:** Did you meet with him on the 14th?

**A:** Yes.

**Q:** Could you tell us what was discussed?

**A:** Tom indicated that production requirements at the plant had grown and that the whole plant had been working a Monday through Friday work week, except that for the last many months—it was almost all of year 1—employees had, in addition to working Monday through Friday, worked every other Saturday or Sunday. So they had been working a six-day work week. There had been a lot of complaints from the employees about the amount of overtime. And, at the same time, even the six-day work week was not sufficient to keep up with production demands. Therefore, the Company needed to go to a seven-day operation.

Tom further pointed out that the existing contract at that time, which expired in June of year 2, provided an option of an eight-hour continuous shift operation, and we discussed the fact that such an operation requires a shift rotation in order to work. Tom indicated the Company would prefer not to have a rotational shift system because then it would be difficult on the employees, and therefore management would come up with an alternative.

**Q:** What do you mean by "rotational"?

A: In most continuous operations with eight-hour shifts there are four groups, often called A, B, C, and D. In order to cover seven days, three shifts per day, with four groups, it requires each group to change its shift every week; one way that would happen would be that Group A would work day shift this week, swing shift next week, graveyard shift the following week, and so on. Additionally, with a rotational system, employees change their days off and have different days off. If the A shift is working Monday through Friday during days this week, somebody has got to work Saturday and Sunday, so another shift would come in and work Saturday through whatever—the next Wednesday.

Q: Did Tom in the December 14th meeting describe the 12-hour operation that the Company was proposing?

A: Yes.

Q: What did he say?

A: On the 14th, Tom laid out what he said the Company was going to propose, at the December 15th labor–management meeting, an arrangement where there would be no shift rotation. Employees would work steady shifts. One group of employees would work the early part of the week, the other would work the latter part of the week, and you would have a day shift group and a night shift group. The specific hours were not determined at that point, and the swing day, that is, the extra day that people would work every other week, was not yet determined. Basically, employees would work four consecutive days, 12 hours a day. They would have four days off and come back and work three days on and three days off.

Q: Was there any mention of holiday pay?

A: Yes. Tom discussed the various contractual benefits and how they would be affected by the 12-hour shift. He indicated that the employees on 12-hour shifts would get the same number of holiday hours per year, 88, as the employees on eight-hour shifts. He said that specifically because at the time that this would be implemented—January 2 or thereabouts of year 2—employees would already have received New Year's Day as their first holiday and would have been given another eight hours as a personal holiday, that those 16 hours would be deducted from the

88, leaving 72 hours, which divides nicely into six 12-hour holidays. Tom indicated the employees in the 12-hour shifts would be allowed to choose which days they wanted off for their six remaining 12-hour holidays.

Q: Did you make any response on behalf of the Union when this was outlined by Mr. Jones on the 14th?

A: No.

Q: And there was a meeting the following day, the 15th?

A: Yes.

Q: Could you identify Joint Exhibit 2?

A: Joint Exhibit 2 is the proposal that was given to us across the table on December 15.

Q: Could you just tell us, what was the Union's response to the proposal management made on the 15th?

A: The Union's response on December 15th was that we felt that because the contract at that point had less than six months to run, it would be beneficial to the parties, rather than to deal with this on a piecemeal basis, to reopen the contract and try to deal with all issues. We indicated if the Company was willing to do that, that we would be willing to deal with this in that context.

Q: Did the Company make a response to that suggestion?

A: Their response was that they were skeptical as to whether they would be able to do that. The Company indicated they needed a few days to consider this and would call and give me their response.

Q: Did you later receive a call?

A: Yes.

Q: From who?

A: Tom Jones.

Q: What was the response?

A: The response was, no, they were not interested in opening up negotiations early.

Q: Did the question of continuous shift come up in January of year 2?

A: No. It was early February.

Q: Was there a meeting in early February between the Company and the Union to have further discussions on the continuous shift question?

A: Yes.

Q: How did that meeting come about?

A: Well, the Company had announced to all employees that it was going to implement an eight-hour continuous shift operation per the contract. The Union members at the plant asked for a Union meeting, and we set one up to discuss the issue. At that meeting, the employees voted to instruct the Union committee to meet with management and present to management a Union proposal for a 12-hour continuous operation. At that point, such a proposal was developed.

**Q:** Was there a meeting on February 10th, year 2?

**A:** Yes.

**Q:** Could you look at Joint Exhibit 5 and tell us what that document is?

**A:** This is notes from that meeting.

**Q:** These are the Company's notes?

**A:** Yes.

**Q:** Have you had a chance to review this?

**A:** Yes.

**Q:** Are these notes accurate?

**A:** Yes.

**Q:** Was there an understanding reached tentatively at the end of the February 10th meeting?

**A:** There was an understanding reached in the sense that there was a proposal from the Company for a 12-hour continuous shift operation. And that proposal was going to be put to a vote of the membership.

**Q:** Is the Company's proposal, Joint Exhibit 6, called a "Proposed Letter of Understanding"?

**A:** Yes.

**Q:** Is this Proposed Letter of Understanding in the Agreement that the Union agreed it would submit to the employees for ratification?

**A:** Yes.

**Q:** Was it, in fact, ratified?

**A:** Yes.

**Q:** When?

**A:** It was ratified a few days later, within the next three or four days.

**Q:** Let me ask you to look at Joint Exhibit 7. Is that the agreement that was ultimately signed on that date, the same as the Proposed Agreement?

**A:** Yes.

**Q:** Let's go back to the February 10th meeting. Was there any discussion at that meeting of what would happen with respect to holiday pay for employees on continuous 12-hour shifts, if they move from one group to another, for example, from A/C to B/D or vice versa, or from either of those back to the eight-hour group?

**A:** No.

**Q:** Look at the Company's response in the fourth paragraph in General Discussion B in Joint Exhibit 5. It begins: "The Company responded that this issue would be resolved by March 15, by trying to look at having each group pick the equivalent of its holidays but this will have to be done by the first group assigned to the 12-hour continuous shifts, and those employees who are assigned later to that shift would have to fit into what the original group chose. This cannot be settled at this meeting but should be settled by March 15." Could you tell me what issue is created by this paragraph?

**A:** The issue created was, because the employees on the 12-hour continuous shifts were going to have the right to select their holidays but not all employees had yet been assigned to the 12-hour shifts, the question was who gets to vote. Does the whole plant vote? Do all the employees who are expected to be on the 12-hour continuous shifts vote? Or do only the employees who are as of this time on the 12-hour shifts get to vote on what the holidays are going to be? And the Company's position, that we concurred with, was that the vote would be conducted only among those employees who were at that time on 12-hour shifts.

**Q:** Was there any discussion at all on the subject of what would happen to an employee's holiday pay if the Company at some point in the future discontinued or started to phase out the 12-hour continuous operation and move people back to eight-hour shifts?

**A:** There was no discussion on that whatsoever.

**Q:** Was there any discussion on that date on the issue I described for you, that is what would happen if the Company decided to phase out the 12-hour continuous operation and involuntarily reassign people back to eight-hour shifts or move them involuntarily from one 12-hour shift to another?

**A:** There was no discussion of that at all.

**Q:** After February 10th, when was the next meeting between the Union and the Company when the holiday schedule for the 12-hour shifts was discussed?

**A:** I believe it was March 9, year 2.

**Q:** Could you look at Joint Exhibit 8, which is the minutes of the March 9th meeting? Have you had a chance to review these?

**A:** Yes.

**Q:** Are these accurate?

**A:** Yes.

**Q:** Let me direct you to Option IV, the last full paragraph, third sentence, which reads, "Once the employees have voted, the holidays would be set, and employees that move around on the 12-hour continuous shift or 8-hour standard shifts could gain or lose holidays depending on the group they change to." Do you remember this part of the discussion on March 9th?

**A:** Yes.

**Q:** Could you tell me how that issue came up and what was said?

**A:** Sure. The Union asked the question because the holidays were just about to be finalized, and we asked the question, "What happens if an employee successfully bids on a move from one shift to another?" There is a lot of bidding that goes on at this plant. There are a lot of different classifications and shifts at this plant. We asked, "How are you going to keep track of the holidays?" The Company's response was that it would be too difficult to try to keep track of the holidays. The Company said that when an employee successfully bids from one job to another and as a result moves to another shift, that employee has the responsibility to know what the holidays are because he or she is making the choice to move, and if an employee chooses to do it, win, lose, or draw, that is the way it comes out.

**Q:** What was the Union's response?

**A:** We felt that was equitable.

**Q:** Was there anything said in the March 9th meeting about what would happen to holiday pay if a group of employees were involuntarily reassigned to a different group?

**A:** No, there was not.

**Q:** Was there any discussion of that issue at any time during any of the meetings in year 2 concerning the implementation of the 12-hour continuous shifts?

**A:** No.

**Q:** When did that question first come up?

**A:** Early in year 3.

**Q:** Could you tell us how it came up?

**A:** On February 16 of year 3, the Company announced at a meeting that, because of production requirements—this time a slow-down in production requirements—that certain departments of the plant were going to be changed from a 12-hour continuous shift back to the 8-hour Monday through Friday shift. The Union claimed that a number of employees would stand to lose holiday pay, potentially, so we raised that issue.

**Q:** Was there a later reassignment of a group of employees from a 12-hour continuous shift to an 8-hour shift that resulted in the loss of some holiday pay?

**A:** Yes.

**Q:** In other words, as a result of the reassignments employees who were covered had a change of their holiday schedule which resulted in less time off than before. Of course the converse also applied.

**A:** Yes.

**Q:** Is it true that the crew schedules did not change but rather employees were affected because they were reassigned to a different crew?

**A:** Yes.

**Q:** That is all.

## b. Cross-Examination by Company Advocate

*Ms. George:*
[to be supplied by student]

5

## 2. Cliff Depin, Chief Shop Steward

### a. Direct Examination by Union Advocate

*Mr. Solly:*

**Q:** Your name and position?

**A:** Cliff Depin, and I am the Chief Shop Steward.

**Q:** How long have you worked at Superior?

**A:** Fifteen years.

**Q:** What department do you work in?

**A:** In-process Control lab.

**Q:** What do they make at Superior?

**A:** All kinds of parts for the aerospace industry.

**Q:** You mentioned you are on the C shift?

**A:** Correct.

**Q:** Is that a 12-hour continuous shift?

**A:** Yes.

**Q:** When the 12-hour shifts were first set up in year 2, were you assigned to one of them?

**A:** Yes.

**Q:** Where did you start out?

**A:** The A/C shift.

**Q:** Did you later move to another shift?

**A:** Yes, the B/D shift.

**Q:** When was that?

**A:** January of year 3, I believe.

**Q:** After that, did you move back to A/C?

**A:** Yes.

**Q:** When the 12-hour continuous shifts were first implemented, was there a communications meeting of the employees in the Company at which the holidays were discussed?

**A:** Yes.

**Q:** What is a communications meeting?

**A:** It is a meeting where all the employees get together and the Company reviews things, talks to us about safety, other issues.

**Q:** This meeting would have been sometime in early year 2?

**A:** Correct.

**Q:** Was there any discussion at that particular meeting of what would happen to holidays if an employee bid from one 12-hour continuous shift to another 12-hour continuous shift?

**A:** Yes.

**Q:** Who was the Company spokesman at the meeting?

**A:** Tom Jones, the Manager.

**Q:** What did he say?

**A:** If you bid to another shift, some would lose and some would gain in response to holiday pay.

**Q:** Did he explain at that meeting what would happen regarding holidays if the company were to phase out the 12-hour continuous shifts and move people back to the 8-hour shifts?

**A:** No.

**Q:** Has that issue ever been brought up at a communications meeting?

**A:** No.

**Q:** When you made your move to a different shift, were these both moves that you initiated through a bid?

**A:** Correct.

**Q:** Did you lose a holiday in both cases?

**A:** Yes.

**Q:** Did you file a grievance?

**A:** No.

**Q:** There was some reference earlier to some changes, I believe in February of year 3 and April of year 3, when people were moved off of the 12-hour continuous shifts. Can you describe what those changes were?

**A:** I do not know.

**Q:** What departments have had 12-hour continuous shifts?

**A:** Towers, IPC labs, mix house, warehouse, maintenance.

**Q:** About how many employees work at the plant?

**A:** Two-hundred.

**Q:** Those departments that have had 12-hour continuous shifts, what part of the 200 is that, approximately?

**A:** About 70.

**Q:** What was the highest percentage of employees on 12-hour continuous shifts at any one time?

**A:** About 90 percent.

**Q:** Did the Company ever move anybody—putting aside the changes made in early year 3—from one shift to another because it needed somebody at one place or another?

**A:** I do not recall that.

**Q:** I have nothing further.

b. Cross-Examination by Company Advocate

*Ms. George:*
[to be supplied by student]


# C. Examination of Company Witness


## 1. Tom Jones, Plant Manager, Operations


### a. Direct Examination by Company Advocate

*Ms. George:*
Q:   What is your name and position, sir?
A:   Tom Jones, Plant Manager, Operations, at Superior.
Q:   Tell us what Superior does.
A:   We prepare materials used in the aerospace industry. P-r-e-p-e-g, one word. We take engineered fabrics, such as fiberglass, quartz, and Kevlar, and coat them with resin systems such as epoxy resins and a few other chemicals I won't go into. The resulting products are then taken and utilized to make composite parts for the aerospace industry. These composite parts are used to replace metal materials.
Q:   Are there various manufacturing departments at your plant?
A:   Yes.
Q:   Can you tell us which ones those are?
A:   Towers, slitter, mix house, hot melt, special processing, warehouse, maintenance, in-process control lab, mechanical labs, chemical labs, raw material testing.
Q:   Do you also have some departments which you call support departments for these manufacturing departments?
A:   Yes.
Q:   Can you tell me which ones those are?
A:   The support groups are the primary support groups, maintenance group, warehouse group. They supply the production organizations.
Q:   I think it's been pretty well discussed that prior to year 2 there was a provision in the Collective Bargaining Agreement that provided for a continuous shift operation. Are you familiar with that provision?
A:   Yes.

Q:   Do you remember having a discussion with Mr. Barsky on or about December 14th, year 1, about the Company's desires with respect to a continuous shift operation?
A:   Yes.
Q:   Tell me what you remember about that conversation.
A:   I was attempting to solicit Moe's input. We had been running at that time for 18 months in an overtime situation, where our employees were basically three shifts of eight-hour employees. I was concerned about the employees, and I wanted a better work schedule for them and was looking to go on a continuous basis because I was concerned about the employees. Also, we were not able to keep up with the business demand.
Q:   Was there an increase in business prior to your discussion with Mr. Barsky?
A:   Yes.
Q:   Did you discuss with him what you had in mind with respect to continuous shift operation?
A:   Yes, I had been researching continuous shift operations of various formats. I myself had managed one that was similar to the one which we later had in our contract, which was discussed earlier.
Q:   Did you tell Mr. Barsky that?
A:   Yes.
Q:   Did you discuss with Mr. Barsky in that December 14th meeting the issue of holidays as it related to your notion of what kind of continuous shift operation you wanted to go to?
A:   Only in the general sense of the overall picture as we were looking at it at that time. I explained to Mr. Barsky that at that time we

had already had some communication meetings, trying to get the employees' input into it and their thoughts about a continuous shift operation. We had discussed the concepts of equivalent holidays for each of the work crews, because we would still have people on the eight-hour shifts. We would have people that would never enjoy holidays if they were on the beginning of the week or end of the week on the 12-hour continuous shifts. So we had to establish holidays for those work crews.

**Q:** You have heard Mr. Barsky's testimony about what occurred after that meeting, and I'm going all the way to February 10th, year 2, when there was a labor-management meeting at which a 12-hour continuous shift operation was discussed. Are you generally in agreement with his description of those events?

**A:** Yes.

**Q:** Do you recall a meeting with the Union on February 10, year 2? Take a look at Joint Exhibit 5 to refresh your memory.

**A:** I remember the meeting.

**Q:** As of that date, had there been a general understanding between the Union and the Company that the Union was willing to discuss a 12-hour continuous shift operation and the ramifications of that?

**A:** Yes.

**Q:** Who called the meeting?

**A:** The Union.

**Q:** What was the purpose of the meeting?

**A:** The Union requested the meeting because they wanted to discuss a 12-hour continuous shift operation, as opposed to the arrangement which was in the contract.

**Q:** Do you recall the Union discussing at that meeting its proposal with respect to how the situation of holidays would be addressed for the 12-hour continuous shift?

**A:** I remember discussing it.

**Q:** Do you remember any discussion as to what, in fact, their proposal was as to how that situation would be handled?

**A:** As the minutes say, they wanted to continue the fixed holidays. I did not consider that a workable solution.

**Q:** Did you tell them that at the meeting?

**A:** Yes.

**Q:** Did you tell Mr. Barsky that?

**A:** Yes.

**Q:** Did you tell him why you did not think it was workable?

**A:** One of the things was Easter Sunday for the A/C group. It is considered a holiday for many people, and they would be unable to have that off, as this proposal was structured.

**Q:** And you used that as an example?

**A:** Yes.

**Q:** Did you offer your own modification with respect to how holidays would be handled under the 12-hour continuous shift operation?

**A:** Yes.

**Q:** Is that the situation that is set forth in General Discussion B, paragraph 4 of Joint Exhibit 5?

**A:** Yes.

**Q:** Was there some discussion by the Company as to why it believed holidays had to be selected by the various groups?

**A:** Yes, we explained that we had three different operating groups that we would be working with, all covered by the same contract but three distinct groups: the beginning-of-the-week group, the end-of-the-week group, and the people that were continuing to work an eight-hour shift.

**Q:** Was it understood in these discussions, in your opinion, by both sides that there would always be a group of employees that would be in the eight-hour group and have the holidays set forth in the Collective Bargaining Agreement of June 8, year 2 in Joint Exhibit 1?

**A:** Yes.

**Q:** Do you recall a further discussion at the meeting of February 10 in response to a Union inquiry about how the holidays would be selected?

**A:** Yes.

**Q:** Take a look in Joint Exhibit 5 in General Discussion B at the Union's point of clarification question on holidays and the Company's response. My question is, do you recall this discussion?

**A:** Yes.

**Q:** Do you recall somebody from the Company making the statement that ''those who come or are assigned later to the shifts will have to fit into what the original group chose''?

**A:** Yes.

**Q:** Who made that statement?

**A:** Most likely, I did.

**Q:** Do you remember in what context that statement was made?

**A:** Specifically in relationship to the fact that not everybody was going to the 12-hour continuous shifts at the same time. We would be phasing people into the 12-hour shifts.

**Q:** You recall some discussion of that point at that meeting?

**A:** Yes.

**Q:** Do you mean an operation that had not been on a 12-hour shift would be converted to a 12-hour continuous shift?

**A:** That is correct.

**Q:** Can you briefly tell us how the phasing worked?

**A:** During year 2 we first brought the 12-hour continuous shift to the towers, part of our mix house which supported the towers, and part of our warehousing operation, and part of our IPC labs to support the tower production area. That was February, of year 2. In the April to May period of year 2, we brought in what we referred to as hot melt production, stretcher polisher area, and the support groups for them. And then on December 31st, year 2, we brought the weaving department onto a 12-hour continuous shift.

**Q:** After the 12-hour continuous shift was brought into these departments, were employees from eight-hour shifts assigned to those departments, both voluntarily and involuntarily?

**A:** Yes. There is a procedure for bid purposes that a person can bid for a position, but we also have a classification called "production workers," where we assign them to different departments on an as-needed basis.

**Q:** In those situations, did those employees receive the holidays for the crew which they went to?

**A:** Yes.

**Q:** Were some employees moved involuntarily from the A/C shift to the B/D shift and vice-versa?

**A:** I believe there most likely were.

**Q:** As far as you knew, they took holidays of whatever crew they were on at a given moment?

**A:** That is correct.

**Q:** Let's say you were phasing in the last operation to go to 12-hour continuous shifts. How did the employees pick what 12-hour shift they would go on?

**A:** Good question. We canvassed all of the employees as to which of the 12-hour continuous shifts they would prefer, but we did ultimately assign the employees on a need basis for smoothness of production of the operation.

**Q:** Do you recall attending a labor–management meeting on March 9, year 2?

**A:** Yes.

**Q:** Do you recall some discussion of the issue of holidays at that joint labor–management meeting?

**A:** Yes.

**Q:** I would like you to refer again to Joint Exhibit 5, the minutes of the meeting of February 10. Does it reflect a discussion regarding the holidays?

**A:** Yes.

**Q:** Do you recall how that issue initially came up?

**A:** A question by the Union as to how holidays were going to be handled.

**Q:** Do you recall specifically the question?

**A:** What happens when an employee moves from one work crew to another? What we said was, depending on where the employee went, they would enjoy the holidays of that work crew.

**Q:** Do you have a recollection of discussing with the Union any concerns management had as to keeping track of holidays as people moved in the plant?

**A:** Yes.

**Q:** What was that discussion?

**A:** The absolute problem of trying to keep track of everybody's hours. There is a lot of other language in the contract that—

**Q:** This was discussed at the meeting?

**A:** Yes. For example, a probationary employee does not get holiday pay. They have to work so many hours the day before or not. It's a nightmare. As a matter of fact, for the Company, it was such a nightmare we had to get a second payroll Company for the employees on the first-of-the-week crew.

**Q:** I am asking you what was said at the meeting with respect to the problem of keeping track.

**A:** It was a nightmare.

**Q:** Do you recall making a statement—that is attributed in the minutes of the February 10 meeting—with respect to employees gaining or losing holidays?

**A:** Yes.

**Q:** What happened early in year 3 that caused the Company to reevaluate its need for a 12-hour continuous shift operation?

**A:** A turndown in business, you know, a slump.

**Q:** Did the Company agree with the Union's position?

**A:** No. The hours gained and lost by employees were equal. There has been no contract violation.

**Q:** Do you recall the Union's complaining some time in February of year 3 about the effect on B/D shift employees specifically?

**A:** Yes.

**Q:** Do you remember what remedy the Union asked the Company to consider at that time?

**A:** Yes.

**Q:** What did they want?

**A:** They wanted effective pay for the employees that they felt were harmed.

**Q:** Did the Company agree with the Union's position?

**A:** No. The Company's position was that the hours gained and lost by employees were equal, and that there had been no contractual violation.

**Q:** Let me show you Joint Exhibit 9. You see just before the selection choices there is a paragraph that says, "The plant will close on the selected holidays and you will receive 12 hours of pay per day" and then it says, "if all other contractual requirements are met." Do you know what the Company's intention was?

**A:** In the contract itself it has very specific methodology as to how a person is compensated relative to working before or after a probationary period. We wanted to make sure in all cases we were meeting the contract requirements.

**Q:** Did you understand that the contract required that the person be scheduled for that holiday?

**A:** The employee only gets the holiday if that employee was going to be working that day.

**Q:** Have you been able to accurately determine as a result of this grievance which employees received more time off than they would have had under Section 8 or which employees received less?

**A:** We have made a summary investigation of the people that were moved back from A/C and B/D to eight-hour shifts, and examined their hours, that is all of those people that did not successfully bid to go someplace else during the year. I mean those subject to involuntary reassignments. It is approximately equal as to the number of hours gained and lost.

**Q:** Do you know how many weeks or months it took you to come up with that estimate?

**A:** We went through it three different times. I would guess the hours involved in coming up with the estimate probably have been between 30 and 40.

**Q:** Did you encounter the administrative nightmare that you thought you were going to realize?

**A:** It was extremely difficult. There was no way we come up with a solution that would not have hurt some employees.

**Q:** I have nothing further.

---

### b. Cross-Examination by Union Advocate

*Mr. Solly:*
[to be supplied by student]

# D. Exhibits

## *JOINT EXHIBIT NO. 1*

COLLECTIVE BARGAINING AGREEMENT

BETWEEN

SUPERIOR PRODUCTS, INC.

AND

LOCAL 11

UNIVERSAL WORKERS AND SPECIALTY UNION

(6/8/02-6/8/05)

· · ·

SECTION 7 - HOURS OF WORK AND OVERTIME

· · ·

H.   Continuous Shift Operation
     A.   8-Hour Continuous Shift Operation

· · ·

     B.   12-Hour Continuous Shift Operation
     A twelve (12) hour continuous shift operation consisting of three (3) or four (4) consecutive twelve (12) hour working days.

     The fourth (4th) paid workday of the work week would be at time-and-a-half.

     All hours worked over ten (10) hours on a workday would be at time-and-a-half.

     Holidays would be chosen by the work crews to be equal to the number of holiday hours granted to eight (8) hour shift employees.

     Vacation and sick leave would be based on the current number of hours earned per month and used on a per hour basis of time off at base pay.

     Funeral leave as outlined in the Contract will be paid at the straight time rate for up to three (3) days.

     Jury duty would be covered . . . .

SECTION 8 - HOLIDAYS

A.   Recognized Holidays

     The following days shall be observed as holidays in which no work is performed:  New Year's Day, Washington's Birthday, Memorial

Day, Fourth of July, Labor Day, Thanksgiving Day, Friday after Thanksgiving, Christmas Day, two (2) Floating Holidays, and one (1) additional personal holiday with pay to be taken on a calendar year basis. Any holiday occurring on a Sunday shall be observed on the following Monday. Holidays falling on a Saturday shall be observed on the preceding Friday.

B.   Holiday Pay

     Employees not required to work on holidays listed above shall be paid an amount equal to eight (8) times their straight time hourly rate including shift differentials during the last pay period, provided they work or have a paid absence on their regularly scheduled workdays immediately preceding and following said holidays. The only exceptions to the above are absences:
     (1)   Approved by the Plant Manager.
     (2)   Due to layoff and/or paid disability, provided the employee has worked at least one (1) full shift during the thirty (30) day period prior to the holiday. The employee's total pay including disability pay shall equal the employee's regular holiday pay.

If an employee is off work when an authorized holiday occurs because of work-connected disability, the employee's total pay including compensation pay shall equal the employee's regular holiday pay. The preceding sentence shall not apply if the disability exceeds three months.

An employee must be on the payroll as of the first workday of the calendar year to be eligible for the personal holiday.

Employees scheduled to work on holidays and who fail to report shall forfeit the holiday pay provided in Paragraph B above. No employee shall be entitled to receive holiday pay, as provided in this Section, until they have completed their probationary period.

C.   Computing Overtime

     A holiday occurring within the work week shall be counted as time worked for the purpose of computing overtime.

## *JOINT EXHIBIT NO. 2*

<u>Management Proposal, December 15, year 1</u>

A.   To add an option of continuous operation based on fixed 12-hour shifts, the fourth day of the work week would be at time-and-a-half.  Holidays would be chosen by the work crews to be equal to the number of holiday hours granted to 8-hour shift employees. Vacation, sick leave and funeral leave would be based on the current number of hours earned per month and used on a per hour basis of time off at base pay. . . .

<u>TYPICAL 12-HOUR WORK SCHEDULE</u>

   1.   FIXED - Mon, Tues, Wed (A & B)
       FIXED - Thurs, Fri, Sat (C & D)
            Alternate Sundays

   2.   FIXED - Sun, Mon, Tues (A & B)
       FIXED - Wed, Thurs, Fri (C & D)
            Alternate Saturdays

   3.   FIXED - Sun, Mon, Tues, (A & B)
       FIXED - Thurs, Fri, Sat (C & D)
            Alternate Wednesdays

All selections provide at least three days off in a row.

Option #1 - A & B have all Saturdays off and every other Sunday.

Option #2 - Everyone alternates Saturday as being off, with A & B working Sundays.

Option #3 - Gives everyone a fixed weekend day off with alternate Wednesdays as the fourth workday.

/s/ John Smith
Assistant Manager

## *JOINT EXHIBIT NO. 3*

GRIEVANCE

<u>Grievant</u>: Local 11 (Class Action)

<u>Date of Grievance</u>: May 1, year 3

<u>Grievance No.</u>: 1234 Class Action

<u>Contract Provision Violated</u>: Sections 7 and 8, and all other relevant provisions of the Agreement.

<u>Request on Behalf of</u>: All employees who lost vacation pay due to their involuntary reassignment from a 12-hour shift to an 8-hour shift.

<u>Remedy</u>: All employees who were harmed by losing vacation because of their involuntary reassignment shall be made whole, plus interest for the hours lost.

/s/ Moe Barsky<br>
Business Agent, Local 11

## *JOINT EXHIBIT NO. 4*

<u>Answer by Company Concerning Grievance No. 1234</u>

May 2, year 3

The grievance is denied. The Company is not responsible for loss of vacation pay.

<u>Appeal</u>

May 10, year 3

The Union appeals Grievance No. 1234 to arbitration pursuant to the fast-track procedure in the Grievance/Arbitration provision of the Collective Bargaining Agreement.

/s/ Moe Barsky<br>
Business Agent, Local 11

### *JOINT EXHIBIT NO. 5*

<u>Labor/Management Meeting February 10, year 2</u>

Attending for the Union:
    Union Committee--Frank Ware, Bonnie John, Al Purdy, and Moe Barsky

Attending for the Company:
    Tom Jones and John Smith

The Union called the meeting to discuss the result of a recent secret ballot taken by the house, whereby the Union Committee was directed to propose to the Company going to a second Continuous Shift Option.

<u>Union Requests</u>

The Union proposed a 4/3, 12-hour shift option:

(a)  The fourth day worked to be paid at 1 and 1/2X

(b)  All hours over 8 on other days to be paid at 1 1/2X except Sunday be paid at 2X

(c)  Continue the 11 holidays as is with those on 12-hour shifts getting paid for 12 hours for each holiday

(d)  Employees off on a holiday would get 12 hours holiday pay

(e)  Vacation pay to be based on weekly schedule for vacation taken and those that work during scheduled vacation week get appropriate pay

(f)  Funeral leave still for 3 days

(g)  Section 7, power failure, modified to effect that if employee loses a day, the employee gets at least 6 hours pay

(h)  Sick leave earned at 6 hours a month

(i)  Attendance Policy modified, with employees not getting 1/2 point until 4 hours of absence

(j)  Job bids to be opened as Company originally proposed

<u>Company Response</u>

The Company responded by asking the Union Committee why a suggestion of Sunday at 2X, when it would be part of the proposed work schedule, not an off day, and that vacation was currently offered on a daily basis if need. The Company asked if the Union was proposing doing away with the daily vacation and the response by the Union was no.

## *JOINT EXHIBIT NO. 5 (continued)*

The Company then stated that at this time it could only offer what was originally outlined in December, with minor changes, because of current time restraints, with February 20, year 2, start date of the Continuous Shift Operation.

The Company outlined the modifications that it could offer as:

    (a)    Allowing employees their choice of shifts may be difficult because of time

    (b)    Funeral leave would be for 3 days

    (c)    Holidays could be selected by the groups and would equal 80 hours but would have to be finalized before March 15, year 2

    (d)    The fourth workday of the work week would be at 1 and 1/2X

### General Discussion A

The Union indicated it recognized the lateness of the hour and stated it had earlier suggested that the parties meet to explore these issues before they occurred.

The Company stated this is what it had been attempting since December but to no avail.

The Union then asked if the Company was prepared to make comments on its proposal or was the issue dead.

The Company stated it would certainly entertain any suggestions that the Union had. Either party could suggest changes on any item.

### Union's Requested Modifications

The meeting reconvened after a break and the Union stated it was prepared to discuss the previous Company proposal except for three modifications which it wanted.

MODIFICATION I:

The weekly minimum to be equivalent to pay for 40 straight time hours. An example was the 3-day work week, where the employees would receive 39 hours pay.

MODIFICATION II:

As to the issue of sick leave, the Union requested that the monthly accumulation be 6 hours instead of the current 4 hours.

MODIFICATION III:

That the Attendance Policy allow an additional four (4) hours before the employee receives a 1/2 point for being off.

Company's Response to the Requested Modifications

The Company responded to the Union's requested modification as follows:

MODIFICATION I:

This issue was covered in the original discussions where it was shown that now an employee averaged 184 hours total pay every four weeks, whereas under the proposed Continuous Shift Operation the employee will average 194 hours of pay in a four-week period.

MODIFICATION II:

With the additional time off under the Company's proposal, use of sick leave would be less, and only used in the future by employees for possible doctor visits or as an insurance policy. The Company could not see a change at this time.

MODIFICATION III:

This is a work rule and not part of the contract. Therefore, this would not be part of the discussion.

General Discussion B

The Union had no other questions on its requests.

The Company stated that the hours for the shifts would be 7:00 a.m.-7:00 p.m. and 7:00 p.m.-7:00 a.m.

The Union asked for a point of clarification on holidays. The question was "How would the Company go about allowing selection of the holidays by group?"

The Company responded that this issue would be resolved by March 15, by trying to look at having each group pick the equivalent of its holidays but this will have to be done by the first group assigned to the 12-hour continuous shifts, and those employees who are assigned later to a shift would have to fit into what the original group chose. This cannot be settled at this meeting but should be settled by March 15.

The Union asked if the Company had a proposal.

## *JOINT EXHIBIT NO. 5 (continued)*

At this time the Company issued a proposal to the Union. (See proposed Letter of Understanding attached.) The Company further stated that it would accept a membership vote at the plant but that it must be ratified within 48 hours of the last vote to switch either to the second Continual Shift Operation or to the 7-day Continuous Shift Operation.

The Union Committee indicated it did not have a ballot box or balloting sheets for the employees. The Company stated it would supply a ballot box and balloting sheets for this use.

The Union Committee members then stated that they could not sign the proposed Letter of Understanding until after the vote was finalized as to the direction they would be directed to go by the Union body. They stated that the vote would act as the Union's acceptance of the proposal if it is in the affirmative. They stated that they would sign the proposed Letter of Understanding at a later date.

A discussion ensued in reference to the voting time and the Union agreed to have the voting over the weekend.

At this time the meeting was closed. The voting will settle the continuous shift issue Monday morning after the final voting at 8:30 a.m.

*JOINT EXHIBIT NO. 6*

2/10/02

PROPOSED LETTER OF UNDERSTANDING

The Company and Union by this letter have jointly agreed to add a Second Continuous Operation Option, as follows:

A.  A 12-hour continuous shift operation consisting of 3 or 4 consecutive 12-hour working days.

B.  The fourth paid workday of the work week would be at time-and-a-half.

C.  All hours worked over 10 hours on a workday would be at time-and-a-half.

D.  Holidays would be chosen by the work crews to be equal to the number of holiday hours granted to 8-hour shift employees. Currently 80 hours a year is paid for scheduled holidays.

E.  Vacation and sick leave would be based on the current number of hours earned per month and used on a per hour basis of time off at base pay.

F.  Funeral leave as outlined in the Contract will be paid at the straight time rate for up to three (3) days.

G.  Jury duty would be covered on days scheduled, for the 12 hours of scheduled work time.

H.  The closed bid procedure of not allowing a successful bidder to make another bid for six months would be set aside as regards bidding on a full shift for continuous operation.

I.  Meal allowance is not applicable to employees working on 12-hour continuous shift.

[unsigned]                              [unsigned]

LOCAL 11                                SUPERIOR PRODUCTS INC.

*JOINT EXHIBIT NO. 7*

2/12/02

<u>LETTER OF UNDERSTANDING</u>

The Company and Union by this letter have jointly agreed to add a Second Continuous Operation Option, as follows:

    A.  A 12-hour continuous shift operation consisting of 3 or 4 consecutive 12-hour working days.

    B.  The fourth paid workday of the work week would be at time-and-a-half.

    C.  All hours worked over 10 hours on a workday would be at time-and-a-half.

    D.  Holidays would be chosen by the work crews to be equal to the number of holiday hours granted to 8-hour shift employees. Currently 80 hours a year is paid for scheduled holidays.

    E.  Vacation and sick leave would be based on the current number of hours earned per month and used on a per hour basis of time off at base pay.

    F.  Funeral leave as outlined in the Contract will be paid at the straight time rate for up to three (3) days.

    G.  Jury duty would be covered on days scheduled, for the 12 hours of scheduled work time.

    H.  The closed bid procedure of not allowing a successful bidder to make another bid for six months would be set aside as regards bidding on a full shift for continuous operation.

    I.  Meal allowance is not applicable to employees working on 12-hour continuous shift.

/s/ Moe Barsky                /s/ Tom Jones
Business Agent                Manager
LOCAL 11                     SUPERIOR PRODUCTS INC.

*JOINT EXHIBIT NO. 8*

<u>Labor/Management Meeting</u>
March 9, year 2
Attending for the Union:

Moe Barsky

Attending for the Company:
Tom Jones

The Union requested the Labor-Management Meeting and presented an agenda.

The first item covered was On-Job Postings and Job Awarding.

Recently some jobs were awarded to grade D-4 employees on qualifications over more senior less qualified employees. The Chief Steward indicated that some people are more qualified for some jobs than some employees with more seniority. The D-4's were more qualified and in this particular case no grievances were filed. The Union wanted to know the Company's position.

The Company referred to Section 4, E, Page 5 of the Collective Bargaining Agreement. As indicated in this section, if a vacancy occurs, the vacancy can be filled by qualified employees. The Company will look at seniority in all job bids but qualifications will also have a bearing in the decision. For example, if two employees were to have equal qualifications, the more senior employee will have first opportunity at the job bid.

The second agenda item was the overtime schedule for the 3/4 continuous shift. The Union referred to a question concerning an upcoming overtime coverage example and asked what the Company's intent for overtime coverage was. Discussions occurred on this subject and the Company met after the meeting, and determined the following tentative options would be available until the entire Plant was on continuous shifts.

OPTION I:

Coverage would occur within the department from a list posted and signed by employees within the department wishing to work overtime.

OPTION II:

Coverage for overtime would come from opposite shifts covering the same time frame (A to B and C to D shifts) to attempt to fill the opening.

OPTION III

Coverage for overtime would come from personnel on the opposite shift (A to C and B to D shift) and would be contacted to fill the opening. All attempts would be made to contact the opposite shift early enough to keep employees from working over 12 hours. However, the first priority is coverage of the employees regularly assigned shift with at least one day break between shifts.

OPTION IV

Personnel on the appropriate 8-hour shift would be contacted in an attempt to fill the opening.

. . .

The fourth item covered the holidays for the 3/4 12-hour continuous shift operation.

A sample copy of the voting sheet was given to the Union. The Union was told that the sheet was in the process of being issued to employees plant-wide for voting purposes. Once the employees have voted, the holidays would be set, and employees that move around on the 12-hour continuous shift or 8-hour standard shifts could gain or lose holidays depending on the group they change to. All sheets were to be returned by March 16, year 2, and evaluated. An announcement would be posted after tabulation of the employees choices. The Company would make the Union aware of the holiday vote outcome.

. . .

The meeting concluded.

## *JOINT EXHIBIT NO. 9*

Sample                          12-HOUR SHIFT HOLIDAYS

March 9, year 2

NAME _____          DATE _____

EMPLOYEE NUMBER _____

All employees will vote for both A/C and B/D shift holidays.

Holidays will start at 7:00 p.m. on the day before, i.e., Sunday holidays start at 7:00 p.m. on Saturday evening.

The Plant will close on the selected holidays and you will receive twelve (12) hours of pay per day if all other contractual requirements are met.

| SHIFTS A/C | SHIFTS B/D |
|---|---|
| Choose 1 of 2 | Choose 1 of 2 |
| Christmas Sunday and Monday December 24 and 25, year 2 _____ | Thanksgiving Wednesday and Thanksgiving November 23 and 24, year 2 _____ |
| Christmas Monday and Tuesday December 25 and 26, year 2 _____ | Thanksgiving Thursday and Friday November 24 and 25, year 2 _____ |
| CHOOSE 3 OF 5 | CHOOSE 3 OF 5 |
| Easter Sunday March 26, year 2 _____ | Easter Saturday March 25, year 2 _____ |
| Memorial Sunday May 28, year 2 _____ | Memorial Saturday May 27, year 2 _____ |
| Independence Tuesday July 4, year 2 _____ | Independence Wednesday July 5, year 2 _____ |
| Labor Sunday September 3, year 2 _____ | Labor Saturday September 2, year 2 _____ |
| New Year's Eve Sunday December 31, year 2 _____ | Christmas Saturday December 23, year 2 _____ |

*JOINT EXHIBIT NO. 10*

COLLECTIVE BARGAINING AGREEMENT

BETWEEN

SUPERIOR PRODUCTS, INC.

AND

LOCAL 11

UNIVERSAL WORKERS AND SPECIALTY UNION

(6/8/01-6/8/02)

. . .

## SECTION 7 - HOURS OF WORK AND OVERTIME

### H.  Continuous Shift Operation

If the Company elects to implement a continuous shift operation, the following will apply:

The work week begins at the start of Monday, 12:01 a.m., and ends at 12:01 a.m. on the following Monday.

On continuous shift operation, eight (8) consecutive hours shall constitute the normal workday per shift.

Workdays will be consecutive, seven (7) day periods followed by two (2) or three (3) days off, as determined by the schedule.  Shifts rotate on a seven (7) day schedule.

Time-and-one-half the regular straight time rate will be paid for all hours over eight (8) per day and over forty (40) hours per week, and for Sundays and for holidays.  (See Section 8-B)

The above provisions apply to those on continuous shift operations only.

### I.  Working Schedules

The Company will endeavor to provide working schedules by shifts one (1) week in advance of the scheduled work.

## SECTION 8 - HOLIDAYS

### A.  Recognized Holidays

The following days shall be observed as holidays in which no work is performed:  New Year's Day, Washington's Birthday, Memorial Day, Fourth of July, Labor Day, Thanksgiving Day, Friday after Thanksgiving, Christmas Day, two (2) Floating Holidays, and one (1) additional personal holiday with pay to be taken on a calendar year basis.  Any holiday occurring on a Sunday shall be observed on the following Monday.  Holidays falling on a Saturday shall be observed on the preceding Friday.

*COMPANY EXHIBIT NO. 1*

May 22, year 2

UNION CONTRACT PROPOSALS

. . .

6. Holidays:

Section 8A - Add one fixed holiday for a total of 96 hours of fixed holidays (8 at 12 hours or 12 at 8 hours) plus one personal holiday at 8 or 12 hours as the case may be. Employees on 12-hour schedules will select fixed holidays for the following year each November; the poll will be conducted by the Labor/Management Committee.

Section 8B - Holiday pay shall be pay for the regularly scheduled hours the employee would have worked.

# Volt Power Company

## Table of Contents

## Table of Contents contd.

## NOTES

# A. Caption

IN THE MATTER OF A CONTROVERSY BETWEEN:

VOLT POWER COMPANY                    )
MILWAUKEE, WISCONSIN         )
                                           )
AND                                   )        RE: Lockout Grievance
                                           )
AMERICAN UNION OF RADIO      )
AND WIRE WORKERS              )
LOCAL 101                         )

Appearances:

For the Union: Jackie Canon

For the Company: Patrick Oyler

Date: June 1, year 3

Place: Milwaukee, Wisconsin

# B. Examination of Union Witnesses

## 1. Richard King, Steward, Fabrication Shop

### a. Direct Examination by Union Advocate

*Ms. Canon:*

**Q:** What is your name?

**A:** Richard King.

**Q:** How long have you been an employee of Volt Power Company, Mr. King?

**A:** Twenty-five years.

**Q:** Do you hold any Union office?

**A:** Yes. Steward in the Fabrication Shop.

**Q:** What is your job classification?

**A:** Spot Welder.

**Q:** Do you work in the Company's Fabrication Shop, in Building 8?

**A:** Yes, I do.

**Q:** Did you work in the Fabrication Shop in Building 8 in November, year 2?

**A:** Yes.

**Q:** For how many years prior to November of year 2 have you worked in the Fabrication Shop?

**A:** For 22 years.

**Q:** Would you identify by groups the employees that work in the Fabrication Shop?

**A:** The Shear Group, the Punch Group, the Brake Group, the Spot Welders group, the Bliss Brake group, the Arc Welders, the Angle Group, and the hourly rated people, like Cranes, Stock Accumulators, and Material Movers.

**Q:** In November of year 1, approximately how many employees were in each of these groups?

**A:** Do you want me to break it down by individual groups?

**Q:** Yes.

**A:** I have a Company record of these numbers and shifts. It's Joint Exhibit 3, I think. Group 20, Punch: ten on the first shift. Group 86, Angle: seven on the first shift, five on the second shift. Group 87, Shear: three on the first, two on the second. Group 89, Punch: eleven on the first, five on the second. Group 90, Brake: two on the first, two on the

second. Numerical Control Punch: three on the first, two on the second. Group 95, Bliss Brake: two on the first. Group 94, Spot Weld: thirteen on the first, eight on the second. Group 92, Arc Weld: ten on the first, five on the second. Group 79, Paint: seven on the first. Represented salaried Expediters, seven on the first. Short Order Shop, direct labor: seven on the first, five on the second, two on the third. Stock, indirect labor: nine on the first, five on the second. Accumulators, indirect labor: two on the first, two on the second. Crane, indirect labor: three on the first, two on the second. Material Movers: three on the first. That's a total of 144, which is the number of employees identified in the grievance.

**Q:** What is the function performed by the Shear group employees?

**A:** They cut the length and the width of the metal as per shop orders.

**Q:** Let me go back for a moment. What is the function of the Fabrication Shop?

**A:** Well, it's the Fabrication Shop's job to fabricate pieces for the assembly floors in Buildings 8 and 10—

**Q:** Now, let's go into each specific group. What does the Shear group do?

**A:** The Shear cuts the length and width of the metal.

**Q:** What does the Punch group do?

**A:** The Punch basically drills holes.

**Q:** What does the Brake group do?

**A:** The Brakes generally bend metal.

**Q:** And the Spot Weld group?

**A:** The Spot Weld will spot weld all types of steel, studs, and nuts.

**Q:** And the Bliss group?

**A:** The Bliss bend metal to a smaller size than the Brake group.

**Q:** And the Arc Weld group?

**A:** The Arc Weld group arc weld frames.

**Q:** And the Angle group?

**A:** The Angle group cuts angles to specified size.

**Q:** What do the employees in the Paint group do?

**A:** The employees in the Paint group will hang steel that the floor coat will paint.

**Q:** What do Expediters do?

**A:** They obtain parts and materials as needed and take them to the floor for processing.

**Q:** What about employees in the Short Order Shop?

**A:** They basically make up shortages that are needed for the floor immediately. Here Fabrication is done more quickly than in the Shop.

**Q:** From where does the Fabrication Shop, or any of the groups in the shop, get its work?

**A:** The paperwork or the physical work?

**Q:** The orders that they are to work on.

**A:** The orders come out of the office and then through the leaders of each group.

**Q:** Is there a work flow that's followed in the Fabrication Shop, as to procedure that is followed in working on any piece of equipment?

**A:** Yes, there is a flow.

**Q:** Normally, into which group will the work first go in the Fabrication Shop?

**A:** The Shear and Angle groups.

**Q:** And after the work is performed by them, where would it then go?

**A:** Then it will go into the Punch group.

**Q:** And after that, where would it go?

**A:** To the Brake.

**Q:** And from the Brake, where would it go?

**A:** From the Brake, it generally goes into accumulation areas on the floor.

**Q:** Okay. After it's placed into the accumulation area, who would next work on it?

**A:** It would either go to the Spot Weld, to the Arc Weld, or directly to Paint.

**Q:** After going to Arc Weld or Spot Weld, where would the product then go?

**A:** To the Paint Shop.

**Q:** And after the Paint Shop?

**A:** It would go to the assembly floors in Buildings 8 and 10.

**Q:** Are these final assembly groups?

**A:** Yes, they are.

**Q:** If work were to start in the Angle group, what is the next step it would follow after that?

**A:** From the Angle group, it would basically go to accumulation.

**Q:** And then, after accumulation, who would work on it next?

**A:** Either Spot Weld or Arc Weld.

**Q:** Then after it's worked on by Spot Weld or by Arc Weld, would it go to the Paint group?

**A:** Yes.

**Q:** And then to the final assembly?

**A:** Yes.

**Q:** Generally, does the work which comes into the Fabrication Shop progress in the manner that you have just described?

**A:** I would say, generally, that's the procedure.

**Q:** When would that procedure not be followed?

**A:** Well, we have engineer-ordered changes that cannot be done, say, in the Short Order Shop, and the engineers would generate the changes in the Fabrication Shop.

**Q:** Generally speaking, how long does it take for the work to progress through the various stages which you have just described, assuming it were to start with the Shear group?

**A:** I would say that the job would take about two weeks.

**Q:** How does a group determine what work it is supposed to do?

**A:** They work from a shop order or worksheet that indicates the number of pieces in the order to be processed.

**Q:** From whom do you, as an employee in Spot Weld, receive these worksheets?

**A:** They are given out by the control cage employees.

**Q:** For the work which you do, are you paid in terms of something other than regular dollars? Are you paid in voucher dollars?

**A:** Yes, voucher money.

**Q:** Would you explain what a voucher dollar is?

**A:** We are piece workers, and a voucher dollar is indirectly money we turn in as piecework pay. We get paid in voucher dollars so much per week, based on a quantity for each piece. The voucher dollars are turned in to the Company as payroll. Of course, the Company pays us in real dollars.

**Q:** Is a voucher dollar more or less than a real dollar, generally speaking?

**A:** I would say it's more.

**Q:** A voucher dollar is more?

**A:** I could be wrong, but I think it's more.

**Q:** I may have confused him. If I have a document which indicates three voucher dollars, for example, how much would that be in real dollars?

**A:** I really don't know. I don't think I want to answer that.

**Q:** All right. Do you use any other kinds of worksheets, other than the one which you have mentioned?

**A:** Engineers sometimes make changes on the work floor. These changes are passed on to the expediter who generates a form to be used by the production workers.

**Q:** Is there an order in which the work flows?

**A:** Yes, if it's done properly.

**Q:** Is a number assigned to each group in the Fabrication Shop?

**A:** Yes, there should be.

**Q:** Do you know which group Group 87 is?

**A:** I think it's the Shears group.

**Q:** And Group 89?

**A:** The Punch.

**Q:** 86 is Angle, is that correct?

**A:** Yes. And 94 is Spot Weld, and 95 is Bliss.

**Q:** What does "Piecework Voucher Generated in Shop" mean?

**A:** It is a form upon which pieceworkers' voucher money is recorded for special jobs. It's generated at the foreman level. They request the work right away, and we do it and are paid.

**Q:** Is this a different kind of work order than the other two which you have previously identified?

**A:** Well, a foreman can issue this whenever he wants. It doesn't have to be pursuant to a shop order.

**Q:** But does this form you described indicate to you that there is work to be done and what the work is?

**A:** Yes, as well as the payment for it.

**Q:** What is tag work?

**A:** It's generally work of a large quantity, generated through tags done by different groups, and there is voucher money connected with it also.

**Q:** How is a weekly payroll sheet used?

**A:** It tracks what work was done and work was not done for a particular week.

**Q:** Are the shop orders written on the payroll sheet?

**A:** Yes.

**Q:** Does the sheet contain many shop order numbers?

**A:** Yes.

**Q:** Is uncompleted work noted on the payroll sheet along with the worth of the uncompleted work?

**A:** Yes, and the worth is in voucher dollars. In some cases the worth may be $2 or $252.

**Q:** When are these weekly payroll sheets prepared?

**A:** During the week on a daily basis.

**Q:** Who prepares them?

**A:** The group's leader.

**Q:** On the basis of your experience, how long would it take for that group to complete $252 in voucher money?

**A:** I would guess about two to three days.

**Q:** Do Stock Shop orders have a particular number?

**A:** Almost all 856 shop orders are Stock Shop orders. The work goes to the Assembly floor, is stocked, and is then used as the Company sees fit.

**Q:** You said that you had been employed in the Fabrication Shop for how many years prior to this incident?

**A:** About twenty-two or twenty-three years.

**Q:** Am I right that on Wednesday, November 18th, year 2, all of the employees in the Fabrication Shop were sent home?

**A:** Yes.

**Q:** Had that ever occurred before in the time that you've worked there?

**A:** No, never everyone.

**Q:** When were you notified that you would be sent home on the 18th?

**A:** About 10:30 that morning.

**Q:** Was the procedure followed on November 18th for sending employees home the same or different than the procedure that

4

had been followed on other occasions? If so, in what respect?

**A:** It was different. Normally when we have a lack of work, the group leader will inform the foreman. If there is any question, the Shop Steward gets involved. On November 18th, at approximately 10:30 in the morning, the foreman, Steve Mann, made a round of the shop and told each employee that he was off that noon.

**Q:** When did you actually go home?

**A:** We went home that morning, at a quarter to twelve.

**Q:** To the best of your knowledge, was there any prior consultation between the foreman and any of the group leaders?

**A:** No.

**Q:** What was your role in this?

**A:** The group leaders came to me, since I was Shop Steward, wanting to know why we were being sent home when there was no lack of work.

**Q:** On those instances in the past where employees in the Fabrication Shop were sent home, was it for half a day or was it for longer?

**A:** Normally, we are off a full day. If there is a lack of work we are informed the day before that we will miss work the next day.

**Q:** After you and the other employees were informed that you would be sent home at 11:45, did you do anything?

**A:** I went to Forman Mann and protested. He told me there was nothing he could do about it. He referred me to the Unit Manager, Joey Cross.

**Q:** Did you see Mr. Cross?

**A:** Yes, I did, at about eleven o'clock. I wanted to know why we were being sent home for a lack of work when we had work to do.

**Q:** What did Mr. Cross say?

**A:** He said something like this, "Well, this is it. These are my orders and you have to go home."

**Q:** Did he indicate to you who had made the decision to send the employees home?

**A:** No, he didn't.

**Q:** Did you ask him on what basis the decision was made?

**A:** No, I didn't ask, and he didn't tell.

**Q:** Who normally makes lay-off decisions?

**A:** As far as I know, the Unit Manager.

**Q:** In preparation for this arbitration, did you have occasion to talk to the various group leaders?

**A:** Yes, I did.

**Q:** Did you make any request that they give you information with regard to the time off which they had during the week in question and the preceding week?

**A:** Yes, I did and I received a memorandum from management.

**Q:** How many days was the Shear group off during the week of November 14th? You can refer to the Joint Exhibit 4, memorandum you received to refresh your memory.

**A:** They were off November 12th and 13th for lack of work.

**Q:** And the Punch group 20?

**A:** The information isn't clear, but I know they worked 24 hours that week.

**Q:** And the Brake group?

**A:** They were off the 9th, 12th, and 13th of November for lack of work.

**Q:** What days was the Spot Weld group off?

**A:** They were off the 10th, 11th, and 12th of November.

**Q:** And the Arc Weld group?

**A:** The group leader couldn't get the records on them.

**Q:** And the Angle group?

**A:** It has off the 10th and the 11th.

**Q:** What about the Punch group 89?

**A:** I think they worked forty hours that week.

**Q:** For the week ending November 21st, Rich, would you tell me what days each of the groups had off?

**A:** The Shear group was only off half of a day on November 18. The Angle group was off the 18th for half of the day. The Brake was off the 16th, the 17th, and half of the 18th. The Spot Weld group was off the 15th and half of the day on the 18th. The Group 20 Punch employees were sent home for half of the 18th. The Group 89 Punch employees were off one unspecified day and half of the 18th.

**Q:** During that two-week period, is there any day, other than the 18th, when all of the employees in all of the groups were off due to lack of work?

**A:** No.

**Q:** Mr. King, on the 18th of November, was there work available for you to do?

**A:** Yes.

**Q:** Had you been given any indication prior to the morning of the 18th that you would be laid off for lack of work?

**A:** No.

**Q:** When did you return to work?

**A:** Friday, the 19th. We worked a full day.

**Q:** Were there any employees in the groups which you mentioned who were still on layoff on Friday?

**A:** No, not to my knowledge.

**Q:** Was there any work performed in the shop between the afternoon of the 18th, when you were laid off, and the 19th, when you returned to work?

**A:** Not to my knowledge. I wasn't there to see any done.

**Q:** No further questions.

### b. Cross-Examination by Company Advocate

*Mr. Oyler:*
[to be supplied by student]

## 2. Garrett Jensen, Acting Group Leader, Brake Department, Fabrication Shop

### a. Direct Examination by Union Advocate

*Ms. Canon:*

**Q:** What is your name?

**A:** Garrett Jensen

**Q:** By whom are you employed, Mr. Jensen?

**A:** Volt Power Company.

**Q:** For how long have you been employed by Volt?

**A:** Approximately thirty-one or thirty-two years.

**Q:** In November of year 2, where did you work?

**A:** The Fabrication Shop, Building 8.

**Q:** For how long prior to November of year 2 had you worked in the Fabrication Shop?

**A:** Thirty years.

**Q:** What group did you work in?

**A:** Group 90. In the Brake Department.

**Q:** Who was the group leader of the Brake Department in November of year 1?

**A:** Technically, there was no group leader.

**Q:** Who was acting group leader?

**A:** I was ex officio group leader, recognized by myself and by the Company, without any differential in pay.

**Q:** Were you performing the functions of a group leader in the Brake group?

**A:** Yes.

**Q:** For how long a period of time had you been doing that?

**A:** Approximately ten years.

**Q:** Who is it that supplies work for the Brake group in the Fabrication Shop?

**A:** 95% of the work comes from the Punch group. I think that's Group 89.

**Q:** And the other 5%?

**A:** It comes in on tags from another area.

**Q:** Generally speaking, how many days in a week does the Brake group work?

**A:** We are scheduled for a five-day week; however, it's rare that everybody works all five. When I say "rare," that's because of a sickness of a member of the group, or a man out for some other reason.

**Q:** When you are scheduled for time off because of lack of work, how is it normally accomplished?

**A:** There's a discussion between myself as acting group leader and the immediate foreman, a day or so prior to the day off. We discuss the volume of work that there is and the volume of work that we need, and if they do not meet, we agree that a day off is necessary. A few times, it had to go above the foreman.

**Q:** What does that mean?

**A:** There were times where we were told by the foreman and the Unit Manager that

6

approval had to come from higher up. I don't know the person's name.

**Q:** In all of the years that you have been working in the Fabrication Shop, can you recall any instance, other than November 18, year 2, where all of the employees in each of the groups were laid off at the same time?

**A:** Never.

**Q:** Do you know whether the Expediters were working a full forty-hour week the week ending November 14, year 2?

**A:** They were.

**Q:** Do you know whether the Short Order group was working a forty-hour week at that time?

**A:** I think they were.

**Q:** What about the Material Movers and the Crane men?

**A:** I think that both were working forty hours.

**Q:** Prior to Wednesday, November 18th, can you recall any instance in which Expediters had been laid off for lack of work?

**A:** For a four-hour basis, never.

**Q:** Do you recall whether they had been laid off for lack of work?

**A:** No, not on a temporary basis. They would be laid off for lack of work and then reassigned to work elsewhere in the plant or be on the street with a layoff notice.

**Q:** Were the Crane Operators ever laid off prior to November 18th?

**A:** No.

**Q:** The Material Movers, were they ever laid off?

**A:** No.

**Q:** Were the Short Order employees ever laid off prior to November 18th?

**A:** Not to the best of my knowledge.

**Q:** When were you advised that the employees of the Brake group would be sent home on the 18th?

**A:** Somewhere between 10:30 and 11:00 a.m.

**Q:** Who advised you of that?

**A:** Foreman Mann.

**Q:** Was there any prior discussion between you and Mr. Mann referring to this incident?

**A:** Absolutely none.

**Q:** Was there work available to be performed by the Brake group employees on the 18th of November?

**A:** Yes, there was.

**Q:** Was there work available to be performed by the Brake group employees on Thursday, the 19th of November?

**A:** Yes, there was.

**Q:** Was it the same or different work than was performed on the 18th?

**A:** The same.

**Q:** On the 19th of November, did you receive any shop orders for work that you did not have on November 18th?

**A:** I don't think so.

**Q:** To the best of your recollection, what was the minimum period of time for which Brake group employees were laid off for lack of work?

**A:** Eight hours.

**Q:** On the day in question, how many hours were you laid off?

**A:** Four hours on each shift.

**Q:** Had that procedure ever been followed in the past?

**A:** No.

**Q:** And am I correct that you returned to work on the 19th?

**A:** That's right.

**Q:** Were you working on the 16th or 17th of November?

**A:** No.

**Q:** What happened?

**A:** We were laid off for lack of work.

**Q:** What was the procedure followed in sending the employees in the Brake group home for lack of work on the 16th and 17th?

**A:** On the 14th or 15th there had been consultations with the Foreman or the Unit Manager. The decision was that there wasn't enough work to warrant our coming in for the following two days.

**Q:** How were you notified when to come in to work, after these two days that you were out?

**A:** Prior to our being off for lack of work, we were told that we would come back on the third day for work.

**Q:** On Wednesday, November 18th?

**A:** That's right.

**Q:** Is that what you had normally done?

**A:** Yes.

**Q:** They would tell you that you would be off for a certain number of days and when to report back?

**A:** Yes.

**Q:** And you reported back and worked for how many hours?

**A:** Four hours.

**Q:** Then they told you that you were off again, is that correct?

**A:** That's right.

**Q:** To the best of your recollection, has it ever happened that you have been laid off for a period of time, you came back, and then worked only four hours before being laid off again?

**A:** Not to my knowledge.

**Q:** Did you work the following Monday, the 23rd?

**A:** Yes, we did.

**Q:** On that particular day, were you performing work pursuant to shop orders which you had in your possession as of the 18th of November?

**A:** That's possible.

**Q:** Well, do you recall exactly?

**A:** I don't recall the specific shop order, but we would have worked some jobs that hadn't been—but could have been—done on the 18th.

**Q:** No further questions.

### b. Cross-Examination by Company Advocate

*Mr. Oyler:*
[to be supplied by student]

## 3. Anthony Prega, Chief Steward

### a. Direct Examination by Union Advocate

*Ms. Canon:*

**Q:** What is your name?

**A:** Tony Prega.

**Q:** By whom are you employed?

**A:** Volt Power Company.

**Q:** What is your job classification?

**A:** Assembler.

**Q:** What building do you work in?

**A:** 10.

**Q:** For how long have you been an employee of Volt Power Company?

**A:** Twenty-three years.

**Q:** Do you hold any Union position?

**A:** Yes, I do.

**Q:** What is it?

**A:** Chief Steward.

**Q:** Were you serving in that capacity in November of year 2?

**A:** Yes, I was.

**Q:** Was there a work stoppage which occurred on Wednesday, November 18th of that year?

**A:** Yes, there was.

**Q:** In Building 10?

**A:** Yes, there was.

**Q:** Were you one of the participants in that work stoppage?

**A:** Yes, I was.

**Q:** What was the nature of the dispute?

**A:** Money.

**Q:** Could you elaborate a little more on that?

**A:** On the bonuses. The bonuses were on the way down, due to parts shortages on the floor and other tie-ups on the jobs.

**Q:** Why were there problems?

**A:** Lack of customer orders and commitments affect our earnings.

**Q:** Was there also a work stoppage in Building 10 on November 10th, year 2?

**A:** Yes, there was.

**Q:** What was the nature of that dispute?

**A:** I don't remember exactly, but I know it was over a grievance we had. It had gone all the way to the level below arbitration, Step 3. There were several of these during that time, so I can't be exact.

**Q:** Was the general matter of the dispute on the 10th the same or different from the matter in controversy on the 17th of November?

**A:** There were two grievances at Step 3, but the subject matter of the grievances was about the same for each, a dispute over wages and bonuses.

**Q:** For how long a period of time, prior to November 18th, had the Union and the Company had this dispute concerning wages and bonuses for the employees?

**A:** I'd say about a year. Maybe a little longer.

**Q:** From where does Building 10 get its work?

**A:** From different shops, like the Copper Shop, the Fabrication Shop, the Compound Section, and the Machine Shop. They all supply parts to be assembled. But the shop order goes from Wage Rate to the floor.

**Q:** Okay. The Fabrication Shop, in Building 8, supplies its work to which particular areas of the Company?

**A:** Assembly area.

**Q:** Do you know which specific ones?

**A:** Well, it would be all of the groups on the floor. From the Fabrication Shop, work first goes to the Paint Shop.

**Q:** After it gets through the paint process, and all of the processes Mr. King testified to, where would it then go?

**A:** It goes to Groups 21, 22, 23, and 24.

**Q:** Where are they located?

**A:** In Buildings 10 and 9.

**Q:** Are there any buildings that are supplied by the Fabrication Shop?

**A:** Yes.

**Q:** What are they?

**A:** 10.

**Q:** Does that Fabrication Shop supply work to any other area of the Company?

**A:** The Shannon Hill location.

**Q:** Okay. Were you present on the Company premises on November 18th?

**A:** Yes, I was.

**Q:** On that date, did you have a conversation with the Unit Manager, Mr. Cross?

**A:** Yes, I did.

**Q:** What did that conversation relate to?

**A:** Well, I received a call at the Union office, saying that there were problems at Building 8. They wanted to send the whole floor home, and people were upset. I proceeded into the plant, to Building 8. Right at the corner, in the aisle, is where members of different groups, group leaders, a Steward, Roken, Foreman Steve Mann, and myself were. Later, Mr. Cross came into the picture.

**Q:** What, if anything, was said to you at that time by either Mr. Mann or Mr. Cross regarding the reason for the employees in Building 8 being sent home from work?

**A:** They said they had orders to send the whole floor home.

**Q:** Who said that?

**A:** At first, it was Mann.

**Q:** Did anybody else say it?

**A:** Later on, when Mr. Cross came into the area, I asked him why they were being sent home, and he said the same thing. I asked him if they had work for these people to perform for that day. He said, "Yes, but I have to send the people home. I have no control over it."

**Q:** What was your response to that?

**A:** I told him that he was locking these people out. And that is why I instructed the Steward, Richard King, to submit a grievance.

**Q:** Did Mr. Cross or Mr. Mann give you any explanation as to why the employees were being sent home?

**A:** They didn't specify.

**Q:** Did you request the information?

**A:** I kept pressuring for an answer, but they never came up with one.

**Q:** No further questions.

### b. Cross-Examination by Company Advocate

*Mr. Oyler:*
[to be supplied by student]

## 4. Joey Cross, Unit Manager (Adverse Witness)

### a. Direct Examination by Union Advocate

*Ms. Canon: I am calling Joey Cross as an adverse witness.*

**Q:** Mr. Cross, are you the Unit Manager over the employees in Building 8?

**A:** No. I'm not the Unit Manager, as of now.

**Q:** Were you the Unit Manager in November of year 2?

**A:** Yes, I was.

**Q:** For how long a period of time had you been the Unit Manager?

**A:** Approximately two and a half years.

**Q:** In what capacity are you presently serving?

**A:** Unit Manager of Top Plate Sub-Assembly.

**Q:** In what group were you the Unit Manager in November of year 2?

**A:** I was the Unit Manager of Metal Clad, Prime Paint and Steel Stock Room.

**Q:** Was the area of your authority coextensive with the Fabrication Shop, as we have described it?

**A:** Yes.

**Q:** I show you an exhibit which has been marked Union Exhibit 1, and ask you what the date in the upper right-hand corner indicates?

**A:** It indicates that this paper was made out on Thursday, 11/19, requesting that these parts be made.

**Q:** How long after that document is made up would it normally get to the Fabrication Shop?

**A:** It could be a period of five or six days, sometimes.

**Q:** Five or six days?

**A:** That's right. It tells you down here that it was priced on 11/21.

**Q:** When you say ''priced,'' what do you mean?

**A:** This paper was upstairs at Wage Rate. They priced it on 11/21, before it came down to the Fabrication Shop.

**Q:** And is the amount of time you just referred to typical?

**A:** In some cases, unless it's a red-hot job.

**Q:** In cases of red-hot jobs, how long would it take?

**A:** Two days.

**Q:** Two days?

**A:** Sometimes.

**Q:** Sometimes less?

**A:** You could do it in a day. It depends on how hot it is.

**Q:** Now, do all of the order sheets—including work authorizations—pass through your hands, or are they reviewed by you?

**A:** Yes. It would come through our control cage.

**Q:** How long is the normal cycle of work through the Fabrication Shop? Let's assume it starts in the Shear Group.

**A:** Approximately three weeks.

**Q:** And during the time that it's in the Fabrication Shop, it will be handled as Mr. King described?

**A:** Yes. It's dispatched to the group leaders by the Dispatch Expediter.

**Q:** If I were to look at these documents, how could I tell whether the whole job, or only part of the job, specified on the worksheet has been completed?

**A:** Well, you can't, other than the fact that this shows that Group 86 was paid for doing their work. Now this could go into next week, when this part might be done.

**Q:** After the employees were sent home in the Fabrication Shop on Wednesday, November 18th, did any other employees work in that shop prior to the 19th?

**A:** No.

**Q:** So the day-shift workers were sent home at approximately 11:45 a.m., is that correct?

**A:** Right.

**Q:** And then were returned to work as of the regular shift time on Thursday, the 19th?

**A:** Yes.

**Q:** And I assume that on the 19th, there was work available for each group to do, is that correct?

**A:** There was work available for the groups, but congestion still persisted in the Fabrication Shop. There was material laying all over the floor, and it was a safety hazard at the time.

**Q:** You mean finished or unfinished material?

**A:** Finished, as far as the Fabrication Shop is concerned. It was waiting to go into Paint and be put into the stock room, where we didn't have room for it.

**Q:** Is that your answer to the grievance in this case?

**A:** Yes.

**Q:** Is that the reason that the employees were given time off on the 18th, as stated in that document?

**A:** Yes.

**Q:** So it is your testimony, Mr. Cross, that the employees were sent home on Wednesday the 18th both because of a lack of work and also because of a lack of storage space?

**A:** Yes.

**Q:** You have a statement here on Joint Exhibit 2 as the answer to the grievance, saying that sufficient work was not available for these employees, is that correct?

**A:** Yes, it is.

**Q:** And is it your testimony that on Thursday the 19th there was sufficient work for these employees to do, but on the 18th there was not?

**A:** There were open orders in the Fabrication Shop at the time.

**Q:** Sufficient to employ these employees in each of the groups for four additional hours on the 18th?

**A:** No. The open orders were being rescheduled.

**Q:** I'm not talking about how you scheduled this. I'm asking whether there were a sufficient number of orders on the 18th so that the employees could have worked for an additional four hours on that date?

**A:** Well, there were open orders in the shop that could have been worked on, except for the fact that we had congestion in the shop such that I had no place to put it. There were orders.

**Q:** Now, whose responsibility was it to clean up this congestion?

**A:** Mine.

**Q:** What classifications of employees actually do the physical work?

**A:** Material Movers and Jitney Drivers. There is also a Sweeper on third shift to sweep the aisles.

**Q:** How many Material Movers are involved?

**A:** There is one in the 8 Building. There is also one Jitney Driver on the day shift and one on the night shift.

**Q:** Were the Material Movers in the Fabrication Shop laid off on the 18th?

**A:** Yes, they were.

**Q:** Did the Jitney Drivers work as part of the Fabrication Shop employees?

**A:** They work as part of the Paint Shop, the Fabrication Shop, and Assembly.

**Q:** Were they laid off on the 18th?

**A:** Not all. One stayed. We had him trying to work around the congestion.

**Q:** So, there was congestion in the Fabrication Shop, but nevertheless, you laid off Material Movers who normally clear up such congestion?

**A:** No. We laid them off because we had no place to move it to.

**Q:** I see. When the employees came back on the 19th, where had you moved the material that was congesting the area on the 18th?

**A:** Well, on the assembly floor. They started to come back. They started to pull jobs, which made room for the other material in our accumulation room.

**Q:** The Assembly floor came back on the 19th?

**A:** That's right.

**Q:** What time did they come back on the 19th?

**A:** A quarter to eight in the morning.

**Q:** When did you receive notification that they were coming back?

**A:** I think we received notice on the afternoon of the 18th. I don't remember exactly.

**Q:** When did you call back the employees in the Fabrication Shop?

**A:** I called them back on Wednesday night.

**Q:** How did you notify them?

**A:** By telephone.

**Q:** You called all 144 of them?

**A:** By telephone. There were a few that we couldn't get a hold of, so we sent them telegrams.

**Q:** And you told them to report at regular time?

**A:** Yes.

**Q:** Now, for my benefit, would you explain how this congestion was cleared up from the afternoon of the 18th to the morning of the 19th?

**A:** When we found out that the Assembly employees were coming back, we had certain jobs that could be pulled and sent onto the floor from our accumulation area. We started moving the material first thing in the morning.

**Q:** What areas do you store material in, other than the accumulation area?

**A:** We have areas right around the Paint Shop and the Steel Stock Room. We don't have enough room there, so we put it in the aisles.

**Q:** Is there any other place that you store material? Have you ever stored material at the Company's Shannon Hill location?

**A:** The only time I recall that happening is when a customer put back an order about eight months. To make room in the stock room, we accumulated this material and sent it out on an overtime basis.

**Q:** The answer to my question, then, is "yes"?

**A:** Yes.

**Q:** Isn't it true that just a week before this incident on the 18th, employees from the Fabrication Shop were working at Shannon Hill?

**A:** No, not to my knowledge.

**Q:** You are positive of that?

**A:** In what kind of capacity were they working there?

**Q:** From the Fabrication Shop?

**A:** Doing what?

**Q:** I'm asking the questions. Do you know of any employees from the Fabrication Shop working in Shannon Hill?

**A:** Not unless I had them out there on white time.

**Q:** What's that?

**A:** Another payment system. You pay them their average earnings since they aren't producing regular piece work.

**Q:** Now, is it your testimony that the materials were pulled out of the accumulation area and brought onto the final Assembly floor on the morning of the 19th, starting at about 7:45?

**A:** That's correct.

**Q:** Don't those materials have to be sent to the Paint Shop first?

**A:** No. It gets painted before it goes into the stock room. We were loaded with the paint work in the Paint Shop, as it was, so we took the material out of the Paint Shop and moved it to the accumulation area, and moved all the material that wasn't painted into the Paint Shop. That removed the congestion from the Fabrication Shop.

**Q:** You moved the materials that were not painted to which area?

**A:** Into the Paint Shop.

**Q:** Where did you move the materials in the Paint Shop?

**A:** Pre-accumulation area.

**Q:** Where is that?

**A:** The further end of the Fabrication Shop.

**Q:** You couldn't do that on the 18th?

**A:** No. It was congested with material already painted.

**Q:** What happened to that?

**A:** We started to pull that out Thursday morning, the 19th.

**Q:** Couldn't that be done on the 18th?

**A:** No, because we didn't know which jobs were going onto the Assembly floor, and there was nobody there to receive them.

**Q:** Where did you take them on the Assembly floor?

**A:** Into various groups. The request tells which job goes where.

**Q:** And how far in advance do you receive these requests?

**A:** About two or three hours.

**Q:** Is it usually more than that?

**A:** No, not usually. If you get hit with five or six requests, of course, it takes longer. It takes an average of three or four hours to accumulate the job. We have jobs pre-accumulated in that area. We got them out in half an hour or an hour by moving them with the jitney. If they are in the stock room, that's a different story.

**Q:** Does the Fabrication Shop do work for the Company's plant in Iowa?

**A:** Not to my knowledge. They might put a job through once in a while, but I never see it or hear about it.

**Q:** Had these congested circumstances that you referred to occurred in the past?

**A:** No, not to the extent that we had on the 18th.

**Q:** What caused the congestion?

A: The material was not being taken off of me as I was making it. The assembly floor was behind.

Q: Did you have an accumulation problem when the Building 10 employees went on strike the previous week?

A: Yes, we did have a problem then too.

Q: Were all of the employees in the Fabrication Shop laid off at that time?

A: Yes, they were.

Q: Every last one of them?

A: Yes.

Q: Including the Crane Operators?

A: The Crane workers were let go, but one Jitney Driver stayed.

Q: How about the Expediters?

A: They were let go.

Q: For how long a period of time?

A: I think half were gone for two days, and half were gone for one, day.

Q: Which days were they?

A: Wednesday and Thursday of the week ending on the 14th, I think.

Q: They were all let go?

A: Yes—all that worked for me.

Q: And on Wednesday the 18th you testify that only one Jitney Driver worked?

A: Well, there was a clerk.

Q: And a clerk?

A: Yes.

Q: Who made the determination to lay the employees off?

A: It was my recommendation to the Manager of Shop Operations, Mr. John Boswell.

Q: Did you normally check with Mr. Boswell before making a determination to send employees home?

A: I always go back to Mr. Boswell, if he's available. If he's not, I make the decision myself.

Q: Did you consult him before the decision was made?

A: Yes, I did.

Q: Before the fact, or after the fact?

A: Before the fact.

Q: Did you have a conversation with Mr. Prega on the 18th?

A: I certainly did not.

Q: Then it is your testimony that the statements made on the witness stand by Union witnesses King and Prega concerning a conversation with you are incorrect?

A: Yes.

Q: Did you talk with any Union representative on the 18th?

A: Yes, I did.

Q: Who was that?

A: Mr. King.

Q: Regarding sending employees home early?

A: Yes.

Q: You did not talk with Mr. Prega, though?

A: No, I did not.

Q: When did you talk with Mr. King?

A: Well, after the men on the floor were told they were being sent home, he came into the office to see about the situation.

Q: But Mr. Prega was not there with him?

A: That's correct.

Q: He didn't come along after the conversation started, or at any time?

A: No.

Q: Who else was present at the meeting on the 18th with Mr. King?

A: He was the only one in the office with me.

Q: No other management representative was there?

A: No.

Q: Is it your testimony that no work could have been done by any of the employees of the groups in the Fabrication Shop on the 18th without creating further accumulation?

A: Yes, it is.

Q: What about Wednesday, 11/11, and Thursday, 11/12, of the preceding week?

A: No work could have been done without creating more congestion and creating a safety hazard.

Q: What was the time at which the determination was made to send these employees home on the 18th?

A: Well, on the 17th of November a meeting was held in Mr. Boswell's office, and I was told to look at what impact the Building 10 Assembly strike would have on the Building 8 Fabrication Shop—the Fabrication Shop personnel were still working at the time—at which time I held a meeting with my supervisor and my foreman and looked over the situation that already prevailed in the Fabrication Shop.

**Q:** This was on the 17th?

**A:** Yes, on the 17th. I had no choice, as of Wednesday, the 18th, but to recommend to Mr. Boswell—because of the congestion—that we had a lack-of-work situation with regard to the Fabrication Shop people.

**Q:** Okay. Why wasn't the decision made on the 17th?

**A:** We had the people working there. I tried everything I could. I looked around the shop. I was trying to find out where I might put some of the material. There just wasn't a place to put it.

**Q:** Didn't you know that as of the 17th, though?

**A:** What time on the 17th, would you say?

**Q:** In the afternoon, maybe?

**A:** No. I didn't know it then because it was already 3:30 p.m. by the time I talked to Mr. Boswell. It was about six or six-thirty when I left the shop.

**Q:** Had you actually made your determination that the employees would be laid off for four hours when you left the plant at six-thirty on the 17th?

**A:** Maybe not at that point. I thought about it that night as I thought about where to put the material.

**Q:** When did the employees get notified?

**A:** Ten-thirty, eleven, the next morning.

**Q:** How much production was actually accomplished in the few hours between 7:45 a.m. and 11:00 a.m.?

**A:** That's hard to say, but not much. I think that can be vouched for. Most of the work done in the daytime is finished up at night, which helps to congest it that much more by Thursday morning. The night shift usually finishes up what the day shift started.

**Q:** Now, you have testified that there was this great amount of congestion in the area as of the 18th, is that correct?

**A:** Yes.

**Q:** And none of that congestion was moved out during the 18th, is that correct?

**A:** There was nothing touched after the men went home.

**Q:** Why, then, did you call the employees back on Thursday, the 19th—the entire shop back on the 19th?

**A:** Like I said before, we had orders that were going to the assembly floor, and we moved out the pre-accumulation jobs, which doesn't take long to do.

**Q:** You did all this after the shift started?

**A:** Yes. A quarter to eight in the morning.

**Q:** Why didn't you wait until some later time to call the employees back?

**A:** That was my decision.

**Q:** Were they all able to start working immediately?

**A:** I can't really say. I may have paid some of them white time to help move material out of there.

**Q:** Could you pay them white time to move the material out of there on the 18th?

**A:** No, I had no place to put it. The assemblers were out on the street. There was nobody there to receive jobs.

**Q:** Were you a Unit Manager for approximately two and a half years in the Fabrication Shop?

**A:** Yes.

**Q:** During that time, was there any instance that you remember that the employees in the Fabrication Shop were all sent home for a half a day?

**A:** Not all, no.

**Q:** And other than the testimony regarding Wednesday or Thursday of the week preceding November 18th, had there been any time when all the employees in the Fabrication Shop had been laid off, in effect, at one time?

**A:** No.

**Q:** And am I correct that there were strikes and walkouts by employees in Building 10 and other areas fed by the Fabrication Shop at other times, both before and after the incident in question?

**A:** It's possible. I can't answer that.

**Q:** You don't remember?

**A:** No, I don't.

**Q:** Isn't it a fact that the areas in and around the Fabrication Shop are always congested?

**A:** No, I wouldn't say that—not to the point where material is piled into the aisles. The only place of congestion was near the Paint Shop, and that's dropped down. There is no other way.

**Q:** How long was the walkout that occurred on Tuesday, November 10th?

**A:** I'm not sure. I think it was two days. That was on the Assembly floor, a week prior to the one in question.

14

**Q:** And what was the first day that the employees in the Fabrication Shop were all laid off? Was it the Thursday after the strike started?

**A:** Certain groups were off Monday and Tuesday and so forth, but I think it was Wednesday and Thursday that the whole shop was off.

**Q:** And your testimony is that the strike lasted two days?

**A:** To the best of my recollection, yes.

**Q:** And was the congestion which existed at that time worse, not as bad, or the same as that which existed on the 18th?

**A:** I would say the same.

**Q:** You knew on November 10th that you had this problem of congestion, so that you wouldn't have any area to put the additional goods into, once the strike arose, right?

**A:** No. The men then returned from the strike, and we moved the material off.

**Q:** Based on your experience with the strike on the 10th, you knew that there would be this problem when the strike occurred on November 17th, right?

**A:** No, I didn't.

**Q:** Why not?

**A:** I had no idea that there was going to be a strike on November 17th.

**Q:** Once it occurred, your problem about the congestion—

**A:** I still worked the people on that day.

**Q:** Which day?

**A:** The 17th.

**Q:** Why did you wait until the afternoon of Wednesday the 18th before furloughing them?

**A:** Like I said, I was trying to figure out where I could put the material; or maybe Building 10 would have come back in on Thursday morning and taken the jobs they took on Friday morning.

**Q:** I have nothing further.

### b. Cross-Examination by Company Advocate

*Mr. Oyler:*
[to be supplied by student]

# C. Examination of Company Witnesses

## 1. Charles Prancer, Former Unit Manager, Final Assembly Operation

### a. Direct Examination by Company Advocate

*Mr. Oyler:*

**Q:** What is your name and current position with the Volt Power Company?

**A:** Charles Prancer. I am Manager of Quality Control for the Motor and Generator Department.

**Q:** How long have you been in that position?

**A:** Three weeks.

**Q:** What was your position prior to that?

**A:** Unit Manager of Final Assembly Operation, Metal-Enclosed Switchgear.

**Q:** How long had you been in that job?

**A:** Approximately three years.

**Q:** And was that your position in November of year 2?

**A:** Yes, it was.

**Q:** What did your responsibilities include in November of year 2?

**A:** Basically the final assembly of the metal-enclosed switchgear and the subassembly floors of Trunnion and Enclosure. I also coordinated manpower, material, and floor space, to construct the switchgear products.

**Q:** What is a metal-enclosed switchgear product?

**A:** The enclosure itself is the housing for, the air circuit breakers, which consist of cubicles roughly three feet wide, eight feet deep, eight feet high, and a hundred to a hundred-fifty feet long. It consists of steel- and copper-compounds. The steel is used for the structural support. The copper is used for the electrical conductants—porcelain and polyester glass are used for insulation.

Q:   Describe for us "metal-clad equipment."

A:   This is a metal-enclosed switchgear. Its width is approximately three feet. Its depth is six to eight feet. Its height is about eight feet. This construction is typical of the product we manufacture.

Q:   What areas were within your responsibility?

A:   The Metal-clad operation for Building 8, Building 10, and the Switchgear Plant.

Q:   And would you identify your areas of responsibility in more detail?

A:   Yes. The final Assembly area; the subassembly area for enclosure; and the trunnion subassembly area were all my responsibility.

Q:   Can you identify by letters and numbers the areas in question?

A:   Yes. Building 10 has the Trunnion Area; Wiring Group 97, which was their workbench area; and Wiring Group 98.

Q:   Charles, were you present at work on Tuesday, November 17, year 2?

A:   Yes, I was.

Q:   Please tell us what happened insofar as your particular area of responsibility was concerned on November 17th?

A:   On Tuesday, November 17, we had some difficulty in work assignments, and the situation culminated in sending home several members of Group 97 for refusal to do work as assigned. At approximately 1:30 p.m. that day, the Shop Steward for that particular group told me that they were going out on strike over two exhausted grievances, not related to that particular situation. And subsequently the members of Group 98 and all the 3901 assembly pieceworkers left the plant.

Q:   Approximately how many people were involved?

A:   About 190 to 195.

Q:   I have no further questions of this witness.

### b. Cross-Examination by Union Advocate

*Ms. Canon:*
[to be supplied by student]

## 2. *John Boswell, Manager, Metal-Enclosed Switchgear Shop*

### a. Direct Examination by Company Advocate

*Mr. Oyler:*

Q:   What is your name and position with Volt Power Company?

A:   John Boswell. I am the Manager of the Metal-Enclosed Switchgear Shop Operations.

Q:   How long have you held that position?

A:   Approximately a year and a half.

Q:   What do your responsibilities include?

A:   In general, the overall responsibility for the direction of the manpower facilities and equipment associated with the production of metal-enclosed switchgear products.

Q:   Would you explain the product flow of the metal-enclosed switchgear product for the

Arbitrator, please? You may wish to refer to Joint Exhibit 5.

A:   Yes. I would like to start out with the Fabrication Shop. The first point at which you start fabrication is where raw steel is brought into the Fabrication Shop at the A Bay, where it's then brought to the Shearing operation. The steel is then progressed into the Shearing operations, where it is cut to size by a particular shop order, or requisition, as we call it.

Q:   What kind of shear is used?

A:   The Cincinnati shear. The bundled steel is progressed into the shear. The next sequence is when the material is transported into the punching operations, where the various notching and piercing operations are performed.

Q: Tell us about the "Punch."

A: There is a lineup of the punches, which are along A Bay. Bundles of material by shop order are progressed down the punch line. The material then is progressed to the brake operations, where the various forming operations are performed.

Q: Describe the "Brake."

A: Two of the three brakes are located in A, B, and C Bays. Material on trucks is taken off and bent by the braking operation. The material at this point will either progress to the Spot Weld and the Arc Weld operations or directly to the prime-paint area.

Q: What is a "Spot Weld"?

A: It means a welding operation using spot weld equipment located in the B Bay. Various subassemblies are spot welded automated spot weld equipment. The material then moves to the Arc Weld area, where reinforcement welds and additional sub-assemblies are welded by hand.

Q: Explain the "Arc Weld" operation.

A: Basic module frames are spot welded, and also some of the larger door sections, with the frames on the right side. Now, after the arch weld phase, material flows out of the Fabrication Shop and goes into the Prime Paint area where material is placed on the paint track and processed through our flow coat operation at that location. Panel sections and frame sections are processed through the flow coat operation.

Q: Then what happens?

A: At this point, instrument doors will be taken off the paint track line and directly moved to the storage area.

Q: Would you describe the area termed Instrument Door Storage?

A: Yes. Doors are prime painted and stored in racks adjacent to the Trunnion wiring area where doors are wired or assembled. The doors are withdrawn from the storage area on demand by the assemblers for a particular requisition and are assembled in an area, marked "Trunnion."

Q: Describe the "Trunnion Wiring" process.

A: Door sections in final assembly in the Trunnion area are wired and placed on a series of trunnions. The completed subassembled doors are then stored in the Completed Instrument Door Storage area, on vertical racks.

Q: What does the "Completed Instrument Door Storage" area look like?

A: The doors are vertically stored when completed; subassemblies are awaiting dispatch to the assembly floor. "Top plate material" progresses through the Prime Paint area to the Top Plate area.

Q: What is the "Top Plate Stockroom"?

A: Subassemblies are stored in that area. The side frames are stored in the C Bay just adjacent to the top plate box and fixture. The frame sections are processed through the Box and Frame Fixture, where they are spot welded and reinforce welded. They then move to the Top Plate Assembly Area.

Q: Please describe the Top Plate Assembly Area.

A: In Top Plate Asembly, subassemblies are mounted on the frame structure. It's one of our basic building blocks for the metal-clad equipment. The top plate modules are then moved, upon completion, into the Completed Top Plate Assembly Storage Area, where they are retained until requested by the final assembly floor.

Q: What is done in the Top Plate Storage Area?

A: A variety of top plate assemblies are stacked two high in the area. This is referred to as "the jungle."

Material also flows from the Prime Paint area into our Steel Stockroom.

Q: What is the Steel Stockroom? Would you please tell me about it?

A: Steel structures which have been removed from the paint track are located in the steel racks by shop order or requisition. Other material will, after being removed from the paint track, go into the Steel Stock area, where it's stored until required for a particular requisition. We also have enclosure steel, which is stored at the end of the Steel Stockroom.

Q: And there is also an Enclosure Steel Storage Area. Would you describe it?

A: Yes. This is under a balcony. This is where we store the front enclosures for our product. It's called a point-of-use storage, in that the operators in the Enclosure Assembly area would withdraw steel as required for a particular shop order. So it's a self-service steel area. The steel withdrawn from the enclosure steel area is then subassembled in the area called Enclosure Assembly.

**Q:** Would you please describe the Enclosure Wiring Area?

**A:** It comprises a series of benches and the enclosure steel which is located in the fixture. This is where the subassembly operations are performed. A variety of devices are added to the enclosure in this operation. Upon completion, the enclosure of steel is then transported at the front of the building to the enclosure storage area. It goes up the aisle and is then stored, at which point it's ready for release to the Assembly floor. The subassemblies are then taken to the Final Assembly floor, where the mechanical assembly and wiring operations are performed.

**Q:** Would you describe the Assembly and Wiring floor?

**A:** This is a typical Assembly floor. Upon completion of a requisition on the Assembly Floor, the subassemblies are then moved by crane and flatbed down the main aisles into the Finish Paint Area.

**Q:** What occurs in the Finish Paint Shop?

**A:** This is a typical splitting section. The subassemblies have been brought in on a flatbed, after which the masking and prime painting and finish painting is performed. The substation is lifted with a crane and dropped down the shipping well to the first floor, in Building 10.

**Q:** All right. Now, John, were you present at work on Tuesday, November 17, year 2?

**A:** Yes, I was.

**Q:** Would you tell the Arbitrator what happened after the walkout of the Assembly area, to the extent that you were directly involved?

**A:** Yes. Shortly after 1:30, on Tuesday the 17th, I had a phone call from Charles Prancer, informing me that there had been a work stoppage in the Final Assembly area. At this point I immediately called the Manager of Manufacturing, and he instructed me to meet him, along with the other subsection managers. After 2:00, we met with George Constantine, Manager of Manufacturing, and the managers

of other subsections—Jim Warren, Manager of Materials; Henry Upps, Manager of Quality Control; Terry Ovens, Manager of Engineering; Mike Winkle, Manager of Shop Operations in the breaker area; and myself. The meeting basically revolved around the present work stoppage situation. Generally, the instructions were for us to evaluate the impact of the work stoppage and reconvene the next morning.

**Q:** What did you do after that meeting?

**A:** I immediately went back to my office to call the Unit Managers. They reported to me.

**Q:** Are these the people that report directly to you?

**A:** Yes. That would be Charles Prancer, Paul Cruz, Joey Cross, and Benjamin Bailey, who actually worked for the materials subsection. We discussed the problem. The instructions I gave were for each of them to evaluate his particular area in terms of impact of the stoppage. We scheduled a meeting for the next morning and then the group left.

**Q:** Did you have a meeting on Wednesday morning, November 18th?

**A:** Yes.

**Q:** Who was present at that meeting?

**A:** All of the gentlemen I just mentioned. We discussed the total impact of the assembly strike and formulated a series of recommendations to present to the Manager of Manufacturing that morning.

**Q:** And did you present those recommendations to him?

**A:** Yes, we did. At the conclusion of the meeting with this particular group, I went to the sixth floor, met with the Manager of Manufacturing, along with several of the Unit Managers that report directly to me, and we laid forth our plans.

**Q:** What did you recommend?

**A:** The recommendation from Paul Cruz's area, the Top Plate Assembly area, was that we would lack work for the indirect personnel. In the Final Assembly area, Charles Prancer's field, we already had a critical imbalance in the Trunnion and Enclosure areas, so we should also "lack of work" the Enclosure and Trunnion and Enclosure groups for the balance of the week. Stuart Duvall's area, which was the Fabrication Shop—the group involved in this arbitration—had an imbalance that it had started the week with. The work stoppage on the Assembly floor also exacerbated the congestion and imbalances in the Fabrication Shop, and the recommendation was to "lack of work" those employees. These were the general comments made to the Manager of Manufacturing. The Manager of Quality Control also evaluated his test load and those jobs that were in process on the floor, and made a recommendation that we "lack of work" the testers and inspectors at final assembly. This is the red group that was out on work stoppage.

**Q:** Could you tell us what happened during Week 47, using your Schedule to refresh your memory?

**A:** Monday, was a normal day. Tuesday, the day of the work stoppage, the Assembly group and the Wire group and the subassembly group in Top Plate were involved in a work stoppage. But the trunnion area enclosure and the balance of the Assembly areas worked a normal day. On Wednesday, the 18th, a lack of work situation became apparent at the Trunnion. Specifically, there was a four-hour lack of work in Trunnion and Enclosure. That is only a single-shift operation. The Paint group was off for lack of work all day Wednesday—first and second shift. And the Door Lineup were involved in half-day lack of work on Wednesday, and second shift, a full shift. Our production men at Top Plate worked. The Expediters in production control worked. The Inspectors worked. Wednesday and Thursday, the Testers were off due to a lack of work. As for the Fabrication Shop, Monday, November 17, was a normal workday. On Tuesday, November 19, some of the imbalances already existing in Fabrication due to the strike by assembly floor employees increased. On Wednesday, November 18, the day after the strike on the Assembly floor, employees were sent home after four hours work. On Thursday, November 19, the employees were called back to work. On that day the Union filed a grievance. We denied it the next day.

**Q:** No further questions.

### b. Cross-Examination by Union Advocate

*Ms. Canon:*
[to be supplied by student]

## 3. Steve Mann, Foreman, Fabrication Shop

### a. Direct Examination by Company Advocate

*Mr. Oyler:*

**Q:** What is your name and position with Volt Power Company?

**A:** Steve Mann, Foreman of the Fabrication Shop.

**Q:** How long have you held that position?

**A:** Presently, I am on second shift. I have been on there about a month. Previously, I was a foreman in the Fabrication Shop on day work. I held that position for roughly 20 to 25 years.

**Q:** Were you present at work on Tuesday, November 17th, and Wednesday the 18th?

**A:** Yes, I was.

**Q:** Did you send home the employees under your direct supervision before the completion of their scheduled shift on Wednesday, November 18th?

**A:** Yes, I did.

**Q:** And do you recall what you told employees when you sent them home?

**A:** That they were temporarily laid off for lack of work, due to the congestion and safety of the area.

**Q:** Did you speak with Richard King, the Shop Steward, concerning the lack of work that day?

**A:** I probably did. I spoke to him in his capacity as an employee. I got the employees together.

**Q:** Did you speak to Richard King individually in his capacity as a Union Steward?

**A:** No.

**Q:** Do you know who Mr. Prega is?

**A:** Yes. He is Chief Steward

**Q:** Did you speak to Mr. Prega that day?

**A:** No.

**Q:** I show you a clock card, with the name Garrett Jensen on it. Is that your signature on the card?

**A:** Yes, it is.

**Q:** What does this clock card show?

**A:** This shows that Mr. Jensen is off on Wednesday, November 18, for lack of work for eight hours.

**Q:** No further questions.

### b. Cross-Examination by Union Advocate

*Ms. Canon:*

[to be supplied by student]

## 4. Stuart Duvall, Former Unit Manager, Fabrication, Prime Paint and Steel Stockroom

### a. Direct Examination by Company Advocate

*Mr. Oyler:*

**Q:** Please give your name and position.

**A:** Stuart Duvall, Unit Manager, Top Plate Subassemblies.

**Q:** In the Fabrication Shop?

**A:** Yes. That's my position now.

**Q:** How long have you held your present job?

**A:** Approximately seven months.

**Q:** And your job prior to that was?

**A:** Unit Manager of Fabrication, Prime Paint and Steel Stockroom.

**Q:** Was that the job you held in November of year 2?

**A:** Yes, it was.

**Q:** What were your responsibilities?

**A:** The Fabrication area, Prime Paint, Short Order Shop, and Steel Stock.

**Q:** Were you present at work on Tuesday, November 17, year 2?

**A:** Yes, I was.

**Q:** Were you present in the Tuesday, November 17th, meeting that Mr. Boswell testified that he held with his staff?

**A:** Yes, I was.

**Q:** What did you do as a result of that meeting?

**A:** After the meeting with Mr. Boswell, I went to the Building 8 Fabrication Shop office and called a meeting with my foremen and the production supervisor. I explained the situation to them and asked them to evaluate what impact the strike that day on the assembly floor would have on us. We actually took a walk around the shop and looked at the orders that were out at that time.

**Q:** What was the situation in Fabrication?

**A:** The situation at the time involved congestion in the aisles, which was causing a safety hazard.

**Q:** Did you attend a meeting on Wednesday, November 18, that Mr. Boswell testified about?

**A:** Yes, I did.

**Q:** Did you report on the Fabrication Shop situation at that time?

**A:** Yes, I did.

**Q:** Did you make any recommendation in that meeting?

**A:** Yes. I recommended that we temporarily "lack of work" the Fabrication Shop because of the congestion situation we had down there.

**Q:** What did you do then, as a result of that meeting?

**A:** After Mr. Boswell had my recommendation, we left the office and went to a meeting with the Manager of Manufacturing. The recommendations given by the Unit Managers were accepted, and I went back and held a meeting with my foremen. I told them we were telling the men that they were going to be off for temporary lack of work due to the congestion in the area.

**Q:** Stuart, other than the lack of work on Wednesday, November 18, did the Fabrication Shop have any other lack-of-work situation close to November 18th—for example, June 25 to December 25, year 2?

**A:** Yes, it did. It was spotty, but there were different groups of employees involved.

**Q:** Would you tell us the reasons for the lack-of-work situations involved during this six-month period, June 25 to December 25?

**A:** The reason is because of the imbalance of the shop orders at that time.

**Q:** Now, on November 18th, did Chief Steward Prega speak to you on the factory floor?

**A:** No, he did not.

**Q:** Did Steward King speak to you on November 18th?

**A:** Yes, he did.

**Q:** Where?

**A:** In my office.

**Q:** What took place in that conversation?

**A:** After King heard about the employees going home, he came to my office and asked me what was going on. At that time, I told him that we were going to have to temporarily "lack of work" the employees because of the congestion in the Fabrication Shop and the safety hazard it was causing. Then King asked me why we couldn't send some of the material to the Shannon Hill plant. I told him that it was not practical and the cost would be exorbitant. He threatened to file a grievance.

**Q:** No further questions.

### b. Cross-Examination by Union Advocate

*Ms. Canon:*
[to be supplied by student]

## 5. Benjamin Bailey, *Former Manager of Production Control for Metal-Enclosed Switchgear*

### a. Direct Examination by Company Advocate

*Mr. Oyler:*

**Q:** What is your name and present position with Volt Power Company?

**A:** Ben Bailey, Unit Manager of Manufacturing, Engineering for Metal-Enclosed Switchgear.

**Q:** How long have you been in that position?

**A:** Since August of this year.

**Q:** What was your position prior to that?

**A:** Prior to that, I was Manager of Production Control for Metal-Enclosed Switchgear.

**Q:** How long did you hold that position in Production Control?

**A:** Three years, approximately.

**Q:** Was that the job you held on November 17th of year 2?

**A:** Yes.

**Q:** What were the responsibilities of the job of Manager of Production Control?

**A:** My responsibilities included ordering and procuring materials, scheduling the shops, customer service, and inventory control.

**Q:** From a production control standpoint, what are the considerations involved in determining whether there is a lack of work in a particular situation?

**A:** Several things are considered: facilities, material availability, manpower, and production balances between contributing shops.

**Q:** Now, Ben, were you present at any of the meetings on November 17th or 18th, which John Boswell testified to earlier?

**A:** Yes, I was.

**Q:** Which ones?

**A:** I was present in the one in Mr. Boswell's office on the afternoon of Tuesday, November 17th. I was also present in his office on the morning of November 18th. I was also present in the meeting on the morning of November 19th.

**Q:** Did you participate in the decision to send several other units, including the Fabrication Shop, home for the lack of work on November 18th?

**A:** Yes, I did.

**Q:** Did you concur in that decision?

**A:** Yes, I did.

**Q:** On what basis?

**A:** On the basis that there was a critical imbalance between the Fabrication Shop and the Assembly Unit.

**Q:** In what way does a production imbalance cause a lack-of-work situation?

**A:** On November 18th, the Fabrication Shop was some two and a half weeks ahead of the Assembly operation.

**Q:** Is that unusual or normal?

**A:** It's highly unusual.

**Q:** Did you make any recommendations, as the Manager of Production Control, with respect to the situation at that time?

**A:** I made recommendations at that time, and I had made recommendations prior to that to Mr. Boswell, that the situation had reached a critical point and that we should curtail certain shop operations in order to rebalance production.

**Q:** No further questions.

### b. Cross-Examination by Union Advocate

*Ms. Canon:*
[to be supplied by student]

22

# D. Exhibits

***Joint Exhibit No. 1***

NATIONAL AGREEMENT

BETWEEN

VOLT POWER COMPANY

AND

AMERICAN UNION OF RADIO AND WIRE WORKERS

YEAR 1-4

. . .

ARTICLE V

Working Hours:   Straight Time -- Overtime

. . .

7.    (b) Report-in Time

Employees who report for work in accordance with their regular schedules, and, without previous notice thereof, neither their regularly assigned nor any reasonably comparable work is available, will receive not less than four hours pay at the rate applicable had they worked.  This subsection (b) shall not be applicable where the inability of the Company to supply work is the result of fire, snow storm, flood, power failure, or work stoppage by employees in the same Company location.  Qualified pieceworkers will be paid at least their anticipated earned rate. Learners on piecework will be paid their average earnings if less than the anticipated earned rate.

. . .

ARTICLE XI

Reduction or Increase in Forces

1.    Whenever there is a reduction in the working force or employees are laid off from their regular jobs, total length of continuous service, applied on a plant, department, or other basis as negotiated locally, shall be the major factor determining the employees to be laid off or transferred (exclusive of upgrading or transfer to higher rated jobs). However, ability will be given consideration.

. . .

23

2.    Since the number of employees in the individual bargaining units covered under this Agreement varies from less than 50 to more than 10,000, each Local shall negotiate with local Management a written Agreement covering the layoff and rehiring procedure for the employees represented by the Local.

      . . .


## ARTICLE XIV

### Strikes and Lockouts


1.    There shall be no strike, sitdown, slowdown, employee demonstration or any other organized or concerted interference with work of any kind in connection with any matter subject to the grievance procedure, and no such interference with work shall be directly or indirectly authorized or sanctioned by a Local or the Union, or their respective officers or stewards, unless and until all of the respective provisions of the successive steps of the grievance procedures set forth in Article XIII shall have been complied with by the Local and the Union, or if the matter is submitted to arbitration as provided in Article XV.

2.    The Company will not lock out any employee or transfer any job under dispute from the local Works, nor will the local management take similar action while a dispute job is under discussion at any of the steps of the grievance procedure set forth in Article XIII, or if the matter is submitted to arbitration provided in Article XV.

      . . .


## ARTICLE XXVIII

### Responsibilities of the Parties

      . . .

4.    (b) (iv) Subject only to any limitations stated in this Agreement, or in any other agreement between the Company and the Union or a Local, the Company and the Union recognize that the Company retains the exclusive right to manage its business, including (but not limited to) the rights to determine the methods and means by which its operations are to be carried on, to direct the work force and to conduct its operation in a safe and effective manner.

*Joint Exhibit No. 1 (continued)*

ARTICLE XXIX

Issues of General Application

This Agreement between the parties is intended to be and shall be in full settlement of all issues which were the subject of collective bargaining between the parties in national level collective bargaining negotiations in year 1.  Consequently, it is agreed that none of such issues shall be subject to collective bargaining during the term of this Agreement and there shall be no strike or lockout in connection with any such issue or issues;. . .

*Joint Exhibit No. 2*

Local 101, AURWW

GRIEVANCE--STEP 3

Date: 11/19/02

Statement of Grievance:

On Wednesday, November 18, year 2, the Company locked the employees out of the Fabrication Shop in violation of Article XIV, after they worked four hours of their 8-hour workday.  The Company also violated Articles V, XI, and Past Practice by taking this action.

Remedy:

The Company refrain from any further lockouts.  Those employees whose wages were affected by the lockout shall be made whole with interest.

/s/ Richard King
Steward, Fabrication Shop

STEP 3 ANSWER

Date: 11/20/02

The employees were sent home due to lack of work.  Moreover, we did not have enough room to store any more pieces on that afternoon.  Grievance denied.

/s/ Joey Cross
Unit Manager

## *JOINT EXHIBIT NO. 3*

Number of Employees in the Fabrication Shop by Group, November year 1

| Group No. | Group Name | Shift | Number of Employees |
|---|---|---|---|
| 20 | Punch | 1st | 10 |
| 86 | Angle | 1st | 7 |
|  |  | 2nd | 5 |
| 87 | Shear | 1st | 3 |
|  |  | 2nd | 2 |
| 89 | Punch | 1st | 11 |
|  |  | 2nd | 5 |
| 90 | Brake | 1st | 2 |
|  |  | 2nd | 2 |
| -- | Numerical Control Punch | 1st | 3 |
|  |  | 2nd | 2 |
| 95 | Bliss Brake | 1st | 2 |
| 94 | Spot Weld | 1st | 13 |
|  |  | 2nd | 8 |
| 92 | Arc Weld | 1st | 10 |
|  |  | 2nd | 5 |
| 79 | Paint | 1st | 7 |
| -- | Represented Salaried Expediters | 1st | 7 |
| -- | Short Order Shop, Direct Labor | 1st | 7 |
|  |  | 2nd | 5 |
|  |  | 3rd | 2 |
| -- | Stock, Indirect Labor | 1st | 9 |
|  |  | 2nd | 5 |
| -- | Accumulators, Indirect Labor | 1st | 2 |
|  |  | 2nd | 2 |
| -- | Crane, Indirect Labor | 1st | 3 |
|  |  | 2nd | 2 |
| -- | Material Movers | 1st | 3 |
| TOTAL |  |  | 144 |

*Joint Exhibit No. 4*

April 10, year 3

MEMORANDUM

To:  Richard King, Steward, Fabrication Shop

From:  Joey Cross, Unit Manager

Re:  Employee time off for lack of work, weeks ending
     November 14, 21, year 2

      You requested information regarding the above.  Please refer
to listings below, as reported by group leaders.

| Group | Days Off | |
| --- | --- | --- |
| | Week Ending Nov. 14th | Week Ending Nov. 21st |
| Shear | 12th, 13th | 18th (1/2 day) |
| Brake | 9th, 12th, 13th | 16th, 17th, 18th (1/2 day) |
| Spot Weld | 10th, 11th, 12th | 15th, 18th (1/2 day) |
| Arc Weld | No information | 15th, 18th (1/2 day) |
| Angle | 10th, 11th | 18th (1/2 day) |
| Punch | | |
| Group 20 | worked 24 hours | 18th (1/2 day) |
| Group 89 | worked 40 hours | one day, 18th (1/2 day) |

*JOINT EXHIBIT NO. 5*

FABRICATION SHOP PRODUCT FLOW FOR METAL-ENCLOSED SWITCHGEAR

Areas

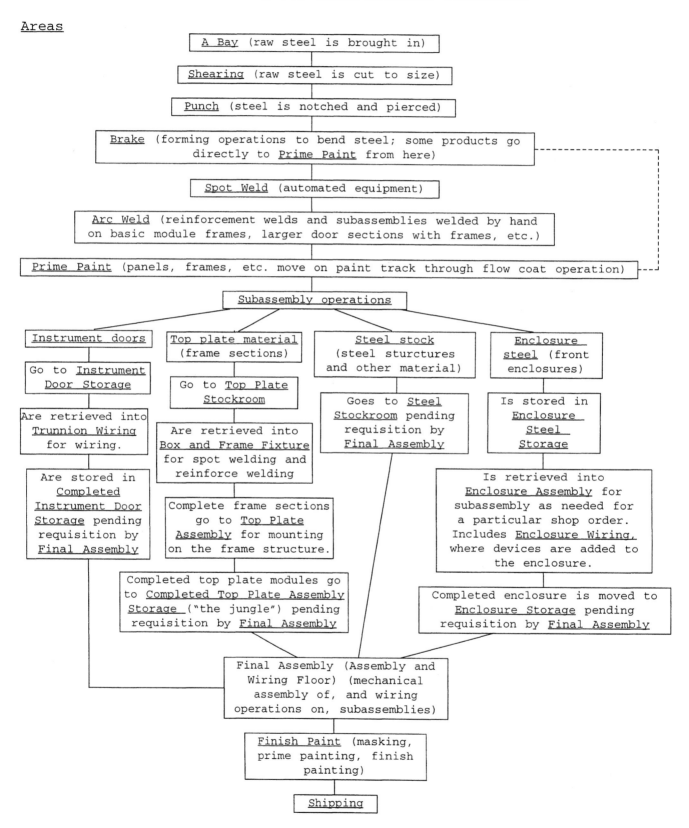

## *Union Exhibit No. 1*

Thursday 11/19/02

(sample)                                ORDER SHEET

<u>Work to Be Performed</u>: Door Molding

<u>Wage Rate</u>: $150   11/21/02

# Price Plastics, Inc.*

## Table of Contents

*Authors' Note: Some of the witnesses in this case are identified by other witnesses as part of their testimony. Participants in this exercise will need to ensure that witnesses providing the identifications are briefed on which individual in the hearing room they are to identify.

## Table of Contents contd.

## NOTES

# A. Caption

IN THE MATTER IN ARBITRATION BETWEEN:

PRICE PLASTICS, INC. )
HAPVILLE, ILLINOIS )
                     )
AND )        RE: Discharge of Five Employees for
                     )            Picket Line Activity
LOCAL UNION NO. 101 )
UNIVERSAL UNION

Appearances:

For the Company: Adam Tackett

For the Union: Robert Shepmanson

Date: January 12, year 8

Place: Hapville, Illinois

## B. Examination of Company Witnesses

## 1. Ronald Hiller, Vice President, Administration and Labor Relations

### a. Direct Examination by Company Advocate

*Mr. Tackett:*

**Q:** State your name and address.

**A:** Ronald Hiller, 6393 Willow Drive, here in Hapville.

**Q:** State your employment.

**A:** I am Vice President of Price Plastics. Primarily in charge of administration and labor relations.

**Q:** How long have you held that position?

**A:** That position I have held for approximately three years.

**Q:** Were you involved on behalf of the Company in the negotiations in year 7?

**A:** Yes, I was.

**Q:** Were you involved in negotiations and prior agreements with this Union?

**A:** Yes, I was involved in the previous agreement.

**Q:** Now, you were present in the room when I made my opening statement, were you not?

**A:** Yes, I was.

**Q:** And my description of the Company, its business and customer relations was heard by you, was it not?*

**A:** Yes, it was.

**Q:** Was it accurate?

**A:** Yes, it was.

**Q:** Now, from the time the strike began on April 7, year 7, until the middle part of May, year 7, the Company operated solely by using some supervisory employees and one or two truck drivers?

**A:** That is correct.

**Q:** What was the nature of the business activities conducted by the Company during that time?

**A:** It was very limited. I would guess a maximum of ten to fifteen percent of normal production.

**Q:** Was production actually being run?

**A:** A little production, yes.

**Q:** Approximately how many people in total were involved in working in the plant during this period of five or six weeks?

**A:** Including the supervision, I would guess approximately thirty people.

**Q:** During this period of five or six weeks did you notice pickets of Local 101 on duty at the plant premises?

**A:** Yes, I did.

**Q:** And where did they picket?

**A:** They picketed at the entrance to the plant just off of Highway 41.

**Q:** How many pickets did you observe at any one time?

**A:** During this period of time it normally ranged from five to eight pickets. Occasionally, there would be a few more.

**Q:** During this period were Company trucks going in and out of the plant?

**A:** Yes.

**Q:** Were there trucks of customers or suppliers similarly leaving and entering the plant?

**A:** Yes.

**Q:** Was there any other, let's say, vehicle traffic?

**A:** Naturally, the employees and customers were going in and out of the plant.

**Q:** Now, was there any interference with the ingress and egress of these people and the Company trucks during the period of five or six weeks?

**A:** There was some, yes.

**Q:** Describe what interference you experienced.

**A:** There were occasions when a supply truck would come up to the picket line and they would stand in front of it and not get out of the way. On some occasions I personally had to go out and get into the truck to help the driver come through the line.

---

*Authors' Note: The Company advocate should have included this background information in the opening statement. This technique is traditional in arbitration.

2

**Q:** Was the picketing line peaceful otherwise?

**A:** Other than what I just described and the conduct of the grievants and a few others, yes, the picketing was peaceful.

**Q:** During the period of time from April 7 through the first two weeks of May, was a decision made by the Company—let's say, initially made by the Company—with respect to whether it would sit out the strike or attempt to hire replacements?

**A:** There was no decision made. No.

**Q:** Was any attempt made by the Company during the first five or six weeks to hire replacements?

**A:** No.

**Q:** Now, subsequently, a decision was made to attempt to hire replacements and get back into operation. Is that correct?

**A:** That is correct.

**Q:** Did you participate in that decision?

**A:** Yes, I did.

**Q:** Would you describe the circumstances which were taken into consideration in making the decision to operate with replacements?

**A:** Two of our largest customers, Standard and Naki Electric, had stated very definitely that unless we began to produce parts they were going to remove their tools and dies from our plant. Two dies accounted for twelve to fifteen percent of our total volume. At that point we decided that we had to do something.

**Q:** Did they give you a deadline?

**A:** They gave us one deadline and had extended it approximately one week at that point.

**Q:** What were the deadlines? If you recall.

**A:** Well, the deadline was approximately—I believe it was Monday, the 21st of May, and then they extended it for three or four days, hoping we could come up with some sort of an agreement with the Union.

**Q:** Were those dies finally pulled?

**A:** Yes, they were.

**Q:** Do you recall the date on which they were recalled?

**A:** No, I do not, specifically.

**Q:** Was it the week of May 21?

**A:** Yes, right.

**Q:** Now, do you recall any negotiating meeting with the Local 101 committee on May 14?

**A:** Yes, I do.

**Q:** Was the Union committee advised that it was likely that some customers would remove their tools and dies?

**A:** Yes.

**Q:** Do you recall what the Union was told about that subject?

**A:** Well, I believe we told them approximately how much business would be lost and how many jobs were involved.

**Q:** Do you recall a meeting with the Union on May 18, year 7?

**A:** Yes.

**Q:** Do you recall specifically anything—any particular thing—the Union was told at that time?

**A:** Nothing other than that the customers were going to pull their dies.

**Q:** Now, at what point was the decision made by the Company to seek to employ replacements and resume operations?

**A:** Well, it was on Monday, May the 21st, that the decision was made.

**Q:** The Union, however, had been advised previously that action was under consideration?

**A:** Yes, they had been.

**Q:** And employees were informed of that possibility in one of the letters sent to them by the Company?

**A:** That is correct.

**Q:** All right. On May 21, what was done by the Company for the purpose of hiring replacements?

**A:** Well, the Company on Monday called the local newspaper and started to run an ad—to place an ad in the newspapers. The ad didn't start until Wednesday of that week, but we were putting the word around that we were going to start hiring replacement employees.

**Q:** Now, I show you Company Exhibit 9, a sheet out of the Hapville *Journal* of Thursday, May 31, year 7, page number 36, and ask you: can you identify your Company's "help wanted" ad on that page?

**A:** Yes, I can.

**Q:** Although that is the newspaper edition of May 31, is that the same ad that began to run on May 23?

**A:** Yes, it is.

**Q:** All right. Now, above the Company's ad on that page is another ad presumably entered by Local 101 stating that the employees are on strike. Do you recall or know when that ad first appeared?

**A:** It appeared approximately two days after our ad appeared in the paper. I assume it was the lead time to get it into the paper, but it was about two days after.

**Q:** Is that Company Exhibit 8?

**A:** Yes.

**Q:** Now, were you at the plant on Monday, May 21?

**A:** Yes, I was.

**Q:** What time did you arrive?

**A:** Approximately seven o'clock in the morning.

**Q:** All right. Were there pickets at the plant that morning?

**A:** Yes, there were.

**Q:** Do you know what time the pickets arrived?

**A:** No, but they were there when I arrived at seven o'clock.

**Q:** At seven o'clock, how many pickets were at the plant?

**A:** I would estimate approximately thirty. It varied during that morning, probably from twenty-five to forty.

**Q:** Describe the manner in which the pickets were picketing when you arrived at seven o'clock.

**A:** Well, they were blocking the entire entrance to the plant area. They did let me through when I drove up and stopped at the picket line. They were yelling and screaming as cars went through.

**Q:** Did they yell and scream at you?

**A:** I don't know. I don't believe they actually yelled and screamed at me, but they were yelling at other cars coming through.

**Q:** Did these pickets maintain their patrolling throughout the entire day?

**A:** Yes, they did.

**Q:** What did you do in the face of this number of pickets?

**A:** Well, the police were called and asked to put someone there at the picket line so we could prevent problems and allow people to come through and leave the plant.

**Q:** Now, how many pickets were at the plant on the 21st day of May? Was there a different number than the thirty or so you described before?

**A:** No.

**Q:** Did any job applicants appear at the plant on May the 21st?

**A:** No.

**Q:** Now, did you go to work at the plant each of the following days of that week?

**A:** Yes, I did.

**Q:** Were there pickets on duty each day when you arrived?

**A:** Yes, there were.

**Q:** What was the smallest number of pickets when you arrived on any one of those days?

**A:** I would guess twenty-five was the smallest.

**Q:** What would you say was the largest number of pickets that were on duty on any one of those days?

**A:** In excess of forty.

**Q:** Now, when did your help-wanted advertisements and notice to the employment offices produce any applicants?

**A:** It was Thursday morning, May 24, that the applicants started to come in.

**Q:** Now, describe what happened that day on the picket line.

**A:** Well, probably the largest number of pickets were present that morning. There were lots of people who were trying to drive into the plant to put in the application, but the pickets were standing at the picket line waving them off. They were telling them they couldn't come in, yelling at the cars, and calling them scabs and such. The applicants were driving by and coming back. The police were there. A couple of times that morning the police asked the pickets to allow the people to come through. But they still were stopping them. I went out to the picket line myself and for a portion of that morning stationed myself out there seeing that applicants' cars were able to come through the picket line. But the minute we stepped away it was completely blocked again.

**Q:** By completely blocked, are you saying the pickets physically positioned themselves so as to block the driveway?

**A:** Yes, they did.

**Q:** Did you observe applicants attempt to turn in and enter the premises?

**A:** Yes, I did.

**Q:** Did the pickets give way and permit them to enter?

A: Sometimes they did and sometimes they did not.

Q: When the applicants passed through the picket line, what did you observe being done by the pickets?

A: They were yelling. I observed some pounding on the cars. Some were kicking the cars as the cars had come through. Cars were scratched as they came through the picket line.

Q: Were you or anyone else able to identify pickets scratching the cars as they passed through the picket line?

A: Yes, and I also observed at least eight or nine cars scratched the entire lengths of their cars. The people who had brought the cars through had said that when they came through the picket line they heard the scraping on the cars.

Q: Now, during the week of the 21st did you have any conversations with the police, asking them to come out and patrol your entrance?

A: Yes, we talked to them several times.

Q: Were you given any advice by the police?

A: On several occasions they asked us to get an injunction to stop the pickets out there.

Q: Did you make the decision or participate in making the decision to refuse to reinstate five employees on strike?

A: Yes.

Q: Would you describe for the Arbitrator how those five employees were selected?

A: Well, we had talked with people; we had made notes of things that had transpired during that week. From this we specifically identified the employees who had in effect violated the right of people coming in and leaving the plant and who were doing damage to property.

Q: Did you personally witness any of the acts which were relied upon in making the decision not to reinstate them?

A: Yes, I did.

Q: What is the name of one of them whose conduct you witnessed?

A: Deborah Matter is one of them.

Q: Would you tell the Arbitrator what Matter did as you observed her?

A: It was Tuesday night of that week, which would have been the 22nd. As one of the employees was leaving the plant in his truck, she walked behind the truck as it stopped at the highway. It had to stop almost right in the midst of the pickets in the line and it was then she threw a glass Coke bottle at the back of the truck. It hit the bed of the truck and dropped to the ground and broke.

Q: Where did it break?

A: Right in the middle of the driveway.

Q: Where were you standing when you observed this?

A: I was standing in the office, which would be 100 feet away from where it happened.

Q: Now, what did you do when you observed this?

A: Well, there were other cars lined up to leave the plant and this glass was right in the middle of the driveway, so I immediately went out and kicked the glass out of the path of the cars trying to leave.

Q: Now, I take it you were acquainted with Matter before you observed this event and you are positive in your identification?

A: Yes. She was an employee.

Q: What is the name of any other employee whose conduct you observed and relied upon in making the decision to refuse to reinstate?

A: Lesley Cole.

Q: What did you observe Cole do?

A: Well, that first morning the applicants started coming in, that Thursday morning, one of the applicants they had turned away drove into Walters' parking lot, which is located next door to us. There had been several people driving into their parking lot. Walters was quite upset about it and had told us to keep the people out of there. Well, the fella stopped his car, got out, and looked around to see what he should do, and I waved to him to turn around and come back through our driveway and I would see that he got through the picket line. The police were stationed there at that time on Walters' parking lot. The applicant pulled out of Walters' parking lot and into our driveway and as he did, he was on the far right-hand side; the police were on the other side of the car on Walters' lot. Cole was standing on the opposite side from the police car and I saw her rear back and with her heels kick into the side of the car. I saw her jar back as she did it, so I know she hit the car.

Q: Where were you standing?

**A:** Halfway between the office and the picket line at that time.

**Q:** So you were approximately fifty feet away?

**A:** Yes.

**Q:** Do you know what time of day that occurred?

**A:** It would have been about nine or ten o'clock in the morning.

**Q:** Approximately how many pickets were on your driveway at that time?

**A:** I'd guess there were thirty to thirty-five at that time.

**Q:** Were you acquainted with Cole before this event occurred?

**A:** I knew her as an employee.

**Q:** You were certain of your identification?

**A:** Yes, I was.

**Q:** No further questions.

### b. Cross-Examination by Union Advocate

*Mr. Shepmanson:*
[to be supplied by student]

## 2. Granville Tomer, Purchasing Agent

### a. Direct Examination by Company Advocate

*Mr. Tackett:*

**Q:** State your name and address please.

**A:** Granville Tomer, 5231 Dogwood Drive, Hapville.

**Q:** Where are you employed?

**A:** Price Plastics.

**Q:** What is your position?

**A:** Purchasing Agent.

**Q:** I take it that is not a position within the bargaining unit represented by Local 101?

**A:** That's right.

**Q:** Did you go to work at the Price plant during the period of the strike?

**A:** I was there every day.

**Q:** Did that include the week of May 21 to 25, year 7?

**A:** Right.

**Q:** Do you know an employee by the name of Deborah Matter?

**A:** I do.

**Q:** Is she present in the room?

**A:** Yes, she is.

**Q:** All right. And maybe it'll help here— would you point her out to the Arbitrator here.

**A:** She's right there.

**Q:** The Arbitrator should note that the witness is pointing at Deborah Matter. Now, did you see Matter on the picket line during the week of May 21 to 25?

**A:** Yes, I did.

**Q:** Did you see her on May 22?

**A:** Yes, I did.

**Q:** Would you tell the Arbitrator what you saw Matter do on May 22?

**A:** She was on the picket line and walked towards the car. She came back down the side of the driveway approximately twenty-five or thirty feet or so. She drew her hand back and threw something on the driveway. At that time I was standing approximately sixty or sixty-five feet from her. Mr. Walts was with me and he got Mr. Hiller. We went down and found tacks strewn completely across the driveway from where she was standing. So we went down and picked up the tacks.

**Q:** Now, from where to where did she walk as you observed her?

**A:** Along the side of the driveway that leads from the road. She was on Company property.

**Q:** And where did you observe her throw something?

**A:** From the side of the drive; she was throwing something directly across the drive.

**Q:** How far from the highway was this?

**A:** I would say approximately thirty feet. It's hard to judge distance at that point.

**Q:** And did you find the tacks in the traveled portion of the driveway?

**A:** Right.

**Q:** Describe the tacks.

A: They were approximately 3/4 of an inch long and looked like carpet tacks.

Q: All right. Now, how do you know the tacks you found had been thrown by Matter?

A: They were scattered from the position she was standing at, all across the driveway.

Q: Do you have any way of knowing that the tacks weren't already on the driveway when you saw her throw something?

A: Yes, I do, because about ten minutes previous to that I had been down on the driveway picking up tacks and other debris. I picked up anything that could get in tires: tacks, wires, small nails, and what have you.

Q: Now, were the tacks you picked up after you saw her throw something capable of puncturing an automobile tire?

A: Yes.

Q: No further questions.

### b. Cross-Examination by Union Advocate

*Mr. Shepmanson:*
[to be supplied by student]

## 3. Oscar Posten, Inventory Control and Assistant Purchaser

### a. Direct Examination by Company Advocate

*Mr. Tackett:*

Q: State your name and address, please.

A: Oscar Posten, Walburg, Illinois.

Q: And by whom are you employed?

A: Price Plastics.

Q: And what is your position?

A: Inventory Control and Assistant Purchaser.

Q: I take it that is a position outside the bargaining unit of Local 101?

A: That is right.

Q: Did you work at Price Plastics' plant during the period of the strike?

A: Yes, sir.

Q: Did you work at the plant during the week of May 21 to 25?

A: Yes, sir.

Q: Did you observe the conduct of Deborah Matter on the 22nd?

A: Yes, I did.

Q: Would you describe to the Arbitrator just what you saw?

A: When I was standing about five feet from Granville Tomer, I saw Matter make a throwing motion with her hand. Immediately after that we went down and found tacks on the driveway about where I had seen her standing and throwing something. This was just after we first cleaned another bunch of tacks off the driveway.

Q: Now, had you been outside with Tomer during the approximately ten-minute interval from the first clean-up until the time you saw the throwing gesture?

A: Yes, sir.

Q: And did you observe anyone else in the vicinity of where you found the tacks the second time?

A: There wasn't anybody up that far on the driveway. Everybody else was down on the other end.

Q: I understand you accompanied Tomer down the driveway and picked up the tacks which Matter threw?

A: Yes.

Q: Who else, if anyone, went with you?

A: Ronald Hiller.

Q: Was there any conversation with any of the pickets when you went to pick up the tacks?

A: I, myself, didn't have any conversation.

Q: Did you hear any conversation?

A: There was some abusive language used by Matter to Hiller.

Q: Now, this was something you heard?

A: Yes.

Q: Did you hear the words she used?

A: I heard them at that time, but I have since forgotten them.

7

**Q:** Had Hiller said anything to her before the remarks you heard her make?

**A:** Not in my presence, no.

**Q:** Did he made any response to the remarks she made?

**A:** No, he did not.

**Q:** Thank you.

### b. Cross-Examination by Union Advocate

*Mr. Shepmanson:*
[to be supplied by student]

## 4. Donna Hippert, Job Applicant During Strike

### a. Direct Examination by Company Advocate

*Mr. Tackett:*
**Q:** Will you state your full name and address for the Arbitrator?

**A:** Donna Hippert, 412 Wimbert Lane, Hapville, Illinois.

**Q:** Are you presently employed?

**A:** No, sir, I am not.

**Q:** And, now, during this past spring did you apply for employment at Price Plastics?

**A:** Yes, I did, on May the 24th.

**Q:** Do you recall what prompted you to go to Price to apply for work?

**A:** An ad in the paper, the Hapville paper.

**Q:** Now, what time of day did you arrive at the plant?

**A:** Approximately ten minutes to eight in the morning. Very early.

**Q:** And you did say that was on the 24th of May?

**A:** Yes, it was.

**Q:** How did you arrive at the plant?

**A:** Alone in my husband's car.

**Q:** Now, when you arrived at the plant, what did you observe?

**A:** Well, at the time, I should say at the time this happened, we lived in Murran, Illinois, thirteen miles southeast of Hapville, and I had come from Murran and I was traveling north on Highway 41. I observed a car traveling south on 41 and it turned in, and there was a group of approximately ten women standing there and there were no police at that time and I didn't know what to think. I thought the strike was over. I wouldn't have been there if I hadn't thought it was over. I've never worked with a Union before, had anything to do with the Union, been around the Union or anything. At the time this happened I was working as a nurse's aide at Hapville Convalescent Center.

**Q:** Now, this car you observed turn in, did it enter the premises?

**A:** Yes, it did. It went through the group of women. There were approximately ten.

**Q:** Now, did you drive into the Company's premises?

**A:** No, I did not at that time. I went up to the Jefferson Shopping Center and turned in there, turned around, came back, and sat at the entrance to that shopping center and watched. I didn't know what was going on or what to think.

**Q:** How long did you sit there and watch?

**A:** Approximately five minutes. Long enough to see another car approaching from the same direction I had come from, and it turned in and went through that group of women.

**Q:** Okay, then what did you do?

**A:** Well, I decided that I'd better go in and ask what was going on.

**Q:** Did you go in?

**A:** Yes, I did.

**Q:** By driving your car into the driveway?

**A:** Yes, I did.

**Q:** What happened as you entered?

**A:** Nothing as I entered, but as I got out of my car someone hollered at me, "You'll be sorry."

**Q:** Do you know who yelled?

**A:** No, I do not. It was someone in that crowd.

**Q:** What did you do then?

**A:** I went into the employment office, but I had to wait.

**Q:** Did you make an application?

**A:** Yes, I did, at the urging of the receptionist.

**Q:** Do you know how long you were in the room there?

**A:** It was less than half an hour. I took an application and sat down and filled it out.

**Q:** Now, when you left the employment office after writing out your application, what did you do?

**A:** By the time I left, the crowd out there had at least doubled. There must have been twenty women out there at least, but they made way for me. They were very peaceful. I went and made a right-hand turn on Highway 41 and went down to another shopping center, Eastview Plaza Shopping Center, and went to the Haller's Drugstore. I pulled up in the fire lane in front of the drugstore.

**Q:** Now, how far is the shopping center or drugstore from the plant?

**A:** I would say four blocks.

**Q:** Now, go on. After you parked your car, what did you do?

**A:** I went into the drugstore and when I came out there was a two-tone brown station wagon sitting so close behind my car that the bumpers were touching and there were three women in that car. One of them on the passenger side leaned out and said, ''Did you just come from Price?'' and I said I did and she said, ''Come over here. We want to talk to you.'' I couldn't get through between the two cars so I walked around the front of my car and then straight back to the driver's side of that Starlight station wagon and I said, ''Yes?'' The woman said, ''Are you going to work at Price?'' and I said, ''Well, no, I just put in an application. I didn't come to go to work.'' She said, ''That's good, 'cause we're here to make sure you don't.'' And all the time she was saying this she had a large allen wrench in her hand. It was approximately twelve inches long and as thick as my thumb, and she was hitting it against the palm of one hand with her other hand all the time she was talking to me. The girl in the middle said to me, ''Do you know what you're doing to us?'' I said, ''No, I don't. I didn't do anything.'' And then she said, ''You've got a Brafford

Company sticker on your car, don't ya?'' I said, ''Yes.'' She said, ''Does your husband work at Brafford?'' I said, ''Yes.'' She said, ''Well, he must not be much if he would let you cross the picket line.'' I said, ''My husband thought the strike was over. I came thirteen miles. I didn't know it wasn't over until I got in there and asked.'' The woman who was driving, had been quiet during all this time and I could see they weren't listening to me. They weren't paying any attention to what I said. I said—I felt like I had to prove to them I wasn't going to work, that I wasn't going back to Price to work, so I said, ''I'm going home now.'' The woman who was driving the car said, ''That's good. That's what we want you to do.'' And I said, ''Oh, why?'' And she said, ''So we can find out where you live and so we can burn your house down.'' So I just—there wasn't any talking to them or reasoning with them so I just turned around and walked away and got in my own car and started to drive off. But, the one thing that was on my mind—the one thought was: don't go home. I wasn't about to.

**Q:** Now, before you continue, can you identify the three people who were in the car? What I'm asking is, are the three people who were in the car on the 24th of May in the room here today?

**A:** I know at least one of them is, and I'm not sure, but I think a couple of the others are here.

**Q:** Can you identify the driver?

**A:** Yes, I can.

**Q:** Will you stand and point her out for the sake of the Arbitrator?

**A:** It's that woman there.

**Q:** The Arbitrator should note that the witness is pointing at Bonnie Mansoney. Now, carefully observing everyone else in the room, is there anyone else you can identify as a person who was in the car on the 24th of May? Point out that person.

**A:** I believe this woman right here is one of them. She certainly looks like the woman who was in the middle. The one who gave me the lecture.

**Q:** The Arbitrator should note that the witness is pointing at Ruth Bert. Are you able to identify anyone else?

**A:** No. I keep wanting to say that woman sitting next to Ms. Mansoney, but I'm not sure.

**Q:** We've identified the driver?

**A:** Definitely, Ms. Mansoney.

**Q:** You got in your car and you left the parking lot?

**A:** Yes.

**Q:** Now, tell the Arbitrator what you did.

**A:** I started driving. I took them on a guided tour of Hapville.

**Q:** By "them" are you referring to the two-tone brown station wagon with the three women in it?

**A:** Yes.

**Q:** What did they do when you drove out of the parking lot?

**A:** They followed me.

**Q:** How close behind you did they follow?

**A:** So close I couldn't see their headlights in my rearview mirror.

**Q:** Where did you drive?

**A:** All around Hapville. I made a right-hand turn onto 36th Street and went down and hit Wiggington Street and made a left on Wiggington Street and came downtown headed out to—made another right and headed out on 41 and headed out towards Carson City.

**Q:** Was there any conversation or any words spoken to you by anyone in that car after you left the shopping center parking lot?

**A:** No. Nobody said anything to me after we left that parking lot.

**Q:** Were there any other occurrences while they were following you?

**A:** When we got out to Carson City, I realized I couldn't get back to Hapville. The Avena Bridge over Brown River was closed or being replaced and the only way I could get to Hapville was to go to Simpson and come back. So I began looking for a wide place in the road to turn around. I knew I couldn't turn around in the middle of Highway 41, so I began looking for a place to turn around. There's a turnoff off the highway and I believe there is a little town there called Benton Village, and as I was turning to cross over the—there's a railroad crossing there—I saw out of the corner of my eye an object come sailing towards the car. This object hit the ground right outside the window where I was sitting in my car, and I looked out the

window and it was a tire tool, an X-shaped metal object.

**Q:** Did you see where it came from?

**A:** It came from behind me and there wasn't anybody else around.

**Q:** Who was behind you at the time?

**A:** That two-tone brown station wagon.

**Q:** Were you moving at the time or were you stopped?

**A:** I was moving.

**Q:** At approximately what speed?

**A:** About five miles an hour or less.

**Q:** Now, I assume you crossed the railroad track?

**A:** Crossed the railroad track and came back to Hapville and kept driving around.

**Q:** Did the station wagon continue to follow you?

**A:** Yes, it did.

**Q:** Okay, now go ahead. What happened after that?

**A:** Well, I decided to head out of town on State Road 17 and I went out State Road 17 doing the speed limit and at all times they were right behind me and so close at times I couldn't see their headlights; just right there. Here I was doing the speed limit and there they were.

**Q:** Do you recall what the speed limit was or how fast you were going?

**A:** Well, when you get out of Hapville, it's fifty-five. Well, there's a turn-off off of State Road 17 that goes over to the intersection of State Road 91 and Highway 41, and I made this turn-off and I got over to the intersection of 91 and 41 and there's a stop sign and I stopped and looked both ways and then went across the highway. I looked in my rearview mirror to see if by chance they had given up the chase and turned left and gone back towards Hapville, but they hadn't, they were still there, and we weren't but about three car lengths off the intersection when something hit the back of the car. It was a very loud noise.

**Q:** Was this before stopping or after starting up again?

**A:** After we had crossed the highway, crossed Highway 41. We were on State Road 91, hadn't gone very far.

**Q:** You said you heard a noise?

**A:** It was very loud and it sounded—well, the first thing I thought of was they had hit me with their car; they had used their car to ram into the back of mine. That's the first thought I had, but, no matter what, I floored it. I didn't look again until I got to the Homer Heights turnoff. There's a housing development called Homer Heights that's on the right about a half a mile down and that's where they quit following me and then I immediately went home. I was just about five minutes from home, although they didn't know it.

**Q:** You went from the apartments where the chase was ended to your home in Murran?

**A:** Yes.

**Q:** Okay, after you got home, what happened?

**A:** Well, I parked the car in the driveway and went into the house and I guess I was as white as a sheet, because my husband knew something was wrong with me. All he had to do was take one look and he said "What happened?" And I took him out and showed him the car.

**Q:** What did you find when you examined the car?

**A:** There was a large place in the middle of the trunk lid that had a dent in it and the paint is all gone.

**Q:** Now, you're indicating an area of three or four inches?

**A:** Right in the middle, yes, three inches. Right smack dab in the middle of the trunk lid. And directly up from that there is a chrome plate or piece about 1/2 of an inch wide that goes around the rear window, and that has a dent in it. That was the damage we found to the car. My husband—to say he was furious has got to be the understatement of the year. Boy, he was mad. Somebody had to pay; somebody was going to pay. And we hid the car. We put it in the garage just in case those women were still looking for me. We got in the truck and we put our two little girls in the camper on the truck, because we have a truck with a camper on it, and we headed back to Hapville by way of 91 and 41. When we got to 91, the allen wrench, which was the same one the woman had in her hand, was lying in the middle of the highway and we stopped and picked it up.

**Q:** Then what did you do?

**A:** We came on in to Price. By the time we got to Price the crowd was huge. A big crowd. There were two police cars sitting in the Walters' parking lot, city police; there had to be at least thirty people out there. We came through. Some of them got in front of the truck. My husband was ready to run over them. He was hoping they would give him the chance.

**Q:** Did he hit anyone?

**A:** No, but he tried. We parked the truck and my husband jumped out of that truck and I couldn't even keep up with him. He went running into the employment office waving that allen wrench like he was ready to knock somebody in the head and he didn't care who. He wanted to know who was going to pay for it and what the hell was going on.

**Q:** Did he talk to someone?

**A:** Well, he talked to Ron Hiller. Hiller came over to me and said, "Is this true, did this really happen?" And I said, "Yes, it is." He said, "Do you know any of those women?" I said, "No, I don't." And then I said, "I'll sure know them again if I see them." And he said, "Did you see any of them as you came in?" And I said, "Yes." We went outside and Hiller said, "Do you see her in that crowd?" I said, "Yes, sir. There she is. That's the woman who was driving the station wagon." And Hiller said that was Bonnie Mansoney and that was the first time I had ever learned her name.

**Q:** Now, the person you pointed to, is that the same person who you pointed to earlier and who is sitting at the table here?

**A:** Yes, she is here. She's the one who was driving the car. Then Hiller asked me if I saw the car anyplace and I looked around and there it sat in the parking lot at Becky's Burgers, a two-tone brown station wagon, and I pointed that out to them. Hiller asked if we wanted him to file charges and my husband said, "You're darn right we do." So we were going to file charges and prosecute to the hilt. And so we went down to the prosecutor's office. Hiller got in his car and my husband and I got in our truck, our pickup truck, and we started out of the lot. Mansoney must have thought we were after her because she ran and got in her car and she drove it over to Dave's Shopping Center parking lot, parked it right in front of the door, and jumped out and ran into the store and we followed her, but there wasn't any doubt in my mind as to that was who it was.

**Q:** You say you followed her, but where?

**A:** We followed her into Dave's parking lot, but we did not go into the store after her and my husband wrote down her license number. It was 3C something or other, I can't remember now. I could have then, but not now.

**Q:** After writing down the license plate number, what did you do?

**A:** We went down to the prosecutor's office. Hiller took us down because we didn't know where to go. We didn't know where the prosecutor was or anything about it, so we went down with him and we did file charges. I did sign papers. I don't know what has happened. We gave the allen wrench to the prosecutor and haven't seen it since. I signed the papers with the prosecutor and nothing has come of that either.

**Q:** You have not been called by the prosecutor?

**A:** Nothing has happened.

**Q:** Were you ever after this date of the 24th offered a job with Price?

**A:** Yes, I was. Sometime around the middle of July. Price called me and said the Union was back. They had an opening and they found my application and was I still interested. I told her, no.

**Q:** Nothing further at this time.

---

### b. Cross-Examination by Union Advocate

*Mr. Shepmanson:*
[to be supplied by student]

---

## 5. Ken Gooch, Vice President of Operations

### a. Direct Examination by Company Advocate

*Mr. Tackett:*

**Q:** State your name and address for the recorder, please.

**A:** Ken Gooch, Rural Route 3, Franck, Illinois.

**Q:** By whom are you employed?

**A:** Price Plastics.

**Q:** What is your position at Price?

**A:** Vice President of Operations.

**Q:** How long have you worked for Price?

**A:** Four years.

**Q:** Were you involved in contract negotiations in year 7?

**A:** Yes, I was.

**Q:** Now, did you work in the Price plant during the period of the strike?

**A:** Some days, yes.

**Q:** And specifically during the week of May 21 to 25?

**A:** Yes.

**Q:** Did you—do you know an employee by the name of Megan Carfield?

**A:** Yes, I do.

**Q:** And is she present here in the room?

**A:** Yes, she is.

**Q:** Could you point at her for the Arbitrator?

**A:** She's sitting right there.

**Q:** The Arbitrator should note that the witness is pointing at Megan Carfield. Now, did you observe her on the picket line during the week of May 21 to May 25?

**A:** Yes, I did.

**Q:** Did you observe her engage in any particular activity which later became the basis for the Company's decision not to reinstate her?

**A:** Yes, I did.

**Q:** Well, would you tell the Arbitrator just what you saw?

**A:** I arrived the morning of the 22nd about 6:30 during the strike, people started to come in at approximately that time and we all tried to arrive by around 7 a.m. if we possibly could. That particular morning, I don't remember any police cars. Normally, we tried to have them at the plant at the time the people tried to come to work. That particular morning Marty Pratter was coming through the picket line. I would judge there were probably twenty, twenty-five pickets out on the line at that time. Pratter started to come in from 41 and the pickets were kind of around the front of his truck and they opened up as he came in at that time. Carfield threw something at the truck and when Pratter came up and parked in the parking lot, he came down to where I was standing outside and he was very upset. He said an egg had been thrown at his truck. I went out and looked at it and there was an egg on the windshield and it had run down onto the hood of the truck and he was pretty upset about it. We had been instructed by the police to report any incidents, so I immediately went in and notified the police of the incident and asked them to come out and look at it. The reason we asked them to come out and look was because he was upset and concerned about the truck and the paint and he wanted to get it off as soon as he could, so we notified the police. The police later came out there and looked at the truck themselves.

**Q:** Did you see this object being thrown by Carfield?

**A:** I saw her hand move and the egg in her hand.

**Q:** You actually saw the object?

**A:** Yes. I did.

**Q:** And where did it strike the truck?

**A:** It was on the windshield on the driver's side, almost in front of the driver.

**Q:** All right. Now—where was she standing when she threw the egg?

**A:** She had just started to move off to the side, and as she moved she threw the egg at that time.

**Q:** Was this out where the highway intersects the driveway?

**A:** Yes.

**Q:** And how far from where she was standing were you standing?

**A:** I was approximately sixty feet, fifty feet away.

**Q:** Away from Carfield?

**A:** Yes.

**Q:** Now, were there any other actions by Carfield that you observed, which were relied upon in deciding not to reinstate her?

**A:** Marty Pratter started to go out in his truck. He stopped briefly for the traffic and the pickets moved out very nicely. Carfield then had moved over into the back of his truck, and she put her hands on his license plate and was trying to bend it. The plate was bent when I looked at it the next morning.

**Q:** Were there traffic problems on 41 such as traffic tie-ups during this week?

**A:** There were tie-ups both from the north and the south.

**Q:** Thank you.

### b. Cross-Examination by Union Advocate

*Mr. Shepmanson:*
[to be supplied by student]

## C. Examination of Union Witnesses

## 1. Earl Bixland, International Representative, Universal Union

### a. Direct Examination by Union Advocate

*Mr. Shepmanson:*

**Q:** Now, during the period of negotiations and during the period of the strike, were you out on the picket line?

**A:** A few times.

**Q:** When you were there, did you see any violence?

**A:** No, I did not. When I was coming down to a meeting or going down to a local Union hall to meet with a committee or to have a meeting, I would stop by if I had time. I would talk to them, but all the times I was there, there were probably at most five or six people there.

**Q:** Did the Company ever complain to you about anything going on on the picket line that they had an objection to?

**A:** Yes, they did. They called me, well it was in May before they got—I believe it was the week they got the injunction. It was one of those days the Company attorney Mr. Tackett told me the Company was upset about all the people and everything out there and asked me if I would look into it. I made a phone call to the president of Local 101 and he told me there were only about six or eight people on the picket line. I never did call Mr. Tackett back and tell him the results of that conversation.

**Q:** Now, prior to May 29, did any Company official ever indicate to you that strikers might be discharged as a result of the strike?

**A:** Actually, no, because from the 18th to the 29th I had not been in contact with them

directly. On the 18th there was no indication there was going to be any. The next time we really had direct contact with them was on the 29th.

**Q:** You worked without a contract until August 29?

**A:** Yes.

**Q:** To your knowledge, were there any arrests made by the city police during the period of the strike?

**A:** Not to my knowledge.

**Q:** Now, before the strike started, you'd been in the plant?

**A:** I'd been in the plant, yes. Not right before the strike started, but I'd been in the plant.

**Q:** Before the strike started? Before at various times?

**A:** Yes.

**Q:** Did you ever see any armed security guards there?

**A:** No. I've never seen any security guards.

**Q:** Since the strike started, have you ever seen any security guards there?

**A:** No, I haven't.

**Q:** No more questions.

### b. Cross-Examination by Company Advocate

*Mr. Tackett:*
[to be supplied by student]

## 2. Sara Manley, Employee

### a. Direct Examination by Union Advocate

*Mr. Shepmanson:*

**Q:** Will you identify yourself to the Arbitrator?

**A:** Sara Manley.

**Q:** And where do you live?

**A:** 611 South Elm Street, Eden, Illinois.

**Q:** And are you an employee of the Company?

**A:** Yes. I'm on leave right now.

**Q:** You're on leave? How long have you been employed by the Company?

**A:** Since November of year 6.

**Q:** And had you been employed by the Company before this?

**A:** Yes.

**Q:** On how many occasions?

**A:** A couple of times, I think.

**Q:** This is your third hitch?

**A:** Yes.

**Q:** Were you working at the plant at the time of the strike?

**A:** Yes.

**Q:** And did you go out on strike with the other employees?

**A:** Yes.

**Q:** Were you on the picket line?
**A:** Only a little. Mainly I was at the Union hall.
**Q:** Now, was there a reason for that?
**A:** I was pregnant.
**Q:** Now, do you know a man by the name of Dave Maps?
**A:** Yes. He works for the Company in the office.
**Q:** And do you know one by the name of Jeff Linker?
**A:** Yes. He works for the Company in the office.
**Q:** Will you tell the Arbitrator what happened to you involving those two men?
**A:** Well, one time when I was at the picket line, Linker hit me with a car and Maps told him to.
**Q:** Now, after you were struck by the car, did either Maps or Linker offer to take you to the hospital?
**A:** No.
**Q:** Then what did you do?
**A:** I went down to the Union hall and called the Local President, Tom Benson, and he told me to press charges. I also called my doctor and made an appointment.
**Q:** You went to see your doctor?
**A:** Yes.
**Q:** Now, about how far along were you in pregnancy?
**A:** About four and a half months, five maybe.
**Q:** Did you file charges with the prosecutor?
**A:** Yes.
**Q:** And what happened to those charges, if you know?
**A:** Nothing that I know of.
**Q:** Now, do Maps and Linker still work at the plant?
**A:** Yes, after the incident they even made Linker assistant foreman on the night shift.
**Q:** Was that as a reward for hitting you or do you know?
**A:** I don't know. I imagine.
**Q:** Now, did you go back after the strike was terminated?
**A:** Yes.
**Q:** And where did you go?
**A:** Out in Finishing.

**Q:** Now, has anything happened to you since you've been back to work?
**A:** Yes, I got a three-day suspension.
**Q:** For what reason?
**A:** They said for harassing the janitor. He hit me in the stomach and I complained about it and they gave me a three-day suspension.
**Q:** Who did?
**A:** Ronald Hiller and Ken Gooch.
**Q:** Who was Ellen Balli?
**A:** She's my boss.
**Q:** What did she do and say?
**A:** She came back there and cussed me and wanted to know why I was harassing her janitor the day after it happened. I didn't know what was wrong with her. She just came back there screaming and carrying on, so I was trying to find out what was wrong with her and then she sent me home and told me to come back in the next day to the office.
**Q:** And they gave you a three-day suspension?
**A:** Yes.
**Q:** Now, was there any water poured on your chair and if so, by whom?
**A:** Well, I don't know who did it. I imagine the janitor, but it was while I was on break.
**Q:** So you don't know?
**A:** When I came back from break my chair was all wet.
**Q:** But you don't know who did it?
**A:** No.
**Q:** Now, although you did most of your duty at the Union hall, were you ever out on the picket line?
**A:** Two or three times.
**Q:** What happened, if you know, concerning the people entering the plant the times you were out there?
**A:** Oh, I wasn't down there very long at a time. I never saw anything out of the way except the day I got hit by the car, those boys came through there cussing; that's why we stopped them when they came out.
**Q:** Who were the boys that were cussing?
**A:** Linker was one of them.
**Q:** Now, do you know a man by the name of Marty Pratter?
**A:** I don't actually know him except when I see him.
**Q:** But if he was here, you could identify him?

**A:** Yes.

**Q:** Is he here?

**A:** No.

**Q:** Now, what happened on the picket line concerning Deborah Matter and Marty Pratter?

**A:** Well, two or three times before that, he had gone out and he had called different ones names, but on one particular time he called Deborah a "bitch." I don't remember the date it was done.

**Q:** No further questions.

### b. Cross-Examination by Company Advocate

*Mr. Tackett:*
[to be supplied by student]

## 3. Lyla Sharp, Former Employee

### a. Direct Examination by Union Advocate

*Mr. Shepmanson:*

**Q:** Will you identify yourself?

**A:** Lyla Sharp, Route 4, Hapville, Illinois.

**Q:** Now, what is your employment date, if you remember?

**A:** January 7 of year 5.

**Q:** Are you now an employee at Price?

**A:** No.

**Q:** Now, when the strike occurred, did you go out with the rest of them?

**A:** Yes.

**Q:** The last day you worked, then, was April 6?

**A:** Yes.

**Q:** Now, where did you do your normal picket duty?

**A:** At the Union hall.

**Q:** Were you out on the line, the picket line, quite a bit or very little?

**A:** Quite a bit.

**Q:** Did you have a conversation while you were out on the picket line with a foreman by the name of Ray Knowles?

**A:** Yes, I did.

**Q:** Will you tell the Arbitrator about it?

**A:** His wife usually drove the car in to bring him to work and then she would leave, leave him at work. She'd come in fast and leave fast and almost hit two or three people. So, one day I stopped her and asked her if she would slow down before she hit somebody. She said a few things that weren't very nice and went on. So, the next day she came in, Knowles was driving the car, so I stopped him and told

him the very same thing. He said, yes, he would make her slow down. Well, when she left after she took him into work, she came out and she struck me.

**Q:** What did you do? You mean she struck you with the car?

**A:** Yes, I was over to the side so she could get out, but it was just like she was coming after me. She just bumped me on the knee; it didn't knock me down, just bumped me. It scared me because I didn't think she would hit me.

**Q:** Now, did anyone else strike you with a car while you were out there on the picket line?

**A:** I was hit by a truck.

**Q:** Who was driving the truck?

**A:** Marty Pratter.

**Q:** Did he stop?

**A:** No.

**Q:** What happened then?

**A:** We were walking across the picket line. I was getting ready to go across when he came through, and I didn't see him because he usually has a camper on the back of his truck and that particular morning he didn't, so I didn't recognize the truck. I just started across and the woman next to me moved out of the way just in time. But she didn't have time to grab me before he hit me and my arm hit the mirror on the side of his truck and he knocked me down.

**Q:** Now, what did you do about it? Did you complain to the police?

**A:** Well, the police saw it happen because the officer was over in Walters' parking lot and he came on over to see if I was all right and then I was taken to the hospital.

**Q:** Did the police do anything?
**A:** It was the very same day they came back and went in to talk to Pratter.
**Q:** No further questions.

### b. Cross-Examination by Company Advocate

*Mr. Tackett:*
[to be supplied by student]

## 3. Megan Carfield, Grievant

### a. Direct Examination by Union Advocate

*Mr. Shepmanson:*
**Q:** Will you identify yourself to the Arbitrator, please?
**A:** My name is Megan Carfield. I live at Rural Route 12, Hapville.
**Q:** What's your marital status, Megan?
**A:** I'm married, four children.
**Q:** How long had you been employed by Price prior to your termination?
**A:** I would have been there fourteen years June the 8th. I was fired May the 30th.
**Q:** You were one of the older seniority people there?
**A:** Yes, second in Finishing; sixth in the whole plant.
**Q:** Since your discharge, have you been able to secure employment?
**A:** No, I have not.
**Q:** Now, your last day working for Price was April 6, before you went on strike?
**A:** Yes.
**Q:** And you haven't been back since?
**A:** No, I haven't.
**Q:** Now, what was your normal picket day duty?
**A:** On Wednesday afternoon from twelve to six, but I was there—after they started hiring new people—I was there about every day.
**Q:** Did you ever physically prevent anyone from entering the plant?
**A:** No, I did not.
**Q:** Did you ever tell any would-be applicant that they ought not go in?
**A:** Well, there were people who came from different places all over to look for a job and they didn't know that we were out on strike. I

told one lady, "I've been here fourteen years and I only make $6.31 an hour" and she said, "My God, I don't want to work here." So she left. We begged them not to come through and take our jobs.
**Q:** Now, did you engage in any violence in the picket line as you understand violence?
**A:** No, I sure didn't.
**Q:** Do you know Marty Pratter?
**A:** Yes, I did. I didn't know him personally, but I sure got to know him when he came through the picket line because he didn't stop for anybody.
**Q:** Did you talk to the police about him?
**A:** Yes, we did. That's one reason I think the police sat over there so much—to watch him, but it didn't do any good.
**Q:** Were you there when Lyla Sharp was struck by him?
**A:** Yes, I was.
**Q:** It's been testified to that on May 22, year 6, that you hit Pratter's windshield or some part of his vehicle with an egg.
**A:** I did. He called me a "bitch" and I would have thrown it in his face if I could have gotten to him. When I asked him what his name was so somebody could talk to him at his home and tell him, ask him not to go in and take our jobs, he said, "Get out of my way, you bitch," and just came right on and when he did, I threw the egg. Someone handed me the egg, I didn't have it, and I threw the egg.
**Q:** Now, it's also been testified to that you bent a license plate.

**A:** Well, someone wanted to know who he was, so I laughed. I said, ''Well, that can be fixed.'' And the license plate was bent double and I just reached over and straightened it out.

**Q:** So you could get the license number?

**A:** So this fella could write down the license plate number.

**Q:** Has anyone from the Company ever talked to you to ask you about these two incidents?

**A:** No, sir, none whatsoever.

**Q:** Who notified you that you'd been discharged?

**A:** Earl Bixland of the Union had my name on a piece of paper.

**Q:** The Company never notified you?

**A:** Company never notified me.

**Q:** That's all.

### b. Cross-Examination by Company Advocate

*Mr. Tackett:*
[to be supplied by student]

## 5. Bonnie Mansoney, Grievant

### a. Direct Examination by Union Advocate

*Mr. Shepmanson:*

**Q:** Will you identify yourself for the Arbitrator?

**A:** I'm Bonnie Mansoney and I live at 571 Nevada Avenue, Hapville, Illinois.

**Q:** What's your employment date, if you remember?

**A:** November 11, I believe, year 3.

**Q:** The last day you worked for Price was April 6?

**A:** Yes.

**Q:** Since your termination, have you been working?

**A:** I went to work on September the 24th at Henley's Grocery.

**Q:** Are you making more or less?

**A:** I'm making much less.

**Q:** What's your marital status?

**A:** I'm married.

**Q:** Children?

**A:** I have six children at home. It takes two salaries to support that size family.

**Q:** You went on strike with the rest of the people?

**A:** Yes, I did.

**Q:** What was your normal picket time?

**A:** It was Thursdays from six in the morning until twelve noon.

**Q:** Now, did you spend any time other than just Thursdays out there?

**A:** I was down a couple of Tuesday mornings because they asked for volunteers, but not over one or two. Mostly it was on Thursdays.

**Q:** Now, during the period you were out there, did you prevent anyone physically from entering the plant or leaving the plant?

**A:** No, sir.

**Q:** Now, what happened on Thursday, May 23, that stands out in your mind?

**A:** Well, that is the day the Company ran the ad in the paper and I guess there were quite a few of us on the picket line. Then this one car came through the line. It was red and as it came through it slowed down and stopped, and then it took off again and it hit Dora Hester, knocking her pocketbook out of her arm and we wrote down the license number. An hour or so later, the car came out of the plant and someone said we should follow it. So two other girls and I followed the car.

**Q:** Where did you follow it to?

**A:** Well, we didn't actually follow it. After we left we found it parked at Eastview Plaza.

**Q:** You went over there?

**A:** Yes, we did.

**Q:** What did you do?

**A:** We waited for her to come out of the drugstore.

**Q:** Did you have a conversation with her?

**A:** Yes, we did.

**Q:** What did the conversation consist of?

**A:** We asked her not to cross the picket line and take our jobs. We told her that she was hurting every employee at the plant. At this point she told us that she had to have the job. She wanted to divorce her husband.

**Q:** That's what she told you?

**A:** That's what she told us.

**Q:** Now, what happened after that?

**A:** Well, she sort of treated it as a big joke and she got in her car, and so we decided to follow her and she led us out around down through Hapville. She then went Highway 41 towards Carson City where she turned. Anyway, we followed her and this time we didn't follow on her tail. She gave us turn signals and let us know when she was going to turn into the Brafford Scarboro Plant.

**Q:** What did she do then?

**A:** There she stopped the car and she wrote a note and she put it in this truck parked at the plant. And she looked at us and said, ''That's my lover.''

**Q:** And then what happened?

**A:** She got back in her car and drove back into town. She went down Main Street to Highway 41. She went down to State Road 91 and she turned off on 91 and we went straight back to the Hapville plant.

**Q:** Now, you heard her testimony?

**A:** Yes, I did.

**Q:** Was she telling the truth?

**A:** No, sir, she was not.

**Q:** Now, did you throw a tire tool at her car?

**A:** No, sir, I didn't.

**Q:** Did you have a wrench?

**A:** No, sir.

**Q:** Was there anyone in your car that had a wrench?

**A:** No, sir.

**Q:** Did you strike her car with an object in any manner?

**A:** No.

**Q:** Now, did the police come to talk to you?

**A:** Yes, they did. They came that same afternoon.

**Q:** What did they tell you?

**A:** They asked me if I had a brown station wagon and if I was driving it that day and in the vicinity of State Road 91 and Highway 41, and I told them I didn't know what they were talking about. They asked me if I would identify the two women with me and which one of them threw something out of my car, a tire tool. They said they would drop all charges against me if I would identify these other two women who were in my car.

**Q:** Did you identify them?

**A:** No, sir. I told him I didn't know what he was talking about. He was a detective in the Hapville Police Department.

**Q:** You weren't going to name the other two women?

**A:** No.

**Q:** You did not know what he was talking about?

**A:** Yes, sir. I did know. I just didn't see the point in involving anyone else.

**Q:** Now, has anyone from the Company ever called you in and asked you about this affair?

**A:** No, sir, they haven't.

**Q:** Who notified you of your discharge?

**A:** Earl Bixland at the Union did.

**Q:** No Company official has ever talked to you?

**A:** No, sir.

**Q:** Now, did Mr. Hiller ever take your license number?

**A:** Yes, sir, that same Thursday, when my picket duty was over. I left the picket line and I had to go into Dave's Drygoods. As I parked my car I saw him in this blue truck turn into Dave's. As I got out and went in, I happened to look back to see what they were doing and he was standing behind my car writing down my license number.

**Q:** He was writing down something?

**A:** Well, I assumed it was my license number. That's where he was standing.

**Q:** Nothing further.

### b. Cross-Examination by Company Advocate

*Mr. Tackett:*
[to be supplied by student]

## 6. Lesley Cole, Grievant

### a. Direct Examination by Union Advocate

*Mr. Shepmanson:*

**Q:** Will you identify yourself to the Arbitrator.

**A:** Lesley Cole, 144 Wald Drive, Hapville.

**Q:** How long have you been employed by the Company?

**A:** Since November of year 5.

**Q:** You're married, you have one child?

**A:** Right.

**Q:** Have you been working since your termination?

**A:** Yes, I worked at Sadie's.

**Q:** What's that?

**A:** A doughnut mill.

**Q:** Do you make more or less money than you did at Price?

**A:** Less.

**Q:** You make less?

**A:** I don't work there now.

**Q:** Oh, you don't work there?

**A:** No.

**Q:** Now the last day you worked at Price was April 6, year 7, is that correct?

**A:** Yes.

**Q:** When the strike was terminated, you were not recalled?

**A:** No.

**Q:** Who told you that you were discharged?

**A:** The Union.

**Q:** Did the Company ever notify you?

**A:** No.

**Q:** Now, have you been to the plant since you were terminated?

**A:** Yes.

**Q:** What happened?

**A:** I called the plant to see if I could bring my I.D. card in and turn it in and they told me yes, so I went in and I turned it in. I asked Hiller's assistant if she could tell me what I was fired for. She said she didn't want to tell me and if I wanted to know, I could ask Hiller. I told her I didn't care who tells me, I would just like to know. So Hiller came out and he told me that I kicked an automobile and he saw me jar or jerk away from the car. I told him that I didn't and he told me he knew I did because he saw me.

**Q:** Did you?

**A:** No, I didn't.

**Q:** What kind of shoes were you wearing that day?

**A:** Tennis shoes with holes in them.

**Q:** Thank you.

### b. Cross-Examination by Company Advocate

*Mr. Tackett:*

[to be supplied by student]

## 7. Alicia Coppan, Grievant

### a. Direct Examination by Union Advocate

*Mr. Shepmanson:*

**Q:** Will you identify yourself to the Arbitrator?

**A:** Alicia Coppan, 760 North Dahl, Hapville.

**Q:** How long have you been employed by Price?

**A:** Five years.

**Q:** What's your marital status?

**A:** Married, with one boy.

**Q:** Since your termination have you been employed?

**A:** Yes.

**Q:** Are you working now?

**A:** Yes.

**Q:** Have you been continuously employed?

**A:** No, I'm on my second job.

**Q:** Are you making more or less?

**A:** Less.

20

**Q:** Now, you went out with the other people when they went on strike?

**A:** Yes.

**Q:** And then the last day you worked at Price was April 6?

**A:** Yes, it was.

**Q:** What was your normal time doing picket duty?

**A:** I went on at midnight Sunday night until six o'clock Monday morning.

**Q:** Were you out there any other times besides your regular duty?

**A:** I was out there on Friday morning, May 25.

**Q:** Outside of that, that was all?

**A:** Yes.

**Q:** Now, did you physically prevent anyone from leaving or entering the plant while you were out there?

**A:** No.

**Q:** Did you engage in any violence while you were on the picket line?

**A:** I scratched a car.

**Q:** How did that happen?

**A:** I was standing there with a nail in my hand and when the car came out someone shoved me and my hand went out and the nail touched the car.

**Q:** How big a scratch?

**A:** A tiny one.

**Q:** Did you scratch more than one car?

**A:** No, I did not.

**Q:** What was the car that you scratched? Do you know which one it was?

**A:** A white station wagon.

**Q:** Who did it belong to?

**A:** A strike breaker.

**Q:** No further questions.

### b. Cross-Examination by Company Advocate

*Mr. Tackett:*
[to be supplied by student]

## 8. Deborah Matter, Grievant

### a. Direct Examination by Union Advocate

*Mr. Shepmanson:*

**Q:** Will you give your name to the Arbitrator?

**A:** Deborah Matter.

**Q:** And what is your address?

**A:** 1732 Gene Drive, Hapville.

**Q:** What's your marital status?

**A:** Divorced.

**Q:** Do you have anyone you are responsible for, any dependent?

**A:** I have a little girl, yes.

**Q:** And you're the sole means of support?

**A:** That's right.

**Q:** When the strike commenced, you went out with the rest of the employees?

**A:** That's right.

**Q:** April 6 was your last day with Price?

**A:** Yes.

**Q:** What was your regular picket duty day?

**A:** From twelve noon on Monday until six o'clock that evening.

**Q:** You've been accused of throwing tacks in the driveway.

**A:** That's right, but I did not do that.

**Q:** You didn't do it?

**A:** I did not.

**Q:** You were also charged with throwing a glass bottle at a truck. Did you do that?

**A:** Yes.

**Q:** When Mr. Hiller came up to you, what did he say to you about tacks on the driveway?

**A:** He was standing in the doorway and came running up to me and said, ''Deborah, did you do this?'' And I looked at him and I said, ''No, I didn't.'' He says, ''Well, I have witnesses that said you did.'' I said, ''Well, I have four or five that said I didn't.''

**Q:** But you did throw the bottle?

**A:** That's right.

**Q:** The truck that you threw the bottle at belonged to Marty Pratter?

**A:** Yes, it had a camper top on top.

**Q:** Now, why did you throw the bottle?

**A:** Because he called me a "bitch." He had no reason to. I didn't do anything to him. I didn't hurt him. I didn't bother him in any way.

**Q:** Did the bottle do any damage to the truck?

**A:** No, it didn't. It broke in the plastic liner.

**Q:** What did Hiller say to you?

**A:** Well, it was after the bottle was thrown. He was picking up some of the glass and kicking other pieces under parked cars. He reached down there and picked up a handful of tacks along with the glass. He looked at me and he said, "And I don't suppose you did this either, did you?" I said, "No, I didn't and don't you accuse me." And I never cussed him or anything else. And he looked at me and said, "Well, I could sue you," but then he said, "Don't worry, Deborah, I'm not going to." Those are the very words he said and then he went in the office.

**Q:** Who notified you that you were being discharged?

**A:** The Union.

**Q:** Did the Company ever ask you if you threw the bottle and the nails? Did they ever ask you to give your side of the story?

**A:** No, sir.

**Q:** Have you been rejected for employment because of your discharge?

**A:** I have.

**Q:** Where?

**A:** Hickman's.

**Q:** What happened?

**A:** Well, I went in to fill my application out, and when I got done with it—and, of course, I didn't want to lie so I put down there I had been discharged from Price—I told her, "There's something I want to explain to you. I want you to know why I was discharged." She previously had told me to put my application in a rack over on the desk. Well, after I told her about this she just took my application and threw it away.

**Q:** You never got hired?

**A:** I sure didn't.

**Q:** No further questions.

### b. Cross-Examination by Company Advocate

*Mr. Tackett:*
[to be supplied by student]

## 9. Ruth Bert, Former Employee

### a. Direct Examination by Union Advocate

*Mr. Shepmanson:*

**Q:** Will you give your name to the Arbitrator, please?

**A:** Ruth Bert, Route 12, Hapville.

**Q:** Are you currently employed at Price?

**A:** No.

**Q:** Now, Ruth, you participated in this strike?

**A:** That's right.

**Q:** And you stayed out until the strike was terminated, did you?

**A:** Right.

**Q:** Now, do you recall the testimony of Bonnie Mansoney that she gave today?

**A:** Yes.

**Q:** Do you know anything about that?

**A:** Yes.

**Q:** What do you know about it?

**A:** Well, this—

**Q:** First of all, were you one of the three women in the car?

**A:** Yes, sir.

**Q:** All right, now, tell the Arbitrator what you remember.

**A:** Well, this girl, the smart aleck there, came through the picket line. When she came through she hit Dora Hester and knocked her purse off her hand and hurt her arm. She went on in and then when she came back out, Bonnie's car was on the picket line, so we got in the car and this woman went over to Haller's drugstore in the shopping center. We wanted to talk to her and ask her not to cross the picket line. She went in the drugstore and when she came back out, we talked to her and asked her not to cross the picket line. She said she wanted to get a job making more money so that she could sue her husband for divorce.

**Q:** The Arbitrator should note that the witness pointed to Donna Hippert. Okay, then what happened?

**A:** Well, she got in her car and we followed her through town to the Brafford plant where she got in a truck and wrote a note and she got back out and smirkingly said to us, "That's my lover, in case you wanted to know." We told her that was her business and we didn't care who it was, that we were just concerned about our jobs. So, then she got in her car and left and we followed her back out to 17 and 41, and we went back to the plant.

**Q:** Did anybody throw anything at her?

**A:** No.

**Q:** From the car you were in?

**A:** No.

**Q:** Did you throw anything at her?

**A:** No.

**Q:** Did you see anyone sitting with you in Bonnie's car throw a wrench or any object?

**A:** No.

**Q:** Did you ever threaten to burn her house down?

**A:** No. I would never think of doing such a thing.

**Q:** Thank you.

### b. Cross-Examination by Company Advocate

*Mr. Tackett:*
[to be supplied by student]

# D. Exhibits

*JOINT EXHIBIT NO. 1*

COLLECTIVE BARGAINING AGREEMENT

BETWEEN

PRICE PLASTICS, INC.

AND

LOCAL UNION NO. 101

UNIVERSAL UNION (Effective 8/29/07)


.  .  .


Article 3.01(b)          The Company has the right and authority to
                         discharge or discipline employees for proper
                         and just cause, subject to their right to
                         grieve such discharge and discipline under
                         the grievance procedure.


.  .  .

---

*JOINT EXHIBIT NO.2*

### E M P L O Y E E (S)   G R I E V A N C E–S T E P 3
Submit to foreman in triplicate.

| Local No. | Unit | Dept. | Date |
|---|---|---|---|
| 101 | | | 9/11/07 |

---

Name of aggrieved employee:
  Bonnie Mansoney, Alicia Coppan,
  Deborah Matter, Lesley Cole, Megan Carfield

---

| Contract Violation: | Article |
|---|---|
| | Article 3.01(b) |

---

| Oral discussion with foreman: | Date | Time | Result |
|---|---|---|---|
| N/A | | | |

---

Detailed reasons for grievance:
The Union and the aggrieved employees contend their termination

for alleged picket line disturbances is not for proper and just

cause. The Company applied disparate treatment. The penalty was

too severe.

---

Specific adjustment requested:
The Union and the aggrieved employees request they be rein-

stated with full seniority and be made whole for any loss

suffered as a result of this termination.

---

Aggrieved signatures:
/s/ Bonnie Mansoney, /s/ Alicia Coppan,

/s/ Deborah Matter, /s/ Lesley Cole, /s/ Megan Carfield

---

Received by Company Official (signature and date)
/s/ Ken Gooch, VP Operations          9/11/07

---

Step 3 Disposition:
The employees listed in the grievance were discharged for mis-

conduct on the picket line.  The Company has witnesses to these

actions and feels justified in not reinstating these employees.

Therefore, grievance must be denied.

---

| Company Official signature: | Date of disposition: |
|---|---|
| | 9/12/07 |
| /s/ Ken Gooch, Vice President, Operations | |

## *COMPANY EXHIBIT NO. 1*

Grievants Discharged:                              5/30/07

1.  Bonnie Mansoney

2.  Alicia Coppan

3.  Deborah Matter

4.  Lesley Cole

5.  Megan Carfield

The parties agree that the discharge of the above-mentioned
grievants shall be arbitrated upon a filing of a Step 3
grievance.


/s/ A. Tackett                      /s/ C. Bixland
    Company Attorney                         International Representative
    Price Plastics, Inc.                     Universal Union

/s/ Adam Shepmanson,
    Union Attorney

**PRICE PLASTICS, INC.**
**8206 South Verdi Drive**
**Hapville, Illinois**

May 15, year 7

Dear Fellow Employees:

We are running out of time.

While you have been on strike we have not been able to meet our customers' demands. Our customers have waited as long as they can. Unless we reach a settlement this week and get back into production, we have been told by several of our large customers that they will pull their dies. As of now these include: Standard 17" cabinet assembly, Norman Electric crisper cover, Liberty 17" front and back, and eight new Liberty panel dies. Approximately 50 employees will be out of work if these tools and dies are pulled. Once these jobs have been pulled, <u>there is no way to get them back</u>. The longer the strike continues, the more we can expect other customers to take their business elsewhere.

Unlike Bradford Company which makes its own products, we are a job shop. We make parts to our customers' orders, using <u>their</u> dies. If we fail to meet our customers' orders, they will simply move their dies elsewhere. We are faced with hundreds of competitors who would like nothing more than to take our customers' dies <u>and your jobs</u>.

On Monday, May 14, the Company representatives met with your bargaining committee for the eleventh time in an attempt to reach a contract settlement. We told your representatives again that the Company's economic offer which is now on the table contains all the Company can agree to pay. The package is a good one. Wages and fringes amount to an increase of <u>more than 11%</u> in the first year alone.

On Monday, we also told your committee the facts discussed above concerning the potential loss of business and jobs. If we fail to reach an agreement this week, the resulting loss of business will eliminate the Company's incentive to reach a settlement. Therefore, as of the end of this week, the company's proposal will be withdrawn.

We know that there is a vocal minority who have undermined every attempt to reach a settlement. We understand these "know-it-alls" have told anyone who would listen that the Company will offer a still larger package if <u>you</u> will just "hold out a little longer." <u>They are absolutely wrong</u>! <u>There is no more money</u>!

<u>*COMPANY EXHIBIT NO. 2 (continued)*</u>

Because of the seriousness of the situation, and because it is your job and the jobs of your friends which are at stake, I thought it necessary to report these facts to you directly. I hope that you will give this problem your most serious thought; I hope you will talk it over with your family; and I hope you will make your views known to your Union representative.

Very sincerely,


/s/ Russell G. Wessell
     President

_COMPANY EXHIBIT NO. 3_

**PRICE PLASTICS, INC.**
**8206 South Verdi Drive**
**Hapville, Illinois**

May 19, year 7

Dear Fellow Employee:

This is to inform you that we are not going to continue holding your job for you.

Our customers need the parts we make for them. We can keep our customers only if we deliver the parts that they need when they need them. Therefore, both you and management have a common obligation to our customers. Management is not willing to have Price Plastics, Inc., go out of business just because you have decided not to work because of the Union's strike.

We need people to run a business. Because of your experience in your job and service to the Company, we would hope that you would return to your job and help us meet our customers' needs. However, if you are unwilling to do so, we are going to find someone to take your place.

For these reasons, we are commencing immediately to hire replacements for all employees who remain on strike. The people we hire will be given permanent employment.

That means that when the strike is over, the Company will not be required to discharge the replacements to make way for strikers. It is entirely possible that strikers who have been replaced will never get their jobs back.

We regret that your Union thought this strike was necessary. We tried in good faith to make a contract with your Union which was both fair and equitable. The Company's offer of wage increases and fringe benefits was larger than most other settlements in the country. Your Union was not satisfied with our offer. The Union decided to call the strike in an attempt to force the Company to agree to completely unreasonable wage demands. The Company could not agree.

We would prefer not having to hire someone to take your place. It will not be necessary if you return to work. You have the right to decide for yourself whether you want to work or strike. No card you have signed, no oath you have taken, and no threat by anyone claiming to act for the Union can take away this right. The law guarantees you the right to choose. We hope you will choose to keep your job.

If you have any questions, please contact me or Mr. Hiller at the plant.

Very sincerely,


/s/ Russell G. Wessel
     President

## COMPANY EXHIBIT NO. 4A

STATE OF ILLINOIS    )
                     )    SS:
COUNTY OF BELL       )

IN THE BELL CIRCUIT COURT

PRICE PLASTICS, INC.,                          )
                                               )
                    Plaintiff,                 )
                                               )
                                               )
        v.                                     )
                                               )
                                               )
UNIVERSAL UNION OF FARM, SPACE, AND            )
AUTO WORKERS, LOCAL UNION 101, FRED            )
RUGMANS, JERI HIGHTE, TONI BENSON,             )
CARLY OTHERR, TAYLOR BORDICK, IRMA             )
PATMAN, EDITH FISHER, LENA EPIRES,             )
LORI MASTERSON, DYLAN ROMBS, TY                )
MARNELL, BELLA O'HARR, MYRNA                    )
STUDDERLAB, BONNIE MANSONEY, ALICIA            )
COPPAN, LESLEY COLE, DEBORAH MATTER,           )
MEGAN CARFIELD, Individually and as            )
representatives of the Universal Union         )
and Local Union No. 101,                       )
                                               )
                    Defendants.                )

## RESTRAINING ORDER

The plaintiff in this action, Price Plastics, Inc., has filed a duly verified Complaint for an Injunction seeking, among other relief, a temporary restraining order without notice. The Court has examined the plaintiff's complaint, has heard the evidence submitted on behalf of the plaintiff in support of its complaint and now finds that a restraining order without notice to the defendants should be entered immediately in this action. The Court has made and filed in the records of this action the findings of fact upon which the restraining order has been entered. The plaintiff has filed its bond, with Amax Casualty & Surety Company as surety thereon, in an amount which has been fixed by the Court and conditioned as required by statute.

## *COMPANY EXHIBIT NO. 4A (continued)*

IT IS THEREFORE ORDERED by this Court that the UNIVERSAL UNION, LOCAL UNION 101, FRED RUGMANS, JERI HIGHTE, TONI BENSON, CARLY OTHERR, TAYLOR BORDICK, IRMA PATMAN, EDITH FISHER, LENA EPIRES, LORI MASTERSON, DYLAN ROMBS, TY MARNELL, BELLA O'HARR, MYRNA STUDDERLAB, BONNIE MANSONEY, ALICIA COPPAN, LESLEY COLE, DEBORAH MATTER, MEGAN CARFIELD, Individually and as Representatives of the Universal Union and Local Union No. 101, all other members of the class comprising members, agents, employees, and representatives of the Universal Union and Local Union and all other persons acting on behalf of or in concert with them are hereby restrained and enjoined until further order of this Court from:


1.   Blocking the driveway and entrances to the place of business of the plaintiff, Price Plastics, Inc., in Hapville, Illinois;

2.   All mass picketing at, upon, or adjacent to the driveway and entrances to the plaintiff's place of business in Hapville, Illinois, which is defined herein as having more than five (5) persons at, upon, or adjacent to any driveway or entrance;

3.   Congregating or loitering at, upon, or about the plaintiff's place of business, on the streets and public right-of-way adjacent thereto or in the immediate neighborhood thereof in such numbers or acting in such manner as to threaten, intimidate, coerce, harass, or interfere with the plaintiff, its employees, or persons lawfully desiring and attempting to do business with the plaintiff;

### COMPANY EXHIBIT NO. 4A (continued)

4. Yelling, screaming, or shaking fists at employees of the plaintiff while they are attempting lawfully to enter or leave its place of business;

5. Pounding on, hitting, kicking, or otherwise touching the automobiles of plaintiff's employees or of any other persons while they are attempting to enter or leave the plaintiff's place of business;

6. Throwing nails, broken glass, or other similar objects in the driveway or entrances to the plaintiff's place of business;

7. Throwing rocks, bottles, or other similar objects at or against the automobiles of plaintiff's employees or of any other persons while they are attempting to enter or leave the plaintiff's place of business;

8. Threatening physical violence or injury to any employee of the plaintiff or to any person doing or attempting to do business with Price Plastics, Inc.;

9. Following any employees of the plaintiff or any person doing business or attempting to do business with the plaintiff for the purpose of threatening, intimidating, coercing, harassing, or otherwise interfering with that employee or person;

10. Trespassing at or upon the private premises or home of any employee of the plaintiff; and

11. Encouraging, aiding, or abetting any person in the commission of any act hereby restrained and enjoined.

## *COMPANY EXHIBIT NO. 4A (continued)*

IT IS FURTHER ORDERED that the plaintiff's application for a temporary injunction is hereby set for hearing at __2:00__ o'clock _p_ m. on the 30th day of May, year 07, and that service of this order will constitute notice to the defendants of the hearing.

IT IS FURTHER ORDERED that this restraining order shall expire and be void after the 30th day of May, year 07.

IT IS FURTHER ORDERED that the Clerk of this Court shall forthwith cause a copy of this restraining order to be served upon each of the named defendants, individually and as representatives of all members, agents, employees, and representatives of the Universal Union and the Local Union and shall deliver copies thereof to the Chief of Police of the City of Hapville, Illinois, the Prosecuting Attorney of Bell County, Illinois, and the Sheriff of Bell County, Illinois.

The Temporary Restraining Order is ENTERED this 25th day of May, year 07, at 6:30 p.m.

/s/ Hector Avariz
Judge, Bell Circuit Court

<u>*COMPANY EXHIBIT NO. 4B*</u>

```
STATE OF ILLINOIS      )
                       )     SS:
COUNTY OF BELL         )
```

IN THE BELL CIRCUIT COURT

```
PRICE PLASTICS, INC.,                         )
                                              )
                      Plaintiff,              )
                                              )
                                              )
          V.                                  )
                                              )
                                              )
UNIVERSAL UNION OF FARM, SPACE, AND           )
AUTO WORKERS, LOCAL UNION 101, FRED           )
RUGMANS, JERI HIGHTE, TONI BENSON,            )
CARLY OTHERR, TAYLOR BORDICK, IRMA            )
PATMAN, EDITH FISHER, LENA EPIRES,            )
LORI MASTERSON, DYLAN ROMBS, TY               )
MARNELL, BELLA O'HARR, MYRNA                  )
STUDDERLAB, BONNIE MANSONEY, ALICIA           )
COPPAN, LESLEY COLE, DEBORAH MATTER,          )
MEGAN CARFIELD, Individually and as           )
representatives of the Universal Union        )
and Local Union No. 101,                      )
                                              )
                      Defendants.             )
```

<u>FINDINGS OF FACT</u>

The above matter having been presented on plaintiff's duly verified complaint and evidence adduced in open court, the Court now, in accordance with the requirements of the statutes and prior to the issuing of a restraining order herein, makes and causes to be filed in the records of this Court the following Findings of Fact:

1. The plaintiff is an Illinois corporation having its place of business at 8206 South Verdi Drive, Hapville, Bell County, Illinois, where it engages in the business of manufacturing and selling molded plastic parts to its customers in the electronic and electric appliance industry and to customers in other industries.

35

## COMPANY EXHIBIT NO. 4B (continued)

2. The defendant Universal Union is a labor organization which transacts business within the state of Illinois and maintains an office at Augustus, Montrose County, Illinois. Local Union No. 101 is a labor organization which transacts business within Bell County, State of Illinois. The individual defendants, and each of them, are members, officers, representatives, and agents of the Universal Union and the Local Union and are made defendants herein both individually and as representatives of a class comprising all members, agents, employees, and representatives of the Universal Union and the Local Union, who are too numerous to be brought before the Court. The following individual defendants hold the offices of the Local Union set opposite their names, respectively:

| | |
|---|---|
| Toni Benson | President |
| Irma Patman | Vice-president |
| Carly Otherr | Financial Secretary |
| Bella O'Harr | Secretary |

At all times mentioned herein the individual defendants acted individually and as agents of the defendant unions.

3. The Universal Union has been, since it was certified by the National Labor Relations Board on October 7, year 1, the exclusive representative for purposes of collective bargaining of a unit of employees of the plaintiff comprising, "employees of the Company at its plant located at Hapville, Illinois, excluding, however, office clerical employees, engineers, professional employees, time study and timekeepers, watchmen and guards, foremen and all other supervisory employees. . . ."

4. Since year 0, the plaintiff has entered into a number of collective bargaining agreements with the Universal Union and its Local Union No. 101 covering the employees in the unit described in the foregoing paragraph 3. The last such contract expired March 31, year 7. Since February 20, year 7, and continuing thereafter to the present, the plaintiff has bargained in good faith with the defendant unions in an attempt to negotiate a new collective bargaining agreement. The last bargaining meeting occurred on May 18, year 7.

5. Commencing on or about April 6, year 7, and continuing to the present, the defendants, and each of them, have engaged in a strike against the plaintiff, and they have picketed and congregated in and about the entrances to the plaintiff's place of business and interfered with the plaintiff's lawful use of and access to the place of business.

6. Since April 6, year 7, the defendants and other persons who were acting on behalf of and in concert with the defendants, but whose identities are not known to the plaintiff, have engaged in the following acts and conduct:

(a) Blocking the driveway and entrances to the plaintiff's place of business by mass picketing, thereby interfering with the rights of the plaintiff, its employees, and other persons lawfully desiring to do business with the plaintiff to enter and leave the plaintiff's place of business;

(b) Yelling, screaming, shaking fists, and otherwise threatening and attempting to threaten employees of the plaintiff and other persons while they were attempting lawfully to enter the plaintiff's place of business through the mass picketing;

## COMPANY EXHIBIT NO. 4B (continued)

(c) Threatening and intimidating employees of the plaintiff by hitting, kicking, and pounding on the automobiles of plaintiff's employees and other persons while they were attempting to enter or leave the plaintiff's place of business through the mass picketing;

(d) Causing damage to the automobiles of the plaintiff, the plaintiff's employees, and other persons while they were attempting to enter or leave the plaintiff's place of business through the mass picketing by throwing rocks, bottles, and other objects at and against the automobiles and by using various sharp objects to scratch the exterior finish of the automobiles;

(e) Threatening physical violence and injury to the plaintiff's employees and other persons who have attempted to work for or to do business with the plaintiff;

(f) Following plaintiff's employees and other persons as they leave the plaintiff's place of business, stopping or blocking them as they attempted lawfully to travel on the public right-of-way, and otherwise interfering with those employees and persons, all for the purpose of threatening, intimidating, and coercing them;

(g) Throwing nails, broken glass, and other similar objects in the driveway and entrances to the plaintiff's place of business;

(h) Congregating and loitering at, upon, and about the plaintiff's place of business, on the streets and public right-of-way adjacent to the plaintiff's place of business and intimidating, coercing, harassing, and interfering with the plaintiff, its employees, and persons lawfully desiring and attempting to do business with the plaintiff.

7. As a result of the mass picketing, threats, vandalism, violence, and other acts and conduct described in the foregoing paragraph 6, the defendants have intimidated and prevented employees of the plaintiff who desire to continue to work for the plaintiff from entering the plaintiff's place of business for the purpose of performing their work. Other persons have been prevented from doing business with the plaintiff. The plaintiff has been prevented from obtaining from vendors, suppliers, carriers, and other persons the goods and services required to carry on the plaintiff's business.

8. Unless the mass picketing, threats, vandalism, violence, and other acts and conduct described in the foregoing paragraph 6 are restrained, substantial and irreparable injury to the plaintiff's property and business will result. Substantial injury has already been done to the plaintiff's property and its business, and the plaintiff has been prevented, and will be prevented, unless the defendants are restrained, from enjoying the full use of and access to its place of business in Hapville, Illinois.

9. As to each item of relief prayed for herein, greater injury will be inflicted on plaintiff by denial of the relief than will be inflicted upon the defendants by granting the relief. The defendants will not be damaged or sustain any injury or be prevented from performing any lawful act by the granting of the relief prayed for herein.

## *COMPANY EXHIBIT NO. 4B (continued)*

10. The plaintiff has no adequate remedy at law.

11. The public officers charged with the duty of protecting the plaintiff's property have been unable to furnish adequate protection.

12. The plaintiff has not failed or refused to comply with any obligation imposed on it by law, nor has the plaintiff failed to make every reasonable effort to settle the labor dispute in question by negotiation by utilizing the aid of all available governmental machinery of mediation.

13. Unless a temporary restraining order without notice is issued, a substantial and irreparable injury to the plaintiff's business and property will be unavoidable.


                                        /s/ Hector Avariz
                                        Judge, Bell Circuit Court


Date:        May 25, year 7

COMPANY EXHIBIT NO. 5

May 30, year 7

Price Plastics, Inc.
Hapville, Illinois

Attention:  Mr. Ronald Hiller
            Executive Vice President
            A&LP

Dear Sir:

This is to inform you that following the acceptance made on 29th May, year 7, of the Company offer of a contract which theretofore had been made, the strike has been terminated and all employee-members have been instructed to report for work at their regular shift times on 31st May, year 7.

Each employee will individually report, but this offer is also made on behalf of each employee-member.

Please let us know when a meeting should be arranged for the formal signing of the agreed contract.

/s/ Earl Bixland
Universal International Representative

_COMPANY EXHIBIT NO. 6_

**PRICE PLASTICS, INC.**
**8206 South Verdi Drive**
**Hapville, Illinois**

August 29, year 7

Mr. Earl Bixland, International Representative
Universal Union and its Local Union No. 101
107 East 81st Street
Augustus, Illinois

    This is to confirm the oral agreement among the
representatives of Price Plastics, Inc., and the and Local Union
No. 101 and the Universal Union concerning the grievances over
conduct, actions, and omissions occurring during the period
between Collective Bargaining Agreements.  Any grievances
protesting the Company's refusal to reinstate a striker or the
discipline of any employee during the period from April 6, to the
effective date of the new agreement, August 29, year 7, if
otherwise properly presented, will be considered timely if
presented to the Company within fifteen calendar days after the
effective date of the Collective Bargaining Agreement and will be
processed in accordance with Step 3 of the procedures established
by Articles 5 and 6 of the Agreement.

                              Sincerely,


                              /s/ Ronald Hiller
                                  Vice President
                                  Administration and Labor Relations

COMPANY EXHIBIT NO. 7

May 30, year 7

Mr. Earl Bixland, Universal Representative
Universal Union and its Local Union No. 101
107 East 81st Street
Augustus, Illinois

Re:  Price Plastics, Inc.

Dear Mr. Bixland:

This is to acknowledge receipt of your letter addressed to Price Plastics, Inc., dated May 30, year 7, terminating your strike against the corporation.  In accordance with the discussion with you and your counsel on May 30, your letter is deemed to be an unconditional offer to return to work on behalf of all striking employees of the corporation.  Consequently, in accordance with that discussion, it will not be necessary for all strikers to present themselves in person to manifest their availability for work.

In accordance with our oral agreement today, strikers will be offered reinstatement in the order of their seniority.

Very truly yours,

/s/ Adam Tackett
Attorney
Price Plastics, Inc.

cc: Robert Shepmanson, Esq.
Ronald A. Hiller

*COMPANY EXHIBIT NO. 8*

```
ANNOUNCEMENTS
PUBLIC NOTICE
PRODUCTION WORKERS
ON ALL SHIFTS AT PRICE PLASTICS
MEMBERS OF LOCAL UNION 101
ARE STILL ON STRIKE
LOCAL UNION NO. 101, UNIVERSAL UNION
```

From Hapville *JOURNAL*

May 31, year 7

Page 26

*COMPANY EXHIBIT NO. 9*

```
HELP WANTED
PRODUCTION WORKERS
ALL SHIFTS

Apply Personnel Office
Price Plastics, Inc.
8206 South Verdi Drive
Hapville, Illinois
```

From Hapville *JOURNAL*

May 31, year 7

Page 36

| DECISION OF APPEALS REFEREE | CLAIM NO. 4/2 83 0 | CASE NO. A-2047 REC. 8-8-07 |
|---|---|---|
| IN THE MATTER OF:  APPELLATE SECTION | SOC. SEC. # 111-222-333 | DATE FILED 6-4-07 |

CLAIMANT:

Megan Carfield
R.R. No. 12
Hapsville, Illinois

| | DEPUTY'S DETERMINATION 8-6-07 |
|---|---|
| | APPEAL FILED 8-7-07 / HEARING DATE 9-10-07 |
| | DECISION MAILED: 9-25-07 |
| | REFEREE Harman / REPORTER Cassette |

EMPLOYER:

Price Plastics, Inc.
8206 South Verdi Drive
Hapsville, Illinois

REFERRED FOR INITIAL DETERMINATION ON:

_Note: the following decision is final unless the claimant, or the employer involved, if any, appeals therefrom to the Review Board in the manner & form provided by law and regulation within 15 days after the mailing date hereof._

STATUTORY PROVISIONS INVOLVED:  Illinois Code YR05, Title V, Article D, Chapter O, Section A, of the Illinois Employment Security Act.  Also, Regulation HBD of the Illinois Employment Security Board.

SUMMARY OF CASE:  This is an appeal by the claimant from the determination that she was discharged on May 30, year 7, for just cause.  Both parties appeared at the hearing scheduled on September 10, year 7.  The claimant was represented by Leonard Myles, attorney.

The weight of the evidence supports the finding that on May 21, year 7, the claimant, while picketing on company premises, bent the license plate of a worker leaving the employer's plant; that on May 22, year 7, again while picketing on company premises, the claimant threw an egg on a worker's car.  She last worked on April 6, year 7.

Her discharge for just cause is held valid under the Code.  It is deemed that the claimant's acts did not fall within the scope of lawful picketing.

### COMPANY EXHIBIT NO. 10 (continued)

DECISION:   The determination of the deputy is modified to show
            that the claimant was discharged on May 30, year 7, but
            effective as of April 6, year 7, the last day worked, and as
            modified is affirmed.   The statutory disqualification is
            imposed.

DATED at Augustus, Illinois this 24th day of September, year 7

                                   /s/ Edgar N. Harman
                                       Referee

## *COMPANY EXHIBIT NO. 11*

| | CLAIM NO. 4/2 83 0 | CASE NO. A-2047 REC. 8-8-07 |
|---|---|---|
| **DECISION OF APPEALS REFEREE** | | |
| IN THE MATTER OF:    APPELLATE SECTION | SOC. SEC. # 222-333-444 | DATE FILED 6-4-07 |
| CLAIMANT: | DEPUTY'S DETERMINATION 8-6-07 | |
| Alicia Coppan 760 North Dahl Hapsville, Illinois | APPEAL FILED 8-7-07 | HEARING DATE 9-10-07 |
| | DECISION MAILED: 9-25-07 | |
| | REFEREE Harman | REPORTER Cassette |
| EMPLOYER: | REFERRED FOR INITIAL DETERMINATION ON: | |
| Price Plastics, Inc. 8206 South Verdi Drive Hapsville, Illinois | *Note: the following decision is final unless the claimant, or the employer involved, if any, appeals therefrom to the Review Board in the manner & form provided by law and regulation within 15 days after the mailing date hereof.* | |

STATUTORY PROVISIONS INVOLVED:  Illinois Code YR05, Title V, Article D, Chapter O, Section A, of the Illinois Employment Security Act.  (See attached page.) Also, Regulation HBD of the Illinois Employment Security Board.

SUMMARY OF CASE:  This is an appeal by the claimant from the determination that she was discharged on May 30, YR07 for just cause.  Both parties appeared at the hearing scheduled on September 10, year 7.  The claimant was represented by Leonard Myles, attorney.

The weight of the evidence supports the finding that the claimant was discharged from her job while she was on the picket line established on company premises and after she had used a sharp object to scratch a company car leaving the premises.  The repairs cost approximately $68.  The claimant last worked on April 6, year 7.

It is deemed that the claimant's acts amounted to misconduct.  Her discharge for just cause is held valid under the Code.

**COMPANY EXHIBIT NO. 11 (continued)**

DECISION:  The determination of the deputy is modified to show
     that the claimant was discharged on May 30, year 7, but
     effective as of April 6, year 7, the last day worked, and as
     modified is affirmed.  The statutory disqualification is
     imposed.

DATED at Augustus, Illinois, this 24th day of September, year 7.

                         /s/  Edgar Harman
                              Referee

# Cardinal Power Company

**Table of Contents**

**Table of Contents contd.**

**NOTES**

# A. Caption

IN THE MATTER OF ARBITRATION BETWEEN:

CARDINAL POWER COMPANY )
BLOOMFIELD, NEW HAMPSHIRE )
  )
  )
  )
AND )      RE: Demotion (Reclassification)
  )
  )
  )
I.P.W.U )
LOCAL UNION No. 19932 )

Appearances:

For the Company: Erik Weigle

For the Union: Janet Alton

Date: April 26, year 4

Place: Bloomfield, New Hampshire

## B. Examination of Company Witnesses

### 1. Donald McFare, General Superintendent

a. Direct Examination by Company Advocate

*Mr. Weigle:*

Q: Will you state your name, please, and where you are from?

A: Donald J. McFare, Ballardsville, New Hampshire.

Q: And your position with Cardinal Power?

A: General Superintendent.

Q: As General Superintendent do you have supervision over the employees Curt Burk and Peter Pious?

A: Yes.

Q: During the time the Company employed Mr. Pious?

A: Right.

Q: Prior to December year 2, who handled substation maintenance within your organization?

A: Three substation foremen: one at Kaswell, one at Napier, and one at Bloomfield.

Q: Were these people classified as Substation Maintenance Working Foremen?

A: Yes.

Q: Did they have crews to supervise?

A: Only the one out of Bloomfield had crews to supervise.

Q: Prior to December year 2, where were Mr. Burk and Mr. Pious stationed?

A: Kaswell and Napier.

Q: And what did their duties include at those posts?

A: To maintain substations, distribution, and primary transmission.

Q: Was there a written job description for Substation Maintenance Working Foreman?

A: Yes.

Q: I hand you what's been marked Company Exhibit 1A and ask whether or not that constitutes that written description?

A: That's correct. It does.

Q: These foremen did not have crews?

A: No.

Q: Why didn't they?

A: There was no need of any added substation personnel in those areas. We were in the period of adding stations and facilities and there weren't enough facilities to justify any other help in those areas.

Q: In December year 2, did management make a decision which changed the use of substation maintenance personnel?

A: Yes. Originally engineering services had the direction of all operations. In October of year 2, the Company separated the engineering department and Mr. Gambel came in as manager of the operations department.

Q: In December year 2, there was a posting for a Substation Maintenance Working Foreman in the Bloomfield area, is that correct?

A: Yes. The vacancy was created when the Substation Maintenance Working Foreman at Bloomfield moved into a supervisory capacity as a transmission supervisor.

Q: At that time, did the Company contemplate any changes in the duties of the replacement?

A: No. The duties were to continue as before.

Q: And what was he to supervise?

A: The Bloomfield area and, in some cases, at Kaswell or Napier.

Q: Would you explain that, please?

A: Most all the heavy equipment that's used for heavy maintenance in our substations is stationed at Bloomfield and the crews would be sent out of here with the equipment. The Substation Maintenance Working Foreman in a lot of cases would go with his crew and do the foremanship work on that particular station. Let me state it this way—we may have some work in the Peterson area, and the substation crew here at Bloomfield would go down to do the work; if the substation man that's located there had an emergency, he was free to get out on that job right away.

Q: Around December year 2, did the Company discuss the efficiency of this system and what would be the most desirable stationing of substation personnel?

**A:** Around that time, the Company upgraded supervisory personnel, split up transmission and substations, divided the organization working arrangements, and put in an electrical supervisor who supervises the substation area.

**Q:** Where did the Company decide was the most efficient location of substation personnel?

**A:** Bloomfield.

**Q:** Was that for all substation personnel?

**A:** No, a portion of them. We were not required to comply with the FPC ruling until June year 3. Until then we made a gradual change in order to get full use out of our personnel and to give the best service possible.

**Q:** Does the stationing of personnel affect concerns of personnel safety or equipment safety?

**A:** No, it doesn't.

**Q:** Why was this move more efficient?

**A:** From central headquarters, orders would be given on a day-to-day basis. Equipment and materials would be located there. We would have better utilization of manpower and vehicles. It would permit better person-to-person contact with our people.

**Q:** Did you receive bids from employees within the Cardinal system to fill the Bloomfield vacancy?

**A:** Yes, we received one bid. Mr. Richard Dixon.

**Q:** What happened?

**A:** We determined that Dixon was not qualified for the position and we contacted an experienced employee, Mr. Pious, about taking the position.

**Q:** What did you tell Mr. Pious?

**A:** We said he could continue to stay at Napier. With the communications systems we have in place, he would perform his supervisory responsibilities from Napier.

**Q:** Why did you allow Mr. Pious to stay in Napier?

**A:** We tried to accommodate his desire to remain living in Napier. Mr. Pious was very well qualified for this position. He had been a Substation Maintenance Mechanic A for years. He was an outstanding employee.

**Q:** I hand you Company Exhibit 1B and ask you whether that constitutes a written description of the Substation Maintenance Mechanic Class A job?

**A:** Yes, it does.

**Q:** When did Mr. Pious assume the vacated position of Substation Maintenance Working Foreman?

**A:** I believe it was in February year 3. I issued an interoffice memo on February 8, year 3, indicating that he would be assuming that position.

**Q:** This has been marked as Company Exhibit 2. Do you recognize this as the memo?

**A:** Yes.

**Q:** What happened to Mr. Pious regarding the duties described in Company Exhibit 2?

**A:** He assumed those duties initially, but in late March or early April year 3 he said he didn't want those duties any longer, after we asked him to relocate to Bloomfield after all.

**Q:** Did he agree to take a pay cut back to Maintenance-Mechanic A if he could stay at Napier?

**A:** Yes, I wrote him a confirmation letter on April 21, year 3.

**Q:** This is Company Exhibit 3. Is this the letter you wrote?

**A:** Yes.

**Q:** Did you then eliminate the position of Substation Maintenance Working Foreman?

**A:** Yes.

**Q:** This arrangement obviously left your Bloomfield position vacant again, correct?

**A:** Yes.

**Q:** What did you do about filling it?

**A:** I wrote a letter to Curt Burk about the position at Bloomfield. If he decided against the Bloomfield position, I offered him the alternative of remaining where he was in Kaswell, as a Maintenance Mechanic Class A, instead of staying there as a Substation Maintenance Working Foreman, since that job was being phased out.

**Q:** That letter has been marked as Company Exhibit 4. Why did you offer him this alternative instead of just assigning him to Bloomfield as a Substation Maintenance Working Foreman?

**A:** In the interest of fairness. If we hadn't offered him the alternative I imagine we would have let him go.

**Q:** Did Mr. Burk accept the Bloomfield position?

**A:** No, he didn't respond to the letter so I assumed that he wanted to stay at Kaswell.

3

**Q:** So your position is that the two grievants, Pious and Burk, voluntarily accepted the classification to Maintenance Mechanic A, the position they held when they filed their qrievance?

**A:** Yes.

**Q:** Did you subsequently send a letter marked Company Exhibit 5 to Mr. Burk on May 19, year 3, regarding a move to Bloomfield?

**A:** Yes. I sent it to Mr. Burk, and the same letter to Mr. Pious, and other substation personnel.

**Q:** Why did the Company make this decision?

**A:** To bring our substation people into Bloomfield and increase efficiency and supervision.

**Q:** Did the Company issue a guideline on June 1, year 3, regarding the move? This is Company Exhibit 6.

**A:** Yes. Effective September 1, year 3, all substation personnel were to work out of Bloomfield.

**Q:** Has this decision been implemented?

**A:** No, this grievance has delayed the implementation.

**Q:** Are you aware of any guarantee made by Cardinal management that the grievants, while in the position of Substation Maintenance Working Foreman, would not be moved?

**A:** No.

**Q:** Is there a specific provision in the Collective Bargaining Agreement which covers demotions?

**A:** No, just promotions.

**Q:** What gave you the right to demote Pious and Burk?

**A:** The employer's inherent right to manage, including the guidelines and job description for the position in question.

**Q:** That is all.

### b. Cross-Examination by Union Advocate

*Ms. Alton:*
[to be supplied by student]

## 2. Sam Gambel, Manager of Operations

### a. Direct Examination by Company Advocate

*Mr. Weigle:*

**Q:** Will you state your name, and address, please?

**A:** Sam Gambel, Bloomfield, New Hampshire.

**Q:** What is your position at Cardinal Power?

**A:** Manager of Operations.

**Q:** Were Mr. Burk and Mr. Pious doing essentially the same work as a Substation Maintenance Mechanic Class A during the time they were listed as, and received the pay of, Substation Maintenance Working Foreman?

**A:** Yes.

**Q:** Why was it that they were listed as Substation Working Maintenance Foremen and yet they were not supervising men?

**A:** When Cardinal started, the plan was to have substation crews at the five major

stations, namely, Kaswell, Peterson, Washington, Finch, and Napier.

**Q:** Was this plan implemented?

**A:** No, we have no major operation at those locations and it would be inefficient for us to have crews located at them.

**Q:** Did you change your plan?

**A:** Yes. We decided that if all of our crews are at one location, we would have more flexibility and centralization. That location would be Bloomfield.

**Q:** So far as you know about the development of Cardinal, now and in the future, you do not see any efficient reason for having a crew at Kaswell for Mr. Burk to supervise?

**A:** It is not economically feasible for us to operate like that.

Q:  And is your judgment the same about having a crew at Napier for Mr. Pious?

A:  Yes.

Q:  I have no further questions.

## b. Cross-Examination by Union Advocate

*Ms. Alton:*
[to be supplied by student]

## C. Examination of Union Witnesses

## *1. Curt Burk, Grievant*

### a. Direct Examination by Union Advocate

*Ms. Alton:*

Q:  Will you state your name, please?

A:  Curtis Burk.

Q:  Where do you live?

A:  Kaswell, New Hampshire.

Q:  And by whom are you employed?

A:  Cardinal Power.

Q:  What is your present job classification?

A:  Substation Maintenance Mechanic Class A.

Q:  What was your prior job classification?

A:  Substation Maintenance Working Foreman.

Q:  When did your classification change?

A:  As of the first of May, year 3.

Q:  When you were hired what pay classification did you receive?

A:  Substation Maintenance Working Foreman.

Q:  Where did the Company assign you?

A:  Kaswell.

Q:  Who was your supervisor?

A:  My immediate supervisor was Don Shole.

Q:  You were to be a Substation Maintenance Working Foreman?

A:  Yes.

Q:  Did you receive any assurances from Cardinal?

A:  At the time I went to Kaswell, I was assured that I would be permanently located in Kaswell. It was important to me because at that time I was paying rent and before I bought a home there I was assured that it would be a permanent location.

Q:  Do you have a house and family at Kaswell?

A:  Yes.

Q:  How long had you been working as a Substation Maintenance Working Foreman before your classification was changed to the lower paying position?

A:  Four years.

Q:  Have your duties substantially changed?

A:  Not particularly, no.

Q:  No further questions.

## b. Cross-Examination by Company Advocate

*Mr. Weigle:*
[to be supplied by student]

## 2. Peter Pious, Grievant

### a. Direct Examination by Union Advocate

*Ms. Alton:*

**Q:** What is your name and address?

**A:** Peter Pious, 615 Arlington, New Town, New Hampshire.

**Q:** How long have you been working at Cardinal Power?

**A:** Four years.

**Q:** And when did you resign?

**A:** September of this year, year 4.

**Q:** What was the classification you had when you resigned?

**A:** Substation Maintenance Mechanic Class A.

**Q:** What was your classification prior to that?

**A:** Substation Maintenance Working Foreman.

**Q:** Where were you stationed?

**A:** I was originally stationed at Finch, and then at Napier, then at Bloomfield, and then back to Napier.

**Q:** What was your classification at all of these locations?

**A:** Substation Working Maintenance Foreman, except for my last stint at Napier.

**Q:** Were you ever given any indication that Napier was a permanent position for you?

**A:** Yes. As a matter of fact, I made this quite clear that, being in the ministry, I could not move from one locality to another, which warranted my resigning from the Company. At the time the Company asked me to move to Napier, I made them put this in writing so that I would not have to move.

**Q:** Who put this in writing?

**A:** Mr. Paul Perley.

**Q:** This is Union Exhibit 1. Is this the letter from Mr. Perley?

**A:** Yes.

**Q:** You resigned two months after you were demoted from Substation Maintenance Working Foreman to Substation Maintenance Mechanic Class A?

**A:** Yes. At the time I was stationed at Napier.

**Q:** No further questions.

### b. Cross-Examination by Company Advocate

*Mr. Weigle:*

[to be supplied by student]

## 3. Herbert Ellio, Union Business Manager

### a. Direct Examination by Union Advocate

*Ms. Alton:*

**Q:** Would you give us your full name?

**A:** Herbert Ellio.

**Q:** Do you have a position in the Union?

**A:** Yes, Business Manager.

**Q:** As Business Manager, would you be in a position to see and review Company proposals?

**A:** Yes.

**Q:** I would show you this document, marked as Union Exhibit 2, and ask if you recognize what it is?

**A:** It's a proposal from the Company to the Union in year 1, for a provision to be put in the Collective Bargaining Agreement which the Union rejected. Neither that proposal nor any similar proposal was put into the Collective Bargaining Agreement.

**Q:** No further questions.

b. Cross-Examination by Company Advocate

*Mr. Weigle:*
[to be supplied by student]

## 4. James Ridge, Union Steward

### a. Direct Examination by Union Advocate

*Ms. Alton:*
**Q:** Will you state your name, please?
**A:** James Ridge.
**Q:** And where do you live?
**A:** Bloomfield, New Hampshire.
**Q:** Where are you employed?
**A:** Cardinal Power.
**Q:** Do you have a position with the Union?
**A:** I'm Steward for outside personnel.
**Q:** In your position as a Steward or in your position as a member of the Union, have there been any discussions over the past two years about moving or about the Company assigning employees to different areas?
**A:** Yes.
**Q:** How long ago?
**A:** It was at a meeting about a month prior to the date on the letter from Mr. Perley to Mr. Pious, which is Union Exhibit 1. It was around June year 1.
**Q:** Who was at that meeting?
**A:** Mr. Perley from the Company, and all outside employees, including Mr. Pious and Mr. Burk and myself.
**Q:** What was the agreement, if any, arrived at during that meeting?

**A:** During the reorganization, Mr. Perley drew up a new schedule or organizational chart for the Company. He said that employees would be requested to move, but that the employees didn't have to move if they didn't want to.
**Q:** Was there any discussion between management and the Union or management and employees about moves after this period of time?
**A:** None whatsoever. The plan presented by Perley was supposed to be the ultimate regroup of Cardinal.
**Q:** What is the basis of the grievance of Pious and Burk and what remedy are they requesting?
**A:** As we indicated in the grievance, the basis of the grievance is the Agreement the Company had with them when they were made Substation Maintenance Working Foremen initially and the absence of contact language to support the Company's demotion of them. As for the remedy, they request to be reinstated as Substation Maintenance Working Foremen at Napier and Kaswell as they had been initially.
**Q:** No further questions.

### b. Cross-Examination by Company Advocate

*Mr. Weigle:*
[to be supplied by student]

## 5. James Hobe, Union Business Representative

### a. Direct Examination by Union Advocate

*Ms. Alton:*
**Q:** Would you state your name, please?
**A:** James Hobe.
**Q:** And your address?

**A:** 113 Maplewood Drive, Clark, New Hampshire.
**Q:** Who is your employer?
**A:** The Union.

**Q:** What is your position?

**A:** Business Representative.

**Q:** Did you represent the Union at any phase of this grievance?

**A:** Yes. The Union business office became involved at the third step, and I was present at the third step meeting.

**Q:** Was there anyone else in the room present at that meeting?

**A:** Mr. Ellio, Mr. Baler, Mr. Burk, Mr. Pious, Mr. Ridge, Mr. Davis, and Mr. Gambel. Mr. McFare was there for part of the time.

**Q:** Did you ask the Company representatives what contractual basis they had for the assignment of personnel and the resulting demotion?

**A:** Yes, I did, and they did not respond to my question.

**Q:** Could they give you any authority whatsoever for what they had done to the grievant?

**A:** Well, at the same meeting they indicated that they had no knowledge of the Company proposal in Union Exhibit 2. They did say the same language was in the Company Personnel Policy Guide.

**Q:** Is the Personnel Policy Guide incorporated into the Collective Bargaining Agreement?

**A:** No, it's not. In fact the Union has never seen it.

**Q:** No further questions.

---

b. Cross-Examination by Company Advocate

---

*Mr. Weigle:*
[to be supplied by student]

8

# D. Exhibits

## *JOINT EXHIBIT NO. 1*

COLLECTIVE BARGAINING AGREEMENT
BETWEEN
CARDINAL POWER COMPANY
AND
I.P.W.U. LOCAL UNION NO. 19932 (8/01/01-8/01/04)

· · ·

10. In filling vacancies or newly created positions, promotions shall be by departments based on seniority, ability and qualifications being sufficient, seniority shall prevail.

(a) If there are no qualified employees in the department under consideration who will accept the promotion, then promotions shall apply to employees in the remaining departments.
   When it is necessary to add employees and employees who have been laid off are called back when they have not lost their seniority, they shall have the right to exercise their seniority over those of lesser seniority in the vacancy to be filled or the new position.

(b) Should an employee deny a promotion, it shall have no effect on his future promotions.

(c) When vacancies occur or when new positions are created within the department the Company will post a notice on bulletin boards for a period of five (5) days (Sundays and holidays excluded) announcing the position open. Employees desiring to be considered shall make written application to the Manager. When necessary, temporary assignment will be made for the period the position is considered open.

11. Within the first six (6) months, after an employee has been promoted to a different classification, the Company may demote the employee to his former job classification if it determines that the employee has not established his ability to meet the job requirement subject to the grievance procedure. In the event an employee is demoted, he shall have included in his seniority in the job classification to which he is returned, the time spent by him in the job classification to which he was promoted.

· · ·

34. (a) Each employee shall supply his own meal, except:

1. When called out with less than one hour notice in advance of their normal starting time.

2. When it is necessary that employees continue work for more than one (1) hour after their regular quitting time, they shall be furnished a meal at the Company's expense and at intervals of not more than five (5) hours thereafter, while they continue to work, with no less pay. When called out more than one (1) hour in advance of normal starting time, employees shall be furnished a meal as soon as possible.

9

3. When required to work outside his headquarters area.

4. When work consists of two (2) or more days, ten (10) or more hours per day the Company reserves the right to decide whether or not the employees shall be returned to working head quarters or housed over night, in which case Company will provide meals and lodging; the employees to be advised before quitting time the day previous that they will be required to remain overnight the following day.

(b) The headquarters areas consist of an area 30 miles in radius from Bloomfield, Napier, Finch, Kaswell, and Henderson; provided, however, that the Union recognizes the right of the Company from time to time during the existence of this contract and as efficient operations make it desirable to so do, to change the headquarters areas established herein.

## CREATION OF JOB CLASSIFICATIONS

• • •

44. The Company agrees to establish job specifications for the job classifications set forth in wage scale TL and wage scale TP (which provides for the wage scale rate) and further agrees to make the job specifications available for inspection by the Union.

In the event that the Company desires to create a new job classification covering work of a kind and character to be performed by Union employees, the Company shall give the Union written notice of its intention after which it may proceed to create, evaluate and establish job specifications for the new job classifications.

The Company shall, after evaluation and establishment of job classifications, give the Union notice thereof along with the wage scale rate for said new job classification and shall review the new job classification with the Union unless the Union waives such review.

If after review of the new job classification and job specifications applicable thereto the Company and the Union are not in agreement as to the wage scale rate for such job classification, then either the Company or the Union at any time within ten (10) days after either of them has given the other written notice of such disagreement, may request in writing that said matter be arbitrated and in such event the matter shall be submitted to arbitration in a manner consistent with Step 4 of Section 12.

### *JOINT EXHIBIT NO. 2*

CARDINAL POWER COMPANY     I.P.W.U. LOCAL UNION 19932

### GRIEVANCE

Complaint: Improper Demotion (Reclassification)

Request: To be made whole.

ANSWER: Grievance Denied.

*COMPANY EXHIBIT NO. 1A*

CARDINAL POWER

JOB SPECIFICATION

SUBSTATION MAINTENANCE WORKING FOREMAN

**DUTIES:**
Under supervision, to direct, oversee and lead in the operations
required in executing assignments for the maintenance, relocation,
rearrangement and assigned phases of the construction of
substations, to read blueprints and wiring diagrams, to handle
arrangements preliminary to execution of field work, to train and
instruct assigned employees, to verify that completed work meets
company requirements and to perform other related work.

1.   Direct and oversee the work of assigned employees grouped at
different working sites and either engaged in maintaining
substation grounds, structures and equipment in operating condition
or in relocating, rearranging or performing assigned construction
work on substation installation, reviewing work order details and
ascertaining related requirements, planning execution of work,
arranging for removal of equipment from service and for proper
clearances and observing that clearances are effective, assigning
work with explanations of hazards, special precautions and unusual
requirements, verifying that instructions are understood and
delegating such of these preliminaries as may be feasible.

2.   Read substation construction blueprints, check circuit and
equipment identification labels and observe accuracy of drawings,
preparing requests for labels, submitting sketches for changes in
drawings and maintaining working files of drawings at specified
locations.

3.   Inspect substation equipment installation assemblies and
equipment parts and circuits, observe indications or evidence of
defects, testing, and check continuity of circuits. Report the
findings and arrange for correction of the defects.

4.   Oversee and engage in the maintenance, repair and replacement
of substation electrical apparatus and associated mechanisms,
dismantling and reassembling the defective units, repairing,
reconditioning or renewing parts and fitting and adjusting these
parts on such equipment items as transformers, air break switches,
oil circuit breakers, lightning arresters, voltage regulators,
apparatus cable, wiring and conduit, bus bars and related
insulators and supports.

## COMPANY EXHIBIT NO. 1B

CARDINAL POWER COMPANY
SUBSTATION MAINTENANCE MECHANIC CLASS A

**DUTIES:**

Under indirect supervision with a minimum of direction, to lead and engage in operations required in maintaining substation sites, structures and equipment in operating condition, to read blueprints and wiring diagrams, to handle as delegated, assigned phases of construction work and arrangements preliminary to execution of field work, to handle service restoration operations, to aid in training and instructing assisting employees and to perform other related work.

1. Handle, in accordance with specific instructions and as delegated, basic arrangements preliminary to the execution of limited field assignments, directing the handling of materials, performing switching when necessary, obtaining clearances, grounding circuits, installing protective devices and placing hold cards and lay out plan of work.

2. Inspect substation equipment assemblies, equipment units and associated wiring and buses, observing indications or evidence of defects, testing and checking circuit continuities, reporting the findings and procceding with, or referring to others, correction of observed defects.

3. Perform, or as required, designate, the sequence of operations required in repairing, replacing and maintaining substation electrical apparatus and associated mechanisms, dismantling and reassembling defective units, reconditioning or renewing parts and fitting and adjusting these parts for such equipment items as transformers, air break switches, oil circuit breakers, lighting arresters, voltage regulators, apparatus cable, conduit and wiring, bus bars and related insulators and supports.

4. Direct or lead in various operations for maintaining substation grounds, fences and structures in proper condition, fertilizing, reseeding and cutting lawn plots, reconditioning crushed stone surfaces, filling holes and depressions, repairing damaged fencing, open closed drains, replacing broken glass, scraping and repainting surfaces and making minor repairs to structures.

5. Perform and lead in a variety of maintenance operations such as changing and filtering oil, changing transformer tap-settings, maintaining supervisory control installations, adjusting contacts, observing assuracy of drawings and wiring diagrams, preparing requests for labels, submitting sketches for drawing changes and field checking completed work.

**SUPERVISOR:** Substation Maintenance Working Foreman

**SUPERVISOR:** Maintenance Superintendent

**DIRECTS:** Substation Maintenance Mechanics Class A

*COMPANY EXHIBIT NO. 2*

**CARDINAL POWER CO.**
**Bloomfield, New Hampshire**

# I N T E R O F F I C E   M E M O

DATE:     February 8, year 3

TO:        ALL CARDINAL PERSONNEL

FROM:     D.J. McFare

SUBJECT:  SUBSTATION MAINTENANCE WORKING FOREMAN

=================================================================
Effective February 14, year 3, Mr. Peter Pious will have the
responsibility as our Substation Maintenance Working Foreman for
CARDINAL properties.  Mr. Pious will be in charge of all
maintenance of our primary and distribution stations.  All
substation maintenance personnel will be under the supervision of
Mr. Pious.

We feel that this will give us better coverage and closer
maintenance on our properties.  Your full cooperation is
expected.

cc:  Mr. Sam Gambel

*COMPANY EXHIBIT NO. 3*

**CARDINAL POWER CO.**
**Bloomfield, New Hampshire**

April 21, year 3

Mr. Peter Pious
R.R. 3
Napier, N.H.

Dear Pete,

    This is to confirm our discussion regarding Cardinal's
request for you to relocate to Bloomfield as Maintenance
Substation Foreman.  In accordance with this discussion, it is my
understanding that you desire to remain at Napier as a Substation
Maintenance Mechanic Class A.  Present wage scale is $9.45 per
hour.
    As per our understanding, this change is to be effective May
1, year 3.

Sincerely,

/s/ D. J. McFare
General Superintendent

DJM/vh
cc:  Sam Gambel

*COMPANY EXHIBIT NO. 4*

**CARDINAL POWER CO.**
**Bloomfield, New Hampshire**

April 20, year 3

Mr. Curt Burk
Box 296
Kaswell, N.H.

Dear Curt,

Subject:  Substation Maintenance Working Foreman, Located at
Bloomfield Hq.

Curt, as you know we have had an opening for Substation
Maintenance Working Foreman in Bloomfield for some time.  To get
our Substation Department in its right perspective our Working
Foreman has to be located out of the Cardinal Headquarters in
Bloomfield.

This letter is to notify you that your services, as Substation
Maintenance Working Foreman, will commence as of May 1, year 2.
You will be working out of our Headquarters at Bloomfield.  Of
course, Cardinal will pay your moving expenses to Bloomfield. You
will continue to receive the rate of pay you are now receiving at
Kaswell.

Curt, if you do not wish to move, you can stay at Kaswell as
Substation Maintenance Mechanic Class A at the going rate of this
position which would be effective as of May 1, year 3. This rate
of pay would be less than what you have been receiving at
Kaswell.

Your reply is expected by April 25, year 3.

Yours Truly,

/s/ D.J. McFare
General Superintendent

CC: Union

**CARDINAL POWER CO.**
**Bloomfield, New Hampshire**

May 19, year 3

Mr. Curt Burk
Box 296
Kaswell, N.H.

Dear Mr. Burk:

After much planning and discussion as to how Cardinal can best
perform the necessary work required in the furtherance of its
objectives, you are hereby advised that all substation personnel
will work out of the Bloomfield headquarters.

This move will become effective on or before September 1, year 3.
It is the policy of Cardinal to pay the moving expense to new
locations when such move is made at the request of Cardinal.

Your cooperation will be appreciated and we stand ready to work
with you in any possible way in order to achieve the above.

Sincerely,

/s/ Sam Gambel
Manager of Operations

SG/re

CC: Union

*COMPANY EXHIBIT NO. 6*

**CARDINAL POWER COMPANY**

**GUIDELINES FOR SUBSTATION PERSONNEL**

The following Guidelines were issued by the Company at a session held on June 1, year 3, at 10:00 a.m. in Bloomfield, New Hampshire:

1.   As of September 1, year 3, all substation personnel will work out of Bloomfield Headquarters.

2.   Driving distance from Headquarters is immaterial.

3.   All Operations Department vehicles will be stationed at Headquarters.

4.   Bloomfield will be substation personnel's headquarters for reporting to and working out of.

5.   Substation personnel will be working in teams a large portion of the time.

6.   Quite frequently substation personnel will be out of Headquarters two or more days per week (which means personnel would be out overnight).

7.   This will mean more versatility in Substation Department manpower-wise and vehicle and equipment-wise.

8.   The prime reason for this decision by Management is that Cardinal Power is not large enough to have personnel working individually in this Department.  It is the prime goal of Cardinal Power to give the best service to its customers at the lowest possible cost.

9.   The Company expects full cooperation from you as individuals on its decision, and if you have any questions, the Company would appreciate hearing from you at this time.

10.  The Company shall discuss with substation personnel any questions on moving and render any assistance on this.

Employees attending this session.

McFare        Burk
Dixon         Brinks
Pious         Skaler

**CARDINAL POWER CO.**
**Bloomfield, New Hampshire**

July 7, year 1

Mr. Peter Pious
R.R. 1
Finch, N.H.

Dear Mr. Pious:

This letter will confirm our discussion in this office concerning your future with Cardinal.

Your job description and future with Cardinal was clarified during this meeting.  Your work will primarily be with substation or related equipment, and occasionally you will assist the line crew at Napier in routine or emergency work.  Pole climbing will not be mandatory.

Your present working attitude, your performance, and your value to Cardinal is satisfactory.

We appreciated your desire to remain with Cardinal and we will assist you in your move to Napier or the vicinity of Napier.

Cardinal will pay for your moving expenses, your automobile expenses, and motel expenses for a night or two as required to get your furniture into your home.

The Napier substation position which we are requesting you to accept is, on the organizational chart, below your present pay scale.  However, at Napier your salary will continue to be based upon the rating you presently hold, Substation Maintenance Working Foreman at Finch.

Very truly yours,

/s/ Paul Perley
Manager Engineering Services

PP/pw

cc: Dave Gerald

17

## *UNION EXHIBIT NO. 2*

### CARDINAL POWER COMPANY TRANSFER PROPOSAL

As extent of operations becomes known and appears stable, work areas will be established and personnel stationed in them.

From time to time, employees may be transferred from areas as job openings or vacancies occur. If Company causes an employee to be transferred, Company will pay moving expenses and provide living quarters expenses for one week while the employee finds suitable living quarters (see limitations on maximum amount).

An employee transferred at the employee's request and for the employee's convenience shall pay his or her own moving expenses.

# Appendixes

# _Appendix A: Pre-Hearing Arbitration Analysis Form_*

Company _____

Union _____

A. Stipulated issue

   If parties fail to stipulate, specify below:
   1. Company's statement of issue



   2. Union's statement of issue



B. Position of Parties
   1. Position of Company



   2. Position of Union



C. Provide details of award desired
   1. Company



   2. Union



D. Points on which Union and Company can agree
   1.

   2.

   3.

   4.

_____

   *Authors' Note: A copy of this form is to be completed at a pre-arbitration meeting by advocates for the parties. Each witness should receive a copy of the completed form for background purposes. Use of this form and those in Appendixes B and C represents adoption of the full-disclosure philosophy. Not all practicing advocates agree with this philosophy. Information disclosed in this form is generally disclosed in the grievance steps of an actual arbitration. This form functions as a substitute for such information. A source of the information is the transcript, including the exhibits.

1

E. Points Union will try to prove

    1.

    2.

    3.

    4.


F. Points Company will try to prove

    1.

    2.

    3.

    4.


G. Contract clause(s) Union will rely on

    1.

    2.

    3.

    4.


H. Contract clause(s) Company will rely on

    1.

    2.

    3.

    4.


I. Past Practice(s) Union will rely on

    1.

    2.

J. Past Practice(s) Company will rely on

    1.

    2.


K. Stipulation on Procedural Arbitrability

## _Appendix B: Pre-Hearing Arbitration Witness Form_*

| Names of Witnesses (in order of appearance) | What the Witness Is Expected to Establish |
|---|---|
| Union Witness | Witness Will Establish |
| 1. | |
| 2. | |
| 3. | |
| 4. | |
| 5. | |
| 6. | |
| 7. | |
| Company Witness | Witness Will Establish |
| 1. | |
| 2. | |
| 3. | |
| 4. | |
| 5. | |
| 6. | |
| 7. | |

---

*_Authors' Note:_ This form should be completed by each of the advocates at the pre-arbitration meeting and then the copies should be exchanged. A copy of the completed forms should be given to each witness for background purposes.

# *Appendix C: Pre-Hearing Arbitration Witness Cross-Examination Form*\*

| Names of Witnesses (in Order of Appearance) | Questions to Ask on Cross-Examination |
|---|---|
| Union Witness | Company Will Ask |
| 1. | |
| 2. | |
| 3. | |
| 4. | |
| 5. | |
| 6. | |
| 7. | |
| Company Witness | Union Will Ask |
| 1. | |
| 2. | |
| 3. | |
| 4. | |
| 5. | |
| 6. | |
| 7. | |

---

\**Authors' Note*: This form may be completed by each of the advocates at the pre-arbitration meeting and then the copies may be exchanged, unless the advocates do not wish to devulge the questions they plan to ask on cross-examination or any part of their arbitration strategies.

# *Appendix D: Sample Post-Hearing Brief*

PROCEEDINGS IN ARBITRATION
THE HONORABLE WALTER DODDY, ARBITRATOR

IN THE MATTER OF THE                        )
                                            )
ARBITRATION BETWEEN LOCAL 22,               )
                                            )
INTERNATIONAL BOXMAKERS                      )
                                            )
AND BOXWORKERS UNION                         )
                                            )
        and                                 )        CASE NO. 222222-93
                                            )
BROWN BOX CORPORATION                        )


BRIEF OF BROWN BOX CORPORATION


                            Donald O. Zipter
                            Its Attorney


OF COUNSEL:
JONES, JONES, JONES & SMITH              January 2, 1996
First City Bank Building
Louisville, Kentucky 40202

## TABLE OF CONTENTS

## TABLE OF CASES

<u>PROCEEDINGS IN ARBITRATION</u>
<u>THE HONORABLE WALTER DODDY, ARBITRATOR</u>

|  |  |  |
|---|---|---|
| IN THE MATTER OF THE | ) | |
| | ) | |
| ARBITRATION BETWEEN LOCAL 22, | ) | |
| | ) | |
| INTERNATIONAL BOXMAKERS | ) | |
| | ) | |
| AND BOXWORKERS UNION | ) | |
| | ) | |
| and | ) | CASE NO. 222222-93 |
| | ) | |
| BROWN BOX CORPORATION | ) | |

I.

<u>PROCEEDINGS</u>

The Employer in this arbitration is Brown Box Corporation (hereafter called the "Company"), a Kentucky corporation with its principal office in Louisville, engaged in the manufacture of shipping containers, primarily, although not exclusively, corrugated boxes. The Company operates box plants in Kentucky, North Carolina and West Virginia. The Union is the International Boxmakers and Boxworkers Union, Local No. 22, AFL-CIO (hereafter called the Union), which represents the Company's employees in the three plants. The grievance involves the return to work of Mr. Robert Schultz, who is employed by the Company as a printing press operator. Mr. Schultz returned to work Monday, September 21, 1995 and was assigned to work in partition assembly the following Monday, September 28, 1995. His grievance for one week's wages (Joint Exhibit 2) was submitted to arbitration, after having been denied at the preliminary steps of the grievance procedure, pursuant to the provisions of Article V, Section 2, of the collective bargaining agreement of the parties, Joint Exhibit 1. The matter was heard by the arbitrator at Louisville, Kentucky on December 3, 1995. Pursuant to arrangements made at the hearing, as modified at the Union's request, the Company herewith submits its brief postmarked not later than January 3, 1996.

## II.

## FACTS

The grievant, Mr. Schultz, has been employed by the Company for almost twenty-nine years. (Tr. Schultz, 50[1]). He has taken a medical leave of absence on three occasions. These leaves of absence were all related and each was made necessary by a nervous condition. (Tr. Schultz, 51).

On June 22, 1995, Mr. Schultz was given a certificate from his personal physician, Dr. Niles, specifying the need for a thirty-day medical leave of absence "Due to a nervous condition." (Union Exhibit 3). On July 18, 1995, Dr. Niles signed a second certificate stating that Mr. Schultz would need an extension of his leave of absence until August 20, 1995. (Union Exhibit 3). Prior to the termination date of his second leave of absence, Mr. Schultz requested that he be allowed to take his vacation. He was allowed to extend his medical leave through August 21 and commenced his four weeks vacation on August 24. (Tr. Union Opening Statement, 6, Tr. Company Opening Statement, 14).

On September 18, 1995, the Company sent a message to Mr. Schultz through his wife, who is also employed by the Company, that he would have to have a release from the Company doctor before he could return to work. (Tr. Schultz, 51-52). Mr. Schultz reported for work on September 21. He was asked if he had a release from the Company doctor. He replied that he did not have one. (Tr. Schultz, 59-60). Then he was asked if he had a release from his personal physician. The only statement he had from his own doctor was the certificate dated July 18. (Tr. Schultz, 60). His supervisor, Mr. Hodge, informed him that he would have to get a

---

[1]*Editors' Note*: In the case of a transcript prepared by a court reporter, the page number is often given.

release from the Company doctor, and suggested Dr. May. Mr. Schultz requested to see Dr. Barnes instead and his supervisor told him that it was all right to see Dr. Barnes. (Tr. Schultz, 62-63).

Mr. Schultz went to see Dr. Barnes the following morning, Tuesday, September 22. (Tr. Schultz, 52-53). Dr. Barnes examined Mr. Schultz and gave him a release "To return to light duty on a trial basis for two weeks—then return to full time regular work." (Union Exhibit 3). On the same day, Mr. Schultz reported for work on the second shift and presented his light duty slip to Mr. Hodge. (Tr. Schultz, 63). He requested that he be permitted to move from operator, his regular job, to first helper on E-35, a printing press. (Tr. Schultz, 63). No other job was mentioned to Mr. Hodge. (Tr. Schultz, 63-64). Mr. Hodge informed Mr. Schultz that no light duty was available. (Tr. Schultz, 54).

Mr. Schultz talked to his Union representative, Mr. Tibbs. (Tr. Schultz, 55). Mr. Tibbs is president of Local 22. Mr. Tibbs informed Mr. Sey, the plant's general manager, of the situation. (Tr. Sey, 35). Mr. Sey consulted the plant's production managers, Mr. Otter and Mr. Hodge. He also consulted the Company's labor relations director, Mr. Handley, in Louisville. Mr. Sey felt that the Company had no obligation under the collective bargaining agreement (Joint Exhibit 1) to get Mr. Schultz back to work but he was uncertain what was meant by "light duty on a trial basis." (Tr. Sey, 37). He called Dr. Barnes the next day, Wednesday, September 24, but was unable to reach him. (Tr. Sey, 37). Mr. Sey sent a letter (Co. Ex. 1) to Dr. Barnes that day and when he did not receive a response, phoned Dr. Barnes' office on Thursday. (Tr. Sey, 38). Mr. Sey was again unable to reach Dr. Barnes. (Tr. Sey, 39).

At about 2:30 on Thursday afternoon, someone from Dr. Barnes' office called Mr. Sey to relay a message from Dr. Barnes (Tr. Sey 39). She informed Mr. Sey that Dr. Barnes wanted Mr. Schultz to have two weeks of light duty under conditions of "no hurry" and "no pressure" to get accustomed to "piecework." (Tr. Sey, 41). Mr. Sey again consulted his associates at the Company and decided that partition assembly would be an appropriate job for Mr. Schultz, since it is "piecework" but there are no mechanical aspects to the job and it is carried on in a manner in which there is "no hurry" or "pressure." (Tr. Sey, 42). Partition work became available on the second shift on the following Monday, September 29. (Tr. Sey, 42). No partition work was available prior to this date, because it is sporadic work which the Company does not have in constant operation. (Tr. Sey, 43).

Mr. Schultz went to work on partition assembly on September 29. (Tr. Schultz, 57). At the end of that week he was asked if he wished to return to his regular job and he replied that he would, and agreed that he was ready to return to this regular work. (Tr. Schultz, 58). Mr. Schultz suffered no adverse consequences when he returned to his regular job and has acted as a temporary supervisor on occasion since that time. (Tr. Schultz, 64-65).

III.

ISSUES AND CONTENTIONS

The Union contends that the Company has discriminated against Mr. Schultz by requiring him to submit to an examination by the Company doctor and obtain a release before he could return to work after a medical leave of absence. The Union contends that it is not Company practice that an employee have a release from a Company doctor before returning to work after a medical leave. It is the Company's position that, while it is not a uniform requirement that an employee obtain a release from the Company physician before returning to work after a medical leave of absence, a medical certificate is frequently required where the duration of the absence or the nature of the illness is such as to leave some doubt as to the physical capabilities of the employee. In the case of an employee who has been away from the plant for a period of three months on the rather vague statement of a "nervous condition" the Company contends that some assurance of the employee's restored health from a physician should precede his return to work.

The Union also contends that the Company was bound to provide work for the grievant instantaneously upon his return to work, even though he was partially disabled, by Article XIV, Section 8 of the collective bargaining agreement (Joint Exhibit 1) which reads as follows:

"Employees unable to perform arduous work because of physical disability may claim such non-production jobs as they are able to perform, provided they furnish a doctor's certificate of disability. In the event no such job is available, such employee may request the bargaining committee and the management to find him a job. Jobs designated as available by mutual agreements between the bargaining committee and management may be claimed by the disabled employee regardless of seniority choices, however, nothing contained in the foregoing shall prohibit an employee from requesting a lower rated job under available jobs. It is further understood that after an employee secures such a job, he shall be governed by the seniority provisions of this Article."

The Union contends that it is the Company's obligation to find a job suitable for a disabled employee. It further contends that a light duty job was available when Mr. Schultz returned to work.

It is the Company's position that Mr. Schultz's rights under the above-quoted article were: first, he could claim a vacant non-production job that was within his physical capabilities to perform; second, if no such job was available then by mutual agreement between the Company and the Union, he could be placed on any suitable job. Mr. Schultz did not claim any suitable, available, non-production job. The Union approached the Plant Manager, and the Company treated this action as a request to find available work for Mr. Schultz. The Company did find available work on Monday, September 28, 1995. Therefore, the Union is really contending that the Company failed to find the work fast enough. It is the Company's position that it acted reasonably and with all deliberate speed, and that it was not obligated to find a partially disabled employee another job *instantaneously* under the collective bargaining agreement.


IV.

ARGUMENT

A. The Company Has Not Discriminated Against Mr. Schultz by Requiring Him to Obtain a Release From the Company Doctor Before Returning to Work in View of the Long Duration of His Illness and the Vague Nature of the Diagnosis.

1. Requiring a Release from a Company Doctor Is Justified When the Employee's Physical Capacity to Perform His Work Is in Doubt. The grievant, Mr. Schultz, seeks to recover one week's wages. Contractually, the problem breaks down into two separate segments: a) Monday, September 21, 1995, when Mr. Schultz first returned to work and b) what occurred the rest of the week. On Monday, September 21, Mr. Schultz did not work because he failed to comply with the Company's request that he produce a doctor's release. Mr. Schultz did not work for the remainder of the week because no work of the nature specified by Dr. Barnes was available.

When Mr. Schultz returned to work on Monday, September 21, he had been absent from the plant for a period of approximately three months. Originally he had been granted a leave of absence because his doctor, Dr. Niles, provided him with a statement specifying the need for a thirty-day medical leave of absence due to a "nervous condition." (Union Exhibit 3). During Mr. Schultz's first thirty-day leave of absence, Dr. Niles changed his mind and issued a second statement, that the grievant needed a leave of an additional thirty days. (Tr. Schultz, 62). These statements signed by Dr. Niles were no more than a doctor's certification that the employee was physically unwell and unable to work. Although they specified that Mr. Schultz needed a leave of absence for a specified number of days, it is clearly indicated from the fact that Dr. Niles had to extend the time specified in the first statement, that these statements were not releases of Mr. Schultz to return to work after his leave of absence. Mr. Schultz offered to the Company no indication that Dr. Niles had examined him again at the end of the second thirty-day leave of absence and his four-week vacation and found him in good health. If a release from a personal physician is to be accepted by the Company, it must be a release which indicates that a doctor has examined an employee and found him in good health and capable of resuming work. The sixty-day-old statement from Dr. Niles that an additional thirty-day leave of absence was required was not a sufficient release.

The Company was faced with a situation in which a doctor had decided that an employee needed thirty days to recuperate from a nervous condition, then changed his mind and decided that thirty days was not sufficient and an additional period of time was necessary. No further release was obtained, and the employee decided that he would take even more time off and take his vacation before returning to work. No indication has been given by Mr. Schultz that he visited a doctor, other than Dr. Barnes, between the dates of July 18 and September 21. So far as the Company knows, Mr. Schultz decided on his own that he was healthy enough to return to work. Mr. Schultz's condition is a recurring nervous condition which has in fact caused Mr. Schultz to need a medical leave of absence on three occasions. (Tr. Schultz, 51). The facts clearly indicated that a physical examination was necessary.

In this situation a company is entitled to some assurance that its employee is physically capable of performing the work assigned to him. Mr. Schultz was informed by the Company that he would need a release from the Company doctor on the Friday before his return to work on Monday, September 21. (Tr. Schultz, 51-52). Mr. Schultz did not obtain such a release. (Tr. Schultz, 59-60). The Company justifiably refused to allow him to return to work without a release. Not only did Mr. Schultz not obtain a release from the Company doctor, he also did not obtain a release from his personal physician, other than a statement, more than two months old, that he needed an additional thirty-day leave of absence after an original thirty-day leave of absence.

The Company's position is reasonable because of the vague nature of Mr. Schultz's ailment. He was suffering from a nervous condition. (Union Exhibit 3). Unlike a broken leg, or a broken finger, or an injured back, a nervous condition is an illness that is not readily apparent. A nervous condition may manifest itself in innumerable ways. A doctor would certainly not be able to prescribe a medicine, a manner of treatment, or even a diagnosis for a disease which is described merely as a "nervous condition." A "nervous condition" could be anything from schizophrenia to hives. When Mr. Schultz did visit the Company doctor, Dr. Barnes specified that he was to return to light duty work on a trial basis. (Union Exhibit 3). The fact that Dr. Barnes stated in his release that Mr. Schultz was not to return to his regular job for two weeks indicates that the Company's precautions were justified. Mr. Schultz was not ready to return to his regular job as a printing press operator.

2. The Decisions of Arbitrators Uphold the Right of the Company to Require a Physical Examination by a Company Doctor of an Employee Returning After an Extended Medical Leave of Absence. In Goodyear Clearwater Mills, 11 LA 364 (1948), Arbitrator Whitley T. McCoy found nothing unreasonable or violative of the collective bargaining agreement involved when the Company required physical examinations of employees returning from extended personal or Union business leaves, although the Company admitted that it had sometimes accepted the certificates of personal physicians after sick leaves. There was no mention of a physical examination as a prerequisite to returning to work in the contract involved.

In Automatic Canteen Co., 47 LA 1 (1966), Arbitrator M. David Keefe found that an employer had the right to require an employee, on leave of absence due to hospitalization for a heart condition, to be examined by the employer's physician before permitting her to return to work, if for no other reason than because the Company was entitled to a detailed confirmation as to the extent of "light work" of which the employee was capable. In that case the employee had had a two-year leave of absence and had suffered recurring heart attacks. The arbitrator held that the employer could not refuse to rehire the employee—after an examination by the Company physician—on the grounds that the employee was a poor health risk, in view of the fact that the Company had made it a practice to assign partially disabled employees to light work assignments. In the present case the Company has not denied Mr. Schultz's right under the collective bargaining agreement to be assigned to light duty work. The Company merely wished to determine the state of Mr. Schultz's health and assign him to work which he was capable of performing. An examination by the Company doctor was necessary to accomplish the desired results in view of the fact that Mr. Schultz had not obtained a satisfactory release from his own personal physician.

A board of arbitrators decided in Southern Connecticut Gas Co., 48 LA 1357 (1967), that an employer had the right to require an employee to take a physical examination prior to assuming a new job already awarded him. In that case, the employer, awarding the position in good faith, had forgotten that the employee had previously had a hernia operation and was concerned about the employee's ability to handle his new job. The Union contended that the Company was discriminating against the grievant in requiring an examination of him which it did not require of other employees. The Board of Arbitrators held that there was no discrimination since the grievant refused to reply to an inquiry as to whether he was capable of performing the work on his new job and refused to submit to a Company demand for a physical examination. The Board concluded that the Company had a good and sufficient reason for requiring the examination.

Similarly, in the present case, the Company had good reason to require Mr. Schultz to take a physical. Mr. Schultz's illness was vaguely described by his personal physician who apparently had not seen him for an extended period of time, and the illness was a recurring one. The Company was naturally concerned and acted in good faith.

3. <u>It Is the Company's Policy to Evaluate Each Case Individually to Determine Whether an Examination and a Release From the Company Physician Is Necessary When an Employee Returns From a Medical Leave of Absence</u>. It is the Company's policy to exercise good judgment in regard to a doctor's release prior to an employee returning to work after a medical leave of absence. (Tr. Sey, 26). There have been many instances in which employees have returned to work with certificates of release from their own physicians. But, there have been many others in which the Company has asked for examination and release from the Company physician. (Tr. Sey, 26). There is no set policy that a person has to have a Company doctor's permit to return to work after a medical leave of absence, but it is not an unusual request.

The Union has demonstrated that in the case of two individual employees, the Company has not required a release from the Company doctor after a medical leave of absence. Both these cases are clearly distinguishable from the present situation. For example, in the case of Union witness Mrs. Pat Brugge, a release signed by Dr. Lang is dated May 28, 1992 and specifies that Mrs. Brugge may return to work on June 2, 1992, a lapse of only five days. (Union Exhibit 2). Another release signed by Dr. Gregg, dated May 1, 1993 states that Mrs. Brugge may return to work May 3, 1993, a lapse of only two days. (Union Exhibit 2). A third release, also signed by Dr. Gregg, is dated December 14, 1994 and states that Mrs. Brugge may return to work December 21, 1994, a lapse of seven days. (Union Exhibit 2). It is apparent in the case of each of these releases that the doctor was familiar with the health of his patient and was obviously capable of saying with a reasonable degree of certainty that his patient was able to return to work. However, in the case of Mr. Schultz, the doctor's release was dated June 18, while Mr. Schultz did not return to work until September 21. The situation of Mr. Schultz is entirely different from that of Mrs. Brugge. The

13

Company was justifiably apprehensive of a doctor's release which was dated so far in advance of the employee's return to work, especially when the illness is a recurring one.

The case of Union witness Peter James, is also clearly distinguishable from the situation of Mr. Schultz. Mr. James suffered a broken leg. (Tr. James, 67). Company officials could determine if Mr. James was fully recuperated by observing Mr. James when he returned to work. This was not the case with Mr. Schultz, who suffered from a "nervous condition." Moreover, Mr. James obtained a release from his personal physician dated November 30, and he returned to work December 1. (Union Exhibit 5). Obviously, requiring a release from a Company doctor in the case of Mr. James would be unnecessary unless he demonstrated some physical incapacity. If he had demonstrated such a physical incapacity, it would have been observable by Company officials and undoubtedly Mr. James would have been asked to submit to some kind of physical. It is also unlikely that Mr. James' condition would have been aggravated if he prematurely returned to work. If his leg had bothered him, the Company could have taken proper action. However, it would be difficult for the Company to detect an aggravation of a nervous condition.

B. <u>Mr. Schultz Received Everything to Which He Was Entitled Under the Collective Bargaining Agreement</u>.

1. <u>There Is No Requirement That the Company Instantaneously Produce Work Other Than the Work Regularly Performed by an Employee When the Employee Becomes Partially Disabled</u>. Article XIV, Section 8 of the collective bargaining agreement (Joint Exhibit 1) provides a procedure under which an employee suffering a physical disability may obtain other work which he is capable of performing. This procedure was not followed in the case of Mr. Schultz. The collective bargaining agreement provides that an employee unable to perform arduous work because of a physical disability may claim a non-production job which he is capable of performing. Mr. Schultz claimed no job which he was capable of performing. The only job which Mr. Schultz requested was that of first helper on E-35, his

regular machine. (Tr. Schultz, 63). The job of first helper was manifestly unsuitable. No other job was mentioned. (Tr. Schultz, 63-64). The first helper has the responsibility of feeding the slotter. (Tr. Schultz, 63). The pace of the work is governed by a machine and, therefore, the job of first helper is not one free from "pressure" and "hurry."

Mr. Schultz did not request the Bargaining Committee and management to find him a job, as provided in Section 8. This section contemplates that such a job must be designated as available by mutual agreement between the Bargaining Committee and management. There was no such agreement in the case of Mr. Schultz. In the opinion of the Company, the first available work which Mr. Schultz was capable of performing was partition assembly and he was immediately assigned to such work when it became available. (Tr. Schultz, 42, 43).

Doctor Barnes requested that Mr. Schultz be assigned to "piecework" under conditions of "no hurry" and "no pressure." (Tr. Sey, 41). The Union contends that the position of janitor met the specifications of Dr. Barnes as light duty work. However, a janitor does not do piecework, and therefore, it did not fall within the criteria set forth by Dr. Barnes. (Tr. Sey, 44). Dr. Barnes specified that Mr. Schultz was to be assigned to light duty work on a "trial basis." (Union Exhibit 3). If the work to which Mr. Schultz was to be assigned was to be on a "trial basis," then it was essential that Mr. Schultz be tested to determine if he was capable of returning to his regular job. In order to test Mr. Schultz's ability it was necessary that he be assigned to some form of piecework since Mr. Schultz's regular job involved piecework. Assigning Mr. Schultz to partition assembly greatly decreased the pressure upon Mr. Schultz and at the same time placed him in conditions reasonably similar to his regular job since partition assembly involves piecework. Mr. Schultz could set his own pace in partition assembly since he would not be paced by a machine. (Tr. Sey, 43-44). While Mr. Schultz could undoubtedly perform the work of janitor, a janitorial position would offer the Company and Dr.

Barnes no opportunity to determine if Mr. Schultz was capable of returning to his regular work, because the two jobs are too dissimilar.

The Company, therefore, fulfilled its obligation under the collective bargaining agreement by finding Mr. Schultz a suitable job at the earliest possible opportunity. Finding a suitable job for Mr. Schultz was not something which the Company could perform instantaneously, nor is it required of the Company under the collective bargaining agreement that an employee with a physical disability be placed at another job instantaneously. It is the clear meaning of the agreement that if an employee with a physical disability claims an available non-production job which he is capable of performing the Company will place him at such job. However, it is evident that the agreement contemplated that the employee would claim work which he was capable of performing and which was available. Mr. Schultz claimed only work which he was not capable of performing, namely, first helper on E-35. It was also contemplated that the Bargaining Committee and management would act upon the request of an employee suffering a physical disability and find him a job by mutual agreement. For the Bargaining Committee and management to come to agreement, some delay is necessary. Therefore, the collective bargaining agreement does not contemplate instantaneous placement of a partially disabled employee at another work assignment.

2. <u>The Company Acted Reasonably Under the Circumstances</u>. Mr. Schultz returned from his vacation and leaves of absence on Monday, September 21. By the following Monday he was working again. (Tr. Sey, 42).

The Company was confronted with an employee who had been absent from work for three months and had been or was still suffering from a nervous condition. They were informed by the Company doctor that Mr. Schultz should be assigned to light duty work on a trial basis. The Company had no way of knowing what was meant by light duty work in the case of an employee who was suffering from a nervous condition. It was apparent that the doctor meant something more than merely light physical work in view of Mr. Schultz's illness.

Mr. Sey was confused as to exactly what to do. (Tr. Sey, 30). He did exactly what would be expected of him under the circumstances. He consulted Mr. Schultz's supervisor and the plant's production managers. (Tr. Sey, 37). He also called Labor Relations in Louisville. (Tr. Sey, 36-37). He then called Dr. Barnes (Tr. Sey, 37). When he could not reach Dr. Barnes he immediately mailed a letter to Dr. Barnes. (Tr. Sey, 38). When he did not receive a response, he called Dr. Barnes on the telephone. (Tr. Sey, 38). He received an explanation from an assistant of Dr. Barnes, that Mr. Schultz was to be placed on light duty work under conditions of "no hurry" and "no pressure" to get accustomed to "piecework." (Tr. Sey, 41). Mr. Sey again consulted with his associates at the Company and determined what job would best suit the framework specified by Dr. Barnes. (Tr. Sey, 41, 42). Having determined what the proper job was, Mr. Sey called Mr. Schultz to tell him he was assigned to partition assembly. (Tr. Sey, 42). Partition assembly work was not available before September 28, when Mr. Schultz was assigned to it. (Tr. Sey, 43). Mr. Schultz has suffered no ill effects since he has returned to work, and he is now working efficiently. (Tr. Schultz, 64). Mr. Schultz has no grounds for complaint. The Company acted as quickly as possible in finding Mr. Schultz suitable work. It has met its responsibility to its employee and under the collective bargaining agreement.

V.

CONCLUSION

The Company has not discriminated against Mr. Schultz by requiring him to obtain a release from the Company doctor before returning to work after an extended medical leave of absence. The Company has also met its obligations under the collective bargaining agreement by finding Mr. Schultz work appropriate to his physical capacity, as quickly as possible under the circumstances. No discrimination or breach of the collective bargaining agreement has been shown. The grievance must be denied.

Respectfully submitted,


/s/Donald O. Zipter
Donald O. Zipter
Attorney for Brown Box Corp.


JONES, JONES, JONES & SMITH                    October 2, 1996
First City Bank Building
Louisville, Kentucky 40202

# *Appendix E: Sample Company Opening Statement*[*]

Mr. Arbitrator, this is an exceedingly meritless grievance both procedurally and substantively.

First, it is untimely. The evidence will establish that the grievant-a teacher assistant/bus aide-had notice of her discharge on June 14, 1991. She received additional notice of this discharge on either July 31 or August 1 of 1991 during a telephone conversation which she initiated.

Despite those notices in June and either late July or early August, this grievance was not filed until September 17, 1991. I would like to direct your attention to Article VII of the parties' collectively bargained grievance procedure. On page 7.2 the grievance procedure provides that, within 20 school days following the occurrence of the event giving rise to the grievance, the employee or the Union may present the grievance in writing to the immediate supervisor.

Article VII, Paragraph A, Paragraph 2, which is on page 7.1, states that failure of an employee or the Union to act on any grievance within the prescribed time limits will act as a bar to any further appeal.

The evidence will establish that the grievant was informed of her discharge on June 14, and again on either July 31 or August 1. Yet no grievance was filed until September 27, three-and-a-half months after the first notification and almost two months after the second notification!

Turning to the merits of the grievance, the evidence will establish as follows: the grievant was hired as a teacher assistant/bus aide in September of 1989. She served some of the neediest children in the School District, special education children from ages 6 to 11 whose predominant language was Spanish. These young students had behavioral disorders or learning disabilities and spoke little English.

---

*By Lawrence J. Casazza, Vedder, Price, Kaufman & Kammholz, Chicago, IL.

1

Grievant's duties and responsibilities were to be on time and on the bus before any of the students were picked up and were on the bus themselves. The reason for this is obvious-safety of these young, needy children who are the District's students and who needed constant supervision while entering, leaving, and riding on the bus.

Grievant was informed of these duties over and over again. She was directed to be on time and told that if she wasn't going to be on time or if she was going to be absent, she needed to telephone the school principal between 6:30 and 7:00 a.m. She was told that this call must be timely so that the principal could get a replacement for the students on the bus.

In 1990-91 alone there were approximately 11 times when grievant was not on the bus and when she never called. Grievant was counseled about this orally. She also was given a written reprimand informing her that her job was in jeopardy-that if she ever did this again, she could lose her job.

And despite all of this counseling, and despite the safety consideration, grievant was tardy four times without calling in during the last two weeks of the school year! As a result, there was no teacher assistant/bus aide on that bus for these children.

The grievant thus gave the District no responsible choice but not to renew her employment contract for the ensuing year.

Now, you're going to hear a very technical defense which the Union will raise on grievant's behalf-that she did not receive an evaluation. And they will undoubtedly direct your attention to Article V, Paragraph D, which is on pages 5.1 and 5.2 of the collective bargaining agreement and refers to annual evaluations. They will claim that grievant should not have been discharged because she did not receive an evaluation that school year.

It is noteworthy, however, that the contract language upon which the Union relies, provides:

"Except in situations involving serious misconduct, no teacher assistant will be dismissed without first having been evaluated."

2

Mr. Arbitrator, nothing can be much more serious than the form of misconduct which we have here. As you will see when you review the grievance history on the issue in question-not reporting absences and tardinesses on a timely basis-grievant had been evaluated time and time again. She had been counseled orally several times and she had been given a forceful, written reprimand telling her that her job was in jeopardy. So, she certainly had been evaluated on that aspect of her job even though such was not required given her serious misconduct.

In summary, we have here a grievant who filed an untimely grievance and who is guilty of grave misconduct involving her utter disregard of the safety of the needy students under her care, utter disregard of the instructions which she received from her teacher, utter disregard of the instruction which she received from the principal, and utter disregard of the responsibilities which were set forth in the job description. In contrast, the only defense that has been or could be submitted by the Union is an attempt to rely upon a hyper-technical point that grievant did not receive a formal evaluation.

We submit that this grievance should be denied as being untimely. Alternatively, it also most assuredly is without merit. The District discharged grievant for grave, dangerous misconduct after ample counseling, warning, and evaluation on the issue in question.

# *Appendix F: Sample Union Opening Statement*

The issue before you, Ms. Arbitrator, is whether the discharge of seven employees and suspension of eight others without pay for 47 days were without cause and unjust in violation of both the collective bargaining agreement between the parties and applicable law.

The burden is on the Employer to prove that the Employer had, prior to January 22, 1992, facts establishing that each employee disciplined had engaged in misconduct warranting the imposition of that discipline.

The Union's position can be simply stated.

(1) There was a collective bargaining agreement in effect between the parties at the time of the alleged misconduct;

(2) The strike activity of the employee was not in violation of that agreement, however, because:

   (a)   The Employer had at least as early as December 1, 1996, repudiated the contract and any obligation to arbitrate grievances, and under Article XXX of the collective bargaining agreement, a work stoppage is permitted in these circumstances.

   (b)   Under Article XXX a work stoppage is permitted until the Employer gives notice to the Union, in which event the employees have 24 hours to abandon the stoppage and return to work. The Employer never gave the notice required by Article XXX.

The work stoppage was therefore entirely lawful and not in violation of the collective bargaining agreement.

(3) The Union does not know what the Employer will present to the Arbitrator to show that it possessed sufficient justification to impose the discipline on each employee. We are prepared to respond to any showing as to any employee to prove:

   (a)   That the discipline imposed was unwarranted without just cause and too severe for any supposed unlawful conduct involved; and

(b) That in the case of each disciplined employee, there were other employees who engaged in similar conduct who were not so disciplined, and that those other nondisciplined employees had not been as active in support of Union causes as those employees whose discipline is on trial here.

In short, Ms. Arbitrator, the Company discriminated against the employees disciplined and treated them in disparate fashion because of their Union activities and their positions with the Union, all in violation of the collective bargaining agreement and applicable law.

The Arbitrator should also notice that the Union brought unfair labor practice charges respecting this discriminatory treatment of these employees for their Union activities and the Board deferred to allow this arbitration to go forward.

It follows that in fashioning a remedy, we are asking that, in addition to reinstatement and back pay, the Arbitrator afford additional appropriate relief as would the National Labor Relations Board in such circumstances.

# _Appendix G: Sample Company Closing Statement_*

As you have heard in the testimony, the Company produces high-quality furniture at its plant. It employs approximately 180 employees. Furniture manufacturing is considered a "High Hazardous Industry" by the Occupational Safety and Health Administration, with a Standard Industry Classification (SIC) of 2511.

The Company's employees use hazardous equipment in the manufacture of its products. It has 150 pieces of equipment, including 12 table saws, 12 lathes, 12 boring machines, 3 rip saws, 3 planers, 5 overhead routers, and 3 semi-automatic shapers. The Company also uses finishing materials involving toxic chemicals, solvents and other dangerous and potentially explosive materials.

In early summer 1995, a group of management employees of the Company met for the purpose of assessing a situation it considered critical for its employees and the Company's future. The factors considered included the following:

(1) A workers' compensation problem of on-the-job injuries that was 44 percent higher than even the dangerous industry it is in.

(2) An absenteeism rate of 10-12 percent—nearly triple the industry average.

(3) At least two employees had entered de-tox programs for drug abuse. And when one of those employees completed de-tox and returned to work, he reported to management that he was approached on his first day back at work by another employee who offered to sell him cocaine.

(4) At least one employee had entered into alcohol abuse rehabilitation.

(5) Several job applicants had tested "positive" in pre-employment drug screening for cocaine and marijuana.

(6) The Employee Relations Director had found a bag of marijuana in the plant.

*By D. Patton Pelfrey, Brown, Todd & Heyburn PLLC, Louisville, KY.

1

(7) Management had found several liquor bottles in the restrooms.

(8) Several supervisors reported their suspicions that drugs were being sold in the plant.

This group decided to draft a substance abuse program that would attack and/or uncover these problems. This, it believed, would create a safer workplace, reduce absenteeism, reduce the appalling injury rate on the job and, when substance abuse was discovered, would aid employees through efforts to rehabilitate them. This was a substance abuse program that would deal with alcohol and licit and illicit drugs in the workplace. Although random testing was preferred—as being fair to all employees and not singling out anyone—it was finally decided to only test on a post-accident basis, i.e., when an employee "is involved in, is the cause of, or is injured in, any accident on the job" <u>or</u> where the accident or injury "causes damage or destruction to Company property which requires more than first aid" <u>or</u> "results in lost working time in excess of one-half hour."

The Company was aware of its probable obligation to bargain over such a policy (notwithstanding Article 39 of the collective bargaining agreement with the Union) under the NLRB's decision in *Johnson Bateman Company* in 1989. The Company offered to negotiate about substance abuse testing on at least three occasions: August 29, 1995; December 7, 1995; and January 2, 1996. The Union refused to negotiate by notice to the Company on September 12, 1995, and January 3, 1996. In addition the Union provided a notice to employees that the Company had offered to bargain but the Union had refused.

On or about January 15, 1996, the Company posted, and distributed with the employees' paychecks, its substance abuse policy. The Company announced the policy would become effective on February 12, 1996. The 30-day notice was to give employees an opportunity to "get clean" and to receive orientation about testing, how it would be done, etc., and to "get ready" for implementation.

This policy was slightly modified on February 2, 1996, because there was a need to provide for a "test" for alcohol. This was

2

accomplished by adding the phrase "<u>or other appropriate test</u>" to the original language providing for urinalysis testing for drugs.

On January 15, 1996, when the Company distributed the policy, it also announced that on January 22 clinical professionals would give orientation sessions. The Union Business Manager was invited to these sessions and did attend. These sessions were conducted by a Corporate Testing Manager of SmithKline/Beecham. All employees received the orientation.

The Company also contracted with a hospital for it to be the collection site for samples. It also contracted with a doctor to be the Medical Review Officer (MRO), who was responsible for checking all positive tests and discussing the results with the employee concerned.

The Company had the right under its collective bargaining agreement with the Union to develop and implement a substance abuse policy. It repeatedly offered to negotiate and bargain with the Union about the entire issue and details of it. The Union repeatedly refused to even discuss it or set dates to bargain. The Company had the right then to unilaterally implement the policy. It did so.

The results have been dramatic. Four of the first eight persons tested, tested positive. All were offered rehabilitation. The Company's lost days caused by accidents have been drastically reduced. The number of reported accidents has gone down dramatically. The absenteeism rate has dropped to approximately 4 percent.

The Company did everything it was required to do—and much, much more—before implementing the policy. It repeatedly offered to bargain over the terms of the policy, but its offer was repeatedly rejected. It narrowly tailored the policy to address its problems by only testing on a post-accident basis. This is the least intrusive and least onerous type of testing. The Company, in short, complied with the NLRA and Article 39 of the collective bargaining agreement with the Union. The policy is reasonable.

The Grievance must be denied.

That completes the closing argument for the Company, Mr. Arbitrator.

3

# *Appendix H: Sample Union Closing Statement*

Madam Arbitrator, you have heard the case. Now you must address and resolve whether the Company had just cause for discharging the grievant, an employee who has worked for the Company for 12 years with but one infraction of the absenteeism rules which occurred one year before the discharge in issue here. The grievant, as testimony has shown, is a single mother who alone supports her only child of five years of age.

The reason for discharge proffered by the Company is for the second infraction of its rule which requires, rigidly and without any exception, that employees notify the Company when, <u>for any reason</u>, they are unable to either be present on the job or anticipate a late arrival.

The Union does not challenge the right of the Company to formulate work rules under the management rights provision of the collective bargaining agreement. It does, however, challenge its right under the contract to apply the work rules in violation of the provision of the contract which expressly requires that discipline or discharge be "for just cause."

It is well established that the Company has the burden of proof in discharge cases and that burden must be sustained by proof beyond a reasonable doubt or, at least, by clear and convincing evidence. This burden of proof is essential to sustaining the economic capital punishment which flows inevitably from the extreme penalty of discharge. The Arbitrator should require such a burden of proof from the Company in this case, which is characterized by gross indifference to the employment history of the grievant and the extreme and unusual circumstance which caused the grievant—as it would have caused any reasonable person—to fail to comply with the rigid, unforgiving absenteeism rule relied upon by the Company to sever the grievant's ability to support herself and her child.

The Union does not dispute the fact that the grievant failed to call her foreman and inform him that she would be absent from work. Her failure to do so was indisputably because her five-year-old child had fallen from a swing and was rendered unconscious, and she accompanied him to the hospital in a distressed state of extreme anxiety for his life and safety.

Would you, Madam Arbitrator, or I, or any reasonable person, be she or he mother or father, have considered compliance with the Company's implacable absenteeism rule over the welfare of the child? I submit the answer is clearly, "No!" The Company chose, nevertheless, to discharge the grievant, as it has apparently done consistently with other employees, in order to maintain its unblemished absenteeism policy.

Such consistency, maintained at the expense of morality and decency in the workplace, especially with respect to a 12-year employee with an almost unblemished record of service to the Company, under extreme and clearly excusable circumstances here presented, should not be sustained. The Company has clearly failed to support the discharge for just cause by even a far lesser burden of proof.

Elementary workplace justice requires that the grievance be sustained. The discharge must be set aside with the grievant being reinstated with full back pay and made whole for all other monetary losses resulting from the discharge.

# *Appendix I: Selected Typical Arbitration Awards*

## 29 LA 77

**MUCON CORP.—**

### Decision of Arbitrator

In re MUCON CORPORATION **and**
RETAIL, WHOLESALE & DEPART-
MENT STORE UNION, DISTRICT 65,
Case No. 56-AS-270, July 11, 1957.

Arbitrator: Arthur Stark, designated
by New Jersey State Board of Mediation.

### DISCHARGE

—Unauthorized leave of absence—
**Propriety of penalty** ▶118.636 ▶106.
**25**

Discharge of employee who left job to
attend week-long religious meeting after
employer had refused to grant leave of
absence for that purpose was justified,
since (1) contract provides for leaves of
absence only with consent of employer,
and (2) employee was warned that she
would be discharged if she did not report
for work. Employer's refusal to grant requested leave was not discriminatory, since
(1) employee had obtained leaves of absence for same purpose in previous years,
(2) employer's refusal was based upon employee's record of absenteeism, and (3)
neither contract nor industrial practice
requires employer to allow its employees
to observe all religious rites of all creeds
and sects.—Mucon Corp., 29 LA 77.

---

## UNAUTHORIZED ABSENCE

STARK, Arbitrator:—A hearing in
this matter was held in Newark, New
Jersey on June 13, 1957. The Company
was represented by M. A. Prince, President, and Joseph S. Oberwager, Counsel. The Union representatives were
Robert M. Burke, General Organizer
and Robert Gibbons, Steward.

### Issue

Jessie Lyle took a leave of absence
without employer consent. Was the
employer justified in terminating employment of Jessie Lyle under the
contract? If not, what shall the
remedy be.

### Background Information

Jessie Lyle has been employed as a
Machine Operator since April 1, 1951.
Her work has been satisfactory.

Mrs. Lyle belongs to a religious
group called Church of God and

## 29 LA 78

Saints of Christ whose members meet
annually in Virginia. On March 25,
1957, she requested a leave of absence
in the following written statement:

"I wish a leave of absence to attend
Passover observed every year by my
church. Starting April 12, to 21, will return to work April 22, 1957.

Thanking you in advance,

(signed) Jessie Lyle

This request was made in accordance with Section 13 of the Contract,
which states:

### Leaves of Absence

With the consent of the Employer
any worker may take a leave of absence, without pay, during the term
of his employment for maternity or
personal reasons, after one year of
service. The length of such leaves
shall be determined by negotiations
between the shop chairman and the
Employer.

During the time that such worker
is away on approved leave, full seniority with all its privileges shall accumulate.

On April 2 the Company told Mrs.
Lyle (and the Shop Steward) that her
request was denied. She asked for reconsideration. On April 4 she learned
the decision would not be changed.
She was told that if she took the time
off anyway, she would be subject to
termination.

On April 12, after Mrs. Lyle failed to
report for work (she had gone to Virginia) the Company discharged her.

Section 17 of the contract deals
with discharge in the following manner:

17a * * * There shall be no dismissals
of any kind because of race, color, creed,
sex, marital status or membership in the
Union * * *

17b. Employees may be discharged or
disciplined by the Employer for just
cause.

The Union's claim that Mrs. Lyle's
discharge was not for just cause is
now before the Arbitrator.

### Position of the Union

The Company has violated Section
17. Mrs. Lyle has attended annual
Spring religious gatherings whenever
she could for the past twenty years.
Her request for a leave was not whim-
sical; it came from profound religious
conviction.

When the leave was denied the Union assured Mrs. Lyle it would fight
her case should she decide to go without permission.

Mrs. Lyle has been a responsible
employee and was entitled to the
leave. The Company knew of her religious beliefs, and granted her permission to attend these services in
the past. By denying this year's request, Management has placed her in
the position of choosing between her
religious convictions and her job. This
is discriminatory and unjust.

Management may not discharge an
employee who has reasonable and excusable grounds for being absent. The
Union compares Mrs. Lyle's April absence to an absence caused by illness.
A deeply religious person has no more
control over his convictions (and re-
sultant actions) than a person who
accidently breaks his leg. Under the
circumstances, it was not even necessary for her to request a leave since
neither maternity nor personal reasons were involved.

If the Company hires and retains
an employee, knowing of his religious
convictions, it is bound to excuse his
absence if caused by religious observance.

Since there was no reasonable
ground for discharging Mrs. Lyle, the

Company should be required to reinstate her with full back pay.

### Position of Management

Section 13 of the contract provides
that an employee may take a leave of
absence only "with the consent of
the Employer." Mrs. Lyle was refused
this consent; therefore the Company
had a right to fire her pursuant to
Section 17b.

Mrs. Lyle took the law (contract)
into her own hands. She had been
warned that she would be fired if she
left without permission. She knew
why her leave was denied.

Mrs. Lyle's attendance record during the past year provided sound basis
for denying the requested leave. The
record shows:

| Month | Days Absent | Reason |
|-------|------------|--------|
| 1956 April | 8 days | Leave of absence to attend Passover observance |
| August | 16 days | Leave of absence to take trip to California |
| Sept.-Oct. | 13 days | Illness |
| Nov. | 1 day | Illness |
| 1957 Jan. | 1 day | Illness |
| Feb. | 1 day | Illness |
| Mar. | 11 days | Parents illness (excused absence) |
| Total | 51 days | |

## 29 LA 79

Religious discrimination is not involved. Mrs. Lyle received permission
to attend this service in the past.
Another plant employee, because of
his fine attendance record, was
granted leave of absence to attend
this year.

The Company is not required to
defend a denial of a leave of absence
It has the absolute right to make this
decision, under the Agreement, and
should not be subject to reversal by
an arbitrator.

The Union is seeking to alter the
clear meaning and intent of the contract. For example:

1. Certain days are set aside as
religious (or national) holidays on
which employees may be off with full
pay. These are the *only* religious holidays recognized by the parties, and
no employee has the right to demand
more or different ones.

2. The "anti-discrimination" clause
is being distorted to cover a situation
for which it was never designed.

### Discussion

The Church of God and Saints of
Christ is a religious group whose members believe themselves to be descend-
ants of the Tribe of Judah. They
observe the Sabbath and refrain from
work on Saturday. In January of each
year they observe Days of Atonement;
in the Spring they celebrate Passover
to commemorate the time when the
children of Israel left Egypt. No
leavened bread is used during this
period, and members of the group who
are physically and financially able
to make the trip, convene in Belleville,
Virginia where services are held each
day during the observance. The
church uses both the old and New
Testaments.

While attendance at the Virginia Passover services is expected of all devout members, about 3,000 attend each year, although total membership is much higher. Mrs. Lyle testified that, although she felt she should go, there have been several occasions on which she did not make the journey. In fact, since 1951, she failed to attend three times—in 1951, 1953 and 1954.

In 1955 and 1956 Mrs. Lyle asked for and was granted permission to take the Passover week off. We may ask, then, somewhat in the vein of that observance, why was this year different from all other years?

The answer lies in the Company's statement that Mrs. Lyle's attendance record was so poor during the previous 12 months, it could not allow her another week away from the job.

Was this decision an interference with the employee's religion? Is it reviewable under the contract?

The text of Section 13 is clear and unambiguous. *With the consent of the Employer* employees may take unpaid leaves of absence; without such consent they may not.

The Union's argument that the "no discrimination" clause implies a tacit agreement that employees must be allowed to observe all the holidays of their chosen religion is without foundation. There are three dominant religious groups in this country, and innumerable smaller ones, each with its holy days and religious practices. The observance of all religious rites, it may be said, is not an employee's contractual right under this contract.

And this makes sense. To hold otherwise is to conjure up a constant parade of workers from various religious backgrounds, coming and going to work on this day or that, depending on their religious beliefs. To prevent situations such as this, the Union and Employer agreed to a set of rules concerning absences of *any* kind whatsoever. And under these rules, Management makes the initial decision.

The Union believes that discharge is too severe a penalty to assess against an employee whose conscience and religious convictions require her to attend Passover services for a week. It argues that an employer should not compel a worker to choose between his job and his religion.

True, this may be a bitter choice. But our society, rightly or wrongly, has subordinated religion to the more mundane aspects of life. It requires citizens to conform to certain accepted practices—not at the peril of their lives, but certainly at the peril of narrowing the area of potential employment. If one's religion should require one to pray between one and three each afternoon, there are a number of jobs one could never hold.

In this case, it is Mrs. Lyle, rather than the Company who created the dilemma. She ignored all Company warnings and without hesitation left for Virginia. Knowledge that she might forfeit her job did not deter her. It is she who must bear responsibility for the outcome.

The Arbitrator, in reviewing the question of "just cause", may determine whether the assessed penalty is

## 29 LA 80

too severe. Criteria such as fairness, reasonableness, equity and the like have been constantly used in this area. Actually, discharge does seem rather strong in view of the employee's obviously sincere convictions. Yet, when asked whether she would do the same thing again if reinstated, Mrs. Lyle answered with a firm "yes". Under the circumstances, there is no point in ordering her back to work, only to defy Management's decisions once more.

While the Arbitrator cannot, under the Agreement find fault with Management's action, nor can he in conscience require the Company to employ Mrs. Lyle, he cannot but pause a moment to admire the unswerving convictions of a woman who places her religion above her livelihood. Truly, Jessie Lyle has crossed her own Rubicon.

---

48 LA 619

## UNIVAC DIV.—

### Decision of Arbitrator

In re UNIVAC DIVISION OF SPERRY RAND CORPORATION and INTERNATIONAL UNION OF ELECTRICAL, RADIO & MACHINE WORKERS, AFL-CIO, L O C A L 165, Case No. AAA PHILA. 1430-0069-67, April 5, 1967
Arbitrator: Sidney L. Cahn

## DISCHARGE

— Insubordination — Reasonableness of rule—Moral scruples ▶ 118.25 ▶ 118.656

Employer was justified in discharging employee, who was assistant minister when not working for employer, for refusing to obey order of employer requiring employees to report to room 15 minutes before close of work day in order to prevent employees from lining up prematurely in order to punch out, notwithstanding employee's claim that this rule conflicted with his moral scruples in that it implied lack of trust and constituted payment for not working. (1) Employer is not required to make exceptions to rules to accommodate employee's personal beliefs; (2) r u l e was reasonable and permissible by right of employer to direct working force; (3) even though grievant was not employee who caused rule to be introduced, he was required to obey; (4) obedience to rule does not require employee to worship "false God," in per-

son of foreman who administers rule; (5) insubordination can be found in refusing to obey reasonable directives which are nonhazardous. (S. Cahn) — Univac Div. of Sperry Rand Corp., 48 LA 619.

---

Appearances: For the employer— David E. Redman, Starr C. Calloway, Senior Labor Relations Representative. For the union—Colostein, Barkan & Brodie, by Lernard L. Barkan, of counsel; Jennie Vincent, President.

## REFUSAL TO OBEY

CAHN, Arbitrator:—The grievant, X— was hired on November 23, 1958 and discharged on January 11, 1967, after three warnings, including a one-day and a three-day disciplinary suspension without pay, for alleged insubordination.

The grievant, an Assistant Baptist Minister, worked in the plant as a janitor, together with several other janitors. His shift and that of the others started at 6 A.M. and continued until 4 P.M.

48 LA 620

Prior to December 1966 janitors received their working instructions in the morning and clocked out at 4 P.M.

In December 1966 the Employer issued a directive which required all janitors on the 8 to 4 shift to report to a specified room at 3:45 P.M. The janitors were kept in this room until

3:55 P.M. and then excused so as to allow them to punch out by 4 P.M.

The testimony as to the purpose of this directive is conflicting, the Company contending that it was to instruct and answer questions concerning special problems involved in the cleaning of the plant as to chemical spillage, etc., while the Union maintained that its sole purpose was to prevent the janitors from prematurely forming a line at the time-clock. In my opinion, because of the reasons hereinafter to be enunciated, the distinction is of no importance.

At first all the janitors complained about this directive but, with the exception of the grievant, finally capitulated.

On December 18, 1966, notwithstanding previous instructions to report to the designated room at 3:45 P.M., the grievant failed to report. He advised his superior that he was of the opinion the Company had no right to put him in a room at 3:45 P.M. and require him to remain there "under guard" until 3:55 P.M. The grievant was then again instructed thereafter to report at 3:45 P.M. and if he failed he would be subject to disciplinary action.

On December 29, 1966 the grievant again failed to report, and when questioned, stated that the Company did not have the right to compel such action unless there was work for him to perform and, accordingly, he would not report in the future. For this violation he received a written warning on December 30, 1966, advising him that any future violation would subject him to severe disciplinary measures, including suspension. This warning was made and issued in the presence of the grievant's Steward.

On January 3, 1967, for failure to report on December 30, 1966, the grievant was suspended without pay for one day, i.e., January 4, 1967, and further given a written warning to the effect that repetition of the offense would lead to more serious disciplinary action.

For failure to report on January 3rd, despite the previous warnings, the grievant was suspended for three days without pay, i.e., January 5th, 6th and 9th, and was given a written warning that repetition of the offense might lead to discharge.

On January 10, 1967, when the grievant returned to work after the three-day suspension, he again refused to report as instructed and was thereupon discharged effective January 11, 1967. The instant grievance is concerned with the aforesaid warnings, lay-offs and discharge.

The grievant's defense concerning his continued refusals to obey supervisor's instructions to attend at 3:45 P.M. was premised upon his alleged religious scruples which he contended, in effect, prohibited him from accepting pay for not working, i.e., from 3:45 P.M. to 3:55 P.M.; that "man cannot order him to do nothing," for to obey that kind of an order was to worship "a false God"; that as a Minister, the other employees looked up to him, and that he believed if he reported at the time in question, he would lose the respect of his co-workers as a Minister; that if the period in question were actually a meeting to receive instructions, he would consider that as part of his duty and would attend; that actually the period was not employed to give instructions but was in fact to prevent early line-up at the time-clock; that he objected to "being placed under guard" for the ten minutes in question for it reflected a Company attitude that he could not be trusted not to queue up before 4 P.M.

It should be emphasized at this point that the Union as such took no position concerning the Company's rights to require attendance at the meeting. It did feel, however, that the Company should respect the religious principles of one of its employees, from which it would follow

that it believed an exception should be made for the grievant.

I have carefully scrutinized the grievant's testimony and fail to find mention of any religious concept as such which would prevent the grievant from obeying the supervisor's directive.

I do find, however, that the grievant had a personal conviction against being asked to remain idle while being paid for not working; that he had scruples against "being placed under guard" (i.e., required to remain in a room for ten minutes) and that emotionally he objected to the implications of lack of trust.

I find nothing in the record which would indicate that the Company, by its actions, required him to "worship a fals⟨ God," for obediance to a direc-

### 48 LA 621

tive of this nature does not and cannot be deemed to require the grievant to "worship a false God," i.e., his foreman. I find nothing in the record, except the grievant's own statement, that in the eyes of his co-workers he would actually lose stature and respect as a Minister by obeying this directive.

The Union's contention that the grievant was not guilty of "insubordination" because insubordination is "the refusal to accept a *work* assignment" and no such work assignment is here involved, must be rejected. Insubordination may very well be found to exist in situations other than a refusal to accept a work assignment, i.e., the refusal to obey any other reasonable and legitimate directive so long as that directive does not involve hazards to the safety and health of an employee beyond that inherent in the job or are clearly and unequivocally demeaning.

The thrust of the grievant's position and the Union's brief to the effect that the requirement to report at 3:45 P.M. constituted a form of "punishment or discipline" which was not warranted insofar as this grievant was concerned must likewise be rejected. The Company's directive was not disciplinary in nature as that term is commonly employed in the field of labor relations. There was nothing of a punitive nature in the directive for the janitors, rather than containing any loss actually gained a ten minute respite at the Company's expense. The company, under its con-

tractual right to manage and direct its working force, had the prerogative to issue the directive and have it obeyed so long as employees were not injured and their contractual rights remained unimpaired. Thus it would make no difference whether the meetings in question were for the purpose of giving instructions to the janitors or whether they were employed to prevent early queuing up at the clock.

While one has great respect for a person who is willing to pay a penalty for his personal convictions, that respect has no bearing on the subject in question. The Company has no contractual or other obligation to honor these personal convictions to the extent that it should be compelled to make an exception for one employee. To compel the Company to do so could, and no doubt would, lead to cause among other employees in the plant who, just as likely, have their own convictions, religious or otherwise, concerning the nature and method of performance of their work. To treat various employees differently because of their individual subjective beliefs would make it impossible to run any industrial plant.

In the Company's third step answer, the Company offered to reinstate the grievant without back pay, providing the grievant agreed to report at 3:45 P.M. each day. This offer was rejected. In the opening statement of Union's Counsel, he alleged that if I were to direct reinstatement on condition that the grievant obey the directive to attend the daily meetings, the grievant would comply. From the standpoint of honoring a "false God," I can see no difference between the foreman's directive and mine, if such were my order. However, the grievant in answer to my specific question, stated that even were I to reinstate him on condition he attend these meetings, he would not do so. Accordingly, in light of my findings, I have no other alternative but to sustain the discharge.

**AWARD**

The undersigned, constituting the duly authorized Arbitrator, in accordance with the above mentioned submission, and to whom was voluntarily submitted the matter in controversy, awards as follows:

X— was discharged for cause. The grievance is denied.

---

### 45 LA 705

**DOVER CORP.—**

**Decision of Arbitrator**

In re DOVER CORPORATION, PEERLESS MANUFACTURING DIVISION [Louisville, Ky.] and INTERNATIONAL MOLDERS & ALLIED WORKERS UNION, Local 214, October 28, 1965

Arbitrator: William F. Dolson, selected by parties

**DISCHARGE**

**—Unauthorized entrance to plant— Propriety of penalty ▶ 118.632**

Employer was not justified in discharging, for "illegal entry," employee who, having reported to work late and finding plant gate locked, climbed plant fence to gain entry to plant, notwithstanding fact that sign on fence read "Warning! private property; only authorized persons are permitted to enter." Plant rule prohibits employees from "leaving or entering plant

through unauthorized entrances or exits," and arbitrator interprets "unauthorized entrances and exits" to mean any unauthorized site of ingress or egress out of plant, including fence; however, employee was "authorized person" within meaning of sign's language, and thus his offense was one of using "unauthorized entrance," for which penalty of written warning for first offense is prescribed by plant rule. (W. Dolson)—Dover Corp. 45 LA 705.

---

## UNAUTHORIZED ENTRY

DOLSON, Arbitrator:—The Grievant, X—, was scheduled to work Saturday, July 17, 1965. The normal starting time for his Department (Weld) was 7 a.m., but during the previous Friday afternoon the foreman of the Department instructed the men to report at 6 a.m. Having been excused from work before this announcement, the Grievant was unaware of the 6 a.m. starting time. Regardless of the starting time, the Grievant reported to work late when he arrived at the plant five minutes after 7 a.m. At that time he found that the plant gate had been locked. He waited for about 20 minutes and then decided to climb over the fence. He believed that the house containing his time card was locked, so he proceeded to his place of work.

The Grievant first punched his card that morning when he left for his lunch break. He punched in after lunch and punched out again at the quitting time 2:30 p.m. However, during the afternoon (about 2 p.m.) Mr. Ralph Lynch, Plant Superintendent, discharged the Grievant.

The Company contends that the Grievant was discharged because of his "illegal entry", that of climbing the fence to gain entry to the plant. It claims that the Grievant's act constituted a violation of the law. The Union contends that the Grievant's offense was merely an infraction of a minor rule which provides for progressive discipline of a written warning; three day suspension; then discharge (Minor offenses rule 6, Union Exhibit # 2). The rule prohibits, "Leaving or entering the plant through unauthorized entrances or exits." The Union would interpret the words "unauthorized entrances or exits" as meaning any site of ingress into or egress out of the plant, —including a fence. The Company interprets these words as meaning established plant openings (a gate, door, and so forth) and therefore not applicable in the present instance where the Grievant entered the plant via a non-opening—a fence.

The Company characterizes the Grievant's act of climbing over the fence as an illegal entry. It asserts that the fence and the 24 hour guard system are present to keep people out of the plant. The Company points to a sign on the fence which reads, "Warning! private property: only authorized persons are permitted to enter!" (Company Exhibit # 4). The Company further claims that it has had an increase in thefts the last few years and therefore is interested in knowing who enters and leaves the plant.

Was the Grievant guilty of an "illegal entry" or a violation of Rule 6? This question can best be answered by examining the act of the Grievant which resulted in his discharge. The discharge was not because he was on the Company's premises without consent, nor because he damaged Company property; rather, it was because he entered the wrong place to get to work—he climbed the fence instead of entering through the gate.

The Company by discharging the Grievant has applied the most extreme penalty in industry to a situation where an employee has not only demonstrated his willingness to work, but used unorthodox means to accomplish this purpose. The Grievant never was warned not to climb the fence during his 17 years as an employee. During this period of time his

### 45 LA 706

most severe discipline has been a written warning. On the day of discharge his foreman, William Harper, rated him as a "good" employee on the termination sheet and recommended that he be reemployed (Union Exhibit #3).

The arbitrator believes that the discharge in this case was not justified. If the Grievant is guilty of any plant rule, it would be Rule 6. This rule is aimed at disciplining employees for "Leaving or entering the plant through unauthorized entrances or exits." The rule is designed to curtail the use of wrong or "unauthorized entrances or exits" by employees authorized to enter and leave the plant. It recognizes that the use of "unauthorized entrances or exits" is a minor offense. A written warning is given for the first offense with progressively severe penalties for further violations. It is undisputed that the Grievant was authorized to enter the plant for work the morning in question. His error was that he climbed over the fence to accomplish this purpose, instead of waiting for the guard to return to the gate. He used the wrong place to gain an authorized entry. The nature of this violation is clearly one which Rule 6 attempts to curtail.

The Company in the past has recognized that the climbing over of a fence is a minor offense. In the only other case of fence climbing brought to the attention of the arbitrator, the discipline was a verbal reprimand. The Company argues that this incident occurred more than four years ago and that security regulations have since been tightened. If the Company has adopted a new

policy concerning the climbing of fences, it has not given notice of such to the employees or Union. The present plant rules were adopted May 6, 1964 (Joint Exhibit #1 and Union Exhibit # 4). These rules reflect no drastic change in the Company's policy toward this problem, except to provide for a written warning in Rule 6 instead of a verbal reprimand for the first offense.

This arbitrator appreciates the Company's concern over the increase in thefts over the past few years. The natural reaction to the problem of theft is to tighten plant security. A part of normal plant security is to prevent unauthorized persons from entering the plant. To prevent such, the Company has posted a sign warning unauthorized persons to keep out. Certainly an entry by an unauthorized person ignoring the warning, would constitute an "illegal entry." Labeling such an act as an "illegal entry" would be consistent with the purpose of the sign and also the general usage of the term. Note that the focus here is not the "place", rather it is the "person"—an unauthorized person.

Keeping in mind the generally accepted concept of "illegal entry" and the purpose of the Company's security program, it cannot be said that the Grievant, an authorized employee, anxious to report to work, committed an "illegal entry" when he climbed over the fence upon finding the gate locked. Under the facts the offense is one of using an unauthorized "entrance." This is not an offense punishable by discharge; rather it is one which Rule 6 is designed to cover. The penalty for the first violation of an "unauthorized entrance" under Rule 6 is a written warning. The arbitrator has no authority to apply any other penalty. (See General Tire and Rubber Co. 6 LA 918 (1947)).

### AWARD

The Grievant's discharge was not for just cause under Article II, section 15 of the Agreement (Joint Exhibit #1). The discharge is reduced to the prescribed penalty for the first violation of Rule 6—a written warning.

It is ordered that the Grievant be reinstated with back pay, less earnings for the period from July 17, 1965, until his reinstatement. His reinstatement shall be without loss of seniority or other contractual rights and benefits. Interest is not traditionally granted in arbitrations and is denied.

## 24 LA 538

### A. C. AND C. CO., INC.—

#### Decision of Arbitrator

In re A. C. AND C. COMPANY, INC.
and UNITED STEELWORKERS OF
AMERICA (CIO), April 21, 1955.

Arbitrator: Israel Ben Scheiber, appointed under rules of American Arbitration Association.

## DISCIPLINE

#### —Evidence — Effect of employer's failure to reveal source of information ▶ 118.313

Written reprimands given employees for alleged sleeping on job which were based solely on charges by fellow worker whose identity employer has refused to reveal shall have no probative value and may not be used by employer as basis for future disciplinary action. Basic concept of our system of jurisprudence is that one accused shall be presumed innocent until proven guilty by competent evidence; mere accusations and unsupported charges are not evidence.—A. C. and C. Co., Inc., 24 LA 538.

#### —Union's right to challenge reprimands ▶ 118.01 ▶ 93.093

Union had right to challenge the propriety of written reprimands given employees, despite employer's claim that right to challenge reprimands arises only after reprimands have been used as basis for disciplinary action. A reprimand is a step in disciplinary procedure and, as with any other disciplinary action, must be based on good and sufficient cause. —A. C. and C. Co., Inc., 24 LA 538.

## DAMAGES

#### —Penalty against employer ▶117.171

Although employer is found to have been unjustified in issuing written reprimands to two employees based solely on charges of fellow worker whose identity employer refused to reveal, union's demand that penalty of $500 payable to charity of union's choice be imposed against employer to insure against repetition of such action must be denied since nothing in contract empowers arbitrator to impose such a penalty.—A. C. and C. Co., Inc., 24 LA 538.

## PROOF OF MISCONDUCT

SCHEIBER, Arbitrator:—By agreement of the parties, a hearing on this matter was held before me as Arbitrator at the Hotel Lincoln, at Reading, Pennsylvania under the procedures of the American Arbitration Association on April 5th, 1955.

### Statement of Controversy

The Union charges the Company with improperly issuing reprimands to employees K— and W—.

The Union demands that this practice cease, and the reprimands issued be retracted and destroyed.

The Union further demands that a penalty of $500.00 payable to a charity of the Union's choice be imposed against the Company to insure against repeat performance.

### Arbitrability of Grievance

The Company has asserted that this grievance is not arbitrable under the terms of the Collective Bargaining Agreement.

Therefore the issue of arbitrability must be decided first.

The Company bases its contention on Section III of the current collective Bargaining Agreement which provides,

#### "Management

"1. Nothing in this Agreement shall limit the Company in the exercise of its function of management in the supervision and control of all operations, under which it shall have, among others, the right to hire new employees and to direct the working forces, to discipline, suspend, discharge for cause, transfer, or lay off employees because of lack of work, or for other legitimate reasons, to require employees to observe Company rules and regulations not inconsistent with provisions of this Agreement, to establish and change shift schedules, to decide the number and location of its plants, products to be manufactured, the methods and schedules of production, technological changes, including the means and processes of manufacture, provided that the Company will not use these rights for the purpose of discrimination, or in any manner which will violate any of the terms of conditions of this Agreement."

Although it is clear that it is the Company's exclusive right to discipline

## 24 LA 539

its employees, that right is not an unrestricted one. The Company cannot discipline for any reason or no reason but *only for cause* which is just and sufficient.

Section III does not deprive the Union of its right to challenge the Company's interpretation of "cause."

The Company further asserts that the Arbitrator has no jurisdiction in this matter since his authority is limited by Paragraph 13 of Section VIII, which provides,

"The impartial umpire shall only have jurisdiction and authority to interpret, apply or determine compliance with the provisions set forth in the Agreement, but the impartial umpire shall not have jurisdiction or authority to add to, detract from or alter in any way the provisions of this Agreement."

However, the Arbitrator is given very broad jurisdiction and authority pursuant to Paragraph I of Section VIII,

#### "Adjustment of Grievances

"1. Should differences arise between the Company and the Union, or its members employed by the Company, as to the meaning and application of this Agreement, or should *any local trouble of any kind* arise in the plant, there shall be no suspension of work on account of such differences but an earnest effort shall be made to settle such differences immediately in the following manner:

"Step 4: *In the event the disputes or differences* shall not have been satisfactorily settled, the matter shall then be appealed to an impartial umpire, to be appointed by mutual agreement of the parties hereto * * *." *

Thus it is the intent of the parties to the Agreement that *"local trouble of any kind"* or *"disputes or differences"* shall be settled through the grievance

*Emphasis is Arbitrator's.

procedure whose final step is arbitration. There can be no question but that the present controversy falls within the meaning of that paragraph.

In deciding this "dispute or difference" between the parties, the Arbitrator would not be adding to or detracting from or altering in any way the provisions of the Agreement. He would be determining compliance with the provision in the Agreement relating to discipline for cause, which is an arbitrable issue.

Therefore, the Arbitrator finds that the dispute is an arbitrable one.

### Factual Background

Reprimands, dated December 10, 1954 were handed to W. K—— and E. W——. The reprimands stated respectively:

"Name of Person Reprimanded—W. K——.

"Reason for Reprimand—It has been brought to the Company's attention that you have been observed sleeping in and around the Brass Valve Stock bins located in the Valve Shipping Department. This is to serve notice that, in the event you are found sleeping by supervision you will be immediately discharged."

"Name of Person Reprimanded—E. W——.

"Reason for Reprimand—It has been brought to the Company's attention that you have been observed sleeping in and around the Valve Shipping Department, also, that you have reported for work smelling of intoxicating drink. This is to serve notice that in the event supervision observes you in either of the alleged conditions you will be discharged immediately."

The Union approached the Company to find out when and by whom they were so observed.

The Company would state only that the information regarding the two men was received by a confidential telephone call from one of the Company's employees. It refused to divulge the name of the informant.

### Union's Position

The Union contends that the actual charges made against the men were not proven in this case. The employees had not been observed violating the rules by any representative of management at any level.

The Union insists that it has a right to challenge any reprimand since it cannot allow the Company to build an "unjustified record" against employees.

Further, the Union asserts that everyone has a right to face his accusers, and the refusal to reveal the names of the accusers will lead to unjust and unfounded charges.

Finally the Union reaffirms that it will not condone any violation of Company rules by its members, but it cannot accept reprimand or discipline of its employees based on unproven charges.

### Company's Position

The Company insists that the issuance of these reprimands is the sole function of management. It further insists that until the Company takes disciplinary action based on these reprimands, the Union has no right to challenge them.

The Company maintains that it must issue these reprimands in order to comply with the arbitrator's decision in Case No. 455. In that case, James J. Healy, the Arbitrator, reinstated an employee who had been dis-

## 24 LA 540

charged for sleeping on the job. Mr. Healy had ruled that discharge was too severe a penalty for the first offense of sleeping, and that the Company in other similar circumstances had given prior warnings to employees before discharging them. Therefore the Company concludes, it is merely protecting itself in issuing these reprimands.

Further, the Company asserts that it cannot reveal the source of its information, since this would quickly dry up that source. Finally the Company states that nothing could be gained by this since it would be just one man's word against another.

### Discussion

The issue resolves itself into a conflict between the Company's undeniable prerogative to keep any records it deems necessary concerning its employees, and, on the other hand, the Union's legitimate interest in records that may be used as evidence in discharge or other disciplinary actions instituted by the Company.

The heart of the issue is the question as to what use will be made of these records.

Although the Company has a right to keep any records of any kind about its employees, the Union has a duty to see that its members live up to the contract and also has a duty to protect its members' good standing with the Company.

In general, the issue of a reprimand, since it may ultimately lead to discharge, is clearly a step in the disciplinary procedure and therefore must be based on good and sufficient cause.

It must likewise be based on good and sufficient evidence.

A basic concept of our American System of Jurisprudence is that one accused shall be presumed innocent until proven guilty by proper and competent evidence.

Mere accusations and unsupported charges are certainly not evidence.

In this issue, the Company has stated that it will use the contested reprimands against the two accused men, should they at any time in the future be again accused of the same offenses, for the purpose of obtaining their discharge.

This obviously threatens the reprimanded men's status as employees of the Company.

It therefore becomes important to examine the basis for this threat.

In response to the Union's repeated offer to withdraw the grievance, if the Company produced a single witness to the acts complained of, the Company witnesses under cross examination stated:

"The 2 packing cases could have been used as beds to sleep in."

"I do not say K—— and W—— actually used them as beds."

"I can't testify that anyone had knowledge of their own, of these offenses."

It should be noted that the reprimands were "based upon a confidential telephone call received by the Company from one of its conscientious employees * * * that he had seen K— and W— sleeping in an isolated location of the Shipping Department and further that W— had been working while giving off an odor of intoxicating drink."

The Company has justified its failure to produce this "conscientious employee" as a witness on the ground that to do so would "place certain conscientious employees in an embarrassing position and would quickly dry up" its sources of information.

An employee who lost his job on the basis of such information and who thereafter found it difficult to get employment elsewhere because of the stigma attached to his discharge would suffer much more than embarrassment.

Likewise, under our American System of Jurisprudence, where these two men could not be convicted of even such minor charges as spitting on the sidewalk or of passing through a red light, without having the chance to face and cross examine the witness to these acts, "confidential telephone calls" are certainly less than sufficient evidence, on which to base reprimands which might at a later date contribute to both their discharge, and to their difficulty in getting future employment.

The livelihood of a worker should certainly not be placed at the mercy of an informer, who because of his personal dislike of the man whom he accuses, or because of the informer's desire to improve his seniority status by the discharge of an accused employee, makes a "confidential telephone call" secure in the knowledge that he will not have to face the man whom he accuses, because of a Company policy not to embarrass him by compelling him to repeat his charges under oath, in the presence of, and to submit to cross examination by, the man whom he has accused.

## 24 LA 541

The Company has correctly recognized the importance of giving a fair warning before resorting to the drastic disciplinary action of discharge.

Certainly a notification that an employee has been charged with an offense, without information as to when the offense was committed, or by whom the charge was first made, and without being given an opportunity to face his accuser, is less than fair.

Also where a man's job depends on it, he should be given a reasonable opportunity to refute the charge. This he may find difficult or impossible to do, if he does not have a chance to marshal his evidence, at the time the charge is made.

To be fair and to have probative value in a subsequent disciplinary proceeding, the written warning delivered to the accused worker must be timely, set forth the nature of the charge, who made it, and when and where the incident occurred.

The Arbitrator was impressed by the repeated assurance of the Union officials that the Union was in complete agreement with the Company in its feeling that it was entitled to a fair day's work for a fair day's pay, and that it would not tolerate sleeping on the job by any of its members, nor defend them when guilty.

No employer can long survive whose employees get paid for sleeping on their jobs.

It therefore narrows the problem down to giving workers so charged a fair warning, after which they would be able to sleep on their own time, when discharged.

### Conclusions

Therefore, the Arbitrator finds that while the Company may keep such records as it deems necessary, any reprimand delivered by it which does not provide complete information as to the circumstances of the alleged offense, that is where and when the alleged offense occurred and by whom it was observed, shall have no probative value and may not be used as the basis for future disciplinary action.

The Union's demand that a penalty of $500.00 be imposed against the Company, is disallowed.

There is no provision in the Contract giving the Arbitrator the authority to impose such a penalty, and the Arbitrator is powerless by his award to write such a provision into the parties' Contract.

### AWARD

It is therefore awarded that the reprimands delivered to employees K— and W— shall have no probative value and may not be used as the basis for future disciplinary action.

It is further awarded that the Union's demand that there be imposed against the Company a penalty in the sum of $500.00 payable to a charity of the Union's choice, be, and the same hereby is, disallowed.

## 25 LA 733

**REPUBLIC STEEL CORP.—**

### Decision of Arbitrator

In re REPUBLIC STEEL CORPORATION and UNITED STEELWORKERS OF AMERICA, LOCAL 4412, Umpire Case Nos. 87 and 88, Grievance Nos. ED-355 and ED-356, June 28, 1955 (hearing date).

Arbitrator: Harry H. Platt, umpire under contract.

### DISCIPLINE

**—Demotion as form of discipline— Careless workmanship ▶118.651 ▶119.101**

Employer may not use demotion as a form of discipline for occasional carelessness or failure to obey instructions in performing work. These are faults which usually can be corrected by a suspension and this type of discipline, rather than demotion, should be applied as long as employee is capable and qualified to do job. Employees who were demoted for these reasons therefore are entitled to be restored to their former jobs, but without back pay. Denial of back pay is justified by the fact that employer has used demotion as form of discipline for this type of offense for many years without previous challenge.—Republic Steel Corp., 25 LA 733.

———

Appearances: For the company—G. R. Rauschenberg, attorney, Cleveland; W. J. Bailey, superintendent, industrial relations, Southern Mines. For the union—Jerome Cooper, attorney; Van D. Jones, Steelworkers Representative; Q. B. Lee, president, Local 4412.

### DISCIPLINE BY DEMOTION

PLATT, Arbitrator: — The above grievances arose during the life of the Labor Agreement between the Company and the International Union of Mine, Mill and Smelter Workers. The employees at the Edwards Mine later changed bargaining representatives and the current Agreement, dated July 1, 1954, is, therefore, between Republic and the United Steelworkers of America.

### Facts

The facts in these cases can be simply stated. At the time in question, James Blakely and Joseph Bonds were Drillers. Blakely had held the classification since 1950 and Bonds since 1952. Supervision regarded both em-

## 25 LA 734

ployees as competent Drillers, well able to perform the duties of that job. They were never before disciplined or disqualified from any job which they held. A few weeks before the grievances arose, it was discovered that the aggrieved and the other Pinning Drillers were not performing their work satisfactorily. Therefore, a campaign was launched to instruct the Drillers in the proper way of doing their work. The involved employees were addressed individually and in groups, at Safety Meetings. They were instruct-

ed in the proper methods of pin-drilling and pin-setting and were cautioned about the hazards of improper pin-setting. And they were warned that they would be removed from their jobs if they proved incapable of doing their work.

On April 20, 1954, Blakely was demoted from a Driller to a Driller Helper, with a consequent rate loss of 17¢ an hour. The next day, April 21, 1954, Bonds was also demoted to a Helper. The reasons for demoting them were that on those days, Blakely set 7 out of 9 pins improperly and Bonds failed to put a rubber hose on his steel to mark the proper depth of pin holes. In a subsequent grievance meeting, when Supervision was asked whether their demotions meant that the aggrieved would be barred from ever asking to participate in that occupation again, they were told "no * * * because we knew that these men had the ability to do the work. They had been doing it. We had tried our best to get them to do it right. And it just looked like they weren't going to do it so we had to take some disciplinary measures." (Tr. pp. 38-39). The grievances of both employees, filed April 26, 1954, protesting their disqualification as Drillers and requesting pay for lost earnings, were denied. Afterwards, on October 13, 1954, a vacancy arose in the Driller classification and Bonds bid for the job and got it. Blakely still occupies the Helper job.

### Position of Parties

The Company claims that the aggrieved were properly disciplined because Blakely "was careless in his work" (Tr. p. 53) and Bonds "was instructed to do his job a certain way and he failed to do it in that way" (Tr. p. 108). And it insists that demotion was a proper form of discipline, under the circumstances. This method of disciplining employees, it urges, has been in vogue at the Edwards Mine for many years, it has never been challenged by the employees or their former bargaining representative, and it has been sustained in two arbitration awards. Moreover, it argues, their demotion did not mean that the aggrieved were forever barred from the Driller classification because they were told they had the right to bid for the job when there was an opening. Accordingly, the Company urges the grievances should be denied.

The Union contends that demotion is not a permissible disciplinary penalty under the contract, where an employee has the requisite ability to satisfactorily perform the duties of his classification. Such penalty, it argues, results in an employee's disqualification from his job for an indefinite period and is an unjust penalty. Also, it "undercuts seniority." And the fact that a former bargaining representative failed to challenge that form of discipline does not give the Company a right to "perpetuate the error." Nor was their demotion defensible even though the aggrieved were told that they could reapply for their jobs if a vacancy

occurred. The grievances were sufficient notice to the Company that the aggrieved deemed their demotion improper and the burden was on the Company to correct its error without waiting for the employees to bid for their jobs. Therefore, the Union claims that the grievances should be granted.

### Discussion

It should be observed at the outset, that the question here is not whether the Company lacks power, under the contract, to demote employees for reasons other than discipline. Management surely has that right when employees are substantially deficient in their work, when they are incapable of performing their work safely, or when their effort and workmanship deteriorate to a point where they no longer keep up with the standard of performance of others in their classification. The demotions of the aggrieved, however, were not for any of those reasons. They lacked neither training, knowledge, or the requisite ability to be Drillers. They had, in fact, been promoted to that classification and Supervision insisted, throughout the hearing, that both Blakely and Bonds knew their work and were capable of doing it satisfactorily. It was only that on the days in ques-

## 25 LA 735

tion, Blakely was careless in the way he set some pins and Bonds neglected to mark his steel in the prescribed manner. And in the view of Supervision, this made them subject to discipline.

I agree with Supervision that the aggrieved's carelessness on the days in question was inexcusable and that they deserved to be disciplined. And I would not hesitate to sustain any reasonable disciplinary penalty, as a corrective measure. But I do not believe that permanent demotion is a proper form of discipline where an employee's capabilities are conceded and his performance is generally satisfactory but where his attitudes of the moment are improper. For improper work attitudes— as evidenced by occasional carelessness and failure to obey instructions—can usually be corrected by suspending or laying off the employee for a reasonable but definite period. That is a form of discipline which does not offend the basic seniority rights of either the disciplined employee or of other employees in the bargaining unit and which does not inflict upon an employee an "indeterminate sentence." Indeed, it has long been recognized that the essential purpose of industrial discipline is not so much to punish workers as it is to correct their faults and behavior and thus to make them better and more productive workers. This belief, which is held by many persons in the Personnel and related fields, has led to the development of the principle of "corrective industrial discipline." It is a concept that calls for lighter penalties for first offenses and progressively harsher penalties for repeated offenses, culminating in discharge when all possibilities of correction have been exhausted.

In the circumstances of these cases, the principle of corrective discipline was applicable. A reasonable layoff penalty thus was justified not, what was in effect, a permanent disqualification for the Driller classification. For although the aggrieved were told they would be given consideration if they reapplied for the Driller's job when a vacancy arose, there was no telling when such an opening would occur and no absolute assurance was given that their bids would be accepted when tendered. Accordingly, I hold that demotion of the aggrieved to Helpers was not proper discipline.

The above holding leads to the inevitable conclusion that the aggrieved employees must be reinstated in their former jobs as Drillers. The further

question is whether they are entitled to compensation for their lost earnings while they remained in the Helper classification.

The evidence is undisputed that for a number of years, Supervision at the Edwards Mine disciplined employees for occasional careless workmanship and for failure to obey instructions by demoting them to lower rated jobs; and neither the employees so disciplined nor their former bargaining representative ever questioned that form of discipline. Moreover, although the form of discipline seems not to have been questioned in two cases that were arbitrated about the same time when Blakely and Bonds were demoted, the awards (of another Arbitrator) in those cases sustained the demotions of employees for substantially the same reasons that Blakely and Bonds were demoted. Under these

circumstances, I cannot say that the Company acted culpably when it demoted the two herein aggrieved employees. And since the question is raised for the first time in the instant cases, while I hold that demotion was not a proper disciplinary penalty under the circumstances, nevertheless I think "the equities of (these) particular cases * * * demand" (Sec. 10D) that the remedy be limited here to the restoration of Blakely and Bonds to their former classification of Drillers.

## AWARD

James Blakely shall forthwith be reinstated in the position of Driller, but without back pay. As Joseph Bonds has held that classification since October 13, 1954, no other relief is warranted as to him.

---

### 73 LA 256

**WESTINGHOUSE ELECTRIC CORP.—**

#### Decision of Arbitrator

In re WESTINGHOUSE ELECTRIC CORPORATION, R & D CENTER and FEDERATION OF WESTINGHOUSE INDEPENDENT SALARIED UNIONS, AAA Case No. 55 30 0166-77, Grievance No. F.A.G. 4581, May 3, 1979
Arbitrator: Peter Seitz

### DISCIPLINE

**—Failure to respond to call-in for snow removal — Protest against assignment ▶ 118.658 ▶ 118.6361**

Employer properly suspended employee who failed to respond to call-in for snow detail because he claimed he did not hear the 62 rings on four separate telephone calls made to reach him, even if it should be accepted that grievant did not and could not hear telephone, since (1) he still is culpable, in that with foreknowledge that snow detail was part of his job duties, grievant could not place himself in position that it would be impossible for employer to communicate with him, (2) evidence establishes that employee merely was continuing his "historic crusade" against call-ins for snow detail and had determined that not answering phone would be effective tactic, and (3) evidence that other employees were exempted from snow detail because one employee was not in condition to perform detail or because employer was not obligated to call every man on roster for detail does not support claim of discrimination.

### ARBITRATION

**—Challenge to arbitrator's impartiality ▶ 94.7055**

Arbitrator retains jurisdiction to determine merits of discipline case in which employer and union clashed on procedure in presenting case but were left relatively free to run arbitration according to style that they preferred, despite charge by union's attorney that arbitrator was not conducting hearing impartially and was interfering with his presentation of case, since (1) review of case supports arbitrator's finding that procedural complaints of union attorney were

without merit, and (2) arbitrator believes that he can issue fair and just decision on dispute.

---

Appearances: For the company — Richard Slosberg, attorney, senior labor counsel. For the union — Albert C. Shapira, attorney, general counsel.

### REFUSING CALL-IN

SEITZ, Arbitrator: — The issue in the dispute to be arbitrated, as agreed to by the parties at the hearings, is: "Did the company have just cause to impose a five-day disciplinary suspension on L— [the grievant]; and if not, what remedy is appropriate.[1]

### 73 LA 257
**Preliminary Remarks**

In this case, Counsel for the Federation, at the opening of the second day of hearings, moved to have the Arbitrator recuse himself on the ground that he was not conducting the hearing impartially and was interfering with the presentation of his client's case. The Company vigorously objected to the Arbitrator withdrawing from the case. After giving each party a full opportunity to be heard on the motion, the Arbitrator expressed the view that he did not regard the facts as supporting the motion and "I can hear this case fairly and issue a just, fair, proper and impartial award; and therefore I suggest that we proceed with the case." Counsel for the Federation continued to argue his position for four additional pages of the transcript; but then proceeded with the case. His motion that the arbitrator withdraw was renewed in a letter he wrote to Mr. John Schano, Regional Director of the American Arbitration Association on March 7, 1979 on the occasion of filing copies of his reply brief.

I have no desire or intention to misuse my office, as Arbitrator, or this Opinion, by carrying on a debate with Mr. Shapira, Counsel for the Federation. An attack has been launched, however, against my professional integrity, impartiality and competence in conducting a hearing. It seems appropriate that I make a few observations on the subject.

In conducting an arbitration hearing (indeed, in conducting a judicial hearing, as well) a situation may arise when two countervailing considerations need to be balanced. First, the arbitrator must afford counsel as much latitude as he can in the organization and presentation of his client's case.[2] The Arbitrator, however, is also under a duty to ensure that the hearing is organized and conducted in an orderly fashion so that the latitude in presentation permitted to one party does not trespass upon the rights of the other party. There are other responsibilities that he bears, as well. Aware as he is that the logotype of the American Arbitration Association (under whose administrative auspices this arbitration is conducted) bears the words "Justice," "Economy" and "Speed," he has the responsibility of running the hearing in such a way as to achieve these objectives. He also has a responsibility to himself and the role he is called upon to play. The difficult decision, ultimately, is his to make, exclusively. He cannot fulfill his duty with excellence (as he hopes to do) unless the hearing and the presentations of the parties develop a coherent, comprehensible and a manageable record that will enable him to make findings of fact and conclusions of law with the proper measure of confidence.

These several considerations — procedural freedom for the party presenting his case on the one hand and protection of the other party, arbitrational econo-

---

[1] In the course of the hearing Counsel for the Union took the position that no just cause for the disciplinary penalty existed; but that if just cause were shown, the Union was not challenging the penalty as excessive.

[2] See "5" of the Code of Professional Responsibility for Arbitrators of Labor-Management Disputes which had been approved by the American Arbitration Association. "5.1.c." of the Code states, "An arbitrator should not intrude into a party's presentation so as to prevent that party from putting forth its case fairly and adequately.

my and speed (to the extent consistent with justice) and the Arbitrator's need for order and a coherent intelligible record on the other hand — are only occasionally in critical opposition in my arbitrational experience spanning several decades. It is only infrequently, as an arbitrator, that I have had to balance the considerations and, by suggestion or by ruling ensure that what I regarded as the priorities be observed. I do not recall any arbitration, prior to this case, in which I was asked to withdraw because an advocate for one party, in mid-hearing, contended that my efforts to conduct a hearing according to the standards and objectives set forth above, disclosed that I lacked fairness and impartiality.

Practice and procedure in arbitration has not developed the relative uniformity that exists in judicial tribunals under codes or procedure and court rules. In my judgment it is fortunate that it has not. The parties, with the assistance of the arbitrator, are left relatively free (excepting for the demands of procedural due process) to run their arbitration according to the style which they prefer. Difficulties arise when one party insists on a particular style of procedure and the other party's preference is in opposition to it — or the arbitrator believes that what is occurring will not furnish him with the kind of record that will enable him, ultimately, to discharge his own duties properly.

Apparently, this was such a case. Mr. Shapira's view of the manner in which he presented the Federation's case clashed with the Company's view of what was appropriate, and the Arbitrator, in an effort to ensure that the Company's rights to fair hearing be not transgressed and that his own duties be properly discharged, made procedural suggestions to Mr. Shapira for his guidance. These suggestions, apparently, were bitterly resented and were the basis for the personal attack on the arbitrator.

On a review of what took place, I find the procedural complaints of Counsel for the Federation to be without merit and his several motions that I withdraw from the case are denied. A decision granting his motions would be unfair

### 73 LA 258

and damaging not only to the Company but to the arbitration process, generally.

Despite the overt hostility to me exhibited by Mr. Shapira, I continue to believe that I can issue a fair and just decision in this arbitration. I trust that this decision I have written meets those requirements.

As indicated above, there are contentions related to arbitrability. These cannot be discussed intelligibly or decided without first setting forth the facts in the case as found by the Arbitrator.

### The Facts

The grievant, L—, was employed in the Plant Service Department at the Company's Research and Development Center since February, 1975. Shortly prior to that date he had been denied promotion to a vacancy in the groundskeeper job (gardener) in that Department because, among other reasons, he

had declared that he would not report for snow detail outside his normal working hours. At this point it seems pertinent to observe that there is a rather long access road on the Company's property leading from the highway to its buildings and the employees' parking lot. When there is a snowfall that is not promptly removed from that access road, during shift change periods, there occurs a considerable congestion of vehicles which backs up to the highway and obstructs traffic thereon. The Company possesses and maintains various kinds of equipment for snow removal. The removal of snow is the responsibility of the Plant Service Department. Employees in the Department are assigned by it to operate the snow-removal equipment and are "called in" prior to their scheduled shift hours should the snowfall occur during the night. For reasons deemed sufficient to it, the Department has exempted some of its employees from such "snow detail." The Department also uses, for snow removal, employees in other departments (or in other unrelated jobs) who volunteer for such "call-in." When the circumstances warrant, it also arranges for snow removal by an independent contractor.

When L— had been denied the promotion in early 1975, it appears that several employees with seniority rights paramount to L—'s had refused the job because they did not desire to or could not perform the snow detail.

L— grieved the denial of the promotion. At a grievance meeting, the Company, having been informed by the Federation that Lamonde would, despite his previous statements, report for snow detail, he was offered the job and he accepted it. Company Exhibit No. 2, dated January 9, 1975, is a memorandum from the Department to L— (with a copy marked for the Federation's representative) which sets forth the "conditions under which you will be continued on the 6CMNO6 Gardener job." The first condition stated is:

"1. You will report for snow detail, including Sunday nights when called."[3]

In November, 1975 L— requested to be relieved of his snow detail for physical reasons and "because it was not mentioned in [his] your job description, and the management cannot force overtime on an employee." (Co. Exhibit No. 6.) The Company responded in the cited exhibit calling attention to the January 9, 1975 memorandum (Co. Exhibit No. 2), referred the question of physical disability to the site medical physician for decision and stated that "fulfilling these job requirements is an absolute necessity if you are to remain so classified" in the job in which he was an incumbent.

Less than a year later, on Monday, November 8, 1976, L— was phoned at his home at 4:30 a.m. to report for snow detail. His wife took the message. He did not report for work, however, until his normal reporting time, 7:30 a.m. When the Department head (DePastino) asked for an explanation, L— responded (according to DePastino) that "neither I or anyone else at the Research and Development Center could make him get out of bed at any hour of

the night, except for his regular starting time, and that no one can make him report for snow duty." (Tr. p. 64.) He was informed that failure to report for snow duty was a grave offense.

As a result of this confrontation, meetings were held with Mr. Regis Hovan, the Federation's representative and Mr. John Daley, Personnel Manager at the Center. Following those meetings a disciplinary penalty of one and one half working days was imposed on L— because of the events of November 8, 1976. Daley then sent a memorandum (Company Exhibit No. 4) dated November 9, 1976 to DePastino with a copy marked for Hovan. It states that Hovan and he (Daley) had agreed as follows with respect to snow detail:

"It is understood that all employes classified as Gardener 06CMN06 will be required to be on the snow detail roster. This is not a *voluntary* duty; the reasoning behind this work assignment is that these employes operate the key pieces of equipment for snow removal."

The memorandum went on to record other agreements reached with respect to snow detail including the fact that

### 73 LA 259

one Snyder had not been called for such detail; that the Union had no objection to the continuation of this practice, but that in "certain situations" that were described, Snyder "would be required to respond for snow detail."

On November 24, 1976 a substitute was issued for Company Exhibit No. 4. This substitute (Company Exhibit No. 5) repeated all of the provisions of Company Exhibit No. 4 excepting those referring to Snyder.

On Monday, November 19, 1976, in the early morning hours, a snow detail was called out but L— was not called because he had a scheduled vacation day on that date and would not be reporting for work at 7:30 a.m.

On November 30, 1976 at about 4:00 or 4:30 a.m. weather conditions again required the calling of a snow detail. The supervisor (Ward) told an employee, Siler (the night shift foreman) to call out eight employees for that detail, including L—. Seven responded and reported for snow detail. Siler reported to Ward that L— had not answered his telephone calls. Ward told Siler to keep calling Lamonde's telephone number and to record the times he called. Siler, in his testimony (which I have no reason to discredit) stated that he had obtained L—'s home telephone number from the snow detail sheet and verified its accuracy by calling the guard at the Center's gate. Siler kept a record of his efforts to reach L— by telephone. When he phoned at 4:47 a.m., he stated, L—'s telephone rang ten times without answer; when he called at 4:55 a.m. it rang 16 times; at 5:00 a.m., 16 times; at 5:15 a.m., 20 times.[4] L— did not communicate with the Center until 7:30 a.m., his regular starting time.

L— told DePastino he did not hear the telephone ring that morning; that a

---

[3] L—'s regular schedule did not call for Sunday night work.

[4] The Company's brief, page 7, sets forth that at 5:15 a.m. Siler let L—'s telephone ring 30 times. This is an error. It is inconsistent with Company Exhibit No. 1, prepared by Siler at the time of his calls.

Thus, according to Siler, excluding his first effort to establish telephone communication with L—, he had his telephone ring 62 times in four calls.

new baby was sleeping in his bedroom; that a vaporizer was in operation; and that the door to his bedroom was closed. The telephone was in another room. DePastino did not credit this explanation in light of his previous experience with L——. On December 1, 1976 a five-day disciplinary suspension from work was imposed. The Company's letter of suspension (Company Exhibit No. 7) refers to the penalty as being based on "Your total record" and at the hearing the Company introduced exhibits and presented testimony with respect to previous disciplinary actions (for offenses unrelated to snow removal). It argues in its brief that L——'s "extremely poor work record, amply support[s] the Company's action in this case."

It seems best to observe at this point that I do not regard the other disciplinary actions or warnings (excepting those related to snow removal detail) as having any relevance in this case. The dispute before me was triggered exclusively by L——'s alleged failures of duty in relation to snow removal detail; and in reaching my conclusions, I do not extend consideration to such other unrelated events and matters.

**Contention of the Parties**

The Company claims that, placed in the context of L——'s previous attitudes and actions regarding snow detail, his explanation for failure to respond to the call-in "is simply incredible," and on the record made, it had just cause for the action grieved.

"THE UNION'S CLAIMS IN THE GRIEVANCE" are tersely set forth on page 2 of its brief, as follows:

"1. On the day he was called to work for snow detail, grievant was on a scheduled day of vacation, and on such a day, he was not subject to any work order. * * *.

"2. The snow detail was being discriminately enforced against grievant, as the Company was excusing other persons similarly situated, from the snow detail. * * *.

"3. Grievant did not hear his phone ring * * * under excusable circumstances. As a result, there was no punishable offense committed."

In its initial brief the Company claimed that the "vacation argument" (Item "1" in the Union's claims, supra) is not for consideration in this arbitration proceeding; and if "arbitrable," is "totally without merit."

On February 26, 1979, following the exchange of the initial post-hearing briefs, Counsel for the Federation wrote to the American Arbitration Association requesting from the Arbitrator "permission to reply to the Company's assertions in its Post Hearing Brief that the Union's 'vacation' arguments are directed to inarbitrable issues." As mentioned above, this requested was granted by the Arbitrator.

The "reply brief" submitted by the Union contains two points. The first is that decisional precedents (which it cites) show that the Company's arguments (with respect to inarbitrability) are "devoid of merit." The second is that the Company's claims "refer to procedural arbitrability only, and the Company is therefore estopped to first raise them in a post-hearing brief."

The "Reply Memorandum of the Company" in its first point argues that the court and arbitration decisions relied upon by the Union "Are Inapplica-

## 73 LA   260

ble to the Case at Hand." In its second point it states that its arbitrability contentions are not in conflict with the Company's contentions that "Any Contract Issues be Resolved in Its Favor."

Before addressing the merits it seems appropriate to consider the "arbitrability" question.

In its initial brief the Company points out that under Paragraph A of Article XV of the collective agreement a request for arbitration must specify which of some 30 "items" (claims of contract violation) the arbitration concerns. The Union had specified Item 30 ("A disciplinary penalty, release or discharge which is alleged to have been imposed without just cause")[5]; but the Company asserts that *no* request was made to arbitrate an alleged violation of the *vacation provisions* of the Agreement in Section XIII thereof and listed in Article XV — A as Item 19.

Then the Company refers to Paragraph B of Section XV — A which forbids arbitration of subjects, "direct or collateral" not involving the disputes described in Paragraph A, "except by mutual written agreement as provided under paragraph H of this Section."[6] The Company states that there was no writing executed pursuant to Paragraph H and that if the Federation desired to challenge the Company's right to call L—— for snow detail on his vacation day, it cannot be done via a grievance protesting a disciplinary suspension; and it must be done by a grievance charging violation of Article XIII of the Agreement. Accordingly, it is said, the matter is not arbitrable.

I have read with care the reply briefs of the parties on the question of arbitrability and the court and arbitration cases cited. Counsel with commendable professional diligence and skilled exercise of the mysteries of hermeneutics have attempted to demonstrate that the cited decisions uphold their own contentions and disprove those of their adversaries. I perceive little profit or utility in launching into my own exegesis of what is represented as Scripture and shall dispose of the problem broadly and briefly.

The grievance filed challenged the position that the Company had just cause to discipline L—— for five days. It protested personnel action taken by the Employer, not its denial of vacation rights reserved to L—— by the Agreement. No one denies that, in the early morning hours of November 30, 1976, L—— was not scheduled for work. The question that arises (in adjudicating whether there was just cause to discipline him) is whether, notwithstanding that he was not in active duty status prior to 7:30 a.m. that morning (and had been on vacation leave during his normal tour of duty on the *previous* day), he was under a duty to respond to a call for snow detail in the pre-shift hours of November 30, 1976.

If the call had been made on a Sunday night or Monday morning (with no vacation leave in the picture) the question

would be the same. Is he under a duty to respond to a call made during hours when he was on off-duty status, or otherwise not scheduled to work? If he was not, a serious question of the existence of "just cause" emerges.

Whether the questions of discipline for just cause and vacation or other leave are "inextricably intertwined," I do not venture to say. It does seem to me, however, that it is consonant with the provisions of the Agreement and with the largest body of arbitral authority that, in challenging the propriety of a disciplinary penalty, the grievant, in the course of explaining or justifying conduct which might be regarded as a violation of duty, can invoke provisions of the Agreement which, he believes, inhibit the Employer from exercising the disciplinary power it claims to possess. An employer claiming "just cause" to discharge or to discipline asserts, in effect, that the employee has breached his job duties and responsibilities. If the employee-grievant justifies his conduct on the ground that the duty and responsibility did not exist (because he was on vacation or was otherwise on leave) a denial of his right to assert it in arbitration, it seems to me, would be grossly unfair to him.

When Mr. Shapira asserted that he was "specifying Item 30 of Paragraph A of Section XV — A" under which a claim is arbitrable if it involves a disciplinary penalty "alleged to have been imposed without just cause," he did all he needed to do in this case; and having done that, when he seeks to explain or justify the charged offense by reference to vacation provisions of the Agreement, he does not, in my opinion, render the dispute or any aspect of it inarbitrable.

In this connection, I only observe, without further comment, that on June 10, 1977, in response to Mr. Shapira's arbitration request of June 1, 1977, the Company wrote to him that it "does not contest arbitrability of the disciplinary suspension given."

Thus, I conclude that the matter under discussion, including the relevance or impact of the vacation provisions, if any, is arbitrable.

## 73 LA   261

**The Merits**

1. However reluctant L—— may have been to be assigned to snow detail — a reluctance he made abundantly clear on a number of occasions — there can be no possible doubt whatever that snow detail was one of the required duties of his job. Company Exhibit No. 2 "defining the conditions" of his continuing in his job states:

"1. You will report for snow detail, including Sunday nights when called."[7]

As stated above, L——'s tours of duties did not normally include Sunday nights. Snow detail, however, was a duty of his job to be performed whenever it snowed and he was called out to help in its removal — and if he could be called for it on Sunday nights, he could also be called for it at any other time when he

---

[5] See letter dated June 1, 1977, Mr. Albert C. Shapira to Mr. R. G. Pumphrey, included in a packet of letters marked Joint Exhibit No. 2.

[6] Paragraph H provides that the parties by mutual consent in writing may waive restrictions and limitations on arbitrability.

[7] The statement in Company Exhibit No. 2, be it noted, does not refer to vacation leave, expressly, as a reason for exemption from snow detail. The Company, however, so far as appears, as a matter of policy respects the convenience of employees on vacation leave.

was off duty because not scheduled for work.[8] The facts in this case and the arguments made involve vacation leave — but they might just as well have involved leave for any other purpose — that is to say, call-in at any time the emergency situations reasonably required it, regardless of his scheduled hours of work.

There is no occasion, in this case, to study the vacation provisions of the Agreement and to determine whether, in the hours that Siler called, he was or was not, actually, on vacation leave according to their terms.[9] Even though it might be argued with some force that his vacation leave applied only to hours that, but for the granting of the leave, he might have been scheduled for work, for the purpose of this discussion it will be assumed that he was on vacation leave from 4:47 a.m. to 5:15 a.m. on November 30. When the snow emergency occurred (a fact that was not challenged) his job duties and responsibilities required him to respond promptly to the call despite the fact that he was being asked to report at a time other than his regularly scheduled tour of duty. This does not mean that the Company is free to call in vacationing employees whose duties include snow detail without regard to their convenience. The Company does not argue here for this claim of power. The record indicates that it did not call for snow detail employees who were known to have been vacationing out of the area. Indeed, it did not call in L— for his pre-shift hours on the previous morning (Monday, November 29) because he was to be on vacation leave that Monday for the hours starting at 7:30 a.m. Thus, had it called him, he would have been on duty removing snow in pre-shift hours and his vacation leave would have started at the hour of his normal reporting time. In exercising its power to call in employees for snow detail, the Company must, of course, act reasonably. It did so in respect of the morning of November 29, in not calling him in. It did so on November 30, when it tried in vain to call him in for pre-shift snow detail inasmuch as he was scheduled to work, in any event, at 7:30 a.m. on that day.

Viewing the case as I do, I find it unnecessary to decide whether or not L— was on vacation leave when Siler tried to reach him by phone; but even if he were, it was his job duty and responsibility to be available for call-in and to respond to a call-in.

---

[8] This statement is tantamount to a job description or specification.

[9] An employee's conception of when he is "on vacation," generally, may not accord with what the collective agreement provides as "vacation" or what is recognized as such in industrial relations practice. An employee is on "vacation," under the agreement, when he absents himself from his customary scheduled hours and days of work with the consent or leave of his employer for "vacation purposes." Thus, for example, if an employee were granted two weeks of "vacation" it cannot be said that he was on approved vacation leave during the week-end intermediate between these two weeks. As a matter of fact and law he does not require his employer's consent to absent himself from work during those days — and, accordingly, although he regards the week-end as a part of his vacation period, it is not a period of vacation provided for in the collective agreement.

Thus, in the early hours of Tuesday, November 30, when L— was called for snow detail, not having had to obtain vacation leave for such hours (and it not having been granted) it cannot be held that he was then on vacation leave.

It is asserted that L— was not culpable in respect of having failed to respond to the call-in because he did not hear his home telephone ring — and that there were special circumstances (such as he described and as are delineated above) which prevented him from knowing that Siler had phoned him on at least five occasions.

This aspect of the case turns, in the greatest part, on the credibility of witnesses.

It has to be acknowledged that it is within the range of the remotely possible and conceivable that L— and his wife and his other children did not hear the telephone ring. But having said this, one must consider the situation against the backdrop of other significant facts in the record.

Despite the fact that the bedroom door was closed on November 8, his wife testified that she heard the telephone ring in the early hours of the morning that day and answered the telephone. This was the day he did not report for the call-in until 7:30 a.m., his regular reporting time. When he did so, he had vigorously challenged the Company's power to call him out for snow detail at hours other than his *regularly sched-*

### 73 LA   262

*uled hours.* To be sure, on November 8, 1976 there was no humidifier in the bedroom; but I have listened (at the hearing) to the humidifier in operation and in my judgment the sound it made while so operating was not such as would explain the fact that the telephone ring was heard on November 8, 1976 but not heard, despite the persistent efforts made by Siler on November 30, 1976. I find it impossible to credit the assertion that nobody, asleep in that house, would fail to hear in excess of 62 rings!

2. It is evident that L— never really accepted the fact that snow-detail call-in was a part of his job duties and responsibilities. He filed a grievance when he was denied the vacancy because he declared he would not peform snow-details; the Company reduced to writing its agreement with the Union that snow-detail call-in was, indeed, a part of his job; he then tried to avoid snow detail by claiming physical disability, and when he was instructed to document his claim by medical certification, apparently, let the matter drop. At the hearing he claimed that he made every reasonable effort on November 8, 1976 to respond to the call-in and that he had been delayed by weather conditions. The record convinces me, however, that when he finally appeared for work at 7:30 a.m., although weather conditions may have been mentioned, his principal point was that he was continuing to challenge the power of the Company to call him in for snow detail outside his regularly scheduled hours.

His attitude, consistently and even obstinately maintained, in reference to his job duties, as described, considered together with the circumstances and facts as I find them to have been, compel the conclusion that credibility cannot be extended to L—'s version of what took place or did not take place on November 30, 1976. I can only conclude, from the record as a whole, that L— was continuing his historic crusade against call-ins for snow detail and had deter-

mined that not answering the phone would be an effective tactic in his Hundred Years War with the Company.

But even if the highly improbable should be factual and true, and L—, under the circumstances that he had described, *did not* and *could not* hear the more than 62 rings on the telephone in more than four separate calls — he is still culpable!

With foreknowledge that snow-detail call-in was a part of his job duties, L— could not, with impunity, place himself so that it would be impossible for the Company to communicate with him for snow-detail call-in. Indeed, under the circumstances, one would think that it was his duty to take such affirmative action as might be necessary to ensure that if he were needed for snow removal, he could be certain that the message would reach him. Instead, if his own version of events be accepted, he created a situation that would enable him to claim that he was unaware of the efforts to reach him. It is impossible to view his actions as anything but a stratagem and a subterfuge to defeat the Company in its position as to his job duties.

Under all of the circumstances, I have to find, not only that the Company was lenient in the discipline imposed, but that it clearly had just cause in suspending the grievant for five days.

3. It is argued that "The discipline here was unconscionably discriminatory in several ways, when the treatment of L—, in relationship to that of Snyder and Cramer, is considered" (Union Brief, p. 15).

The Union devotes 15 pages in its brief to the point that, requiring L— to report when called for "snow detail" and exempting Snyder and Cramer (who were incumbents of the same job title or classification) amounts to "insidious discrimination" [sic] which answers the Company's position that it had just cause under the Agreement for the disciplinary penalty imposed on L—. The Company's brief does not address itself, so far as I can see, to this aspect of the Union's case.

Snyder, it appears, "had a serious physical situation"[10] and the Company claims that it had exempted him from snow detail for that reason. In the first memorandum dated November 9, 1976 memorializing the agreement reached between Daley and Hovan (Company Exhibit No. 4) it was stated that the Union had "no objection" to that exemption with the proviso that in the event of an "extreme snowfall or lack of availability of qualified operators" Snyder would be required to respond for snow-detail." In the revision of that memorandum dated November 24, 1976, all references to Snyder in connection with snow detail were exercised. So far as appears, the Company never called him for snow-detail. Snyder was hospitalized on or about November 29, 1976 and died early in 1977.

Cramer, according to the Company, had a disability resulting from a back injury. He had been sent to a lower coded job because of the disability. In 1976 he was regarded as having recovered and was "repromoted" to the gardener's job; but so far as appears, had not been called for snow detail.

---

[10] Testimony of John Daley, Tr. 244.

The Federation's brief emphasizes that the exemption of both Snyder and

### 73 LA    263

Cramer from snow detail was not based upon the certification of physicians but by the judgment of management.

I find no merit in the Federation's argument on discrimination against L— in the respects discussed.

First, it is extremely rare in our industrial society to find that all incumbents of a job classification have absolute or ideal equality of treatment in the assignments made to them or the tasks they are called upon to perform.[11] Unless there is some explicit provision in the contract providing to the contrary, management, in making assignments, often gives consideration to the relative seniority, skills and physical and mental capacities of those in the same job classification. I have been directed to no such provision in the governing Agreement, here. The memorandum of November 24, 1976 (Company Exhibit No. 5), however, does announce agreement that all in the Gardener job will be required to be on the snow detail roster. Thus, *as of that date* the Company had committed itself to include Snyder and Cramer among those subject to call-in on the snow detail roster.

The Federation's brief, at various points, stresses that the discriminatory treatment it calls "insidious"[12] occurred both before and after the agreement of November 24, 1976. If there occurred discriminatory treatment prejudicial to L—'s rights prior to the making of that agreement the reason for complaining about it in this case is obscure. Such discriminatory treatment, I assume, could have been the subject of a grievance in which the remedy requested would be the inclusion of Cramer and Snyder in the snow detail roster. So far as appears, no such grievance was filed. It seems inappropriate, then, to complain of such discriminatory treatment before November, 1976 in connection with the question whether the Company had just cause to discipline Lamonde for the events of November 30, 1976.

If the discriminatory treatment complained of is the Company's failure, notwithstanding the agreement of November 24, 1976, to call in Snyder and Cramer for snow detail on November 30, as it had called in L—, there are several considerations to canvass.

a) Snyder having entered the hospital on November 29, 1976, apparently, it must be assumed he was not in condition to perform snow detail, if called, on November 30, 1976.

b) Although the agreement of November 24, 1976 required Cramer to be included on the snow detail roster

there is nothing to show that the Company was under a legal duty to call *every* man on that roster for the snow detail for which L— failed to report on November 30, 1976. Placing Cramer's name on the roster means to me that snow detail was included in his job responsibilities; but it does not mean that if the Company on a particular day calls in L— and not Cramer for reasons it considers sufficient, that there has been some invidious or offensive discrimination against L— that shields him from disciplinary action for failure to perform *his own* duty.

c) Discriminatory or disparate treatment might have been a relevant consideration in this case had L— and another Gardener both failed in their duty to respond to call-ins for snow detail and, without a reasonable basis, therefore, *L— had been given a more severe penalty than the other Gardener.* Disparate treatment of those similarly situated who have committed the same infraction is unfair and wrong unless a rational and persuasive basis for the difference in treatment is demonstrated.

This is *not*, however, the kind of disparate treatment or "discrimination" with respect to which the Federation complains.

The fact is that it is as clear as can be that snow detail was a duty that *L—* was obliged to perform. Under the circumstances of this case and on the kind of record made he cannot, to avoid culpability, avail himself of the argument that someone else had not been called on that day. The argument assumes a disparity of treatment in the imposition of penalties, which is contrary to fact. If the Federation believed that the Agreement was violated in that the Company was making assignments of job duties in a classification, that objection should have been raised in a grievance directed to that violation. It has no place in this grievance protesting discipline for failing to perform what was clearly a job duty of the grievant.

In this decision I have attempted to deal with what seemed to me the points raised by the parties which they regarded of paramount importance. There are other arguments in the briefs which I have not addressed. I have read the briefs with care and I find that there would be little utility or purpose in setting forth more than I have as the basis for the accompanying Award.

Since having prepared a draft of this Opinion and Award, I have received from the American Arbitration Association Mr. Albert C. Shapira's letter of April 9, 1979 and Mr. R. A. Edwards' letter of April 10, 1979.

I have read Mr. Shapira's letter with care. I find nothing in it that requires

### 73 LA    264

amendment or revision of my previously prepared draft.

Mr. Shapira, in his second paragraph, seems to complain of the Arbitrator's

order which had provided that after he had filed the Reply Brief (for which permission had been granted to him on his express request) the Company was given an opportunity to answer the Union's Reply Brief. He states that the Arbitrator's order "precludes any response to it by us * * *." I find no merit in this objection. As I see it, it would have been grossly unfair to the Company to have granted Mr. Shapira's request to file a reply brief without also having afforded the opportunity to the Company to comment on it. Aside from the question of unfairness to the Company, I believed that the proper discharge and fulfillment of my own responsibilities as arbitrator indicated the desirability of having both parties state their position on the matter that would be placed in Mr. Shapira's Reply Brief.

Second, inasmuch as Mr. Shapira claims that the Company's argument in its Reply Brief has nothing to do with "arbitrability," he asks the Arbitrator "to apply the proper sanction of returning that brief to Mr. Edwards without considering it" and he asks "for such a ruling upon this Motion."

The motion for said sanction is denied.

Third, the position of Mr. Shapira's letter marked "(2)" consists of Mr. Shapira's passionate and unrestrained rhetorical defense against what he considers to be a personal attack on him by Mr. Edwards — this, despite the fact that he states "I find it unnecessary to defend myself against the gutter-sniping venom of Mr. Edwards' last letter, and I do not."

The tone and content of this portion of the letter is most unfortunate and inappropriate in a lawyer's communication to an arbitrator. I find distasteful, particularly, the statement that "the continued showering of the arbitrator [by the Company] with loving embrace almost to the point of lewdness, comprises a sordid picture, so foreign to the principles of this forum."

This, and other remarks by Mr. Shapira, in his letter, can only be read to reflect upon the integrity of the Arbitrator. It suggests that the Arbitrator has either encouraged or has willingly accepted a relationship with the Company that is highly improper.

Arbitrators have no means available to them to protect or to defend themselves from this kind of personal attack except to deny, with such dignity as they may still possess, any real basis for the assault. Accordingly, I must be content to declare, only, that the attack was wholly unjustified; and that I consider it deplorable when an advocate in an arbitration proceeding indulges himself in such reckless and opprobrious abuse of his adversary and the Arbitrator as I find in Mr. Shapira's letter.

### AWARDS

The grievance of L— is denied.

---

[11] Excepting, perhaps, in simple machine operations or in unskilled jobs.

[12] Tr. pp. 42 and 45. I am assuming that this is a typographical error and "invidious" was intended.

## 65 LA 435

### YALE UNIVERSITY—

#### Decision of Arbitrator

In re YALE UNIVERSITY and FEDERATION OF UNIVERSITY EMPLOYEES, LOCAL 35, September 2, 1975

Arbitrator: Peter Seitz

#### ELIMINATION OF JOBS

**— Change of duties — New job**
▶ **117.334**

Employer had right to eliminate job of head waitress/waiter and to require dining room desk attendant to assume duties following conversion of its dining room food service to cafeteria-style operation in which customers are asked to place their used dishes and trays in designated areas, notwithstanding union's contention that contract provision giving employer right to change job descriptions requires "freezing" of existing jobs as of date negotiations are completed, since contract provision not only contemplates possibility of changes in job duties but also sets forth procedure to be followed to adjust compensation for such changes. Grievances are sustained to extent that new job title of dining room desk attendant shall be evaluated at level of Labor Grade 3 instead of Labor Grade 2.

---

Appearances: For the employer — Robert B. Snow, Jr., attorney. For the union — Norman Zolot, attorney.

#### Opinion

SEITZ, Arbitrator: — The parties, having experienced difficulty, at the hearing, in agreeing on a statement of the issue to be resolved, delegated that responsibility to the Arbitrator.

On the basis of the exhibits offered, the testimony given and the briefs presented, I perceive the issue to be as follows:

In revising the content of job description, changing the job title and assigning a new labor grade to Head Waitress/Waiter as set forth in Joint Exhibit 6, dated January 24, 1975, is the University violating Section 2.9 and Section 21.3 of the Agreement; and if so, what remedy is appropriate?

The University operates some 26 food service locations for students, faculty, employees and others. The Union represents employees in these facilities.

This dispute arose when Mr. Albert R. Dobie, Director of the Department of Dining Halls, wrote as follows to Mr. Vincent J. Sirabella, Business Manager of the Union, on January 24, 1975:

"During the past academic year, the Department of Dining Halls completed the process of converting all dining halls on campus to self-bussing. We now have the experience of one complete year under the new system and have been able to evaluate its effectiveness.

"As a result of this evaluation, it has become apparent to us that the duties and responsibilities set forth in the job description for Head Waitress no longer applies to the work required to be performed by the present incumbents. Therefore, we seek to revise the content of the job description, change the job title and assign the job to a new

## 65 LA 436

labor grade more in keeping with the responsibilities of the job as now performed. Such revised job description is to be reclassified in labor grade 2 and retitled Dining Hall Desk Attendant. A copy of the revised job description is attached to this letter. Please contact me directly if you have any questions.

"It is our intent to affect this change as soon as possible, but no later than March 9, 1975."

Attached to Mr. Dobie's letter was a document (marked "J-7") dated March 9, 1975 [1] which consists of a job description of "Dining Room Attendant," Labor Grade 2. The Union resists and challenges the elimination of the job title "Head Waitress/Waiter" (Labor Grade 4), the establishment of a new title "Dining Room Attendant" (Labor Grade 2) and the assignment of incumbents of the first named job title to the second named job title at reduced hourly rates.

In brief, the parties signed their extant collective agreement (entered into as of July 10, 1974) on November 19, 1974. That Agreement contained a Schedule A with job titles in the bargaining unit, the labor grades assigned to them, and the rates of pay applicable to each title in July, 1974, 1975 and 1976. The list includes

Assistant Head Waitress/Waiter (L. G.2)

Head Waitress/Waiter (L.G.4)

and other job titles. These labor grades and rates were negotiated at the sessions preceding the signing of the contract (as they had been, apparently, in the past) on the basis of job descriptions which had been drafted by the University and accepted, either explicitly or implicitly by the Union as the underpinnings for Schedule A of the Contract.

The wage structure of the University, under this Agreement, is not based upon any systematic ranking of jobs according to factor evaluation. Jobs are given titles, the job duties and responsibilities are described and the parties reach agreement as to whether the jobs, as performed and described, belong in one established labor grade or another.

It should also be observed that there seems to be no absolute uniformity in all of the food-service facilities in their operation or in the performance of jobs. There is diversity in the physical aspects of the facilities and in the manner of performing jobs from one to another of them.

For some time, moreover, the University has been engaged on a program of simplification of operations in its facilities. Prior to 1970 the method of operation, generally, required the services of waitresses, assistant head waitresses and head waitresses, among others in the work force. The gradual substitution of cafeteria operation for waitress service changed the system materially; and in 1971 the University started the elimination of "bussing" (removal of dirty dishes and trays by wait-

---

[1] Probably it bears this date (later than that of the letter) because this is the date on which the University proposed to put the changes in effect.

resses) and gradually developed a system of "self-bussing" under which customers removed their dirty dishes and trays to designated areas. These developments took place over time. Self-bussing was started first in three professional school dining halls; then, in 1972 it was extended to twelve undergraduate student dining halls; and in 1973 the program was virtually completed.

This change from a dining room to a cafeteria-style operation involved the phased and staged elimination of employees engaged in dining-room style service. In the course of the development of the program Assistant Head Waiters were eliminated completely. The Director of Labor Relations testified that at the 1974 negotiations the University was "aware" that the Head Waiter's job was "affected" by self-bussing; but nothing was said at those negotiations as to the changes which were the subject of Mr. Dobie's letter of January 24, 1975.

The program of the University, represented by Mr. Dobie's letter, envisaged the elimination of some supervisory functions and activities of present incumbents of Head Waitress/Waiter and the addition of some clerical and bookkeeping or quasi-accounting activities. After an evaluation (unilateral) of the job responsibilities of the newly described job (Dining Hall Desk Attendant) the University reached the conclusion that employees transferred to that job from Head Waitress/Waiter (to be abolished) would be entitled to compensation at the rate appropriate to Labor Grade 2. This represents, for such employees, a reduction of two labor grades.

The Union's principal argument, as expressed in the able brief of its Attorney, is that Section 2.9 of the agreement "freezes the existing jobs as of the time the negotiations are completed" and that the cited section "relates to changes which occur dur-

## 65 LA 437

ing the contract term and does not relate to changes which occurred prior to the current agreement with which the University was fully aware but which it elected not to bring to the bargaining table." (U. Brief p. 8.)

Section 2.9 has two subsections. Subsection (a) provides that the job descriptions "shall be used as guides in hiring, training, promoting, assigning and evaluating performance." Subsection (b), more pertinent here, provides:

"The University shall notify the Union of any changes in the job descriptions set forth in Exhibit C at least ten (10) working days prior to the effective date of any such change. The Union shall have the right to challenge, through the grievance procedure the content of any new or revised job description or the labor grade assigned to any new or re-evaluated job title. Until such challenge is agreed to by the University or sustained by arbitration, the new or revised job description or the new or reevaluated labor grade assignment shall be held in abeyance."

This provision, unmistakably, supplements and gives support to the provisions in Article XXI - Management, which give express recognition to the University's power to exercise "the regular and customary functions of management including, among other things, the direction of the working forces; [and] the establishment of methods of operation." So far as appears, there is nothing in this collective agreement which distinguishes it from that vast majority of collective labor agreements under which the employer, as entrepreneur, determines what work is to be done and how and when. The Union's right limits the exercise of the University's prerogatives as to the appropriateness of the compensation for the work the University assigns to be performed and, of course, the conditions under which it is to be performed.

Excepting for the last sentence of 2.09(b) (which provides that challenged new or revised job descriptions or new or reevaluated labor grades shall be held "in abeyance" until the challenge is ended by agreement or arbitration award) there is nothing in the contract which "freezes" job descriptions or assigned labor grades during its term. That is to say, of course, the job descriptions and compensation agreed upon in the Agreement are binding on the parties, as a part of the bargain expressed in the document so long as the work (job responsibilities and duties) remains substantially unchanged. The provision cited, however, clearly contemplates the possibility of changes in the job duties during the life of this multi-year contract and sets forth elements of the procedures to be followed in order to adjust compensation, if need be, to such changes. To find otherwise would mean that job duties and responsibilities and the way in which work is to be performed can only be changed when the collective agreement is renegotiated at the end of its term. It is doubtful that any business could survive such a strangulating procedure. If a provision of such a character had been agreed to, of course, it would have to be enforced because, as both parties in this case have taken the trouble to admonish me, I cannot rewrite the contract by addition to or subtraction from its terms or to impose my personal brand of industrial jurisprudence. However, absent an explicit prohibition of changes in work assignments and duties and in light of the recognition of "changes" in Section 2.9 I see no basis on which it can be found that work, job assignments and compensation can be glaciated for the term of the Agreement.

On behalf of the Union, its counsel argues skillfully and eloquently that the circumstances here justify a departure from the rule as stated above. Although the University's program of "bussing" and "self-bussing" had been in evolutionary progress for some years, nothing was said about the changes in work and compensation grieved here at the negotiations (which eventuated in a contract signed in November, 1974) about the University's plan to change work and compensation after the bargain had been struck and the contract signed; and the notice of the changes was given in January to be effective in March, 1975. According to the argument, the parties having reached agreement on work and compensation when the contract was signed, and the arrangements then in effect having been continued up to the date of the notice, the University was not free, in January, to disavow it. It is said that to permit "changes" at any other place but the bargaining table "would be to permit the University to conceal from the Union vital decisions * * * which were not intended to be subject to the more costly and non-voluntary process of arbitration as required by the contract."

It is not the function or the responsibility of the arbitrator to make observations or findings or to ad-

## 65 LA 438

monish the parties as to the quality of their relationship or the extent to which candor should govern their dealings. His duty is to decide disputes. In the instant case if the facts warranted it, he would not hesitate to invoke equitable remedies such as estoppel to prevent a party from enjoying the fruits of its deliberate deceit. There is nothing in the record of this case to justify a finding that such deceit has been practiced. The failure of the University to take the Union into its confidence as to the progress of its program, at negotiations, is unexplained on the record of this case; but, on the other hand, it asserts that it served its notice to be effective at a time when some measure of uniformity of action could be undertaken in its several facilities and it considered that the time was ripe to make the changes desired. Head Waitresses who had been performing for some time under the old job descriptions could only have been advantaged by the delays in concluding the final steps in the program.

This is not a case in which it can be said that the parties negotiating their agreement had failed to address their attention to the problem involved in a change of work that would affect the rate of compensation. If Section 2.9(b) does not spell out and elaborate in detail all of the aspects and incidents of the procedure agreed to, it tells enough to make the reader confident that the approach and manner of handling such a problem is clearly laid out.

The cited section, by stating when the notice of change is to be given, can only be read to mean that change in work, job description and compensation might occur during the term of the Agreement [2] and was within the contemplation of the signatories.

[2] There would be no need, conceivable, to provide that "changes in the job descriptions set forth in Exhibit C" in the Agreement could take place only on the renegotiation of the Agreement at its term's end, as the Union argues. When the contract is at an end anything that is in the area of negotiable items can be changed.

It then tells us that the Union has the right to challenge changed job descriptions and assigned labor grades related to such changes. Finally, it says that until agreed to or sustained by arbitration the changes shall be held in abeyance.

This may not be a model of draftsmanship, but its meaning and consequences are unmistakable. The Union has the power to challenge in arbitration

a) the accuracy of the new or revised job description as reflecting changes in job duties and responsibilities which the University has placed into effect following due notice under Section 2.9(b); and

b) the evaluation of such new or revised job description in terms of compensation and the assignment of a labor grade.

If the Union may make such a challenge in arbitration, what can the provision mean but that, in arbitration, a decision can be made as to the accuracy of the job description and the fairness of the job evaluation and compensation to be paid for the changed duties?

To declare this is not to say (as the University, apparently, would have me hold) that it is free of all restraints in the reordering and rearranging of work and compensation, on the one hand; nor to say, on the other hand (as the Union, apparently, would have me hold) that work and compensation are "frozen" for the duration of the contract. This decision holds, to the contrary, that the Agreement permits the University to change work duties and responsibilities (and the job specifications describing them) during the term of the contract as its conception of its entrepreneurial duties to operate efficiently and economically, seem to require; and that the Union may challenge the changed job description as not reflecting, properly, the actualities in the University's job structure; and that the Union may challenge the evaluation of the University of the changed job and the appropriateness of the labor grade assigned; and finally, that the Arbitrator has the responsibility of judging the merits of such challenges.

The University's program contemplates the elimination of the job title Head Waitress/Waiter, the creation of the new job of Dining Room Desk Attendant, the assignment of Grievants to the new job and the evaluation of that job at the level of Labor Grade 2.

It is found the University is well within its powers to reorganize work and reallocate tasks as contemplated in the job descriptions submitted.

The Union argues that this involves the performance of some tasks by non-bargaining unit employees, previously performed by bargaining unit employees (tantamount to forbidden sub-contracting) and, conversely, the performance by bargaining unit em-

## 65 LA 439

ployees previously performed by non-bargaining unit employees. I do not regard these claims as coming within the compass of the grievances or the issues in this case as perceived by me. At any rate, it is impossible, on the record made in this case,[3] to make a responsible decision as to such matters. Accordingly, such claims are dismissed without prejudice and with full freedom to the Union to press these arguments in connection with any other grievance that may be filed.

The Union, as the University observes in its brief, presented no witnesses at the hearings. The facts on which its case relies, are to be found in the exhibits and the testimony given on cross-examination of the University's witnesses. The record as made does not furnish facts which could serve as a foundation for findings that the reorganization of work involved in the case was "arbitrary,

---

[3] The testimony was general in character. There is insufficient proof that identified managerial employees are doing bargaining unit work.

capricious or discriminating" (Section 213).

This leaves for consideration the question of the merits of evaluating the changed job to which the grievants are to be assigned as being at Labor Grade 2. There has been a wealth of detail elaborated by both parties to support their respective positions—that the grievants should be retained in Labor Grade 4 (as argued by the Union); and that the new job has been properly evaluated at Labor Grade 2. I shall not undertake to analyze the facts and arguments presented. To do so would require me to write a book — a task which I have not been requested to undertake[4] and which, if attempted, is not likely to satisfy the advocates for either party. I have carefully considered all that has been presented on the subject and content myself with the concluding statement that in my judgment a proper evaluation of the new job would result in placing

---

[4] Cf. "If they Asked Me I Could Write A Book"; Rodgers and Hart, Pal Joey.

it in Labor Grade 3. Perhaps it would have been more desirable that the parties had jointly negotiated the appropriate rate for the new job, when installed, in the bargaining leading up to the signing of the Agreement. Instead of doing this, however, the University chose not to make its plans the subject of bargaining and the union, after the receipt of the notice of the changes, chose to take the position that the changes could not be made at all. In consequence the matter had to be determined in what may be the least satisfactory forum for such a dispute: arbitration.

## AWARD

The grievances are denied to the extent that they challenge the University's power to rearrange work among job titles, eliminate and abolish the job title of Head Waitress/ Waiter and install a new job title of Dining Room Desk Attendant. The grievances are sustained to the extent that the new job title shall be installed at the level of Labor Grade 3 instead of Labor Grade 2.

---

## 41 LA 905

### BENDIX CORP.—

#### Decision of Arbitrator

In re BENDIX CORPORATION, KANSAS CITY DIVISION and INTERNATIONAL ASSOCIATION OF MACHINISTS, DISTRICT LODGE, No. 71, October 19, 1963
Arbitrator: Carl A. Warns

#### SUBCONTRACTING

**—Absence of contractual restrictions — Limitations — In-plant work**
▶ 117.381

Although contract contains no limitation or restriction upon subcontracting, contract read as a whole, including management rights, recognition, union security, and seniority clauses, bars employer from bringing employees of others into its plant to perform services normally performed by its own employees solely because other employees will work at a cheaper rate. However, employer has right to subcontract work to be performed on its premises in such special circumstances as (1) order or project requires skills not possessed by work force, (2) special tools or equipment are required and capital investment would be unreasonable under circumstances, or (3) employer's present work force cannot meet time limitations. (C. Warns)—Bendix Corp., 41 LA 905.

---

Appearances: For the company — J. A. Pope, director of industrial relations. For the union—George Christensen, associate counsel.

#### IN-PLANT SUBCONTRACTING

WARNS, Arbitrator:—This arbitration involves eight grievances filed in March and April, 1962 by Bendix Millwrights A—, B—, C—, D—, E—, F—, G—, and H—. With the exception of the D— Grievance, all are

individual complaints by laid off Bendix millwrights over Company assignment during their layoff of in-plant maintenance work which the grievants contend they could and have performed, to outside contractors. The eighth grievance, filed by millwright steward D—, was a general grievance over performance by outside employees of in-plant maintenance work normally performed by Bendix millwrights.

The relief requested in the general grievance is that Bendix be directed to cease contracting for performance by outside contractor employees of any in-plant maintenance work customarily performed by Bendix millwrights. The relief requested by the individual grievants was recall to the millwright classifications plus reimbursement for wage losses for all hours either not worked or worked at rates less than the millwright rate for period extending from thirty days prior to the filing date of each of the seven grievances to the date of recall. All seven individual grievants have since been recalled as millwrights.

#### Contract Provisions

It is briefly the Union's substantive position that the Company violated the intent, purpose and spirit of the collective agreement, and particularly the recognition, seniority, wage, union security, and other conditions thereof, by without prior notice contracting for and causing in-plant maintenance work regularly performed by Bendix millwrights to be performed by outside contractor employees at rates of pay, hours and conditions other than those of Bendix millwrights, meanwhile laying off Bendix millwrights and maintaining them in layoff status during the

period the outside contractor employees performed their work in the plant. The Company's response is that the Agreement is clear and unambiguous on its face and it does not prohibit or restrict the Company in its right to subcontract; second, the history of collective bargaining negotiations which resulted in the present contract demonstrates that the Company has the right to subcontract; and third, if any reference to past practice is necessary, past practice conclusively demonstrates the propriety of the Company's action. The contract contains a Management Clause:

"Except as specifically limited by this Agreement, the management of the Company and the direction of the working forces, including but not limited to, the products to be manufactured, the location of plants, the schedules and fair standards of production, the schedules of hours and shifts, the methods, processes and means of manufacturing, the right to hire, promote, demote and transfer employees, to establish rules of conduct, to discharge or discipline for cause, and to maintain discipline and efficiency of employees, are the sole and exclusive rights and responsibilities of the Company."

A Recognition Clause:

"The Bendix Corporation, Kansas City Division, recognizes District Lodge No. 71 of the International Association of Machinists as the exclusive representative as

## 41 LA 906

certified under the decision of the National Labor Relations Board, for the purpose of collective bargaining with respect to rates of pay, wages, hours of employment and other conditions of employment in accordance with the terms of this Agreement and within the scope of the Labor-Management Relations Act of 1947 (as amended) for all production and maintenance employees . . ."

A "zipper" clause:

"c. The parties acknowledge that during negotiations which resulted in this Agreement, each had the unlimited right and opportunity to make demands and proposals with respect to any subject or matter not removed by law from the area of collective bargaining, and that the understandings and agreements arrived at by the parties after the exercise of that right and opportunity are set forth in this Agreement. Therefore, the Company and the Union, for the life of this Agreement, each voluntarily and unqualifiedly waives the right and each agrees that the other shall not be obligated to bargain collectively with respect to any subject or matter referred to or covered in this Agreement, or with respect to any subject or matter not specifically referred to or covered in this Agreement, even though such subjects or matter may not have been within the knowledge or contemplation of either or both of the parties at the time they negotiated or signed this Agreement."

The contract also contains a Seniority Clause, a Union Security provision, and the usual limitations on the power of the Arbitrator not to change the parties' negotiated agreement.

**Arbitration Awards**

Both sides cited arbitration cases in support of their positions, including one reported and one unreported by the present Arbitrator. In this regard, a remark by Arbitrator Kadish in a recent contracting out case involving KVP Sutherland Paper Company and United Papermakers and Paperworkers, 40 LA 737 is appropriate:

"After examining these studies (on contracting out) and many of the decisions discussed, it is fair to conclude that no one, whatever his initial inclinations or prejudices, will go away from them without finding something he likes. Like the town fair, there is something for everyone."

The Company referred to an unpublished decision written by me between the Dayton Steel Foundry Company and the United Steelworkers of America, decided in 1962. That case involved a challenge to the Company's contracting out janitorial services. I repeat some of the reasoning in that case:

"The Company cited several recent cases involving the contracting out of janitorial services. I have read these cases carefully. After reading these cases and many others and after a careful study of this problem extending over a number of cases, I must agree with the arbitrator in Olin Mathieson Chemical Corporation 36 LA 1147 (cited by the Company in its brief) that 'there is no general agreement as to the basic principles which should serve as the guide to a fair and equitable decision'. The Arbitrator is speaking of the issue of contracting-out where the contract is 'silent' as to the point in question. The earlier decisions did to a large extent lay down the principle that absent an express limitation, the Company could contract-out if done in good faith. But then as the Arbitrators acquired more experience with the practical application of this broad doctrine, implied limitations appeared. In the janitor cases, we find statements that the Company could contract-out janitorial services if no bargaining unit employee was laid off, or if only a few were laid off, or if the 'equities' supported the Company. The Arbitrators are not in agreement on whether such contracting-out violates the 'Recognition' clause or the seniority provisions. Some

Arbitrators, consistent with the argument advanced by Management here, consider a relevant factor any history or past practice on contracting-out in the plant and bargaining table discussions on the subject. All in all, this is indeed a complex problem. Before relating the appropriate factors to the facts of this case, let me list some of the important considerations. It is fundamental to good management that decisions which lead to maximum production with minimum cost are 'sound'. This applies to any aspect of management's decision-making, whether it be the hiring of janitors or planning production schedules. On the other hand, this sound principle of management in its more immediate aspects is sometimes limited by contracts with other companies; if, for example, the Company enters into an exclusive agreement to purchase all of its raw materials from another employer, it cannot force the renegotiation of that agreement, simply because it later found a supplier who could 'beat the rate'. The traditional sanctity of contract forbids this. It is this basic principle of law that I find as the real implied limitaton on the Company in this kind of case; it is the 'Recognition' clause which impliedly codifies this doctrine. This is not to say that the status quo is frozen in all aspects because a collective agreement is signed. Under external compelling circumstances, jobs and classifications can be changed with an appropriate change in rate consistent with normal principles of job evaluation. But in a purely static situation where there is no change in equipment, process or operation, to say that the Company can bring onto the premises someone to do the work performed by the unit where there is no evidence of a special needed skill, or evidence of a time factor, or any other special equity other than the perfectly legitimate motive of saving money could, all other factors being equal, be considered as violative of the Recognition Clause."

## 41 LA 907

As the stream of court decisions on a given point may reflect through the years greater insight by the judges into significance of the facts as they relate to legal principle, so may arbitrators' decisions become more perceptive when they move from the flat perspective of the early cases to the wisdom of the later decisions on the same issue. Standing alone, the Recognition Clause confirms the Company's obligation to bargain with the Union regarding the employees in the unit. The Union Security clause speaks for itself as does the "zipper" clause. The Management Clause needs no interpretation. The subject matter of contracting out is not expressly mentioned in the foregoing or in any of the other provisions of the contract. But interpreting contracts as a whole is not new in the law. As the 10th Circuit remarked in United Steelworkers versus New Park Mining Company, 273 F.2d 353, 45 LRRM 2158, cited by the Union, implied limitations on the right of the Company to contract out are consistent "with the implied covenant in every contract 'that neither party shall do anything which will have the effect of destroying or injuring the rights of the other party to receive the fruits of the contract.' . . . 3 Williston (Rev. Ed., 1936, Section 670.)" So the balance of interests of the parties as reflected in their negotiated agreement (the Management clause as against the Union seniority,

recognition and other limitations on the Company) demands that each case of contracting out be examined in the light of its own facts. These interests, viewed separately are legitimate. The Company has the right to get the job done as efficiently and with as low a cost as possible. The employees as individuals can insist that they receive the "fruits of the contract" as negotiated. The Union can assume that the contract it negotiates for the bargaining unit will not be bypassed in regard to anticipated benefits unless reasonable men would agree that the larger interests of the Company's relationship with the market place at the moment compel the use of other employees in place of its own. But such compelling circumstances must be viewed closely. The Company has no right to unilaterally reduce the negotiated wages of its employees because of the pressure of competition. Similarly, the Company has no right to bring the employees of others on its premises to perform services normally done by its own employees absent certain special circumstances to be discussed solely because the other employees will work at a cheaper rate. There is no difference in principle between holding that the Company cannot reduce wages unilaterally and denying the Company the right to bring outsiders into the plant for customary services solely on the basis of lower costs. Both would be a violation of Williston's implied covenant; the first of course, would also be an express violation of the wage provisions. In evaluating the contract "as a whole," we cannot ignore the Company's responsibilities to its stockholders, its customers, present and intended, and in some cases, its obligations to the Federal and State governments. A particular order or plant project may require skills that the Company does not possess in its work force, and the circumstances may indicate that it would be unreasonable to expect the Company to employ or train employees in those special skills. Clearly, then, in the absence of stated contractual limitations, the Company would have the right to contract out the work even though performed on the premises. Certain orders or projects may require the use of tools and equipment which the Company does not possess and the capital investment would be unreasonable under the circumstances. Here again the Company would have the right under its Management Clause to contract out this work. Still another order or project may have a time limitation which the present work force cannot meet, either because it is too small, is busy on regular work and overtime would not be feasible, or simply because it lacks the efficiency of the contractor who is a specialist in the area under consideration to meet the time limits imposed. Contracting out would be authorized in this case. There may be more illustrations where factors other than the saving of money arising from lower labor costs justify the use of outside contractors in providing services on Company property customarily performed by the Company's employees. The preceding variables, not argued by either party in the hearing before me, must be examined before a fair decision can be reached as to whether the Company violated its implied obligations to continue to direct the "fruits of the contract" to the employees or whether the Company had the right to bypass the contract because of

## 41 LA 908

legitimate business reasons. It becomes apparent then that I do not agree, as a matter of basic contract interpretation, with the broad, general positions of either the Company or the Union, that is, that under the contract before me as written, the Company has the right to contract out because there is no express limitation on that right, or that alternatively the Company cannot under any circumstance assign to non-employees work in the plant customarily performed by the grievants.

### Bargaining Duty

Before reaching a final decision on this case, there remains for consideration whether the contract requires the Company to bargain with the Union on contracting out in all cases. In addition, the impact of Atomic Energy regulations, as well as the negotiations leading to the current contract, together with the influence of possible past practice, must be examined. At the outset, I do not agree with the Union that the contract as a whole, obligates the Company to bargain with the Union or even to notify it in all cases of contracting out. This is an area of the parties' relationship covered by public law rulings and it is to the forum of the public law that the redress of the Union should be sought regarding refusal to bargain. I do not agree with the Company that AEC regulations require the Company to breach its agreement with the Union in contracting out cases. As to the effect upon the interpretation of the contract as a whole on the broad issue of contracting out, by the Union's proposal on this subject in the 1960 negotiation, a withdrawal of prior grievances, I find no admission or mutuality of agreement with the Company that would foreclose the Arbi-

trator finding that under some conditions, contracting out may or may not be permissible. The Union proposed and the Company rejected:

SUB-CONTRACTING

A) The Company agrees that it will not remove any machinery, tools, or work from the Plant, including manufactured parts, tool making, machine repair, tool designing or contractors to perform any work in the Plant, where such removal or contracting would directly necessitate the reduction of hours below the normal work week for any of its Employees, or would necessitate the reduction of manpower. The Company recognizes its obligation to utilize the service of its Employees to the fullest capacity possible. Machinery and tools, and equipment may be removed from the Plant after written agreement with the Union.

The above is general and without exception. The Company rejected it and it is not therefore the governing criterion on this subject. What does govern the parties is a reasonable interpretation of the contract as a whole as finally agreed upon. I have previously stated my interpretation. The Company introduced evidence of contracting out from April 22, 1949 to the date of the hearing. The work ranged from general c o n s t r u c t i o n and sprinkler installation to office rearrangement. The record does not show in any specific way the circumstances under which these various contracts were let, that is, whether they were the result of a "crash program" with insufficient time to utilize the existing work force, whether insufficient skills were present in the plant, whether special e q u i p m e n t was needed, or whether the contractor employees did in fact replace the grievants. To be specific, it can be reasonably concluded, at least from the record discussion of the rehabilitation contract at the former Westinghouse plant, that the contractor who did the work including the original installation of the Henges wall panel had the entire rehabilitation contract in the area before Bendix actually took over the plant. This raises a further point of analysis. It may be that the Company has the right to contract out a given project, for example, the installation of a water sprinkler system assuming for the sake of illustration that the Company employees may lack the skill and the equipment to do the work. This may also involve the cutting and threading of pipe, work that can be done in the plant. Unless the

contract is severable, and it is customary to separate the authorized from the unauthorized work, the Company violates no implied obligation to the employees by signing a contract for the work as a whole. I cannot tell from the Company's list of examples of contracting out how many if any of the projects fit into this category. In brief, I cannot conclude that the Union has acquiesced in the contracting out to the extent that they are foreclosed in the present arbitration from claiming a violation at least of their rights to work customarily performed in the absence of the special circumstances previously enumerated. The evidence is convincing, however, that some of the work done by the contractors in the period thirty days prior to the grievances (See Grievance Procedure) consisted of removal and replacement of partitions, general

## 41 LA 909

painting, carpentry and duct work, breaking and replacement of existing flooring, and other work generally associated with the work of the grievants.

Lacking specific evidence by which to determine the extent to which the contracting out thirty days prior to the grievances was authorized within the criteria set forth in this decision, I am returning the case to the parties for an administrative determination of this issue. I will retain jurisdiction of the matter for a period of sixty (60) days from the date of the decision, and if the parties mutually agree, a further hearing may be agreed upon determining the remedy.

### AWARD

The grievance is upheld in part and denied in part as to the principle relied upon by the Union. Lacking specific evidence by which to determine the extent to which the contracting out thirty days prior to the grievances was authorized within the criteria set forth in this decision, I am returning the case to the parties for an administrative determination of this issue. I will retain jurisdiction of the matter for a period of sixty (60) days from the date of the decision, and if the parties mutually agree, a further hearing may be agreed upon in determining the remedy.

---

92 LA 374

**BOSTON EDISON CO. —**

**Decision of Arbitrator**

In re BOSTON EDISON COMPANY and UTILITY WORKERS UNION OF AMERICA, LOCAL 387, AFL-CIO, AAA Case No. 1130-2055-87, November 11, 1988
Board of Arbitration: George Nicolau, impartial chairman; Robert A. Scannell, company member; Francis J. Toland, union member.

**DRUGS AND ALCOHOL**

— **Drug testing — Selection for promotion or transfer** ▸124.60 ▸119.128 ▸120.03

Mandatory drug testing of applicants for promotion or transfer is unreasonable, since fact that employer is public utility does not confer any special status or greater need for drug-testing program, majority of workforce is clerical, program is not testing for fitness but for off-duty drug use, employer made no prior attempt to determine extent of drug use among employees, drug testing is an invasion of privacy, and employer has other means of achieving its objective.

— **Denial of promotion — Suspension — Drug testing** ▸119.121 ▸124.60 ▸118.653

Denial of promotion and suspension because of results of without-cause drug test violated contract, since mandatory drug testing of applicants for promotion or transfer is unreasonable.

**REMEDY**

— **Denial of promotion — Drug test** ▸119.121 ▸124.60

Employee who was improperly denied promotion because of results of without-cause drug test is ordered to be placed in position and is awarded back pay, benefits, and seniority.

---

## WITHOUT-CAUSE TESTING

### The Background in Brief

NICOLAU, Arbitrator: — The Company is a public utility supplying electricity to residential and commercial customers in the Boston area. The employees represented by Local 387, some 950 in number, are in what is known as the Office and Clerical Unit. Approximately 700 of the 950 are clerks, i.e., file clerks, contact clerks, typists, stenographers, word processors, bookkeepers, etc. The remaining unit members are drafting technicians (75), meter readers (125), collectors (27), right-of-way agents (5), and district sales representatives (7).[1]

The clerks and drafting technicians work primarily at the Company's main offices; the others are field employees who are not directly supervised at their work sites.

The Company unilaterally promulgated the challenged Alcohol and Drug Policy in February 1984. The Union thereafter filed a written protest in which it expressed opposition to "the Company's approach that *all* offenses [were] cause for discharge" and its belief that each case should be "treated on an individual basis".

Under the Policy, employees seeking promotion or transfer are now subject to drug testing as part of a previously-required physical examination. Those who fail the test are subject to discipline and are required, under penalty of discharge, to undergo rehabilitation. Though the written Policy is not explicit on this point, they are also denied their requested promotion for at least a year and are subject to random testing for the same period.[2]

In October 1985, B___, a Pay Grade IV Clerk in the Collections Division who had been employed by the Company since 1981, applied for the posted position of Meter Reader. At the time of her application, the posting required a Massachusetts drivers license and successful completion of "Company-approved tests," including a test measuring driving competence and ability.

B___ was interviewed and subsequently advised that she had been approved for the promotion pending medical examination results. That examination took place on October 23. One week later, she was advised that she had tested positive for cocaine, that she would not be promoted, and would have to participate in a rehabilitation program. She was also told that her failure to do so or her subsequent use of illegal substances would result in her discharge. On her initial

### 92 LA 375

refusal to participate, she was suspended for five days, pending her compliance with the rehabilitation program. The Union immediately

protested the Company's actions and ultimately filed a Demand for Arbitration asking that the suspension be rescinded and that she be placed on the Meter Reader Roster with "all seniority and back pay." At some point, B___ did participate in EAP counseling sessions and the Company thereafter rescinded her suspension. However, it continued to deny her the promotion.

Long after the Demand, the job posting for the Meter Reading position was changed. The re-posting stated that the "selection procedure" involved "medical clearance including testing for illegal drugs" and that "evidence of illegal drug use will disqualify a candidate."

* * *

Though the Demand speaks in terms of B___'s suspension and promotion, it is evident that the matters in question here are broader. At the hearing, the Parties could not agree on the phrasing of the specific issues to be submitted and have left that to the Board's determination. On reading the Record and the briefs of the Parties, it can fairly be said that the issues properly before the Board are as follows:

1. Did the Company's unilateral implementation of its Alcohol and Drug Policy in February 1984 violate the collective bargaining agreement? If so, what shall be the remedy?

2. Did the Company violate the collective bargaining agreement by requiring, pursuant to Paragraphs 2 and 6 of its Alcohol and Drug Policy, a drug screen as part of the physical examination of an applicant for transfer or promotion within the bargaining unit? If so, what shall be the remedy?

3. If the answer to Question 1 or 2 is not in the affirmative, does the Union's challenge to the Company's determination that B___ was not qualified for the position of Meter Reader based on the asserted results of a drug screen raise an arbitrable issue or must such a claim be resolved under the procedures set forth in Article XXVIII?

### The Contract

The contract provisions of relevance to those issues read:

#### "ARTICLE I

##### Recognition and Representation

1. The Company recognizes the Union and the Local as the exclusive representative for the purpose of collective bargaining with respect to rates of pay, wages, hours of employment or other conditions of employment of all employees of the Company in the Office and Clerical Unit as certified by the National Labor Relations Board in Case No. 1–RC–1638 on August 3, 1950."

#### "ARTICLE IV

##### Mutual Obligation

The Company recognizes an obligation to promote the welfare of the employees by maintaining rates of pay, wages, hours of employment and other conditions of employment that are equitable, reasonable and fair; and the Union and the Local recognize the obligation of the Company to furnish adequate uninterrupted service to the public and to maintain such earnings as will enable the Company adequately to perform its duties. The Company nor the Local will unlawfully discriminate against an employee because of race, color, religion, sex, national origin, age or handicap."

#### "ARTICLE V

##### Management Rights

1. The Union and the Local recognize the right and power of the Company to select and hire all employees; to promote employees; to determine the necessity for filling a vacancy; to transfer employees from one position to another; to suspend, discipline, demote or discharge employees; to assign, supervise, or direct all working forces and to maintain discipline and efficiency among them, to lay off employees and to stagger employment when required because of lack of work or curtailment of work; and generally to control and supervise the Company's operations and to exercise the other customary functions of Management in carrying on its business without hindrance or interference by the Union, the Local, or by employees. If the Local claims that the Company has exercised the right to suspend, discipline, demote, or discharge employees in an unjust or unreasonable manner, such claim shall be subject to the Grievance Procedure in Article XXXI and Arbitration under Article XXXII. If the Local claims that the Company has "exercise any of the foregoing rights in a capricious or arbitrary manner, such claims shall be subject to the Grievance Procedure in Article XXXI and Arbitration under Article XXXII.

2. The Company, the Union and the Local recognize the responsibility of the employees to comply with reasonable rules, regulations and practices prescribed by the Company which do not conflict with the provisions of this Agreement."

#### "ARTICLE IX

##### Conformation to Laws, Regulations and Orders

1. It is understood and agreed that all agreements herein are subject to all applicable laws, now or hereafter in effect and to the lawful regulations, rulings and orders of regulatory commissions having jurisdiction. If any of said laws, regulations, rulings or orders shall conflict with any provision of this Agreement, the parties shall confer in an effort to negotiate a lawful substitution or modification; but if as a result of such conference no substitution or modification is agreed upon, the disagreement shall not affect the remaining provisions of

### 92 LA 376

this Agreement and shall not constitute a question subject to the Grievance Procedure in Article XXXI or Arbitration under Article XXXII."

#### "ARTICLE XVII

##### Seniority

1. The following provisions as to seniority were first established as of December 5, 1950 and have been amended by subsequent Agreements between the Company and the Union, and the Local, and by this Agreement. As so amended, "they shall continue in effect.

* * *

10. In increasing and reducing forces, in making promotions or demotions, and in making appointments to fill vacancies in existing ratings and in newly created ratings, the Company shall determine the fitness and ability of all applicants for the new or different positions, and its decisions shall be final except as follows: (a) if the Local claims that the Company has exercised its rights in making promotions or in making appointments to fill vacancies in existing ratings and in newly created ratings in an unjust or unreasonable manner, or that such action was due to discrimination against an employee because of his membership in or his lawful activity in behalf of the Union, such claim shall be subject to the Grievance Procedure in Article XXXI and Arbitration under Article XXXII; (b) If the Local claims that the Company has exercised any of its other rights set forth in

---

[1] The numbers are approximate.
[2] The transcript is in two volumes. The above reference is to the 2nd volume, and Mr. Godfrey is the Company's Manager of Labor Relations.

this paragraph in a capricious or arbitrary manner, such claim shall be subject to the Grievance Procedure in Article XXXI and Arbitration under Article XXXII."

## "ARTICLE XXVIII

### Medical Examinations

The Medical Director shall examine and pass upon the physical fitness of:

1. Employees at their request, annually or by arrangement.

2. Employees returning to work upon recovery from incapacity for ten (10) working days or more.

3. Employees returning from leave of absence of more than four (4) weeks. However, the Business Agent or Acting Business Agent "returning from leave of absence, under Article VIII, of this Agreement, will be examined in accordance with Article VIII, Section 8.

4. Employees requesting transfer to new positions.

5. When it is obvious, or if either the Company or the Union has information that the physical condition of an employee is such that it would be injurious to himself, his fellow employees or the public, he may also be required to take a physical examination.

6. An employee upon whom his own physician has placed restrictions shall be subject to examination until the restriction is removed. If any such employee is not satisfied with the conclusions arrived at by the Medical Director, he may at his own expense submit a report from a doctor of his own choosing for consideration by the Company. Should any conflict result between the examination reports of the doctors involved, the Local and the Company shall by agreement select a third doctor who shall be a Specialist certified by his respective Board who will consider the case submitted to him and render a decision within one (1) week from the date he receives the case, and his decision will be binding upon the parties hereto.

Should the Company and the Local be unable to agree upon a third doctor then the matter will be referred to the Massachusetts Medical Society for the selection of the third doctor who shall be a Specialist certified by his respective Board who will consider the case and his decision will be binding upon the parties hereto.

Each party shall compensate the doctor chosen by it for the time spent and expenses incurred in the case, and the parties shall share equally in paying the compensation and expenses of the third doctor."

## "ARTICLE XXXII

### Arbitration

1. * * *

(g) No Board of Arbitration or arbitrator shall have the power to add or subtract from or modify any of the terms of this Agreement or to pass upon or decide any questions except the grievance submitted to the Board in accordance with the foregoing provisions."

## "ARTICLE XXXIII

### Amendments

1. This Agreement is intended to cover the entire subject matter of the Company's relations with its employees as defined in Article I; except as provided in the Stipulations attached hereto, and except as provided for in the Article IX entitled 'Conformation to Laws, Regulations and Orders,' no party shall have the right without consent of the other parties to insist upon any addition thereto, change therein or deletion therefrom. Amendments to this Agreement may be made, however, and amendments proposed in writing by one party shall be considered by the others and discussed by the parties jointly; but, if as a result of such negotiations no amendments are agreed to, the disagreement shall not

constitute a dispute subject to the Grievance Procedure in Article XXXI or to Arbitration under Article XXXII."

## The Alcohol and Drug Policy

"Boston Edison Company
Alcohol and Drug Policy

Boston Edison Company, in keeping with its long standing and strong commitment to safety and health, establishes this policy statement regarding drug and/or alcohol use and the effect of each on work performance. This policy does not change in any way the Company's existing policy regarding the drinking of alcoholic beverages, which remains in force, unchanged.

The Company, while it respects the privacy of its employees and does not wish to intrude into their private lives, nevertheless recognizes that employee involvement with

### 92 LA 377

drugs/alcohol off the job, as well as on the job, can have an impact on work, on safety, and on the general performance of its employees.

Employees who voluntarily request assistance in dealing with a personal drug/alcohol problem may participate in the Company's Employee Assistance Program provided they are not under investigation at the time they request assistance, and stop any and all involvement with drugs or alcohol. The Company's Medical Department will refer employees to an appropriate treatment resource. Volunteering to participate in the Rehabilitation Program will not prevent disciplinary action for those detected in violation of this policy or for future violations. Confidentiality will be maintained in accordance with the practices of the Company's Rehabilitation Program.

#### I Illegal Drugs

1. The illegal use, sale, or possession of narcotics, drugs or controlled substances while on the job, or on Company property, is a dischargeable offense. Any illegal substances will be turned over to the appropriate law enforcement agency and may result in criminal prosecution.

2. Off-the-job illegal drug use which could adversely affect an employee's job performance, or which could jeopardize the safety of other employees, the public, or Company equipment, is proper cause for administrative or disciplinary action, up to and including termination.

3. Employees who are arrested for off-the-job drug activity may be considered in violation of this policy. In deciding what action is to be taken, the Company will take into consideration the nature of the charges, the employee's present job assignment, the employee's record with the Company, and other factors relative to the impact of the employee's arrest upon the conduct of Company business.

4. Some of the drugs which are illegal under federal, state, or local laws include, among others, marijuana, heroin, hashish, cocaine, hallucinogens, and depressants and stimulants not prescribed for current personal treatment by a licensed physician.

* * *

6. The Company reaffirms its right to perform necessary physical examinations to determine drug use as part of all physical examinations, including pre-employment, promotion, and transfer; it further reaffirms its right to search any and all Company property at any time.

#### II The Alcoholic Beverages Rule

The Company policy regarding alcoholic beverages, dated April 1, 1974, remains in effect unchanged, as stated on the following page.

#### III Chronic Alcohol Problems

Employees who are not affected by the Alcoholic Beverages Rule, but whose use of alcohol after working hours may nevertheless have a profound effect on their work performance and their fitness for duty, may

be subject to disciplinary action; such employees should contact the Company Employee Assistance Program for assistance with their alcohol problem.

#### The Alcoholic Beverages Rule

Drinking of alcoholic beverages by any employee during the employee's working hours, including overtime periods, is prohibited. In addition, in the interests of safety and the avoidance of adverse public relations, employees in any of the following categories are prohibited from drinking alcoholic beverages during meal periods or other authorized interruptions of work occurring during the span of their working hours, including overtime periods:

(1) All Management and Confidential personnel.

(2) Employees on designated job assignments where consideration of safety or public relations are deemed to be controlling.

(3) Employees whose duties include the operation of a motor vehicle.

Nothing herein shall be construed to diminish the responsibilities of employees pertaining to fitness for duty and efficient work performance."

### The First Issue

### The Background

Though the above-cited Policy speaks of the Company reaffirming its right to "perform necessary physical examinations to determine drug use," it is conceded that there was no drug testing procedure or drug policy prior to February 1984. Nor was there ever, or is there now, an alcohol testing procedure. There was an Alcoholic Beverages Rule. It is identical to that incorporated in the present Policy and was unilaterally promulgated in the 1960's (Godfrey).[3] There was also, as there is now, an EAP.

The present Policy was formulated by the Company with the aid of outside consultants and made known to the Union and its sister locals at a Company-called meeting on February 22, 1984, just days before its effective date of March 1. Though the Policy was explained at that meeting, there was no bargaining, either then, prior thereto, or thereafter.[4] In fact, it appears from an examination of the Policy brochure that the document had already been printed before the aforesaid meeting took place. In any event, the Policy, which was evidently not preceded by any study of the incidence of drug use by Company employees, was presented to the locals as a "finished product" (Godfrey).

The Union's reaction on receiving a copy was to write Vice President of Employee Relations Parry on March 16, 1984. The letter reads:

"This Local is in receipt of a letter and booklet containing the Health and Safety Information on Alcohol and Drug Abuse.

### 92 LA 378

Part of the booklet contains the Boston Edison Alcohol and Drug Policy. While we do not condone nor support the use or sale of drugs on the job or on Company property, we are totally opposed to the Company's approach that all offenses are cause for discharge. We believe that each case should be treated on an individual basis.

Local 387 will react to any action that the Company takes in the future based on our duty to fairly represent our Members, and

---

[3] Since the Alcoholic Beverages Rule's re-issuance in 1984, the portions limited to certain categories of employees have been made applicable to all employees (Godfrey).
[4] Mr. Faherty is Local 387's President.

we are saying now that before the Company takes the final step, that proof beyond a reasonable doubt must be the criteria."

Though President Faherty testified that he requested "discussion or negotiation" over the Policy by contacting Vice President Parry as well as Mr. Godfrey; Labor Relations Administrator Scannell; and the Company's Medical Directors, there is nothing in writing to that effect and Godfrey testified that Faherty did not even seek to "discuss" the Policy as such until sometime in 1985. (The first written indication of such a request in this Record is a December 9, 1985 letter from Faherty to Scannell, dealing, in other respects, with the B— grievance.)

## The Contentions of the Parties

The Company points out that the question posed by the first issue, i.e., the Company's right to implement the Policy unilaterally, is not statutory, but contractual. It notes that this matter is not here on deferral from the National Labor Relations Board and that the Union has never even filed a refusal to bargain charge under the Act. As a consequence, the Company maintains, the question is not what the Board might rule if such an issue were presented to it, but what the Contract requires.

The Company characterizes the Policy as a "set of work rules governing employee conduct" and finds support for its promulgation in the management rights clause, particularly Section 2 of Article V, in which the Union" . . . recognize[s] the responsibility of the employees to comply with reasonable rules, regulations and practices prescribed by the Company . . ." and in past practice. In this regard, the Company cites numerous unilaterally promulgated rules involving safety, including the mandatory reporting of accidents, as well as the prohibition against the carrying of firearms on Company premises, rules governing telephone use, sexual harassment and the aforementioned ban on alcoholic beverages.

None, the Company maintains and the Union concedes, were bargained. All were formulated and implemented by the Company acting alone. In the Company's view, the Policy at issue here is of the same nature and similarly within the Company's authority to enact.

The Company reinforces its position by pointing to the various provisions requiring it to bargain with the Union on certain contingent events. These include the requirement to agree on the seniority status of an employee promoted out of the unit and subsequently returned to it (Article II, Section 3); the proper pay for an employee performing emergency work (Article VII, Section 1); the replacement of provisions declared illegal (Article IX); and changes in job specifications occasioned by the introduction of new equipment or systems (Article XII, section 2[b]). Had the Parties intended, the Company maintains, to require bargaining prior to the implementation of new or expanded rules, they would have written that requirement into Article V, just as they wrote such a requirement into the above-cited provisions. The fact that they did not,

must be taken as convincing evidence that bargaining prior to the implementation of work rules was not their intention.

The Union vigorously disagrees on all counts. While conceding that the issue is contractual rather than statutory, it cites as instructive the September 8, 1987 guideline memorandum issued by the General Counsel of the NLRB in which she concluded that drug testing was presumptively a mandatory subject of bargaining and that the addition of a drug test to an existing program of mandatory physical examinations was a significant change in conditions of employment, bargainable on demand.

The Union also argues that the Policy is far more than a "set of work rules" of the kind that falls within a management rights clause, in that mandatory drug testing, unlike ordinary work rules, fundamentally alters a number of previously-bargained provisions, including the seniority clause, the medical examination provision and the requirement of just cause.

With respect to the seniority provision, the Union points out that the Parties negotiated a means of posting and filling vacancies; that they pledged, in Article XVII, Section 1, to continue such provisions except as amended by agreement; that the Company specifically asked in the 1983 negotiations and the Union specifically agreed to the Company's use of a particular Edison Electric Institute (EEI) test to determine the fitness and ability of Meter Reader applicants (the Company's proposal to that effect is in evidence as Union Exhibit 15), and

### 92 LA 379

that the Company, having bargained over job qualifications and qualifying tests, cannot now implement additional "fitness for duty" tests on its own.

The Union's argument with respect to the medical examination provision is in the same vein. It maintains that the Parties bargained over and agreed to the specific circumstances in which medical examinations would be given or required; that those examinations were limited to determining an employee's physical ability to do the job and that the Company cannot now turn those examinations into a "surveillance device" designed to search for off-premises conduct without regard to its effect, if any, on work performance.

The Union contends that the propositions it advances are not just a matter of federal doctrine, but have been accepted by a number of arbitrators, whose opinions it cites as evidence thereof.

The Company, for its part, cites authorities to the contrary. It also argues that even if the Contract were found to contain an obligation to bargain, the Union's conduct constituted a waiver of any such requirement. Here, the Company places its reliance on the previously-mentioned memorandum of the General Counsel, particularly the portion on page 10 thereof stating that, to avoid a Board finding of Union waiver or acquiescence, a mere protest of the change is not enough, but that there must have been a "timely" and "reasonably clear" request to bargain over the matter.

The Company maintains that there was no such request here, but only a protest and a vow to contest individual cases, with the request to discuss the Policy's implementation, such as it was, coming more than a year after the Policy's effective date.

The Union, in response, also cites the above-referenced memorandum, noting the General Counsel's observation that a request for bargaining need not be made if the employer's notice of the change is insufficiently in advance of implementation to allow time for bargaining or is no more than "a mere announcement of a *fait accompli*." Since, the Union contends, the Company's announcement of its new Policy left no time for bargaining and was, by Company admission, the unveiling of a "finished product," any "technical" argument concerning "the form of the Union's bargaining demand" is without merit.

### Discussion and Analysis

In considering this first issue, the reasonableness or unreasonableness of the Company's Policy is irrelevant. The question is whether the Company has the right to take unilateral action.

That question, as the Parties recognize, is contractual. While Board law and the opinions of the General Counsel, which are not Board law, may be instructive, they are not controlling. What controls is the Parties' collective bargaining agreement.

In approaching this matter, it should be said at the outset that the Chairman is not unmindful of the drug scourge or the Company's interest, both direct and indirect, in contributing to its eradication. No reasonably knowledgeable person in the United States can be unaware of the toll drugs exact physically, mentally and financially. Yet, what an employer can do is limited by its contractual rights or by the agreements it can make with the representative of its employees. This is right and proper, for if the employees or the Union have certain rights under the collective agreement, those rights cannot be abridged simply because it is felt that something should be done.

That having been said, what leaps out of this Record is the fact that the Company's drug testing procedure and drug Policy of February 1984 was completely new. Unlike *Bath Iron Works*,[5] on which the Company mistakenly relies, there was no prior rule against the use of drugs, either on or off Company premises, or any pre-existing requirement, as there was in that case, to "submit to a test administered by the Medical Department" to determine if one was under the influence of drugs. Here, there was no drug policy; no drug testing requirement of any kind.

Absent any pre-existing policy or requirement, the February 1984 Policy cannot be viewed as a refinement of

---

[5] *Local 6 & 7, IUMSWA and Bath Iron Works* (June 30, 1986). Because of the pre-existing rules, the arbitrator in that case, Dean Eric Schmertz, held that the testing program there at issue was a "particularization and methodological implementation of managerial authority . . . implicit" in the prior rules and, thus, not a matter requiring bargaining under the Act. (The Union points out that the General Counsel has declined to defer to that decision and has issued a refusal to bargain charge against Bath.)

what went before, as was the case in *Bath*. Rather, there can be no real doubt that it embodied a sea change from the past; a substantial transformation of the rules of the game and a significant alteration of the conditions of employment, not only by making drug testing mandatory in certain circumstances, but by dictating adverse consequences, in the form of discipline

### 92 LA 380

and forced medical treatment on particular results. One does not need the General Counsel's opinion to conclude that the Policy constitutes more than a mere work rule and that its testing procedure is not a rule, as that term is properly defined, but a means of enforcing a rule.

A change of that magnitude goes far beyond that ordinarily contemplated by the "rule, regulation and practice" phraseology of Article V, Section 2 and cannot properly come within its ambit.

Even if that Section could be said to encompass a change of this nature, that, in my opinion, would not be enough to insulate it from a successful challenge. Under Section 2, a rule is not valid if it conflicts with other provisions of the Agreement and the above-outlined Union arguments that this "rule" fails that test with respect to the seniority and medical examination provisions, because it goes beyond what was previously negotiated, is powerful and persuasive. Under the seniority provisions, the Parties, as already mentioned, have agreed upon qualifying tests. It would seem that the unilateral imposition of a significant new test, one not inextricably linked to the ability to perform particular tasks, is simply inconsistent with their prior understandings. Similarly, they have agreed, in the medical examination clause, to limit the circumstances, the scope and the purpose of examinations. An examination that goes beyond that limited purpose, one not designed to test "physical fitness" to perform particular work, but to determine whether an employee uses drugs, irrespective of their impact on his or her ability or performance, is of an entirely different character and has a completely different objective than those tests on which they have previously agreed.

Contrary to the Company's argument, limitations on its unilateral authority need not be expressed solely in the form of affirmative obligations to bargain. They can be inferred from the scope and character of previous bargains. In this instance, that inference, is, in the Chairman's view, compelling.

This conclusion, however, does not end the matter, for there is a serious question of waiver here, arising, not from agreements made or actions not taken before the Policy's promulgation, but from what occurred or failed to occur thereafter. It is quite apparent that the Union did not seek bargaining, at least in writing, until long after the Policy's implementation; a year, perhaps even longer. The issue is

not of an inartful demand. There was no demand; certainly none suspectible of proof by the ordinary means of documentary evidence. The March protest, the only formal 1984 response of the Union, did not hint at a bargaining request or even begin to suggest a general challenge to the Company's authority.

I am mindful of the NLRB cases cited by the General Counsel in her September 8, 1987 memorandum and the fact that the time between the Company's announcement and the Policy's effective date was short and that the purpose of the February 22 meeting, from the Company's perspective, was to present a "finished product." Given those factors, the Board, if faced with this issue, might not find a waiver. However, given other Board precedents, such as *Citizens National Bank of Willmar* (245 NLRB 389 [102 LRRM 1467] [1979], enf. 106 LRRM 2816 [D.C. Cir. 1981]), the absence of a timely demand on the Union's part, coupled with the absence of any refusal to bargain charge, might impel a different result.

Whatever the NLRB might have done, I find the Union's failure to act difficult to ignore. But, in the final analysis, the lack of a timely bargaining request is of little practical consequence in this proceeding. For, even if the first issue were to be answered, "yes, but ...", i.e., "the Company's unilateral implementation of the Alcohol and Drug Policy did violate the collective bargaining agreement, but the Union waived its right to object ...", I am persuaded that the Union must still prevail. The reason lies in the answer to the second issue, which, in my judgment, must be "yes."

### The Second Issue

Unlike the previous issue, the issue here — whether the required drug screen violates the Contract — embodies a reasonableness test. This stems, not just from general principles of industrial relations and the balancing of interests inherent therein, but from the specific provisions of the Parties' collective agreement.

If the Company's policy of testing on promotion or transfer is thought of as an Article V, Section 2 rule, then, pursuant to that Section, the rule must be "reasonable." If the Policy is considered a means by which the Company determines an applicant's fitness and ability pursuant to the promotion pro-

### 92 LA 381

visions of the seniority clause (Article XVII, Section 10), the Union may challenge any action that, in its view, has been" ... exercised ... in an unjust or unreasonable manner." If the Policy is approached from the perspective of discipline, it must meet the standard of just cause, for that standard necessarily implicates the reasonableness of any rule or procedure on which the Company relies.

No matter, then, how the Policy is viewed, its reasonableness is properly in contest.

### The Contentions of the Parties

The Company contends that the basic purpose of the Policy is to create a

"drug free environment at Boston Edison," and that this objective serves to override any other considerations. It notes that it is a public utility held to a higher standard than an ordinary industrial enterprise; that drugs, unlike alcohol, are illegal; that the use of drugs can affect job performance and lead to accident or injury; that drug use is progressive and that increased or proliferating user can lead to particularly severe consequences, such as theft, use or sale on Company premises and, in extreme cases, death.

Its testing program, designed for its protection and the protection of its employees and limited to "pre-employment, promotion and transfer," is, in the Company's view, preventive; and its underlying goal, rehabilitative, not punitive. As such, the Company argues, it is reasonable, both on its face and in application, and should be sustained.

While conceding the dangers of drugs and a Company interest in their eradication, the Union contends there is no justification for a "broad-scale drug screening of office and clerical workers, meter readers, and draftsmen where there is no indication that Edison has a 'drug problem' and there is no individualized suspicion that the particular employees tested have taken drugs which impair job performance." In every reported case, the Union argues, there was at least a "colorable claim" that the jobs at issue were sensitive or dangerous, but there can be no such claim here. Thus, in the Union's view, the Company's interest, given the nature of the work force and the absence of reported drug use, is minimal at best and cannot serve to offset the rights and reasonable expectations of its employees.

The Union further maintains that drug testing turns the contractual assurances of just cause and the contractually-required "reasonable" exercise of the Company's power of promotion "on their head," since employees who could not be disciplined in the absence of just cause or denied promotion in an "unjust or unreasonable manner" are "investigated (for the purposes of possible disciplinary action) for no cause."

Apart from asserted flaws in the testing procedure, which it also raises, the Union further contends that the Company's concerns are purely speculative; that the testing program is not related to legitimate management objectives, such as job performance or determining fitness for duty, but to the discovery of off-duty behavior, irrespective of its impact, if any, on an employee's capabilities. As such, the Union concludes, it can hardly be approved as a reasonable exercise of managerial discretion.

### Discussion and Analysis

The Parties well recognize that there are competing interests here and that, in deciding the reasonableness of the Company's testing program, those interests must be evaluated and an appropriate balance struck.

The Company's interest in providing a drug-free environment cannot be gainsaid; nor can the interest of employees in their contractual rights and their expectations of privacy.

In balancing these interests, one must examine a number of factors. Included, along with other elements, are the nature of the enterprise; the nature of the workforce; the jobs that workforce performs; the nature and extent of the threat to productivity, safety and health; the availability of alternative, less intrusive means of protection, if any; and the relationship of the conduct at issue to the enterprise.

In the Chairman's view, the fact that the Company is a public utility, while a factor to be considered, does not confer any special status. Completely private or unregulated enterprises or certain governmental entries might have a greater objective need for a drug testing program than Boston Edison.

Irrespective of the Company's status, the nature of the workforce affected by its Policy heavily militates against the position it has taken here. While the Company sought to show use of machinery (in the duplicating room) and the driving of vehicles by meter readers and some others, thus raising the possibility of danger to the employee and others, the fact is that the great bulk of the unit is composed of clerks, whose work is not dangerous,

### 92 LA 382

sensitive or particularly unique. Moreover, the work of the meter readers and other non-clerks cannot begin to compare with that of munitions workers, chemical workers and nuclear power plant workers. Yet, as the Union points out, other arbitrators have firmly held without cause testing of such workers unreasonable.

It must also be remembered that the program in question is not testing for fitness as such; it is testing for off-duty drug use. The Company seeks to blur this distinction or bridge it by suggesting an "irrebuttable presumption" that such drug use does affect performance and that there are "no circumstances" under which such an employee "would be able to come to work unimpaired" (Godfrey). But saying this does not make it so. Moreover, we all know that present technology does not and cannot test impairment, but only tells us, with regard to impairment, of the presence of drug metabolics in the body, some of which can linger for significant periods of time.

Also of significance is the fact that the Company made no attempt to determine the extent of drug use among its employees before embarking on without cause testing of those employees seeking upward mobility. While a

detailed survey may not be required, some greater awareness of the nature of the threat would appear to be in order.

It is not enough, in my view, to justify the intrusion of testing on generalized notions of the "integrity" of the work place. As was noted by the court in *Guiney v. Roache*, the Boston Police case, that argument proves too much and could justify any intrusion, including the search of homes and personal property wherever it might be found.

There can be no mistake, it must be said, that drug testing is an intrusion and invasion of privacy, one that goes beyond the taking of a urine sample during the Company's usual medical examination. In the first place, urine testing for drugs is accompanied, more often than not, by someone's observation of the evacuation. Secondly, the invasion of privacy is not solely in that observation, but in the involuntary taking of urine that can reveal personal habits and considerable physiological information.

In addition to weighing the foregoing factors and the need and the gain, as it were, one should examine the loss. A company's inability to test without cause does not leave it defenseless with respect to suspected drug use. Certainly, not this Company. According to the materials supplied in this case, its supervisors have already been schooled in the signs of drug use and possible impairment. Drug users whose conduct directly affects their performance can be spotted and identified and actions taken against them, as the Union suggests, based on probable cause or even reasonable suspicion.

When all the relevant factors are weighed, I'm persuaded that the balance here must be in favor of the employees. While the Company's motivation is completely understandable, it's my considered judgment, given the nature of the workforce, the available alternative means at the Company's command of achieving its objectives, and the other factors cited herein, that the intrusion inherent in a program of without cause testing goes too far and is unjustified under the Parties' Agreement. I find, therefore, that the Company's without cause drug testing of applicants for promotion or transfer is unreasonable and violative of Article XXVIII; that its denial of B—'s promotion was a violation of Article XVII, and that her suspension was unjust and unreasonable and violative of Article V.

\* \* \*

This disposition of the matter makes it unnecessary to consider the details of the testing procedure, the fact that B— may not have been specifically ap-

prised of the consequences of her drug test or the uses to which that test would be put. It is also unnecessary, given the formulation of the questions to be addressed and this ruling, to deal with the third issue.

What remains is the scope of the remedy.

### The Remedy

There is no need here to formally rescind B—'s suspension, as the Company did that long ago and made her whole for the five days and two hours pay lost. Because that suspension stemmed from a test not permitted under the Agreement, it should not be considered or referred to in any subsequent proceedings. However, I shall not require that the records of Grievant's participation in the Employee Assistance Program be expunged.

As to the denied promotion, the remedy is to place B— on the Meter Reader roster as of October 23, 1985 with appropriate back pay, benefits and seniority attendant thereto.

The major remedial issue is with the Alcohol and Drug Policy itself. The Union asked that it be rescinded and declared void in its entirety. I cannot agree. Although the Union occasionally discussed the Policy as a whole, the

### 92 LA 383

focus of its attack was on the testing of applicants for promotion or transfer as set forth in Paragraph 6 thereof. It is that aspect of the Policy toward which the Award is directed. Its other aspects, not directly at issue here, can await other cases should they arise.

### AWARD

The Company's without cause testing of applicants for promotion or transfer pursuant to Paragraph 6 of its Alcohol and Drug Policy is unreasonable and a violation of Article XXVIII of the Contract between the Parties. That portion of Paragraph 6 is hereby declared void.

The Company's denial of a promotion to Grievant B— subsequent to such a test was a violation of Article XVII and its suspension of Grievant was unjust and unreasonable and a violation of Article V.

Grievant shall be placed on the Meter Reader roster as of October 23, 1985 with appropriate back pay, benefits and seniority and her suspension, already rescinded by the Company, shall not be considered or referred to in subsequent proceedings.

At the request of the Union, the Board shall retain jurisdiction of the cause for a period of sixty (60) days in order to resolve any disagreements as to the remedies ordered herein.

## 46 LA 335

**FMC CORP.—**

### Decision of Arbitrator

In re FMC CORPORATION, JOHN BEAN DIVISION, LANSING PLANT [Lansing, Mich.] and UNITED AUTOMOBILE, AEROSPACE AND AGRICULTURAL IMPLEMENT WORKERS OF AMERICA, LOCAL 724, March 23, 1966

Arbitrator: Richard Mittenthal

## WORKING CONDITIONS

**—Observance of workers by closed circuit television—Management right ▶ 124.01 ▶ 24.35**

Employer did not violate any provision of contract by installing closed circuit television camera in order to observe employees in receiving room, from which employer believed it was losing material through theft. Employer's failure to use TV surveillance of employees in the past cannot be considered as mutually agreed-upon binding past practice that would bar such action. Surveillance is not "an infringement of the workers' basic rights of privacy," since actions of employees at work are not private actions, and, in any event, use of TV cameras to observe employees is not basically different from traditional use of supervisors for that purpose. (R. Mittenthal)—FMC Corp., 46 LA 335.

Appearances: For the company—Ken H. Moore, personnel manager; Tracy Carrigan, division manager; Arthur F. David, manufacturing manager. For the union—Edmund Johnson, international representative; Neal Dukes, chairman, bargaining committee; J. V. Earls, committeeman.

## CLOSED CIRCUIT TV

MITTENTHAL, Arbitrator: — The grievance in this case protests Management's action in "unilaterally install[ing] closed circuit television within the plant" for the purpose of observing employees. The Union claims this conduct constitutes a violation of the Agreement. It asks that Management be ordered to discontinue this use of television.

The Lansing Plant produces farm machinery, fire-fighting equipment, and automotive parts. There are approximately 450 employees in the bargaining unit. Sometime ago Management noted a loss of material and equipment from the Receiving Department. It believed the loss was attributable to theft and decided the problem might be solved by placing a closed-circuit television system in the plant. It informed the Bargaining Committee in early 1965 that it intended to install such a television system in the receiving room. There was no agreement at that time regarding the use of television. The Union says Management sought "mutual agreement"; the Company denies this and says it was the Bargaining Committee which sought "a Memorandum of Understanding concerning the use of TV."

The closed-circuit television system was installed on October 7, 1965. A camera was placed in the receiving room to provide a picture of any activity there. This picture does not encompass the entire room. Two monitors were used to receive the

## 46 LA 336

picture.[1] One was located in the front guard house where a plant guard is stationed; the other was located in the radio control room, a short distance from the receiving room, where a salaried employee works. The latter employee helps control the flow of material through the plant by radio contact with the lift trucks. Employees are aware of the television camera and of the possibility that they are being observed at any given moment by the plant guard or the salaried person. Management, on the same day the television system was installed, gave the Bargaining Committee a "Memo of Understanding" which read:

"To avoid any misunderstanding concerning the use of television cameras in our plant, the Company hereby states that these cameras are being installed to assist in the detection of pilferage and theft and also to assist in regulating traffic to more economically handle materials in our manufacturing processes."

The Union complained that the introduction of the television system was a violation of the Agreement. Its grievance (No. 388) alleges that employees "working without cameras focusing on their every move" was a beneficial "working condition," that the installation of the television camera and monitors eliminated this "working condition," thus imposing a "serious burden" on the employees, that this action interfered with "the employees' right of privacy," and that Management failed to establish any "problems of supervision or change in methods that would warrant its action."

**Discussions and Findings**

The union emphasizes its opposition to "surveillance, whether by machine recording device, motion picture camera, listening device, closed-circuit television, or otherwise . . . as an encroachment on the human dignity of workers."[2] But the issue in this case is not whether closed-circuit television is a reprehensible method of observing employees. My authority as arbitrator is set forth in the Agreement. Article III, Section 3 says the arbitrator's decision "shall be *limited* to the controversies arising out of the *interpretation* or *application* of this written *Agreement* . . . and shall be within the scope thereof." Thus, the real issue here is whether the unilateral installation of closed-circuit television was a violation of the *Agreement*. My personal views as to the propriety of television as a means of overseeing workers are not relevant.

The Union contends first that Management's use of television is contrary to past practice. It states that there has been "a clear and consistent practice of at least twenty-five years of no T.V. installation on the premises." It believes this practice has become a binding condition of employment, arguing that "the contract represents an agreement incomplete in many specific areas, but complete in the sense that the parties have *impliedly agreed* on their *general conduct* for a stated period." Its position, in other words, is that the parties have impliedly agreed that the conduct of the business would not include television surveillance of employees for the life of the Agreement.

Past practice may be important and even decisive in applying provisions of the Agreement. It may serve to clarify or implement contract language. But these are not its only functions. Sometimes an established practice may, apart from any basis in the Agreement, be regarded as a distinct and binding condition of employment which can only be changed by the mutual consent of the parties. It is this principle which the Union stresses in arguing that the practice of no television surveillance of employees has become in effect a binding condition of employment.

Even though the principle may be correct,[3] there remains the crucial problem of determining under precisely what circumstances a practice may by implication become an integral part of the Agreement. The Union seems to say that if a given course of conduct qualifies as a practice, it must automatically be considered a binding condition of employment. That is not so. For a practice, to be enforceable, must be supported by the *mutual agreement* of the parties.[4] Its binding quality is due not to the fact that it is past practice but rather to the agreement on which it is based. Yet, there are

## 46 LA 337

many practices which are not the result of joint determination at all. Umpire Harry Shulman, in a Ford Motor Company-UAW case, explained the point in these words:

"A practice thus based on mutual agreement may be subject to change only by mutual agreement. . . . But there are other practices which are not the result of joint determination at all. They may be mere happenstance, that is, methods that developed without design or deliberation. Or they may be choices by Management in the exercise of managerial discretion as to convenient methods at the time. In such cases, there is no thought of obligation or commitment for the future. Such practices are merely present ways, not prescribed ways, of doing things. The relevant item of significance is not the nature of the par-

---

[1] They receive a picture but not the sounds (conservation, etc.) of the area.
[2] See Union Exhibit No. 1, a resolution adopted by the International Union at its last convention.

[3] I shall assume, for purposes of this case, that the principle is sound and does not conflict with the terms of the Agreement. There is no need to make a decision on this point.
[4] This mutual agreement may be express or implied—that is, an actual joint understanding or a course of conduct from which such an understanding can reasonably be implied.

ticular method but the managerial freedom with respect to it. Being the product of managerial determination in its permitted discretion such practices are, in the absence of contractual provision to the contrary, subject to change in the same discretion. . . . But there is no requirement of mutual agreement as a condition precedent to a change of a practice of this character." [5]

Thus, there are different kinds of practices. Only those which are supported by mutual agreement may, apart from any basis in the contract, be regarded as binding conditions of employment. They must be continued for the life of the contract unless changed by mutual consent. To treat all practices as binding conditions of employment, without regard to the matter of mutuality, would be to place past practice on an equal footing with the written Agreement, a result which these parties could hardly have contemplated. There is, after all, no provision in this Agreement which specifically requires the continuance of existing practices. And the arbitrator certainly has no authority to write a "past practice" clause into the Agreement under the guise of contract interpretation.

It is true that there had been no closed-circuit television in this plant in the past. But nothing in the evidence indicates that this practice—this absence of television—was in any way based upon the mutual agreement of the parties. Management had never agreed not to install such a television system. The matter had never been discussed prior to 1965. The fact that television had not been used to watch employees was not the result of design or deliberation. Nowhere does the record suggest that Management had ever before considered installing closed-circuit television. Traditional methods of supervision had been followed in the receiving room for years. Nowhere does it appear that these methods were the subject of Union-Management discussion or negotiation. Nor does Management appear to have committed itself to freeze all working conditions in the receiving room or to abstain from any innovations in the supervision of the work force. Hence, when material and equipment began to disappear from the receiving room, Management decided that the loss was most likely due to theft and that closed-circuit television might be an effective means of eliminating the problem. Clearly, the claimed practice lacks the requisite

mutual agreement. The Union's position therefore must be rejected.[6]

The Union also maintains that Management had "an obligation to secure an agreement from the Union . . . as a prelude to the installation of the T.V." It alleges that Management acknowledged this obligation by seeking "mutual agreement" on the use of television at a meeting in early 1965. It states that there was no such agreement and that Management's use of television was hence an improper unilateral action.

This argument is not convincing. The use of television to watch employees concerns the subject of supervision. A decision as to how employees are to be supervised and what are the proper methods of supervision is a normal function of Management. Nothing in the Agreement suggests that this function can be exercised only with the prior consent of the Union. Management has the right to change its methods, procedures and operations without "mutual agreement"—so long as the change does not result in a contract violation. Article VI, Section 5 broadly states: ". . . All the powers and authority the Company had prior to

### 46 LA 338

the signing of this Agreement, except those specifically modified or delegated hereby, are retained by the Company." As for the parties' discussions in early 1965, there is considerable disagreement as to what happened. The Company says it simply informed the Union that it intended to install the television system later in the year with the Union thereupon requesting "a Memorandum of Understanding concerning the use of TV." The Union says Management sought "mutual agreement" on its proposed use of television. In face of these conflicting statements, I cannot find that Management conceded it had no right to install the television without the Union's agreement.

The Union finally asserts that

closed-circuit television represents "an infringement of the workers' basic rights of privacy." Its claim refers to no provision of the Agreement.

The right of privacy concerns an individual's right not to have his statements, actions, etc. made public without his consent. But this serves only to protect him against the publication of his *private* statements or *private* actions. It should be evident that an employee's actions during working hours are *not private* actions. Management is properly concerned with the employee's work performance, what he does on the job and whether he obeys the plant's rules and regulations.[7] This and other information about employees is obtained through line supervisors. One of the supervisor's principal functions is to observe the employees at work. Surely, such supervision cannot be said to interfere with an employee's right of privacy. The same conclusion should apply in this case. For all the Company has done is to add a different method of supervision to the receiving room—an electronic eye (i.e., the television camera) in addition to a human eye. Regardless of the type of supervision (a camera, a supervisor, or both,) the employee works with the knowledge that supervision may be watching him at any time. He has a much better chance of knowing when he is being watched where there is no camera. But this is a difference in degree, not a difference in kind. For these reasons, I find there has been no interference with the employees' right of privacy.[8]

My conclusion is that the installation of the closed-circuit television system in the receiving room was not a violation of the Agreement.

**AWARD**

The grievance is denied.

---

5 Opinion A-278, September 4, 1952. Reported at 19 LA 237, 242 (1952).

---

6 The Union cited Electronic Instrument Company, Inc. (EICO), 44 LA 563 (1965), a case in which the arbitrator held that the installation of closed-circuit television was a contract violation. But that case is clearly distinguishable, the arbitrator there basing his decision upon a contract clause which guaranteed the continuation of beneficial conditions of employment unless good cause was shown for their withdrawal. The arbitrator held that not being watched by television was a beneficial condition of employment. The contract clause stated in part: ". . . any conditions of employment not covered by this agreement which are beneficial to employees and which are now in effect as regular company practice shall be continued during the period of this agreement . . ." There is no such "past practice" clause in the instant Agreement.

---

7 See, for example, the following provisions in Article VI: "Any employee of the plant whose conduct is such as to interfere with harmonious relationship between the Company and its employees shall be subject to discipline" (Section 4); "The Union . . . agrees that it will fully cooperate with the Company to assure a full day's work on the part of all its members for a full day's pay" (Section 7); "Any employee . . . violating any of the terms of this Agreement shall be subject to discipline up to and including discharge" (Section 8).

8 I need not decide here whether information secured through the use of close-circuit television is admissible in evidence in a disciplinary dispute. This raises a slightly different question, namely, whether the arbitrator may—absent a constitutional right or a contract right—reject evidence because the manner in which it is obtained is reprehensible to him or because sound labor-management relations would in his opinion be better served by such exclusion.